Adobe® InDesign®
CS2 Bible

Galen Gruman

WILEY

Wiley Publishing, Inc.

Adobe® InDesign® CS2 Bible

Published by
Wiley Publishing, Inc.
111 River Street
Hoboken, NJ 07030-5774
www.wiley.com

Copyright © 2005 by Wiley Publishing, Inc.

Published simultaneously in Canada

Library of Congress Control Number is available from the publisher.

ISBN: 0-7645-8812-5

Manufactured in the United States of America

10 9 8 7 6 5 4 3 2 1

1O/RV/QU/QV/IN

For general information on our other products and services or to obtain technical support, please contact our Customer Care Department within the U.S. at (800) 762-2974, outside the U.S. at (317) 572-3993 or fax (317) 572-4002.

Wiley also publishes its books in a variety of electronic formats. Some content that appears in print may not be available in electronic books.

Library of Congress Cataloging-in-Publication Data: 2005923241

About the Author

Galen Gruman is principal at The Zango Group, an editorial and marketing consulting firm, and senior editorial associate at BayCreative, a creative consultancy, as well as editorial director at EmergeMedia, publisher of *IT Wireless.* Currently a frequent contributor to *SBS Digital Design*, *Macworld*, *CIO*, and *InfoWorld*, he has also been editor of *Macworld* and *M-Business*, executive editor of *Upside*, West Coast bureau chief of *Computerworld*, and vice president of content for ThirdAge.com. He is coauthor of 18 other books on desktop publishing. Gruman led one of the first successful conversions of a national magazine to desktop publishing in 1986 and has covered publishing technology since then for several publications, including the trade weekly *InfoWorld*, for which he began writing in 1986, *Macworld*, whose staff he joined in 1991, and most recently *SBS Digital Design*. Originally a newspaper reporter in Los Angeles, Gruman got caught by the production-technology bug in 1979 and hasn't recovered.

Credits

Acquisitions Editor
Michael Roney

Project Editor
Cricket Krengel

Technical Editor
Jonathan Q. Woolson

Editorial Manager
Robyn Siesky

Vice President and Executive Group Publisher
Richard Swadley

Vice President and Publisher
Barry Pruett

Project Coordinator
Erin Smith

Graphics and Production Specialists
Sean Decker
April Farling
Lauren Goddard
Denny Hager
Joyce Haughey
Jennifer Heleine
Barry Offringa
Heather Ryan
Ron Terry
Erin Zeltner

Quality Control Technician
John Greenough
Brian H. Walls

Proofreading and Indexing
TECHBOOKS Production Services

To Barbara Assadi, my longtime friend, writing partner, and valued colleague.

Foreword

If you're anything like me, switching from one desktop publishing application to another seems like an enormous undertaking. You grow comfortable and confident with one program's features, all the ins and outs, and its capabilities, only to start all over again. But in making the move to InDesign, Adobe has made the transition an easy one. If you've ever used any other Adobe products, some of the features and tools might seem vaguely familiar and intuitive. However, I'm the first to admit it's still a slightly scary and very daunting experience. Your sense of control and ease of maneuverability have suddenly vanished, and you start to feel awkward and maybe even a little flustered and frustrated with the simplest of tasks. Yet, while you may hold fast in your knowledge that answers come from trial and error or in the user's guide, frankly there are times when you just find yourself up against a wall and need to ask for help.

Whether you're a beginner, an advanced user, or somewhere in between, the *Adobe InDesign CS2 Bible* is the most comprehensive guide out there to understanding and using InDesign. When I was seeking to expand our coverage of InDesign in *SBS Digital Design*, a magazine that features expert advice and how-to for designers, I turned to Galen because his previous *Adobe InDesign CS Bible* was clearly superior to any other book on the market. As a relatively new user myself, I found his background in both QuarkXPress and InDesign especially helpful, and his approach to be refreshingly straightforward, well organized, and complete. At *SBS Digital Design,* we strive to give our readers that same practical advice that takes users to the next level. Galen seemed the most natural fit, and now he consistently dispenses expert advice in hands-on, insightful how-to articles for *SBS Digital Design*.

So the next time you need a quick answer or would like to engage in a little discussion, you'll find that the *Adobe InDesign CS2 Bible* is the quintessential reference book you'll always want to keep within reach. Trust me.

Jennifer Reding
Editor
SBS Digital Design

Preface

I've spent two decades working with page-layout software, heading one of the first efforts by a national magazine to go from traditional tools to electronic ones in 1986. Over the years, I've also reviewed all the page-layout tools for various magazines, including *InfoWorld* and *Macworld*. For the first five years, I felt that Ventura Publisher was the best page-layout program available, and in the 1990s, I judged QuarkXPress to be the best. During that time, I saw PageMaker sink into irrelevance because of neglect by Adobe and, more recently, I saw QuarkXPress follow a similar path of complacency. So I was excited in 1999 by the first version of InDesign but disappointed that it had several drawbacks that could have been avoided considering it came so many years after Ventura Publisher, PageMaker, and QuarkXPress had addressed most users' needs. The promise was strong, but the product was still very rough around the edges. Users saw that and didn't widely adopt InDesign. Version 2 corrected many of the deficiencies, and user adoption of InDesign accordingly skyrocketed in 2002. In late 2003, InDesign CS (version 3) put InDesign clearly in the lead, and began a sea change in the publishing market away from the dominant QuarkXPress. For example, major magazine publishers such as Hearst and Meredith have now standardized on InDesign.

The newest version on InDesign — version 4, known as InDesign CS2 — does something that's particularly hard; it extends a great product even more. InDesign CS2 is not a huge leap, as InDesign CS was from InDesign 2, but it is a significant leap nonetheless. Its changes come down to two types: continued refinement of InDesign's many powerful features and extension of the program into new areas, such as word-processing-type capabilities. Adobe was smart to bring to InDesign some of the features we've all long had in Microsoft Word but not in mainstream page-layout programs, including automatic bullets, footnotes, and anchored items. There are other new capabilities such as object styles that make it easier to produce standards-based layouts and experiment with changes across multiple objects simultaneously.

Layout artists have an incredibly powerful tool in the form of InDesign to let them deliver on their creative aspirations and vision. I can only hope that this book helps you achieve those ambitions.

Acknowledgments

Thanks to the development and product marketing staff at Adobe for providing early versions of the InDesign CS2 software and listening to suggestions on making it even better. Thanks to the editors and production staff at Wiley Publishing for their efforts in making this book possible, especially to project editor Cricket Krengel and technical reviewer Jonathan Woolson for their improvements to the book's content and clarity. And thanks to designer John Cruise, who provided much of the insights in Chapters 25 and 26.

The `www.InDesignCentral.com` Web site and its contents are copyrighted by The Zango Group.

The Adobe Open Options user guides and FAQs were designed by BayCreative LLC and copyrighted by Adobe Systems Inc. The *IT Wireless Essential Products Guide* was designed by Galen Gruman and copyrighted by EmergeMedia Inc. The YMCA of Oakville brochure examples were designed by Branimir Zlamalik of Gb.com and copyrighted by the YMCA of Oakville, Ontario. The Jackson County (Ore.) Library Foundation brochure is designed and copyrighted by designer Shawn Busse of Kinesis. The *In the Footsteps of Paul* workbook is designed and copyrighted by Ronald Lanham. The Zango Group marketing collateral examples are copyrighted by The Zango Group. Original photographs are copyrighted by Galen Gruman and Ingall W. Bull III, unless otherwise credited.

All materials are used by permission.

Contents at a Glance

Contents

PART II: Document Fundamentals   115

Chapter 4: Creating, Opening, and Saving Documents 117

Chapter 5: Working with Pages 135

PART III: Object Fundamentals   211

Chapter 9: Adding Text Frames, Graphics Frames, and Lines 213

Chapter 10: Manipulating Objects 225

PART VII: Specialty Publishing Techniques   659

Chapter 32: Book and Long-Document Publishing 661

Chapter 33: Interactive Document Setup 687

Chapter 34: Working with XML 701

PART VIII: Introduction to Publishing   747

Chapter 38: The Publishing Environment 749

Chapter 39: Layout Theory and Practice 763

Introduction

Welcome to the *Adobe InDesign CS2 Bible* — your personal guide to a powerful, full-featured publishing program that offers precise but flexible control over all aspects of page design. My goal is to guide you each step of the way through the publishing process, showing you how to make Adobe's InDesign CS2 — also known as InDesign 4 — work for you. You'll also learn tips and tricks about publishing design that you can use in any document, whether it was created in InDesign or not.

Taking the best from the two schools of thought on desktop publishing, InDesign merges the highly structured approach of programs such as QuarkXPress and Ventura Publisher with the more naturalistic approach of Adobe PageMaker, which InDesign all but replaced in 1999. Thus, InDesign offers a wide range of desktop-publishing capabilities for sophisticated designers who develop magazines, books, ads, and product brochures. It also gives the power of the press to individuals and groups who use the program's impressive set of publishing tools to communicate their thoughts, dreams, and philosophies.

Version CS2 of InDesign takes that strong basis and makes it even better, often in subtle ways meant to make the workflow process easier and more intuitive. (Its features could be hard to find and awkward to use because of a slavish mirroring of the Adobe Photoshop and Illustrator user interfaces. Although InDesign adheres strongly to that core Adobe interface, it's been tweaked to work more naturally for a layout artist's needs.) While InDesign's abundance of features necessarily makes its interface complex, Adobe continues to find ways to simplify it. And it has also added new features, from small enhancements in cut and paste to significant additions like object styles, as well as missing-for-too-long features such as saving to the previous version.

InDesign can also lets you take advantage of modern electronic publishing's full range. Not only can you produce high-quality, lively flyers, newsletters, magazines, and similar publications in InDesign, you can also create rich, colorful documents that can be viewed on the Web, distributed by CD, or set directly to a printing press for faithful print reproduction.

In a nutshell, InDesign is meant to help those who educate, inform, and document the world in which we live. Join me in learning how to use this powerful program.

What This Book Offers

So, because InDesign comes with good documentation that is full of examples, why do you need this book? To see the bigger picture. Publishing design involves much more than understanding a particular program's tools — it involves knowing when, how, and, most important, *why* to use them. In this book, I help you realize the potential of InDesign by applying its tools to real-world publishing design needs. I also identify any weaknesses and explain how to overcome them — something that vendor manuals rarely do.

Some desktop publishers have years of high-end creative, design-intensive experience. Others are just getting started in publishing, perhaps by producing simple newsletters or flyers to advertise a community event. Not a few are exploring the brave new world of Web publishing.

Desktop publishers fall into several classes:

+ Designers new to InDesign but familiar with other desktop publishing software

+ Designers familiar with print publishing but new to electronic publishing

+ Experienced designers new to desktop technologies

+ Novice designers new to desktop technologies

No matter which class you're in, you'll find that this book addresses your needs. You don't need a degree in design or ten years' experience producing national ad campaigns — you can use this book if you're responsible for developing and implementing the look of documents, whether a four-page company newsletter or a four-color billboard ad. The basic techniques and issues are the same for both ends of the spectrum. And this book, of course, covers in detail the specialized needs — such as table creation, image control, color output, and electronic publishing — of specialty designers. (If you're just learning such advanced techniques, be sure to read the sidebars that explain the underlying issues.) Regardless of your level of experience with desktop publishing, this book will help you use InDesign.

What distinguishes this book from the rest is that it does not attempt to substitute for the documentation that accompanies InDesign. Instead, it guides you through the *process* of publishing a document, regardless of whether that document is your first or your thousandth.

How to Read This Book

The *Adobe InDesign CS2 Bible* is made up of 42 chapters and seven appendixes divided into nine parts, in addition to the QuickStart that appears just before Part I begins. If you're a novice InDesign user but familiar with desktop publishing, I suggest you read the book in order, because the process of page design is presented in the typical publishing workflow. You first learn how (and why) to create basic pages, containers, placeholders, and templates; then you learn how to work with specific elements (such as text and graphics); and finally, you learn how to use special effects and deal with prepress issues (such as output control, image manipulation, trapping, and printing).

If you're experienced with InDesign, read the book in any order you want — pick those sections or chapters that cover the InDesign implementation issues you want to know more about. You should also find the exhaustive index a real aid in finding what you're looking for.

If you're new to publishing, be sure to start with Part VIII: "Introduction to Publishing," which teaches novice publishers the basics. And experienced publishers should at least skim this part as well — you're likely to find new ideas and perspectives on how you approach your work.

Whether you're reading the book sequentially or nonsequentially, you'll find the many cross-references helpful. Publication design is ultimately successful because the result is more than the sum of its parts — and the tools used to create and implement your designs cannot be used in isolation. Because this is true, having one "right" order or grouping of content is impossible. The cross-references let you know where to get additional information when what you're seeking to understand or learn doesn't fit the way I've organized this book.

Following is a brief description of the parts you will find in the *Adobe InDesign CS2 Bible*.

InDesign QuickStart

This guide walks you through the creation of a document to give you a quick tour of the program, from creation to printing. It's a convenient way to see the main InDesign features in action and quickly get a sense of how they work, whether you're new to publishing or new to InDesign.

Part I: Welcome to InDesign

This part walks you through the initial steps of using InDesign to create your publications. I give you a basic introduction to InDesign itself, explaining the concepts it uses in its layout approach. I also highlight what's special about InDesign in general and about InDesign CS2 in particular.

Part II: Document Fundamentals

This part explains how to create the basic containers — documents, pages, and layers — of a publishing project and how to set the standards for your documents, from master pages, libraries, and templates to guides and colors. InDesign comes with a set of tools that lets you automate repetitive work, apply common elements to a range of pages, and customize page settings, among other capabilities. This part walks you though the ins and outs of all of them.

Part III: Object Fundamentals

This part explains how InDesign's frame and line tools work so you can create and manipulate layout objects. With these building blocks, you construct almost all the components in a layout, from the frame containers that hold text and pictures to original artwork you create in InDesign. You'll also learn how to move, group, copy, and lock such objects and how to automate repetitive object actions to save time.

Part IV: Text Fundamentals

This part shows you how to import and work with text files, including the application of typographic features to really jazz up your layout. You'll also learn how to create tables and how to set up styles to automate the application of typography to document text.

Part V: Graphics Fundamentals

This part discusses how to use InDesign to manipulate and work with pictures and images in your layout, whether imported from another program or created within InDesign. Although text carries the message, a picture is what gets your attention — and often can say more than any collection of words. This part helps you get the most out of your images in InDesign. It also shows you how you can use the tools in InDesign to create a variety of shapes that can be used as original artwork or as specialty containers for text and images.

Part VI: Output Fundamentals

This part walks you though the output steps of publishing. This part shows you what you need to be aware of as well as show you how to output your documents for printing or for use in the Adobe Portable Document Format (PDF), which is often used for network- and CD-based documents, as well as for Web-based documents.

Part VII: Specialty Publishing Techniques

This part expands your horizons. Very few publishers work by themselves, and most have a whole raft of tools to work their miracles. The chapters in this part expose you to key insights in working beyond InDesign, covering workgroup issues, the use of plug-ins to add new capabilities, and the use of scripts to automate your work. You'll also learn how to use the book-publishing features meant to standardize the production of multi-chapter projects. And you'll learn how InDesign can help you create interactive documents — those that take advantage of multimedia files, page actions, and forms — that are distributed as PDF files or as an eBook. Finally, you'll learn the basics of working with XML, the structured content system widely used by Web-oriented content engines. InDesign can both create XML files and use XML files to turn templates into completed InDesign documents for automated publishing systems.

Part VIII: Introduction to Publishing

This part is a quick tour of publishing fundamentals for new and experienced users alike. I cover the essential tools for a complete publishing environment, show you how to use special characters in your documents, define the terms used in publishing, and explain the basic principles to good layout, typography, and color usage.

Part IX: Appendixes

The appendixes in this book take you through the ins and outs of how to install Adobe InDesign, what is new in version CS2, how QuarkXPress and PageMaker users can more easily make the switch to InDesign, and how to use the optional InCopy CS2 group-editing tools. You'll also find an appendix with all the shortcuts in one place, and another that previews the companion Web site www.InDesignCentral.com.

Conventions Used in This Book

Before I begin showing you the ins and outs of InDesign, I need to spend a few minutes reviewing the terms and conventions used in this book.

InDesign commands

The InDesign commands that you select by using the program menus appear in this book in normal typeface. When you choose some menu commands, a related pull-down menu or a pop-up menu appears. If this book describes a situation in which you need to select one menu, and then choose a command from a secondary menu or list box, it uses an arrow symbol. For example, "Choose Layout ➪ Margins and Columns" means that you should choose the Margins and Columns command from the Layout menu.

Like most modern programs, InDesign has an interface feature that has proved to be quite popular called *tabbed panes*. This is a method of stuffing several dialog boxes into one dialog box. You see tabs, like those in file folders, and by clicking a tab, the pane of options for that tab comes to the front of the dialog box. You can even move tabs from one dialog box to another to create the arrangement that best suits your work style. This book will tell you to go to the pane, which you do by clicking the tab where the name of the pane is to display the pane. For example, "Go to the General pane" means click the General tab in the current dialog box.

Mouse conventions

Because you use a mouse to perform many functions in InDesign, you need to be familiar with the following terms and instructions. And, yes, when I say *mouse,* I also mean other pointing devices, such as trackballs and pen tablets.

✦ **Pointer:** The small graphic icon that moves on the screen as you move your mouse is a pointer (also called a *cursor*). The pointer takes on different shapes depending on the tool you select, the current location of the mouse, and the function you're performing.

✦ **Click:** Most Mac mice have only one button, but some have two or more; all PC mice have at least two buttons. If you have a multibutton mouse, quickly press and release the leftmost mouse button once when I say to click the mouse. (If your mouse has only one button — you guessed it — just press and release the button you have.)

✦ **Double-click:** When I say to double-click, quickly press and release the leftmost mouse button twice (if your mouse has only one button, just press and release twice the button you have). On some multibutton mice, one of the buttons can function as a double-click (you click it once, the mouse clicks twice); if your mouse has this feature, use it — it saves strain on your hand.

✦ **Right-click:** A Windows feature since Windows 95, right-clicking means clicking the right-hand mouse button. On a Mac's one-button mouse, hold the Control key when clicking the mouse button to achieve the right-click effect. On multibutton Mac mice, assign one of the buttons to the Control+click combination. (Mac OS X automatically assigns the right-hand button to Control+click.)

✦ **Drag:** Dragging is used for moving and sizing items in an InDesign document. To drag an item, position the mouse pointer on it. Press and hold the mouse button, and then slide the mouse across a flat surface to drag the item. Release the mouse button to drop the dragged item in its new location.

Dealing with Computer-Platform Appearance Issues

InDesign CS2 runs on Mac OS X 10.2.8 (Jaguar), Windows 2000 with Service Pack 2 or later installed, and Windows XP, as well as later versions of these operating systems. Most desktop publishers use Apple Computer's Macintosh, and thus most readers of this book will likely be Mac-based. That's why I use Mac screenshots in the illustrations throughout this book. (Plus, Adobe uses Windows screen shots in its documentation.) But the minority in publishing who use Microsoft's Windows continues to grow, especially for business-oriented and personal publishing, so I do show Windows screenshots when notable differences exist. Adobe has done a good job of ensuring that the interface for InDesign is almost identical — within the natural differences between Mac and Windows — on the two platforms.

Keyboard conventions

This book provides both the Macintosh and Windows shortcuts throughout, with the Mac shortcut first. In most cases, the Mac and Windows shortcuts are the same, except for the names of the keys, as follows:

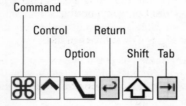

- ✦ The Mac's Command key (⌘) is the most-used shortcut key. Its Windows equivalent is Ctrl.

- ✦ Shift is the same on the Mac and Windows. In many Mac program menus — including InDesign — Shift is displayed by the symbol ⇧.

- ✦ The Option key on the Mac is usually the same as the Alt key in Windows. In many Mac program menus — including InDesign — you'll see the symbol ⌥ used.

- ✦ The Control key on the Mac has no Windows equivalent (it is *not* the same as the Windows Ctrl key). Many Mac programs — including InDesign — indicate it with the symbol ⌃ in their menus.

- ✦ The Tab key is used both to move within fields in panes and dialog boxes and to insert the tab character in text. InDesign and many other Mac programs indicate it in menus with the symbol ⇥.

- ✦ The Return key (Mac) or Enter key (Windows) is used to apply a dialog box's settings and close the dialog box (equivalent to clicking OK or Done), as well as to insert a hard paragraph return in text. In InDesign and many other Mac programs, it is indicated in menus by the symbol ⏎. Note that there is another key labeled Enter on most keyboards, in the numeric keypad. This sometimes works like the regular Return or Enter, but in InDesign text, it inserts a column break. I refer to it as *keypad Enter* in this book.

- ✦ The Delete key (Mac) and Backspace key (Windows) deletes text, one character at a time, to the left of the text-insertion point. Windows also has a separate Delete key that deletes text, one character at a time, to the *right* of the text-insertion point. The Mac's Clear key, although in the same position on the keyboard, does not delete text.

If you're supposed to press several keys at the same time, I indicate that by placing plus signs (+) between them. Thus, Shift+⌘+A means press and hold the Shift and ⌘ keys, then press A. After you've pressed A, let go of all three keys. (You don't need to hold down the last letter in the sequence.)

I also use the plus sign (+) to join keys to mouse movements. For example, Option+drag means to press and hold the Option key while dragging the mouse on the Mac, and Alt+drag means to press and hold the Alt key while dragging the mouse in Windows.

Also note that InDesign lets you change the shortcuts associated with menu and other commands (by choosing Edit ⇨ Keyboard Shortcuts). Throughout the book, I assume the shortcuts in use are the default ones and that you haven't altered them.

Icons

You'll notice special graphic symbols, or *icons,* used throughout this book. I use these icons to call your attention to points that are particularly important or worth noting:

The New Feature icon indicates a technique or action that is new to InDesign CS2.

The Tip icon indicates a technique or action in InDesign that will save you time or effort.

The Note icon indicates information that you should remember for future use — something that may seem minor or inconsequential but will, in reality, resurface.

The Caution icon is used to warn you of potential hang-ups or pitfalls you may encounter while using InDesign (and how to avoid them).

The Cross-Reference icon points you to different parts of the book that contain related or expanded information on a particular topic.

The Platform Difference icon alerts you to differences using InDesign on the Macintosh versus in Windows.

The QuarkXPress User icon alerts QuarkXPress users who are switching to InDesign to significant differences in function and approach between the two programs.

InDesign QuickStart

Although InDesign is a complex program that lets you do everything from designing a fashion magazine to indexing a book to generating separation plates for professional printing, you can get started building documents with just a few simple skills. If you're in a hurry to get started on a document — or you have a job interview tomorrow based on your proficiency in InDesign — work through the steps in this section. You'll learn the basic building blocks of documents (frames and lines) and the two primary tools (Selection and Direct Selection).

By all means, do not assume that these steps provide all you need to know about InDesign. From here, head to related sections of the book and explore the full functionality of the program. If you're not sure where to start, figure out what you'll be doing the most. For example, if you'll be flowing text into a newsletter template, head to Part IV, "Text Fundamentals."

To create the sample document shown in Figure QS-1 — an annual compendium of case studies from a publication called *IT Wireless* — you'll need InDesign, a text file from a word processing program such as Microsoft Word, a graphic file such as a TIFF file, and a laser or inkjet printer. You can follow the steps exactly (substituting your own text, graphic, and fonts), or you can vary the design as much as you want. (You can download the text and graphics used in this QuickStart example at www.InDesignCentral.com/QS.html. You'll have to supply your own fonts, however.)

In This QuickStart

Creating a new document

Working with frames

Working with lines

Working with text and graphics

Creating and applying colors

Printing a composite

Figure QS-1: Combining formatted text and several graphics with a few simple frames and lines produces a completely designed magazine article.

Creating a New Document

When you create a new document in InDesign, you're actually specifying the final size and setup of the pages in the document. Note that in this QuickStart, I provide measurements in picas, which is a more standard measure in the layout world, and then provide the equivalent measurement in inches.

1. **Start InDesign.**

2. **Choose File ⇨ New ⇨ Document, or press ⌘+N or Ctrl+N.** The New Document dialog box appears (see Figure QS-2).

3. **In the Page Size pop-up menu, choose Letter.**

4. **Select the Facing Pages option.** Because this is a magazine printed on two sides, you need both left- and right-page versions.

5. **Select the Master Text Frame option.**

6. **Set the number of columns to 2, with a gutter width of 1p6 (0.25 in).**

7. **Set the margin guides at 4p6 (0.75 in) for the top and inside, 3p6 (0.583 in) for the bottom, and 3p (0.5 in) for the outside.** Note that in this example InDesign has been set with picas as the default measurement for vertical and horizontal measurement, one of two typical settings for publications. (The other is to set horizontal at picas and vertical measurements at inches.)

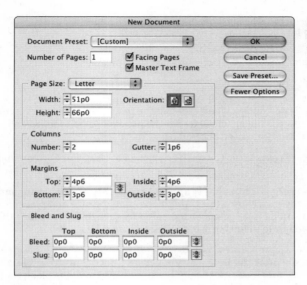

Figure QS-2: Set up the page size and other attributes for your document in the New Document dialog box.

8. **Click Save Preset, and give these specifications a name.** Assigning a name to these specifications lets you select these exact settings for future documents for this publication by choosing the Preset name from the Document Preset pop-up menu.

9. **Click OK to create the new document's new layout.** InDesign creates one 8½-x-11-inch page.

10. **Choose File ⇨ Save As, or press Shift+⌘+S or Ctrl+Shift+S.**

11. **In the Save As field, type** ITW Case Studies 2005.indd, **as shown in Figure QS-3.** Choose a location for the file, and then click Save.

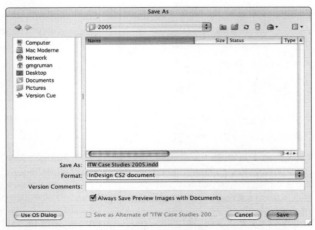

Figure QS-3: Use the Save As dialog box to name a new document.

Cross-Reference For more information about creating a new document, see Chapter 4.

Working with Frames

By using the Master Text Frame option when creating the new document, you've already created the frame, or container, for the article text. But the article has colored frames at the top for the story title that need to be created via frames.

1. **Select the Rectangle Frame tool.** To see the names of tools, point at them until a Tool Tip appears.

2. **Click and drag to create a frame that is approximately 21p (3.5 in) wide and 4p (0.667 in) tall, as shown in Figure QS-4.** You'll fine-tune the size and placement in the next steps. The new frame is selected, as indicated by the white handles. If the frame becomes deselected in the following steps, click on it to select it.

3. **Highlight the X field in the Control palette (Window ➪ Control, or Option+⌘+6 or Ctrl+Alt+6), which specifies the item's origin across (placement from the left edge of the page); type** 4p6 **in this field.** Make sure the upper-left square is black (in the grid of nine squares)at the left of the palette; this controls what the coordinates are based on. Click that square to make it black (active) if it's not already black.

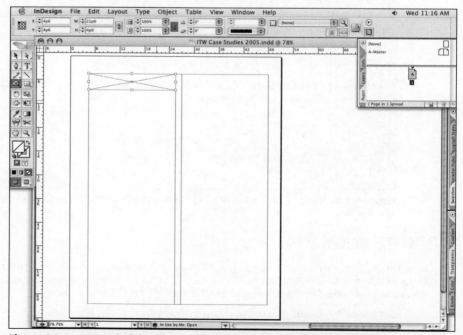

Figure QS-4: Use any of the frame tools to create background shapes into which you will import a picture. Use the Control palette (at the top) to precisely control its position and size.

4. **Tab to the Y field, which specifies the item's origin down (placement from the top of the page); type** 4p6 **in this field.**

5. **Tab to the W field, which specifies the item's width; type** 21p **in this field.**

6. **Tab to the H field, which specifies the item's height; type** 4p **in this field.**

7. **Press Return or Enter to reposition and resize the frame according to the values typed.**

8. **Choose Item ⇨ Duplicate, or press Option+Shift+⌘+D or Ctrl+Alt+Shift+D.** If necessary, first click on the new frame to select it.

9. **Highlight the X field in the Control palette, and then type** 25p6.

10. **Tab to the Y field, and then type** 4p6.

11. **Tab to the W field, and then type** 22p6.

12. **If the H field is not already set to 4p, type** 4p **in its field.**

13. **Press Return to reposition and resize the second frame, as shown in Figure QS-5.** Later, you will add color to this frame.

Cross-Reference   For more information about working with frames, see Chapters 9 and 10.

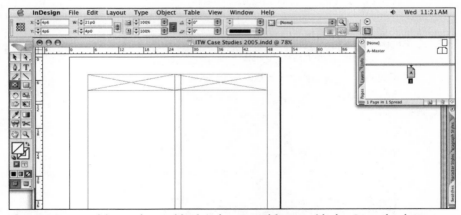

Figure QS-5: Resizing and repositioning the second frame with the Control palette

Working with Text

In InDesign, text goes inside a text frame. You can type text into the frame or import a text file in various formats. Once text is inside the frame, you can change the font, size, color, and many more options. First, you'll create text frames and type text into them.

1. **Select the Type tool.** You can also use the Rectangle tool or the Rectangular Frame tool.

2. **Click and drag to create a frame that is approximately 45p (7.5 in) wide and 6p (1 in) tall, as shown in Figure QS-6.** Select the new frame with the Selection or Direct Selection tool, as indicated by the white handles. If the frame becomes deselected in the following steps, click on it to select it.

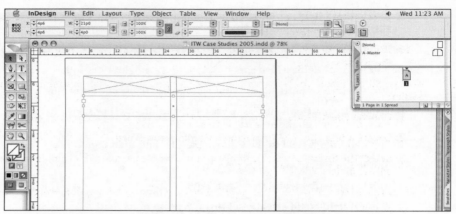

Figure QS-6: Use the Type tool to create a container for text.

3. **To size and place the frame precisely, type the following values in the Control palette: X: 4p6, Y: 9p6, W: 43p6, H: 5p0.**

4. **Select the Type tool, and then click in the new frame that will hold the story's headline.**

5. **Type the words** Public Safety's Second Wireless Wave **in the frame.**

6. **Highlight the entire phrase and choose a different font from the Control palette's Font menu (the example uses Frutiger).**

7. **Choose a typestyle from the Type Style menu (the example uses 65 Bold).**

8. **Choose 28 pt from the Font Size menu, as shown in Figure QS-7.**

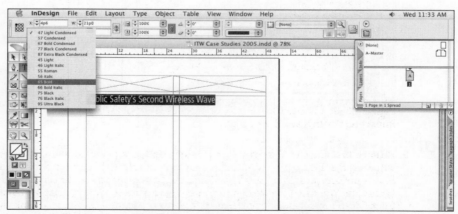

Figure QS-7: When text is highlighted, you can format it using controls on the left side of the Control palette.

9. **In the frame at upper right, enter two paragraph returns and type the phrase** CASE STUDY **(in all caps).**

10. **Highlight the text** *CASE STUDY* **and apply the font Frutiger 76 Black Italic to it; make the point size 12 pt.**

Now you'll put text in the text frame that was created through the Master Text Frame feature earlier:

1. **Choose File ➪ Place, or press ⌘+D or Ctrl+D.** The Place dialog box appears.

2. **Locate a text file in a format such as Microsoft Word.**

3. **Select the Show Import Options option.** The file used in the example has just two style sheets in use: Normal and Headline 2.

4. **Click to select the text file, and then click Open.** The Microsoft Word Import Options dialog box appears, as shown in Figure QS-8.

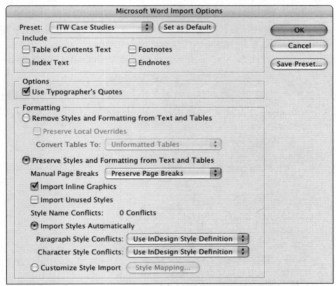

Figure QS-8: Choose File ➪ Place, or press ⌘+D or Ctrl+D, to import text from a word processor.

5. **Be sure that the Use Typographer's Quotes option is selected.** In most cases, you will want the Import Styles Automatically option selected, with both the Paragraph Style Conflicts and Character Style Conflicts pop-up menus set to Use InDesign Style Definition. You can save Word import settings for reuse later by clicking Save Preset. Click OK to import the file. InDesign will show the loaded-text icon (it looks like a tiny paragraph) that indicates a file ready to be placed into a frame. (If you do not have a text file to import, simply type another sentence in the frame.)

Note

If the text file you import does not fit in the frame, a red square in the lower-right corner indicates that text is overflowing. There is no need to worry about that for these purposes.

6. **Click the two-column master text frame to pour the text into it.** Figure QS-9 shows the result.

7. **Because the first page of the article has the two empty frames at the top as well as the headline frame, you'll want to resize the master text frame for this page so the story text doesn't overprint the other frames.** (You can also set text wrap for each of those frames using the Text Wrap pane, covered later in this QuickStart.) To resize, use the Selection tool to drag the middle frame handle at the top of the frame, and drag the frame's top down below the three other frames.

With the text placed, you now need to format it. Follow these steps:

1. **With the Type tool, click anywhere in the text and highlight all the text using ⌘+A or Ctrl+A.**

2. **Choose Type ➪ Character, or press ⌘+T or Ctrl+T, to open the Character pane and select a font (the example uses ITC Veljovic), select a typestyle (Book, here), set the point size to 9.5 pt, and set the leading to 11 pt.** You can also use the Control palette to set these settings (be sure to click the A icon to see its character settings). Figure QS-10 shows the pane and the results.

3. **Make sure all the text is still selected, and choose Type ➪ Paragraph, or press Option+⌘+T or Ctrl+Alt+T, to open the Paragraph pane.**

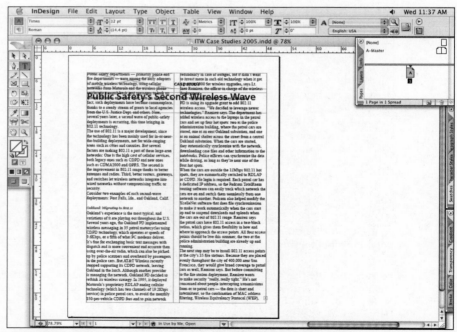

Figure QS-9: When text is placed into the master text frame, it overprints other frames that overlap it.

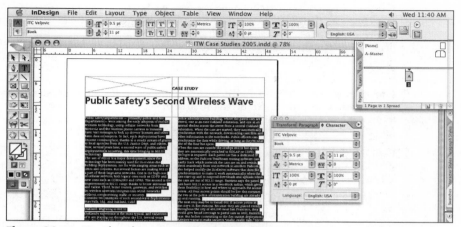

Figure QS-10: Use the Character pane or Control palette to set the font, typestyle, point size, and leading.

4. **Make sure the alignment is set to Justified, the first-line indent to** 0p10, **and the Hyphenate option is selected, as shown in Figure QS-11.** You can also use the Control palette; just be sure to click the ¶ icon to see its paragraph settings.

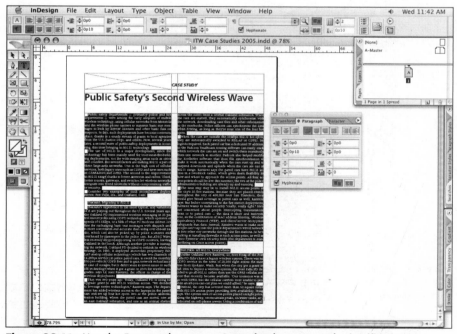

Figure QS-11: Use the Paragraph pane or Control palette to set the justification.

5. **For the first paragraph, add a drop cap by clicking the paragraph with the Type tool and choosing Drop Caps & Nested Styles from the Paragraph pane's palette menu or by pressing Option+⌘+R or Ctrl+Alt+R.** Type **4** in the Lines field and **1** in the Characters field. Click OK. In the Paragraph pane, change the first-line indent to 0p. Highlight the first letter in this paragraph, and then go to the Character pane and change the font to **Frutiger** and the typestyle to **65 Bold**.

6. **Find the internal section headlines in the story and format them to be left-aligned, hyphenation turned off, the first-line indent set to 0p, space above to 1p, space after to 0p3, the point size to 11 pt, and the font to** Frutiger 65 Bold **using the Paragraph and Character panes or by using the Control palette.**

7. **Find the paragraphs that immediately follow the internal headlines and change the first-line indent to 0p using the Paragraph pane.** Figure QS-12 shows the results of all this text formatting.

8. **If you will be creating pages with the same type specifications, create styles from the formatted text:**

    a. **Start with the drop cap: Highlight the text with the Type tool, and then choose New Character Style from the Character Style pane's palette menu.** (Choose Type ➪ Character Styles or press Shift+F11.) Provide a name at the top of the New Character Styles dialog box, verify the attributes in the Basic Character Formats pane, and then click OK.

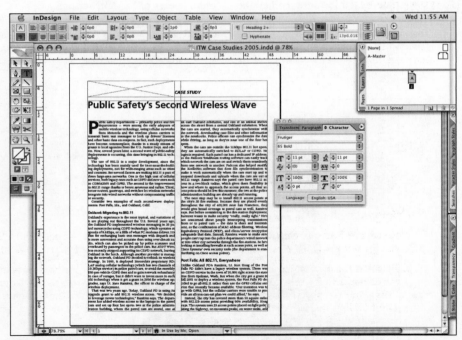

Figure QS-12: Your document should look something like this.

b. **Now, click anywhere in the regular story text with the Type tool, and then choose New Paragraph Style from the Paragraph Styles pane's palette menu.** (Choose Type ⇨ Paragraph Styles, or press F11, to open the pane.) Provide a name at the top of the New Paragraph Style dialog box, and then verify the attributes in the Basic Character Formats, Indents and Spacing, Hyphenation, and Justification panes. (For the drop cap paragraph style, you'll also use the Drop Caps and Nested Styles pane; select the drop cap character style you created earlier in the Character Style pop-up menu.) Click OK when done. You should end up with one character style (it could be called Drop Cap) and five paragraph styles (they could be called Main Headline, Internal Headline, Body Text, Drop Cap Body Text, and First Body Text).

c. **Apply these styles to your text by clicking anywhere in a paragraph, and then clicking the appropriate name in the Paragraph Styles pane.** To apply a character style (such as to the drop cap), select the appropriate text, and then click on the appropriate name in the Character Styles pane.

9. **Choose File ⇨ Save, or press ⌘+S or Ctrl+S to save your work.**

Cross-Reference

For more information about typing, importing, and formatting text, see Part IV, "Text Fundamentals."

Working with Lines

You can create lines of any shape and size, and then change the style, width, and color. Here, I'm adding a line to the document's master page, so it appears on all pages. To work on a master page, double-click a master page icon in the Pages pane (Window ⇨ Pages or F12). Figure QS-13 shows the pane.

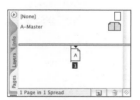

Figure QS-13: The Pages pane lets you work on master pages, as well as create new pages.

1. **Select the Line tool.**

2. **Be sure the Stroke button in the Tools palette is set to black—click the button, open the Swatches pane (Window ⇨ Swatches or F6), and finally click the [Black] swatch.**

3. **Position the mouse where you want to draw the line (below the master text frame for this example), and then click and drag to create a line, as shown in Figure QS-14.** Press Shift while you drag to constrain the tool to drawing a horizontal or vertical line. The new line is selected, as indicated by the white handles. If the line becomes deselected in the following steps, click on it to select it.

4. **Precisely place and size the line using the Control palette, as follows: for the right page: X: 55p6, Y: 63p9, L: 43p6; for the left page: X: 3p, Y: 63p9, L: 43p6.**

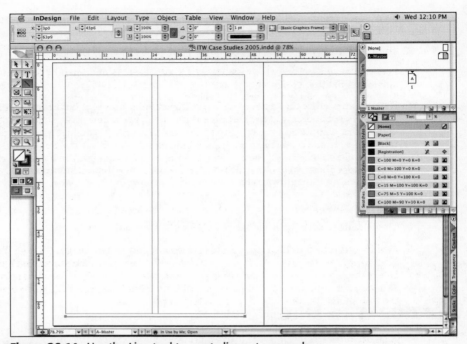

Figure QS-14: Use the Line tool to create lines at any angle.

5. **Make the stroke 1 pt, also in the Control palette.**

6. **Return to the story page you worked on previously by double-clicking its icon in the Pages pane.**

7. **Choose File ⇨ Save, or press ⌘+S or Ctrl+S, to save your work.**

Cross-Reference

For more information about working with lines, see Chapter 10.

Working with Graphics

In InDesign, any image that you import into a layout — whether it's a digital photograph, chart, or line drawing — is referred to as a graphic. Graphics go inside graphics frames — either one you create before you place a graphic, or one that InDesign creates automatically when you import a graphic when no frame is selected. Once a graphic is inside a frame, you can change its size and placement.

1. **Click and hold on the Rectangle Frame tool.**

2. **Position the pointer on the page, and then click and drag to create a rectangular graphic frame of any shape.** The new frame is selected, as indicated by the white handles. If the frame becomes deselected in the following steps, click on it to select it.

3. **To size the frame precisely, type the following values in the Control palette: X:** 22p8, **Y:** 30p8, **W:** 25p4, **H:** 25p4.

4. **To import a graphic, choose File ⇨ Place, or press ⌘+D or Ctrl+D.**

5. **Locate a graphic file such as a TIFF, JPEG, GIF, or EPS as shown in Figure QS-15; select it and click Open.**

6. **If necessary, click the graphic with the Direct Selection tool, and then highlight the Scale X Percentage field in the Control palette.** Type a new scale such as **80%**. This resizes the graphic while leaving the frame unchanged. (If you had used the Selection tool, this action would resize both the frame and its graphic.) The Scale Y Percentage field should change to the same value as long as the two fields are locked (a chain–button appears to their right; if the chain is open, click the button to lock the two fields).

 Tip   You can also resize the image to fit the frame by choosing Object ⇨ Fitting ⇨ Fit Content Proportionally (Option+Shift+⌘+E or Ctrl+Alt+Shift+E).

7. **Add a runaround to the image so text does not run to the image.** Choose Window ⇨ Text Wrap, or press Option+⌘+W or Ctrl+Alt+W, to get the pane shown in Figure QS-16. Select the graphic with the Selection tool and then click the Text Wrap pane's Wrap Around Bounding Box button (the second from the left), and set the wrap margins in the four fields (there's one for each side) to **0p6**.

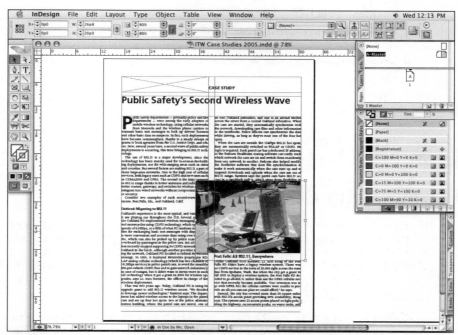

Figure QS-15: Choose File ⇨ Place, or press ⌘+D or Ctrl+D, to import graphics into frames.

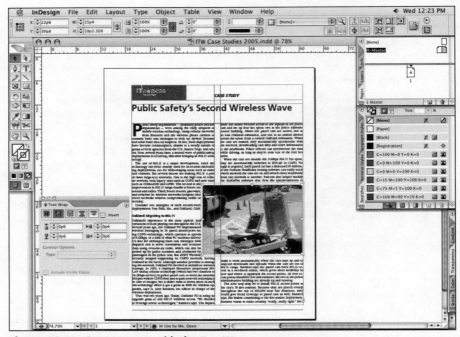

Figure QS-16: Set text wrap with the Text Wrap pane.

8. **Import a logo graphic for the first frame you created and size it to fit, as shown in Figure QS-16.** It doesn't have to fill the whole width of that frame.

Cross-Reference

For more information about working with graphics, see Part V, "Graphics Fundamentals."

Creating Colors

To apply the color you want to an item or text, first create that color. By default, InDesign provides a few colors: cyan, magenta, yellow, [Black], red, blue, green, [Paper] (white), [None], and [Registration]. (The names that InDesign puts in brackets are colors that cannot be deleted or modified.) In most cases, you'll be creating additional colors to suit your documents.

1. **Choose Window ⇨ Swatches or press F5 to open the Swatches pane.** Here, you create, modify, and apply colors. You'll create a color based on a color in our imported logo.

2. **Select the Eyedropper tool, and then click on the background color in that logo.** For the *IT Wireless* magazine logo shown in Figure QS-16, the color is a medium blue.

3. **Choose New Color Swatch from the pane's palette menu.**

4. **From the Color Mode pop-up menu, choose CMYK.** This creates a color based on the four process colors widely used in commercial printing: cyan, magenta, yellow, and

black. Because you selected a color with the Eyedropper tool, the New Color Swatch dialog box shows the values, as seen in Figure QS-17. If you had not first selected a color with the Eyedropper tool, you would type values or click and drag the four sliders to select a desired color. If the Name with Color Value option is selected, InDesign names the color automatically; if it is not selected, you can give it a more memorable name such as Bright Navy.

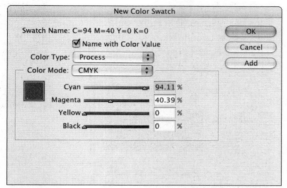

Figure QS-17: Create a CMYK color by first selecting a color from an object in the layout with the Eyedropper tool or by selecting the proportions of the constituent colors in the New Color Swatch dialog box.

5. **Click OK to create the color and close the dialog box.** If you want to create more colors, click Add. Click OK only when you want to close the dialog box.

Cross-Reference For more information about creating colors, see Chapter 8.

Applying Colors

InDesign's Swatches pane, combined with the Tools palette, makes it easy to experiment with different colors. You can apply colors to frame backgrounds, lines, strokes, some imported images, and text.

1. **Be sure the Swatches pane is open (Window ⇨ Swatches or F5).**

2. **Click on the two frames at the top of the page with the Selection tool.** To select both, click one, and then Shift+click the other.

3. **Make sure the Fill button is selected in the Tools palette, as seen in Figure QS-18.** This tells InDesign what you want to color the object, not any strokes it may have.

4. **Click the name of the color you created in the previous section.** The selected frames will now fill with the color.

5. **Using the Type tool, highlight the text *CASE STUDY* in the upper-left frame.**

Fill icon

Figure QS-18: Click a color to apply it to the background of a frame.

6. **Again ensuring the Fill button is selected in the Tools palette, click the [Paper] color in the Swatches pane.** This makes the text white.

7. **Choose File ➪ Save, or press ⌘+S or Ctrl+S, to save your work.**

Cross-Reference   For more information about applying colors, see Chapters 10 and 27.

Printing a Composite

Whether you're designing a document for black-and-white photocopying, color printing, professional printing, or even for PDF, you'll need to review drafts. By default, InDesign is set up to your system's default printer with just a few clicks.

1. **Choose File ➪ Print, or press ⌘+P or Ctrl+P.**

Tip   If you press Return or Enter as soon as the Print dialog box appears, chances are that InDesign will print a usable draft on your laser printer. However, if you've selected a different page size, orientation, or other option, you may want to confirm the other settings.

2. **At the top of the dialog box, the Printer pop-up menu is usually set to your system's default printer.** You can leave this setting or locate and select the printer you're actually using. It's best to select your actual printer.

3. **Go to the Output pane and make sure the Color pop-up menu is set to Composite Grayscale if you're printing to a black-and-white laser printer and to Composite CMYK if you're printing to a color inkjet or laser printer.**

4. **Look at the page preview at the lower left of the dialog box and make sure the page (indicated by a light-gray rectangle) fits within the printer paper (indicated by a blue line), as shown in Figure QS-19.**

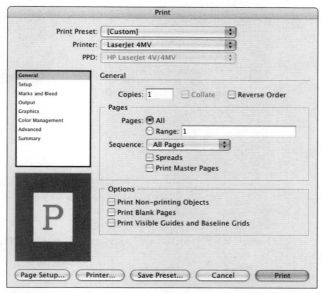

Figure QS-19: The Print dialog box lets you confirm that your document fits on the paper in the selected printer, as well as set the appropriate print settings for your document and target printer.

5. **Click Print.**

Cross-Reference For more information about printing, see Part VI, "Output Fundamentals."

✦   ✦   ✦

Welcome to InDesign

What InDesign Can Do for You

Although Adobe InDesign is a relatively new desktop-publishing program, its history actually spans more than 16 years; it succeeds the venerable Adobe PageMaker, the first popular desktop-publishing program. InDesign *is* an all-new program — make no mistake about that — but it draws on the experience and design of PageMaker, which Adobe Systems acquired in 1994 and significantly modified in the intervening years. As Adobe's entry into the professional, more-creative publishing space that has been dominated by QuarkXPress, the developers of InDesign also learned a lot of lessons from QuarkXPress. They responded by offering many comparable features, plus a whole raft of unique ones, in a way that fits the InDesign publishing workflow model.

Why does this history matter? Because chances are you already use PageMaker or, more likely, QuarkXPress and are switching to InDesign or adding InDesign to your software toolkit. You'll find a lot of familiar things in InDesign, but InDesign does borrow extensively from PageMaker and other Adobe products, as well as from its chief rival, QuarkXPress. It also adds new components of its own. So draw on your experience with PageMaker, QuarkXPress, or other Adobe software, but don't let that experience fool you into thinking you can run InDesign on autopilot. Instead, be sure to really learn InDesign's approaches.

Of course, if you're an experienced user of previous InDesign versions, you already know the InDesign approach. That's great — you're a step ahead! Feel free to skip this chapter or just skim it for a refresher.

Cross-Reference If you're switching to InDesign from QuarkXPress or PageMaker, be sure to check out Appendix C or Appendix D. These appendixes will help you translate your QuarkXPress and PageMaker expertise into InDesign's frame of reference.

Note My book *QuarkXPress to InDesign: Face to Face*, also published by Wiley Publishing, provides a detailed step-by-step transition guide for QuarkXPress users.

So what can InDesign do for you? A lot. For years, layout designers had to choose between a free-form but manual approach to layout (PageMaker) and a structured but easily revised approach (QuarkXPress). Most chose the latter. With InDesign, you can choose both. That's important for both novice and experienced users because it isn't a one-size-fits-all answer. Sometimes (for example, if your project is a one-time publication or an experimental effort), creating a layout from scratch — almost as if you were doing it by hand on paper — is the best approach. And sometimes using a highly formatted template that you can modify as needed is the best approach because there's no need to reinvent the wheel for common documents.

InDesign can handle sophisticated tasks such as magazine and newspaper page layout, but its simple approach to publishing also makes it a good choice for smaller projects such as flyers and newsletters. InDesign is also a good choice for corporate publishing tasks such as proposals and annual reports. Plug-in software from other vendors adds extra capabilities; for example, Virginia Systems offers several plug-ins that make InDesign a good tool for books and academic papers.

Cross-Reference   For more on plug-in software, see Chapter 36.

But that's not all. InDesign is not merely a merger of QuarkXPress and PageMaker — though it will seem that way to experienced users. It is designed from the ground up as an *electronic* publishing tool. That means documents can easily be sent to service bureaus and printing presses for direct output, saving you lots of time and money. It also means you can create documents for electronic distribution, particularly using the Adobe Portable Document Format (PDF). These electronic files can include interactive features such as forms and sounds.

Cross-Reference   For more in-depth coverage of output and interactive-document fundamentals, see Chapter 33.

This chapter details the wide range of uses and features of InDesign, points out the ways in which InDesign can be useful to you, and describes the basic metaphor on which the program is based. I also provide a comprehensive list of the terms — clearly and concisely defined — that I use throughout the book. So whether you're an expert or novice, read on and prepare yourself for a great InDesign adventure.

What Makes InDesign Special

The release of PageMaker in 1986 launched the desktop-publishing revolution, and in the following years, PageMaker and its competitors added tons of cool features. It may be hard to imagine that there's anything new to add to this publishing toolkit.

Well, InDesign's creators have managed to add a few new features. Following are the significant additions to the desktop-publishing toolkit, courtesy of InDesign (note that this list doesn't include enhanced versions of features found in competitors such as QuarkXPress or in PageMaker):

✦ **Paragraph composer.** This lets InDesign adjust the spacing and hyphenation over an entire paragraph at once — rather than the typical one-line-in-isolation of other programs — to achieve the best possible spacing and hyphenation. (See Chapter 17.)

✦ **Optical margin alignment.** This actually moves some characters past the margin of your columns to create the optical illusion that all the characters line up. It works because some characters' shapes fool the eye into thinking they begin before or after where they really do, so although technically aligned, they appear not to be. Optical margin alignment fixes that. (See Chapter 17.)

✦ **Optical kerning.** This adjusts the spacing between characters based on their shapes, which provides for the most natural look possible without resorting to hand-tuning their spacing. (See Chapter 17.)

✦ **A menu for inserting special characters.** This makes it so you no longer have to remember codes or use separate programs like the Mac's Character Palette or the Windows Character Map to add special symbols like bullets (•) and section indicators (§). Your word processor has likely had this feature for a few years, but this is a first in desktop publishing. (See Chapter 14.)

✦ **Glyph scaling.** This lets InDesign stretch or compress characters to make them fit better on a line. (A *glyph* is a character.) This works in addition to tracking and kerning, which adjust the spacing between characters to make them fit better on a line. (See Chapter 17.)

✦ **Custom strokes for characters.** This lets you change the look of characters by making their outlines thicker or thinner. You can also give the part of the characters inside the outlines a different color to create an outline effect. (Typically, the part inside the stroke is the same color as the stroke, so the reader sees a normal, solid character.) (See Chapter 17.)

✦ **EPS display.** This feature allows you to see the detailed contents of an EPS file rather than rely on a poor-quality preview image or, worse, see an X or gray box in place of the image. (See Chapter 21.)

✦ **Illustrator and Photoshop file import.** This lets you place these graphics files directly in your layout. (See Chapter 22.)

✦ **Multiple views of the document.** This lets you have several windows open for the same document, enabling you to see different sections at the same time. (See Chapter 3.)

✦ **Custom drop-shadow creation.** This lets you create exactly the kind of drop-shadow effect you want and not be stuck with a canned option. (See Chapter 10.)

✦ **Transparency.** This lets you make objects fade to create special effects as they overlap or for ghost-like visuals. (See Chapter 10.)

✦ **Automated spell-checking and text correction.** This is similar to Microsoft Word's noninvasive correction tools. (See Chapter 14.)

There are also a few features that aren't new in desktop publishing history but have not been available to major programs for many years since Ventura Publisher bowed out:

✦ **Object styles.** This lets you apply a range of attributes, such as fill and stroke, to an object and reuse those same settings on other objects. (See Chapter 11.)

✦ **Footnotes.** This is similar to how word processors handle this annotation method. (See Chapter 32.)

✦ **Follow-me anchored objects.** This lets you keep items such as figures and sidebars with text as it flows throughout a document. (See Chapter 11.)

Discovering the InDesign Approach

Publishing programs, although similar in many ways, differ in their approach to the publishing task. One way to describe a program's approach to publishing is to talk about its *metaphor*, or the overall way that it handles publishing tasks. Some programs use a *free-form metaphor*, which means that the method used to assemble a document is based on assembling page elements as you would if they were placed on a pasteboard until ready for use (this is also called the *pasteboard metaphor*, although that's a less precise term because software using other metaphors can still include a pasteboard). PageMaker is the best-known example of the free-form approach. Other programs approach page layout using a *frame-based metaphor,* in which frames (or boxes) hold both the page elements and the attributes that control the appearance of those elements. QuarkXPress is the best-known example of the frame-based approach. InDesign uses both the free-form metaphor and the frame-based metaphor.

The frame-based metaphor

Under a frame-based metaphor, you build pages by assembling a variety of frames that will contain your text and graphics. First, you set up the basic framework of the document — the page size and orientation, margins, number of columns, and so on. You then fill that framework with text, pictures, and lines.

Note   These frames and lines need not be straight or square. With InDesign, you can create frames that are shaped by Bézier curves. (In the 1970s, French engineer Pierre Bézier created the mathematics that make these adjustable curves work.)

There are several reasons to use frames:

✦ **To create a template for documents such as newsletters and magazines that use the same basic elements for many articles.** You create the frames and then add the text and graphics appropriate for each specific article — modifying, adding, and deleting frames as necessary for each article.

✦ **To get a sense of how you want your elements to be placed and sized before you start working with the actual elements.** This is similar to creating a pencil sketch on paper before doing a formal layout.

✦ **To ensure specific size and placement of elements up front — in this case, you're often working with a template or guidelines that limit size and placement of elements.** In many cases, you can copy an existing frame because its size is one you're using in several locations of your layout. For structured or partly structured documents like newsletters and magazines, I find setting up my documents up front so elements are sized and placed correctly easier than resizing elements one at a time later.

Note   Bear in mind that whether you start by creating frames in which you will later place graphics or text or you simply place the text and graphics directly on your page, you're using frames. In the case of direct placement of elements on the page, InDesign creates a frame automatically for each element. The difference is that the frame InDesign creates is based on the amount of text or the size of the graphic, rather than on your specific specifications. Of course, in either case, you can modify the frames and the elements within them.

The free-form metaphor

Under a free-form (pasteboard) metaphor, you draw the pages' content as if you're working on paper. Depending on how long you've been in this business, you may well remember paste-up boards with strips of type, camera-ready line drawings, and halftone pictures strewn about, sticking to pasteboard thanks to the wax on their backs. You would then assemble all those pieces until you got the combination that looked right to you. The free-form metaphor encourages an experimental approach, which is particularly well suited to one-of-a-kind documents such as ads, brochures, annual reports, and marketing materials.

In a frame-based approach, you can certainly experiment by using the frames as placeholders for actual text and graphics. But visual thinkers like to work with actual objects, and that's why the free-form metaphor works much better for them. With InDesign, you pick the metaphor that works for your style, your current situation, and your mood. After all, both approaches can lead to the same design.

Understanding Global and Local Control

The power of desktop publishing in general, and InDesign in particular, is that it lets you automate time-consuming layout and typesetting tasks while letting you customize each step of the process according to your needs. This duality of structure and flexibility — implemented via the dual use of the frame-based and free-form layout metaphors — carries over to all operations, from typography to color. You can use *global* controls to establish general settings for layout elements and then use *local* controls to modify those elements to meet specific publishing requirements. The key to using global and local tools effectively is to know when each is appropriate.

Global tools include:

✦ General preferences and application preferences (see Chapter 3)

✦ Master pages (see Chapter 7)

✦ Text styles (see Chapter 19)

✦ Object styles (see Chapter 11)

✦ Sections of page numbers (see Chapter 5)

✦ Color definitions (see Chapter 8)

✦ Hyphenation and justification (see Chapter 17)

✦ Libraries (see Chapter 7)

Styles and master pages are the two main global settings that you can expect to override locally throughout a document. You shouldn't be surprised to make such changes often because, although the layout and typographic functions that styles and master pages automate are the fundamental components of any document's look, they don't always work for all of a publication's specific content.

Local tools include:

✦ Frame and shape tools (see Chapters 9, 10, 11, 20, and 24)

✦ Character and paragraph tools (see Chapters 16, 17, 18, and 19)

✦ Graphics tools (see Part V)

Knowing which tools to use

In many cases, it's obvious which tool to use. If, for example, you maintain certain layout standards throughout a document, then using master pages is the obvious way to keep your work in order. Using styles is the best solution if you want to apply standard character and paragraph formatting throughout a document. When you work with special-case documents, such as a single-page display ad, it doesn't make much sense to spend time designing master pages and styles — it's easier just to format one-of-a-kind elements on the fly.

In other cases, deciding which tool is appropriate is more difficult. For example, you can create *drop caps* (large initial letters set into a paragraph of type, like the drop cap that starts each chapter in this book) as a character option in the Character pane, or you can create a *character style* (formatting that you can apply to any selected text, ensuring the same formatting is applied each time) that contains the drop-cap settings and apply that style to the drop cap. Which method you choose will depend on the complexity of your document and how often you'll need to perform the action. The more often you find yourself doing something, the more often you should use a global tool (such as character styles).

Fortunately, you don't have to decide between global and local tools right away while designing a document. You can always create styles from existing formatting later or add elements to a master page if you find you need them to appear on every page.

Specifying measurement values

Another situation in which you can choose between local or global controls is specifying measurement values. Regardless of the default measurement unit you set (and that appears in all dialog boxes, panes, and palettes), you can use any unit when entering measurements in an InDesign dialog box. If, for example, the default measurement is picas, but you're accustomed to working with inches, go ahead and enter measurements in inches.

InDesign accepts any of the following codes for measurement units (replace x with your measurement value):

✦ xi or x inch or x" (for inches)

✦ xp (for picas)

✦ $x$pt or 0px (for points)

✦ xc (for ciceros)

✦ $x$cm (for centimeters)

✦ $x$mm (for millimeters)

InDesign Vocabulary 101

InDesign comes with its own terminology, much of it adopted from other Adobe products. The general terms include the following:

✦ **Frame.** The container for an object, whether text, graphic, or color fill.

✦ **Link.** The connection that InDesign makes to an imported file; the link contains the file's location, last modification date, and last modification time. A link can reference any image or text file that you have imported into a layout. InDesign can notify you when a source text or graphics file has changed, so you can choose whether to update the version in your layout. (A *hyperlink,* often also abbreviated to *link* in casual conversation, connects elements in a Web page to other Web pages or other resources such as PDF files.)

✦ **Package.** The collecting of all files needed to deliver a layout for printing or Web posting.

✦ **PDF.** The Adobe Portable Document Format is the standard for electronic documents. No matter what kind of computer it is viewed on (Windows, Macintosh, Palm, or Unix), a PDF document retains high fidelity to the original in typography, graphics representation, and layout. InDesign can both place PDF files as if they were graphics and export its own pages as PDF files.

✦ **Place.** To import a graphic or text file.

✦ **Plug-in.** A piece of software that loads into InDesign and becomes part of InDesign, to add more capabilities.

✦ **Stroke.** The outline of an object (whether a graphic, line, or individual text characters) or frame.

✦ **Thread.** The links between text frames that route stories among them.

Not too long ago, only a few publishing professionals knew—or cared about—what the words *pica, kerning, crop,* or *color model* meant. Today, these words are becoming commonplace because almost everyone who wants to produce a nice-looking report, a simple newsletter, or a magazine encounters these terms in the menus and manuals of their layout programs. Occasionally, the terms are used incorrectly or are replaced with general terms to make nonprofessional users feel less threatened, but that substitution ends up confusing professional printers, people who work in service bureaus, and Internet service providers. For a primer on publishing terms, see Chapters 39, 40, and 42.

Tip It doesn't matter whether you put a space between the value and the code: *1inch* and *1 inch* are the same as far as InDesign is concerned.

Tip You can enter fractional picas in two ways: in decimal format (as in *8.5p*) and in picas and points (as in *8p6*). Either of these settings results in a measurement of 8½ picas (there are 12 points in a pica).

Summary

InDesign offers a strong set of features for professional publishers working on brochures, magazines, advertisements, and similar publications. Although it lacks specialized tools for database publishing (such as for catalogs), it offers many unique features such as a multilane composer, glyph scaling, and customer character strokes.

InDesign's use of both the free-form and structured layout metaphors makes it very flexible, letting you pick the layout style that works best for you and for your document's specific needs.

✦　　✦　　✦

A Tour of InDesign

The first time you use a program, it can be overwhelming. You're not sure what you can actually do with the program, and each program has its own idiosyncrasies. InDesign is no different. If you're familiar with other Adobe applications, such as PageMaker or Photoshop, the InDesign software interface will be familiar to you. Even if you've been using QuarkXPress, you'll be able to translate much of what you see in InDesign to QuarkXPress terms.

But because every program is unique, each has its own style and approaches. So now that you're ready to start using InDesign, follow through this chapter to find out where InDesign puts its capabilities and how to access them. When you first launch InDesign, you see the Tools palette on the left, and you may see several other palettes on the right. InDesign is ready and waiting for you to open a document and start working.

However, taking a few minutes to familiarize yourself with the interface is invaluable to learning new software. After all, without a basic understanding of what you're looking at on-screen, it's difficult to begin working in InDesign.

Note InDesign lets you change the shortcuts associated with menu and other commands. (Chapter 3 covers this feature in more detail.) Throughout the book, I assume the shortcuts in use are the default ones.

Cross-Reference If you've used previous versions of InDesign, you'll be familiar with the basic InDesign CS2 interface, so you can skim this chapter. But you may want to know specifically what is new in InDesign CS2. Appendix B lists all the changes in one convenient place.

The InDesign Application Folder

Often, users simply launch an application from an alias or shortcut and never even look in the application folder. This is just fine, until it comes time to install a new plug-in or to share important information with other users. Familiarizing yourself with the basic contents helps ensure that you're not throwing away anything important and that you're working with the correct files and folders.

◆   ◆   ◆   ◆

In This Chapter

Discovering what's inside the application folder

Exploring the document window

Using tools, panes, and palettes

Reviewing menu commands

◆   ◆   ◆   ◆

If you locate the InDesign application folder on your hard drive and open it, you'll see it's chock-full of stuff you may not even recognize. The three folders you need to know about in this folder are the Presets folder, the Plug-ins folder, and the Required folder.

The Presets folder

The Presets folder contains four kinds of standards: shortcut sets, color swatch libraries, scripts, and workspaces. InDesign lets you create shortcut sets so different users can have their own shortcut definitions; these preferences are stored in the InDesign Shortcut Sets folder in the Presets folder. The Swatch Libraries folder contains color-swatch libraries — both those that come with InDesign and any you might add yourself. The Scripts folder contains scripts that appear in the InDesign Scripts pane. Finally, the Workspaces folder contains workspace definitions; a *workspace* is a set of palettes and palette positions that you can save (for example, you can have all text-editing palettes appear when you're working on text).

Cross-Reference   I cover shortcut sets and workspaces in Chapter 3. I cover swatch libraries in Chapter 8. I cover scripts in Chapter 37.

The Plug-ins folder

The Plug-ins folder in the InDesign folder contains small software modules, called *plug-ins,* that add both core features and additional, optional features to InDesign. The Plug-ins folder contains a variety of subfolders such as Dictionaries, Filters, and Graphics that make locating files easy.

To install additional plug-ins from Adobe or other companies, add them to the Plug-ins folder. Follow the instructions provided by each vendor — some have an installation program, while others have you copy the plug-in file to the Plug-ins folder.

To remove a plug-in, simply click and drag it out of the subfolder of the Plug-ins folder and store it someplace else or delete it.

Tip   To keep track of required files and plug-ins versus optional ones, you may want to create an Optional Plug-ins folder and install any optional plug-ins there rather than in the existing folders in the Plug-ins folder.

You also use the Plug-ins folder to get access to any customizations you make to the spelling or hyphenation dictionaries in InDesign. These custom settings are saved in the files inside the Dictionaries folder. If you're in a workgroup, the only way to ensure that everyone is working with the same spelling and hyphenation standards — so that text flows the same way on everyone's computer — is to share the dictionary files.

Cross-Reference   See Chapter 35 for more information on maintaining standards across workgroups. See Chapter 36 for details on managing plug-ins.

The Required folder

The Required folder is similar to the Plug-ins folder in that it contains components of InDesign. The difference is that the components in the Required folder are necessary for InDesign to function, so you should not modify this folder or its contents.

Exploring the Document Window

When you're running InDesign, the first thing to do is create a new, empty document by choosing File ➪ New ➪ Document, or pressing ⌘+N or Ctrl+N, and clicking OK immediately. This gives you a document window so you can start exploring the application. (Never mind the settings for now — you're just exploring.)

No matter what size document you're dealing with or how many pages it has, all documents are contained within a standard window. The window provides controls that help in creating and placing objects, changing the view scale, and navigating between pages. Figure 2-1 shows all the standard elements of a new document window.

Title bar

The bar across the top of the window is known as the *title bar*. InDesign's title bar not only reports the name of the document, but also the magnification at which you're viewing it. For example, the words "Herb Article @ 68%" centered in the title bar mean that you're looking at an InDesign document file called "Herb Article" and you're viewing it at 68 percent — a typical percent value you'll land at when choosing View ➪ Fit Page in Window (⌘+0 [zero] or Ctrl+0 [zero]) on a 17-inch monitor. The title bar also includes three boxes for manipulating the document window, as shown in Figure 2-1.

Tip   Double-clicking the document title bar on the Mac minimizes the window. In Windows, it maximizes the window (or restores the window if it is already maximized).

Slight differences exist between the Macintosh and Windows interfaces for document windows. The Windows controls for window sizing appear in the upper-right corner rather than in the upper-left corner. In Windows, the Maximize button performs the same role as the Mac's Zoom button. Note that the Maximize button becomes the Restore button when the document window is *maximized* (made to fill the screen); the Restore button returns the window to its previous size. Also, in Windows, you can resize a window by clicking and dragging any side or corner, not just by clicking the Size button at the lower right. Figure 2-2 shows the Windows window-sizing controls.

New document windows always display a horizontal ruler across the top and a vertical ruler down the left side. The horizontal ruler measures from the top-left corner of the page across the entire spread; the vertical ruler measures from the top to the bottom of the current page.

You can use these rulers to judge the size and placement of frames and lines on your page. Although InDesign provides more precise methods for placing objects — such as the Transform pane and Control palette, in which you can enter exact values — designers often use the rulers for rough placement while they experiment with a design, as shown in Figure 2-3.

By default, both rulers display increments in picas, but you can change the measurement system for each ruler in the Units & Increments pane of the Preferences dialog box (choose InDesign ➪ Preferences on the Mac or Edit ➪ Preferences in Windows, or press ⌘+K or Ctrl+K). If you do this while no documents are open, the rulers in all new documents will appear in your preferred measurement systems. If a document is open, the rulers are changed only in that document.

Tools palette

Control palette

Zero point (ruler origin)

Close button

Minimize button   Title bar   Page margins   Palette menu

Zoom button   Rulers   Page boundary   Palette   Docked palettes

Pane tabs   Pane

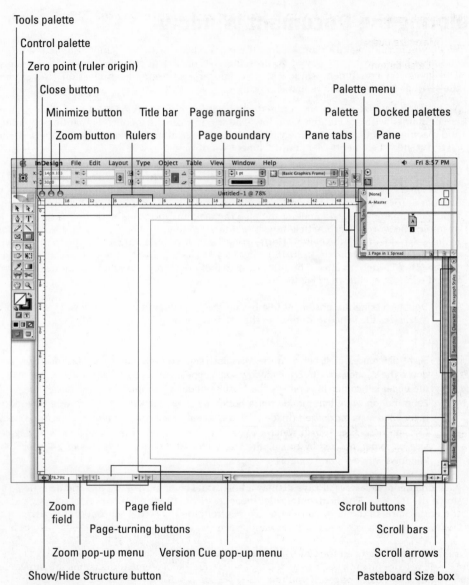

Zoom
field

Page field

Page-turning buttons

Zoom pop-up menu   Version Cue pop-up menu

Show/Hide Structure button

Scroll buttons

Scroll bars

Scroll arrows

Pasteboard Size box

Figure 2-1: The standard document window provides controls for managing documents on-screen, changing the view scale, displaying different pages, and placing objects on pages.

Figure 2-2: The Windows window-sizing controls

Minimize button

Maximize button

Close button

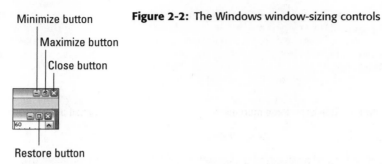

Restore button

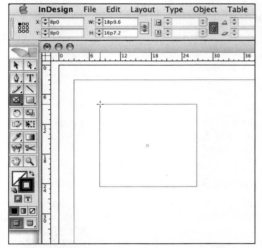

Figure 2-3: This box's top is aligned with the 8-pica mark on the vertical ruler.

Cross-Reference Chapter 3 explains ruler increments in more detail.

If you need more space on-screen or want to preview a design without all the layout tools, you can hide the rulers by choosing View ➪ Hide Rulers, or by pressing ⌘+R or Ctrl+R. Most users show the rulers all the time out of habit, but the rulers aren't really necessary in template-driven documents such as magazines where all the placement decisions are indicated by guides and master pages. If you're editing text on a smaller monitor, you might appreciate the space gain of not having rulers, minimal though it might be.

Zero point

The intersection of the rulers in the upper-left corner of the page is called the *zero point*. Known as the *ruler origin* in other applications, this is the starting place for all horizontal and vertical measurements. If you need to place items in relation to another spot on the page (for example, from the center of a spread rather than from the left-hand page), you can move the zero point by clicking and dragging it to a new location. The X and Y values in the Transform pane and Control palette update as you click and drag the zero point so you can place it precisely. The zero point is document-wide, so it changes for all pages or spreads in the document. To restore the zero point to the upper-left corner of the left-most page, double-click the intersection of the rulers in the upper-left corner.

After the zero point is moved, all the objects on the page display new X and Y values even though they haven't moved. Objects above or to the left of the zero point will have negative X and Y values, and the X and Y values of other objects will not relate to their actual position on the page or spread.

All this can be confusing, especially in a workgroup when other users may change the zero point and forget to restore it to the upper-left corner. To solve this problem, you can lock the ruler origin, making it more difficult for users to change it. Control+click or right-click the ruler origin and choose Lock Zero Point from the contextual menu. Granted, the Unlock Zero Point command is right there as well, so users can just as easily unlock it. But even though unlocking it is easy to undo, it's still worth using this feature, because some users won't know how to unlock it and others will be reminded that you don't want them messing with the zero point.

Scroll bars

Standard scroll bars run down the right side and across the bottom of the document window. As in most applications, you can either click and drag the scroll boxes or click the scroll arrows to move around on a page or move to other pages in the document.

Pasteboard, pages, and guides

Inside the rulers, you'll see a white area surrounding the black, drop-shadowed outlines of your pages (see Figure 2-1). The work area surrounding the page is called the *pasteboard,* and it's designed as a workspace for creating, experimenting with, and temporarily storing objects. You can also use the pasteboard to bleed objects off a page so they'll print to the edge of a trimmed page. Unlike PageMaker (and like QuarkXPress), each page or spread in InDesign has its own pasteboard. There's 1 inch of pasteboard above and below each page, and a space equal to the page width to the left and right of each page or spread. For example, a spread consisting of two 4-inch pages will have 4 inches of pasteboard to the left and 4 inches of pasteboard to the right.

Pages, drawn with black outlines, reflect the page size you set up in the New Document dialog box (File ➪ New ➪ Document, or ⌘+N or Ctrl+N). If it looks like two pages are touching, you're looking at a multipage spread. By default, you'll see magenta lines across the top and bottom of each page showing the top and bottom margins you specified when you created the document. Violet-colored lines indicate the left and right margins (for single-page documents) or inside and outside margins (for facing-page documents). These lines are nonprinting guides that can help you position objects.

You can change the placement of these guides by choosing Layout ➪ Margins and Columns, and you can create additional guides by clicking and dragging them off the horizontal and vertical rulers.

 Cross-Reference   I cover guides in detail in Chapter 4.

If you can't see the guide colors well, you can change them for all new documents. When no documents are open, choose new colors in the Guides & Pasteboard pane of the Preferences dialog box (choose InDesign ➪ Preferences on the Mac or Edit ➪ Preferences in Windows, or press ⌘+K or Ctrl+K). The Margins color changes the horizontal guides and the Columns color affects the vertical guides.

Show/Hide Structure button

The dual-arrow button at the bottom of the document window (see Figure 2-1), called the Show/Hide Structure button, opens and closes the XML Structure window, which is used in Web-oriented documents based on the Extensible Markup Language (XML).

Cross-Reference

I cover XML in Chapter 34.

Zoom field and pop-up menu

The lower-left corner of the document window contains the Zoom field and pop-up menu that lets you change the document's view scale. The view scale can be as small as 5 percent and as large as 4,000 percent, and you can modify it in 0.01 percent increments. You have three options for using the Zoom field and pop-up menu:

✦ To change the view to a preset value, click the arrow on the field and choose an option from the pop-up menu, as shown in Figure 2-4.

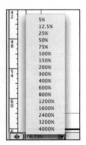

Figure 2-4: You can choose from a list of preset view percentages using the list in the Zoom pop-up menu.

✦ To change the view to a specific value, highlight the value in the field, type a new value, and press Return or Enter.

✦ To jump into the field quickly and type a specific value, press Option+⌘+5 or Ctrl+Alt+5, type a new value, and press Return or Enter. (This method lets you change the view without taking your hands off the keyboard.)

Version Cue pop-up menu

As Figure 2-5 shows, InDesign can show you the status of your document in the Version Cue version-management system that comes with InDesign CS2 and other Creative Suite 2 programs.

New Feature

This pop-up menu is new to InDesign CS2. Chapter 35 covers Version Cue in detail.

Version Cue is now turned on by default, which changes all dialog boxes for opening, importing, exporting, and saving files to let you access files in Version Cue folders, in which you can save multiple versions of the same file. As part of this, InDesign CS2 also adds the Version Cue pop-up menu that lets you see other versions and alternates, revert to the project's version of the file, and show the source file in the Adobe Bridge browser window or in the Finder (Mac) or Explorer (Windows) interface. At left is an information display that indicates the document's current Version Cue status.

If Version Cue is not enabled, or if the current document has not been saved to a Version Cue folder, most options will be grayed out.

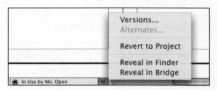

Figure 2-5: An unlabeled pop-up menu at the bottom of the document window lets you open other versions or alternates of your document, find the file in the Adobe Bridge browser or in the Mac Finder or Windows Explorer, or revert to the project's master version. To the left of this pop-up menu, InDesign displays the document's current Version Cue status.

Page controls

InDesign has several controls for maneuvering through pages: page-turning buttons, and the Page field and pop-up menu. There are also controls for entering prefixes for sections' page numbers and for indicating absolute page numbers in a document that contains multiple sections.

Page-turning buttons

Next to the Zoom pop-up menu, you'll find a combined page-number field and pop-up menu encased by two sets of arrows, shown in Figure 2-6. These arrows are page-turning buttons, which let you turn pages sequentially or jump to the first or last page in the document. From left to right, clicking these arrows takes you to the first page, the previous page, the next page, and the last page.

Figure 2-6: Buttons on the bottom of the document window (at right) let you flip from page to page. You can also use the Page pop-up menu to select a specific page.

Page field and pop-up menu

The document window also provides a control for jumping to a specific page or master page in a document. To jump to a specific page number, highlight the current number in the page number field, type a new page number, and press Return or Enter. A shortcut to highlighting the field is ⌘+J or Ctrl+J.

To jump to a master page, type the first few characters of the master page's name in the field. Jumping to document pages can be a little more complicated. Because the page number that displays and prints on the document page does not have to match the position of the page in the document — for example, the third page might be labeled *iii* instead of *3* — there are two methods for entering the page number you want to jump to: section page numbers and absolute page numbers.

You can also use the pop-up menu to the right of the page-number field to get a list of available pages, including master pages (see Figure 2-6).

Page navigation menus and shortcuts

InDesign also offers several menu commands and keyboard shortcuts to quickly navigate your layout, as Table 2-1 details.

Table 2-1: Page Navigation Menus and Shortcuts

Navigation	Menu Sequence	Macintosh Shortcut	Windows Shortcut
Go to first page	Layout ⇨ First Page	Shift+⌘+PgUp	Ctrl+Shift+Page Up
Go back one page	Layout ⇨ Previous Page	Shift+PgUp	Shift+Page Up
Go forward one page	Layout ⇨ Next Page or Layout ⇨ Go Forward	Shift+PgDn or ⌘+PgDn	Shift+Page Down or Ctrl+PgDn
Go to last page	Layout ⇨ Last Page	Shift+⌘+PgDn	Ctrl+Shift+Page Down
Go to last page viewed	Layout ⇨ Go Back	⌘+PgDn	Ctrl+PgDn
Go forward one spread	Layout ⇨ Next Spread	Option+PgDn	Alt+Page Down
Go back one spread	Layout ⇨ Previous Spread	Option+PgDn	Alt+Page Up

Section page numbers

A *section page number,* specified through the Numbering & Section Options dialog box (choose Layout ⇨ Numbering & Section Options or choose Numbering & Section Options in the Pages pane's palette menu) is a customized page number. You use section numbers if your document needs to start on a page other than 1 — for example, if you're working on a magazine and each article is saved in a different document. You can also split a single document into separate sections of page numbers, and use section page numbers to change the format of numbers to Roman numerals, letters, and so on.

To jump to or print a page with a section page number, you need to indicate which section it is and what page number appears on the page. InDesign provides a default name for sections, starting at Sec1. When you enter a section page number, you must separate the section name and the page number with a colon. For example, if you start the page numbering on page 51, you'll need to type **Sec1:51** in the page number field to jump to that page. Having to include this undisplayed section information makes this option fairly unappealing, so you may prefer to use absolute page numbers (see the following section).

Absolute page numbers

An *absolute page number* indicates a page's position in the document, such as 1 for the first page, 2 for the second page, and so on. To specify an absolute page number in the page number field or other dialog box (such as Print) that involves selecting pages, you type a plus sign before the number that represents the page's position. For example, the first page in the document is always +1, the second page is always +2, and so on. If you don't type a plus sign, the first page with the number 1 is what InDesign will assume you mean — although this may not be the first page in the document. For example, perhaps you have a 5-page section with Roman numerals followed by a 30-page section with Arabic numerals; type just **1** will go to the first page in the Arabic-numbered section, while entering **+1** will go to the first page in the document (*i*, in this case).

Using Tools

InDesign always displays a floating palette called the Tools palette (also sometimes referred to as the Toolbox by InDesign documentation), which contains 30 tools plus 13 other functions. It appears by default at the upper-left of the screen (see Figure 2-7). The tools let you create and manipulate the objects that make up your pages. The tools work similarly to those in other Adobe products (such as Photoshop, Illustrator, and PageMaker), and they work somewhat like the tools in QuarkXPress. But the tools do not work like the toolbars in your word processor, which are more like macros that make something happen. With InDesign's tools, for the most part, you select the tool and do something with it — draw a new frame, rotate a line, crop an image, and so on.

With so many tools, all of which perform limited functions, understanding what each tool does is imperative. When it comes to tools, InDesign has little intuition — it requires you to select the precise tool for the action you want to complete. The software is unable to predict that you might want to make a box slightly larger while you're editing text, or that you might want to reshape a frame at the same time you're resizing it. You need to learn which tool to use and get used to switching tools — a lot.

QuarkXPress User
The limited functionality of each tool may be familiar to PageMaker users but is likely to drive a QuarkXPress convert crazy. In recent years, QuarkXPress has made tools more flexible so users don't have to switch as often when they go from, for example, editing content to resizing the frame to better fit that content. If you're a QuarkXPress user, pay special attention to the tool definitions that follow so you can translate the InDesign tools to tools that you understand.

Using Tool Tips and keyboard shortcuts

To start getting familiar with the tools, first make sure that the Tool Tips pop-up menu is set to Normal or Fast in the General pane of the Preferences dialog box (choose InDesign ⇨ Preferences on the Mac or Edit ⇨ Preferences in Windows, or press ⌘+K or Ctrl+K). Point at each tool to learn its official name, as shown in Figure 2-7; let the pointer rest on the tool for a few seconds (if Tool Tips is set to Normal) and a Tool Tip appears, telling you the name and shortcut key of that tool. Knowing the actual name is the key to learning about any tool — after all, neither the InDesign documentation's index nor this book's index lists tools by the way they look (for example, little black pointer or empty square); instead, if you want to look up a tool, you need to know the tool's name (Selection tool or Rectangle tool, for example).

While you're learning the tool names, you'll notice a single letter in parentheses next to each tool name. This is the shortcut key to selecting that tool. For example, the (T) next to the Type tool indicates that pressing T selects the Type tool. The Tools palette's shortcuts don't use modifier keys like ⌘ and Ctrl. If you're editing text or otherwise have the Type tool selected — or if you're in a text-entry field in a pane or dialog box — typing these shortcuts will simply insert the text where your cursor is.

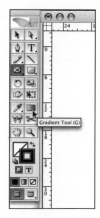

Figure 2-7: Tool Tips provide the names of tools along with the shortcut key (in parentheses) that you can use to select that tool.

Caution   If you're not careful, you can type nonsense text in your articles because of the way the Tools palette's shortcuts work (without having to press ⌘ or Ctrl). This shortcut makes no sense in a program that includes significant text-handling functionality. Adobe's graphics programs, such as Photoshop and Illustrator, use such single-letter shortcuts, which does make sense because artists rarely used text in them. Adobe has decided to standardize the interface across all its products, which in this case results in an unintuitive and potentially damaging approach.

Tip   To avoid typing these extra letters into your text, always use ⌘+click or Ctrl+click to click any-where on the page or pasteboard. This "releases" the live text that you were working on *before* typing a single-letter keyboard shortcut.

After you learn all the keyboard commands, you can create and refine a layout without ever reaching for the Tools palette. In no time, you'll be switching from the Scale tool to the Rotate tool with a quick punch of the R key, and then hitting T to add a text frame. Now, obviously, you can't use the keyboard commands for selecting tools while typing or editing text, but they are worth remembering for switching tools while designing a layout. In many production environments, copy editors handle text changes, while layout artists handle design issues. In such environments, the layout artists would learn these shortcuts, while the copy editors would avoid them.

Opening and closing the Tools palette

Opening and closing the Tools palette is easy. One method of opening (or closing) the Tools palette is to choose Window ➪ Tools. The other method of opening (or closing) the Tools palette is more obscure: Pressing the Tab key (with any tool but the Type tool selected) closes all open palettes, including the Tools palette. To reopen those palettes, press Tab again. To reopen just the Tools palette, choose Window ➪ Tools.

You can reposition the Tools palette by clicking and dragging it to a new location on-screen — make sure you drag it by its title bar. You can also change its orientation and appearance by double-clicking the title bar. The first double-click converts the Tools palette to be one icon wide rather than the default two icons wide. The second double-click rotates the Tools palette to horizontal orientation. A third double-click restores it to the standard two-icon-wide vertical orientation. (You can also set the display in the General pane of the Preferences dialog box, using the Floating Tools Palette pop-up menu.) Figure 2-8 shows the three options.

Figure 2-8: By clicking the Tools palette's title bar (in which there is no title), you can change its appearance and orientation.

Selecting tools

To select a tool and start using it, click it in the Tools palette. As long as you're not using the Type tool, you can also press a keyboard shortcut displayed in parentheses in the Tool Tips.

In addition to the tools you can see, the Tools palette contains a few hidden tools that are consolidated into little pop-out menus. Any tool with a small arrow in its lower-right corner is hiding one or more similar tools, as shown in Figure 2-9. To access hidden tools, click and hold on a tool that has a pop-out indicator. When the pop-out displays, click one of the new tools to replace the standard tool with the pop-out tool.

Note   Many of the pop-out tools also have keyboard shortcuts, as Figure 2-9 shows.

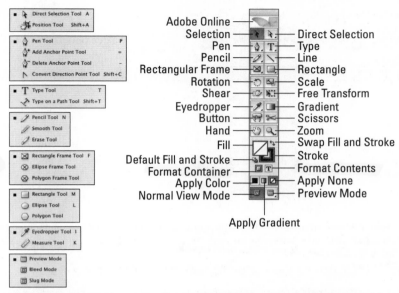

Figure 2-9: The Tools palette. If a small triangle appears in the lower-right corner of a tool, you can click and hold on it to display pop-out tools. Pop-outs are shown for all tools that have them, with the tool at the top the one that is the default tool for the Tools palette.

Tool definitions

In real life, you can often get by using the wrong tool for a job—using a flat screwdriver instead of a Phillips, or a shoe instead of a fly swatter. This won't work in InDesign. Whether you're typing text, reshaping an object, or applying a color, there's one—and only one—tool for each job. Loosely organized with the most commonly used tools at the top, the Tools palette includes tools for creating and manipulating frames and lines—the objects that make up your designs (see Figure 2-9).

Note   Frames are shapes and containers that you can size, position, and reshape with precision. InDesign has three types of frames: empty (unassigned) frames for blocks of color, text frames for type, and graphics frames for imported images. By default, most frames are empty but can be easily converted to text or graphics frames. Other frames are created specifically as text or graphics frames.

Adobe tool

In the Adobe world of software, the first item of the Tools palette is actually a big button that takes you to the Adobe Web site. A fairly large, prominent tool for something you can do just as easily many other ways, the Adobe tool does show the product icon so you always know from the Tools palette that InDesign is active.

Selection tool

The Selection tool (shortcut V) lets you select objects on the page and move or resize them. You might want to rename this tool in your mind to the Mover tool because it's the only tool that lets you drag objects around on-screen.

QuarkXPress User   Think of the Selection tool as half your Item tool.

Tip   If you're working with text and have the Type tool selected, you can switch to the Selection tool by holding down ⌘ or Ctrl, instead of using the Tools palette.

Here's how the Selection tool works:

✦ **To select any object on a document page,** click it. If you can't seem to click it, it might be an object placed by a *master page* (a preformatted page used to format pages automatically) or it might be behind another object.

✦ **To select an object placed by a master page,** press Shift+⌘ or Ctrl+Shift while you click.

✦ **To select an object that is completely behind another object,** ⌘+click it or Ctrl+click it.

✦ **To select multiple objects,** click and drag around the objects or Shift+click them individually. Because you need to press the Shift key anyway while selecting objects placed by master pages, you can always multiple-select those objects.

✦ **To move selected objects,** click somewhere within the objects and drag the mouse.

✦ **To resize a selected object,** click and drag any handle. Press Shift+⌘ or Ctrl+Shift while you drag to maintain the proportions of the object.

✦ **To resize both a selected frame and its graphic,** press ⌘ or Ctrl while you drag. Press Shift+⌘ or Ctrl+Shift to keep things proportional.

Tip   To resize multiple objects simultaneously, you must first group them (choose Object ➪ Group, or press ⌘+G or Ctrl+G). Otherwise, only the object whose handle is being dragged will resize. Ungroup by choosing Object ➪ Ungroup, or Shift+⌘+G or Ctrl+Shift+G.

Direct Selection tool

The Direct Selection tool (shortcut A) lets you select individual handles on objects to reshape them, and it lets you move graphics independently of their frames.

QuarkXPress User   Think of the Direct Selection tool as the other half of your Item tool and also as the Content tool for pictures.

Here's how the Direct Selection tool works:

✦ **To select an object to reshape it,** click it to display anchor points on the edges (the anchor points are hollow handles that you can select individually, as shown in Figure 2-10). You can drag the anchor points to reshape the object.

✦ **To select objects placed by a master page,** Shift+⌘+click or Ctrl+Shift+click, as with the Selection tool. The Direct Selection tool lets you easily select objects behind other objects and to select items within groups.

✦ **To select multiple objects,** click and drag around the objects or Shift+click them. Because you need to press the Shift key anyway while selecting objects placed by master pages, you can always multiple-select those objects.

✦ **To move a graphic within its frame,** click inside the frame and drag the graphic.

✦ **To move a frame leaving the graphic in place,** click an edge of the frame and drag it.

In addition to using the Selection tool for *threading* (linking) text frames (see Chapter 16), you can use the Direct Selection tool. This is one of the few cases where you have more than one tool to handle a task.

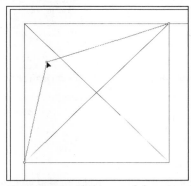

Figure 2-10: Clicking and dragging a hollow anchor point with the Direct Selection tool lets you reshape items.

Position tool

The Position tool is a renamed version of PageMaker's Crop tool. You access it from the pop-out menu in the Direct Selection tool. The Position tool combines some aspects of the Selection tool with some aspects of the Direct Selection tool:

✦ As with the Selection tool, you can resize an object's frame by dragging its handles.

✦ As with the Direct Selection tool, you can click a graphic and reposition it (crop it) within the frame by dragging.

The InDesign CS2 Tools palette adds the Position tool.

Pen tool

The Pen tool (shortcut P) lets you create paths consisting of straight and curved segments. Modeled after the pen tools in Illustrator and Photoshop, this is the tool for creating simple illustrations within InDesign.

If a path you create with the Pen tool is left open, the object is essentially a line that you can color or adjust stroke settings for. If the path is closed, the object is basically an empty frame. You can import text or graphics into the paths using the Place command (choose File ➪ Place, or press ⌘+D or Ctrl+D) or you can type into the path using the Type tool. If you decide to place text or graphics in an open path, the path closes automatically and becomes a frame. (To place text on a path, first select the Type on a Path tool [shortcut Shift+T], and then click the path.)

Here's how the Pen tool works:

✦ **To create straight segments of a path,** click to establish an anchor point, move the mouse to the next location, click again, and so on. To move an anchor point after clicking, press the spacebar and drag the segment.

✦ **To create curved segments of a path,** click and drag, and then release the mouse button to end the segment.

✦ **To close a path and create a frame,** click over the first anchor point created (the hollow one).

✦ **To leave a path open and create a line,** ⌘+click or Ctrl+click away from the path or select another tool.

The Pen tool includes a pop-out menu containing three additional tools for reshaping lines and frames: Add Anchor Point (shortcut =), Delete Anchor Point (shortcut - [hyphen]), and Convert Direction Point (shortcut Shift+C).

Cross-Reference   For more information about using these tools, see Chapters 25 and 26.

Type tool

The Type tool (shortcut T) lets you type, edit, and format text. The Type tool also lets you create rectangular text frames as you need them.

QuarkXPress User   Think of the Type tool as a combination of the Rectangle Text Box tool and the Content tool for text — except remember that by itself, it doesn't let you do anything else such as resizing a frame. However, if you press and hold the ⌘ or Ctrl key, the frame's control points will appear, allowing you to resize it. When you are done resizing it, release the ⌘ or Ctrl key to return to editing text in the frame.

Here's how the Type tool works:

✦ **To create a rectangular text frame,** click and drag; hold the Shift key to create a perfect square.

✦ **To begin typing or editing text,** click in a text frame or in any empty frame.

✦ **To highlight text so you can format it,** cut and paste it, drag-move it, and so on.

✦ **To select a word,** double-click anywhere in the word.

✦ **To select a paragraph,** triple-click anywhere in the paragraph.

✦ **To select all the text in a *story* (a series of threaded text frames),** choose Edit ➪ Select All or press ⌘+A or Ctrl+A.

You can place or drag and drop text files, and you can *thread* (link) text frames with either of the selection tools, but they won't let you touch the text.

Type on a Path tool

The Type tool has a pop-out menu to select the Type on a Path tool (shortcut Shift+T), which lets you select a path or frame and type text onto it so it follows the path or frame's outline.

Line tool

The Line tool (shortcut E) lets you draw free-standing lines (rules) on your page. To use this tool, simply click it and drag the mouse. You can use the rulers, the Control palette, or the Transform pane to size and position the line precisely. Pressing the Shift key while you click and drag constrains the line angle to 45-degree increments, which is useful for creating straight horizontal and vertical lines.

Frame tools

There are three frame tools — Rectangle Frame (shortcut F), Ellipse Frame, and Polygon Frame — in InDesign. Their icons are distinguished by a large *X* inside. The latter two tools, which have no shortcuts, are available from the Rectangle Frame tool's pop-up menu. The frames created by these tools are meant to hold either pictures or text. To create frames with these tools, click and drag using the rulers or information in the Transform pane or Control palette to judge the size and placement. To create a perfect circle with the Ellipse Frame tool or a perfect square with the Rectangle Frame tool, press the Shift key while you click and drag.

You can fill and stroke the empty frames for use as design elements or you can import text and graphics into them using the Place command (File ⇨ Place, or ⌘+D or Ctrl+D). You can also click in an empty frame with the Type tool to begin typing in it.

QuarkXPress User The InDesign frame tools are the same as picture- and text-box tools in QuarkXPress, except that InDesign's frames can hold either type of content, so there are not two variants of these tools in InDesign as there are in QuarkXPress.

To create a rectangle or ellipse, you click somewhere in the document window and drag the mouse to another location. The rectangle or ellipse fills the area. But creating a polygon frame works differently:

1. **Double-click the Polygon tool to display the Polygon Settings dialog box, shown in Figure 2-11.**

2. **Type a value between 3 and 100 in the Number of Sides field to specify how many sides you want on your polygon.**

3. **If you want to create a star shape, use the Star Inset field to specify the size of the spikes.** The percent value specifies the distance between the polygon's bounding box and the insides of the spikes (for example, typing **50%** creates spikes that are halfway between the bounding box and the center of the polygon).

4. **Click OK to close the Polygon Settings dialog box.** The settings are saved with the active document for the next time you use the Polygon tool.

5. **Click and drag to create the polygon, using the rulers or the Transform pane or Control palette to judge the size and placement.**

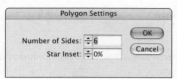

Figure 2-11: Double-clicking the Polygon tool displays the Polygon Settings dialog box, which you can use to specify the number of sides on a polygon, as well as any starburst spike settings.

Tip

To create a symmetrical polygon, in which all the sides are the same size, press the Shift key while you click and drag the Polygon tool.

Shape tools

If you'd rather create actual shapes, use the Rectangle (shortcut M), Ellipse (shortcut L), or Polygon tools. (The Ellipse and Polygon tools are pop-out tools available from the Rectangle tool.) The tools are meant to create shapes that you will use as artwork, rather than as containers. But you can place text or graphics into one of these shapes the same way as you would a frame. Essentially, the shape tools are superfluous and can be ignored.

Rotate tool

The Rotate tool (shortcut R) lets you change the angle of selected items visually. To use the Rotate tool, first select an item with the Selection tool or the Direct Selection tool, and then select the Rotate tool. Or ⌘+click or Ctrl+click an object with the Rotate tool. Click and drag in any direction. The object rotates from the default location of the control point, as shown in Figure 2-12.

The control point is indicated through the nine boxes in the upper left of the Control palette or Transform pane—the black square is the current control point from which the rotation will pivot and from which all coordinates originate. Just click whatever square you want to be the control point. You can also click and drag the control point to a new location for a custom rotation.

Tip

To rotate an object in 45-degree increments, press the Shift key while you click and drag.

Scale tool

The Scale tool (shortcut S) lets you grab any object and resize it horizontally, vertically, or proportionally. When you scale text or graphics frames, the size of the text and image are resized as well. As with the Rotate tool, the Scale tool doesn't let you select items to scale. You either need to select an object first with a selection tool, or ⌘+click or Ctrl+click it with the Scale tool.

The Scale tool works as follows:

✦ **To make an object wider,** click and drag to the left.

✦ **To make an object narrower,** click and drag to the right.

✦ **To make an object taller,** click and drag down.

✦ **To make an object shorter,** click and drag up.

✦ **To resize an object both horizontally and vertically,** click and drag up or down diagonally.

✦ **To resize an object proportionally,** press Shift while you drag.

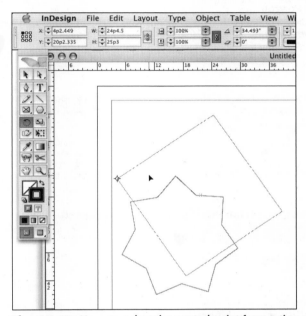

Figure 2-12: You can select the control point for rotating items, not just use the center of an object. Here, the upper left control point is selected in the Control palette.

Shear tool

The Shear tool (shortcut O) works much the same as the Scale tool. Instead of resizing the object and contents, the Shear tool slants selected objects in the direction you drag. But it also rotates the object, creating a more 3D-like perspective effect.

Free Transform tool

The Free Transform tool (shortcut E) is handy because it lets you move, rotate, and reshape objects all with one tool. If you click and hold the mouse within the object, you can drag it. If you click any of the handles on the object frame, you can resize it. If you click and hold on any edge (except where there is a handle) or anywhere outside the object, you can rotate the object.

Measure tool

The Measure tool, which has no shortcut, opens the Info pane and lets you draw a line whose dimensions appear in that pane so you can measure an arbitrary distance. You can see objects' dimensions in the Control palette and in the Transform and Info panes, but the value of the Measure tool is in determining the distance between objects rather than the dimensions of objects. It can also come in handy when measuring the distance across multiple objects.

Scissors tool

The Scissors tool (shortcut C) lets you cut paths into separate paths. When you cut an open path (a line), you get two separate lines. When you cut a closed path in one place, you get an open path. When you cut a closed path (a frame) in two places, you get two closed paths containing the same contents. Note that you cannot cut paths containing text.

To use the Scissors tool, ⌘+click or Ctrl+click an object to select it. Then do the following:

✦ **To cut a path,** click anywhere on the path. The path will not appear to be cut until you click and drag an anchor point with either the Selection tool or the Direct Selection tool.

✦ **To divide a frame into two separate frames,** click two different locations on a path.

Eyedropper tool

The Eyedropper tool (shortcut I) displays the color settings for the object at the location you click with it. This is handy way to find out the color makeup of imported graphics so you can then create a color swatch that matches it exactly.

 Cross-Reference   I cover color and gradients in Chapter 8.

Gradient tool

The Gradient tool (shortcut G) lets you change the direction of existing gradient fills or strokes applied to objects. To apply gradients to objects, you use the Gradient pane (accessible by clicking Window ➪ Gradient) as discussed in Chapter 8.

To change the gradient direction, follow these steps:

1. **Select an object.**

2. **Click either the Fill button or the Stroke button (immediately below the Gradient tool) to indicate the location of the gradient you want to change.**

3. **Select the Gradient tool.**

4. **Click within the object at the start point, and then drag to the end point.** You can drag from the inside out, from top to bottom, from left to right, and so on, depending on the effect you want to achieve.

Button tool

The Button tool, which has no shortcut, creates rectangular frames that are used as buttons in Acrobat forms, which you can create in InDesign.

Hand tool

The Hand tool (shortcut H) lets you scoot pages around to view a different portion of a page or another page entirely. The Hand tool is an entirely visual method of scrolling, allowing you to see the page contents at all times. To use the Hand tool, click and drag in any direction. You can access the Hand tool temporarily without actually switching tools by pressing Option+spacebar or Alt+spacebar.

Zoom tool

The Zoom tool (shortcut Z) lets you increase and decrease the document view scale. You can highlight a specific area on a page to change its view or you can click on-screen to change the view scale within InDesign's preset increments (shown in the Zoom field and pop-up menu in the lower-left corner of the document window).

The Zoom tool works as follows:

✦ **To increase the view scale by a preset increment,** click on-screen.

✦ **To increase the view scale of an area,** click and drag around it.

✦ **To decrease the view scale by a preset increment,** Option+click or Alt+click on-screen.

✦ **To decrease the view scale of an area,** press Option or Alt while you click and drag around it.

Tip

You can access the Zoom tool temporarily without actually switching tools by pressing ⌘+spacebar or Ctrl+spacebar to zoom in and Option+⌘+spacebar or Ctrl+Alt+spacebar to zoom out.

You can also use ⌘+-- or Ctrl+-- to zoom in and ⌘+- (hyphen) or Ctrl+- (hyphen) to zoom out, or choose View ➪ Zoom In or View ➪ Zoom Out.

Color buttons

The bottom portion of the Tools palette contains buttons for applying colors to the edges of objects (strokes) and the insides of objects (fills). You use these buttons with the Stroke, Color, Gradient, and Swatches panes to apply and experiment with the colors applied to objects. See Figure 2-9 for an illustration of these buttons.

Here's how the color buttons work:

✦ **To modify the fill (or background) of the selected object,** click the Fill button.

✦ **To modify the stroke (or outside edges) of the selected object,** click the Stroke button. (The shortcut X toggles between the Fill and Stroke buttons.)

✦ **Once you've clicked the Stroke or Fill button, use the Color, Swatches, or Gradient panes to apply a new color or gradient.**

✦ **To switch the color and/or gradient of the stroke and fill,** click the Swap Fill Stroke button or use the shortcut Shift+X.

✦ **To revert the selected object to InDesign's default of a white fill and a black stroke,** click the Default Fill/Stroke button or use the shortcut D.

✦ **To apply the last color used in the Swatches or Color pane,** click the Color button or use the shortcut <, (comma).

✦ **To apply the last gradient pattern used in the Swatches or Gradient pane,** click the Gradient button or use the shortcut , (comma).

✦ **To remove the stroke or fill from an object,** click None or use the shortcut /.

View buttons

At the very bottom of the Tools palette are the two view buttons: Normal View Mode and Preview Mode. The first shows the pasteboard, margins, and guidelines, while the second hides those to give an unadorned preview of the final document.

There are two preview options available via a pop-up menu in the Preview Mode button: Bleed mode and Slug mode. Bleed mode shows any objects that bleed beyond the page boundaries, while Slug mode shows the space reserved for information such as crop marks and color separation names used in final output. You set these up when you create new documents or by choosing File ➪ Document Setup.

Working with Palettes and Panes

Initially, software developers used floating palettes to provide convenient access to commonly used options such as colors, fonts, and styles. Palettes provide a more interactive method of working with features, because the screen is not obscured by a large dialog box and you can access the controls quickly. Eventually, palettes started to move away from serving as a convenient alternative to commands and became the primary method — often the *only* method — for performing many tasks.

Panes versus palettes

Using an approach pioneered by Photoshop, InDesign's palettes are often composed of multiple panes. Each pane has a tab (like a file folder does) that you click to switch to that pane. InDesign lets you drag panes from one palette to another, as well as to anywhere on-screen (creating a new palette with just the one pane). That makes the distinction between a palette and a pane somewhat artificial. In this book, I use *palette* to refer to the entity that holds one or more panes, or for entities like the Tools and Control palettes that are self-contained floating objects. I refer to *panes* as anything that can be made a pane, even if you might have made it into its own palette (for example, I still call the Transform pane the *Transform pane*, even if I move it into its own palette).

Almost every palette (whether it contains one pane or many panes) has a palette menu that provides a pop-up menu of options specific to that pane. (It is much like a contextual menu.) The palette menu's options are specific to the current pane.

Note   The word *pane* has another use in InDesign. A pane is also a specific area in a dialog box. Such multipane dialog boxes also have tabs (and in some cases, option lists) that let you switch among the panes. Having multiple panes in a dialog box lets Adobe fit more functionality into the same space on-screen.

There are so many panes in InDesign — even more than in previous versions — that you might want to consider hooking up a second monitor for displaying them. And break out the computer glasses and your decoder ring, because the panes are small and laden with mysterious icons.

As with the tools, if you make sure Tool Tips is selected in the General pane of the Preferences dialog box (choose InDesign ➪ Preferences on the Mac or Edit ➪ Preferences in Windows, or press ⌘+K or Ctrl+K), you'll get some pretty good hints as to what the pane icons and fields do.

Managing palettes

Because there are so many panes in InDesign CS2—26 standard palettes including the Tools palette and *not* including any libraries or any of the 12 panes you might make into their own palettes—you're not going to want them all open all the time. In fact, the palettes would more than fill an entire screen if they were all open. Therefore, you might have some palettes you leave open all the time, some you open only while formatting text, and some that you open and close for one-time uses. As you become familiar with the palettes, you'll discover which ones you want to keep open.

New Feature InDesign CS2 adds the PageMaker Toolbar palette, which is covered in Appendix D, and the Quick Apply palette, which is covered in Chapters 11 and 19, as well as the Object Styles pane (covered in Chapter 11) and the Data Merge pane (covered in Chapter 15).

Many palettes actually consist of multiple panes, such as the default combination of the Transform, Character, and Paragraph panes. You can create different combinations of panes to customize the palettes.

Tip To try to gain some control over InDesign's palette profligacy, you can create *workspaces,* which are essentially memorized palette collections. Display the palettes you want, where you want them, and create a new workspace by choosing Window ➪ Workspace ➪ Save Workspace. Give it a name that makes sense, such as Text Palettes. That workspace is now available by clicking Window ➪ Workspace ➪ *workspace name,* automatically displaying just those saved palettes in their saved locations. By having several such workspaces, you can quickly switch among collections of palettes based on the tasks you're focused on.

Here's how panes work in InDesign:

✦ **To open a pane,** choose its menu command (such as Window ➪ Swatches). Some panes have keyboard shortcuts, as indicated in the menu. Opening a pane will open a palette, which might contain other panes. If a palette containing the desired pane is already open, InDesign will make the desired pane active in that open palette.

✦ **To close a floating palette,** click its Close box in the upper-left corner (Macintosh) or upper-right corner (Windows). This closes all the panes in the palette. (You can't close a pane that's part of a palette with other panes. To get rid of such a pane, you either close the palette and all its panes, or you drag the pane to its own palette and then close that new palette.)

✦ **To shrink a floating palette down to the names of the panes within it,** click its Zoom button (Macintosh) or Minimize button (Windows).

✦ **To shrink a docked palette,** double-click any of its tabs.

✦ **To move a palette,** click and drag its title bar. (A docked palette can only be moved up or down along the screen side on which it is docked.)

✦ **To select a different pane in a palette,** click its tab.

✦ **To combine the panes of different palettes,** drag and drop a pane's tab into another palette.

✦ **To pull a pane out of a palette into its own,** drag and drop its tab out of the palette into its own palette.

Note
A few palettes contain arrows in the lower-right corner that you can click and drag to resize the palette, and some palette menus let you change the orientation of the palette from horizontal to vertical.

A few palettes also use a double-arrow character next to the pane name to indicate that there is more to the pane than may be displayed; click the pane title to expand or collapse those extra options.

You can dock panes to either side of the monitor, not just the right side, as Figure 2-13 shows. To collapse a pane into a side tab, click on the palette's tab and drag it to an edge of your screen. To open the pane, click its tab. To collapse the pane, double-click its tab. To separate a pane from the screen edge, drag the tab out from the side of your screen or move it into a palette.

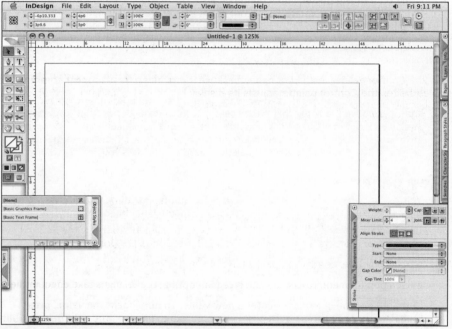

Figure 2-13: The side-tabs feature lets you dock pane tabs at the sides of the monitor window and click the tab names to open them when needed.

When you install InDesign, three palettes are placed along the right side of your screen by default; they contain the Pages, Layers, and Info panes; the Swatches, Character Styles, and Paragraph Styles panes; and the Stroke, Color, Transparency, and Gradient panes. If you open other panes, they will open as floating panes rather than be aligned to the side of the screen, but you can always move them to a screen edge if you prefer that placement.

Marrying and Divorcing Palette Panes

Although it may seem as if combining and splitting panes is the antidote to InDesign's palette-itis, the resulting palettes can be difficult to work with. Combined panes can become cumbersome: If you combine panes that have different default sizes or orientations, each time you click a different pane the palette changes its size — this can be fairly disorienting. Plus, you can't see and reach for different types of options as easily, because you have to activate different panes. On the other hand, splitting panes into too many separate palettes can leave you with an overwhelming number of palettes.

In general, you'll want to split palettes that you use often and combine or close panes that you use rarely. And you might change the palette configuration based on the type of document. If you're working on a movie poster, you'll definitely want the Navigator pane but might have little use for the Pages pane. Or if you're laying out a newsletter that is formatted exclusively with styles, you might as well close the Character and Paragraph panes.

Use the workspaces feature to save different pane and palette configurations for different points in the workflow or for different kinds of documents.

Also use the Control palette instead of panes because it provides access to most common functions. Even better, the Control palette adjusts its display based on what the current object is, so you get just the relevant options. For example, when you select a text frame, the Control palette provides the most functions of the Transform, Character Style, Character, Paragraph, Paragraph Styles, and Stroke panes.

Using panes

To use a pane, first you need to activate it. You can do this by clicking its tab (if the palette containing it is open) or by choosing its menu command in the Window menu (if the pane is not open or if another pane in that palette is active). You'll need to be on the lookout here — if a menu command brings a pane forward in a palette, you might not even notice.

When a pane is active, controls in panes have the following characteristics:

✦ Click a pop-up menu to display and select an option; the changes take effect immediately.

✦ Highlight a value in a field to enter a new value. To implement the value, press Shift+Return or Shift+Enter. Or you can press Tab to move to the next field or Shift+Tab to the previous field. Or just click in a different field or elsewhere in the document. To get out of a field you've modified, leaving the object unscathed, press Esc.

✦ Some fields include up and down arrows that you can click to increase or decrease the value in the field.

✦ Fields accept values in all different measurement systems. (I discuss this in detail in Chapter 3.)

✦ In addition to typing values in fields, you can enter calculations. You can add to, subtract from, multiply, and divide values in fields using the following operators: +, −, * (multiply), and / (divide). For example, to reduce the width of a frame by half, you might type **/2** next to the current value of 4.5 inches in the Width field. Or, to increase the length of a line by 6 points, you can type **+6** next to the current value in the Length field.

Tip You can also use percentages in fields, such as **50%**, which adjusts the current value by that percentage.

✦ Most panes provide a full menu that you can display by clicking the arrow in the upper-right corner. The *palette menu* provides commands related to the current pane's contents (for example, the Object Styles pane provides a command for creating a new style, as shown in Figure 2-14).

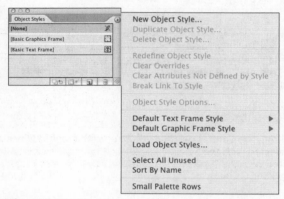

Figure 2-14: Most panes include palette menus that provide access to related features.

Checking out the panes

Like the tools in InDesign, each pane has a distinct function. The use of each pane is covered in detail in the appropriate chapters throughout this book (for example, the Layers pane is covered in Chapter 6). But with the help of Tool Tips and a quick introduction to their primary purpose, you can start using many of the panes to start performing basic functions.

Tip All but one of the text-oriented panes are available from the Type menu: Character, Character Styles, Glyphs, Index, Paragraph, Paragraph Styles, Tabs, and Table. (The Table pane is not available here, but that's because it has its own Table menu for access to its controls.) This provides faster access than accessing them through the Window ➪ Type & Tables submenu.

Here is a quick summary of the InDesign palettes and panes (all available through the Window menu unless otherwise indicated). Note that in the figures of the various panes, the full pane is shown for any that have the option of showing just some options; these panes have a double-arrow to the right of the pane name.

✦ **Tools palette.** As covered earlier in this chapter, this palette is the mechanism by which you select the appropriate tool to accomplish various layouts tasks.

✦ **Control palette (Option+⌘+6 or Ctrl+Alt+6).** This is one of the most useful features in InDesign. It combines many attributes about the currently selected object so you can minimize the use of other panes and menu items. The palette changes based on what is selected, as seen in Figure 2-15.

QuarkXPress User

The Control palette by default is docked to the top of the screen. QuarkXPress users might want to float it at the bottom to mimic QuarkXPress's interface.

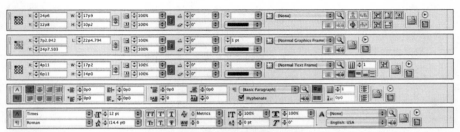

Figure 2-15: From top to bottom, the Control palette for frames with graphics, lines and text paths, frames with text selected with the Selection or Direct Selection tool, frames and text paths with text selected with the Type tool (with each of the two variations of the Control palette for text displayed)

✦ **Links pane (shortcut Shift+⌘+D or Ctrl+Shift+D).** The Links pane shows the original location of imported graphics and text files (see Figure 2-16).

✦ **Character pane (Window ➪ Type & Tables ➪ Character, or press ⌘+T or Ctrl+T).** Use this pane (shown in Figure 2-18) to change common attributes of highlighted text such as the font, size, leading, kerning, tracking, and scaling.

✦ **Paragraph pane (Window ➪ Type & Tables ➪ Paragraph, or press Option+⌘+T or Ctrl+Option+T).** Use this pane (shown in Figure 2-17) to change common attributes of selected paragraphs such as the alignment, indents, space before and after, and hyphenation.

✦ **Character Styles pane (Window ➪ Type & Tables ➪ Character Styles or press Shift+F11).** Use this pane (shown in Figure 2-18) to create and apply styles consisting of character-level formats.

✦ **Paragraph Styles pane (Window ➪ Type & Tables ➪ Paragraph Styles or press F11).** Use this pane (shown in Figure 2-18) to create and apply styles consisting of paragraph-level formats.

✦ **Object Styles pane.** Use this pane (shown in Figure 2-18) to create and apply styles for frames, lines, and other objects.

New Feature

The Object Styles pane is new to InDesign CS2.

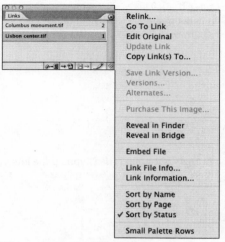

Figure 2-16: The Links pane

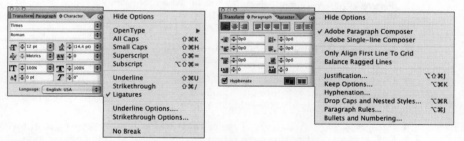

Figure 2-17: The Character pane (left) and the Paragraph pane (right)

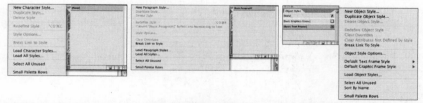

Figure 2-18: The Character Styles pane (left), Paragraph Styles pane (center), and Object Styles pane (right)

✦ **Tabs pane (Window ⇨ Type & Tables ⇨ Tabs, or press Shift+⌘+T or Ctrl+Shift+T).**
This pane (shown in Figure 2-19) lets you create tab stops for selected paragraphs; you can also specify alignment, position, and leader characters for the tabs.

✦ **Story pane (Window ⇨ Type & Tables ⇨ Story).** It's small but important — the Story pane (shown in Figure 2-19) lets you specify hanging punctuation for all the frames in a story by checking Optical Margin Alignment. You can also change the type size if the need arises.

Figure 2-19: The Tabs pane (left) and the Story pane (right)

✦ **Glyphs pane (Window ⇨ Type & Tables ⇨ Glyphs).** The Glyphs pane lets you access special characters within a font. Figure 2-20 shows the Glyphs pane.

Figure 2-20: The Glyphs pane

✦ **Text Wrap pane (shortcute Option+⌘+W or Ctrl+Alt+W).** The Text Wrap pane (shown in Figure 2-21) provides intuitive buttons for controlling how text runs around selected objects.

✦ **Transform pane (Window ⇨ Object & Layout ⇨ Transform or press F9).** This pane (shown in Figure 2-21) lets you specify size, placement, scale, rotation, and shear of selected objects.

✦ **Align pane (Window ⇨ Object & Layout ⇨ Align or -Shift+F7).** The Align pane (shown in Figure 2-21) provides buttons that let you evenly distribute or realign multiple-selected objects with one click.

Figure 2-21: The Text Wrap pane (left), the Transform pane (center), and the Align pane (right)

✦ **Pages pane (shortcut F12).** Use this pane (shown in Figure 2-22) to create master pages and to add, rearrange, and delete document pages. You can also create sections of page numbers using the Pages pane's palette menu.

✦ **Layers pane (shortcut F7).** The Layers pane (shown in Figure 2-22) provides access to vertical slices of a document that you can use to control the stacking order of objects, to isolate specific portions of a design, or to store revisions of the same document.

✦ **Navigator pane (Window ➪ Object & Layout ➪ Navigator).** The Navigator pane (shown in Figure 2-22) shows a color proxy version of pages and lets you isolate a portion of any page to display in the document window.

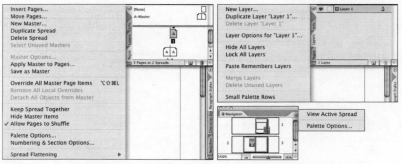

Figure 2-22: The Pages pane (left), the Layers pane (upper right), and the Navigator pane (lower right)

✦ **Swatches pane (shortcut F5).** The Swatches pane (shown in Figure 2-23) lets you create named colors such as those using Pantone, Focoltone, and Toyo inks, and apply the colors to text, strokes, and fills.

✦ **Stroke pane (shortcut F10).** Use the Stroke pane (shown in Figure 2-23) to outline the edges of frames and lines; you have control over the thickness and the pattern of the outlines.

✦ **Color pane (shortcut F6).** The Color pane (shown in Figure 2-23) lets you create LAB, CMYK, and RGB colors, and apply the colors to text, strokes, and fills. (LAB, CMYK, and RGB are all composite color models, in which all colors are made by mixing a small number of primary colors. Chapters 8 and 42 describe these models in detail.)

✦ **Gradient pane.** Use the Gradient pane (shown in Figure 2-23) to create a stroke or fill consisting of a graduated blend between two colors.

✦ **Attributes pane.** The Attributes pane (shown in Figure 2-23) lets you specify that the stroke or fill in selected objects overprints the background.

✦ **Table pane (Window ➪ Type & Tables ➪ Table or Shift+F9).** The Table pane (shown in Figure 2-24) lets you adjust table settings.

✦ **Index pane (Window ➪ Type & Tables ➪ Index or Shift+F8).** The Index pane (shown in Figure 2-24) lets you add and manage index and table-of-contents entries.

✦ **Data Merge pane (Window ➪ Automation ➪ Data Merge).** The Data Merge pane (shown in Figure 2-24) lets you import data for use in form letters, labels, and other documents that use the same layout for variable text.

New Feature

The Data Merge pane is new to InDesign CS2.

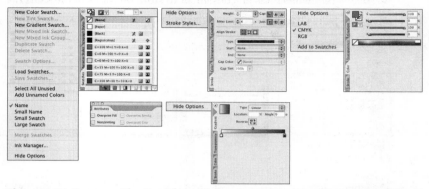

Figure 2-23: Top row: The Swatches, Stroke, and Color panes. Bottom row: The Attributes and Gradient panes

Figure 2-24: The Table pane (left), the Index pane (center), and the Data Merge pane (right)

✦ **Scripts pane (Window ➪ Automation ➪ Scripts).** The Scripts pane (shown in Figure 2-25) shows available AppleScripts and Java scripts in the Scripts folder in the InDesign folder.

✦ **Script Label pane (Window ➪ Automation ➪ Script Labels).** The Script Label pane (shown in Figure 2-25) lets you change the label of an object for use by scripts.

Figure 2-25: The Scripts pane (left) and the Script Label pane (right)

✦ **Pathfinder pane (Window ➪ Object & Layout ➪ Pathfinder).** This pane (shown in Figure 2-26) lets you manipulate paths, such as combining, separating, and otherwise working with open and closed paths. It also now lets you convert shapes.

The ability to convert shapes is new to InDesign CS2.

Figure 2-26: The Pathfinder pane

✦ **Transparency pane (shortcut Shift+F10).** This pane (shown in Figure 2-27) lets you adjust the solidity of images to create fading and overlap effects.

✦ **Flattener Preview pane (Window ➪ Output ➪ Flattener).** This pane (shown in Figure 2-27) lets you see what page items (typically those with transparency) are *flattened* (made solid) during printing or exporting to Encapsulated PostScript (EPS), Scalable Vector Graphics (SVG, a vector format for the Web), or Portable Document Format (PDF) formats. Flattening occurs for printing devices and graphics export formats that don't support transparency.

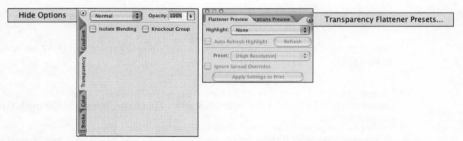

Figure 2-27: The Transparency pane (left) and the Flattener Preview pane (right)

✦ **Separations Preview pane (Window ➪ Output ➪ Separations or Shift+F6).** This pane (shown in Figure 2-28) lets you see page items with various color plates enabled, as well as preview the effects of different ink densities.

✦ **Trap Presets pane (Window ➪ Output ➪ Trap Presets).** The Trap Presets pane (shown in Figure 2-28) lets you set and apply different trapping settings to objects, which controls how abutting and overlapping objects print to avoid gaps caused by paper-feed variations during printing.

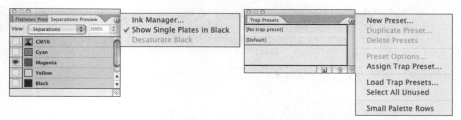

Figure 2-28: The Separations Preview pane (left) and the Trap Presets pane (right)

✦ **Info pane (press F8).** This pane (shown in Figure 2-29) shows some of the characteristics — such as size, position, and cropping — of selected objects.

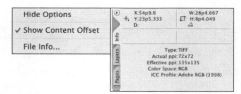

Figure 2-29: The Info pane

✦ **Bookmarks pane (Window ➪ Interactive ➪ Bookmarks).** This pane (shown in Figure 2-30) creates the bookmarks used in PDF files to create clickable indexes and tables of contents.

✦ **Hyperlinks pane (Window ➪ Interactive ➪ Hyperlinks).** The Hyperlinks pane (shown in Figure 2-30) lets you set up hyperlinks from and to document objects and pages, as well as to World Wide Web locations.

✦ **Tags pane.** The Tags pane (shown in Figure 2-30) lets you add XML tags and map them to paragraph and character styles. XML tags determine the formatting for XML data sources used in XML documents.

✦ **States pane (Window ➪ Interactive ➪ States).** This pane (shown in Figure 2-30) sets button actions for both Web pages and PDF files.

✦ **Quick Apply palette (Edit ➪ Quick Apply, or ⌘+Return or Ctrl+Enter).** This palette (shown in Figure 2-31) lets you access paragraph, character, and object styles from a single location; plus it lets you use the keyboard to select and apply them, making it easier to apply styles to text when editing with the keyboard (no need to switch to the mouse and back).

New Feature

The Quick Apply palette is new to InDesign CS2. Chapters 11 and 19 cover its use.

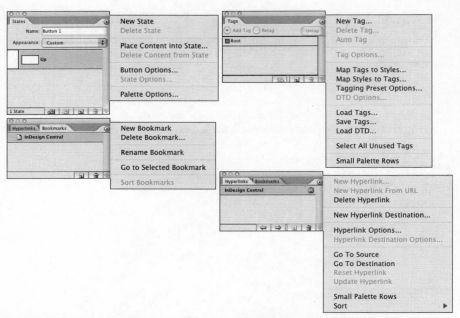

Figure 2-30: Top row: The States and Tags panes. Bottom row: The Bookmarks and Hyperlinks panes

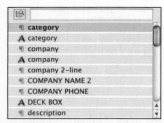

Figure 2-31: The Quick Apply palette

Reviewing Menu Commands

With so many palettes and panes, menu commands take on a more secondary function in InDesign. Many menu commands do nothing but display a palette or bring a pane of a palette forward. But to get comfortable in InDesign, you need to know the basic function of each menu.

QuarkXPress User

If you're switching from QuarkXPress, you might get lost in the menus, so charts in Appendixes C and D of this book — which cover how to make the move from QuarkXPress or PageMaker to InDesign — show the equivalent menus.

InDesign menu

Available only on Mac OS X, the InDesign menu, shown in Figure 2-32, contains preference and plug-in settings, as well as the command to exit the program and to hide it. The Services menu option contains Mac OS X functions, not any InDesign-specific options.

 The InDesign menu is available only on the Mac. In Windows, the About InDesign and Configure Plug-ins menu options reside in the Help menu, the Preferences menu option resides in the Edit menu, and the Quit InDesign menu option resides in the File menu. The other InDesign menu options are Mac OS X–specific.

Figure 2-32: The InDesign menu (in Mac OS X only)

File menu

The File menu (shown in Figure 2-33) lets you perform actions on entire documents, libraries, and books, including creating, opening, saving, closing, and printing. The Place command lets you import graphics and text files, and the Export command lets you save documents in different formats such as EPS, HTML, and PDF. The Windows version also includes the Quit menu option.

Edit menu

InDesign's Edit menu (shown in Figure 2-34) provides access to its invaluable multiple undo and redo features, as well as the standard Cut, Copy, Paste, and Clear commands. You'll find Duplicate, and Step and Repeat here, even though you might be searching the Object menu for them. The Edit menu also provides commands for searching and replacing text and formats, checking spelling, and editing spelling and hyphenation dictionaries, as well as for opening the new Story Editor text-editing feature. It also provides access to color settings and keyboard shortcut preferences. The Windows version also contains the Preferences menu option.

 The Edit menu has several new options, including Paste without Formatting, Edit Original, and Quick Apply. Also, Check Spelling and Dictionary have been made submenus of the new Spelling menu option.

File	Edit	Layout	Type	O
New				▶
Open...				⌘O
Browse...				⌥⌘O
Close				⌘W
Save				⌘S
Save As...				⇧⌘S
Save a Copy...				⌥⌘S
Save a Version...				
Revert				
Place...				⌘D
Import XML...				
PDF Export Presets				▶
Export...				⌘E
Document Presets				▶
Document Setup...				⌥⌘P
File Info...				
Preflight...				⌥⇧⌘F
Package...				⌥⇧⌘P
Package for GoLive...				
Print Presets				▶
Print...				⌘P

Figure 2-33: The File menu

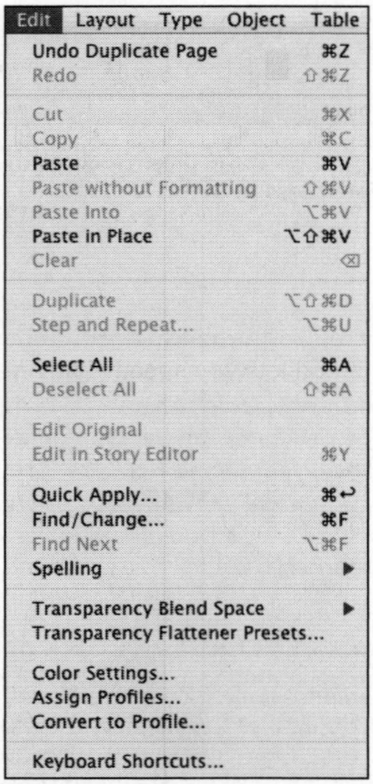

Edit	Layout	Type	Object	Table
Undo Duplicate Page				⌘Z
Redo				⇧⌘Z
Cut				⌘X
Copy				⌘C
Paste				⌘V
Paste without Formatting				⇧⌘V
Paste Into				⌥⌘V
Paste in Place				⌥⇧⌘V
Clear				⌫
Duplicate				⌥⇧⌘D
Step and Repeat...				⌥⌘U
Select All				⌘A
Deselect All				⇧⌘A
Edit Original				
Edit in Story Editor				⌘Y
Quick Apply...				⌘↵
Find/Change...				⌘F
Find Next				⌥⌘F
Spelling				▶
Transparency Blend Space				▶
Transparency Flattener Presets...				
Color Settings...				
Assign Profiles...				
Convert to Profile...				
Keyboard Shortcuts...				

Figure 2-34: The Edit menu

Layout menu

With the Layout menu (shown in Figure 2-35), you can change the position of the column and margin guides you established in the New Document dialog box, create guides at specific locations, and resize an entire document proportionally. You can also turn pages in a document and insert automatic page numbers using Layout menu commands. Finally, this menu contains the commands for setting up tables of contents.

Figure 2-35: The Layout menu

 New Feature The Layout menu adds the Pages menu option, which duplicates some page creation, movement, and deletion functions of the Pages pane, for easier access to them.

Type menu

The Type menu (shown in Figure 2-36) provides all your controls for formatting text—character formats, paragraph formats, tabs, and styles. The Story command lets you specify hanging punctuation for all the frames in a story. You can also convert text to a frame and insert special characters using a dialog box rather than keyboard shortcuts.

 New Feature The Type menu adds two new menu options to accommodate InDesign CS2's new footnotes capabilities: Insert Footnote and Document Footnote Options.

Object menu

Use the Object menu (shown in Figure 2-37) for layout functions such as controlling the stacking order of lines and frames, grouping objects together, locking objects to the page, and wrapping text around objects. You can manipulate objects, such as changing the number of columns and text inset in the Text Frame Options dialog box or fine-tuning the corners of a frame using the Corner Effects dialog box. For working with graphics, the Object menu lets you fit graphics to frames and frames to graphics, create clipping paths, merge and separate paths, convert shapes, apply colors to some types of images, and create drop shadows. It also lets you insert movies and audio files for interactive PDF documents.

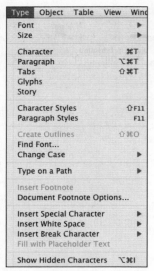

Figure 2-36: The Type menu

Figure 2-37: The Object menu

New Feature   The Object menu adds several new menu options to accommodate new InDesign CS2 capabilities: Anchored Object, Object Layer Options, and Convert Shape. It also replaces the Reverse Path menu with the Paths menu whose submenu contains three options: Open Path, Close Path, and Reverse Path.

Table menu

The Table menu (shown in Figure 2-38) contains the controls to create and edit tables. Using commands from this menu, you create tables, modify them, convert text into tables and vice versa, manage table cells, and control row and column spacing.

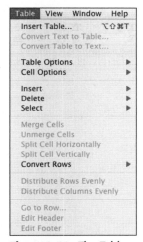

Figure 2-38: The Table menu

View menu

With the View menu (shown in Figure 2-39), you can change the view scale of the document, choose whether objects placed by master pages appear, and specify which layout tools are visible: *threads* (links between text frames), the edges of frames, rulers, guides, the baseline grid, and the document grid. You can also specify whether guides are locked and whether items snap to guides and the document grid.

Tip   If you're expecting to use the View menu to show and hide invisible characters such as spaces and tabs, look in the Type menu instead.

New Feature   The View menu consolidates several options into the new Grids & Guides menu.

Window menu

For the most part, the Window menu (shown in Figure 2-40) opens palettes or brings panes of palettes forward. Other commands let you manage document windows, opening additional windows for the same document and redistributing document windows on-screen. Currently open documents are listed at the bottom of the menu.

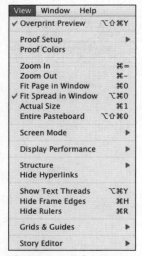

Figure 2-39: The View menu

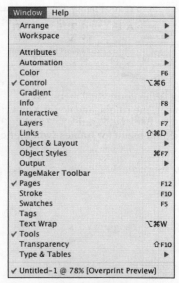

Figure 2-40: The Window menu

The Window menu adds several menu options to consolidate existing and new features: Automation (which replaces the Scripting menu and adds the New Data Merge option), Object & Layout (which consolidates the Align, Navigator, Pathfinder, and Transform menu options as submenus), and Output (which replaces the Output Preview menu and consolidates the Flattener, Separations, and Trap Presets menu options as submenus). The Object Styles and PageMaker Toolbar menus are completely new.

The Text Wrap menu option has moved back to the Window menu, up from being a submenu in the Type & Tables menu.

Help menu

The Help menu (shown in Figure 2-41) contains links to Adobe's HTML help files, as well as to Adobe's program update function. The Windows version also contains the About InDesign and Configure Plug-ins menu options.

Figure 2-41: The Help menu

The Help menu adds three new menu options. Two — Activate and Transfer Activation — accommodate InDesign CS2's new activation requirement to reduce piracy. One — Updates — lets you check for software updates and lets you set automatic update settings, which had been handled by a preferences pane in InDesign CS.

Contextual menus

The last interface element you'll find useful in InDesign is the contextual menu. By Control+clicking or right-clicking the document, an object, the rulers, and so on, you can display a menu of options for modifying whatever it is you're clicking. Figures 2-42 and 2-43 show the seven contextual menus: two variants of one contextual menu for frames (whether containing text or graphics), two variants when using the Type tool, one for when nothing is selected, and two affecting the rulers.

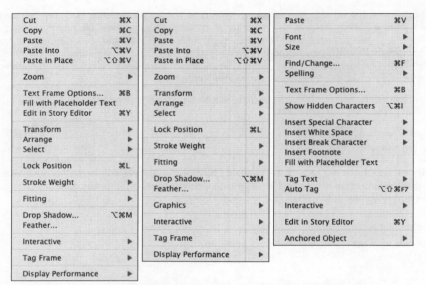

Figure 2-42: From left to right, the contextual menus for a text frame, a graphics frame, and for a text-insertion point

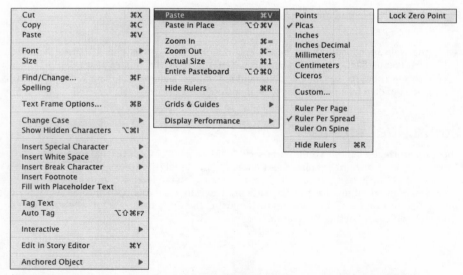

Figure 2-43: From left to right, the contextual menus for a selection of text, for when nothing is selected, for rulers, and for the zero point

Summary

InDesign stores its preferences in a file that you can copy and send to other users to ensure standard interface in workgroups. It offers its functionality through a variety of interface methods: tools, palettes, menu options, and contextual menus, as well as through some navigation controls in the document window. Panes are the primary vehicle for accessing InDesign features, while tools are the primary vehicle for determining what actions are possible.

The variety of panes can be overwhelming, so InDesign lets you save different workspace sets that let you specify which panes to display and where in each set. You can move pane tabs to the side of your monitor screen to keep them accessible but less distracting. You can also move, separate, and combine panes into palette groups of your choice. New panes are Data Merge and Object Styles, and there is also the Quick Apply palette for style selection and the PageMaker Toolbar palette for PageMaker users. The Control palette is a great timesaver, grouping many functions into one palette, showing only the relevant options for different kinds of objects.

✦   ✦   ✦

Getting InDesign Ready to Go

Although you may not realize it, Adobe has made a variety of educated guesses about the way you work. For example, it assumes you work in picas, that you prefer low-resolution previews of images, and that you use typographers' quotes. Adobe has also made decisions about the default properties of text, the default color swatches included with documents, and the default attributes of some objects. In all cases, Adobe tried to make the defaults appropriate for most publishers.

But no matter how much thought Adobe put into making these educated guesses, they won't work for everybody. In fact, it's unlikely that every single setting will work for you. So no matter how tempted you are to jump in and start working, take a minute to prepare InDesign for the way you actually work. Otherwise, you'll end up conforming the way you work to InDesign's decisions, making it more difficult to learn the program and get your work done; or you'll end up making the same changes to document after document, wasting time in the process.

Working with Preferences Files

InDesign stores preferences in several places. Some are stored in the documents themselves, so they work as expected as they are moved from user to user. Others are stored in files on your computer and affect only you.

InDesign Defaults file

The preferences you set in InDesign, from measurement units to color-calibration settings, are all stored in the InDesign Defaults file. On the Mac, this file is in the `Users:current user:Library: Preferences:Adobe InDesign:Version 4.0` folder on the drive that contains the Mac OS X System folder. In Windows, it is in the `\Document and Settings\current user\Application Data\Adobe\ InDesign\Version 4.0` folder on the drive that contains Windows.

To specify these defaults, you modify settings in the Preferences dialog box when no documents are open. All new documents you create are based on these settings.

Because some of the information affects how text flows and how documents look, you may want to standardize it for a workgroup by setting preferences once and sharing the InDesign Defaults file. (Sharing the file is a simple matter of giving copies of the file to other InDesign users to place in the appropriate system folder.)

You can delete the InDesign Defaults preference files when opening InDesign: Press Control+Option+Shift+⌘ or Ctrl+Alt+Shift when launching InDesign.

 If you make changes to preferences while a document is open, the change is saved with that document and not in the InDesign Defaults file. The document remembers its own preference settings so it will look the same when it's opened on other computers running InDesign.

Presets folder

The Presets folder in your InDesign application folder contains four kinds of standards: shortcut sets, color-swatch libraries, workspaces, and scripts. InDesign lets you create shortcut sets, so different users can have their own shortcut definitions; these preferences are stored in the InDesign Shortcut Sets folder in the Presets folder. The Swatch Libraries folder contains color-swatch libraries, both those that come with InDesign and any you might add yourself. The Workspaces folder contains workspace definitions; a *workspace* is a set of palettes and palette positions that you can save so, for example, you can have all text editing palettes appear when you're working on text. Finally, the Scripts folder contains your scripts.

Using the Preferences Dialog Box

Preferences are settings that affect an entire document — such as what measurement system you're using on rulers, what color the guides are, and whether substituted fonts are highlighted. In InDesign, you access these settings through the Preferences dialog box (choose InDesign ➪ Preferences on the Mac or Edit ➪ Preferences in Windows, or press ⌘+K or Ctrl+K). They are stored in the InDesign Defaults files in your InDesign application folder.

InDesign has two methods for changing preferences: You can change preferences when no documents are open to create new settings for all future documents, or you can change preferences for the active document, which affects only that document. Your strategy for changing preferences depends on the way you work and the needs of specific documents. For example, if you generally prefer to work in points, you might change the default measurement system to points with no documents open. However, you might have a design such as an envelope that makes more sense in inches, so you can change the measurement system for that specific document.

The Preferences dialog box provides 14 types of settings divided into panes: General, Type, Advanced Type, Composition, Units & Increments, Grids, Guides & Pasteboard, Dictionary, Spelling, Autocorrect, Story Editor Display, Display Performance, Appearance of Black, and File Handling. The steps for setting preferences stay the same, regardless of the changes you need to make.

 The Type and Advanced Type panes are new, taking the place of the Text pane in InDesign CS and expanding its controls. The Appearance of Black pane takes the Print Options section from the old General pane and adds additional controls. The Autocorrect pane is entirely new to InDesign CS2. The Updates pane has gone away, and its settings are now handled by clicking Preferences in the Updates dialog box (Help ➪ Updates).

When using the Preferences dialog box:

1. **Determine whether the change is for a specific document or for all future documents, and then open or close documents accordingly.** If no documents are open, the changes are stored in your preferences file and will be remembered for all new documents. If a document is open, the changes are in effect for that document only.

2. **Choose InDesign ➪ Preferences on the Mac or Edit ➪ Preferences in Windows, or press ⌘+K or Ctrl+K, to open the General pane.** Alternately, you can select a specific command from the Preferences submenu. For example, you might choose InDesign ➪ Preferences ➪ Composition on the Mac or Edit ➪ Preferences ➪ Composition in Windows. (There are no shortcuts for these submenus.)

3. **To switch to a specific pane, click an option from the list at the left of the dialog box, as shown in Figure 3-1.**

4. **Change any settings in any of the panes, and then click OK.** The changes are saved with the active document or in the InDesign Defaults file.

This section takes a comprehensive look at all the preferences in InDesign. Preferences that affect specific features are often discussed again in the relevant chapters. For example, Dictionary preferences are covered in Chapter 14.

Unlike most actions you perform in InDesign, you cannot reverse changes to preferences using the Undo command (choose Edit ➪ Undo, or press ⌘+Z or Ctrl+Z). If you change your mind about a preference setting, open the Preferences dialog box and change the setting again.

General preferences

Options in the General pane (see Figure 3-1) affect the operation of several InDesign features.

Page Numbering area

In the Page Numbering area of the Preferences dialog box, the View pop-up menu controls how page numbers appear in the fields such as the page number field on the document window. Here are the controls:

See Chapter 2 for information about the difference between section page numbers and absolute page numbers.

✦ **Section Numbering.** This is the default setting, which means that InDesign shows the page numbers according to the information in the Section Options dialog box accessed through the Pages pane's palette menu. When Section Numbering is selected, by default you need to type section page numbers, such as **Sec2:3**, in fields.

✦ **Absolute Numbering.** This option, which I prefer, shows page numbers according to each page's position in the document. For example, the first page is 1, the second page is 2, and the third page is 3, even if the pages display the Roman numerals i, ii, and iii. When this option is selected, you can always jump to the first page in a document by typing **1** in the Page Number box.

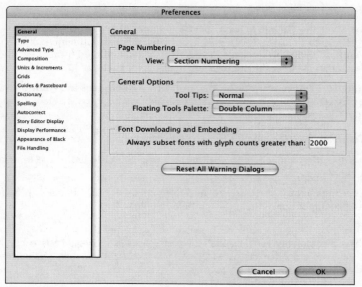

Figure 3-1: The General pane of the Preferences dialog box

General Options area

InDesign has two options in the General Options section over tool display. The Tool Tips pop-up menu has three options: Normal, Fast, and None. None turns off *Tool Tips,* the labels that pop up when the mouse hovers over a pane's icons. Fast makes the labels appear faster, which is best for new users learning the interface. Normal is the default setting and is the best for experienced users because it waits a bit before displaying the label so they don't pop up if you're just moving the mouse slowly.

The second option is the Floating Tools Palette pop-up menu, which lets you set the Tools palette as single-column width, single row, or the default double-column width. This is a matter of personal preference.

Font Downloading and Embedding area

The Always Subset Fonts with Glyph Counts Greater Than field is used for OpenType fonts that have many special characters, such as accented letters, symbols, and diacritical marks. To prevent output files from getting clogged with very large font files, this option lets you set the maximum number of characters (glyphs) that can be downloaded from a font file into an output file. Any characters actually used are always downloaded; the reason you might want to download an entire font is so someone could edit the file as a PDF or EPS file and have access to all characters in the proper fonts for such editing.

Reset All Warning Dialogs button

Use this button to turn on warning dialogs you may have turned off. Most warning dialog boxes have an option to turn off future warnings, and this resets them so they all appear again.

Type preferences

Options in the Type pane of the Preferences dialog box, shown in Figure 3-2, affect how several character formats work, whether you use typographer's quotes, and how text appears on-screen.

Type Options area

The first four of the seven Type Options that control different aspects of InDesign's character handling are selected by default.

✦ **Use Typographer's Quotes.** When you press the quote key on the keyboard with Use Typographer's Quotes selected, InDesign inserts the correct typographer's quotes (often called *curly quotes*) for the current language in use. For example, for U.S. English, InDesign inserts typographic single quotes (' ') or double quotes (" ") rather than straight quotes. For French, InDesign inserts double angle quillemets (« »). InDesign knows what language's characters to use based on the Language pop-up menu in the Character pane (choose Window ➪ Type & Tables ➪ Character, or press ⌘+T or Ctrl+T), or in the Paragraph Style and Character Style dialog boxes' Advanced Character Formats pane (choose Window ➪ Type & Tables ➪ Paragraph Styles, or press F11, and choose Window ➪ Type & Tables ➪ Character Styles, or press Shift+F11, respectively).

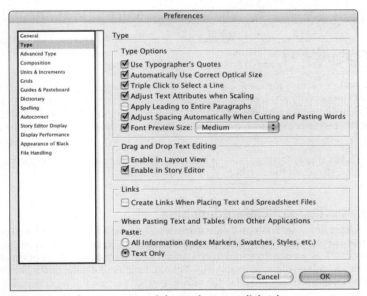

Figure 3-2: The Type pane of the Preferences dialog box

✦ **Automatically Use Correct Optical Size.** Use this option when selected, automatically accesses OpenType and PostScript fonts that include an optimal size axis, which ensures optimal readability at any size.

✦ **Triple Click to Select a Line.** When this option is selected, InDesign lets you triple-click anywhere in a line to select the whole line. This used to be a standard shortcut in Mac applications but has fallen into disuse recently.

✦ **Adjust Text Attributes when Scaling.** If selected, this option lets InDesign change text size and proportional scaling when you resize the text box or path that contains the text. If deselected, the text formatting is untouched. It makes sense to click this option if you're working on display ads and other materials where you are sizing text visually and interactively; it does not make sense in magazines, books, and other structured projects where the text attributes are standardized and changes to objects' size are meant to change the containers' size, not the text's size. Even if you deselect this option, you can still scale the text by pressing and holding ⌘ or Ctrl while you resize a text frame.

✦ **Apply Leading to Entire Paragraphs.** If selected, InDesign applies leading changes to the entire paragraph as opposed to the current line. In most cases, you want the leading to be applied to all paragraphs, so I recommend that you click this option (it is *not* selected by default in InDesign).

QuarkXPress User

Like other layout programs, QuarkXPress rightfully treats leading as a paragraph attribute, so be sure to select the Apply Leading to Entire Paragraph option in InDesign to make it work like it should. But note that InDesign does not support QuarkXPress's additive leading capability (where you type **+2 pt** to make the leading 2 points more than whatever the current point size is), so leading in InDesign will never exactly match the QuarkXPress approach.

✦ **Adjust Spacing Automatically When Cutting and Pasting Words.** This option is selected by default and adds or deletes spaces around words when you cut and paste, so words don't abut or have too many spaces next to them.

✦ **Font Preview Size.** If selected, a preview displays in all menus in which lists of fonts appear. The preview shows the actual font so you can see what you'll get before selecting the font. The pop-up menu at right lets you select the size of the preview. Figure 3-3 shows an example. Note that if you have lots of fonts, the preview menu size quickly gets unwieldy.

New Feature

The Adjust Spacing Automatically and the Font Preview Size options are new to InDesign CS2.

Drag and Drop Text Editing area

The options here control whether you can drag and drop text selections within a document. By default, Enable in Story Editor is selected while Enable in Layout View is deselected. These default settings mean you can drag and drop text in the Story Editor but not when working on a layout, the rationale being that a layout artist could inadvertently move text if it were enabled for the layout view.

New Feature

The Drag and Drop Text Editing options are new to InDesign CS2.

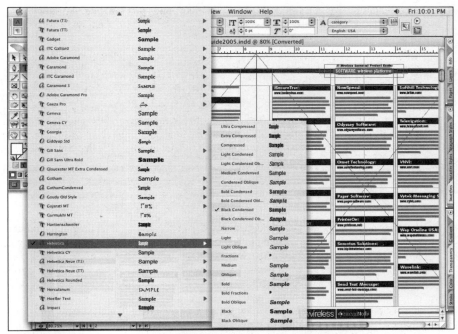

Figure 3-3: Example of a font menu that appears when Font Preview Size is selected and set to medium size

Links area

The Create Links When Placing Text and Spreadsheet Files option creates links to your source text files. InDesign can alert you when those files change so you can reimport them if desired. (InDesign always does this for graphics files.) Select this option if you want InDesign to track such links in the Links pane.

When Pasting Text and Tables from Other Applications area

This area gives you a choice as to how formatting is handled when you paste textual objects from other applications: For the Paste radio buttons, you click either All Information or Text Only. The default is Text Only. This can be helpful or a pain, depending on whether you want copied text to preserve its formatting or you prefer copied text to take on the formatting of the destination location's text. The right answer will depend on your specific layouts.

New Feature The Paste options in the When Pasting Text and Tables from Other Applications area is a renamed and enhanced version of InDesign CS's Preserve Text Attributes When Pasting option.

Advanced Type pane

The Advanced Type pane includes additional typographic settings, as seen in Figure 3-4.

New Feature In InDesign CS2, the Advanced Type pane's settings have been moved from the Text pane (retitled the Type pane in InDesign CS2).

The palette menu on the Character pane (Window ➪ Type & Tables ➪ Character, or ⌘+T or Ctrl+T) lets you format highlighted characters as Superscript (reduced and raised above the baseline), Subscript (reduced and dropped below the baseline), or Small Caps (reduced versions of capital letters). Note that Superscript, Subscript, and Small Caps characters do not need to be reduced — they can actually be enlarged instead. The controls in the Advanced Type pane govern precisely how these characters are placed and resized, as well as control the handling on non-Latin text entry.

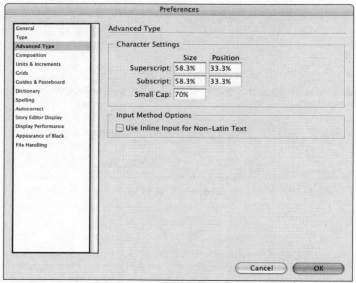

Figure 3-4: The Advanced Type pane of the Preferences dialog box

Character Settings area

This area controls the size of subscripts, superscripts, and small caps:

✦ The Size fields let you specify how much to scale these characters. The default is 58.3 percent, but you can type a value between 1 and 200 percent. I prefer 60 or 65 percent, depending on the type size and font.

✦ The Position fields let you specify how much to shift Superscript characters up and Subscript characters down. The default is 33.3 percent, but you can type a value between –500 and 500 percent. I prefer 30 percent for subscripts and 35 percent for superscripts.

✦ The Small Cap field lets you specify the scale of Small Caps characters in relation to the actual capital letters in the font. The default is 70 percent, but you can type a value between 1 and 200 percent.

See Chapter 40 for information about using the *true small caps* variation of a typeface, when available, rather than the Small Cap character format.

Input Method Options area

The Use Inline Input for Non-Latin Text option enables input method editors (IMEs) from Microsoft, Apple, or other companies, if installed on your computer, for typing Chinese, Japanese, and Korean (CJK)–language characters on non-CJK operating systems. It's meant for the occasional use of CJK characters. If you publish regularly in these languages, you should use the appropriate CJK version of InDesign instead.

 In InDesign CS2, the Input Method Options area has been moved to the new Advanced Type pane.

Composition preferences

In general, preferences in the Composition pane, shown in Figure 3-5, affect entire paragraphs rather than individual characters.

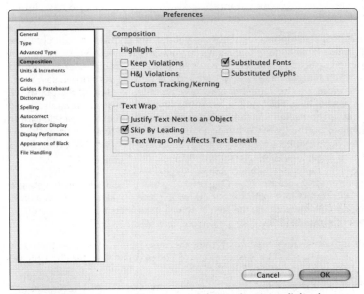

Figure 3-5: The Composition pane of the Preferences dialog box

Highlight area

The options in the Highlight area control whether InDesign calls attention to possible typesetting problems by drawing a highlighter pen effect behind the text.

✦ **Keep Violations.** This option is deselected by default and highlights the last line in a text frame when it cannot follow the rules specified in the Keep Options dialog box in the

Paragraph pane's palette menu (Window ➪ Type & Tables ➪ Paragraph, or Option+⌘+T or Ctrl+Alt+T). For example, if the Keep Options settings require more lines to stay together than fit in the text frame and thus bump all the text in a frame to the next text frame in the chain, the Keep Options rules are violated and the last line of text is highlighted so you know to change the frame size or the Keep Options rules for that text.

✦ **H&J Violations.** When selected, H&J Violations uses three shades of yellow to mark lines that might be too loose or too tight due to the combination of spacing and hyphenation settings. The darker the shade, the worse InDesign considers the problem to be. H&J Violations is deselected by default; you might want to select it while fine-tuning type, and then deselect it when you're finished.

✦ **Custom Tracking/Kerning.** If this option is selected, it highlights custom tracking and kerning (essentially, anywhere you override the defaults) in a bluish green. It's handy for copy editors to quickly find such overrides to make sure they're not too tight or loose for readability reasons.

✦ **Substituted Fonts.** This option is selected by default and uses pink highlight to indicate characters in fonts that are not available to InDesign. InDesign actually uses Adobe Sans MM or Adobe Serif MM to create a replacement for missing fonts, so the text looks close to the actual font. For editing purposes, the substituted fonts work fine, although the pink highlight can be distracting. But for output purposes, it's important that you have the correct fonts, so you may want to live with the irritation and have InDesign highlight substituted fonts for you.

✦ **Substituted Glyphs.** This option highlights in yellow any glyphs (special characters) that are substituted. This usually occurs when you have multiple versions of the same font, with different special characters in each version. For example, a file using the euro (€) currency symbol might have been created in the newest version of, say, Syntax. But a copy editor working on the same file may have an older version of Syntax that doesn't have the euro symbol in it. Selecting Substituted Glyphs ensures that such a problem is highlighted. Substituted Glyphs also highlights characters of an OpenType font that have been changed on the fly by turning on some OpenType features from the Control palette's or Character pane's palette menu, such as Discretionary Ligatures, Swashes, Small Caps, Slash Zero, and so on. I recommend you select this option.

Note   InDesign is hypersensitive to fonts (see Chapter 14), so you'll get such highlighting even when you have the correct font installed but the wrong face applied to it (such as Normal rather than Regular); in these cases, the font style will have brackets ([ ]) around it in the Character pane or Control palette.

Text Wrap area

As the label makes clear, the three options here affect how text wraps:

✦ **Justify Text Next to an Object.** If this option is selected, it overrides any local justification settings that justify text that wraps around an object. That means the text will smoothly follow the object's shape, rather than keep any ragged margins that can make the wrap look strange. This option comes into play when you wrap ragged (left-aligned or right-aligned) text around objects; I recommend that you avoid wrapping text on its ragged side because it looks awkward. Although this option eliminates the awkwardness of ragged text that wraps around an object, it presents a different awkwardness: having some text ragged (that which is not wrapping) and some text justified (that which is wrapping).

✦ **Skip by Leading.** When selected, this option uses the text's leading to determine how much space follows an object that it is wrapping. This has an effect only if you choose the Jump Object text-wrap option in the Text Wrap pane. (See Chapter 24 for more on text wrap.)

✦ **Text Wrap Only Affects Text Beneath.** If selected, this option has only text below an object wrap around that object. This allows some text to overlap an image and some text to overwrap it, depending on the text's location in the stacking order.

Units & Increments preferences

The measurement systems you use for positioning items and the way the arrows on the keyboard increase or decrease settings are controlled by settings in the Units & Increments pane shown in Figure 3-6.

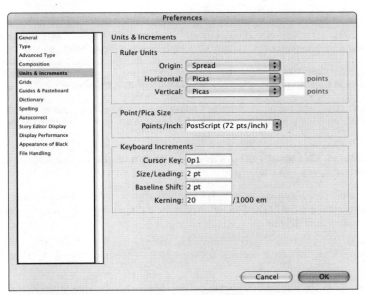

Figure 3-6: The Units & Increments pane of the Preferences dialog box

Ruler Units area

The Ruler Units area affects three things: the origin point (by page, by spread, or by the spine), the measurement system displayed on the horizontal and vertical ruler on the document window, and the default values in fields used for positioning objects.

The Origin pop-up menu determines the zero point (typically, the upper-left corner of the page) for object positions. If you choose Page, objects' positions are relative to each page's upper-left corner. If you choose Spread, objects' positions are relative to the current spread's upper-left corner. If you choose Spine, objects' positions are relative to the binding spine of each spread — the very top and center of where the two pages meet.

With the Horizontal and Vertical pop-up menus, you can specify one measurement system for the horizontal ruler and measurements and specify another measurement system for the vertical ruler and measurements. For example, you might use points for horizontal measurements so you can use the rulers to gauge tab and indent settings, while using inches for vertical measurements. If you use Inches for both the Horizontal and Vertical Ruler Units, not only do the rulers display inches, but the X, Y, W, and H fields on the Control palette or Transform pane (choose Window ➪ Object & Layout ➪ Transform or press F9) display values in inches as well.

Note   To display the document ruler, choose View ➪ Show Ruler, or press ⌘+R or Ctrl+R.

Tip   The default horizontal and vertical measurement system is picas. If you aren't accustomed to working in picas, be sure to change the default Horizontal and Vertical Ruler Units when no documents are open. This ensures that all future documents use your preferred measurement system. (If you make the change with a document open, the change applies only to the open document.)

To specify the measurement systems you want to use, click an option from the Horizontal pop-up menu and from the Vertical pop-up menu. The following options are available:

✦ **Points.** A typesetting measurement equal to ¹⁄₇₂ of an inch. To enter values in points, type a **p** before the value or **pt** after the value (p6 or 6 pt, for example).

Tip   InDesign doesn't care if you put spaces between numbers and the abbreviations in your measurements — **3 p** is read the same as **3p**, and **0.4inch** is read the same as **0.4 inch**, for example.

✦ **Picas.** A typesetting measurement equal to ⅙ of an inch. To enter values in picas, type a **p** after the value (for example, 6p).

✦ **Inches.** An English measurement system that is divided into sixteenths. To enter values in inches, type **i**, **in**, **inch**, *or* " after the value. For example, 3i, 3in, 3 inch, and 3" are all read by InDesign as 3 inches.

✦ **Inches decimal.** Inches divided into 10ths on the ruler rather than 16ths. To enter values in inches decimal, include a decimal point as appropriate and type **i**, **in**, **inch**, or " after the value.

✦ **Millimeters.** A metric measurement that is ¹⁄₁₀ of a centimeter. To enter values in millimeters, type **mm** after the value. For example, 14mm.

✦ **Centimeters.** A metric measurement that is about ⅓ of an inch. To enter values in centimeters, type **cm** after the value. For example, 2.3cm.

✦ **Ciceros.** A European typesetting measurement that is slightly larger than a pica. To enter values in ciceros, type **c** after the value. For example, 2c.

✦ **Custom.** This option lets you set a custom number of points as your measurement unit, placing a labeled tick mark at every point increment you specify. You get to customize the number of tick marks between the labeled marks by typing a value in the Points field. For example, if you type *12* in the field, you get a tick mark at each pica, because there are 12 points in a pica.

Despite the Ruler Units you specify, you can type values in any fields using any supported measurement system. For example, if you're working in picas, you can type an inch value in the Width field by typing **1 in**. InDesign will automatically convert the value to picas for you. You can type values in picas and points by placing a *p* between the two values. For example, typing **1p2** indicates 1 pica and 2 points.

Point/Pica Size area

The Point/Inch pop-up menu lets you specify how a point is calculated. The default is PostScript (72 pts/inch). You can also select Traditional (72.27 pts/inch), which had been the standard before electronic publishing took hold in the 1980s, as well as 72.23 and 72.3. You can also enter a value of between 60 and 80. Leave this at PostScript (72 pts/inch) unless you or your service bureau have a reason to select a different option.

The ability to define a point's value is new to InDesign CS2.

Keyboard Increments area

The arrow keys on the keyboard let you move selected objects right, left, up, or down. You can also use the arrow keys and other keyboard shortcuts to change some text formatting. You can customize the way these shortcuts work, for example, by specifying how far each click of an arrow key moves an item.

These preferences are not used consistently to modify the arrow keys or keyboard shortcuts. Basically, the Cursor Key field works with all four arrow keys. The Size/Leading value works with the up and down arrow keys for leading, while the Kerning field works with the left and right arrows. Meanwhile, the Size/Leading value works with a regular keyboard shortcut, and the Baseline Shift field works only while pressing the arrow keys when the Baseline Shift field is highlighted on the Character pane.

The options are:

✦ **Cursor Key field.** When you select an object with the Selection tool or the Direct Selection tool, you can move it up, down, left, or right using the arrow keys on the keyboard. By default, the item moves 1 point. You can change the increment to a value between 0 (which would be useless) and 100 points (equal to 8p4 or1.3888 inches). For example, if you're using a document grid, you might change the increment to match the grid lines.

If you press the Shift key while you press an arrow key, the object moves ten times the amount specified in the Cursor Key field. Holding the Option or Alt key while you press an arrow key creates a copy of the selected object at the distance specified in the Cursor Key field. Holding the Shift key with the Option or Alt key while you press an arrow key creates a copy of the selected object spaced at ten times the amount specified in the Cursor Key field. This last combination is a very simple and quick way to create a grid of text or graphics frames with equal spacing between them.

✦ **Size/Leading field.** The value you type in this field, which is 2 points by default, speci-fies how much point size or leading is increased or decreased when implemented with keyboard commands. You can type a value between 1 and 100.

Tip

To increase the point size of selected text, press Shift+⌘+. (period) or Ctrl+Shift+. (period); to decrease the point size, press Shift+⌘+, (comma) or Ctrl+Shift+, (comma). Add Option or Alt to the combination to multiply the increment by five. To modify leading for selected text, Option+click or Alt+click the up or down arrow on the keyboard.

✦ **Baseline Shift field.** You can shift the baseline of highlighted text up or down by click-ing in the Baseline Shift field on the Character pane, and then pressing the up or down arrow on the keyboard. You can change the default value of 2 points to any value between 1 and 100. If you press Shift while clicking, the increment is multiplied by five.

✦ **Kerning field.** To kern text with keyboard commands, you position the cursor between two letters, and then Option+click or Alt+click the right arrow key to increase kerning or the left arrow to decrease kerning. By default, each click changes kerning by $^{20}/_{1000}$ of an em. You can change this value to anything between 1 and 100. Hold the ⌘ or Ctrl key to multiply the increment by five.

Grids preferences

Grids preferences let you set up a baseline grid, commonly used to space text evenly across columns, and a document-wide grid, which you can use for positioning or drawing objects. If you're planning a structured design that will use a grid, you'll want to set it up before you start working in the document. It's likely that each design you create will have different grid settings based on its individual content, so you probably won't change Grids preferences with no documents open. The Grids pane is shown in Figure 3-7.

Note

By default, both the baseline grid and the document grid appear on every spread behind all objects; the document grid appears on the pasteboard as well. Both grids cover the entire document and cannot be associated with a specific master page or layer. You can have grids appear in front by deselecting the Grids in Back option.

Baseline Grid area

You can specify the color of the baseline grid, where it starts, how far apart each grid line is, and when it appears. To display the baseline grid for a document, choose View ➪ Grids & Guides ➪ Show Baseline Grid, or press Option+⌘+' (apostrophe) or Ctrl+Alt+' (apostrophe). You have the following options:

✦ **Color pop-up menu.** The default color of the baseline grid is Light Blue. If this color is difficult for you to see, or if you're accustomed to the pink lines in QuarkXPress, you can select a different color from the Color pop-up menu. Choose Other to access the system color picker and create your own color.

✦ **Start field.** This value specifies how far down from the top of the page the grid starts. The Start value, which defaults to 3p0, usually matches your top margin.

✦ **Relative To pop-up menu.** InDesign lets you set where the grid starts: at Top of Page or Top Margin.

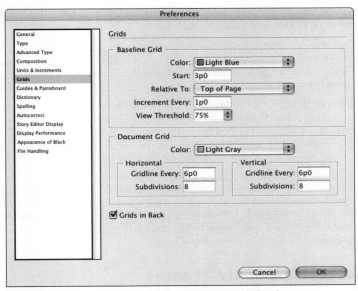

Figure 3-7: The Grids pane of the Preferences dialog box

New Feature

The Relative To pop-up menu is new to InDesign CS2.

✦ **Increment Every field.** The amount of space between grid lines is specified in the Increment Every field. The default value of 1p0 is usually changed to match the leading of your body text so text aligns with the grid.

✦ **View Threshold pop-up menu.** You can prevent the baseline grid from appearing when you decrease the view percentage. If you use the default setting, the baseline grid will not appear at views below 75 percent. You can type a value between 5 and 4,000 percent.

Tip

You might want to change the View Threshold to match the document's most common Fit Page in Window view. For example, a magazine page on a 15-inch monitor in a full window might display at around 65 percent when you choose View ⇨ Fit Page in Window. Usually you use Fit Page in Window to get an overall look at the page, and the baseline grid is simply in the way. (You can also choose View ⇨ Fit Spread in Window, which has the shortcut Option+⌘+0 [zero] or Ctrl+Alt+0 [zero], that you might want to use to change the View Threshold to match instead.)

Document Grid area

The document grid consists of intersecting horizontal and vertical gridlines, forming a pattern of small squares that you can use for object placement and for drawing symmetrical objects. You can customize the color and spacing of the grid lines. To display the document grid, choose View ➪ Grids & Guides ➪ Show Document Grid, or press ⌘+' (apostrophe) or Ctrl+' (apostrophe). You have the following options:

✦ **Color pop-up menu.** The default color of the document grid is Light Gray. Although this light shade is unobtrusive, you might want to change it to something brighter or darker so you can see it better. You can choose a different color from the Color pop-up menu or choose Other to create your own.

✦ **Gridline Every field.** The major grid lines, which are slightly darker, are positioned according to this value. The default value is 6p0; in general, you'll want to specify a value within the measurement system you're using. For example, if you're working in inches, you might type **1 inch** in the Gridline Every field. That way, the gridlines match the major tick marks on the ruler. You set the horizontal and vertical settings separately.

✦ **Subdivisions field.** Although this is a number and not a measurement, it ends up specifying the amount of space between grid lines. The major grid lines established in the Gridline Every field are divided according to the value you type here. For example, if you type **1 inch** in the Gridline Every field, and you type 4 in the Subdivisions field, you will get a gridline at each quarter-inch. The default number of subdivisions is 8. You set the horizontal and vertical settings separately.

Guides & Pasteboard preferences

When you create a new document, you set up margins in the New Document dialog box (File ➪ New ➪ Document, or ⌘+N or Ctrl+N). For more alignment options within a document, you can create guidelines by clicking and dragging them off the rulers or clicking Layout ➪ Create Guides. Settings in the Guides & Pasteboard pane, shown in Figure 3-8, control the color and other attributes of the margins and guides.

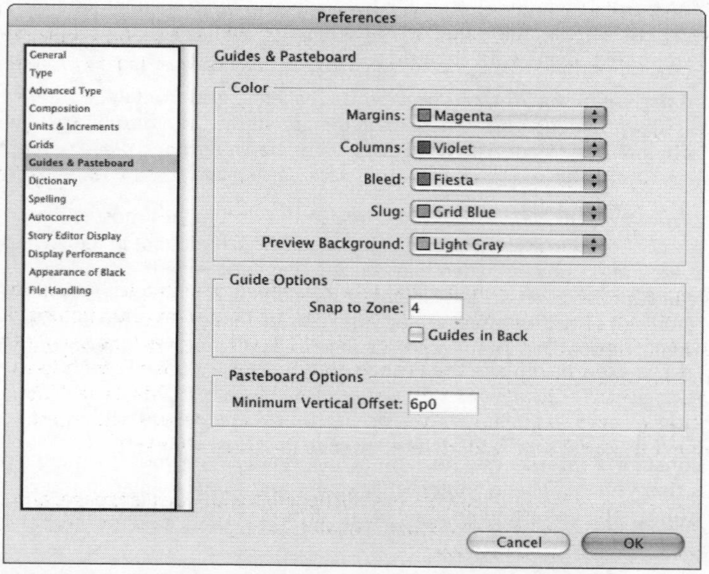

Figure 3-8: The Guides & Pasteboard pane of the Preferences dialog box

Color area

In the Color area, the Color pop-up menus for Margins, Columns, Bleed, Slug, and Preview Background (a new name for the previous version's Pasteboard option) let you select a color other than the defaults. If you want to make your own color, choose Custom to access the system color picker. The Margins color, Magenta by default, displays on all horizontal guides; the Columns color, Violet by default, displays on all vertical guides. To display guides in a document, choose View ➪ Grids & Guides ➪ Show Guides, or press ⌘+; (semicolon) or Ctrl+; (semicolon).

Guide Options area

This area controls guide snap-to and placement:

✦ **Snap to Zone.** This field's value specifies how close you need to drag an object to a grid line or guideline to make it *snap to* the line (think of it as the line's magnetic field). The default Snap to Zone value is 4 pixels, but you can type a value between 1 and 36. You enable snapping to the grid through the Snap to Document Grid and Snap to Guides commands in the View menu.

✦ **Guides in Back.** By default, margins and guides appear in front of all objects. If you prefer to have objects obscure margins and guides, select the Guides in Back option in the Guide Options area. Note that baseline grids and document grids always appear behind all objects, regardless of this setting.

QuarkXPress User

This Guides in Back option is for those QuarkXPress 3.3 users who never figured out how to change the unfortunate default of placing guides in back, and are therefore accustomed to working with guides this way.

Pasteboard Options area

The Pasteboard Options area has the Minimum Vertical Offset field, where you specify the amount of pasteboard to appear above and below your pages. The default is 6p0 (1 inch).

Dictionary preferences

The Dictionary pane, shown in Figure 3-9, sets options related to hyphenation and spelling dictionaries, as well as to quotation marks.

Language area

The Language area begins with a pop-up menu that lets you select a language. You choose a language when you want to replace the existing, or add new, hyphenation and spelling dictionaries for that language. (This lets you control the dictionaries used by each language separately.) For example, if you want to replace the French dictionaries, choose French in the pop-up menu, and then select the new French dictionaries elsewhere in this pane. The current dictionaries for the selected language are shown in the window beneath it, and there are four buttons to (from left to right) link, add, delete, or save dictionary files.

New Feature

InDesign CS2 now lets you associate multiple user dictionaries with each language, and the list of such dictionaries is new to this version. Chapter 14 explains how to create, edit, remove, and otherwise manage dictionaries.

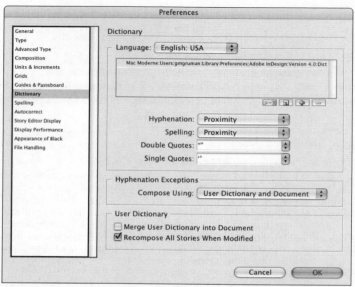

Figure 3-9: The Dictionary pane of the Preferences dialog box

In addition, the Language area offers these controls over dictionaries:

✦ **Hyphenation.** This pop-up menu lets you choose from any hyphenation dictionaries installed for the selected language. Typically, there is only the default dictionary, such as Proximity, in this pop-up menu.

✦ **Spelling.** This pop-up menu lets you choose from any spelling dictionaries installed for the selected language. Typically, there is only the default dictionary, such as Proximity, in this pop-up menu.

How to Install Dictionaries

To install different dictionaries, place them in the Dictionaries folder inside the Plug-ins folder (inside your InDesign folder). Press Option+⌘+/ or Ctrl+Alt+/ to update the pop-up menus in the Dictionary pane without restarting InDesign. (In a workgroup, it's important that everyone use the same dictionaries.)

Eventually, you may be able to purchase third-party spelling or hyphenation dictionaries for InDesign—although no third-party commercial dictionaries have been released since InDesign was created in 1999. For example, you might be able to purchase a different Traditional German dictionary with more words than the one InDesign has. In that case, when you check the spelling of a word with Traditional German as its language format, InDesign would consult the third-party dictionary rather than the default. More likely, you will use this feature to create your own project-specific dictionaries.

The Language area also lets you set the quotation marks you want use. Different languages use different quotation marks, and InDesign adjusts the quotation marks automatically when you switch the language. However, there may be some cases where you might want to override the languages' default quotation-mark settings, which you can do in the Double Quotes and Single Quotes pop-up menus.

Note that changing the quotation-mark options for one language does not affect the settings for others. Each language can have independent settings for the quotation marks used.

Caution   After you change a language's quotation-mark settings, there's no way to reset them to the language defaults except to choose the proper options from the pop-up menus. That means you need to remember or record what the original, correct setting was.

Hyphenation Exceptions area

The Compose Using pop-up menu has three options that specify what to use for hyphenation exceptions, which override the language dictionary's hyphenation rules. For example, you may choose not to hyphenate a short word like *preset* that has a legitimate hyphenation *(pre–set)*. And you may correct the hyphenation of specialized terms not in the language's dictionary.

The options here dictate how you manage those exceptions. By default, InDesign stores hyphenation exceptions in an outside file, so multiple users can standardize on the same exceptions list. But you can also store exceptions in a document, perhaps for unique needs. The Compose Using pop-up menu lets you select from Document, User Dictionary, and User Dictionary and Document options. Choose User Dictionary if you want to override any exceptions stored in the document — perhaps they're wrong or the copy editors want to rely only on a standard exception list. Choose Document if you want to ignore exceptions stored in an outside file. Choose User Dictionary and Document if you want to use both.

User Dictionary area

This area has two options that are selected by default and should stay that way:

✦ **Merge User Dictionary into Document.** If selected, this option copies the user dictionary file into the document, so if the file is sent to someone else who doesn't have access to that dictionary, the hyphenation in the document is preserved. The main reason to deselect this option is if you need to keep your files to a minimum size; otherwise, selecting this option prevents reflow when you pass a document to a service bureau or another designer, especially if you have *any* custom hyphenations.

✦ **Recompose All Stories When Modified.** If selected, this option redoes the document's hyphenation to reflect the changed user dictionary.

Spelling preferences

The Spelling pane, shown in Figure 3-10, lets you control what the InDesign spell checker examines when it checks spelling in a document.

Spelling area

There's little reason not to select all four options in this area — Misspelled Words, Repeated Words, Uncapitalized Words, and Uncapitalized Sentences. Note that Uncapitalized Words checks for known proper nouns that aren't capitalized.

Dynamic Spelling area

This area lets you set the colors used in InDesign to indicate the four types of spelling and capitalization areas that InDesign CS2 can now display in your layout as you type and after you import text. Select the desired color from the appropriate pop-up menu.

 Dynamic spelling is new to InDesign CS2. Chapter 14 covers this new capability in detail.

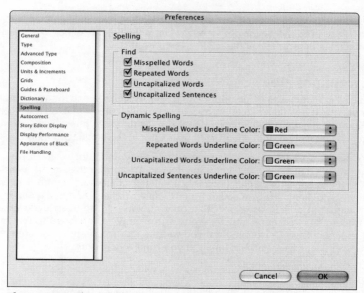

Figure 3-10: The Spelling pane of the Preferences dialog box

Autocorrect preferences

This pane, shown in Figure 3-11, lets you turn on automatic text correction and specify which words are to be replaced in the list below. Click Add to add a misspelled word and its correction; you can also use this to add codes or other keystrokes that you want changed to something else. For example, you could type @@-- and tell InDesign to convert it to an em dash (—).

 Automatic text correction is new to InDesign CS2. Chapter 14 covers this new capability in detail.

Story Editor Display preferences

The Story Editor Display pane controls how the Story Editor displays text and the text cursor. Figure 3-12 shows the pane.

 Chapter 14 covers the Story Editor in detail.

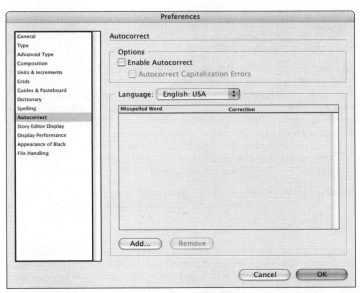

Figure 3-11: The Autocorrect pane of the Preferences dialog box

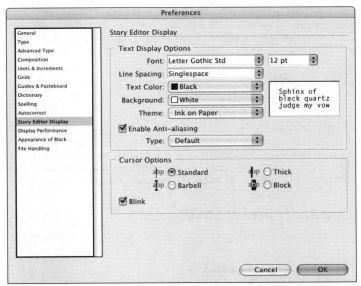

Figure 3-12: The Story Editor Display pane of the Preferences dialog box

Text Display Options area

The Text Display Options area determines how text displays in the Story Editor. All are meant to make it easy to edit text on-screen.

The first set of options lets you customize the text itself in the Story Editor. The Display Font pop-up menu lets you choose a font that is easy to read — you can use any active font available on your computer — as well as a point size (the default of 12 points is usually quite readable, but you may want to enlarge or reduce that in specific cases). The Line Spacing pop-up menu lets you change the default of single-spaced presentation to 150%, Doublespace, and Triplespace. You may prefer 150% or Doublespace if you have a wide Story Editor window to help make reading the text easier. Finally, the Enable Anti-aliasing option lets you smooth on-screen font display, which can make text hard to read for some fonts, especially at small sizes, or make it easier to read for some fonts, especially at medium and large sizes.

Two pop-up menus control the basic display: Text Color and Background. You'll rarely want to change either of these from the default of black for the text color and white for the background. (You might want to choose a light yellow or green as a background color to be a bit easier on the eye.)

The Theme pop-up menu has four predefined text color/background combinations that override any changes you make to the Text Color and Background pop-up menus. Of those four themes, you'll want to keep Ink on Paper, which is simply black text on a white background. The other three options provide hard-to-read displays modeled after the very first computer displays in the 1970s and early 1980s.

The Enable Anti-aliasing option, if selected, smoothes text display for better readability in the Story Editor. You choose the smoothing type — Default, Best for LCD Display, or Soft — you prefer in the Type pop-up menu. Note that both Windows and the Mac OS offer similar capabilities systemwide, so you may not want to set anti-aliasing in InDesign if you have already set it for your whole computer.

 New Feature   The ability to turn on anti-aliasing is new to InDesign CS2.

Cursor Options area

InDesign gives you a choice of the text cursor that appears in the Story Editor. In the Cursor Options area, choose whichever looks best on-screen and is easy to find without obscuring the text under it. That will vary based on the font and point size chosen. If you want the text cursor to blink — that helps some people find it more easily — be sure to select the Blink option.

Display Performance preferences

The Display Performance pane, shown in Figure 3-13, controls how images and text appear on-screen.

Options area

In the Default View pop-up menu in the Options area, you can choose from three view settings: Typical, Fast (which used to be called Optimized), and High Quality. These affect only what appears on-screen, not what is printed. The three options correspond to how you set the options in the Adjust View Settings area of this pane.

If selected, the Preserve Object-Level Display Settings option overrides any global view settings here with those you have set for specific images. Images that have no individual view settings set will still take on the settings in this pane. (You set view settings for individual images by selecting them in your layout and then choosing Object ⇨ Display Performance.)

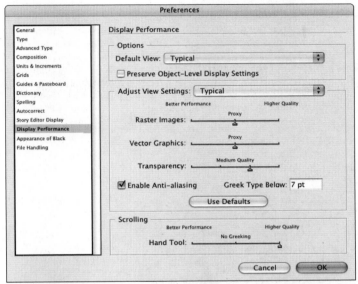

Figure 3-13: The Display Performance pane of the Preferences dialog box

Adjust View Settings area

Use the Adjust View Settings area to determine what Typical, Optimized, and High Quality should mean in your copy of InDesign. Click the tick mark for the quality level you want to set in each of the three graphical view aspects (Raster Images, Vector Images, and Transparency). You can also click and drag the sliders to the desired tick mark. Note that you must move the slider all the way to a tick mark; you cannot choose a setting in between tick marks.

For raster (bitmap) images and vector images, you have three options: Gray Out, Proxy, and High Resolution. Proxy means a low-resolution version (72 dpi). For transparency, there are three quality levels available — Low, Medium, and High — as well as Off, which doesn't display objects behind transparent portions of an image.

The Adjust View Settings area also has two controls for text:

✦ **Enable Anti-aliasing.** When this option is selected, it smoothes text display. Note that you may already have set anti-aliasing in your Windows or Mac OS X systemwide display preferences, in which case you probably don't need to also set them in InDesign.

✦ **Greek Type Below.** This field is where you set at what size text appears as gray lines rather than as actual characters.

Click Use Defaults to return to InDesign's default setting for this pane.

Scrolling area

You can adjust screen refresh while scrolling by setting your preferred options in the Hand Tool slider. Either click the desired tick mark or move the slider to the desired tick mark.

Selecting the leftmost tick mark means you will see less detail appear as you scroll. This can speed up scrolling in complex documents. It has no effect on image preview when you stop scrolling, nor on printing quality.

New Feature The image-quality control for scrolling is new to InDesign CS2.

Appearance of Black preferences

InDesign CS2 lets you control how black appears on-screen and when printing, as seen in Figure 3-14.

New Feature The Appearance of Black pane is new to InDesign CS2. The Overprinting of Black section had been handled in InDesign CS's General pane.

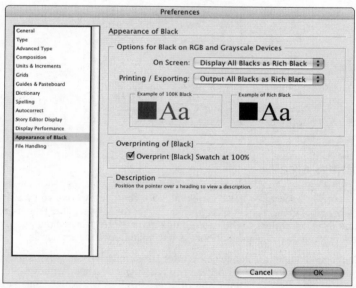

Figure 3-14: The Appearance of Black pane of the Preferences dialog box

Options for Black on RGB and Grayscale Devices area

This area enables you to control the display of blacks, as well as the printing and exporting to PDF. Using the On Screen and Printing/Exporting pop-up menus, you can choose Display All Blacks Accurately or Display All Blacks as Rich Black. *Rich black* (also called *superblack*) is created by combining black and magenta to create a darker appearance. Chapter 8 covers this concept in more detail.

Overprinting of [Black] area

By default, the Overprint [Black] Swatch at 100% option is selected so that any black text, strokes, or fills overprint. This usually results in clearer text and lines. (This option applies to the [Black] color in the Swatches pane, rather than, say, a black swatch that you create.) If you deselect Overprint [Black], all black text, strokes, and fills knock out of their backgrounds, which results in a lighter black and could cause some misregistration when printing.

Cross-Reference See Chapters 8 and 28 for more details on creating colors and trapping colors, respectively.

File Handling preferences

The File Handling pane, shown in Figure 3-15, controls how recovery files and document previews are handled. It also controls the pasting of PDF files to the Clipboard and of formatted objects from other applications.

New Feature In InDesign CS2, the Clipboard area has been moved from the General pane.

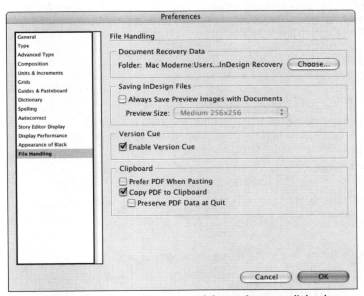

Figure 3-15: The File Handling pane of the Preferences dialog box

Document Recovery Data area

In this area, InDesign lets you specify the folder that contains autorecovery files, which are files that let you recover most or all of your work in case of a program or system crash. You can click Choose to select an alternate directory, but there's really no reason to change the default, which places the recovery folder safely inside your System folder's InDesign preferences folder on the Mac and in your Application Data folder's InDesign subfolder in Windows.

Saving InDesign Files

The Always Save Preview Images with Documents option, if selected, enables InDesign to save a thumbnail view of the document's first page. Select a preview size from the Preview Size pop-up menu. That preview appears in the Open dialog box instead of the InDesign logo when you select a file. It's handy when you've got a ton of files in a folder and can't remember which is which.

New Feature   The Preview Size pop-up menu is new to InDesign CS2.

Version Cue area

The Enable Version Cue option, if selected, turns on Adobe's Version Cue file-management system. This changes your Open a File, Save, Place, Export, and similar file-handling dialog boxes to allow the saving of multiple versions of the same document for workflow publishing.

New Feature   Although Adobe introduced Version Cue with InDesign CS, InDesign CS2 lets you turn it on from within each Creative Suite 2 program, not just from a Windows or Mac control panel. Chapter 35 covers Version Cue in more detail.

Clipboard area

The Clipboard area controls how image and text formatting are handled when copying elements to the Clipboard (choose Edit ⇨ Copy, or press ⌘+C or Ctrl+C, and choose Edit ⇨ Cut, or press ⌘+X or Ctrl+X). There are three options:

✦ **Prefer PDF When Pasting.** Selecting this option converts items copied from Adobe Illustrator into PDF files so that transparency objects, blends, and patterns are preserved during the paste operation into InDesign.

✦ **Copy PDF to Clipboard.** Selecting this option creates a temporary PDF file when you copy items from InDesign for pasting into applications such as Illustrator.

✦ **Preserve PDF Data at Quit.** Selecting this option keeps any pasted PDF information in the Clipboard's memory when you quit InDesign. You usually won't need to select this option.

New Feature   The Preserve PDF Data at Quit option is new to InDesign CS2.

Setting Other Global Preferences

There are several global preferences handled outside the Preferences dialog box.

Setting up automatic program updates

The Adobe Updater Preferences dialog box, shown in Figure 3-16, lets you decide whether to let InDesign connect automatically to Adobe's servers over your Internet connection to download and install product updates.

To open this dialog box, choose Help ➪ Updates, and then click the Preferences button in the resulting dialog box (you will have to wait until InDesign completes looking for any current updates before the Preferences button appears). The Adobe Updater Preferences dialog box will appear, displaying the Adobe Updater Preferences pane.

New Feature InDesign CS's Updates pane has been moved from the Preferences dialog box to the separate Adobe Updater Preferences dialog box in InDesign CS2.

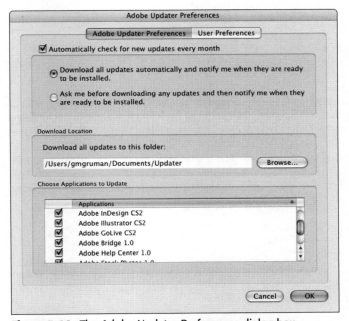

Figure 3-16: The Adobe Updater Preferences dialog box

In this pane, select the Automatically Check for New Updates Every Month option to enable this feature. You can also determine whether to have InDesign install the updates after they are downloaded or to ask you for permission first. You can also change the download folder for updater files, and select which Adobe applications are updated. (This lets you conveniently set automatic updating for all your Adobe applications without having to go to this dialog box in each application.)

The User Preferences pane lets you control Internet proxy server access, for which your network administrator will provide the right settings if this is needed on your network. Most users never have to use this pane.

Customizing keyboard shortcuts

InDesign provides keyboard shortcuts for accessing most tools and menu commands, and for many pane options. For the most part, the keyboard shortcuts selected by Adobe either match platform standards — such as ⌘+X or Ctrl+X for Edit ➪ Cut — or they're based on keyboard shortcuts in PageMaker, Photoshop, and Illustrator. Fortunately, you're not stuck with the keyboard shortcuts Adobe decided on — and I say fortunately because a few decisions and omissions are a little odd.

QuarkXPress User

You can choose to use shortcuts based on QuarkXPress 4.0 shortcuts, or you can modify a copy of the QuarkXPress set. Note that the QuarkXPress 4.0 set is not a perfect match for *every* keyboard shortcut in QuarkXPress 4. I cover this topic in more depth later in this chapter.

I recommend not using QuarkXPress shortcuts in InDesign. Using those QuarkXPress shortcuts will just prolong the necessary adaptation to InDesign's native interface.

The Keyboard Shortcuts dialog box (choose Edit ➪ Keyboard Shortcuts), shown in Figure 3-17, provides all the tools you need for modifying keyboard shortcuts.

To Customize or Not to Customize

The ability to customize keyboard shortcuts, letting you work the way you want, is great — or is it? Maybe it is only if you work alone and never talk to others about your work or their work. Modified keyboard shortcuts can lead to confusion when discussing techniques, reading documentation, or sharing computers. While modifying keyboard shortcuts — or even while considering it — keep the following in mind:

✦ You can specify keyboard shortcuts for specific fonts and faces that you use frequently, such as a shortcut for Gill Sans Bold Italic. For the font to be listed in the Commands area, you'll need to make sure it's available to InDesign when you open the Keyboard Shortcuts dialog box.

✦ Don't change systemwide conventions such as the shortcuts for New, Open, Save, and Print.

✦ Don't change common keyboard commands to harmful shortcuts — for example, don't use ⌘+F or Ctrl+F for changing leading rather than invoking Find/Change.

✦ If you share computers in any way — even just another user reaching over your shoulder to provide assistance — adding keyboard shortcuts is safer than changing them. Your shortcuts will be slightly customized, but other users will be able to use your copy of InDesign without unexpected results.

✦ If you're at a 24-hour production shop in which two or three people share computers, each person can have his or her own set of named keyboard shortcuts. But this requires each user to remember to activate his or her own set.

✦ You can't export keyboard shortcuts to share with other users. If consistency is important, make sure everyone creates the same set.

✦ Don't modify keyboard shortcuts for computers in public places such as training centers or photocopy centers.

✦ QuarkXPress users coming to InDesign have to learn new software anyway, so they might benefit — in the long run — from learning new keyboard shortcuts as well. Even though using your old shortcuts will ease the initial transition, the frustration caused by missing or different shortcuts can be worse than learning new ones.

✦ When you're specifying keyboard shortcuts, remember to use a modifier key or keys: ⌘, Option, Shift, or Control on the Mac and Ctrl, Alt, or Shift on Windows. Single-letter or single-number commands (which Adobe uses for selecting tools) obviously can't be used while you're editing text.

If all this makes me seem negative about customizing keyboard shortcuts, I'm really not. Just consider all the ramifications before you do any customizing.

Using and modifying default shortcuts

When you first launch InDesign, you're using the default set of shortcuts, which you can view in menus, in some Tool Tips, and in your documentation. (This book lists default shortcuts as well.) You cannot modify the default set, but you can create a new set based on it, and then modify the shortcuts in that set.

The Keyboard Shortcuts dialog box (Edit ➪ Keyboard Shortcuts), shown in Figure 3-17, provides all the tools you need for modifying keyboard shortcuts. To use the standard keyboard shortcuts after switching to another set, choose Default from the Set pop-up menu at the top of the dialog box, and then click OK.

Here's how to create a new set:

1. **Choose Edit ➪ Keyboard Shortcuts.**

2. **Click New Set.**

3. **In the New Set dialog box, choose Default from the Based On Set pop-up menu.**

4. **Type a different name for the set in the Name field, and then click OK to create the set.**

5. **To start modifying the commands, select a menu or type of shortcut to change from the Product Area pop-up menu.** For example, you can choose File Menu, Object Editing, or Typography.

6. **Scroll through the Commands area, and click to select a command so you can change its shortcut.** The Current Shortcuts area shows you the command's existing shortcut (if there is one).

7. **Click in the Press New Shortcut field. You have three options at this point:**

   - If a keyboard shortcut exists for this command, you can click Remove to delete it and free it up for another command.

   - If no keyboard shortcut exists for this command, you can press the actual modifier keys and command, and then click Assign.

   - If a keyboard shortcut exists for this command, but you want to override it, you can press the actual modifier keys and command, and then click Assign. (The shortcut you are overriding is shown below the Assign button.)

8. **Click Save after modifying a shortcut.**

9. **When you're finished editing keyboard shortcuts, click OK to save them.** For the shortcuts that don't appear in menus, you can print a list to use as a reference. See the section "Viewing and printing shortcuts" later in this chapter.

Tip You might consider adding a keyboard shortcut for Layout ➪ Create Guides, such as the unused Option+Shift+G or Alt+Shift+G. Another command sorely in need of a keyboard shortcut is Type ➪ Insert Glyphs. Try the unused Option+Shift+I or Alt+Shift+I.

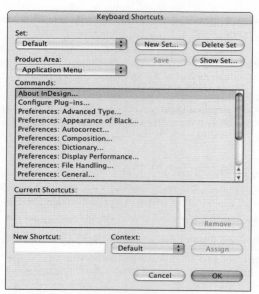

Figure 3-17: The Keyboard Shortcuts dialog box lets you create new sets of keyboard shortcuts.

Using and modifying QuarkXPress shortcuts

If you're switching to InDesign from QuarkXPress—and are not accustomed to using Photoshop or Illustrator—the keyboard shortcuts in InDesign may seem odd. To ease the transition to InDesign, Adobe has provided a set of keyboard shortcuts based on those in QuarkXPress 4.0. I say based on because some QuarkXPress commands don't have equivalents and some work very differently, while other QuarkXPress shortcuts conflict with long-established Adobe shortcuts. And commands unique to InDesign still have their own keyboard shortcuts—for example, you can still select tools with the single letters shown in the Tool Tips.

Among the shortcuts you'll miss or be confused by are the following:

✦ Option or Alt for the Page Grabber Hand is missing (use the Navigator pane instead).

✦ ⌘+K or Ctrl+K for deleting selected objects is missing (you can always use the Delete key unless the Type tool is selected). (Even though InDesign's QuarkXPress 4.0 shortcut set maps the Preferences dialog box to QuarkXPress 4's ⌘+Y or Ctrl+Y shortcut, it also retains the standard Adobe shortcut of ⌘+K or Ctrl+K to open the Preferences dialog box.)

If you want to use the QuarkXPress set of keyboard shortcuts, choose Set for QuarkXPress 4.0 from the Set pop-up menu at the top of the Keyboard Shortcuts dialog box (Edit ➪ Keyboard Shortcuts). You might want to print out the list of keyboard shortcuts and review them so you know what's available and what's different. (See the section "Viewing and printing shortcuts" later in this chapter.)

If you decide to use the QuarkXPress set of keyboard shortcuts, you might want to create a copy and modify some of them. For example, you can assign ⌘+K or Ctrl+K to Clear because you're used to using it for deleting items (rather than leave it set to open the Preferences dialog box). You can also repair the incorrect commands, although in many cases they're assigned to other commands and must be replaced.

Viewing and printing shortcuts

After you modify keyboard shortcuts, you may need a list for reference. (In addition, reviewing the entire QuarkXPress set before you start editing it is helpful.)

Click Show Set in the Keyboard Shortcuts dialog box (Edit ⇨ Keyboard Shortcuts) to view a list of shortcuts for the currently selected set. The shortcuts appear in TextEdit (on the Macintosh) or in WordPad (in Windows). You can then print the list from that application.

Color management settings

You can customize the way color management works. The Color Settings dialog box (choose Edit ⇨ Color Settings) lets you customize the default color transformations used for viewing and outputting colors.

Cross-Reference   See Chapter 28 for details on color management and how to set the defaults.

Modifying Defaults for Documents, Text, and Objects

When you create a new document, start typing, or create a new object, it is based on default settings that you can change. For example, by default, a new document is always letter-sized, but if you design only CD covers, you can change the default.

You may need to work with InDesign for a while to determine which of these settings to change and what settings you prefer. When you identify a problem—for example, you realize that you always end up changing the inset for text frames—jot down a note about it or close all documents right then. When no documents are open, change the setting for all future documents.

Document defaults

You can modify the default size, margins, and columns in new documents; the default attributes of guides; and the way layouts are adjusted. To modify document defaults, choose the following with no documents open:

✦ **File ⇨ Document Setup (Option+⌘+P or Ctrl+Alt+P).** The Document Setup dialog box, shown in Figure 3-18, lets you modify the default settings in the New Document dialog box for the Number of Pages, Page Size, Facing Pages, and Master Text Frame, as well as for bleeds and slugs if you click the More Options button.

✦ **Layout ⇨ Margins and Columns.** The Margins and Columns dialog box, shown in Figure 3-19, lets you modify the default settings in the New Document dialog box for the Margins and Columns areas.

✦ **Layout ⇨ Ruler Guides.** This adjusts the View Threshold and Color for all new guides. It opens the Ruler Guides dialog box, which is shown in Figure 3-20.

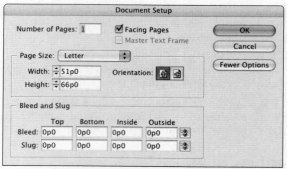

Figure 3-18: When no documents are open, the Document Setup dialog box lets you customize default settings in the New Document dialog box.

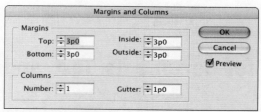

Figure 3-19: Use the Margins and Columns dialog box — when no documents are open — to establish default margins and columns.

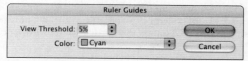

Figure 3-20: When no documents are open, the Ruler Guides dialog box lets you customize default settings for ruler display.

✦ **Layout ➪ Layout Adjustment.** The Layout Adjustment dialog box, shown in Figure 3-21, lets you resize entire layouts and customize how they are resized.

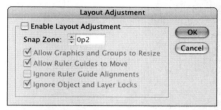

Figure 3-21: Use the Layout Adjustment dialog box — when no documents are open — to establish default layout-adjustment settings.

Text defaults

When you start typing in a new text frame, the text is formatted with default Character formats, Paragraph formats, and Story attributes. You can also choose to show invisible characters such as spaces and tabs by default; otherwise you'll need to activate it in each text-heavy document. To modify text defaults, choose:

✦ **Window ➪ Type & Tables ➪ Character (⌘+T or Ctrl+T).** Select default options for character formats such as Font, Size, and Leading from the Character pane. (You can also choose Type ➪ Character.)

✦ **Window ➪ Type & Tables ➪ Paragraph (Option+⌘+T or Ctrl+Alt+T).** Select defaults for paragraph formats such as alignment, indents, spacing, and so on from the Paragraph pane. (You can also choose Type ➪ Paragraph.)

✦ **Window ➪ Type & Tables ➪ Paragraph Styles (F11).** Select defaults for the [Basic Paragraph] style, which is what all unstyled imported text, as well as text typed in a new text frame in InDesign, will use. (You can also choose Type ➪ Paragraph Styles.)

✦ **Window ➪ Type & Tables ➪ Story.** This lets you activate Optical Margin Alignment by default. (Because Optical Margin Alignment works best for display type rather than body type, it's unlikely that you'll do this.)

✦ **Type ➪ Show Hidden Characters (⌘+Option+I or Ctrl+Alt+I).** Select this option if you often edit in InDesign and always end up turning on Show Hidden Characters.

You can also edit the spelling and hyphenation dictionaries while no documents are open by choosing Edit ➪ Spelling ➪ Dictionary. However, because all the edits are saved in the same file, it doesn't matter whether documents are open.

Object defaults

When you create new objects, they're based on some default settings. For example, you can specify how text wraps around objects. To modify object defaults, use the following commands:

✦ **Object ➪ Text Frame Options (⌘+B or Ctrl+B).** The Text Frame Options dialog box, shown in Figure 3-22, lets you specify the default Columns, Inset Spacing, First Baseline, and Ignore Text Wrap settings for new text frames.

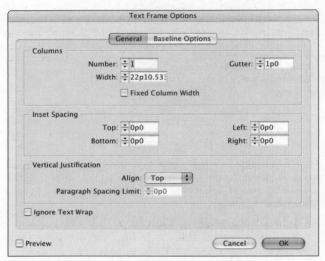

Figure 3-22: Use the Text Frame Options dialog box to specify default attributes of new text frames.

✦ **Window ➪ Object Styles (⌘+F7 or Ctrl+F7).** Select defaults for the [Normal Graphics Frame] and [Normal Text Frame] styles, which are what all new frames created in InDesign will use.

✦ **Window ➪ Text Wrap (⌘+Option+W or Ctrl+Alt+W).** The Text Wrap pane lets you specify how text will wrap around all new objects.

✦ **Object ➪ Corner Effects (⌘+Option+R or Ctrl+Alt+R).** The Corner Effects dialog box lets you choose a style for the corners of all new frames except those created with the Type tool.

✦ **Object ➪ Clipping Path (Option+Shift+⌘+K or Ctrl+Alt+Shift+K).** The Clipping Path dialog box lets you specify the default attributes of clipping paths imported into graphics frames.

✦ **Window ➪ Stroke (F10), Window ➪ Swatches (F5), Window ➪ Gradient (F6), and Window ➪ Attributes.** These let you specify other default properties of objects. For example, if all objects you create are stroked (framed), specify a weight in the Stroke pane.

✦ **Double-click the Polygon tool to open the Polygon Settings dialog box (there is no menu command or keyboard shortcut),** which lets you specify the default number of sides and the inset for the first new polygon in a new document.

Modifying Defaults for Views

Another way to customize your copy of InDesign is to specify which layout tools appear by default. The lower two-thirds of the View menu, shown in Figure 3-23, lets you do this. If you'd prefer not to view the edges of frames, you can hide them by default. Or if you always want to start with a document-wide grid, you can show it by default. To modify viewing defaults, choose the appropriate menu options. Note that the menu names will toggle between Show and Hide each time you select them. (Therefore, if the menu option begins with Hide, that means that attribute is currently being displayed; if it starts with Show, that means the attribute is currently not being displayed.)

Figure 3-23: The View menu commands that are available when no documents are open

✦ **View ➪ Show/Hide Text Threads (Option+⌘+Y or Ctrl+Alt+Y)** to show or hide the links between text frames.

✦ **View ➪ Show/Hide Frame Edges (⌘+H or Ctrl+H)** to show or hide the edges of frames.

✦ **View ➪ Show/Hide Rulers (⌘+R or Ctrl+R)** to show or hide the horizontal and vertical ruler.

✦ **View ➪ Grids & Guides ➪ Show/Hide Guides (⌘+; [semicolon] or Ctrl+; [semicolon])** to show or hide margin, column, and layout guides.

✦ **View ➪ Grids & Guides ➪ Show/Hide Baseline Grid (Option+⌘+' [apostrophe] or Ctrl+Alt+' [apostrophe])** to show or hide the baseline grid established in the Grids pane of the Preferences dialog box (choose InDesign ➪ Preferences ➪ Grids on the Mac and Edit ➪ Preferences ➪ Grids in Windows).

✦ **View** ➪ **Grids & Guides** ➪ **Show/Hide Document Grid (⌘+' [apostrophe] or Ctrl+'
[apostrophe])** to show or hide the document-wide grid established in the Grids pane of
the Preferences dialog box.

In addition to changing which layout tools appear by default, you can control some of their
default behavior. Choose the appropriate menu options to enable or disable them. Note that if
currently enabled, a check mark will appear next to the menu option's name, in which case
choosing it again disables this option and the check mark will disappear.

✦ **View** ➪ **Grids & Guides** ➪ **Lock Guides (Option+⌘+; [semicolon] or Ctrl+Alt+; [semi-
colon]).** Disabled by default, when you choose this option to enable it, all ruler guides
are locked in place.

✦ **View** ➪ **Grids & Guides** ➪ **Lock Column Guides.** Enabled by default, when you choose
this option to disable it, all column guides are no longer locked in place.

✦ **View** ➪ **Grids & Guides** ➪ **Snap to Guides (Shift+⌘+; [semicolon] or Ctrl+Shift+; [semi-
colon]).** Enabled by default, when you choose this option to disable it, aligning objects
with guides is more difficult, but positioning objects *near* guides is easier.

✦ **View** ➪ **Grids & Guides** ➪ **Snap to Document Grid.** Disabled by default, when you
choose this option to enable it, objects are easy to align with document grid lines
whether or not they're showing.

**New
Feature**

The Lock Column Guides option is new to InDesign CS2.

Several View menu options have been moved to the new Grids & Guides submenu in
InDesign CS2.

Color and Style Defaults

If you find yourself creating the same colors, paragraph styles, character styles, and object
styles over and over again, create them with no documents open. They will be available to all
future documents. To create these elements, use the New command in the palette menus for
the following panes: Swatches (F5), Character Styles (Shift+F11), Paragraph Styles (F11), and
Object Styles (⌘+F7 or Ctrl+F7). You can also use the palette menus' Load commands to
import colors and styles from existing documents instead of creating them from scratch.

Reverting Preferences and Defaults

If you inherit a copy of InDesign from another user, or if you've been changing preferences
and defaults at random and are unhappy with the results, you can revert InDesign to all its
default settings. You will particularly want to do this if you're learning InDesign using tutorial
files or in a class setting.

Tip

To revert all preferences and defaults, deleting the InDesign Defaults preference files when
opening InDesign, press Control+Option+Shift+⌘ or Ctrl+Alt+Shift when launching
InDesign.

Note

Keep in mind that you will need to re-enable any custom keyboard shortcut set you were
using by choosing it from the Set pop-up menu in the Keyboard Shortcuts dialog box (Edit ➪
Keyboard Shortcuts).

Changing Views

Customizing also involves the way you look at your work. InDesign provides a variety of options for magnifying and displaying your work. Understanding these ahead of time and memorizing the ones that work best for your type of work, your eyesight, and your monitor will help you get started with InDesign.

Desktop publishing pioneers in the late 1980s often worked on publications using 9-inch black-and-white monitors, and they spent as much time zooming in, zooming out, and pushing oversized pages around on undersized screens as they did formatting text and modifying pictures. The best present you could give yourself — or your employer could give you — is a large monitor (two large monitors aren't bad, either). In this era of proliferating panes, there's no such thing as too much screen space. But even if you have a huge monitor, you're going to find yourself zooming in and out and using InDesign's other display-related features to control what you see on-screen and help you work more efficiently.

Zooming and scrolling

When you begin building a page, it's often easiest to display the entire page (choose View ⇨ Fit Page In Window, or press ⌘+0 [zero] or Ctrl+0 [zero]) or spread (choose View ⇨ Fit Spread in Window, or press Option+⌘+0 [zero] or Ctrl+Alt+0 [zero]) and work somewhat roughly — creating the required objects and positioning them more or less where you want them. After you add text and pictures to your frames, you'll probably want to begin polishing the page by modifying individual objects. At this point, seeing a reduced view of an entire page or spread isn't the best way to work. If you need to work on details, it's best to pull out a magnifying glass. With InDesign, this means tapping into the program's view-magnification capabilities.

You can zoom in to magnifications up to 4,000 percent and zoom out to magnifications as small as 10 percent. Like many other features, you have several options for changing view magnification. You can zoom in and out using:

✦ The Zoom tool

✦ The zoom commands in the View menu

✦ The Zoom pop-up menu or the accompanying box at the bottom left of the document window

The Zoom tool

If you're the type of designer who prefers the click-and-drag solution when it's available, you'll probably use the Zoom tool to enlarge a portion of a page. Here's how it works:

1. **Select the Zoom tool or press Z if the Type tool is not selected.**

2. **At this point you have two options:**

   • **You can move the Zoom pointer over the area you want to see and click the mouse.** Each click enlarges the view to the next preset magnification percentage. (To display these percentages, click the pop-up menu next to the Zoom field at the bottom-left corner of the document window.)

- **You can click and drag a rectangle that encloses the area you want to see.** When you release the mouse, the area is centered in the document window. (When you hold Option or Alt, the plus sign in the Zoom pointer changes to a minus sign. Clicking or clicking and dragging in this situation will zoom out instead of in.)

Tip   You never have to actually select the Zoom tool. Instead, use its keyboard shortcuts: ⌘+spacebar or Ctrl+spacebar (for zooming in) and ⌘+Option+spacebar or Ctrl+Alt+space-bar (for zooming out).

Zoom options in the View menu

The third group of commands in the View menu, shown in Figure 3-24, lets you change the view magnification. Here's a brief description of each command:

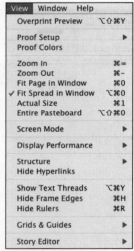

Figure 3-24: The zoom commands in the View menu

- ✦ **Zoom In (⌘+= or Ctrl+=).** This enlarges the display magnification to the next higher percentage. (When no objects are active, the Zoom In command is also available in the contextual menu.)
- ✦ **Zoom Out (⌘+– [hyphen] or Ctrl+– [hyphen]).** This reduces the display magnification to the next lower percentage. (When no objects are active, the Zoom Out command is also available in the contextual menu.)

Tip   If an object is active when you choose Zoom In or Zoom Out or use the Zoom field or pop-up menu, the object is centered in the document window after the view changes.

✦ **Fit Page in Window (⌘+0 [zero] or Ctrl+0 [zero]).** This reduces or enlarges the display magnification of the currently displayed page (the current page number is displayed in the page number field at the lower left of a document window) so that the entire page is visible (and centered) in the document window.

✦ **Fit Spread in Window (Option+⌘+0 [zero] or Ctrl+Alt+0 [zero]).** This is similar to Fit Page In Window, except you use it if you're working on a facing-page document and want the entire spread to be on-screen.

✦ **Actual Size (⌘+1 or Ctrl+1).** This displays the document at 100 percent magnification. When you choose Actual Size, a pica is a pica and an inch is an inch — if your monitor is appropriately configured.

Tip Double-clicking the Zoom tool is the same as choosing View ↪ Actual Size; it displays a document at 100 percent magnification.

✦ **Entire Pasteboard (Option+Shift+⌘+0 [zero] or Ctrl+Alt+Shift+0 [zero]).** Reduces the display magnification so that the current page or spread and its surrounding pasteboard are visible within the document window.

Tip To switch back and forth between the last two magnification percentages, press Option+⌘+2 or Ctrl+Alt+2.

The Zoom field

The Zoom field in the bottom-left corner of the document window and its accompanying pop-up menu, shown in Figure 3-25, offer two additional methods for changing display magnification. To use the field, simply type a value between 5 percent and 4,000 percent, and then press Return or Enter. To use the pop-up menu, click the arrow, and then choose one of the preset magnification values.

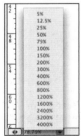

Figure 3-25:
The Zoom field
and its pop-up
menu

Tip If an object is active when you click Zoom In or Zoom Out (from the View menu) or use the Zoom field or pop-up menu, the object is centered in the document window after the view changes.

Pushing a page around with the Hand tool

Sometimes after you've zoomed in to work on a particular object, you'll want to work on a portion of the page that's not currently displayed. You can always zoom out, then use the Zoom tool or the zoom commands to zoom back in, or you can "push" the page around within the window until you can see the portion of the page you want to work on. To scroll, you can use the scroll bars and boxes on the right and bottom of the document window, or you can use the Hand tool (press H if the Type tools is not selected). Simply select it, and then click and drag to move the currently displayed page or spread around within the document window. When you can see what you want, release the mouse.

Tip   To temporarily access the Hand tool when the Type tool is not selected, press the spacebar. The hand pointer appears. Click and drag to move the page within the document window. (This is one of InDesign's most useful keyboard shortcuts!)

Changing the view with the Navigator pane

The Navigator pane (Window ⇨ Object & Layout ⇨ Navigator), shown in Figure 3-26, is the home of several display-related features, most of which are available elsewhere (and which I've already covered in this chapter).

Figure 3-26: The Navigator pane

Tip   If you choose View All Spreads from the Navigator pane's pop-up menu, the page area at the top of the pane displays all of the document's spreads. The more spreads in a document, the smaller each one appears in the Navigator pane when View All Spreads is selected.

Object display options

Generally, you're going to want to display the objects you've placed on your pages. After all, what's displayed on-screen is what gets printed, right? Not exactly. For example, text and graphic frames are displayed on-screen with blue borders, even if they're empty, but the borders don't print. In addition to the six zoom commands (covered earlier in this chapter), there are two other commands that affect how objects appear:

✦ **View ⇨ Show/Hide Frame Edges (⌘+H or Ctrl+H).** When you click Hide Frame Edges, text and graphics frames are not displayed with a blue border. Additionally, an *X* does not appear in empty graphics frames when frame edges are hidden. You might want to hide frame edges to see how a page will look when printed.

Tip   When you move an object by clicking and dragging, you have the choice of displaying the entire object (including the contents of a frame) or displaying only the bounding box. If you begin dragging immediately after clicking to select an object, only the bounding box appears as you drag. If you pause after clicking an object until the stem of the arrow pointer disappears and then begin dragging, the entire object appears.

✦ **In the Pages pane's palette menu, View ➪ Show/Hide Master Items.** When you choose Show Master Items, any objects on the currently displayed document page's master page are appear. When you choose Hide Master Items, master objects on the currently displayed page are hidden. This command is page-specific, which lets you show or hide master objects on a page-by-page basis.

Opening Multiple Document Windows

Like most programs, InDesign lets you open several documents at once. It also takes this concept one step further by letting you open multiple windows simultaneously for individual documents. Earlier in this chapter, I recommended using the largest monitor you can get your mitts on. A large monitor makes this feature even more useful. By opening multiple windows, you can:

✦ **Display two (or more) different pages or spreads at once and work on them at the same time.** Well, you still have to work on them one at a time, but no navigation is required—you have only to click within the appropriate window.

✦ **Display multiple magnifications of the same page.** For example, you can work on a detail at high magnification in one window and display the entire page—and see the results of your detail work—at actual size in another window.

✦ **Display a master page in one window and a document page based on that master page in another window.** When you change the master page, the change is reflected in the window in which the associated document page is displayed.

To open a new window for the active document, choose Window ➪ Arrange ➪ New Window. The new window appears in front of the original window. To show both windows at once, choose Window ➪ Arrange ➪ Tile. When you click the Tile command, all open windows are resized and displayed side by side. (If you choose Window ➪ Arrange ➪ Cascade, all open windows appear stacked and staggered on top of each other. The frontmost document window is visible; the title bars of the other windows are visible above the frontmost document.)

When multiple windows are open, clicking on a window's title bar or anywhere within the window activates it. Also, the names of all open documents appear at the bottom of the Window menu. Choosing a document name from the View menu brings that document to the front. If multiple windows are open for a particular document, each window appears (they're displayed in the order in which you created them) in the Window menu.

Tip   When you open a document, it appears in the last window you used before you last saved it. Any other windows that were open when you saved the document are not saved.

Ending the Exposé Conflict

The Mac OS X Exposé utility usurps three commonly used InDesign shortcuts: F10 (which opens the Stoke pane), F11 (which opens the Paragraph Styles pane), and F12 (which opens the Pages page). Exposé provides a quick way to change your display of windows on-screen, but its usage of keyboard shortcuts long employed by other programs is annoying.

I recommend that you change the Exposé shortcuts to ones that won't interfere with InDesign and other programs. To change the shortcuts, open the System Preferences dialog box (➪ System Preferences), double-click the Exposé button, and change or disable the Exposé shortcuts in the Keyboard section of the Exposé dialog box.

To close all windows for the currently displayed document, press Shift+⌘+W or Ctrl+Shift+W. To close all windows for all open documents, press Option+Shift+⌘+W or Ctrl+Alt+Shift+W.

Summary

InDesign provides extensive controls for setting preferences for everything from how objects appear on-screen and how text is managed for spelling and hyphenation to how keyboard shortcuts work and how color is handled. You can also reset all preference changes to their defaults with just one command.

✦   ✦   ✦

Document Fundamentals

Creating, Opening, and Saving Documents

You're pumped up. You've purchased a copy of InDesign, installed it, checked out the interface, and now you're ready to put the program to work. So, what's next? Launch the application and start clicking? Hardly. Creating a publication with InDesign is much like going on a trip. You won't reach your destination unless you've prepared a plan for getting there. And you'll reach your destination more quickly and more easily if your plan is a sound one.

Remember, too, that most trips don't go exactly according to plan. InDesign is both versatile and forgiving. As you create a publication, you should feel free to change your mind, experiment, and let your creativity roam. As long as you reach your destination (on time!), taking a few detours is acceptable, and encountering a few roadblocks (small ones, you hope) is inevitable.

Before You Begin

Before you launch InDesign, open a new document, and begin working, you must answer several fundamental questions about the publication you'll be producing:

✦ What is the basic nature of the piece? Will it be printed, or will it be distributed over the Internet or an intranet? Is it going to be published as both a print and PDF piece?

✦ What are its dimensions?

✦ How many pages will it have? If it will be a multipage publication, will it have facing pages like a book or a catalog, or will it be single-sided like a flip chart?

✦ How many columns will each page have? How wide will the margins be?

✦ Does the budget allow for the use of color? If so, how many colors? What kind of paper will it be printed on? What kind of printer or printing press will be used?

✦ How will the publication be distributed? Under what circumstances will it be read? What's the life expectancy of the publication?

✦ If the publication is bound for the Internet, will you create an HTML file (which can be viewed by anybody with a Web browser) or a PDF file (which requires viewers to have the free Adobe Reader application or browser plug-in)?

✦ And what about the content of your publication? What programs were used to create the text files and graphic files your publication will contain? Did you create the content yourself, or did others? What file formats were used for text and graphic files? What is the most effective way to present the content given the production requirements and budget?

As you answer these questions, a rough image of your publication will begin to take shape in your mind. When you're ready to begin turning your ideas into an actual publication, you have a couple of choices. Many designers whose skills date back to the days of traditional paste-up still prefer to use traditional tools — a drawing pad and colored markers or pencils in this case — to create rough sketches before they fire up their page-layout or illustration program. Other designers who were never exposed to such archaic tools are comfortable doing their brainstorming and sketching on the fly, using their favorite software. Whatever method suits you is fine. Keep in mind that, at this early stage, you shouldn't be spending much time fine-tuning details. You can do that later with InDesign.

An overly careful person can plan forever — in which case, nothing actually gets done. At some point, when the image you have of the publication you're creating is clear enough in your mind to begin work, it's time to create a new InDesign document.

Setting Up a New Publication

After you launch InDesign, you have two options: You can choose the Open command (File ➪ Open, or ⌘+O or Ctrl+O) to open a previously created document or template (more on opening documents and templates later in this chapter), or you can choose File ➪ New ➪ Document, or ⌘+N or Ctrl+N, to create a new document.

When you create a new document, the New Document dialog box shown in Figure 4-1 appears. It is here that you implement many of the decisions — including page size, number of pages, number of columns, and margin width you arrived at during the planning stage. Although you're free to change your mind later, you'll save yourself time and potential headaches by sticking with the basic page parameters you establish in the New Document dialog box.

Tip   To change the measurement units displayed in the New Document dialog box, choose InDesign ➪ Preferences ➪ Units & Increments on the Mac or Edit ➪ Preferences ➪ Units & Increments in Windows, or press ⌘+K or Ctrl+K, and then choose the measurement system you want from the Horizontal and Vertical pop-up menus in the Ruler Units area. If you change preferences when no documents are open, your changes are applied to all subsequently created documents.

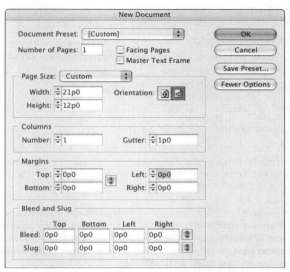

Figure 4-1: The settings you make in the New Document dialog box establish the basic framework for the pages in your publication. This example shows the settings used to create a standard 21p-×-12p (3½-×-2-inch) business card. Notice that the Facing Pages and Master Text Frame options are not selected because they're not necessary for a one-page document.

Creating new documents

Here's how to create a new document:

1. **Choose File ➪ New ➪ Document or press ⌘+N or Ctrl+N.**

2. **If you know exactly how many pages your publication will have, type the number in the Number of Pages field.** If you don't know for sure, you can always add or delete pages later as needed.

3. **Select the Facing Pages option if you're creating a multipage publication that will have a spine, such as a book, catalog, or magazine.** You do not need to select this option if you're creating a one-page document, such as a business card, an ad, or a poster. Some publications, such as flip charts, presentations, and three-ring bound documents, have multiple pages but use only one side of the page. For such documents, don't select the Facing Pages option, either.

4. **If you want to flow text from page to page in a multipage document, such as a book or a catalog, select the Master Text Frame option.** (See Chapter 15 for more information about using master text frames.) When you select this option, InDesign automatically

adds a text frame to the document's master page and to all document pages based on this master page. This saves you the work of creating a text frame on each page and manually threading text through each frame.

5. **In the Page Size area, you can choose one of the predefined sizes from the pop-up menu.** Your options are Letter (8.5" × 11"), Legal (8.5" × 14"), Tabloid (11" × 17"), Letter Half (5.5" × 8.5"), Legal Half (7" × 8.5"), A4 (210mm × 297mm), A3 (297mm × 420mm), A5 (148mm × 210mm), B5 (176mm × 250mm), Compact Disc (4.7222" × 4.5"), or Custom. If you choose Custom, you can type values in the Width and Height fields—and if you type values in those fields, the Page Size automatically changes to Custom. The minimum height and width is 1 pica (0.1667"); the maximum is 216". Clicking the Portrait icon next to Orientation produces a vertical page (the larger of the Height and Width values is used in the Height field); clicking the Landscape icon produces a horizontal page (the larger of the Height and Width values is used in the Width field). You can also specify Height and Width values by clicking the up and down arrows associated with these fields.

Tip

When you specify page size, make sure the values you type in the Height and Width fields are the size of the final printed piece—and not the size of the paper in your printer. For example, if you're creating a standard-sized business card, type **3.5i** in the Width field and **2i** in the Height field. If you want to print *n-up*—meaning several "pages" on one sheet, such as several business cards on an 8½-x-11-inch sheet of paper—you can create a letter-sized document (8.5" × 11"), but you'll have to arrange the business cards within the page boundary and add your own crop marks for each card.

6. **Specify margin values in the Margins area.** The *margin* is the white area around the outside of the page within which page elements—text and pictures—are placed. A document doesn't have to have margins (you can type **0** into these fields), and if you want you can place text and pictures in the margin area. If the Facing Pages option is selected, Inside and Outside fields are available in the Margins area. Designers often specify larger inside margins for multipage publications to accommodate the fold at the spine. If Facing Pages is not selected, Left and Right fields replace the Inside and Outside fields. You can also specify margin values by clicking the up or down arrows associated with the fields.

7. **Type a value in the Columns field to specify how many columns your pages have.** You can also specify the number of columns by clicking the up or down arrows associated with the Column field.

8. **Specify a gutter distance (the gutter is the space between columns) in the Gutter field.** You can also specify a gutter width value by clicking the up/down arrows associated with the Gutter field.

9. **If you click More Options, the Bleed and Slug area of the New Document dialog box appears (refer to Figure 4-1).** The More Options button provides options to set bleed and slug areas. A *bleed area* is a margin on the outside of the page for objects you want to extend past the edge of the page—you want them to extend at least ⅛ inch so if there is any shifting of the paper during printing, there's no white space where the image should be (touching the edge of the page). The *slug area* is an area reserved for printing crop marks, color plate names, and other printing information—some output devices cut these off during printing unless a slug area is defined. For both bleed and slug areas, you can set the top, bottom, left, and right margins independently.

10. **Click OK to close the New Document dialog box.** When you do, your new, blank document appears in a new document window. Figure 4-2 shows the window of a newly created document (a business card) that uses the settings shown in Figure 4-1.

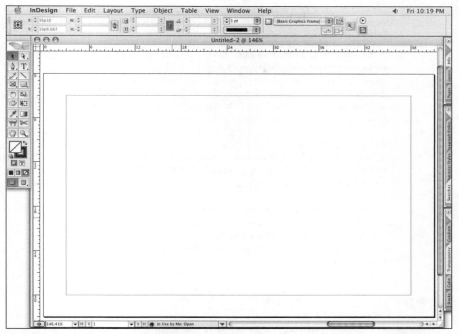

Figure 4-2: The business card settings in the New Document dialog box shown in Figure 4-1 resulted in the document you see here. The view percentage field in the lower-left corner of the document window shows that the business card is currently displayed at 146.41 percent of actual size.

Tip

You can bypass the New Document dialog box by pressing Shift+⌘+N or Ctrl+Shift+N. When you use this method, the most recent settings in the New Document dialog box are used for the new document.

Creating your own document types

InDesign lets you create predefined document types, called document presets, to supplement the standard ones such as Letter.

There are three ways to create document presets:

✦ You can save these new-document settings by clicking Save Preset in the New Document dialog box. These saved settings will then appear in the Document Style pop-up menu in the future.

✦ You can add custom pages by editing the New Doc Sizes.txt file in the Presets folder (in the InDesign applications folder) and adding a new line for each document style as follows: name→width→height. For example: Business card→3.5"→2". (The → character here indicates a tab; you should press the Tab key.) This is a handy way to distribute document styles to multiple users. An example would be building a document style for every standard ad size for a magazine or newspaper to ensure correct dimensions on new ad documents.

✦ You can choose File ⇨ Document Presets ⇨ Define to create (by clicking New) a new document style or import (by clicking Load) one from another document. It opens the dialog box shown in Figure 4-3.

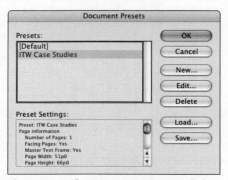

Figure 4-3: The Document Presets dialog box lets you create, import, edit, and delete document styles.

Opening Documents and Templates

Opening documents with InDesign is pretty much the same as opening documents with any program. Simply choose File ⇨ Open or press ⌘+O or Ctrl+O, locate and click the document on which you want to work, and then click Open. But InDesign offers a few options for opening documents you don't find in every program. For example, you can:

✦ Open more than one document at a time.

✦ Open a copy of a document instead of the original. This keeps the original file from being overwritten accidentally — very helpful if you're making several variations of one document.

✦ Open a template under its own name. This makes editing templates easier than it is with other programs, specifically QuarkXPress.

✦ Open documents created with some versions of PageMaker and QuarkXPress.

New Feature   InDesign CS2 can now open QuarkXPress Passport 3.3–4.1 files (the multilingual format) in addition to the standard single-language QuarkXPress 3.3–4.1 formats, plus it can now open PageMaker Version 6.0 files, not just versions 6.5 and 7.0. Also, the ability to open GoLive section and PDF creation setting (job option) files is new to InDesign CS2.

Tip   InDesign's File menu displays the names of the five most recently saved documents in the Open Recent submenu that appears under the Open option in the File menu after you have opened a file.

To open a file:

1. **Choose File ➪ Open, or press ⌘+O or Ctrl+O.** The Open a File dialog box shown in Figures 4-4 and 4-5 appears. The Open a File dialog box differs based on whether you are using Adobe's Version Cue file-management system or not, as covered in Chapter 35. (This book's screen shots have Version Cue enabled because that is InDesign's default setting.)

New Feature

InDesign CS2 gives you two ways to work with files, through the standard Windows and Macintosh folder structures or through the Adobe Version Cue structure, which is designed to help multiuser environments work in shared folders. Version Cue is enabled by default in InDesign CS2. See Chapter 35 for more information on using this feature.

Tip

One downside to the use of the Version Cue dialog boxes is that you won't see image previews when placing graphics in their default views, as you will with the standard Mac and Windows dialog boxes. To see image previews in Version Cue dialog boxes, choose Thumbnails, Icons, or Tiles from the Version Cue dialog box's View menu, as explained in Chapter 35.

2. **Locate and open the folder that contains the document(s) you want to open.** Click a filename or press and hold ⌘ or Ctrl and click multiple filenames. In Windows, the Files of Type pop-up menu offers several options: PageMaker 6.0–7.0 files, QuarkXPress 3.3–4.1 files, InDesign files, InDesign Interchange, GoLive Section, Adobe PDF Creation Settings Files, and All Formats. Choose any of these options to display a specific file format in the file list. Note that InDesign CS2 can open files created by any previous version of InDesign, in addition to CS2-created files. The InDesign Interchange format is a variation of the standard InDesign CS2 format that lets InDesign CS read your CS2 file, minus any CS2-specific formatting.

   On a Mac, the Open a File dialog box displays any supported file formats that have a Mac icon, and the dialog box includes a Preview pane that displays a thumbnail version of the selected file or, more commonly, its icon.

Platform Difference

In Windows InDesign, use All Files in the Files of Type pop-up menu to display files with no extensions. In Macintosh InDesign, use All Documents in the Enable pop-up menus to display files without the InDesign icons.

3. **Click Open Normal if you want to open the original document (rather than a copy of the document); click Open Copy to open a copy of a document.** When you open a copy of a document, it's assigned a default name (Untitled-1, Untitled-2, and so on). If you want to use a template to create a new version of a publication, click Open; InDesign will create a document based on the template. To open a template under its own name so that you can edit it, click Open Original. Templates are explained in the following section, "Opening documents versus opening templates."

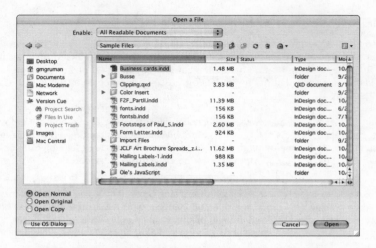

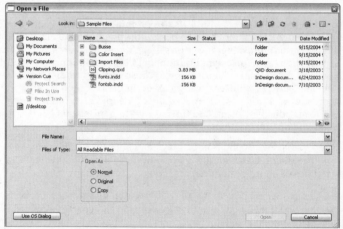

Figure 4-4: With Version Cue enabled, the Mac (top) and Windows (bottom) versions of the Open a File dialog box differ slightly. When you open a file, you have the option to open it normally (Open Normal), open the original copy of a template (Open Original), or open a copy of the file (Open Copy).

4. **Click Open to close the dialog box and open the selected file.** Each document you open appears in a separate document window. The page and view magnification displayed when a document was last saved is used when you open the document.

Tip

You can also open an InDesign document or template by double-clicking its file icon. If InDesign is not running, double-clicking a document or template file — as long as it has the proper icon on the Mac or file extension (.indd for documents and .indt for templates) in Windows — will launch the application and open the document/template. If InDesign is already running, the document appears in a new window.

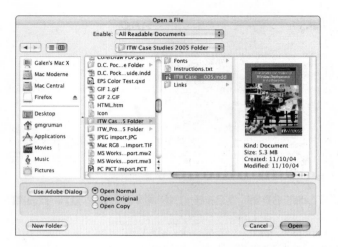

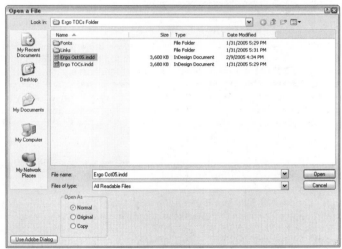

Figure 4-5: With Version Cue disabled, the native Mac (top) and Windows (bottom) versions of the Open a File dialog box also differ slightly from each other.

Opening documents versus opening templates

Whenever you save a document, you have the option of saving a standard document file or a template (more on saving templates later in this chapter). A *template* is an InDesign file that's used to create multiple iterations of the same publication. For example, if you produce a monthly newsletter, you'll save gobs of time and ensure consistency from issue to issue by using a template as the starting point for each edition of the newsletter. A template is essentially the shell of a publication that contains the basic framework—page layout, master pages, styles, and so on—but doesn't contain any actual content.

For more information about creating templates, see Chapter 7.

When you open a template, you have two choices: You can either open a copy of the file and use it to create a new publication, or you can open the original file, make changes, and then save an updated version of the template. If you want to use a template as the starting point for a new publication, choose File ➪ Open or press ⌘+O or Ctrl+O, locate and select the template, and make sure Open Normal is selected in the Open a File dialog box (refer to Figure 4-4) before you click Open. If you want to modify a template, click Open Original. If Open Normal is selected, clicking Open opens a new document window and assigns the document a default name, Untitled-1, Untitled-2, and so on. If Open Original is selected, the original file opens and the original name appears in the title bar.

Converting documents created with other programs

One of InDesign's hallmarks is its ability to open documents from other programs and convert them to InDesign documents. You can open PageMaker 6.0–7.0 and QuarkXPress and QuarkXPress Passport 3.3–4.1 documents. (Adobe has no plans to support files in the version 5 or 6 formats of QuarkXPress.)

Well, *most* of the time you can open PageMaker and QuarkXPress documents. Because the other programs' formats are so different from InDesign's, and their capabilities differ as well, the chances of being able to import a foreign document and have it flawlessly convert to InDesign are small. So use this feature to do the first step in the conversion process, but expect to spend time cleaning up the converted files by hand. In some cases, you may see that the amount of cleanup work is more than simply re-creating the document in InDesign from scratch — don't panic when that's the case. And be happy when your documents convert effortlessly.

InDesign alerts you to any import issues of PageMaker and QuarkXPress files with a dialog box that appears after the import is complete (see Figure 4-6).

InDesign cannot import PDF files, but it can bring in PDF files as graphics for placement in your document. Chapter 22 covers this process in detail. However, InDesign can open GoLive section files, a format for XML-based Web documents; Chapter 34 covers this in more detail. Finally, it can also import PDF job-option files, so you can reuse the same settings already developed for Adobe Acrobat Distiller when you export to PDF, as Chapter 31 covers.

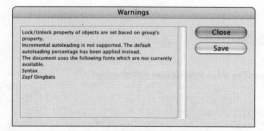

Figure 4-6: InDesign shows a Warnings dialog box if there are any conversion issues when importing foreign file formats.

QuarkXPress

InDesign can read QuarkXPress and QuarkXPress Passport files from versions 3.3, 4.0, and 4.1. Because there are so many differences between QuarkXPress and InDesign, it's impossible to predict all the conversion issues that may arise. The good news is that a great many things work well, but some don't. Here are some common conversion issues to which you should pay attention:

✦ If your QuarkXPress document relies on XTensions (a type of plug-in) to add capabilities (such as table creation), it will not convert correctly into InDesign and may not even import at all. Examples include any documents built with QuarkXPress's indexing and book features.

✦ QuarkXPress's leading model is different than InDesign's, so expect leading to sometimes vary significantly, especially if you use additive leading as the automatic leading method in QuarkXPress.

✦ InDesign won't retain kerning-table adjustments in QuarkXPress files. (It does retain any kerning applied manually, which InDesign 2 did not.)

✦ The customizable dashes in QuarkXPress are converted to solid and dashed lines (note that stripes do convert properly).

✦ Special gradient blends, such as the diamond pattern, are converted to linear blends or circular blends.

✦ Text on a curved path is converted to regular text in a rectangular frame, even though InDesign supports text on paths.

✦ H&J sets don't have an equivalent in InDesign, so they do not convert, although any H&J settings are carried over into the converted paragraph styles.

✦ Libraries won't convert.

✦ Printer styles won't convert.

Appendix C covers other issues in moving from QuarkXPress to InDesign.

PageMaker

InDesign can read PageMaker 6.0, 6.5, and 7.0 files. Because PageMaker and InDesign offer many of the same features, there are fewer translation issues between them. Some to take note of include:

✦ Fill patterns aren't supported.

✦ Libraries won't convert.

✦ Printer styles won't convert.

Appendix D covers other issues in moving from PageMaker to InDesign.

Importing text files

In addition to letting you open InDesign, PageMaker, and QuarkXPress files, InDesign also lets you work with text files created with word processing programs. However, you can't open word processing files using the Open command (File ➪ Open, or ⌘+O or Ctrl+O). Instead, you must place, or import, text files using the Place command (File ➪ Place, or ⌘+D or Ctrl+D).

You can use the Place command to import Rich Text Format (RTF), Microsoft Excel, Microsoft Word, and text-only (ASCII). For Word and Excel, InDesign supports all Mac versions since version 98 and all Windows versions since version 97.

InDesign also supports two proprietary text formats: Tagged Text, a way of coding text files with InDesign formatting information; and InDesign Interchange, a format that lets InDesign CS and InDesign CS2 users work on the same files.

Cross-Reference

For more information about importing text files and on Tagged Text, see Chapter 13.

In addition to letting you import text files, InDesign lets you export text files. See the section "Saving files in other formats" later in this chapter for more information.

Recovering a document after a crash or power failure

InDesign includes an automatic recovery feature that protects your documents in the event of a power failure or a system crash. As you work on a document, any changes you make after saving it are stored in a separate, temporary file. Under normal circumstances, each time you choose Save, the information in the temporary file is applied to the document. The data in the temporary file is important only if you aren't able to save a document before crashing. A word of warning: Although InDesign's automatic recovery feature is a nice safety net, you should still be careful to save your work often. Here's how it works:

1. **Relaunch InDesign or, if necessary, restart your computer and then launch InDesign.**

2. **If automatic-recovery data is available, InDesign automatically opens the recovered document and displays the word "Recovered" in the document's title bar.** This lets you know that the document contains changes that were not included in the last saved version.

3. **If you want to save the recovered data, choose File ➪ Save; "Recovered" is removed as part of the filename, and InDesign asks if you want to overwrite the old file.** Overwriting the old file is easier than using File ➪ Save As and typing a name—unless you do want to save a copy of the file in case you want to go back to the old version later. If you want to use the last saved version of the document (and disregard the recovered data), close the file (File ➪ Close, or ⌘+W or Ctrl+W) without saving, and then open the file (File ➪ Open, or ⌘+O or Ctrl+O).

Note

Sometimes, InDesign can't automatically recover the documents for you. Instead, it gives you the choice of recovering any files open during a crash or power outage, saving the recovery data for later, or deleting the recovery data. You'll typically want to recover the files immediately.

Saving Documents and Templates

When you open a new document, it's assigned a default name—Untitled-1, Untitled-2, and so on—and the first page appears in the document window. At this point, you're like a painter standing in front of a blank canvas. But painters don't have to worry about system crashes and power failures; you do. Make sure that when you work on InDesign documents, you follow the first rule of safe computing: Save early and often.

The second group of commands—Close, Save, Save As, Save a Copy As, Save a Version, and Revert—in InDesign's File menu provides options for saving the active/front most document. Here's a rundown of what each command does:

✦ **Close (⌘+W, or Ctrl+W or Ctrl+F4).** This closes the active document. If the document has never been saved or if it's been changed since it was last saved, a dialog box appears that lets you save, close without saving, or cancel and return to the document.

✦ **Save (⌘+S or Ctrl+S).** This saves changes you've made to the active document since you last saved. If you choose Save for a document that hasn't yet been saved, the Save As dialog box appears. This dialog box lets you name and choose a storage folder for the document.

Tip
If you have more than one document open, you can save them all at once by pressing Option+Shift+⌘+S or Ctrl+Alt+Shift+S.

Note
As with the Open a File dialog box, the Save dialog box's appearance will differ slightly depending on whether you are using Version Cue or not.

✦ **Save As (Shift+⌘+S or Ctrl+AltShift+S).** This lets you save a copy of the active document in a different (or in the same) folder using a different (or the same) name. When you choose Save As—and when you choose Save for an unsaved document—the Save As dialog box (see Figure 4-7) appears.

✦ **Save a Copy (Option+⌘+S or Crtl+Alt+S).** This lets you create a copy of the active document in a different (or in the same) folder using a different (or the same) name. When you use the Save a Copy command, the original document remains open and retains its original name. It differs from Save As only in that it keeps the original document open.

✦ **Save a Version.** This saves the current document as a version with a Version Cue project. This latest save will be considered a version of the previously saved file.

Cross-Reference
Version management is covered in Chapter 35.

✦ **Revert.** This undoes all changes you've made to a document since you last saved it. There is no way to undo this and reinstate all your changes after you revert, so be careful.

New Feature
InDesign CS2 also adds a Save as Alternate option if you are using the Version Cue–enabled Save dialog box. This option is covered in Chapter 35.

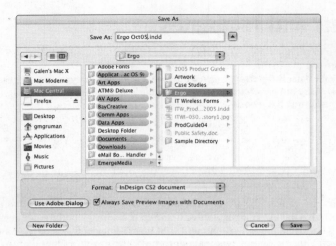

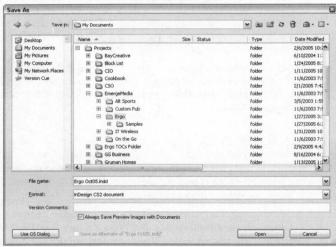

Figure 4-7: The Mac version of the Save As dialog box (top) and the Windows version (bottom) are slightly different. If Version Cue were disabled, they would also look slightly different as well (compare Figures 4-4 and 4-5).

Tip   InDesign's Save, Save As, and Save a Copy commands let you save only InDesign documents and templates. If you want to save a document as an Encapsulated PostScript (EPS), InDesign Interchange, Scalable Vector Graphics (SVG), Extensible Markup Language (XML), or Adobe Portable Document Format (PDF) file, you should use the Export command (File ➪ Export), which is explained later in this chapter.

Saving documents versus saving templates

Whenever you save a document for the first time or you use the Save As or Save a Copy As command, the Save As dialog box lets you save a standard InDesign document file or a template.

In an ideal world, you would create a finished template, save it, and then open a copy of the template and use it to create an actual publication. In the real world, however, templates are often created by yanking the content out of a finished publication and then saving the gutted file as a template. Regardless of how you create your templates, make sure you remember to select the InDesign CS Template option in the Save As dialog box. On the Mac with Version Cue enabled, use the Enable pop-up menu; on the Mac with Version Cue disabled, use the Format pop-up menu; and in Windows, use the Save as Type pop-up menu.

If you forget to save a document as a template, it will open under its actual name. If you then make any changes and choose File ➪ Save (⌘+S or Ctrl+S), the changes are saved with the original document. If this happens, simply save the document again and choose the InDesign CS Template option.

Tip   Choosing File ➪ Package lets you save a copy of a document along with all files — linked graphics, fonts, and ICC color profiles — required to print the document. This feature is particularly handy if you intend to send an InDesign document to an output provider. (See Chapter 29 for more information about the Package command.)

Note   Choosing File ➪ Package for GoLive collects all the document's image files and creates an XML document for use in creating a Web version of your InDesign document in Adobe GoLive 7 or later — it does *not* create an HTML version of your InDesign document that can be used in any other Web-creation program.

Knowing how to *not* save changes

As mentioned earlier in this chapter, InDesign is a very forgiving program. If you make a mistake, change your mind, or work yourself into a complete mess, you don't have to remain in your predicament or save your work. InDesign offers several escape routes. You can:

✦ **Undo your last action.** Do this by choosing Edit ➪ Undo or pressing ⌘+Z or Ctrl+Z. (Some actions, particularly actions such as scrolling that do not affect any items or the underlying document structure, are not undoable.) You can undo multiple actions in the order they were done by choosing Edit ➪ Undo or pressing ⌘+Z or Ctrl+Z — each time you undo, the previous action is undone.

✦ **Redo an action you've undone.** Do this by choosing Edit ➪ Redo or pressing Shift+⌘+Z or Ctrl+Shift+Z. Alternately choosing Undo and Redo is a handy way of seeing a before/after view of a particular change. As with undo, you can redo multiple undone actions in the order in which they were undone.

✦ **Revert to your last saved version.** To do this, choose File ➪ Revert. This will undo all changes you made since last saving a document. There is no way to undo this and reinstate all your changes after you revert, so be careful.

Tip   If you perform an action, and then change your mind while InDesign is completing the action, pressing Esc cancels the operation.

Tip   To undo any changes you make after opening a dialog box, press Option or Alt, which changes the Cancel button into a Reset button, and then click Reset. (This feature is not available in all dialog boxes.)

Saving files in other formats

InDesign's Save commands (File ➪ Save, File ➪ Save As, and File ➪ Save a Copy) let you save documents and templates using InDesign's native file format. The Export command (File ➪ Export) lets you save the stories — and in some cases stories and whole layouts — in InDesign documents in several formats:

✦ **InDesign CS format.** InDesign CS2 can create files readable by InDesign CS users. The trick is to export — not save as — their files to the InDesign Interchange format. (There is no way to save the file in a version readable by InDesign 2.)

**New
Feature**   The ability to create files compatible with a previous version is new to InDesign CS2.

✦ **Word processing formats.** If you place the text cursor into a story, you can export its text (select a range of text if you want to export only that selection) into one of three formats: RTF for import into word processors with only basic formatting retained and Text Only for import into word processors that don't support RTF (no formatting is retained).

Note   You can save only one text file at a time. If you need to export several stories from the same document, you must do so one at a time.

✦ **InDesign workflow formats.** If text is selected using the Type tool, you can save the story in the InDesign Tagged Text format (for editing in a word processor and later re-import into InDesign with all InDesign formatting retained) or in the InDesign CS Interchange format (for import into InDesign CS).

✦ **Production formats.** Whether text is selected using the Type tool or the Direct Selection tool, you can save the document — not just the story — as EPS or PDF files for use by prepress tools and service bureaus or for import into other applications as pictures.

✦ **Online formats.** Whether text is selected using the Type tool or the Direct Selection tool, you can save the document — not just the story — in XML format for use in online database-oriented content-management systems, as well as a specific page, spread, or text selection into JPEG bitmap or SVG vector formats for use as online graphics.

When exporting a file, choose a format from the Format pop-up menu (called the Save as Type pop-up menu in Windows when you aren't using Version Cue) in the Export dialog box.

Summary

When you're ready to begin working on a new document, choose File ⇨ New ⇨ Document, and then use the controls in the New Document dialog box to specify the page size, margins, column format, and any bleed and slug areas for the document. You can also save these settings for easy future use as document styles from the New Document dialog box.

After opening a new document, choose File ⇨ Save to save a standard InDesign document file or a template file. (A template is a preconstructed document that you use to create multiple versions of a publication.) You can choose File ⇨ Save As to save a copy of the current document, or you can choose File ⇨ Revert to discard your most recent round of changes. If you want to work on a document you've previously saved, choose File ⇨ Open.

In addition to opening InDesign documents and templates, you can open QuarkXPress and QuarkXPress Passport 3.3, 4.0, and 4.1 documents, as well as PageMaker 6.0, 6.5, and 7.0 documents. Choosing File ⇨ Export lets you save InDesign documents as EPS, PDF, XML, JPEG, and SVG files, as well as save text in RTF, text-only, InDesign Tagged Text, and InDesign Interchange formats. (With the InDesign Interchange format, InDesign CS2 can now export in a format readable by a previous version of InDesign.) Last, you can create XML files optimized for Adobe GoLive by using File ⇨ Package for GoLive.

✦   ✦   ✦

Working with Pages

It's a rare InDesign user who creates only one-page documents. Even if business cards, ads, and posters are your bread and butter, you'll probably produce at least a few multipage documents. If you'll be creating newsletters, newspapers, books, catalogs, or any other such multipage publications, you need to know how to add pages to your document, move pages around if you change your mind, and delete pages if necessary.

In addition to letting you create multipage documents — something that most illustration and image-editing programs don't — InDesign lets you divide multipage documents into independently numbered sections. As documents grow in size, your ability to navigate quickly to the page you want to work on becomes an important consideration. The longer you spend getting to the page you want, the less time you have to work on it. Fortunately, InDesign provides several navigation aids that make it easy to move around on a page or in a document.

Working with Multipage Documents

If you intend to create a multipage document, you should select the Facing Pages option in the New Document dialog box (File ➪ New ➪ Document, or ⌘+N or Ctrl+N) when you create the document. You'll also want to display the Pages pane (Window ➪ Pages or F12), shown in Figure 5-1, because it provides the controls that let you add pages (document and master), delete and move pages, apply master pages to document pages, and navigate through a document.

Cross-Reference For more information about using the Pages pane to work on master pages, see Chapter 7.

Note The overwhelming majority of multipage documents are facing-page publications such as books, catalogs, and magazines. Some exceptions are flip charts, Web pages, and three-hole-punched publications printed on only one side. In this chapter, the figures show examples of a facing-page document. If you're creating a single-sided multipage document, the techniques are the same as for facing-page documents, but the icons in the Pages pane will show only single-sided page icons (the icons aren't dog-eared).

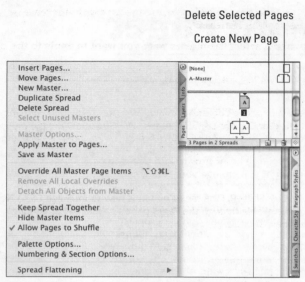

Figure 5-1: The Pages pane and its palette menu. This is how the pane looks when you open a new, facing-page document (here, it happens to have one page).

Adding pages

A document can contain as many as 9,999 pages, although you'd never want to create a document nearly that long. In general, try to break up long publications into logical pieces. For example, if you're creating a book, it's a good idea to create separate documents for the front matter, each chapter, the index, and any other parts (appendixes and so on). Also, if you're producing a long document, you'll want to take advantages of master pages (covered in Chapter 7), which save you the work of building each page from scratch.

When you create a multipage document, you're free to add however many pages you want. But be careful. Even though InDesign will let you create a seven-page newsletter, in real life, facing-page publications always have an even number of pages — usually a multiple of 4 and often a multiple of 16 because of the way printers arrange multiple pages on a single sheet of paper.

Here's how to add pages to a document:

1. **If it's not displayed, open the Pages pane by choosing Window ➪ Pages or pressing F12.**

2. **From the Pages pane's palette menu, choose Insert Pages.** The Insert Pages dialog box, shown in Figure 5-2, appears.

3. **In the Pages field, type the number of pages you want to add.**

4. **Select an option from the Insert pop-up menu: After Page, Before Page, At Start of Document, or At End of Document.** Be careful: If you've already started working on page 1, for example, make sure you add new pages after page 1. Otherwise, it won't be page 1 anymore and you'll have to move the objects you already created.

5. **Type a page number in the field next to Insert or use the arrows to increase or decrease the value in one-page increments.**

6. **From the Master pop-up menu, select the master page you want to apply to the new pages.**

7. **When you're finished, click OK to close the dialog box.**

New Feature

In InDesign CS2, there is a faster way to add and manipulate pages if you don't happen to have the Pages pane already open: Choose Layout ➪ Pages, and then select the appropriate option, such as Add Pages, from the submenu. The resulting dialog boxes match those accessed from the Pages pane.

Tip

If you want to quickly add just one page after the current page, click Layout ➪ Pages ➪ Add Page, or press Shift+⌘+P or Ctrl+Shift+P. (The menu option is new to InDesign CS2.) Note that this menu shortcut is not available through the Pages pane's palette menu, although, of course, you can use the keyboard shortcut at any time.

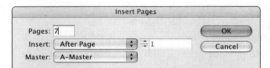

Figure 5-2: The Insert Pages dialog box

You can also add new pages or spreads — spreads are added if a spread is selected in the Pages pane — one at a time at the end of a document, by clicking the Create New Page button at the bottom of the Pages pane. When you use this method, the master page applied to the last document page is applied to each new page. Pages are added after the currently selected page in the pane.

You can also click and drag a master page icon (or both pages in a facing-pages spread to add a spread) from the top of the Pages pane to add a page using a master page's settings (use the [None] page for a plain page) between any pair of document page spreads or to the right of the last document spread. If a vertical bar appears when you release the mouse button, the spread is placed between the spreads on either side of the bar. If a vertical bar does not appear between document page spreads when you release the mouse button, the new spread is placed at the end of the document.

Tip

When you insert new pages, existing pages are automatically changed from left-hand (verso) pages to right-hand (recto) pages, and vice versa, as needed when individual pages are added and removed in a facing-pages document. You can prevent that for selected spreads by first selecting them in the Pages pane and then by clicking Keep Spread Together in the palette menu. You might do this for a spread, such as a two-page table, that you don't want to have broken apart when other pages are added or deleted. Of course, for proper printing you may need to move that spread so it follows a complete spread when you're done adding or deleting pages.

Copying pages

You can copy pages from one document to another by clicking and dragging the page icon from the source document's Pages pane to the target document's Pages pane. Any master page(s) associated with the copied document pages(s) are copied as well.

You can also duplicate the current spread within the current document by clicking Duplicate Spread from the Pages pane's palette menu or by choosing Layout ➪ Pages ➪ Duplicate Spread.

Deleting pages

InDesign offers several choices for deleting pages from a document. You can:

✦ Select one or more page icons in the Pages pane and either click and drag them to the pane's Delete Selected Pages button (the trashcan icon) or simply click the Delete Selected Pages button. Click a spread's page numbers to select both pages. You can click a page icon or spread number and then Shift+click another page icon or spread number to select a range of pages. Hold down the ⌘ or Ctrl key and click page icons or spread numbers to select multiple, noncontiguous pages.

✦ Select one or more page icons in the Pages pane and then click Delete Page(s) or Delete Spread(s) from the pane's palette menu.

✦ Choose Layout ➪ Pages ➪ Delete Pages. Any page(s) or spreads(s) selected in the Pages pane will be deleted. (If one or more spreads are selected, the menu option will be Delete Spreads.) This is not a terribly useful option because you have to have the Pages pane open and thus may as well just use its palette menu to delete.

Moving pages

Although you can move pages around in a document, this is something you should do with great care — if at all. Generally, if you want to move the objects on one page to another page, it's safer to cut or copy (Edit ➪ Cut, or ⌘+X or Ctrl+X, or Edit ➪ Copy, or ⌘+C or Ctrl+C) the objects than to move the page, which might cause subsequent pages to shuffle. If you absolutely need to move a single page, it's safer to move its spread. (Of course, if you're working on a single-sided facing-page document, shuffling is not an issue.)

To move a page, click its icon, and then drag the hand pointer between two spreads or between the pages of a spread. A vertical bar indicates where the selected page will be placed. Release the mouse button when the vertical bar is where you want to move the page. To move a spread, click the page numbers beneath the icons (rather than on the page icons).

 New Feature InDesign CS2 adds a new palette menu option — Move Pages — to the Pages pane.

Alternatively, you can select the page(s) you want to move in the Pages pane and then click Move Pages from the Pages pane's palette menu. (If you don't want to work through the Pages pane, you can also choose Layout ➪ Pages ➪ Move Pages.) You'll get the dialog box shown in Figure 5-3, where you can specify where to move the page(s): after a specific page, before a specific page, at the beginning of the document, or at the end of the document.

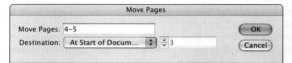

Figure 5-3: The Move Pages dialog box

Starting documents with a left page

By default, InDesign starts all documents with a right-hand page. As a default, that makes sense, because the first sheet in a document always is a right-hand page. But sometimes, you want documents to start on a left-hand page, particularly if they are a chapter or section in a larger document. For example, magazine articles often start on a left age, giving the introduction a full spread. To start a document on a left page:

1. **Select the first page in the Pages pane and then choose Numbering & Section Options from the pane's palette menu or choose Layout ⇨ Numbering & Section Options.**

2. **Select the Start Section option.**

3. **Select the Start Page Numbering at option and enter an even number such as 2 in the field to its right.**

4. **Click OK.**

5. **The Pages pane will update, showing the start page on the left of the spine.**

6. **You may not want to assign a starting page number (for example, if the starting page number is unknown because the number of pages that precede this document is unknown, and you are letting the Book feature determine the page numbers later).** In this case, repeat Step 1 but deselect Start Section. This will leave the page as a left-hand page but let the Book feature figure out the page number.

QuarkXPress User

The preceding technique will be familiar to you, except that QuarkXPress does not let you remove the section start—as soon as you do, QuarkXPress would make the page a right-hand page again. InDesign does not.

Cross-Reference

For more on the Book feature, see Chapter 32. Sections are covered in more detail later in this chapter.

Creating gatefold spreads

Have you ever seen a publication—a magazine, perhaps—that had a foldout page? Often such pages are ads (publishers love advertisers who buy multipage ads) or special sections. Or maybe you've seen a two-sided, multifold brochure with several panels, each the same size. A multipage spread of this type is often called a gatefold or accordion page, or (in earlier versions of InDesign) an *island spread.*

When you designate a spread a gatefold spread, the spread's pages don't move if you add or delete any document pages in front of it. (Normally, when you add or delete pages, all subsequent pages are bumped backward or shuffled forward.)

When you create a gatefold spread of three pages in a facing-page publication, you should always create them in pairs because, in an actual printed publication, if you add a third page to a two-page spread, the backside of the page becomes the third page in another three-page spread. Along the same lines, if you create a four-panel, trifold brochure, both the front and the back have four panels.

One last word about gatefold spreads: They require special care throughout the production process, and they'll cost you extra at the printer and bindery. If you're creating a modest, black-and-white newsletter for a local nonprofit organization, throwing in a three-panel gatefold probably isn't an option. On the other hand, if you can find an advertiser with deep pockets, InDesign lets you create gatefold spreads with up to ten pages.

To create a gatefold spread, first select the pages in the existing spread that you want to make into a gatefold, and then select the Keep Spreads Together option from the pane's palette menu. (When you designate a spread to be kept together, the page numbers below the spread in the Pages pane are displayed in brackets.) To add pages to a gatefold spread, click and drag a document page icon (a master page icon won't work) next to or between the pages of an island spread. A vertical bar indicates where the page will be placed. When the bar is where you want to place the page, release the mouse button. To clear agatefold, select it in the Pages pane and then deselect the Keep Spreads Together option in the pane's palette menu. Figure 5-4 shows a pair of three-page gatefold spreads in a facing-pages publication.

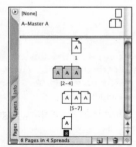

Figure 5-4: In this example, pages 2, 3, and 4 are a gatefold, as are pages 5, 6, and 7. The extra page in each spread is based on the A-Master master page.

Tip   You may want to create a section out of the extra pages in a gatefold so that you can number them separately from the surrounding pages. Sections are covered later in this chapter.

QuarkXPress User   The InDesign gatefold spread is similar to QuarkXPress's ability to place several pages on one spread to create foldouts. Both use the same process: clicking and dragging a page next to a page in the spread to which you want to add the page. The difference is that in QuarkXPress you don't have to first select the pages and then tell QuarkXPress to keep them together, as you do in InDesign.

Working with Page Numbers

Pages are numbered automatically starting at 1 based on the order in which they appear in the Pages pane. But you can change the page numbering from Arabic numerals to Roman numerals or letters, as well as change the start page to be something other than 1. To do so, select the first page in the document in the Pages pane and choose Layout ➪ Page Numbering & Sections or choose Numbering & Section Options from the Pages pane's palette menu. You'll get the dialog box shown in Figure 5-5. To change the initial page number, select the Start Page Numbering at option and type a new starting page number in its field. To change the page numbering style from the default of Arabic numerals (1, 2, 3, 4, . . .), use the Style pop-up menu and choose from I, II, III, IV, . . .; i, ii, iii, iv, . . .; A, B, C, D, . . .; and a, b, c, d, ...

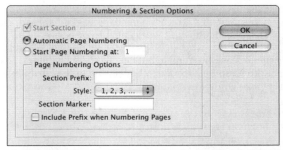

Figure 5-5: The Numbering & Section Options dialog box lets you change the starting page number and the types of numerals used.

Tip To have a facing-pages document start on a left-hand page, you must have the starting page number be even.

Entering page references in text

You'll often want page references in text — the current page number in a folio, for example, or the target page number for a "continued on" reference. You could type in a page number manually on each page of a multipage document, but that can get old fast. As I mentioned earlier in this chapter, if you're working on a multipage document, you should be using master pages. And if you're using master pages, you should handle page numbers on document pages by placing page-number characters on their master pages.

If you want to add the current page number to a page, you can choose Type ➪ Insert Special Character ➪ Auto Page Number or press Option+Shift+⌘+N or Ctrl+Shift+Alt+N whenever the Type tool is active and the text cursor is flashing. If you move the page or the text frame, the page-number character is automatically updated to reflect the new page number.

To create "continued on" and "continued from" lines, choose Type ➪ Insert Special Character ➪ Next Page Number to have the next page's number inserted in your text, or choose Type ➪ Insert Special Character ➪ Previous Page Number to have the previous page's number inserted. That next or previous page will be the next or previous page in the story.

Tip   One flaw in InDesign's continued-line approach is that the text frames must be linked for InDesign to know what the next and previous pages are. Thus, you're likely to place your continued lines in the middle of your text. But if the text reflows, so do the continued lines. Here's a way to avoid that: Create separate text frames for your continued-on and continued-from text frames. Now link just those two frames, not the story text. This way, the story text can reflow as needed without affecting your continued lines.

Dividing a document into sections

Some long documents are divided into parts that are numbered separately from the other parts. For example, the page numbers of the front matter of books often use Roman numerals, while standard Arabic numerals are used for the body of the book. If the book has appendixes, a separate numbering scheme could be applied to these pages. In InDesign, such independently numbered parts are referred to as *sections*.

A multipage document can contain as many sections as you want (a section has to contain at least one page). If each section of a document uses a different page layout, you'll probably want to create a different master page for each section. Here's how to create a section:

1. **If it's not displayed, open the Pages pane by choosing Window ➪ Pages or pressing F12.**

2. **Click the icon of the page where you want to start a section.**

3. **Choose Numbering & Section Options from the pane's palette menu.** The Numbering & Section Options dialog box, shown in Figure 5-5, appears. (You can also create a section starting at the current page in your document by choosing Layout ➪ Numbering & Section Options.) By default, the Start Section option is selected. Leave it selected.

4. **In the Section Prefix field, type up to eight characters that identify the section in the Page field at the lower-left corner of the document window.** For example, if you type Sec2, the first page of the section will be displayed as Sec2:1 in the Page field.

5. **From the Style menu, choose the Roman numeral, Arabic numeral, or alphabetic style you want to use for page numbers.**

6. **For Page Numbering, select the Automatic Page Numbering option if you want the first page of the section to be one number higher than the last page of the previous section.** The new section will use the specified style; the previous section may use this style or another style.

7. **Select the Start Page Numbering at option and type a number in the accompanying field to specify a different starting number for the section.** For example, if a book begins with a section of front matter, you could begin the body section of a book on page 1 by choosing Start At and typing **1** in the field. If you select Continue from Previous Section, the first page of the body section would begin one number higher than the Roman numeral on the last page of the front matter.

8. **In the Section Marker field, type a text string that you can later automatically apply to pages in the section.** You might want to enter something straightforward like **Section 2** or, if the section is a chapter, the name of the chapter.

Tip   You can insert the section marker name in folios, chapter headings, and story text by choosing Type ➪ Insert Special Character ➪ Section Marker. This is a great way to get a chapter name (if you use it as the section marker) in your folio or to have cross-references in text to a section whose name might later change.

9. **Click OK to close the dialog box.**

Targeting Versus Selecting Spreads

Depending on the task you're working on, you may want to use the Pages pane to *target* a spread or to *select* a spread. The choice you make determines the actions you can perform.

A target spread is the spread to which copied objects will be placed when you choose Paste, or to which library objects will be placed when you choose Place Items from a library pane's palette menu. The target spread is the one that's in the center of the document window and is indicated by the page number displayed in the page-number field at the lower-left corner of the document window. Only one spread can be the target spread at any one time. At reduced magnifications, it's possible to display several spreads in the document window. In this case, the number in the page-number field indicates the target spread.

When you select one or more spreads, you can then perform several page-level modifications, such as adjusting margin and column guides, applying a master page, or deleting the pages, in a single operation.

There are several ways to target a spread. You can:

✦ Modify an object on the spread or its pasteboard.

✦ Click on a spread or its pasteboard.

✦ In the Pages pane, double-click the page numbers below the spread's page icons. (This also moves you to the document pages in the spread.)

You also have several options for selecting a page or spread:

✦ Click once on a page icon to select one page of a spread; click the page numbers to select both pages. If you click twice, the page or spread is selected and targeted.

✦ Click a page icon or spread number and then Shift+click another page icon or spread number to select a range of pages.

✦ Hold down ⌘ or Ctrl and click page icons or spread numbers to select multiple, noncontiguous pages.

In the Pages pane, the page numbers of the target spread are displayed reversed, white numbers in a black rectangle, while the page icons are highlighted in a light-blue color.

When you create a section, it's indicated in the Pages pane by a small, black triangle over the icon of the first page in the section, as shown in Figure 5-6. (If you move the mouse pointer over the black triangle, the name of the section appears.) The page-numbering scheme you've specified is reflected in the page numbers below the page icons. When you begin a section, it continues until the end of the document or until you begin a new section.

Tip   By default, the Pages pane displays section numbers beneath the icons of document pages. If you want to display absolute page numbers—the first page is page 1 and all other pages are numbered sequentially—you can do so by choosing InDesign ⇨ Preferences ⇨ General on the Mac or Edit ⇨ Preferences ⇨ General in Windows, or by pressing ⌘+K or Ctrl+K, and choosing Absolute Numbering from the View pop-up menu.

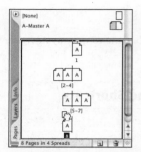

Figure 5-6: The small
triangle above a page
icon (page 1, here)
represents a section start.

Removing a section

If you decide that you want to remove a section, navigate to the page that begins the section, choose Numbering & Section Options from the Pages pane's palette menu, or choose Layout ⇨ Numbering & Section Options, and deselect the Section Start option.

Navigating Documents and Pages

Moving from page to page in a long document and scrolling around a large or magnified page are among the most common tasks you'll perform in InDesign. The more time you spend displaying the page or page area you want to work on, the less time you have to do the work you need to do. Like most trips, the less time you spend between destinations, the better.

For navigating through the pages of a document, the Pages pane (Window ⇨ Pages or F12) offers the fastest ride. For navigating around in a page, you may want to switch to the Navigator pane (Window ⇨ Object & Layout ⇨ Navigator).

Navigating with the Pages pane

When the Pages pane appears, you can use it to quickly move from page to page in a multi-page document and to switch between displaying master pages and document pages. To display a particular document page, double-click its icon. The selected page is centered in the document window. To display a master spread, double-click its icon in the lower half of the pane.

Tip   The Fit Page in Window command (View ⇨ Fit Page in Window, or ⌘+0 or Ctrl+0) and Fit Spread in Window command (View ⇨ Fit Page in Window, or Option+⌘+0 or Ctrl+Alt+0) let you enlarge or reduce the display magnification to fit the selected page or spread in the document window. Related view options are View ⇨ Fit Spread in Window, or Option+⌘+0 or Ctrl+Alt+0, and View ⇨ Entire Pasteboard, or Option+Shift+⌘+0 or Ctrl+Alt+Shift+0. (Note that the shortcuts use the numeral 0, not the letter O.)

Navigating with the menus and shortcuts

InDesign also offers several menu commands and keyboard shortcuts to quickly navigate your layout, as Table 5-1 details.

Table 5-1: Page Navigation Menus and Shortcuts

Navigation	Menu Sequence	Macintosh Shortcut	Windows Shortcut
Go to first page	Layout ▷ First Page	Shift+⌘+PgUp	Ctrl+Shift+Page Up
Go back one page	Layout ▷ Previous Page	Shift+PgUp	Shift+Page Up
Go forward one page	Layout ▷ Next Page or Layout ▷ Go Forward	Shift+PgDn or ⌘+PgDn	Shift+Page Down or Ctrl+keypad PgDn
Go to last page	Layout ▷ Last Page	Shift+⌘+PgDn	Ctrl+Shift+Page Down
Go to last page viewed	Layout ▷ Go Back	⌘+PgUp	Shift+Page Up or Ctrl+keypad PgUp
Go forward one spread	Layout ▷ Next Spread	Option+PgDn	Alt+Page Down
Go back one spread	Layout ▷ Previous Spread	Option+PgUp	Alt+Page Up

Using the Navigator pane

Although it's possible to use the Navigator pane (Window ▷ Object & Layout ▷ Navigator) to move from page to page in a long document, the Pages pane is better for this task. The Navigator pane is more useful for scrolling within a page, particularly for doing detail work on a page that's displayed at a high magnification. If you're an Illustrator, PageMaker, or Photoshop user, you may already be familiar with the Navigator pane, which works the same in all three applications.

Figure 5-7 shows the Navigator pane and its palette menu.

Figure 5-7: The Navigator pane and its palette menu

Changing view magnification

You can use the Navigator pane to zoom in or zoom out on the current spread. You have several options for zooming in and out:

✦ Click the handle on the zoom and drag left to zoom out or right to zoom in.

✦ Click the zoom-out icon to the left of the zoom slider to zoom out; click the zoom-in icon to the right of the zoom slider to zoom in.

✦ Type a view percentage in the field at the bottom right of the Navigator pane. Type a smaller value to zoom out; type a larger value to zoom in. Type 100% to display the page at actual size.

Tip   You can also use the Zoom tool or its keyboard shortcuts to zoom in or out (⌘+spacebar or Ctrl+spacebar to zoom in, Option+⌘+spacebar or Ctrl+Alt+spacebar to zoom out).

Scrolling with the Navigator pane

The rectangle displayed in the Navigator pane (on the actual screen it should appear in red) indicates the area that's currently displayed in the document window. When you change the display magnification, the rectangle changes size (it gets larger as you zoom out and smaller as you zoom in). You can display a different area in the currently displayed spread by clicking and dragging the rectangle or by clicking outside it. If you click outside it, the point where you click is centered in the document window.

Other options in the Navigator pane

If red isn't your favorite color, you can change the color of the rectangle displayed in the Navigator pane by choosing Palette Options from its palette menu, and then choosing a different color from the Color pop-up menu in the Palette Options dialog box.

If you choose Show All Spreads from the Navigator pane's palette menu, all the document's spreads appear in the pane. The more spreads you have, the smaller they appear and the smaller the rectangle becomes that indicates the area that's displayed in the document window. By clicking and dragging the rectangle from page to page you can navigate to a particular area on a page while remaining at the current display percentage. This can be a handy way of navigating, but if you're working on a document that has many pages, the page icons and rectangle can become too small to work with easily. Figure 5-8 shows the Navigator pane with the View All Spreads option selected.

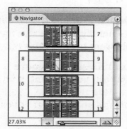

Figure 5-8: The Navigator pane with View All Spreads selected

Tip   You can also use the scroll bars at the right and bottom of the document window to move to different areas of a page or to a different page in a document or the keyboard shortcut. (Hold down the spacebar, and then click and drag the hand pointer. Make sure the Type tool is deselected or else this feature will not work.)

Adjusting Page Layouts and Objects

If you've ever created and worked with a document all the way to the finishing touches, and then discovered that the page size was wrong from the beginning, you know the meaning of frustration. Manually adjusting the size and placement of all the objects in a document is an ugly chore, one you want to avoid at all costs. However, should the unthinkable happen — you have to modify the size, orientation, or margins of a document that is partially or completely finished — InDesign automatically resizes and repositions objects when you change its basic layout.

For example, maybe you've created a magazine for an American audience that subsequently needs to be converted for publication in Europe. Most newsletters in the United States use letter-sized pages (8½ × 11 inches), while in Europe the standard page size for such publications is A4 (210 × 297 mm), which is slightly narrower and slightly taller than U.S. letter size. Of course, you'll have to change *color* to *colour, apartment* to *flat,* and so on. But you'll also have to both squeeze (horizontally) and stretch (vertically) every item on every page to accommodate the A4 page's dimensions. The Layout Adjustment command (Layout ➪ Layout Adjustment) gives you the option of turning this chore over to InDesign, which will automatically adjust object shape and position according to the new page size, column guides, and margins.

The Layout Adjustment dialog box lets you turn layout adjustment on or off and specify the rules used to adjust objects when you change page size or orientation (via the Document Setup dialog box; File ➪ Document Setup or Option+⌘+P or Ctrl+Alt+P) or margins or columns (via the Margin and Columns dialog box, accessed via Layout ➪ Margins and Columns). To adjust a layout:

1. **Choose Layout ➪ Layout Adjustment to display the Layout Adjustment dialog box, shown in Figure 5-9.**

2. **Select the Enable Layout Adjustment option to turn on the feature; deselect it to turn it off.**

3. **In the Snap Zone field, type the distance within which an object edge will automatically snap to a guideline when layout adjustment is performed.**

4. **Select the Allow Graphics and Groups to Resize option if you want InDesign to resize objects when layout adjustment is performed.** If you don't select this option, InDesign will move objects but not resize them (the preferred option).

5. **Select the Allow Ruler Guides to Move option if you want InDesign to adjust the position of ruler guides proportionally according to a new page size.** Generally, ruler guides are placed relative to the margins and page edges, so you'll probably want to select this option.

6. **Select the Ignore Ruler Guide Alignments option if you want InDesign to ignore ruler guides when adjusting the position of objects during layout adjustment.** If you think that objects may snap to ruler guides that you don't want them to snap to during layout adjustment, select this option. If selected, InDesign will still snap object edges to other margin and column guides.

7. **Select the Ignore Object and Layer Locks option to let InDesign move locked objects (either objects locked directly via Object ➪ Lock Position, or via ⌘+L or Ctrl+L, or objects that reside on a locked layer).** Otherwise, locked objects will not be adjusted.

8. **When you're done, click OK to close the dialog box.**

The Layout Adjustment feature works best when there's not much work for it to do. But if you radically change a document that you've already done considerable work on, the Layout Adjustment feature usually creates more work than it saves. For example, the switch from a

U.S. letter-sized page to an A4-sized page is a relatively minor change and the layout adjustments will probably be barely noticeable. But if you decide to change a tabloid-sized poster into a business card in midstream, well, you're probably better off starting over.

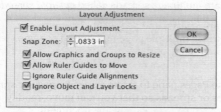

Figure 5-9: The Layout Adjustment dialog box

Here are a few things to keep in mind if you decide to use InDesign's Layout Adjustment feature:

✦ If you change page size, the margin widths (the distance between the left and right margins and the page edges) remain the same.

✦ If you change page size, column guides and ruler guides are repositioned proportionally to the new size.

✦ If you change the number of columns, column guides are added or removed accordingly.

✦ If an object edge is aligned with a guideline before layout adjustment, it remains aligned with the guideline after adjustment. If two or more edges of an object are aligned with guidelines, the object is resized so that the edges remain aligned with the guidelines after layout adjustment.

✦ If you change the page size, objects are moved so that they're in the same relative position on the new page.

✦ If you've used margin, column, and ruler guides to place objects on pages, layout adjustment will be more effective than if you've placed objects or ruler guides randomly on pages.

✦ Check for text reflow when you modify a document's page size, margins, or column guides. Decreasing a document's page size can cause text to overflow a text frame whose dimensions have been reduced.

✦ Check *everything* in your document after the adjustment is complete. Take the time to look over every page of your document. You never know what InDesign has actually done until you see it with your own eyes.

Tip If you decide to enable layout adjustment for a particular publication, you may want to begin by using the Save As command (File ➪ Save As, or Shift+⌘+S or Ctrl+Shift+S) to create a copy. That way, if you ever need to revert back to the original version, you can simply open the original document.

Summary

If you're working on a multipage document, you'll want to display the Pages pane. It lets you add, move, and delete document pages as well as create multipage spreads called *gatefold spreads*.

If you're working on a long document with multiple parts, and you want to number each part separately, you can create sections to manage these multiple page-numbering schemes within the document. You can also have InDesign automatically add the correct page numbers for folios and continued lines, as well as section names in folios and other text.

As you work on a long document, you can use the Pages pane to target a specific page or spread in the document window; to select multiple pages or spreads so that you can move, modify, or delete them collectively; and to navigate from page to page in a multipage document. If you're doing detail work or working on a large page, you can use the Navigator pane to scroll around the page and to change the view magnification.

If you decide to change the layout of a publication after you've started work, you can use the Layout Adjustment feature to automatically adjust the size and position of objects and guidelines when you change the document's page size, margins, or columns.

✦   ✦   ✦

Working with Layers

Publishers seem to spend a lot of time doing the same things: creating several different versions of the same ad for different markets or flowing text in another language into a design. The goal of software is to automate the predictable so you have more time for creativity. Toward this goal, InDesign provides a method for preserving the time you put into creating and editing a layout that is used for more than one purpose: *layers*.

If you've ever seen a series of clear plastic overlays in presentations, understanding layers is easy. In one of those old overhead presentations, the teacher might have started with one overlay containing a graphic, then added another overlay with descriptive text, then added a third overlay containing a chart. Each overlay contained distinct content, but you could see through each one to the others to get the entire message. InDesign's layers are somewhat like this, letting you isolate content on slices of a document. You can then show and hide layers, lock objects on layers, rearrange layers, and more.

Understanding Layers

Each document contains a default layer, Layer 1, which contains all your objects until you create and select a new layer. Objects on the default layer — and any other layer for that matter — follow the standard *stacking order* of InDesign. (The first object you create is the backmost, the last one you create is the frontmost, and all the other objects fall somewhere in between. See Chapter 11 for complete information about stacking order.)

Like the clear plastic overlays, the order of the layers also affects the stacking order of the objects. Objects on the bottom layer are behind other objects, and objects on the top layer are in front of other objects. In Figure 6-1, the Background Images layer toward the bottom of the list contains the business card's standard graphics and the main text. Two additional layers contain different sets of contact information, in separate text frames, for different people.

Although layers are often compared to plastic overlays, there's one big difference: Layers are not specific to individual pages. Each layer encompasses the entire document, which doesn't make much difference when you're working on a 1-page ad but makes a significant difference when it comes to a 16-page newsletter. When you create layers and place objects on them, it's important that your strategy considers all the pages in the document.

The Layers pane (Window ⇨ Layers or F7) is your gateway to creating and manipulating layers (see Figure 6-2). As with other panes, when Tool Tips are turned on via the Tool Tips pop-up menu in the General pane of the Preferences dialog box (choose InDesign ⇨ Preferences on the Mac or Edit ⇨ Preferences in Windows, or press ⌘+K or Ctrl+K), you can learn what controls do by pointing at them. If you know what the controls do, you can intuit a great deal of how to work with layers.

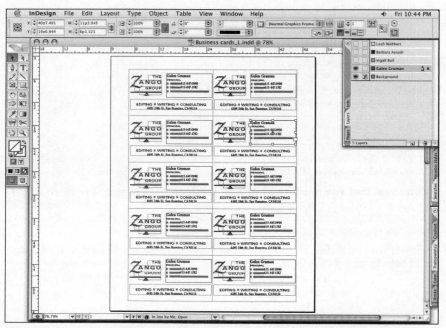

Figure 6-1: A business card with different layers for each person's card. The graphics common to all cards are on their own layer.

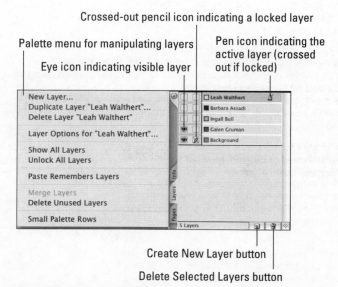

Figure 6-2: The Layers pane

When, Where, and Why to Use Layers

The layers feature is one that you can honestly ignore. If you never looked at the Layers pane, you could continue to do your work in InDesign. But take a look at the possibilities and see if they fit into your workflow. In the long run, using layers can save you time and help you prevent mistakes that can result when you need to track changes across multiple documents.

Say you've created an ad with the same copy in it but a different headline and image for each city where the ad runs. You can place the boilerplate information on one layer and the information that changes on other layers. If any of the boilerplate information changes, you only need to change it once. To print different versions of the ad, you control which layers print.

You might use layers in the following situations:

✦ **A project with a high-resolution background image.** For example, a background such as a texture might take a long time to redraw. You can hide that layer while designing other elements, and then show it occasionally to see how it works with the rest of the design.

✦ **A document that you produce in several versions.** For example, a produce ad may have different prices for different cities or a clothing catalog may feature different coats depending on the climate in each area. You can place the content that changes on separate layers, and then print the layers you need.

✦ **A project that includes objects you don't want to print.** If you want to suppress printout of objects for any reason, the only way you can do this is to place them on a layer and hide the layer. You might have a layer that's used for nothing but adding editorial and design comments, which can be deleted when the document is final.

✦ **A publication that is translated into several languages.** Depending on the layout, you can place all the common objects on one layer, and then create a different layer for each language's text. Changes to the common objects only need to happen once—unlike if you created copies of the original document and flowed the translated text into the copies.

✦ **To experiment with different layouts of the same document.** You can show and hide layers to present different options to your supervisor or client. This strategy lets you use common elements, such as the logo and legal information, in several versions of the same design.

✦ **A complex design with overlapping objects, text wraps, and grouped objects.** Say the background of a page consists of a checkerboard pattern made up of filled, rectangular frames. You don't want to accidentally select the blocks while you're working with other objects. If you isolate complex objects on their own layer, you can show only that layer to work on it, hide that layer to concentrate on other layers, lock the layer so objects can't be selected, and otherwise manipulate the layer.

✦ **To create bulletproof templates.** Locked layers are a great way to decrease the possibility of items in a template being moved or deleted. Move all the objects you don't want moved or deleted on a layer and lock the layer. Although a layer can be unlocked, it will keep the people who use the template from accidentally moving or removing anything too quickly.

When determining whether objects should go on a layer, remember that layers are document-wide and not page-specific.

Creating Layers

Each document contains a default layer, Layer 1, which contains all the objects you place on master pages and document pages — until you create and activate new layers. You can create as many layers as you need; the number of layers in a document is limited only by the RAM available to InDesign. Once you create a new layer, it's activated automatically so you can begin working on it.

Creating a layer

The Layers pane (Window ⇨ Layers or F7) provides several methods for creating new layers. It doesn't matter which document page is displayed when you create a layer because the layer will encompass all the pages in the document. To create a layer, do one of the following:

✦ To create a new layer *on top of all existing layers*, click the New Layer button on the Layers pane to get the New Layer dialog box. The layer will get the default name of Layer *x*.

✦ To create a layer *above the selected layer*, ⌘+click or Ctrl+click the New Layer button. The layer will get the default name of Layer *x*.

✦ To create a new layer *on top of all existing layers but customize its name and identifying color*, Option+click or Alt+click the New Layer button. Use the New Layer dialog box to specify options for the layer. (The New Layer dialog box — set with a custom name and color — is shown in Figure 6-3.)

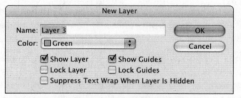

Figure 6-3: The New Layer dialog box

Note   You can create a layer while a master page is displayed. Objects you create on a layer while a master page is displayed will be placed on all pages based on that master page. However, the layer is not specific to that master page. It is available for all document pages — even those based on other master pages — and you can place objects on it.

Customizing layers

A dialog box lets you customize the name, identifying color, guides, and lock status of objects on a new or existing layer. If you choose to customize the layer when you create it (by Option+clicking or Alt+clicking the New Layer button), the New Layer dialog box appears. If you choose to customize an existing layer, double-click it to display the Layer Options dialog box. (You can also choose Layer Options for *Name of Layer* from the Layers pane's palette menu.)

Whether you're using the New Layer dialog box shown in Figure 6-3 or the nearly identical Layer Options dialog box, the options all work the same:

✦ **Name field.** Type a descriptive name for the layer. For example, if you're using layers for multilingual publishing, you might have a U.S. English layer, a French layer, and a German layer. If you're using layers so you can hide background objects while you're working, you might have a Background Objects layer.

✦ **Color pop-up menu and button.** A layer's color helps you identify which layer an object is on. The color appears to the left of the layer name in the Layers pane and appears on each object on that layer. The color is applied to frame edges, selection handles, bounding boxes, text ports, and text wraps. Note that the display of frame edges is controlled by the View ➪ Show/Hide Frame Edges command (also available through the shortcut ⌘+H or Ctrl+H). By default, InDesign applies a different color to each new layer, but you can customize it to something meaningful for your document and workflow. Choose a color from the list or double-click the color swatch to use from the operating system's color picker.

✦ **Show Layer option.** Selected by default, this control lets you specify whether objects on a layer display and print. If you want to suppress printout of the objects on a layer (for example, to hide a different version of a document or to hide pictures while proofing), deselect Show Layer. The Show Layer option has the same effect as clicking the Eye icon on the Layers pane.

✦ **Lock Layer option.** Deselected by default, this option lets you control whether objects on a layer can be edited. Select Lock Layer if you don't want to be able to select items and modify them. For example, in a document containing multiple versions of text on different layers, you might lock the layer containing background images and other objects that stay the same. The Lock Layer option has the same effect as clicking the Pencil icon on the Layers pane.

✦ **Suppress Text Wrap When Layer Is Hidden option.** Deselected by default, this new option prevents text wrapping around the layer's objects when the layer is hidden. Be sure to select this option when you use multiple layers for variations of the same content—such as multilingual text or different contacts for business cards. Otherwise, your layer's text cannot display because it is wrapping around a hidden layer with an object of the same size in the same place.

✦ **Show Guides option.** This lets you control the display of guides that were created while the selected layer was active. When selected, as it is by default, you can create guides while any layer is active and view those guides on any layer. When deselected, you cannot create guides. Any guides you create while that layer is active are not displayed, but you'll still be able to see guides created while other layers were active. Note that when guides are hidden entirely (View ➪ Grids & Guides ➪ Hide Guides, or ⌘+; [semicolon] or Ctrl+; [semicolon]), this command has no apparent effect.

✦ **Lock Guides option.** This works similarly to Show Guides in that it only affects guides that are created while the layer is active. When deselected, as it is by default, you can move guides on any layer for which Lock Guides is deselected. When selected, you cannot move guides created while that layer was active. You can, however, move guides on other layers for which Lock Guides is deselected. Note that when all guides are locked (View ➪ Grids & Guides ➪ Lock Guides, or Option+⌘+; [semicolon] or Ctrl+Alt+; [semicolon]) this command has no apparent effect.

Tip   You can multiple-select layers and customize them all at once. Because each layer must have a different name, the Name field is not available in the Layer Options dialog box when multiple layers are selected.

Working with Objects on Layers

Whether you're designing a magazine template from the ground up or modifying an existing ad, you can isolate specific types of objects on layers. You can create objects on a layer, move objects to a layer, or copy objects to a layer.

The active layer

The *active layer* is the one on which you're creating objects — whether you're using tools, importing text or graphics, clicking and dragging objects in from a library, or pasting objects from other layers or other documents. A Pen icon to the right of a layer's name means it's the active one (refer to Figure 6-2). Although more than one layer can be selected at a time, only one can be active. To switch the active layer to another layer, click to the right of the layer name that you want to be active; the Pen icon moves, making that the new active layer. Keep in mind that to activate a layer, it must be visible.

Regardless of which layer is the active layer, you can select, move, and modify objects on any visible, unlocked layer. (The display and locking of layers is controlled by the Eye and Pencil icons on the Layers pane, respectively, and by the Show Layer and Lock Layer options in the Layer Options dialog box.)

Selecting objects on layers

Regardless of the active layer, you can select, move, and modify objects on any visible, unlocked layer. You can even select objects on different layers and manipulate them.

The Layers pane (Window ➪ Layers or F7) helps you work with selected objects in the following ways:

✦ To determine to which layer an object belongs, match the color on its bounding box, handles, and so on, to a color to the left of a layer name.

✦ To determine which layers contain active objects, look to the right of the layer names. A small box next to a layer name (refer to Figure 6-2) indicates that it contains an active object.

✦ To select all the objects on a layer, Option+click or Alt+click the layer's name in the Layers pane. The layer must be active, unlocked, and visible.

Tip   To select master-page objects as well as document-page objects on a layer, you need to Option+Shift+click or Altl+Shift+click the layer name.

Placing objects on layers

To place objects on a layer, the layer must be active as indicated by the Pen icon. To place objects on the layer, use any of these options:

✦ Use any tools to create paths and frames.

✦ Use the Place command (File ➪ Place, or ⌘+D or Ctrl+D) to import graphics or text.

✦ Use the Paste command (Edit ➪ Paste, or ⌘+V or Ctrl+V) to paste objects from the Clipboard onto the layer.

✦ Click and drag objects to the layer from a library or another document.

Note When you create objects on master pages, they are placed on the default layer and are therefore behind other objects on document pages. To create objects on master pages that are in front of other objects, place the objects on a different layer while the master page is displayed.

Note You can cut and paste objects from one page to another, but have the objects remain on their original layer — without concern about the active layer. To do this, use the Paste Remembers Layers command in the Layers pane's palette menu before choosing Edit ➪ Paste, or pressing ⌘+V or Ctrl+V. You might do this if you're moving the continuation of an article from one page to another but you want the text to remain on the same layer. (For example, if you're working on a multilingual document with separate layers for English, French, and Spanish text, using Paste Remembers Layer ensures that text frames cut or copied from the French layer are pasted onto the French layer on the new location.)

Moving objects to different layers

Once an object is on a layer, it isn't stuck there. You can copy and paste objects to selected layers, or you can move them using the Layers pane. When you move an object to a layer, it's placed in front of all other objects on a layer. To select multiple objects, remember to Shift+click them, and then move them in one of the following ways:

✦ **Paste objects on a different layer.** First cut or copy objects to the Clipboard. Activate the layer on which you want to put the objects, and then use the Paste command (Edit ➪ Paste, or ⌘+V or Ctrl+V). This method works well for moving objects that are currently on a variety of layers.

✦ **Move objects to a different layer.** Click and drag the active object box (to the right of a layer's name) to another layer. When you use this method, it doesn't matter which layer is active. However, you can't move objects from multiple layers to a single layer using this method. (If you select multiple objects that reside on different layers, dragging the box moves only objects that reside on the first layer on which you selected an object.)

✦ **Move objects to a hidden or locked layer.** Press ⌘ or Ctrl while you click and drag the active object box.

✦ **Copy rather than move objects to a different layer.** Press Option or Alt while you click and drag the active object box.

✦ **Copy objects to a hidden or locked layer.** Press Option+⌘ or Ctrl+Alt while you drag the active object box.

Tip After designing a new template, you might realize that working with it would be easier if you had isolated certain objects on layers. You can create new layers, then move objects to them at this point. Just make sure the layers are in the same stacking order as the original objects.

Manipulating Layers

Using the Layers pane, you can select and manipulate entire layers. These changes affect all the objects on the layer — for example, if you hide a layer, all its objects are hidden; if you move a layer up, all its objects appear in front of objects on lower layers. Functions that affect an entire layer include hiding, locking, rearranging, merging, and deleting.

Selecting layers

The active layer containing the Pen icon is always selected. You can extend the selection to include other layers the same way you multiple-select objects: Shift+click for a continuous selection and ⌘+click or Ctrl+click for a noncontiguous selection. When layers are selected, you can move them within the stacking order of layers, modify attributes in the Layer Options dialog box, merge them, or delete them.

Hiding layers

When you hide a layer, none of the objects on that layer displays or prints. You might hide layers for a variety of reasons, including to speed screen redraw by hiding layers containing high-resolution graphics, to control which version of a publication prints, and to simply focus on one area of a design without the distraction of other areas. To show or hide layers using the Layers pane, do one of the following:

✦ Click the Eye icon in the first column to the left of a layer's name. When the Eye's column is blank, the layer is hidden. Click in the column again to show the layer. You can also double-click a layer and select or deselect the Show Layer option in the Layer Options dialog box.

✦ If no layers are hidden, you can show only the active layer by choosing Hide Others from the palette menu.

✦ Regardless of the state of other layers, you can show only one layer by Option+clicking or Alt+clicking in the first column next to its name. All other layers will be hidden.

✦ If any layers are hidden, you can show all layers by choosing Show All Layers from the palette menu. You can also Option+click or Alt+click twice in the first column to show all layers.

Note When you use the Package command (File ➪ Package, or Option+Shift+⌘+P or Ctrl+Alt+Shift+P) to prepare a document for a service bureau, InDesign includes only visible layers. This lets you hide the layers containing different versions of the document to ensure that they aren't accidentally printed.

QuarkXPress User You cannot print hidden layers in InDesign as you can in QuarkXPress 6. You must make them visible before printing.

Locking objects on layers

When you lock a layer, you cannot select or modify objects on it — even if the locked layer is active. You might lock a layer containing boilerplate text or a layer containing a complex drawing that you don't want altered. Locking and unlocking layers is easy, so you might lock one layer while focusing on another, and then unlock it. To lock or unlock layers using the Layers pane, do one of the following:

✦ Click the blank box in the second column to the left of a layer's name. When the Pencil icon appears, the layer is locked. Click the Pencil icon to unlock the layer. You can also double-click a layer and select or deselect the Lock Layer option in the Layer Options dialog box.

✦ If no layers are locked, you can lock all but the active layer by choosing Lock Others from the palette menu.

✦ If any layers are locked, you can unlock all layers by choosing Unlock All Layers from the palette menu.

✦ You can toggle between Lock Others and Unlock All Layers by Option+clicking or Alt+clicking the blank box or the Pencil icon.

Note   When you lock an object to a page (Object ➪ Lock Position, or ⌘+L or Ctrl+L), the object's position stays locked regardless of its layer's lock status.

Rearranging layers

Each layer has its own front-to-back stacking order, with the first object you create on the layer being its backmost object. You can modify the stacking order of objects on a single layer using the Arrange commands in the Object menu. Objects are further stacked according to the order in which the layers are listed in the Layers pane. The layer at the top of the list contains the frontmost objects and the layer at the bottom of the list contains the backmost objects.

If you find that all the objects on one layer need to be in front of all the objects on another layer, you can move that layer up or down in the list. In fact, you can move multiple-selected layers up or down, even if the selection is noncontiguous. To move layers, click the selection and drag it up or down. When you move layers, remember that layers are document-wide so you're actually changing the stacking order of objects on all the pages.

Note   You might be accustomed to moving objects to the front of the stacking order to make them easily editable. Working this way, you might be tempted to bring a layer up to the top of the layer stacking order so you can edit it easily, and then move it back to its original location. Try to get out of that habit, though, and into the habit of simply showing the layer you need to work on and hiding the others.

Combining layers

If you decide that all the objects on one layer belong on a different layer — throughout the document — you can merge the layers. When you're learning about the power of layers, it's easy to create a document that is unnecessarily complex (for example, you might have put each object on a different layer and realized that the document has become difficult to work with). The good news is that you can also merge all the layers in a document to *flatten* it to a single layer. To flatten all layers:

1. **Select the *target layer* (where you want all the objects to end up) by clicking it.**

2. **Select the *source layers* (which contain the objects you want to move) in addition to the target layer.** Shift+click, or ⌘+click or Ctrl+click, to add the source layers to the selection.

3. **Make sure the target layer displays the Pen icon and that the target and source layers are all selected.**

4. **Choose Merge Layers from the Layers pane's palette menu.** All objects on the source layers are moved to the target layer, and the source layers are deleted.

Note   When you merge layers, the stacking order of objects does not change, so the design looks the same — with one notable exception: If you created objects on a layer while a master page was displayed, those objects go to the *back* of the stacking order with the regular master-page objects.

Deleting layers

If you've carefully isolated portions of a document on different layers and then find that you won't need that portion of the document, you can delete the layer. For example, if you have a U.S. English and an International English layer, and you decide that you can't afford to print the different versions and one dialect's readers will simply have to suffer, you can delete the unneeded layer. You might also delete layers that you don't end up using to simplify a document.

When you delete layers, all the objects on the layer throughout the document are deleted. To ensure that you don't need any of the objects before deleting a layer, you can hide all other layers, and then look at the remaining objects on each page. If you think you might need them later for this or another document, you can click and drag them to the pasteboard or place them in a library.

Using the Layers pane, you can delete selected layers in the following ways:

✦ Click and drag the selection to the Delete Selected Layers button.

✦ Click the Delete Selected Layers button. (The current layer — the one with the Pen icon — will be deleted.)

✦ Choose Delete Layer from the Layers pane's palette menu.

If any of the layers contain objects, a warning reminds you that they will be deleted. And, of course, the ubiquitous Undo command (Edit ➪ Undo, or ⌘+Z or Ctrl+Z) lets you recover from accidental deletions.

Tip   To remove all layers that do not contain objects, choose Delete Unused Layers from the Layers pane's palette menu.

Summary

If you take the time to integrate layers into your workflow, you can save time and effort in creating multilingual publications, produce multiple versions of a document, and benefit from greater flexibility with objects. Until you create new layers, all the objects are placed on the default layers. Although each layer has its own stacking order, the order of layers also affects stacking order.

You can create objects on the active layer, and you can move objects to different layers. Even though objects are on layers, you can continue to select and modify them as you normally would — provided that the layers are visible and unlocked. Hiding layers suppresses the printout of objects, in addition to preventing their display. To streamline a document, you can merge and delete layers.

✦　　✦　　✦

Creating Layout Standards

Think for a moment about the publications you produce. Chances are that most of your work involves creating multiple iterations of a basic set of publications, and each publication looks more or less the same from issue to issue. For example, periodicals such as newsletters, magazines, and newspapers don't change much from one issue to the next (disregarding the occasional redesigns that all publications undergo). The ongoing uniformity of such things as page size, margins, page layouts, text formats, even the tone of the writing, gives each publication a unique look and feel.

If you had to start from scratch every time you created a publication, you'd spend the bulk of your time setting up your documents and have little time left to attend to the appearance of the content (you'd probably get terribly bored, too). Few things are less rewarding than doing the same job over and over. Fortunately, InDesign includes several extremely useful features that let you automate repetitive tasks. This chapter focuses on three of them: master pages, templates, and libraries:

+ A *master page* is a preconstructed page layout that you can use when adding pages to a multipage document. With master pages, you can design a single background page and then use it as the basis for as many document pages as you want. Without master pages, you would have to create every page from scratch.

+ A *template* is a preconstructed document that's used to create multiple iterations of the same design or publication. A template is a shell of a document that contains everything in a publication — except content. Each time you need to create a new version of a repeatedly produced publication, you open its template, save as a new document file, add the content (text and pictures), tweak as desired, and then print. Next issue, same thing.

+ As its name suggests, a *library* is a place where you store things. Specifically, InDesign libraries are files for storing objects that you create in InDesign and that you intend to use repeatedly in multiple documents.

When you combine master pages, templates, and libraries with the ability to create character and paragraph styles (see Chapter 19) and object styles (see Chapter 11), you have a powerful set of automation tools. Styles automate text and object formatting; libraries automate object creation; master pages automate page construction; and templates automate document construction.

How and to what extent you use these features depends on your personal preferences and the publications you produce. You might think that something as small as a business card wouldn't benefit from any of these features, but if it's a business card for a corporate employee, the chances are that, other than the personal information, it's exactly the same as business cards of every other employee. By creating and saving a business-card template, you can quickly build cards for several or several hundred new employees. All you have to do is open the template; add the name, title, and phone number of the new employee; and then print.

For other publications, you might use several — perhaps all — of the aforementioned timesaving features. A good newsletter template, for example, contains a set of styles for formatting text, probably a master spread or two (depending on whether all pages share exactly the same design), and perhaps an associated library of frequently used objects — house ads, corporate logos, boilerplate text, and so on.

Tip   Although this chapter begins with master pages, this doesn't mean that you should begin work on a publication by creating master pages. You may prefer to work on text-formatting tasks first and build styles before turning your attention to page-layout and document-construction tasks. One of the best things about InDesign is that it lets you perform tasks in whatever order makes most sense to you. Over time, you'll develop a personal modus operandi for creating publications. Whatever style you develop, make sure that you make full use of styles, libraries, master pages, and templates.

Note   In this chapter, the terms *master page* and *master spread* are used interchangeably. If you're working on a facing-pages document, you'll use facing-pages masters that have both left- and right-hand pages. These are master spreads. For single-sided documents, a master page has only a single page.

Creating and Applying Master Pages

Before the arrival of personal computers, publications were created by graphics designers who leaned over light tables and — armed with matte knives and waxing machines — stuck galleys of type, halftones, and plastic overlays onto paste-up boards. The paste-up boards were usually oversized sheets of white card paper on which was printed a grid of light blue lines. The blue guidelines indicated such things as the edge of the final, trimmed page; the margins in which text and pictures were placed; column boundaries; and so on. These guidelines helped the designer position elements on a page and also helped ensure consistent placement of repeating page elements, such as page numbers.

Although there are no paste-up boards in the electronic publishing world, the concept has survived in the form of *master pages*. A master page is a building-block page that you can use as the background (that is, as the starting point) for document pages. The master pages themselves don't print, but any pages that use them will print the items they derive from the master page, in addition to any unique elements you add to those pages. Typically, master pages contain text and graphic elements such as page numbers, headers, footers, folios, and so on, that appear on all pages of a publication. And like their paste-up board ancestors, master pages also include guidelines that indicate page edges, column boundaries, and margins, as well as other manually created guidelines to aid page designers in placing objects. By placing items on master pages, you save yourself the repetitive work of placing the same items one by one on each and every document page.

By default, every InDesign document you create contains a master page. Whether you use the master page or create and use additional master pages depends on the kind of publication you're creating. If it's a single-page document, such as a business card or an advertisement, you don't need to worry about master pages at all. (Generally, master pages are of little use for one-page documents.) However, if you're creating a multipage document like a newsletter, a book, or a catalog, using master pages will save you time and help ensure design consistency. It's impossible to overstate the importance of master pages. They're one of InDesign's most powerful features.

The Pages pane

When you work on multipage documents, you'll probably want to display the Pages pane (Window ➪ Pages or F12), which is shown in Figure 7-1. The Pages pane displays an icon-based view of document pages (bottom) and master pages (top) in the current document. The controls in the Pages pane and its accompanying pop-up menu let you perform several master page-related tasks, including creating and deleting master pages, applying master pages to document pages, and creating master pages out of document pages. The Pages pane also lets you add and remove document pages.

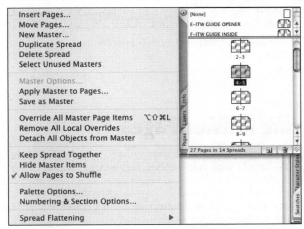

Figure 7-1: The Pages pane. The document page icons at the bottom of the pane show that the publication has 27-pages. The master-page icons at the top show the default document's master pages: [None], E-ITW Guide Opener, and F-ITW Guide Inside.

Cross-Reference See Chapter 5 for more information about adding and removing document pages.

Here's a quick rundown of the controls available in the Pages pane and the commands in its pop-up menu:

✦ The page icons at the top of the pane represent master pages. Every document includes a master page called [None], which includes only margin guidelines, and A-Master, which reflects the margin and column settings you specify in the New Document dialog box when you create the document. If a letter appears on a master page icon, it indicates that the master spread is based on another (parent) master page; for example, if you have a master page named C-Master and the icons for C-Master have the letter *A,* then C-Master is based on A-Master. A master page's name appears below its icon. If a master page and its name are highlighted, it means that the master page appears in the document window. If a master page name appears in reverse type, it's currently displayed in the document window.

✦ The page icons at the bottom of the pane represent document pages. Dog-eared icons represent left and right pages in a facing-pages document. The letter displayed on a page icon indicates the master page it's based on. (If no letter appears, the page is based on the blank master page.) The numbers below the page icons indicate the page numbers, including section numbering, if any (sections are covered in Chapter 5). If a page and its number are highlighted, it means that page currently appears in the document window. If a page number appears in reverse type (that is, white characters on a black background), it means that it's currently displayed in the document window.

✦ The Create New Page button (notepad icon) at the bottom of the pane lets you add a new page with a mouse click.

✦ The Delete Selected Pages button (trashcan icon) lets you delete document and master pages.

New Feature   InDesign CS2 adds a new palette menu option — Move Pages — to the Pages pane.

✦ The Move Pages palette menu command lets you move document pages using a dialog box in which you specify which pages to move and where to move them. You can also simply click the pages to select them and drag them to their new location within the Pages pane.

✦ The Insert Pages palette menu command lets you add pages to a document and specify the master page on which they're based.

✦ The New Master palette menu command lets you add a new master page.

✦ The Duplicate Spread and Duplicate Page palette menu commands do exactly what the names say. They let you duplicate a page or a facing-pages spread. The name of the command depends on whether a page or spread is highlighted in the pane.

✦ The Delete Page, Delete Spread, Delete Master Page, and Delete Master Spread palette menu commands let you delete single pages and facing-pages spreads (both document pages and master pages). Again, the menu name will change based on what is selected in the pane.

✦ The Select Unused Masters palette menu command selects all unused master pages and spreads, so you can easily identify and perhaps delete them.

✦ The Master Options palette menu command is used for changing master-page attributes, including name and parent master page (if you want to base a master page on another master page).

✦ The Apply Master to Pages palette menu command is used for applying a master-page layout to one or more document pages.

✦ The Save As Master palette menu command lets you convert a document page into a master page.

✦ The Override All Master Page Items palette menu command lets you have any local changes to the selected pages override the master-page settings. This command moves all master items to the document page on the selected pages.

✦ The Remove All Local Overrides and the Remove Selected Local Overrides palette menu commands return master objects that you've modified on specific document pages to their original condition. If no object is selected, the menu command is Remove All Local Overrides; if one or more objects are selected, the menu command is Remove Selected Local Overrides.

✦ The Detach Selection from Master palette menu command removes any master page items that had been modified on the selected pages from the master page *for those selected document pages* only. Essentially, this command prevents you from using the Remove All Local Overrides or Remove Selected Local Overrides commands for these document pages, permanently changing the master pages for them.

✦ The Keep Spread Together palette menu command ensures that pages are not split apart as you add pages. Normally, adding a single page shuffles all subsequent pages so they form new spreads. With this command, existing spreads are maintained, so adding an odd number of pages will not cause them to be reshuffled.

✦ The Hide Master Options palette menu command will hide in your document any master-page items. (The menu option then becomes Show Master Options so you can redisplay them.)

New Feature

InDesign CS2 has moved the Hide/View Master Options command from the View menu to the Pages pane's palette menu.

✦ The Palette Options palette menu command controls icon size, position, and other Pages pane display settings.

✦ The Numbering & Section Options palette menu command lets you establish independently numbered sections in a single document. For example, you can create a section if you want to use a different numbering scheme (Roman numerals, perhaps) for the front matter of a book than for the body.

Cross-Reference

See Chapter 5 for more information about sections.

✦ The Spread Flattening palette menu command lets you control image flattening for specific spreads. *Flattening* is InDesign's term for reducing the resolution of graphics to save disk space and speed output time. Typically, you'd flatten images for Web-oriented documents because the Web displays images at the relatively low resolution of 72 dpi. You might also flatten high-resolution graphics when printing a draft version to speed up printing.

Chapter 30 covers flattening in more detail.

Creating a new master page

If all the pages in the publication you're creating share essentially the same page design, you don't need to create a new master page. Instead, you can simply use the default master page called A-Master that every document has. But if you intend to use more than one page layout in your document — maybe you're building a magazine and you want some pages to use a three-column format and others to use a two-column format — you'll need to create additional master pages.

Before you create a new master page, you should have a general idea of how you want it to look. In particular, you should know where you want to place margins, column boundaries, and repeating elements, such as page numbers. (Laying out master pages is covered later in this section.) When you're ready to create a new master page, follow these steps:

1. **If the Pages pane is not displayed, choose Windows ⇨ Pages or press F12.**

2. **From the Pages pane's palette menu, choose New Master.** You can also press Option+⌘ or Ctrl+Alt and click the Create New Page button at the bottom of the pane. The New Master dialog box, shown in Figure 7-2, appears.

Figure 7-2: The New Master dialog box

3. **In the Prefix field, specify a one-character prefix that's attached to the front of the master page name and appears on associated document page icons in the Pages pane.** The default is a letter such as B, C, or D.

4. **In the Name field, type a name for the master page.** Use something descriptive, such as "3-column Layout," "Front Matter Layout," or "Chapter Title Pages."

5. **If you want to base the master page on another master page you've already created, select the parent master page from the Based on Master pop-up menu.** Basing a master page on another master page is covered in more detail later in this section.

6. **In the Number of Pages field, type the number of pages you want to include in the master spread.** Typically, you'll type 2 for a facing-pages document and 1 for a single-page document.

7. **When you finish specifying the attributes of the new master page, click OK to close the dialog box.**

After you create a new master page, it appears in the document window. (When a master page is displayed, its name appears in the Page field in the bottom-left corner of the document window.) You can modify any of a master page's attributes at any time by clicking its icon at the top of the Pages pane, choosing Master Options from the pane's palette menu, and then changing any of the settings in the Master Options dialog box, which is identical to the New Master dialog box.

Basing a master page on another master page

If you find that a particular publication requires more than one master page, you may want to first lay out a base master page (you can use the default A-Master) and then create additional master pages that share the same basic layout but are slightly different. For example, if the magazine you're working on uses two-, three-, and four-column page layouts, you can create the two-column master spread first and include all repeating page elements. You can then create two additional master-page spreads, base them on the two-column master, and specify different column formats. The two *children* masters are identical to the parent except for the number of columns. If you subsequently decide to modify, move, or delete a repeating page element, such as the issue date in the folio, you can make the change on the parent master and it is automatically applied to the children masters.

When you create a new master page, the New Master dialog box provides the option to base it on an existing master page. You can also choose or change a master spread's parent by:

✦ Choosing Master Options in the Pages pane's palette menu and then choosing a master page from the Based on Master pop-up menu.

✦ Dragging and dropping the icon of a master spread (the parent) onto the icon of another master spread (the child). Be careful if you use this method. It's possible to base only one page of a master spread on another, but in most cases you'll want to base both pages of the child master on both pages of the parent master. To do so, make sure that when you release the mouse button both pages of the child are highlighted.

✦ Clicking the master spread you want to be the child, and then pressing Option or Alt and clicking the master spread you want to be the parent.

When you base a master page on another master page, the prefix of the parent appears on the page icon of the child.

Tip

If you base a master spread on another master spread, you can still modify the master objects (that is, the objects inherited from the parent master) on the child master page. As with regular document pages, you have to Shift+⌘+click or Ctrl+Shift+click on the object inherited from a parent master to release it before you can edit it on a child master.

In QuarkXPress, one master page cannot be based on another. As a result, InDesign users who are used to QuarkXPress might ignore this feature, but they shouldn't. This feature has the same power that based-on formatting provides styles in QuarkXPress and InDesign.

Creating a master spread from a document spread

Generally, if you need a new master spread, you'll begin by choosing New Master from the Pages pane's palette menu. But you can also create a master spread from a spread of document pages. To do so, highlight the spread of document pages by clicking the page numbers below the page icons in the Pages pane, then choose Save as Master from the Pages pane's palette menu. The new master is assigned a default name and prefix. If you want to modify any of its attributes, click its name in the Pages pane, and then choose Master Options from the pop-up menu.

Duplicating a master

You can create a copy of a master spread by clicking its icon and then choosing Duplicate Master Spread from the Pages pane's palette menu or by clicking and dragging its onto the Create new page button, and releasing the mouse. If you duplicate a master spread, there is not a parent/child relationship between the original master and the copy (as there is when you base a master on another master).

Deleting a master

To delete a master page, click its name and then choose Delete Master Page from the Pages pane's palette menu. You can also click the master-page icon, and then click the Delete Selected Pages buton (trashcan icon) in the Pages pane or click and drag the master-page icon directly to the Delete Selected Pages button.

Laying out a master page

Because a master page is similar to a document page, you can use the same approach for building both master and document pages. Some designers prefer to do a preliminary sketch on paper and then re-create the design in InDesign. You may like to do your creative brainstorming at your computer, in which case you can use InDesign as your sketchpad. The main difference between document pages and master pages is that master pages don't contain any content (other than elements that appear on every page). So, when you're building a master page, you should be thinking more about the page's overall infrastructure than about details.

Here are a few things to keep in mind when designing master pages:

✦ If you're working on a facing-pages document (most multipage publications have facing-pages), you'll create facing-pages master spreads. The left-hand page (used for even-numbered document pages) and right-hand page (used for odd-numbered document pages) of the master spreads you create will be — more or less — mirror opposites of each other. For example, page numbers are generally placed near the outside edge of facing pages so that they're visible when a reader thumbs through the pages. Or you may decide to place the publication name on one side of a spread and balance it by placing the date of publication in the same position on the other side.

✦ If you want to automatically place page numbers on document pages, you should add a page number character on each page of your master spreads. To add a page number character, draw a text frame with the Type tool, and then choose Type ➪ Insert Special Character ➪ Auto Page Number or press Option+Shift+⌘+N or Ctrl+Alt+Shift+N. The prefix of the master page (A, B, C, and so on) is displayed on the master page, but on document pages, the actual page number is used. When you add a page number to a master page, make sure to format the numbers as you want them to look on document pages.

✦ Perhaps the most important elements of a master page are the margins and column guides. To specify margins and columns for a master page, make sure the page appears in the document window, and then choose Layout ➪ Margins and Columns. The Margins and Columns dialog box, shown in Figure 7-3, appears. The controls in this dialog box let you specify the position of the margins, the number of columns, and the gutter width (space between columns).

New Feature InDesign CS2 lets you lock column guides independently of ruler guides. Choose View ➪ Grids & Guides ➪ Lock Column Guides to ensure they can't be moved. Choose View ➪ Grids & Guides ➪ Unlock Column Guides to make them movable again.

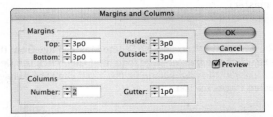

Figure 7-3: The Margins and Columns dialog box

Tip When placing text elements on master pages, you may want to use placeholder text instead of actual text. For example, if you produce a monthly magazine and you want to include the name of the month on each spread (perhaps opposite the name of the newsletter on the facing page), you can use placeholder text like *Name of month* or *Add month here*. If you use placeholder text, format it as you want the actual text to appear on document pages. Of course, be sure to replace the placeholder text with the actual text in your final document.

Cross-Reference Note that you can use the Section Marker feature in some cases to have InDesign automatically enter text, such as the issue month. See Chapter 5 for more details.

✦ If you want to place additional guidelines on a master page, you can add as many custom guidelines as you want. (Guidelines are covered later in this chapter.)

✦ Like objects on document pages, the objects you place on master pages have a stacking order. On document pages, all master objects remain beneath any objects you add to the page.

Figure 7-4 shows a typical master-page spread for a newsletter. Whenever you want to make a change to a master page, double-click its icon in the Pages pane to display it in the document window.

Tip

To copy a master page from one document to another, display the source document, click the master's name in the Pages pane, drag it to the window of the target document, and then release the mouse button.

QuarkXPress User

The ability to move master pages from one document to another, or even from one layout to another in a QuarkXPress 6 project, does not exist in QuarkXPress. So QuarkXPress users may be in the habit of using libraries to transfer master-page items from one document to another. In InDesign, you don't need to take this circuitous route.

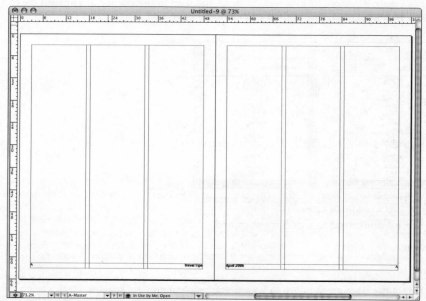

Figure 7-4: A typical three-column master layout for a newsletter. The footer at the bottom of the left- and right-hand pages includes a page-number character on the outside. On a master page, the page number appears as the master page's prefix (A, in this case).

Applying a master page to document pages

After you've built a master page, you can apply it to new document pages as you add them or to existing pages. (See Chapter 5 for information about adding and removing document pages.) For facing-pages documents, you can apply both pages of a master spread to both pages of a document spread, or you can apply one page of a master spread to one page of a document spread. For example, you can apply a master page with a two-column format to the left-hand page of a document spread and apply a master page with a three-column format to the right-hand page.

To apply only one page of a master spread to a document page, click the icon of the master spread and then drag it onto the icon of the document page you want to format. When the target document page is highlighted (framed in a black rectangle as shown in the left side of Figure 7-5), release the mouse button. If both document pages are highlighted, both sides of the master spread are applied to the document spread.

To apply both pages of a master spread to both pages of a document spread, drag the master spread's icon onto the document spread's page numbers (under its page icon). When both pages of the target document spread are highlighted, as shown in the right side of Figure 7-5, release the mouse button. (You'll need to move the icon to the corner of a spread for the spread to be highlighted, rather than an individual page.)

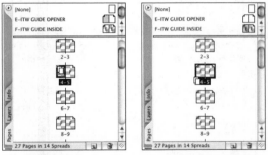

Figure 7-5: Left: Applying a single page of a master spread to a document page. Right: Applying both pages of a master spread to a document spread.

InDesign also lets you apply a master page to multiple document pages in a single operation. You can:

✦ **Select the document pages to which you want to apply a master.** Click a page then Shift+click another page to select a range of pages, or you can press ⌘ or Ctrl and click pages to select nonconsecutive pages. After you select the document pages, press Option or Alt and click the master page you want to apply.

✦ **Choose Apply Master to Pages from the Pages pane's palette menu.** The Apply Master dialog box, shown in Figure 7-6, appears. Choose the master page you want to apply from the Apply Master pop-up menu, and specify the pages to which you want to apply it in the To Pages field. Use commas to separate page numbers; use a hyphen to specify a range of pages. For example, type **2, 4-6, 8** to apply the selected master to pages 2, 4, 5, 6, and 8.

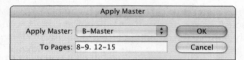

Figure 7-6: The Apply Master dialog box

You can also use these techniques to apply a different master page to a document page. If you want to disassociate a document page from its applied master page, you can apply the default [None] master page the same way you apply any other master page.

New Feature In InDesign CS2, you can apply a master page to the currently displayed page(s) by choosing Layout ➪ Pages ➪ Apply Master to Page(s).

Modifying master items on document pages

As you work on a document page that's based on a master, you may find that you need to modify, move, or delete a master object. For example, you might apply a master to the first page of a newsletter and then decide that the page number you've placed on the master page isn't necessary for page 1. In this case, you'd select the master object on the document page and delete it. Any change you make to a master object on a local page is referred to as a *local override*.

If you remove a master object from a document page, you sever the object's relationship to the master-page object for that document page only. If you subsequently move or modify the object on the master page, it won't affect the deleted object on the document page—it remains deleted on that particular document page.

However, you can modify a master object on a document page without completely breaking its relationship to the corresponding object on the master page. For example, if you change the size, position, or content of a master object on a document page, any subsequent size, position, or content change you make to the object on the master page does not affect the object you modified. But any changes you make to the stroke or fill of the object on the master page are applied to the overridden master object on the document page. Similarly, if you use any of the transformation tools or the corresponding controls in the Transform pane to modify a master object on a document page, any similar transformation applied to the corresponding object on the master page is not applied to the overridden object.

In other words, any type of attribute applied to the item on a particular document page prevents any changes to the same attribute on the master page from affecting that document page.

Tip The Show Master Items command (choose Show Master Items in the Pages pane's palette menu) lets you show or hide master objects on document pages. (The name of the menu option changes to Show Master Items when items are hidden; if items are not hidden, the option would be Hide Master Items.)

To modify a master object on a document page, you must select it. However, master objects behave slightly differently than other objects on document pages. Specifically, to select a master object on a document page, you press Shift+⌘ or Ctrl+Shift when you click the object with one of the selection tools. After you select a master object on a document page, you can modify it in the same manner as you modify nonmaster objects.

If you modify one or more master objects on a document page and then decide you want to revert back to using the original master objects, you can remove the local overrides. To do so, display the document page that contains the master objects you've modified, select the objects, and then choose Remove Selected Local Overrides from the Pages pane's palette menu. If no objects are selected, the command name changes to Remove All Local Overrides (if the selected spread doesn't have any modified master objects, the command is not available).

Using Templates

A template is a preconstructed InDesign document that you can use as the starting point for creating multiple versions of the same design or publication. For example, if you are assigned the task of creating a dozen testimonial ads that share the same layout but use different pictures and text, you begin by creating a template that contains all the elements that are the same in every ad — placeholder frames for the pictures and text, guidelines, and so on. Along the same lines, if you produce periodicals like a newsletter or a magazine, you should create a template for each one.

The process of creating a template is much the same as creating a document. You create the required character and paragraph styles, master pages, repeating elements (for example, the nameplate on the first page and mailing information on the back page), and so on. The only thing you don't add to a template is actual content.

It would be nice if designers had the luxury of creating a template for each new publication they produced. But in the real world, templates are often created by gutting an existing document. The first time you create a publication such as a newsletter, the main goal during production is getting a finished document to the printer — hopefully on time. After you finish the first issue of a publication (or a prototype), you can open the file, remove all objects and content that aren't repeated in every issue, and then save the gutted file as a template. This is probably how you'll build many of your templates.

Here are the steps in creating a template:

1. **Choose File ➪ Save As or press Shift+⌘+S or Ctrl+Shift+S to display the Save As dialog box shown in Figure 7-7.**

2. **Choose a storage folder and specify a name for the file.** It's not a bad idea to add the word Template to the filename, if possible. It lets whoever uses the file know its purpose.

3. **On a Mac, choose InDesign CS Template in the Format pop-up menu. On a PC, choose InDesign CS Template from the Save as Type pop-up menu.** If you are saving the template in a Version Cue workspace, the pop-up menu is called Format on both the Mac and Windows.

4. **Click Save to close the Save As dialog box and save the template.**

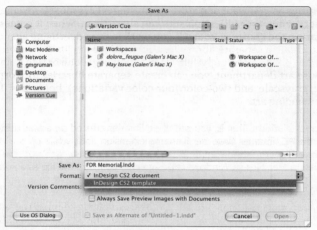

Figure 7-7: Saving templates

Tip   If you're designing a template that will be used by others, you might want to add a layer of instructions. When it's time to print a document based on the template, simply hide the annotation layer. (See Chapter 6 for more information about working with layers.)

A template is almost exactly the same as a standard InDesign document with one major exception: A template is slightly protected from being overridden. When you open a template, it's assigned a default name (Untitled-1, Untitled-2, and so on). The first time you choose File ⇨ Save, or press ⌘+S or Ctrl+S, the Save As dialog box appears.

Note   As you use a template over time, you're likely to discover that you forgot to include something — perhaps a style, a repeating element on a particular master page, or an entire master page. To modify a template, you must open it, make your changes, and then use the Save or Save As command to save the file in the same place and with the same name as the original.

Storing Objects in Libraries

If you're a savvy InDesign user, you'll never build the same document twice. After all, that's what templates are for. Along the same lines, you never have to create the same object twice; that's what libraries are for. An InDesign library is a file — similar in some ways to a document file — in which you can store individual objects, groups and nested objects, ruler guides, and grids (ruler guides and grids are covered in the next section). For example, if you create a logo in InDesign and you want to use it in other documents, you can place it in a library. Once you save an object in a library, it's as though you have an endless supply of copies. Every time you need a copy, all you have to do is click and drag one out of the library.

Creating a library is easy: Choose File ⇨ New ⇨ Library, choose a location to save the library in, give the library a name, and click Save.

You can create as many libraries as you want and store them wherever is most convenient, including on a networked server so other InDesign users can share them. When it comes to naming and organizing libraries, the choice is yours. If you work for an advertising agency, for example, you may decide to create a separate library for each client; each library can contain logos, images, boilerplate text (disclaimers, copyright information, legal blurbs, etc.), and so on. If you work for an in-house art department, you can create separate libraries for corporate logos (black-and-white, grayscale, and two-color/four-color variations), house ads, frequently used pictures, and standing art.

Tip   InDesign libraries are cross-platform. That is, you can open libraries created on a Mac using a PC and vice versa. On the PC, libraries have the filename extension .indl, while on the Mac they don't have to have a filename extension. In a cross-platform environment, add the PC filename extensions even to Mac files so Windows InDesign will recognize the file as a library.

After you create a new library, an empty library pane is displayed, as shown in Figure 7-8. The name you assigned is displayed in its title bar. You add items by dragging them to the pane. You can group the pane with other panes (by dragging its tab onto another pane) or close it by clicking its close box or choosing Close Library from its pop-up menu.

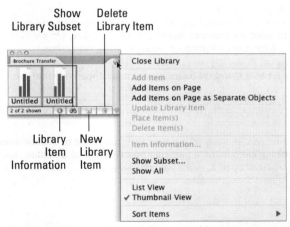

Figure 7-8: A new (empty) library and its accompanying palette menu

At this point, you're ready to begin placing objects into the library, after which you can begin copying the objects into other documents. Before we look at moving items into and out of libraries, here's a brief description of the controls in a library pane and the commands in the accompanying palette menu (refer to Figure 7-8):

✦ **Numbers in the lower-left corner of the pane.** These indicate the number of objects currently displayed in the pane (although not necessarily visible, depending on the size of the pane) and the number of objects in the library. Search capabilities let you display a subset of the entire library.

✦ **Library Item Information.** Clicking this button displays the Item Information dialog box, shown in Figure 7-9. Here you can assign a name, type, and description to a library object. (You can search for library objects based on these attributes.)

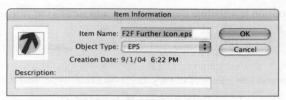

Figure 7-9: The Item Information dialog box

✦ **Show Library Subset.** Clicking this button displays a dialog box that lets you locate and display objects that meet certain search criteria.

✦ **New Library Item.** This lets you add a selected object on a document page to a library.

✦ **Delete Library Item.** Clicking this button lets you delete highlighted objects in the library.

✦ **Close Library.** This palette menu command does the same thing as clicking a library pane's Close button.

Note

If a library pane is part of another palette, if it is the frontmost palette, and if you close that palette, the library pane also closes. But if the library pane is not the frontmost pane in the palette, the library remains open when you close the palette.

✦ **Add Item and Add All Items on Page.** These commands let you add a selected item or all items on a document page to a library. You can also simply click and drag items into the pane.

✦ **Update Library Item.** Although you might think this menu option only updates the library item to reflect any changes made to the original item, that's not true. What this command really does is let you replace a library object, either a modified version of the original item or a completely different object. After you select the library object you want to replace, click whatever object you want to replace it with in your layout, and then choose Update Library Item.

New Feature

The Update Library Item option is new to InDesign CS2.

✦ **Place Item(s).** This command lets you place copies of selected library objects into a document.

✦ **Delete Item(s).** This command lets you remove selected library objects from the library.

✦ **Item Information.** This command displays the Item Information dialog box (refer to Figure 7-9).

✦ **Show Subset.** This command opens the same dialog box that appears if you click the Show Library Subset button. The dialog box lets you locate and display objects that meet certain search criteria.

✦ **Show All.** This command displays all library objects (rather than a subset identified by a previous search).

✦ **List View.** When this option is selected, library objects appear in a list rather than as Thumbnails.

✦ **Thumbnails View.** When this option is selected, each library object appears in its own thumbnail window.

✦ **Sort Items.** This command lets you sort library items by name, type, and date.

To open an existing library, choose File ➪ Open or press ⌘+O or Ctrl+O.

Note Multiple users can share a library, but only if it's locked (meaning people can use items in the library but not add new ones). To lock a library on the Mac, locate the library file in the Finder, select it, choose File ➪ Get Info, and select the Locked option. In Windows, locate the library file in its current folder, right-click the filename or icon, and then select Read-Only from the Properties contextual menu's General pane.

To delete a library, you must delete the file. Either click and drag the file icon to the Trash (Mac) or move the file icon to the Recycle Bin (Windows).

Adding and deleting library objects

In addition to placing individual objects, such as text and graphics frames, into a library, you can also place multiple-selected objects, groups, nested frames, ruler guides, guidelines, and all objects on a page.

There are several ways to add objects to a library. You can:

✦ Select one or more objects and then drag and drop them into an open library pane.

✦ Select one or more objects and then click the New Library Item button at the bottom of an open library pane.

✦ Select one or more objects and then choose Add Item from the pop-up menu of an open library pane.

✦ Choose Add All Items on Page from the pop-up menu of an open library pane to add all objects on the current page or spread.

Tip If you press and hold Option or Alt when adding an object to a library using any of the preceding methods, the Item Information dialog box appears. This dialog box lets you add searchable attributes to the object.

To delete a library object, click and drag its icon to the Delete Library Item button (trashcan icon) at the bottom of the pane. You can also click on the object once and then choose Delete Item(s) from the library pane's palette menu or just click the Delete Library item button. You can select a range of objects by clicking on the first one and then Shift+clicking on the last one. You can select multiple, noncontiguous objects by pressing and holding ⌘ or Ctrl and clicking on each icon that you want to delete.

When you place an object into a library, all its attributes are saved. For example, if you import a picture into a document and then place a copy of the picture into a library, the path to the original picture file is saved, as are any transformations you've applied to the picture or its frame (scale, rotation, shear, and so on). If you save text in a library, all formats, including styles, are retained.

Library Caveats

Because the attributes of the original object are retained when you place a copy in a library, there are some pitfalls you have to watch out for:

✦ If you move, modify, or delete the original graphic files associated with a picture you've placed in a library and then copy the library object into a document, the Links pane will report that the graphics file is modified or missing (just as it would if you imported the picture then moved, modified, or deleted the original). It's a good idea to store graphics files used in libraries in a common location, such as in a Standards folder on the network, so the graphics files aren't accidentally moved or deleted when you delete or archive a set of project files that happen to contain objects placed in libraries.

✦ If you copy a text frame from a library onto a document page, any character styles, paragraph styles, or colors in the library object that have the same name as character styles, paragraph styles, or colors in the target document are replaced by those in the target document. If the target document does not contain character styles, paragraph styles, or colors in the placed text, they're added to the document.

✦ If you copy a text frame from a library onto a document page, make sure that the fonts are available. If they're not available, you'll have to select alternate fonts.

Cataloging library objects

If your libraries contain only a few objects, finding the one you're looking for won't be very hard. But a library can hold as many objects as you want, and as a library becomes bigger, locating a particular object gets increasingly difficult. To make library objects easier to find, InDesign lets you tag them with several searchable attributes.

To tag a library element, select it and then choose Item Information from the library pane's palette menu. You can also display the Item Information dialog box by double-clicking on a library object or by clicking once on a library object and then clicking the Library Item Information button at the bottom of the library pane. (Figure 7-9 shows the Item Information dialog box.) Now specify a Name, Object Type, and/or Description. In the Description field, it's a good idea to type one or more keywords that describe the object so that you can easily find it later. Click OK to close the dialog box and return to the document.

InDesign lets you search for library objects based on the information specified in the Item Information dialog box. For example, if you've placed several different corporate logos into a library that includes many other objects, you could search for the term *logo* in the Name or Description field. If you used the word *logo* in either of these fields for your logos, a search of these fields for the word *logo* will identify and display your logos. The ability to search for library objects based on name and description is a good reason to name your library objects carefully and consistently and to specify keywords in the Description field of the Item Information dialog box. Follow these steps:

1. **Choose Show Subset from a library pane's palette menu or click the Show Library Subset button (glasses icon) at the bottom of the pane.** The Subset dialog box, shown in Figure 7-10, appears.

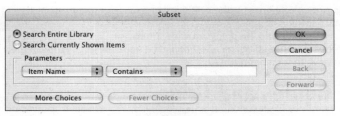

Figure 7-10: The Subset dialog box

2. **To search the entire library, click Search Entire Library; to search only the objects currently displayed in the page, click Search Currently Shown Items.**

3. **From the leftmost pop-up menu in the Parameters area, choose the Item Information category you want to search: Item Name, Creation Date, Object Type, or Description.**

4. **From the next pop-up menu choose Contains if you intend to search for text contained in the chosen category; choose Doesn't Contain if you want to exclude objects that contain the text you specify.**

5. **In the rightmost field, type the word or phrase you want to search for (if Contains is selected) or exclude (if Doesn't Contain is selected).**

6. **To add more search criteria, click More Choices; to reduce the number of search criteria, click Fewer Choices.** You can add up to five levels of search criteria.

7. **To display objects that match all search criteria, select Match All; to display objects that match any of the search criteria, select Match Any One.** These options are available only if two or more levels of search criteria are displayed.

8. **Click OK to conduct the search and close the dialog box.**

All the objects that match the search criteria appear in the pane. The pane is empty if no objects match the search criteria. If you want to display all objects after conducting a search, choose Show All from the library pane's palette menu.

Tip   The Sort Items command in a library pane's palette menu lets you sort objects by Name, Oldest, Newest, and Type. If you sort by Oldest or Newest, items are arranged based on the order in which they were placed into the library.

Copying library objects onto document pages

Once you place an object into a library and, optionally, specify item information for the object, you can place copies of the library object into any document or into another library. To place a copy of a library object onto the currently displayed document page, click the object's icon in the library pane and drag it onto the page. As you drag, the outline of the library object appears. Release the mouse button when the outline is positioned where you want to place the object. You can also place a library object onto a document by clicking its icon and then choosing Place Item(s).

Tip   You can copy an object from one library to another by clicking and dragging its icon from the source library pane and dropping it onto the target library pane. If you press and hold Option or Alt when dragging and dropping an object between libraries, the original object is removed from the source library (in effect moving it from one library to the other).

Using Ruler Guides and Grids

If you've ever seen a carpenter use a chalked string to snap a temporary line to use as an aid for aligning objects, you understand the concept behind guidelines. They're not structurally necessary and they don't show in the final product, yet they can still make your work easier. InDesign lets you create and display three types of nonprinting guidelines:

✦ **Ruler guide.** These are moveable guidelines that you can create by hand or automatically. They're helpful for placing items precisely and aligning multiple items.

✦ **Baseline grid.** This is a series of horizontal lines that help in aligning lines of text and objects across a multicolumn page. When displayed, a baseline grid makes a page look like a sheet of lined paper.

✦ **Document grid.** This is a crisscross of horizontal and vertical lines that aid in object alignment and placement.

✦ **Frame-based grid.** This is like a page's baseline grid except that it is just for a specific text frame.

New Feature   Frame-based baseline grids for text frames are new to InDesign CS2. You set it as part of your text frame options by choosing Object ⇨ Text Frame Options, or by ⌘+B or Ctrl+B, and going to the Baseline Options pane. Setting up a frame-based grid is otherwise just like setting up a page's baseline grid.

InDesign's grids and guides capabilities verge on overkill. Chances are you'll end up using a combination of ruler guides and the baseline or ruler guides and the document grid, but using all four is more complicated than necessary.

Ruler guides

InDesign lets you create individual ruler guides manually or a set of ruler guides automatically with the Create Guides command (Layout ⇨ Create Guides).

Creating ruler guides manually

To create manual ruler guides, go to the page or spread onto which you want to place ruler guides. (If the rulers do not appear at the top and left of the document window, choose View ⇨ Show Rulers or press ⌘+R or Ctrl+R.) Now click the horizontal ruler or vertical ruler, and drag the pointer onto a page or the pasteboard. Release the mouse button when the guideline is positioned where you want it. If you release the mouse when the pointer is over a page, the ruler guide extends from one edge of the page to the other (but not across a spread). If you release the mouse button when the pointer is over the pasteboard, the ruler guide extends across both pages of a spread and the pasteboard. If you want a guide to extend across a spread and the pasteboard, you can also press and hold down ⌘ or Ctrl as you drag and release the mouse when the pointer is over a page.

Tip   You can place both a horizontal and vertical guide at the same time by pressing ⌘ or Ctrl and dragging the ruler intersection point onto a page.

Ruler guides are cyan in color (unless you change the color using Layout ⇨ Ruler Guides) and are associated with the layer onto which they're placed. You can show and hide ruler guides by showing and hiding the layers that contain them. You can even create layers that contain nothing but ruler guides and then show and hide them as you wish.

Tip   You can also place a guide that extends across the page or spread and pasteboard by double-clicking the vertical or horizontal ruler.

Tip   If you want to create ruler guides for several document pages, create a master page, add the guides to the master page, and then apply the master to the appropriate document pages.

Creating a set of guides automatically

Follow these steps to create a set of ruler guides:

1. **If the document contains multiple layers, display the Layers pane (Window ⇨ Layers or F7) and click the name of the layer to which you want to add guides.**

Cross-Reference   See Chapter 6 for more information about layers.

2. **Choose Layout ⇨ Create Guides.** The Create Guides dialog box, shown in Figure 7-11, appears. Select the Preview option if you want to see the guides on the current document page as you create them.

3. **In the Rows and Columns areas specify the number of guides you want to add in the Number fields and, optionally, specify a Gutter width between horizontal (Rows) and vertical (Columns) guides.** Type **0** in the Gutter fields if you don't want gutters between guides.

4. **In the Options area, click the Margins option to fit the guides in the margin boundaries; click the Page option to fit the guides within the page boundary.**

5. **Click the Remove Existing Ruler Guides option to remove any previously placed ruler guides.**

6. **When you're done specifying the attributes of the ruler guides, click OK to close the dialog box.**

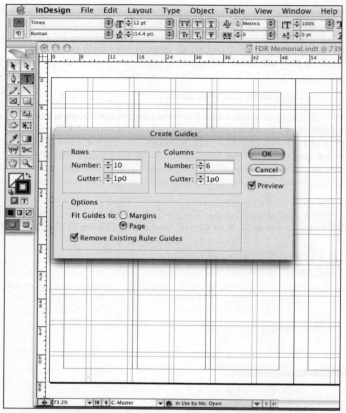

Figure 7-11: The Create Guides dialog box, along with the guides it created

Working with ruler guides

Once you've created ruler guides, you can show or hide them, lock or unlock them, and select and move, copy and paste, or delete one or more guides at a time. Here are a few pointers for working with ruler guides:

✦ To display or hide ruler guides, choose View ➪ Grids & Guides ➪ Show/Hide Guides or press ⌘+; (semicolon) or Ctrl+; (semicolon).

✦ To lock or unlock all ruler guides, choose View ➪ Grids & Guides ➪ Lock Guides or press Option+⌘+; (semicolon) or Ctrl+Alt+; (semicolon). (If the Lock Guides option is selected, ruler guides are locked.)

✦ To select a ruler guide, click it with a selection tool. To select multiple guides, press and hold down Shift and click them. The color of a selected guide changes from blue to the color of its layer. To select all ruler guides on a page or spread, press Option+⌘+G or Ctrl+Alt+G.

✦ To move a guide, click and drag it as you would any object. (You can also change its coordinates in the Control palette or Transform pane.) To move multiple guides, click and drag them. To move guides to another page, select them, choose Edit ➪ Cut, or ⌘+X or Ctrl+X, or Edit ➪ Copy, or ⌘+C or Ctrl+C, display the target page, and then choose Edit ➪ Paste, or ⌘+V or Ctrl+V. If the target page is the same shape as the source page, the guides are placed in their original position.

✦ To delete ruler guides, select them and then press Delete or Backspace.

✦ To change the color of the ruler guides and the view percentage above which they're displayed (the default view threshold is 5 percent), choose Layout ➪ Ruler Guides. The Ruler Guides dialog box, shown in Figure 7-12, appears. Modify the View Threshold value and choose a different color from the Color pop-up menu, and then click OK. If you change the settings in the Ruler Guides dialog box when no documents are open, the new settings become defaults and are applied to all subsequently created documents.

✦ To display ruler guides behind objects instead of in front, choose InDesign ➪ Preferences ➪ Guides & Pasteboard on the Mac or Edit ➪ Preferences ➪ Guides & Pasteboard in Windows, or press ⌘+K or Ctrl+K, and check Guides in Back in the Guide Options section of the dialog box's Guides & Pasteboard pane.

✦ If the Snap to Guides command (View ➪ Grids & Guides ➪ Snap to Guides, or Shift+⌘+; [semicolon] or Ctrl+Shift+; [semicolon]) is selected, object edges will snap to ruler guides when you drag them in the snap zone. To specify the *snap zone* (the distance — in pixels — at which an object will snap to a guide), choose InDesign ➪ Preferences ➪ Guides & Pasteboard on the Mac or Edit ➪ Preferences ➪ Guides & Pasteboard in Windows, or press ⌘+K or Ctrl+K, and type a value in the Snap to Zone field in the Guide Options section of the dialog box.

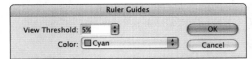

Figure 7-12: The Ruler Guides dialog box

Working with the baseline grid

Every new document you create includes a baseline grid. If the document you're working on uses a multicolumn page layout, a baseline grid can be helpful for aligning text baselines across columns and for ensuring that object edges align with text baselines. Baseline grids aren't much use for small documents — business cards, ads, and so on — and one-column designs. Here's how to create them:

1. **Choose InDesign ➪ Preferences ➪ Grids on the Mac or Edit ➪ Preferences ➪ Grids in Windows, or press ⌘+K or Ctrl+K and choose the Grids pane.** The Grids pane, shown in Figure 7-13, appears.

2. **Choose a color from the Color pop-up menu in the Baseline Grid area.**

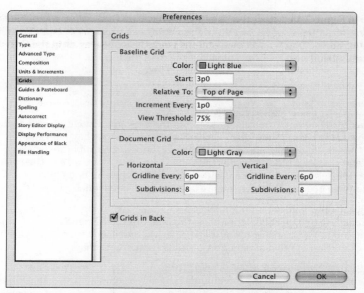

Figure 7-13: The Grids pane of the Preferences dialog box

3. **In the Start field, type the distance between the top of the page and the first grid line.** If you type **0**, the Increment Every value determines the distance between the top of the page and the first grid line.

4. **Type the distance between grid lines in the Increment Every field.** Generally, the value you type in this field will be the same as the leading value you use for the publication's body text.

5. **Choose a View Threshold percentage from the pop-up menu or type a value in the field.** Generally, you don't want to display the baseline grid at reduced view percentages because grid lines become tightly spaced.

6. **Click OK to close the dialog box and return to the document.**

A baseline grid is document-wide (that is, you can't change it from page to page), and grid lines are displayed behind all objects, layers, and ruler guides. The default baseline grid begins ½ inch from the top of a document page, the grid lines are light blue lines and placed 1 pica apart; and grid lines are displayed at view percentages above 75 percent. If you change any of these settings when no documents are open, the changes are applied to all subsequently created documents; if a document is open, changes apply only to that document.

Tip   The Show/Hide Baseline Grid command (View ➪ Grids & Guides ➪ Show/Hide Baseline Grid, or Option+⌘+' [apostrophe] or Ctrl+Alt+' [apostrophe]) lets you display and hide a document's baseline grid.

You set the baseline grid for a text frame in a very similar way. After selecting the text frame, choose Object ➪ Text Frame Options (⌘+B or Ctrl+B), and then go to the Baseline Options pane, shown in Figure 7-14. Select the Use Custom Baseline Grid option to enable the grid for this text frame, and then choose the rest of the settings as appropriate to it. The Offset, Start, Relative To, Increment Every, and Color options work the same way as in the Grids pane of the Preferences dialog box.

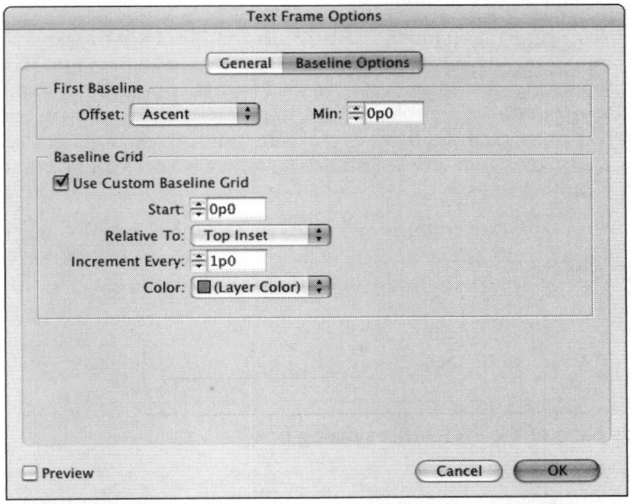

Figure 7-14: The Baseline Options pane of the Text Frame Options dialog box

Working with the document grid

Like the baseline grid, every document includes a default *document grid,* which is a set of horizontal and vertical lines. And like baseline grids, you may or may not find the document grid to be a useful aid for laying out pages. If you like working on graph paper in the real world, the document guide may be just your cup of tea. On the other hand, you may find document grids to be too constricting and opt not to use them. If you want to use document grids, follow these steps:

1. **Choose InDesign ➪ Preferences ➪ Grids on the Mac or Edit ➪ Preferences ➪ Grids in Windows, or press ⌘+K or Ctrl+K.** The Grids pane appears (refer to Figure 7-13).

2. **Choose a color from the Color pop-up menu in the Document Grid area.**

3. **Type the distance between grid lines in the Gridline Every field.** If your basic measurement unit is an inch, you'll probably want to use the default value of 1 inch.

4. **Type the number of divisions between grid lines in the Subdivisions field.** If your basic measurement unit is an inch, you can specify a value of 6 to subdivide the grid into 1-pica squares. Or, if you prefer, you can type a value of 4, 8, 16, and so on to subdivide the grid into standard divisions of an inch.

5. **Click OK to close the dialog box and return to the document.**

Tip   The Show/Hide Document Grid command (View ⇨ Grids & Guides ⇨ Show/Hide Document Grid or ⌘+' [apostrophe] or Ctrl+' [apostrophe]) lets you display and hide the document grid.

Summary

If you want to be a true InDesign expert, you must take advantage of three of its most powerful features: master pages, templates, and libraries. All these features save time and ensure design consistency across documents. A master page is a preformatted page design that you can apply to document pages in a multipage publication; a template is a preconstructed document that serves as the starting point when you need to create multiple versions of the same publication; and a library is a storage file in which you can save any object you've created with InDesign for use in other publications.

To help you place and align objects, InDesign lets you create three types of guidelines: ruler guides, the baseline grid, and the document grid. You can show or hide guidelines, and you have the option to snap object edges to guidelines when you click and drag them in the specified snap zone.

✦   ✦   ✦

Defining Colors and Gradients

Although color is most widely used by high-end publishers — people producing magazines and catalogs — color is becoming more accessible to all publishers thanks to the recent emergence of inexpensive color printers, color copiers, and leading-edge desktop-publishing programs. Whether you want to produce limited-run documents on a color printer, create newsletters using spot colors, or publish magazines and catalogs using process colors and special inks, InDesign offers the tools that you need to do the job well.

You can use color in your graphics or apply colors to text and layout elements (such as bars along the edge of a page). Or you can use color in both ways. To a great extent, where you define and apply color determines what you can do with it.

Chapter 28 covers color matching and other high-end color-output issues in depth. This chapter concentrates on how to create and apply colors within InDesign.

Defining Colors

InDesign comes with a few predefined colors: black, registration (black on each negative for the printing press), paper (white), none (transparent), cyan, magenta, yellow, red, green, and blue. So you'll likely want to add a few of your own.

Before you can apply any colors — whether to bitmap images or to layout elements such as strokes, text, frames, and shapes — you must first define the colors. InDesign CS2 offers three ways to create colors: via the Swatches pane, via the Colors pane, and by double-clicking the Fill or Stroke button on the Tools palette. You can also import colors from other Adobe programs and from some color images.

No matter how you define colors, you have a couple of decisions to make first:

  ✦ Do you want to create your own color by mixing basic colors like red, green, and blue (called RGB and typically used for screen display), or cyan, yellow, magenta, and black (called CMYK or *process colors*, and typically used for printing presses)?

✦ Do you want to use a color from an ink maker like Pantone or Toyo? These colors — called *spot colors* — are typically used as an extra ink on your document but can also be converted to the standard four-process colors and so are handy when you'll know the color you want when you see it.

All of InDesign CS2's color-creation tools support both process and spot colors. And all have access to the predefined colors like Pantone and Toyo as well as to the free-form color pickers for mixing CMYK or RGB colors. If you plan to print the color on its own plate, you need to use a predefined color, so you know the printer can reproduce it. If you plan to color-separate a color into the four CMYK plates, then it doesn't matter whether you use a predefined color or make one of your own. One advantage to using a predefined color is that it's easy to tell other designers what the color is; another is that you will get very close matches if you start with a predefined color and then end up having it color-separated in some documents and kept as a spot color in others.

Creating colors the ideal way

The best way to create colors in InDesign is to use the Swatches pane. All colors in this pane get a unique name and are tracked by InDesign. That means each such color is available to be used on any object in your document, with no risk of having slightly different variants. Plus, you can modify a swatch and ensure that all objects using that swatch are updated, and you can delete a swatch and tell InDesign which color to use in its place. Furthermore, when you print, you have control over how each color is handled (whether it is printed to its own plate, whether it is printed at all, and whether there should be any adjustments to its ink density or screening angle.) Figure 8-1 shows the Swatches pane.

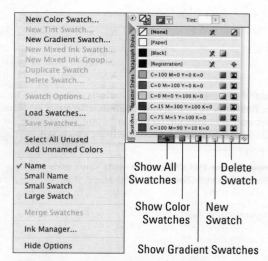

Figure 8-1: The Swatches pane and its palette menu

Note   If no document is open when you create, edit, or delete colors, the new color palette becomes the default for all future documents.

Tip

You can change the appearance of the entries in the Swatches pane by using the three options in the Swatches pane's palette menu: Name (the default), Small Name (a tighter list view), Small Swatch (no names, just small icons), and Large Swatch (no names, just larger icons). Also, use the Hide Options menu to suppress display of the Stroke, Fill, Formatting Affects Container, and Formatting Affects Text buttons and the Tint field and pop-up menu; Show Options brings them back. Finally, you can use the Show All Swatches, Show Color Swatches, and Show Gradient Swatches at the bottom of the pane to control which swatches appear.

To create your own color, go to the Swatches pane (Window ⇨ Swatches or F5) and select New Color Swatch from the palette menu. You'll get the New Color Swatch dialog box shown in Figure 8-2. Now follow these steps:

1. **In the Swatch Name field, give your color a name that describes it, such as Lime Green or Bright Purple.** You can also select the Name with Color Value option, which uses the color values to make up the color name as done for the colors under [Registration] in Figure 8-1. This option is available only for CMYK, RGB, and LAB colors, not for swatch-based colors such as Pantone.

2. **In the Color Type pop-up menu, choose from Process or Spot.** These are covered later in this chapter; leave the color type at Process if you're not sure.

3. **In the Color Mode pop-up menu, choose the mixing system or swatch library (both are considered to be** *color models***) you will use:**

   - **CMYK:** Cyan, magenta, yellow, and black are the colors used in professional printing presses and many color printers.

   - **RGB:** Red, green, and blue are the colors used on a computer monitor, for CD-based or Web-based documents, or for some color printers.

   - **LAB:** Luminosity, *A* axis, *B* axis, is a way of defining colors created by the international standards group Commission Internationale de l'Éclairage (the CIE, which translates to International Commission on Illumination in English).

   - **A swatch-based model:** Sets of premixed colors from various vendors, including ANPA, DIC, Focoltone, HKS, Pantone, Toyo Ink, and Trumatch for print documents, as well as a Web-specific set and sets specific to Windows and the Mac OS for on-screen documents. InDesign also has the Other Library from which you can select any swatch library file in Adobe Illustrator format.

4. **For the CMYK, RGB, and LAB models, use the sliders to create your new color.** A preview appears in the box at left. For the swatch-based models, scroll through the lists of colors and select one.

5. **If you want to create multiple colors, click Add after each color definition and then click Done when done.** To create just one color, click OK instead of Add. You can also click Cancel to abort the current color definition.

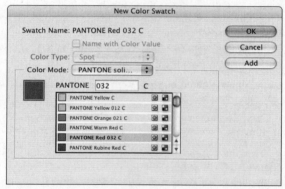

Figure 8-2: The New Color Swatch dialog box lets you define colors. (At top is the dialog box for CMYK color mixing; at bottom is the dialog box for the swatch-based Pantone colors.) An identical dialog box named Swatch Options lets you edit them.

Tip

Because regular black can appear weak when it's overprinted by other colors, many designers create what printers call *superblack* or *rich black* by combining 100 percent black and 100 percent magenta. (Some use cyan instead of magenta.) You can define superblack as a separate color or redefine the registration color as 100 percent of all four-process colors, and use that as a superblack. Note that superblack should be used only in large areas — using it on type or small objects increases the chances of registration problems for those items.

How to Decide on a Color-Naming System

You can name a CMYK, RGB, or LAB color anything you want. (Colors defined in other models will use their official names, such as Pantone 147U or ANPA 1732-4 AdPro.) To make it easier to remember what a defined color looks like, you should use either descriptive names (such as Grass Green or Official Logo Blue) or use names based on the color settings. Choose one naming convention to keep things consistent.

The benefit of using descriptive names is that they have intrinsic meaning, which helps designers choose the right one. For example, there's no confusion that Official Logo Blue is the color to be used for the company logo, but the proper usage of the same color using a name based on its color values won't be so obvious.

The benefit of using color-value names is that designers who do a lot of color work will know what that color is. Grass Green could be any of several colors, but C=30 M=0 Y=50 K=5 can be only one color.

A good strategy is to use the color-value names for all colors — with a twist: For colors that have specific usage, add that to the color name. For example, you might use a grassy green for a feature article, so you would just name it based on its color values (for example, C=30 M=0 Y=50 K=5). But your magazine logo color would be named something like Logo C=100 M=100 Y=20 K=25, so you have a reminder of this swatch's designated usage.

InDesign will name colors based on their values automatically if you select the Name with Color Value option and choose Process as the Color Type when you define the color. For example, if you create a color in the CMYK model, you might give it a name based on its mix, such as *55C 0M 91Y 0K* for that grass-green color — composed of 55 percent cyan, 0 percent magenta, 91 percent yellow, and 0 percent black. (Believe it or not, this naming convention is how professionals specify colors on paste-up boards.) InDesign's Name with Color Value option would name this color *C=55 M=0 Y=91 K=0*. The same system applies to the RGB, HSB, and LAB models.

The most popular swatch libraries used by North American professional publishers are those from Pantone, whose Pantone Matching System (PMS) is the de facto standard for most publishers in specifying spot-color inks. The Pantone swatch libraries come in several variations, of which InDesign includes four:

✦ **Pantone Process Coated:** Use this when you color-separate Pantone colors and your printer uses the standard Pantone-brand process-color inks. (These colors will reproduce reliably when color-separated, while the other Pantone swatch libraries' colors often will not.) Colors in this variant will automatically have the code *DS* (digital SWOP, or Specifications for Web Offset Publications) prefixed to their names and *C* (coated) appended.

✦ **Pantone Solid Coated:** Use this when your printer will use actual Pantone inks (as spot colors) when printing to coated paper stock. Colors in this variant will have the code *C* (coated) appended to their names.

✦ **Pantone Solid Matte:** Use this when your printer will use actual Pantone inks (as spot colors) when printing to matte-finished paper stock. Colors in this variant will have the code *M* (matte) appended to their names.

✦ **Pantone Solid Uncoated:** Use this when your printer will use actual Pantone inks (as spot colors) when printing to uncoated paper stock. Colors in this variant will have the code *U* (uncoated) appended to their names.

QuarkXPress User

Unlike InDesign, both PageMaker and QuarkXPress support more Pantone color swatches — such as metallics and pastels — and QuarkXPress also supports the high-fidelity Pantone Hexachrome colors. Check out www.InDesignCentral.com for Pantone library sources for InDesign.

Tip

When printing on uncoated paper stock with any colors designed for use on coated stock (which is glossier and shinier), you will usually get weaker, less-saturated color reproduction. That's because the colors designed for uncoated stock are a little richer to make up for the fact that some of the ink gets absorbed into the paper. In uncoated stock, there is much less absorption because the coating acts as a barrier. A matte finish is not as glossy as coated stock but more glossy than uncoated paper.

The other swatch libraries available in InDesign are:

✦ **ANPA.** The color library defined by the Newspaper Association of America (formerly called the American Newspaper Publishers Association, thus the acronym ANPA). Its colors are based on LAB values.

New Feature

Support for the ANPA color model is new to InDesign CS2.

✦ **DIC Color.** The Dainippon Ink & Chemical library, used mainly in Japan.

✦ **Focoltone.** A CMYK-based library from Focoltone, used mainly in Asia.

✦ **HKS.** Used in mainly Germany and other European countries, with variants for industrial printing such as on plastics, it uses various combinations of cyan, magenta, and yellow with black overlays to achieve different shades.

✦ **System.** InDesign has two system libraries, one for Macs and one for Windows. Both are sets of RGB colors available on all Macs or PCs for on-screen publications such as CD-based presentations.

✦ **Toyo.** A spot-color model from Toyo Ink, used mainly in Japan.

✦ **Trumatch.** A CMYK-based library from Trumatch, used mainly in Europe.

✦ **Web.** A set of RGB colors that all Mac and PC browsers display consistently, for use in Web documents.

Note

Several of the swatch library names are in all uppercase in InDesign's menus and dialog boxes. That's because they're trademarked names, which some people (such as those at Adobe) like to indicate by using all caps. That's just a convention and means nothing per se. (Legally, the word need only be treated as a proper adjective, though the owner needs to use the ® or ™ symbols in its own materials to assert ownership.)

Tip

Color swatches based on the CMYK colors—such as Focoltone, Pantone Process, and Trumatch—will accurately color-separate and, thus, print accurately on a printing press because a printing press uses the CMYK colors. Other swatches' colors often do not color-separate accurately because they are supposed to represent special inks that may have elements like metals and clays designed to give metallic or pastel appearances that simply can't be replicated by combining cyan, magenta, yellow, and black. Similarly, some colors (like several hues of orange and green) can't be accurately created using the CMYK colors.

Other ways to create colors

Many people will try to use the Color pane (Window ➪ Color or F6) to define colors, but that can be a mistake. At first, you may not realize you can create colors from the Color pane. It shows a gradation of the last color used and lets you change the tint for that color on the current object. But if you go to the palette menu and choose a color model (RGB, CMYK, or LAB), you'll get a set of mixing controls (refer to Figure 8-3).

So what's the problem? Colors created through the Color pane won't appear in your Swatches pane and so can't be used for other objects. Called *unnamed colors* because they don't appear anywhere, these can be dangerous for publishers to use. (Adobe added them to InDesign to be consistent with how Illustrator defines colors—a foolish consistency.)

First, you can't modify them later in the Swatches pane if you want to adjust the color for all objects using them.

Figure 8-3: The Color pane

Second, you can't specify the color to print as a spot color, which you might later decide is how you want to print a particular color. They will print only as process colors and will not show up in the list of colors in the Color pane of the Print dialog box (see Chapter 30 for more details on this).

Fortunately, there is a way to fix unnamed colors: If you go to the Color pane and modify a color without thinking about it, choose Add to Swatches from the palette menu to add the modified color to the Swatches pane. Of course, if you forget to do this, you'll have an unnamed color, so it's best to think *Swatches pane* when you think about adding or editing colors instead of the more obvious *Color pane*. If you do forget, you can use the Add Unnamed Colors menu item in the Swatches pane's palette menu to add the colors to the Swatches pane.

**New
Feature** InDesign CS2 now lets you double-click the Stroke and Fill buttons on the Tools palette to create colors, using a Photoshop-style color picker. You can add any colors created this way to the Swatches pane using the Add Swatch button. Otherwise, you run the same risk as creating colors through the Color pane.

Creating tints

A *tint* is a shade of a color. InDesign lets you create such tints as separate color swatches, so they're easy to use for multiple items. The process is easy:

1. **In the Swatches pane, just select a color from which you want to create a tint.**

2. **Using the palette menu, select New Tint Swatch.** You'll get the New Tint Swatch dialog box shown in Figure 8-4.

3. **Click and drag the slider to adjust the tint, or type a value in the field at right.**

4. **Click Add to create another tint from the same base color, and then click OK when you're finished.** (If you're adding a single tint, there's no need to click Add; just click OK when done.) Click Cancel to abort the current tint. Any new tint will have the same name as the original color and the percentage of shading, such as Leaf Green 66%.

Note You can create a tint from a tint, which can be confusing. Fortunately, InDesign goes back to the original color when letting you create the new tint. Thus, if you select Leaf Green 66% and move the slider to 33%, you'll get a 33 percent tint of the original Leaf Green, not a 33 percent tint of the Leaf Green 66% (which would be equivalent to a 22 percent tint of the original Leaf Green).

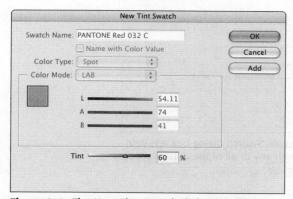

Figure 8-4: The New Tint Swatch dialog box lets you define colors; a nearly identical dialog box named Swatch Options lets you edit them. The difference is that, when editing, you can change all the other color values, not just the degree of tint.

Creating mixed colors

InDesign offers another type of color: mixed-ink color. Essentially, a mixed-ink color combines a spot color with the default process colors (cyan, magenta, yellow, and black) to create new color swatches. For example, you can combine 38 percent black with 100 percent Pantone 130C to get a darker version of Pantone 130C (called a *duotone,* though InDesign doesn't limit you to mixing spot colors with just black, as traditional duotones do).

To create a mixed-ink swatch, select the spot color you want to begin with and then choose New Mixed Ink Swatch from the Swatches pane's palette menu. You get the dialog box shown in Figure 8-5, in which you select the percentages of the spot color and any or all of the default process colors you want to mix. You also give the new color a name. Click Add to add another mixed-ink swatch based on the current spot color, and then click OK when you're finished. If you're creating just one color, click OK instead of Add. You can click Cancel to abort the current mixed-ink color definition.

 Tip
Be sure to test such mixes by creating a color proof first. They may not look as you expect when actually printed because of how printing presses handle a color overlapping other colors.

There's more to mixed-ink colors than creating them one by one. InDesign lets you create mixed-ink groups, which are a series of colors based on a spot color and one or more default process colors. Figure 8-6 shows the New Mixed Ink Group dialog box, in which you select the colors to mix as you do in the New Mixed Ink Swatch dialog box. This feature is handy to create a palette of colors within a color range.

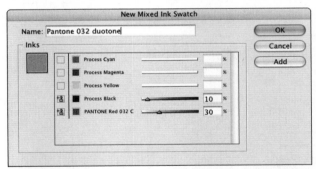

Figure 8-5: The New Mixed Ink Swatch dialog box lets you mix a selected spot color with any or all of the default process colors to create new shades and variations.

But you do more than simply mix the colors. In this dialog box, you specify an initial tint for each color you want to mix, then how many times you want to create a color using it, as well as the increment of color for each creation. This can be confusing, so let's walk through the options in Figure 8-6.

Process Black is chosen with an Initial value of 10%, a Repeat setting of 3, and an Increment of 2.5%. Also chosen is the spot color Pantone Red 032 C, with an Initial value of 50%, a Repeat setting of 5, and an Increment of 10%. This combination will create 24 mixed-ink swatches, as shown in the Swatch Preview section (click Preview Swatches to display the preview colors in the Swatch Preview section of the dialog box).

InDesign uses the settings and first mixes 50 percent of Pantone 032 with 10 percent of process cyan. That's one swatch. Then it mixes 50 percent of Pantone 032 with 12.5 percent of black (adding the increment of 2.5%). It does so two more times, for 15 percent and 17.5 percent of black mixed with the 50 percent of Pantone 032 because there was a Repeat setting of 3. Note that InDesign stops at 100 percent saturation even if the Increment results in a higher number.

So that's four mixed-ink swatches based on 50 percent of Pantone 032. InDesign now repeats this mixing with the next increment of Pantone 032 (60 percent, based on the Increment value of 10% for that color). That's four more. The process is repeated four more times, one for 70 percent, one for 80 percent, one for 90 percent, and one for 100 percent of Pantone 032, to meet the Repeat setting of 5.

Tip　To figure out how many swatches you can create using this feature, add 1 to the number in each of the Repeat fields, and then multiply the values. In the preceding example, you get 24 — (3+1) × (5+1), or 4 × 6, or 24. That's because the Repeat setting indicates how many more variations to create *in addition to* those with the base (Initial) value.

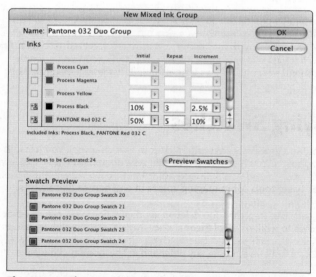

Figure 8-6: The New Mixed Ink Group dialog box lets you mix a selected spot color with any or all of the default process colors in user-defined increments to create a range of new shades and variations.

Editing Colors and Tints

Editing colors is pretty easy in InDesign: For any color in the Swatches pane, just double-click the color or its name, and the Swatch Options dialog box (which is the same as the New Swatch dialog box shown previously in Figure 8-2) appears. Make any adjustments and click OK when you're done. Voilà! Your color is now changed.

Similarly, if you double-click a tint swatch, you get the Swatch Options dialog box, which lets you change the tint percentage.

Caution   When editing a tint, the Swatch Options dialog box also lets you change the other attributes of the color. It's key to remember that if you change those settings in the tint, all other tints based on the original color, as well as the original color, are changed accordingly. If you want to change a setting of just the tint — such as making it a spot color while leaving the original color a process color — you need to duplicate the original color and make a tint from that duplicate.

In addition to double-clicking a swatch to edit it, you can select Swatch Options from the palette menu, but why bother?

To help work with swatches, you can have InDesign show just color and tint swatches, just gradient swatches, or all swatches by using the icons at the bottom of the Swatches pane. Figure 8-1 illustrates which icon does what.

InDesign also lets you merge swatches — select multiple swatches and then choose Merge Swatches from the Swatches pane's palette menu — but I suggest you avoid this. When InDesign merges swatches, it tries to calculate a new value based on the swatches' values, essentially weighting the CMYK values (RGB and other values are converted to CMYK first). But it's a crapshoot: You are not likely to get the color you expect. If you want a shade between two colors, I recommend you create it as a new swatch, manually entering the desired CMYK (or RGB or LAB) values.

Deleting and Copying Swatches

When you create colors, tints, and gradients (described later in this chapter), you'll find it easy to go overboard and make too many. You'll also find that different documents have different colors, each created by different people, and you'll likely want to move colors from one document to another. InDesign provides basic tools for managing colors in and across documents.

Note   Remember that when selecting swatches for deletion or duplication, you can ⌘+click or Ctrl+click multiple swatches to work on all of them at once. Note that Shift+clicking selects all swatches between the first swatch clicked and the swatch that you Shift+click, whereas ⌘+click or Ctrl+click lets you select specific swatches in any order and in any location in the pane.

Deleting swatches

InDesign makes deleting swatches easy: Just select the color, tint, or gradient in the Swatches pane. Then choose Delete Swatch from the palette menu, or click the Delete Swatch button at the bottom of the Swatches pane.

Well, that's not quite it. You'll then get the dialog box shown in Figure 8-7, which lets you assign anything using the deleted swatch to a new color (the Defined Swatch option) or leave the color on any object that happens to be using it, but delete the swatch from the Swatches pane (the Unnamed Swatch option). (As explained earlier in this chapter, unnamed colors should be avoided, so if your document is using a color, keep its swatch.)

Caution   If you delete a tint and replace it with another color, any object using that tint will get the full-strength version of the new color, not a tint of it.

Likewise, if you delete a color swatch that you've based one or more tints on, those tints will also be deleted if you replace the deleted swatch with an unnamed swatch. However, if you delete a color swatch and replace it with a defined swatch, any tints of that deleted swatch will retain their tint percentages of the replacement-defined swatch.

Tip   InDesign offers a nice option to quickly find all unused colors in the Swatches pane — the palette menu's Select All Unused option. Then you can just delete them in one fell swoop.

Figure 8-7: The Delete Swatch dialog box lets you replace a deleted color with a new one or leave the color applied to objects using it.

Tip   If you delete a swatch and replace it with an unnamed swatch, you can recapture that deleted swatch later by choosing the Add Unnamed Colors menu item in the Swatches pane's palette menu.

Copying swatches

To duplicate a swatch, so you can create a new one based on it, use the Duplicate Swatch option in the Swatches pane. The word *copy* will be added to its name, and you edit it — including its name — as you would any swatch.

Tip   A quick way to import specific colors from another InDesign document or template is to click and drag the colors from that other file's Swatches pane into your current document or template.

Importing swatches

You can also import colors from other InDesign, Illustrator, and Illustrator EPS files by choosing Load Swatches from the Swatches pane's palette menu. Plus, you can now also import colors from Adobe Swatch Exchange library files this way. From the resulting dialog box, navigate to the file that contains the colors you want to import, select that file, and click Open.

QuarkXPress User When you import color swatches from other documents or Adobe Swatch Exchange files, InDesign brings in all the colors. You cannot choose specific colors to import, as you can in QuarkXPress.

InDesign CS2 lets you save swatches into color library files for use by other Creative Suite 2 users. Just select the colors you want to save, and then choose Save Swatches from the Swatches pane's palette menu. You'll be asked to give the Adobe Swatch Exchange file a name before you save it.

New Feature The ability to import and save Adobe Swatch Exchange files is new to InDesign CS2.

Finally, when you import a graphic file in EPS format or in PDF, any named colors (swatches) in that file are automatically added to the Swatches pane.

Spot Color versus Process Color

Earlier in this chapter, I mentioned briefly that there are two types of colors that InDesign works with: spot and mixed (which includes process colors). Understanding how these differ is key to using them effectively and saving hassles and money when printing your documents.

Several forms of color are used in printing, but the two basic ones are *process color* and *spot color.*

Process color refers to the use of four basic colors—cyan, magenta, yellow, and black (known as a group as *CMYK*)—that are mixed to reproduce most color tones visible to the human eye. A separate negative is produced for each of the four process colors. This method, often called *four-color publishing,* is used for most color publishing.

Note Like CMYK, RGB and LAB are also created by mixing colors, so InDesign refers to all such colors as *mixed colors,* leaving the term *process color* for CMYK because that's an industry-standard term for CMYK.

Spot color refers to any specific color ink—whether one of the process colors or some other hue—used for specific elements in a document. For example, if you print a document in black ink but print the company logo in red, the red is a spot color. A spot color is often called a *second color* even though you can use several spot colors in a document. Each spot color is output to its own negative (and not color-separated into CMYK).

Using spot color gives you access to special inks that are truer to the desired color than any mix of process colors can be. These inks come in several standards, with Pantone being the most popular. Trumatch, ANPA, Focoltone, HKS, Toyo, and DIC are less popular but still common standards, with ANPA used mainly by newspapers, Trumatch used mainly in Asia, Focoltone and HKS used mainly in Europe, and Toyo and DIC used mainly in Japan. InDesign supports all seven spot-color standards.

Spot-color inks can produce some colors that are impossible to achieve with process colors, such as metallics, neons, and milky pastels. You even can use various varnishes as spot colors to give layout elements a different gleam from the rest of the page. Although experienced designers sometimes mix spot colors to produce special shades not otherwise available, it's unlikely that you will need to do so.

Tip   If you create spot colors, I suggest that you include the word *Spot* as part of the name, so you can quickly tell in a palette or menu whether a selected color will print on its own plate or be color-separated. InDesign does use an icon to tell you whether a color is process or spot, as well as what color model (CMYK, RGB, or LAB) in which it was defined (refer to Figure 8-1), but using the word is often more visible than looking for a tiny icon.

Note   Adobe programs, including InDesign, show spot colors like Pantone, Toyo, and DIC as being based on the CMYK color model, even though they're not. It doesn't really matter, because if you print them as a spot color, they get their own plate and your printer will use the actual Pantone, Toyo, or DIC ink. And if you color-separate them into process colors, you'll get the CMYK values shown in the Swatch Options dialog box or by holding the mouse over the color name in the Swatches pane (if the Tool Tips option is enabled in the Preferences dialog box, as described in Chapter 3).

Some designers use both process and spot colors in a document—known as *using a fifth color.* Typically, the normal color images are color-separated and printed via the four process colors while a special element (such as a logo in metallic ink) is printed in a spot color. The process colors are output on the usual four negatives; the spot color is output on a separate, fifth negative and printed using a fifth plate, fifth ink roller, and fifth inkwell. You can use more than five colors; you're limited only by your budget and the capabilities of your printing plant.

No matter whether you set a color to be a spot color, you still have the option when you output to convert all spot colors to process (see Chapter 30). What you can't do when printing is select specific spot colors to be output as process colors (be color-separated) and let others remain spot colors. If you're going to color-separate some colors and have others print as spot colors, you must be sure to set them up properly in the Swatch Options dialog box.

InDesign can convert spot colors to process colors, and vice versa. This handy capability lets designers specify the colors they want through a system with which they're familiar, such as Pantone, without the added expense of special spot-color inks and extra negatives.

You can convert a color defined in any model to the CMYK, RGB, or LAB models simply by selecting one of those models when editing the color. Just use the Color Mode pop-up menu in the Swatch Options dialog box.

Caution   Colors defined in one model and converted to another may not reproduce exactly the same because the physics underlying each color model differ slightly. Each model was designed for use in a different medium such as paper or a video monitor.

Although conversions are almost never an exact match, there are guidebooks that can show you in advance the color that will be created. With Pantone Process variation (which InDesign supports), designers can pick a Pantone color that will color-separate predictably. Focoltone and Trumatch colors were created by mixing process colors, so all can reliably be color-separated into CMYK.

Tip   If you use Pantone colors, I suggest that you get a copy of the *Pantone Process Color Imaging Guide: CMYK Edition* swatchbook, available from several sources, including art and printing supply stores, mail-order catalogs, and Pantone itself. This swatchbook shows each Pantone color and the CMYK equivalent so that you can see how accurate the conversion will be and, thus, whether you want to use the actual Pantone ink on its own negative or convert to CMYK.

Working with Color Pictures

When you work with imported graphics, whether they are illustrations or scanned photographs, color is part of the graphic file. So the responsibility for color controls lies primarily with the creator of the picture. It is best to use color files in CMYK EPS or DCS format (for illustrations) or CMYK TIFF format (for scans and bitmaps). These standards are de facto for color publishing, so InDesign is particularly adept at working with them. (See Chapter 21 for details on preparing graphics files for import.)

Note   RGB is the standard color model used by scanners and graphics software because monitors use red, green, and blue electron guns to display images. The dilemma most designers face is that an RGB image displays properly on-screen but may appear with slightly adjusted hues in print, while a CMYK image may print correctly but appear incorrectly on-screen. Most designers get good at mentally shifting the colors from one model to another as they see the results of their work in print over time. Until that happens, rely on color proofs from your printer to see what your images actually look like when printed.

Caution   Color files pasted via the Clipboard should print properly after they're pasted into an InDesign graphics frame. But problems, such as dropped colors or altered colors, sometimes occur depending on the applications involved and the amount of memory available. If you click and drag files from Photoshop or Illustrator directly into InDesign rather than using copy and paste, you should have no such problems.

Working with EPS files

InDesign automatically imports color definitions from EPS files, so any spot colors you see in them show up in your Swatches pane and in menus and dialog boxes that display color lists.

Note   If you create files in EPS format, do any required color trapping in the source application— InDesign offers only basic trapping capabilities (see Chapter 28).

Not all programs encode color information the same way. If you create EPS files in some illustration programs, colors may not print as expected. One of three things can happen:

✦ Each color prints on its own plate (as if it were a spot color), even if you defined it as a process color.

✦ A spot color is color-separated into CMYK even when you define it as a spot color in both the source program and in InDesign.

✦ A color prints as black.

There is no easy solution because the problem is in how the illustration program manages color internally. The only safe bet is to use a program that uses standard color-definition methods; these include the latest versions of Adobe Illustrator, CorelDraw, and Macromedia FreeHand.

Working with TIFF files

Color TIFF files do not cause such peculiarities because they don't use spot colors — by their very nature, they are broken down into RGB or CMYK when they are created.

InDesign can color-separate RGB TIFF files as well as CMYK TIFF files. You may notice a color shift for color-separated RGB images, or for RGB images printed on a CMYK proofing printer. The degree of shift depends on the device and whether any color-management system (CMS) plug-ins were used in creating the image, and whether the same one is active in InDesign for printing.

Cross-Reference   Chapter 28 covers color-management in more detail.

Working with PDF files

InDesign accurately imports any colors used in a PDF file.

Caution   Even though InDesign doesn't support Hexachrome colors, it does retain any Hexachrome colors in the PDF file and retains them for output *only* if you export the InDesign file as a PDF. Otherwise, the Hexachrome colors are converted to CMYK when you print or generate a PostScript file from InDesign. Many Hexachrome colors do not print properly when converted to CMYK, so you should always export InDesign files using Hexachrome PDF images to PDF for output. If that's not possible, edit the original image in the program that generated the PDF or in a program like Illustrator that can edit PDF files, and choose CMYK colors instead. Then re-export the PDF image.

Working with Gradients

A technique that has increased in popularity is the gradient, which blends two or more colors in a sequence, going from, say, green to blue to yellow to orange. InDesign has a powerful gradient creation feature that lets you define and apply gradients to pretty much any object you create in InDesign: text, lines, frames, shapes, and their outlines (strokes).

Note   Gradients go by several names among artists. Included among them are *blends* and *graduated fills.*

Creating gradients

In the Swatches pane, where you define colors and tints you can also define gradients: Just use the New Gradient Swatch option in the palette menu. You'll get the dialog box shown in Figure 8-8. The first two options are straightforward:

✦ **Type a name for the gradient in the Swatch Name field.** Picking a name is a bit more difficult than for a color, but use something like "Blue to Red" or "Bright Multihue" or "Logo Gradient" that has a meaning specific to the colors used or to its role in your document.

✦ **In the Type pop-up menu, choose Linear or Radial.** A linear blend goes in one direction, while a radial blend radiates out in a circle from a central point. (Later in this section, Figure 8-11 shows some example gradients.)

Now it gets a little tricky. Follow these steps:

1. **Select a stop point — one of the squares at the bottom of the dialog box, on either side of the gradient ramp that shows the gradient as you define it.** The stop points are essentially the from and to colors, with the from being the stop point at left and the to being the stop point at right. With a stop point selected, you can now define its color.

2. **Choose what color model you want to define the color in — select from CMYK, RGB, LAB, and Swatches in the Stop color pop-up menu.** The area directly beneath the pop-up menu changes accordingly, displaying sliders for CMYK, RGB, and LAB, as well as a list of all colors from the Swatches pane for Swatches.

3. **Create or select the color you want for that stop point.**

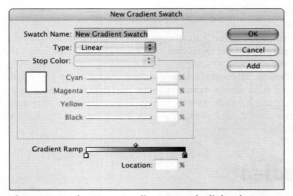

Figure 8-8: The New Gradient Swatch dialog box

Tip   You can select the [Paper] swatch — essentially, transparency or no color — as a stop point in a gradient. You can also click and drag swatches from the Swatches pane to the gradient ramp.

   4. **Repeat Steps 1 and 2 for the other stop point.** Note that the color model for the two stop points don't have to be the same — you can blend from a Pantone spot color to a CMYK color, for example.

You now have a simple gradient. But you don't have to stop there. Here are your options:

   ✦ You can change the rate at which the colors transition by sliding the diamond icon at the top of the gradient ramp.

   ✦ You can create additional stop points by clicking right below the gradient ramp. By having several stop points, you can have multiple color transitions in a gradient. (Think of them like tab stops in text — you can define as many as you need.) You delete unwanted stop points by clicking and dragging them to the bottom of the dialog box.

Notice that there's a diamond icon between each pair of stop points — that means each can have its own transition rate. Figure 8-9 shows a complex gradient being defined.

Tip   When you create a new gradient, InDesign uses the settings from the last one you created. If you want to create a gradient similar to an existing one, click on that existing gradient before selecting New Gradient Swatch from the palette menu. InDesign copies the selected gradient's settings to the new one, which you can then edit. One reason to use this is to create, say, a radial version of an existing linear gradient.

QuarkXPress User   InDesign's gradient controls are much more sophisticated than QuarkXPress's simple two-color blend controls. Plus, InDesign lets you save your gradient settings as swatches for easy reuse; QuarkXPress does not.

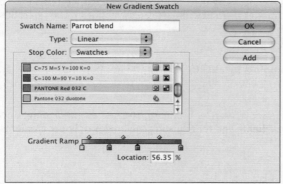

Figure 8-9: A complex, multihued gradient being defined

The Swatches pane shows the actual gradient next to its name. You'll also see the pattern in the Fill box or Stroke box in the Tools palette if that gradient is currently selected as a fill or stroke, as well as in the Gradient box in that palette, whether or not it's currently applied as a fill or stroke.

Note If a gradient mixes spot colors and process colors, InDesign converts the spot colors to process colors.

Tip If you want to share your settings with others, you can give them the color definitions for each stop point, as well as the exact location of each stop point and transition control — notice the Location field at the bottom of the dialog box. As you click each control and stop point, it shows the current setting. You can also adjust the settings for the select control or stop point by changing the value in the field, rather than sliding the control or point.

Creating unnamed gradients

Just as it does with colors, InDesign lets you create *unnamed gradients* — gradients that have no swatches. My caution on using this feature for colors applies less for gradients because all colors in a gradient are converted to process colors and/or use defined spot-color swatches — so there are no unnamed colors in their output. Here's how it works:

1. **Select the object to which you want to apply the gradient.** Make sure the stroke or fill, as appropriate, is active in the Tools palette.

2. **Go to the Gradient pane (Window ⇨ Gradient), shown in Figure 8-10.**

3. **Select a stop point.**

4. **Now go to the Color pane or Swatches pane.** The Color pane is usually in the same palette as the Gradient pane, but choose Window ⇨ Color or press F6 to display it if not. Open the Swatches pane by choosing Window ⇨ Swatches or pressing F5.

5. **In the Colors pane, create a color using the CMYK, RGB, or LAB models.** (Use the palette menu to choose the model.) Or click and drag a swatch from the Swatches pane onto the stop point.

6. **Repeat Steps 2 through 5 for the other stop point.**

7. **Create any additional stop points by clicking below the gradient ramp, and adjust the transition controls as desired.**

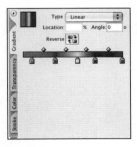

Figure 8-10: The Gradient pane is used for creating unnamed gradients and for adjusting the angles of linear gradients.

Editing gradients

Editing a gradient is as simple as double-clicking its name in the Swatches menu or selecting it and choosing Edit Gradient Swatch. You'll get the Gradient Options dialog box, which is nearly identical to the New Gradient Swatch dialog box in Figures 8-8 and 8-9.

What's different in the Gradient Options dialog box is the Preview option, which lets you see a gradient change in a selected object (if it's visible on-screen, of course) as you make changes in the Gradient Options dialog box. The Gradient pane used to create unnamed gradients also has a use for gradient swatches. After you apply a linear gradient—whether via a gradient swatch or as an unnamed gradient—you can change the angle of the gradient, as done with the bottom middle gradient in Figure 8-11 (compare it to the otherwise identical object at the bottom right). Just type a value in the Angle field to rotate the gradient's direction.

You can't rotate a radial gradient because it's circular and, thus, any rotation has no effect. That's why InDesign grays out the Angle field for radial gradients. But you still can adjust the location of a radial gradient—as well as that of a linear gradient—using the Gradient tool in the Tools palette. After applying a gradient to an object, select the Gradient tool and draw a line in the object, as shown in Figure 8-12:

✦ For a linear gradient, the start point corresponds to where you want the first stop point of the gradient to be, while the end point corresponds to the last point. This lets you stretch or compress the gradient, as well as offset the gradient within the object. Also, the angle at which you draw the line becomes the angle for the gradient.

✦ For a radial gradient, the line becomes the start and end point for the gradient, in effect offsetting it, as done in the upper-left gradient in Figure 8-11 (compare it to the standard gradient setting for the same object at upper-right).

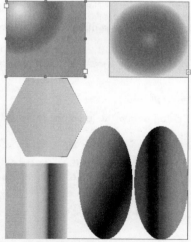

Figure 8-11: Examples of gradients

Figure 8-12: The Gradient tool lets you set the offset, adjust the gradient length, and (for gradient blends) adjust the gradient angle.

Applying Colors

Applying colors, tints, and gradients to objects in InDesign is easy. Select the object, then click the Formatting Affects Text button or Formatting Affects Container button in the Swatches or Gradient pane as appropriate for what you want to apply the color to, and then click the appropriate swatch.

Another way to apply colors, tints, and gradients is by selecting the object and using the Formatting Affects Text, Formatting Affects Content, Fill, or Stroke buttons in the Tools palette to determine what part of the object you want to color. You can use the Swatches or Gradients panes to select a swatch, or pick the last-used color and gradient from the Apply Color and Apply Gradient buttons on the Tools palette. Figure 8-13 shows the palette.

For tints, you can use a tint swatch, or you can simply apply a color from the Swatches pane and enter a tint value in the pane's Tint field. You would use a swatch for tints you want to use repeatedly in your layout (such as for the background tint in sidebar boxes), to ensure consistency. You would use the Tint field for tints you are applying on the fly, typically for one-time use.

You can also apply colors and tints to gaps in strokes through the Stroke pane's palette options menu (select Show Options and select a gap color).

Figure 8-13: The Tools palette lets you choose what part of an object you want to color, as well as to apply the last-used color or gradient.

Summary

InDesign uses swatches to contain defined colors (including colors made up of other colors), tints, and gradient blends; the use of swatches lets you apply colors repeatedly with the assurance it's the same color each time, much as character and paragraph styles assure consistent text formatting. Although you can also apply colors without using these swatches, doing so can cause output problems, especially when you're using color separations.

To maintain consistency of colors, InDesign can import colors from other InDesign documents, as well as from Adobe swatch files known as Adobe Swatch Exchange files. InDesign also imports colors used in EPS and PDF files.

Key to defining colors is choosing the appropriate color model: spot or process. A spot color prints on its own plate, while a process color is separated into the four basic colors used in traditional color publishing. If you define too many colors as spot colors, you're likely to create an impossible-to-print or a very expensive-to-print document. InDesign lets you convert colors from spot to process and vice versa, so you can choose the right output options for each document. Similarly, it's best to create color images in the color model you intend to use for output: CMYK for traditional printing and RGB for on-screen display.

A powerful feature in InDesign is its ability to create gradient blends that can contain blends among multiple colors. No other layout program offers this level of control or flexibility on gradients, although image editors such as Photoshop go even further than InDesign does.

✦   ✦   ✦

Object Fundamentals

◆ ◆ ◆ ◆

In This Part

◆ ◆ ◆ ◆

Adding Text Frames, Graphics Frames, and Lines

When you create a new InDesign document, you make several important decisions — including the page size, number of columns, and gutter width — that determine the basic structure of your publication. After you click OK in the New Document dialog box (File ⇨ New ⇨ Document, or ⌘+N or Ctrl+N), you're greeted with a blank first page. Much like an artist confronting an empty canvas, it's now time for you to add the text, pictures, and graphic elements (shapes and lines) that make up the final piece.

InDesign uses *objects* as the building blocks you manipulate to create finished pages. An object is a container that can (but doesn't have to) hold text or graphics, as well as attributes such as color, strokes, and gradients; when an object contains an imported graphic or text, or if an object is created as a placeholder for a graphic or text, it's referred to as a *frame*. A frame looks and behaves much the same as an object but has some additional properties:

✦ If you change the size or shape of a frame that contains text, you affect the flow of text in the frame and in any subsequent frames of a multiframe story.

✦ If you change the size or shape of a frame that contains an imported graphic, you also change the portion of the graphic that's visible.

Designing pages in InDesign is largely a matter of creating and modifying frames and modifying the text and graphics the frames contain. If, for example, you're creating a simple, one-page publication such as a business card, an advertisement, or a poster, you'll likely add several text frames to the page; each text frame will hold a different piece of textual information. In the case of a business card, text frames would contain the company name, the name and title of the cardholder, the company address and phone numbers, and so on. If you want to include pictures or computer-generated illustrations in your piece — maybe you want to add an EPS version of a corporate logo to your business card or a scanned image to an ad — you must also add graphics frames. A graphics frame serves as the cropping shape for the image within.

In this chapter, I show you how to create and modify basic text frames, graphics frames, and straight lines. After you create a text frame, you can type text directly into it or you can place a text file from a word processing program. (For information about importing, formatting, and flowing text through a document, see Part IV.) After you create a graphics frame, you can import a graphic into it and then crop, scale, or apply other effects to the graphic. (For more information about importing and modifying graphics, see Part V.)

The Control palette provides the basic controls for objects all in one place. Chapter 10 covers this versatile palette in more depth, although you can get a glimpse of it in several figures in this chapter.

This chapter focuses on creating simple frames and straight lines. You can also create complex shapes and convert them to frames for holding text and pictures. For more information about using InDesign's Pen tool to create free-form shapes and curved lines, see Chapters 25 and 26.

Chapter 11 shows you how to use the new ability to anchor frames to text, so frames follow the text as it reflows, a useful feature for figures, tables, and sidebars. Finally, InDesign CS2 now lets you save object styles so you can apply the same settings to multiple frames and keep them in synch; Chapter 11 also covers this new feature in more detail.

Creating a Text Frame

All the text blocks in an InDesign document are contained in text frames. Unlike a word processing program, which doesn't let you do anything but type text, InDesign requires you to create a text frame before you can add text to a page using the keyboard. (If you want to import the text from a word processing file onto a page, you don't have to create a text frame before you import.) After you create a new text frame, you can type and format text, move or resize the frame, and add graphic effects to the frame edge and the frame background.

For information about importing text, see Chapters 13 and 14.

The Tools palette contains several tools for creating both shapes and graphics frames, and because any shape or graphics frame can be converted into a text frame, you can use any of these tools to create a container that you intend to fill with text. However, in most cases, your text will be contained within simple, rectangular text frames, and the quickest and easiest way to create such a frame is with the Type tool (it's the tool with a big T on it).

If you want to place a particular piece of text on every page in a multipage publication (for example, the title of a book or the name of a magazine), you should place the text frame on a master page.

For more information about placing text frames on master pages, see Chapter 7.

Here's how to create a text frame:

1. **Select the Type tool by clicking it or by pressing T.**

2. **Move the I-beam pointer anywhere within the currently displayed page or on the pasteboard.**

3. **Click and hold the mouse button, and while holding down the mouse button, drag in any direction.** As you drag, a cross-hair pointer appears in the corner opposite your starting point; a colored rectangle indicates the boundary of the frame, as shown in Figure 9-1. (The color will be blue for objects on the default layer; objects on other layers will have that layer's color. See Chapter 6 for more on layers.) You can look at the width and height values displayed in the Control palette or the Transform pane as you drag to help you get the size you want. Holding down the Shift key as you drag creates a square.

Figure 9-1: Creating a text frame with the Type tool is a simple matter of clicking and dragging until the rectangle that appears as you drag is approximately the size and shape of the intended text block.

4. **When the frame is the size and shape you want, release the mouse button.** The flashing cursor appears in the finished frame, indicating that you can use the keyboard to type new text. Don't worry too much about being precise when you create a text frame: You can always go back later and fine-tune its size and position.

When you create a text frame with the Type tool, you can align the frame edge with a guideline by clicking within the number of pixels specified in the Snap to Zone in the Guides & Pasteboard pane of the Preferences dialog box (InDesign ➪ Preferences on the Mac or Edit ➪ Preferences in Windows, or ⌘+K or Ctrl+K).

To create nonrectangular text frames, select the appropriate frame shape (ellipse or polygon), as described in the next section for graphics frames. Then click in the frame with the Type tool to type text, or select the frame with the Selection, Direct Selection, or Type tool, and import text by choosing File ➪ Place or pressing ⌘+D or Ctrl+D.

At this point, you can begin typing, or you can click and drag elsewhere on the page or pasteboard to create another text frame. To add text to the frame, you can also:

✦ Choose File ➪ Place to import a word processing file. (If no text frame is selected, InDesign will let you select a frame or it will create a text frame for you if you click outside of a frame.)

QuarkXPress User

InDesign does not require that you create a frame before importing text, unlike QuarkXPress.

✦ Paste in text that you've cut or copied from another InDesign document or from a document created with another program.

New Feature

If you paste text that's been cut or copied from another program, you'll lose any formatting applied to the text. But if you cut or copy text from within InDesign, you have two options for pasting it: File ➪ Paste (or ⌘+V or Ctrl+V) or the new File ➪ Paste without Formatting (or Shift+⌘+V or Ctrl+Shift+V). This lets you choose each time you paste text whether to preserve formatting or not. If you want InDesign CS2 to remove formatting when you choose File ➪ Paste, rather than having to remember to use File ➪ Paste without Formatting, go to the File Handling pane of the Preferences dialog box and select the Text Only option for the Paste setting.

✦ Drag and drop text highlighted from text from another frame or document. If you press and hold Option or Alt while dragging, you'll drag a copy of the selected text rather than move the original text.

Note

You need to set whether drag-and-drop text movement works in Story Editor windows and layout windows in the Type pane of the Preferences dialog box, accessed through InDesign ➪ Preferences on the Mac or Edit ➪ Preferences in Windows, or ⌘+K or Ctrl+K.

Tip

There are a couple of other ways to place text on a page: (1) You can drag the icon of a text file or a supported word processing file directly from the Windows Explorer (desktop or folder) or from the Mac Finder (desktop or folder) onto an InDesign page. (2) You can use your operating system's drag-and-drop text feature to drag highlighted text from a document created with another program (Microsoft Word, for example) into an InDesign document window. In both cases, a new text frame is created.

Whenever the Type tool is selected, you can create as many new text frames as you want. Just make sure not to click in an existing text frame when your intention is to create a new one. If you click within an existing frame when the Type tool is selected, the flashing cursor appears and InDesign thinks you want to type text.

In addition to adding text to a newly created text frame, you can also move, resize, delete, or add a border (called a *stroke*) or a colored background. But you can't do any of these things when the Type tool is selected. You have to switch to the Selection tool or the Direct Selection tool. (See Chapter 10 for more about modifying frames and Chapter 8 for more on creating colors.)

Tip If you accidentally use the Type tool to create a frame that you want to use as a container for a graphic, you can change it to a graphics frame by choosing Object ⇨ Content ⇨ Graphic or simply by importing a graphic into it.

Note Because InDesign lets you convert any empty shape into a text frame or a graphics frame and convert any text or graphics frame into an empty shape, it doesn't really matter what tool you use to create a particular shape. However, you have to be careful when working with shapes and frames. For example, using the Place command (File ⇨ Place, or ⌘+D or Ctrl+D) to place an imported image into a text frame produces different results (placing an image in a text frame with an active text-insertion point creates an anchored graphic within text, which limits your ability to size, position, and otherwise modify it) than placing an image within a graphics frame (you have nearly unlimited control over its attributes).

Creating a Graphics Frame

Although you can use InDesign's illustration features to create the kind of vector graphics that can be created with dedicated illustration programs such as Illustrator, FreeHand, and CorelDraw, you may find yourself needing to import an illustration that you or somebody else created using another program. You may also want to add other kinds of digital images to a publication, such as a scanned photograph, a piece of clip art stored on a CD-ROM, or a stock photograph that you've downloaded from the Internet.

In InDesign, all imported images are contained within graphics frames. The Tools palette contains three tools for drawing graphics frames:

✦ **Ellipse Frame.** This tool lets you create oval and round frames.

✦ **Rectangle Frame.** This tool lets you create rectangular and square frames.

✦ **Polygon Frame.** This tool lets you create equilateral polygons and starburst-shaped frames.

The first time you use InDesign, the Rectangle Frame tool is displayed in the Tools palette, as is the Rectangle tool for creating frames that hold neither text nor graphics. (The frame tools have an *X* through their icons.) To access the other frame tools, click and hold on the Rectangle Frame tool to display a pop-up menu with the Ellipse Frame and Polygon Frame tools. Drag and release to select a different frame tool. When you do, it replaces the Rectangle Frame tool in the Tools palette until the next time you change the tool.

Tip If you accidentally use the Ellipse, Rectangle, or Polygon tool (instead of the frame version of these tools) to create an object that you subsequently want to use as a graphics frame (or a text frame for that matter), you can change the object to a frame via Object ⇨ Content. Choose Graphic from the submenu to make the frame hold a graphic, Text to make the frame hold text, or Unassigned to keep it empty. Or just place or paste the desired object (text or graphic) into the object to have InDesign change it to a frame automatically.

You can create a graphics frame using any of the frame tools, and then use the Place commands (File ⇨ Place, or ⌘+D or Ctrl+D) to import an image into the selected frame, or you can use the Place command to import an image directly onto a page without first creating a graphics frame. In this chapter, you'll learn how to create basic graphics frames into which you can then import an image. (See Part V for more information about importing images using the Place command and modifying images.)

Tip

Whether you use the Place command to import an image into a selected frame or you place an image directly onto a page, the results are similar: A frame surrounds the picture and also serves as the picture's cropping shape.

QuarkXPress User

InDesign does not require that you create a frame before importing a graphic, unlike QuarkXPress.

Here's how to add a new graphics frame:

1. **Select the Ellipse Frame tool, the Rectangle Frame tool (or press F), or the Polygon Frame tool.**

2. **Move the cross-hair pointer anywhere within the currently displayed page or on the pasteboard.**

3. **Click and hold the mouse button, and while holding down the mouse button, drag in any direction.** As you drag, the cross-hair pointer appears in the corner opposite your starting point and a blue shape indicates the boundary of the frame. You can look at the width and height values displayed in the Control palette or Transform pane as you drag to help you get the size you want. Holding down the Shift key as you drag creates a circle if the Ellipse Frame tool is selected, a square if the Rectangle Frame tool is selected, and an equilateral polygon or starburst if the Polygon Frame tool is selected.

4. **When the frame is the size and shape you want, release the mouse button.** Don't worry too much about being precise when you create a graphics frame. You can always go back later and fine-tune it. Figure 9-2 shows an oval graphics frame.

Note

When you release the mouse button after creating a graphics frame, the frame you created is active. If the Selection tool was previously selected, the frame is displayed within its bounding box, which contains eight resizing handles. If the Direct Selection tool was previously selected, moveable anchor points are displayed at each vertex of the frame. In both cases, you have to change tools if you want to change the shape or size of the bounding box or the frame. The Selection tool lets you change the shape of the frame's bounding box by dragging any of the resizing handles; the Direct Selection tool lets you change the shape of the frame itself by moving the frame's anchor points.

Cross-Reference

Chapter 10 explains how to resize a frame with the Selection tool; see Part V for information about modifying the shape of a frame using the Direct Selection tool.

Tip

When you create a graphics frame with any of the frame tools, you can align the frame edge with a guideline by clicking within the number of pixels specified in the Snap to Zone in the Guides & Pasteboard pane of the Preferences dialog box (choose File ➪ Preferences on the Mac or Edit ➪ Preferences in Windows, or press ⌘+K or Ctrl+K). When the cross-hair pointer is near a guideline, a small, hollow arrowhead appears below and to the right of the cross hair.

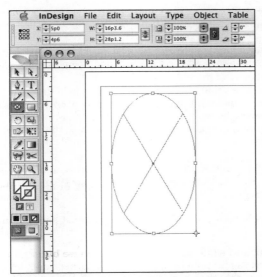

Figure 9-2: Creating a graphics frame with any of the frame-creation tools is the same as creating a text frame with the Type tool. Choose the appropriate frame tool, and then click, drag, and release. In this example, an elliptical graphics frame has just been created; its bounding box appears with resizing handles.

If you've gone to the trouble of creating a graphics frame, chances are that sooner or later you'll want to place an image within it. To add a picture to a graphics frame, you can:

✦ Use the Place command (File ➪ Place, or ⌘+D or Ctrl+D) to import a graphic file in any supported format.

✦ Paste in a graphic that you've copied from within InDesign.

Tip   You can also place an image on a page—and automatically create a new graphics frame—by clicking and dragging a supported graphic file directly from Windows Explorer (desktop or folder) or the Mac Finder (desktop or folder) onto an InDesign page.

Cross-Reference   See Part V for more information about importing images and modifying imported images.

Modifying Frames

When a frame is active, you can modify it by adding a stroke to its edges or a background color, by rotating, skewing, or shearing it, and so on.

Caution   Don't try to click a frame handle when a frame-creation tool is selected. Instead of moving the handle you are clicking, you'll end up creating a new frame. You have to switch to one of the selection tools to move or resize a graphics frame.

You can configure the Polygon tool and the Polygon Frame tool to create either regular polygons or starburst shapes. Double-click either of the Polygon tools to display the Polygon Settings dialog box, shown in Figure 9-3. The value in the Number of Sides field determines how many sides your polygons will have. If you want to create a starburst shape, specify a value in the Star Inset field. As you increase the percentage value, the spikes become longer and pointier. When you change the values in the Polygon Settings dialog box, the new values are used for both versions of the polygon tool.

Note   You cannot modify an existing polygon's attributes by selecting the polygon and then opening the Polygon Settings dialog box. You must either edit its shape with the Direct Selection tool, as covered in Chapter 25, or change attributes in the Polygon Settings dialog box and create a new polygon.

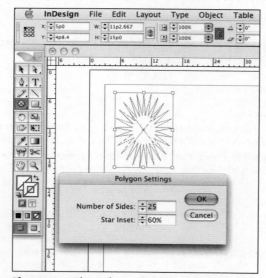

Figure 9-3: The Polygon Settings dialog box lets you specify the number of sides your polygons will have and, optionally, create starburst shapes by specifying a Star Inset value. Shown above the dialog box is a starburst created with the settings shown in the dialog box.

When any of the frame-creation tools is selected, you can create as many new frames as you want. Simply keep clicking, dragging, and releasing. After you create a graphics frame, you can modify it (without changing tools) by adding a border or a colored background or by applying any of the effects — such as rotation, shear, and scale — in the Control palette or Transform pane. You can also move or resize a graphics frame, but you have to switch to the Selection tool or the Direct Selection tool to do so.

Tool Differences: Selection versus Direct Selection

For QuarkXPress users, the difference between the Selection tool and the Direct Selection tool takes some getting used to. In terms of working with content, the Direct Selection tool is much like QuarkXPress's Content tool, but it also lets you edit the frame as if it were a Bézier object.

For example, if the Direct Selection tool is selected and you drag a point on the frame, you'll move that point and thus change the shape of the object—a rectangle would be converted into a polygon because the lines immediately adjacent to the moved point will move with the point, while the rest of the frame will not be affected.

In QuarkXPress, if the Content tool is selected and you drag a point on the frame, you'll resize the frame (perhaps nonproportionally) but the entire side(s) adjacent to the point will move with the point, so a rectangle would still be a rectangle. To change a frame in the way that QuarkXPress does with both the Content and Item tools, use the Selection tool in InDesign.

Finally, the new Position tool in InDesign lets you crop and resize a frame by dragging its handles (like the Selection tool) or drag an object to reposition it (like the Direct Selection tool).

Cross-Reference   See Chapter 10 for more about modifying frames and Chapters 25 and 26 for sophisticated shape creation and manipulation techniques.

Drawing Straight Lines

Although they're not as flashy or versatile as graphic shapes and frames, lines can serve many useful purposes in well-designed pages. For example, plain ol' vertical rules can be used to separate columns of text in a multicolumn page or the rows and columns of data in a table. Dashed lines are useful for indicating folds and cut lines on brochures and coupons. And lines with arrowheads are handy if you have to create a map or a technical illustration.

InDesign lets you create straight lines with the Line tool and zigzag lines, curved lines, and freeform shapes with the Pen tool. In this chapter, I keep things simple and limit the discussion to the Line tool.

Cross-Reference   For information about using the Pen tool, see Chapter 25

To draw a straight line:

1. **Select the Line tool (or press \).**

2. **Move the crosshair pointer anywhere within the currently displayed page or on the pasteboard.**

3. **Click and hold the mouse button, and while holding down the mouse button, drag in any direction.** As you drag, a thin, blue line appears from the point where you first clicked to the current position of the cross-hair pointer. Holding down the Shift key as you drag constrains the line to horizontal, vertical, or a 45-degree diagonal.

4. **When the line is the length and angle you want, release the mouse button.** Don't worry too much about being precise when you create a line. You can always go back later and fine-tune it. Figure 9-4 shows a new line.

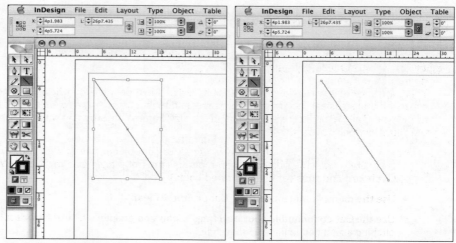

Figure 9-4: After you create a line with the Line tool, the active line appears either within a rectangular bounding box that has eight resizing handles (if the Selection tool was previously selected; left) or with anchor points at both ends (if the Direct Selection tool was previously selected; right).

When you release the mouse button after creating a line, the line is active. If the Selection tool was previously selected, the line appears within a rectangular bounding box, which contains eight resizing handles. If the Direct Selection tool was previously selected, moveable anchor points appear at the end of the line. In both cases, you have to change tools if you want to change the shape or size of the bounding box or the line. The Selection tool lets you change the shape of the line's bounding box (which also changes the angle and length of the line) by dragging any of the resizing handles. The Direct Selection tool lets you change the length and angle of the line itself by moving anchor points on the frame.

Chapter 10 explains how to resize lines with the Selection tool; see Part V for information about modifying shapes using the Direct Selection tool.

When you create a line, it takes on the characteristics specified in the Stroke pane (Window ➪ Stroke or F10). When you first open a document, the default line width is 1 point. If you want to change the appearance of your lines, double-click the Line tool and adjust the Weight in the Stroke pane that will appear. If you make this adjustment when no document is open, all new documents will use the new line settings.

When the Line tool is selected, you can create as many new lines as you want. Simply keep clicking, dragging, and releasing. After you create a line, you can modify it (without changing tools) by changing any of the attributes — including weight, style, and start/end shapes — in the Stroke pane.

Cross-Reference See Chapter 10 for more about modifying lines.

Deleting Objects

There are several ways to delete objects in InDesign. Most people either have favorites or use a method that's easiest to adopt in their current state (such as using a mouse action to delete a frame when they're using the mouse already to size frames). Be sure you select an object with the Selection tool. The methods are:

✦ Use the keyboard shortcuts ⌘+X or Ctrl+X to cut objects; use ⌘+Delete or Backspace to delete (clear) the object. (Cleared objects are not placed into the Mac or Windows Clipboard and thus cannot be pasted back.)

✦ Use the menu commands Edit ➪ Cut or Edit ➪ Clear.

✦ Use the Cut command in the contextual menu you get when Control+clicking or right-clicking an object.

✦ Drag the object to the Mac's Trash or the Windows Recycle Bin.

Summary

Empty objects, frames that hold text and pictures, and lines are the fundamental building blocks of pages. InDesign's Tools palette contains several tools for creating these objects. The easiest way to create a text frame is by clicking and dragging a rectangle with the Type tool. After you create a text frame, you can type text directly into it or import a text file, then modify the appearance of the frame or the text within. Similarly, after you create a graphics frame, you can import a picture into it and then crop, scale, or apply other effects to the graphic or modify the frame. The Line tool lets you draw straight lines, which you can modify by changing color, width, and style.

✦ ✦ ✦

InDesign Color Techniques

Adobe InDesign offers a strong set of tools for color creation and control, as Chapters 8 and 29 show in detail. This special eight-page color section shows some of these tools in action, using InDesign's actual capabilities. Most images in this section are color photographs scanned in at 24-bit RGB files at 600 dpi and converted to CMYK TIFF images in Adobe Photoshop. I also adjusted brightness, sharpness, and color balance as needed.

Color Models

Color is made up of light, but the printing model and computer-monitor models act very differently. Color printing is based on how light reflects off paper through inks — the standard inks in printing are cyan, magenta, yellow, and black (CMYK), although there are specialty inks such as Pantone, Toyo, and Trumatch. The ink absorbs all colors but the one you see; for example, your eyes can see cyan because the ink has absorbed all the other colors that light would normally pick up. That's why mixing several inks produces a dark brown or gray — most of the light is absorbed by the multiple inks. By contrast, computer monitors use a model based on how the three colors of light — red, green, and blue (RGB) — combine. All three combine to make white, while having none gives you black. Because the physics of the two models is different, what you see on-screen — or what your scanner or digital camera sees when capturing an image — won't necessarily match what is printed.

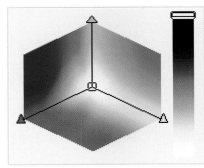

The CMYK model

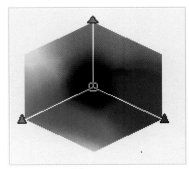

The RGB model

CMYK color (far left) and RGB color (immediate left). For CMYK, the cube shows how cyan, magenta, and yellow combine in various percentages; the slider at the cube's right adds black, which has the effect of darkening the combination shown. In RGB, there's no slider since the three colors combine to produce all color shades (white is the absence of all colors). Below are example inks from specialty color libraries.

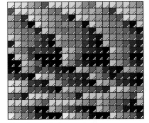

Pantone ink swatches

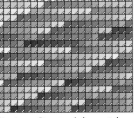

Pantone Process ink swatches

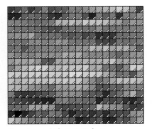

Pantone ink swatches

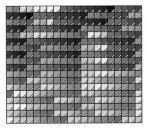

Pantone ink swatches

Colors on the Web

Although the Hypertext Markup Language (HTML) supports thousands of colors, you can only count on 216 colors to display properly on popular Macintosh and Windows Web browsers. That's because most browsers play it safe and assume that people have just the basic video support on their computers: 8-bit color depth, which permits 256 colors. Of those 256, Windows reserves 40 for its interface, leaving 216 for the browser to use. Understanding this, InDesign comes with a Web swatch library that has only the Web-safe colors.

The InDesign swatch library at right shows all Web-safe colors; compare that to the very partial (about 2 percent) listing of print-oriented colors shown in the swatches on the preceding page.

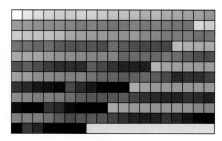

The examples below show how print-oriented colors are typically shifted when viewed in a Web browser.

Photo by Ken Marquis

Photograph in print

Photo by Ken Marquis

Photograph on the Web

Gradient in print

Gradient on the Web

CAFÉ
Solid color in print

CAFÉ
Solid color on the Web

Copying Colors from an Image

Even if you have an excellent sense of color, matching colors by eye can be difficult. Because you may want to use a color from an image in your document — as a text color or for lines or strokes — an accurate color matching tool is a necessity. Fortunately, InDesign has the Eyedropper tool to sample a color and add it to an object or to text.

Photo by Galen Gruman

The color-selection process is simple: Select the Eyedropper tool, then click on any colored object in your document. If another object is currently selected (via the Selection tool), that object will take on the clicked color. You can also Option+Shift+click or Alt+Shift+click an unselected object to apply the color to its background fill.

To add the color to your Swatches pane, select New Color Swatch from the Swatches pane's palette menu, then provide a name and choose Spot or Process from the Color Type menu, and click OK to save it.

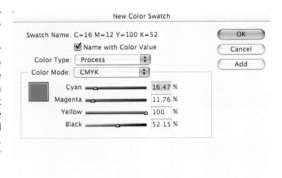

After clicking a color with the Eyedropper tool, the Eyedropper tool changes to the Stroke Marker tool, which lets you change the color of text's *stroke* (outline) by highlighting the text with the Stroke Marker tool (click and drag over the text whose stroke you want to color). The Stroke Marker tool is shown at left.

Applying Color Tints

Adding color to an image, whether at full strength or as a lighter tint, can greatly change its character. The examples here show how you can apply color to an object to give your grayscale images a new look. To do more-complex colorizing, use an image editor like Adobe Photoshop or Corel Photo-Paint.

The original grayscale image is at upper left; the others all have a tint applied.

To change an image's foreground color (normally black), select the image with the Direct Selection tool and apply a color or tint swatch.

Note that you cannot change the background color (the white part) by applying a fill to the graphics frame — not even if your image has a transparent background.

Photo by Charlotte Walthert

Working with Gradients

Gradients (also called blends) add a sense of motion or depth to a background or image. An image editor or illustration program such as Photoshop, Photo-Paint, Illustrator, or CorelDraw gives you very fine control over gradients, letting you control their shape and pattern. InDesign approaches the ability of such programs, and in some cases surpasses them.

Two-color linear gradient **Two-color radial gradient**

Example gradients (at left), using various settings for the stop and start colors, as well as for the gradient midpoint and, for linear gradients, the angle. Below are examples of more-complex gradients. (Chapter 28 explains how to apply these settings.)

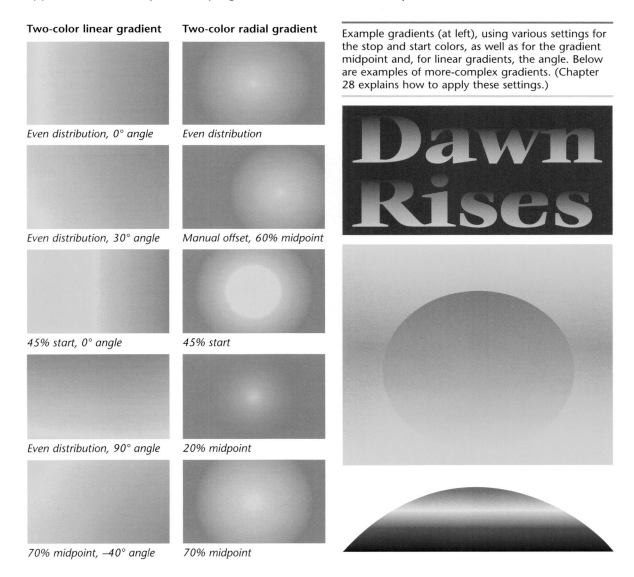

Even distribution, 0° angle *Even distribution*

Even distribution, 30° angle *Manual offset, 60% midpoint*

45% start, 0° angle *45% start*

Even distribution, 90° angle *20% midpoint*

70% midpoint, −40° angle *70% midpoint*

The Effects of Color Profiles

Like most professional design tools, InDesign uses color profiles to help ensure that your output will match as closely as possible the original image's colors (the capabilities and limits of your output device ultimately determine how close you can get). By applying color profiles and using InDesign's Rendering Intent color settings, you can change the output character of your images.

Compare the original image against the modified insets. The original uses the Generic CMYK color profile and is set with a Rendering Intent of Perceptual (Images), the default for photograph-like images.

In the top row, the insets all use the Generic CMYK profile but different Rendering Intent settings: from left to right, Saturation (Graphics), Relative Colorimetric, and Absolute Colorimetric.

The remainder of the inset images use the Rendering Intent setting of Perceptual (Images), but different profiles. In the second row, I applied the three Kodak SWOP Proofer CMYK profiles: from left to right, Coated, Uncoated, and Newspaper.

Finally, I applied the Color LW 12/600 PS profile (for an Apple color laser printer) in the third row and the 3M Color Matchprint Euro profile to the inset image in the final row.

Photo by Galen Gruman

Working with Traps

If you don't have your InDesign documents output to negatives or directly to plate and have them printed on a standard web offset press (SWOP), you don't need to worry about trapping. But if you do such professional output, trapping is an issue you should be aware of. InDesign lets you control trapping in some situations, based on what kind of output device you are using. These controls are global — affecting everything in the document — so if you want to set specific trapping settings for graphics, for example, you'll need to do so as part of creating the illustration in a program like Illustrator or CorelDraw. The one local control InDesign does offer is whether strokes and fills overprint or trap.

Photo by Galen Gruman

At right: The various trapping methods you can use in InDesign. Except for overprinting, each method is applied to every object in your document.

Knockout (no overlap of abutting colors)

Overprint

Centering (light color and dark color each move into each other)

Choke (dark color moves into light color)

Spread (light color moves into dark color)

InDesign lets you control on an object-by-object basis whether fills and strokes overprint or trap. In the images at left, I applied different settings. The text in the top image has the fill overprint and the stroke trap; the text in the middle image has the stroke overprint and the fill trap; the text in the bottom image has both traps (the default).

Working with Clipping Paths

InDesign can import clipping paths — invisible outlines — in images created in such programs as Photoshop. It can also create clipping paths from images placed in InDesign. However they are generated, the clipping paths become InDesign frame boundaries. Using clipping paths, you can create close-fitting text wraps or create masks in images through which other objects can appear.

Photo by Laura Antolovich

At top left is a picture imported with the clipping path ignored, while at top right is the same image with the path enabled. That let me put a gradient in the frame behind it to create a new background.

The set of bottom images is similar, except that in this case I created a clipping path that excluded the soccer ball so I could colorize it in InDesign by having a colored frame behind it.

InDesign can also create its own clipping paths by ignoring image areas that have less than a certain hue (see Chapter 25). This is less exact than in a program like Photoshop where you can specify the actual path, but it does work for simpler images.

Photo by Angela Burgess

Manipulating Objects

The primary purpose of the text frames and graphics frames that you add to the pages of your InDesign documents is to hold text and pictures, and much of the time you spend using InDesign will involve modifying the appearance of the text and pictures you put in your frames. However, like real-world containers — bags, boxes, cartons, and cans — text frames and graphics frames exist independently of their contents (they don't even have to have any contents), and you can modify the position, shape, and appearance of frames without affecting the text and pictures within.

In this chapter, you learn how to manipulate the frames and lines that you add to your pages. If you've ever worked with a page-layout or illustration program, many of the basic techniques for manipulating objects will seem very familiar:

+ **If you want to move or modify an object, you must first select it.**

+ **If you want to select an object, you must first choose a selection tool.** InDesign offers two tools for selecting objects — the Selection tool (the solid arrow pointer; shortcut V) and the Direct Selection tool (the hollow arrow pointer; shortcut A). These tools are explained in the section "Selecting Objects" later in this chapter.

+ **When an object is selected, commands and controls for changing its position and appearance become available.**

Cross-Reference For information on working with the text within a frame, see Part IV; for information on working with imported pictures, see Part V.

Selecting Objects

All InDesign objects — unassigned shapes, text and graphics frames, and straight and curved lines — have at least two levels of selection. You can select the object itself, or you can select the rectangular bounding box that encloses the object. (For rectangular objects, the bounding box and the shape are the same.) The tool that you choose — either the Direct Selection tool or the Selection tool — determines what you can do to the object you select:

+ **Direct Selection tool.** This tool lets you select any of the individual anchor points (and direction handles of free-form shapes and curved lines) on an object. If you click with the Direct Selection tool on an object that has a bounding box, the shape within is selected; the bounding box is not selected. You use this tool to work on the object independently of its container frame. You can also move a graphic within its frame by clicking within the object with the Direct Selection tool and then dragging the graphic.

✦ **Selection tool.** This tool lets you select an entire object by clicking anywhere in the object. This is the best tool to use if you want to move or resize an object's container. For a text object, resizing the frame will not affect the text size, but for a graphics object, both the frame and graphic are resized. (You can also resize objects with the Direct Selection tool.) When you click an object with the Selection tool, the object's bounding box is selected.

The difference between the Selection tool and the Direct Selection tool takes some getting used to for QuarkXPress users. In terms of working with content, the Direct Selection tool is much like QuarkXPress's Content tool, but it also lets you edit frames as if they were Bézier objects. For example, if the Direct Selection tool is selected and you click and drag a point on the frame, you'll move that point and, thus, change the shape of the object. A rectangle would be converted into a polygon because the lines immediately adjacent to the moved point move with the point, while the rest of the frame will not be affected. In QuarkXPress, if the Content tool is selected and you click and drag a point on the frame, you'll resize the frame (perhaps nonproportionally), but the entire side(s) adjacent to the point will move with the point, so a rectangle would still be a rectangle. To change a frame in the way that QuarkXPress does with both the Content and Item tools, use the Selection tool in InDesign.

You'll find more information about using the Direct Selection tool to select and change the shape of objects by dragging anchor points and direction handles in Chapter 26.

There's also a new way to work with objects: the Position tool. (To access it, click and hold on the Direct Selection tool until the pop-up menu appears, and then choose the Position tool.) Essentially a renamed version of PageMaker's Crop tool, the Position tool combines some aspects of the Selection tool with some aspects of the Direct Selection tool:

✦ As with the Selection tool, you can resize an object's frame by clicking dragging its handles.

✦ As with the Direct Selection tool, you can click a graphic and reposition it (crop it) within the frame by dragging.

Unless you're a PageMaker user totally mystified with the InDesign Selection and Direct Selection tools, you'll likely never use this new tool.

The Position tool is new to InDesign CS2.

Here's how to select a frame or line with the Selection tool:

1. **Select the Selection tool by clicking it or, if the Type tool is not selected, by pressing V.**

2. **Move the pointer anywhere within an object, and then click and release.** To select an unassigned shape with no background color, you must click its edge. If you click within the shape, the object is not selected.

When you release the mouse button, the object you clicked — or the object's bounding box if it has one — appears with a blue outline (the color will be different if it is on a layer other than the default layer) and eight resizing handles (four on the corners and four on the midpoints of the sides), as shown in Figure 10-1. Figure 10-2 shows the same graphics frame selected using the Direct Selection tool, with one of the points being dragged to reshape the frame.

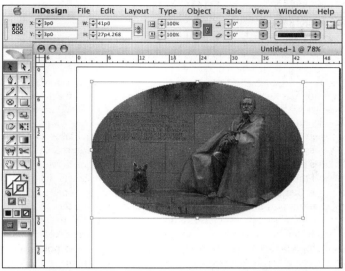

Figure 10-1: When you select a frame with the Selection tool, in this case an oval graphics frame, the bounding box appears with eight resizing handles.

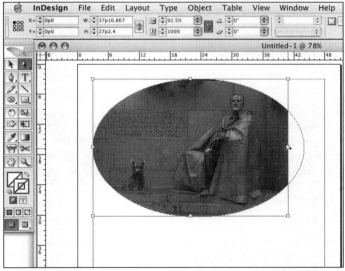

Figure 10-2: When you select a frame with the Direct Selection tool, in this case an oval graphics frame, the frame's control points, or nodes, appear. Here, I am moving one of those points. Note how it reshapes — not resizes — the frame.

You can also select an object with the Selection tool by clicking and dragging a rectangle. Simply click in an empty portion of the page or pasteboard near the object you want to select and drag out a rectangle that intersects the object. (You don't have to enclose the entire object.) Clicking and dragging is a handy way to select multiple objects.

You can also select an object with the Selection tool by clicking and dragging a rectangle. Simply click in an empty portion of the page or pasteboard near the object you want to select and drag out a rectangle that intersects the object. (You don't have to enclose the entire object.) Clicking and dragging is a handy way to select multiple objects.

Selecting overlapping objects

You'll often have multiple objects overlapping in your layout, with some objects completely obscured by others. So how do you select them? By using the Select submenu option in the Object menu. Figure 10-3 shows the Select submenu and its options.

The first four options let you select another object relative to the currently selected object:

✦ **First Object Above** (Option+Shift+⌘+] or Ctrl+Alt+Shift+]) selects the topmost object.

✦ **Next Object Above** (Option+⌘+] or Ctrl+Alt+]) selects the object immediately on top of the current object.

✦ **Next Object Below** (Option+⌘+[or Ctrl+Alt+[) selects the object immediately under the current object.

✦ **Last Object Below** (Option+Shift+⌘+[or Ctrl+Alt+Shift+[) selects the bottommost object.

If no objects are selected, InDesign bases its selection on the creation order.

You can also access these four selection options by Control+clicking or right-clicking an object and choosing the Select menu from the contextual menu.

The Select submenu has four other options:

✦ If an object has content (text or graphic) and you've selected its content, choose Object ➪ Select ➪ Container to choose the frame. This is the same as selecting it with the Selection tool.

✦ If an object has content (text or graphic) and you've selected its frame, choose Object ➪ Select ➪ Content to choose the content within the object. This is basically the same as selecting it with the Direct Selection tool.

✦ If you have selected an object in a group of objects, using the Direct Selection tool, choose Object ⇨ Select ⇨ Previous Object in Group to navigate to the previous object in the group.

✦ Similarly, if you have selected an object in a group of objects, using the Direct Selection tool, choose Object ⇨ Select ⇨ Next Object in Group to navigate to the previous object in the group.

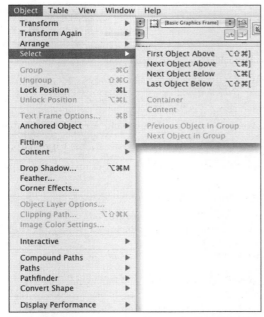

Figure 10-3: The Select submenu in the Object menu

Note   Object creation order determines what is "previous" or "next" in a group.

Control Palette Selection Options

The Control palette also provides icons to select the next or previous object, as well as to select the content or container (frame). These icons appear only if you have selected a group. The icons for selecting the next or previous object appear only if you are using the Direct Selection tool, while the icons for selecting the content or container appear whether you are using the Selection or Direct Selection tool. The figure below shows the icons.

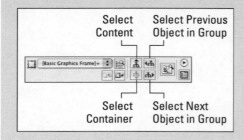

Selecting multiple objects

When an object is selected, you can move or modify it. When several objects are selected, you can move or modify all the objects at once, saving you the time and drudgery of selecting and performing the same modification to several objects one at a time. You have several options for selecting multiple objects. You can:

✦ Choose the Selection tool and hold down the Shift key while clicking in succession on the objects you want to select.

✦ Choose either the Selection tool or the Direct Selection tool, then click in an empty portion of the page and drag a rectangle around any portion of each object you want to select. Make sure you don't click an item or you'll move it when you drag.

  • If you use the Selection tool, the bounding box of each item is selected. You can resize any of the bounding boxes, but the anchor points and direction lines of the shapes within are not selected and cannot be moved.

  • If you use the Direct Selection tool, the anchor points and direction handles of the shapes in the bounding boxes are selected. You can change the shape of any of the objects by dragging an anchor point or direction handle.

✦ If you want to select all items on a page or spread, choose Edit ⇨ Select All or press ⌘+A or Ctrl+A. (If the Type tool is selected and a text frame is active when you choose Select All, you'll highlight all the text, if any, in the frame.) If the Direct Selection tool is selected when you choose Select All, the anchor points and direction handles of the shapes in the selected objects' bounding boxes are selected. If any other tool is selected when you choose Select All, the bounding boxes of the objects are selected.

Tip To select a master item on a document page, you must hold down Shift+⌘ or Ctrl+Shift as you click it. For more information about using master pages, see Chapter 7.

Deselecting objects

A selected object remains selected until you cause it to become deselected, and there are many reasons you might want to deselect an item. For example, you might want to deselect a text frame if you want to see how it looks when displayed without the frame's in and out ports visible. Or you might want to simply "let go" of an object you just finished working on. There are several ways to deselect a selected object. You can:

✦ Click in an empty portion of the page with either of the selection tools selected.

✦ Press and hold down the Shift key with either of the selection tools selected and click the object you want to deselect.

✦ Choose any of the object-creation tools (the Pen tool, the Line tool, or any of the shape- and frame-creation tools), and then click and drag to create a new object.

✦ If you want to deselect all items on a page or spread, choose Edit ➪ Deselect All or press Shift+⌘+A or Ctrl+Shift+A. (If the Type tool is selected and a text frame is active when you choose Deselect All, you'll deselect any text that's highlighted in the frame.)

Moving, Copying, Resizing, and Deleting Objects

One of the great things about using computers to create publications is that it's easy to change your mind. For example, if you don't like where you've placed an object, it's easy to move it or remove it altogether. When you combine this flexibility with InDesign's option to undo as many previous actions as you want, you're free to experiment to your heart's content.

Cross-Reference Chapter 12 covers techniques to batch-duplicate and align objects.

Moving and copying objects

Before you can move or copy an object, you must first select it. Once an object is selected, InDesign provides several methods for moving or copying it.

You can move a selected object by:

✦ **Clicking and dragging it to a different location.** When you drag an object, you can move it anywhere within the current page or spread, into an open library (see Chapter 7 for more information about libraries), or into another document (if another document is open and its window is visible). If you drag an object from one document to another, a copy of the object is placed in the target document and the original object remains unchanged in the source document.

Tip   Press and hold down the Shift key as you drag to restrict the angle of movement to the nearest 45-degree angle based on the direction in which you're moving your mouse.

✦ **Pressing any of the arrow keys.** Each time you press an arrow key, the object is nudged by the distance specified in the Cursor Key field in the Units & Increments pane of the Preferences dialog box (choose File ➪ Preferences on the Mac or Edit ➪ Preferences in Windows, or press ⌘+K or Ctrl+K). The default nudge value is 1 point. If you press and hold the Shift key when using arrow keys, the nudge increment is 10 points.

✦ **Changing the X and Y values in the Control palette or in the Transform pane.** These values determine the distance between an object's point of origin and the ruler origin, where the horizontal and vertical rulers intersect (usually the upper-left corner of a page or spread). (If the Control palette is not displayed, activate it by choosing Window ➪ Control or pressing Option+⌘+6 or Ctrl+Alt+6. If the Transform pane is not displayed, activate it by choosing Window ➪ Object & Layout ➪ Transform or pressing F9.) Figure 10-4 shows the Control palette and Transform pane and their controls. If you want, change the object's point of origin — where the X and Y coordinates refer to.

New Feature   InDesign CS2 has moved the Transform menu option into the new Object & Layout submenu of the Window menu.

Note   The grids of small, white squares in the far left of the Control palette and in the upper-left corner of the Transform pane let you specify the point on the object used to position the object relative to the page origin. If a shape or curved line is selected, all nine squares are selectable for the point of origin; if a straight line is selected, six of the small squares are grayed out and only three squares are selectable for the point of origin. Click a white square to change the point of origin. (The current point of origin is indicated by a black square rather than a white square.)

Each of the preceding methods for moving objects has its merits. The method you choose depends on how you prefer to work.

Copying objects

Copying objects in InDesign is very similar to moving them:

✦ You can create a *clone* (that is, an exact duplicate) of an object when you move it by pressing Option or Alt as you drag with a selection tool. Not only is this a handy way to create a duplicate, it's also a great way to experiment: You can practice on a clone without jeopardizing the original.

✦ If you press and hold Option or Alt as you nudge an object with the arrow keys, a clone of the selected object is created.

✦ To create a clone of an object, press Option+Return or Alt+Enter after changing the X and/or Y value in the Control palette or Transform pane.

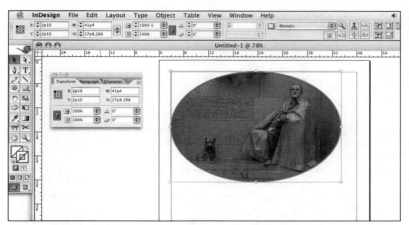

Figure 10-4: Use the Control palette or Transform pane to move objects and perform other modifications. The Control palette is more flexible, providing different options based on what is selected. At left are the position (X and Y) fields.

You also have the standard ability to copy objects by selecting them and choosing Edit ⇨ Copy, or pressing ⌘+C or Ctrl+C), and then selecting Edit ⇨ Paste, or pressing ⌘+V or Ctrl+V, to copy the object to a new location. You'll usually need to then modify the location as described in the previous section.

Plus, there's the faster method of choosing Edit ⇨ Duplicate, or pressing Option+Shift+⌘+D or Ctrl+Alt+Shift+D, on a selected object. This makes a copy immediately, offsetting the duplicate from the original so you can more easily select the duplicate and then position it where you want it.

New Feature InDesign CS2 now will offset a duplicate by whatever settings are in the Step and Repeat dialog box *or* by the distance and direction of the last Option+drag or Alt+drag copying of an object. InDesign CS2 takes the last offset from whichever operation was last performed and uses that as the new default for a Duplicate operation.

Cross-Reference Chapter 12 covers techniques to batch-duplicate objects, such as step-and-repeat.

Resizing objects

After you create a shape, frame, or line, you may find that it's too big or too small for your design. No problem. Resizing objects is as easy as moving them. And as is the case with re-positioning objects, you have multiple options for resizing. You can:

✦ **Click and drag an object's bounding box using the Selection tool.** To change the width and height, drag a corner handle. To change only the width or height, drag a mid-point handle. If you press and hold Shift as you drag, the object's original proportions are retained.

Tip   When you resize a graphics or text frame by clicking and dragging a handle, the graphic or text within isn't affected unless you hold down ⌘ or Ctrl as you drag. Holding down ⌘ or Ctrl and dragging changes the content's scale as well as the size of the frame.

Tip   If you drag immediately after clicking a handle, only a frame's bounding box is displayed as you drag. If you click and then pause until the pointer changes, the contents within are displayed as you drag.

✦ **After selecting the object with either selection tool, modify the horizontal and/or vertical scaling by changing the width and/or height values in the Control palette or Transform pane.** It's best to use the Direct Selection tool, as explained in the sidebar "Tips and Gotchas When Scaling Objects."

Tips and Gotchas When Scaling Objects

You can also resize an object by selecting it and then changing the values in the Scale X Percentage and Scale Y Percentage fields in the Control palette or Transform pane. If you scale a graphics frame with the Selection tool, both the frame and the picture within are scaled. If you scale a picture with the Direct Selection tool, only the picture size changes. If you scale a text frame with either selection tool, both the frame and its text are scaled. (By the way, if you resize an object by scaling it, you can return to its original size by choosing 100% from the Scale X Percentage and Scale Y Percentage pop-up menus.)

When you scale an object with the Control palette or Transform pane, the tool you use affects the display:

✦ If you use the Selection tool, the scale displayed in the Scale X Percentage and Scale Y Percentage fields always reverts to 100%, even though the size has clearly changed. That happens because the Selection tool is actually working on the frame (which is usually 0 points wide, so any resizing has no effect on it), and the contents simply go along for the ride. Because scaling a 0-point frame doesn't change the frame's stroke width, the Control palette and Transform pane show the size still at 100%.

✦ But if you use the Direct Selection tool, which works only on the frame's contents, the Control palette and Transform pane shows the actual resizing percentage applied. That means to set the contents back to 100%, you need to first select the object with the Direct Selection tool.

There is a way to display the actual resizing percentage no matter what tool you select the object with: In the palette menu of the Control palette or Transform pane, be sure to select Scale Strokes. Then the Selection tool reports the scale of the stroke, which is the same as the contents. Of course, scaling the stroke may cause problems if you use strokes on your frames, because the frame strokes will no longer stay the same size as you resize the frames.

Also, note that you can flip the contents of a graphics frame or text frame by dragging a bounding box handle across and beyond the opposite corner or edge. Although this isn't a scaling operation, you accomplish it by dragging a handle as if you are resizing.

Tip

If you want to have the X and Y values change by the same amounts when you enter a new value for either, be sure the Constrain Proportions for Scaling button shows a solid link in the Control palette or Transform pane. If the icon is of a broken link, each dimension is scaled independently.

Note

If the Direct Selection tool is selected when you click an object, the object's anchor points and direction handles appear. Clicking and dragging a point or a handle changes the shape of the object. For more information about changing the shape of objects, see Chapter 26.

Deleting objects

Alas, not all the objects you create survive all the way to the final version of your publication. Some wind up on the cutting room floor, so to speak. You can always move an object to the pasteboard if you're not sure whether you want to get rid of it altogether (objects on the pasteboard won't print). But when it's time to ax an object, oblivion is just a keystroke or two away. If you delete a text or graphics frame, the contents are removed as well as the frame.

Here's how to delete objects: Using either selection tool, click the object you want to delete, and then press Delete or Backspace. You can also delete a selected item by choosing Edit ➪ Clear.

QuarkXPress User

If you're a QuarkXPress user, you may find yourself instinctively pressing ⌘+K or Ctrl+K to delete an object. In InDesign, this shortcut displays the Preferences dialog box. Even if you use Edit ➪ Keyboard Shortcuts to switch to InDesign's built-in QuarkXPress shortcuts, the ⌘+K or Ctrl+K shortcut won't work to delete items. However, you can create a new set of shortcuts (by making a copy of the QuarkXPress set if you want) and assigning ⌘+K or Ctrl+K to the Clear command.

Tip

Choosing Edit ➪ Cut, or ⌘+X or Ctrl+X, also removes a selected object. However, in this case a copy of the object is saved to the Clipboard (and can be pasted elsewhere with Edit ➪ Paste, or ⌘+P or Ctrl+P) until you cut or copy something else or you shut down your computer.

Adding Strokes, Fills, and Other Effects

When you create a new frame, there's not much to it. It has no content, no color (it's transparent — or *none-colored* in InDesign's vocabulary), and no border. If you print a page with an empty frame, you'll get a blank page. Of course, when you place text or a picture into a frame, it springs to life. But whether a frame is empty or filled, InDesign lets you change its appearance in several ways. You can:

✦ Add a border, or *stroke,* around a frame's perimeter and apply a solid color, a tint, or a gradient to the stroke.

✦ Add a solid color, a tint, or a gradient to the frame's background.

✦ Apply any of several corner effects.

✦ Scale, rotate, and/or *shear* (skew) the frame using tools or the Control palette or Transform pane.

Note Choose View ⇨ Show Frame Edges, or press ⌘+H or Ctrl+H, to see frame edges if they aren't already visible.

Adding strokes

In the old days of traditional paste-up, adding a simple, black border around a sidebar or a thin keyline around a picture was a tedious and time-consuming process of laying out adhesive tape and then hoping that your meticulously placed rules remained straight and your perfectly square corners remained tight long enough to make it to the printer. If you were unlucky, your rules wound up on the floor or stuck to somebody's elbows. Nowadays, computers make adding borders to shapes an easy task. InDesign lets you quickly apply strokes to the shapes you create and modify the thickness, color, and style of strokes.

To add a stroke to a frame:

1. **Select either of the selection tools and click the frame to which you want to add a stroke; then click the Stroke button in the Tools palette (see Figure 10-5).**

2. **You now can click a color, tint, or gradient from the Swatches pane, or click one of the three buttons at the bottom of the Tools palette, which (from left to right) let you use the last-selected color, last-selected gradient, or None (this removes the stroke's color, tint, or gradient).**

Cross-Reference For information about adding colors to the Swatches pane, see Chapter 8.

When you add a stroke to a frame, it's assigned a width of 1 point. You can change the width and several other characteristics of a stroke using the controls in the Stroke pane. You can also change the stroke width and type in the Control palette.

Tip You can type percentages in pane fields for size- and scale-oriented items such as stroke widths. For example, to change a 1-point stroke to a hairline (0.25 points), you can type **0.25 pt** or **25%**.

Tip The controls in the Color pane (Window ⇨ Color or F6) let you change the tint of the color applied to a stroke, but I recommend you use the tint control on the Swatches pane (Window ⇨ Swatches or F5) instead, so you don't accidentally use unnamed colors (see Chapter 8 for more information on this issue). The Gradient pane (Windows ⇨ Gradient) gives you the option to apply either a linear or radial gradient. For linear gradients, you can specify the angle using the Angle field.

When using the Stroke pane to modify a stroke:

1. **Select either of the selection tools and click the object whose stroke you want to modify.**

2. **If the Stroke pane is not displayed, show it by choosing Window ⇨ Stroke or pressing F10.**

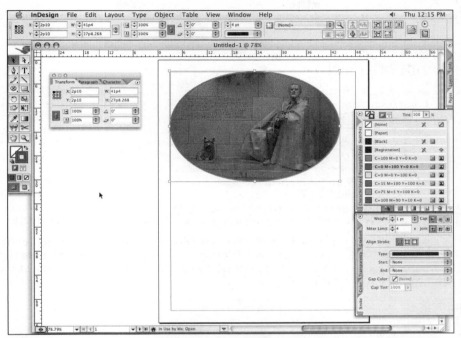

Figure 10-5: The color tools at the bottom of the Tools palette offer the quickest and easiest method of applying the last-used color or gradient to objects, or removing a color, tint, or gradient.

3. **To change the width of stroke, enter a new value in the Weight field.** You can also change the Weight value by choosing a new value from the field's pop-up menu or by clicking the up and down arrows. (Each click increases or decreases the stroke by 1 point.)

4. **Set the Miter Limit.** The default of 4 is fine for almost all frames.

Note

The value in the Stroke pane's Miter Limit field determines when a corner point switches from *mitered* (squared off) to beveled. You'll rarely use this feature; it's useful when you have thick lines joining at sharp angles. In such cases, the lines may extend farther than needed, and the miter value (1 to 500, with 1 being the most conservative setting and 500 the most forgiving) tells InDesign when to change the squared-off corner to a beveled one, which prevents the problem.

5. **Click any of the three Cap button to specify how dashes will look if you create a dashed stroke (covered in Step 9).** Figure 10-6 shows how each of the cap styles affect a dashed stroke.

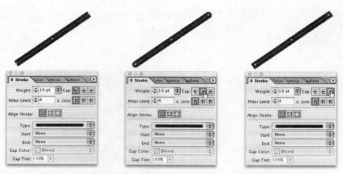

Figure 10-6: The line in this illustration was selected with the Direct Selection tool. Each of the three available endcap styles— butt (left), round (center), and projecting (right)—is shown.

6. **Click any of the three Join buttons to specify how corners are handled.** Figure 10-7 shows how each of the join styles affects a corner.

7. **Choose an Align Stroke option.** The default is the first button, Align Stroke to Center, which has the stroke straddle the frame. You can also choose Align Stroke to Inside, which places the entire thickness inside the frame boundary, or Align Stroke to Outside, which places the entire thickness outside the frame boundary.

8. **You can also choose endpoints for your strokes (this affects lines only, not rectangles, ellipses, and other closed-loop shapes) using the Start and End pop-up menus.** Figure 10-8 shows the options.

Figure 10-7: The Stroke pane lets you apply mitered (left), rounded (center), and beveled (right) corners to shapes.

Figure 10-8: The Start options in the Stroke pane. (The End options are identical.)

9. **To create a dashed line instead of a solid line, choose an option from the Type pop-up menu.** (These are also available from the Control palette.) You'll see 16 types of pre-defined dashes and stripes, as shown in Figure 10-9. The Gap Color and Gap Tint fields at the bottom of the Stroke pane become active as well and let you choose a specific color and tint for the gaps in dashes and stripes.

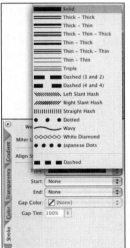

Figure 10-9: The predefined dash and stripe options in the Stroke pane's Type pop-up menu

Tip

To see the full Stroke pane, choose Show Options in the pane's palette menu. By default, the pane shows only the Weight, Cap, Miter Limit, and Join options.

Creating stroke styles

InDesign lets you create custom strokes, known as stroke styles, in any of three types: dashed, dotted, and striped lines. To create custom dashes or stripes, choose the Stroke Styles option in the Stroke pane's palette menu. Figure 10-10 shows the Stroke Styles dialog box from which you can create new strokes, edit or delete existing ones, and import (load) strokes from a stroke styles file which you create by saving a document's strokes as a separate file for import into other documents by using the Save button; stroke style files have the filename extension .inst.

QuarkXPress User The InDesign Stroke Styles feature looks and works very much like the QuarkXPress Dashes & Stripes feature. The major difference is that InDesign has a separate option for dotted lines.

Note that you cannot edit or delete the seven default stripe patterns shown in the figure, nor can you edit or delete the default dash patterns — they're not even available in the dialog box. When you edit or create a stroke pattern, you get the New Stroke Style dialog box, shown in Figure 10-11. In the Name field, type a name for your stroke. In the Type pop-up menu, you can choose to create (or convert a stripe you are editing to) a dashed, dotted, or striped stroke.

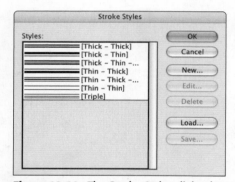

Figure 10-10: The Stroke Styles dialog box

For dashes, you can resize the dash component by clicking and dragging the down-pointing triangle at the end of the dash in the ruler section. You can add dash segments by simply clicking on the ruler and dragging a segment to the desired width. Or you can use the Start and Length fields to manually specify them. The Pattern Length field is where you indicate the length of the segment you're defining; this is then repeated to fill the frame or line the stroke is applied to. In the Corners pop-up menu, you tell InDesign whether to adjust how the dashes and gaps are handled at corners; the default is Adjust Dashes and gaps, a setting you should keep — it will make sure your corners have dash segments that extend along both sides of the corner, which looks neater. (Your other options are Adjust Dashes, Adjust Gaps, and None.) You can also choose a cap style and the stroke weight. The preview section of the pane lets you see your dash as you create or edit it.

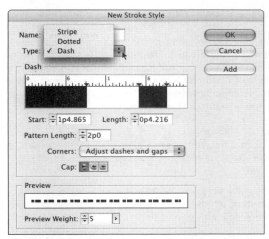

Figure 10-11: The dashes version of the New
Stroke Style dialog box

For dots, you get a dialog box similar to dashes, as Figure 10-12 shows. The Start and Length
fields disappear, replaced with the Center field that determines where any added dots are
placed on the ruler. (The initial dot, shown as a half-circle, starts at 0 and cannot be moved or
deleted.) The Caps field is also gone.

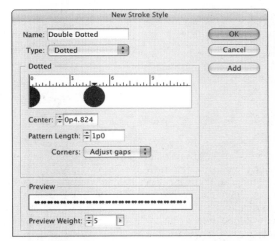

Figure 10-12: The dotted-line version of the New
Stroke Style dialog box

To delete a dash or dot segment, just click and drag it off the ruler to the left.

For stripes, you get the dialog box shown in Figure 10-13. The principle is the same as for dashes: You create segments (in this case vertical, not horizontal) for the stripes by dragging on the ruler. However, the stripes version of the dialog box expresses its values in percentages because the actual thickness of each stripe is determined by the stroke weight — the thicker the stroke, the thicker each stripe is in the overall stroke.

In all three versions of the New Stroke Style dialog box, you click Add to add the stroke to your document, and then you can create a new one. When you're done creating strokes, click OK. (When editing a stroke, you won't have the Add button available.)

Note the use of the preview Weight slider in Figure 10-13. This is available in all three versions of the New Stroke Style dialog box, which lets you increase or decrease the preview size so you can better see thin or small elements in your stroke.

Adding fills

The option to add a stroke to any shape becomes even more powerful when combined with the option to fill any shape with a color or tint. For example, adding a stroke around a text frame is an effective way to draw attention to a sidebar. Adding a fill to a shape is much like adding a stroke, and the options available for specifying color and tint are identical. The only difference is that you click the Fill button in the Tools palette rather than the Stroke button.

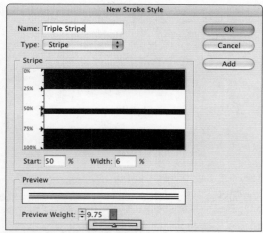

Figure 10-13: The stripe version of the New Stroke Style dialog box

If you really want to turn eyes, you can create reversed text within the frame by adding a fill color and lightening the text. But remember: Reversed text is harder to read, so keep the text size on the large side, and use this effect sparingly. You'll often want to make the reversed-out text boldface to aid in its readability.

Adding special effects to corners

Anytime you're working on an object that has any sharp corners, you have the option to add a little pizzazz to the corners with InDesign's Corner Effects feature (Object ⇨ Corner Effects). Five built-in corner styles, shown in Figure 10-14, are available. Note that if the shape contains only smooth points, any corner effect you apply won't be noticeable.

 Caution   A word of caution about adding fancy corners: These effects are handy for such things as certificates and coupons, but don't get carried away and use them for everyday tasks such as frames for pictures and text unless you have a good reason. Few things kill a design like too much graphic embellishment.

 QuarkXPress User   The corner-style feature in InDesign is similar to the text-box and picture-box variants in QuarkXPress, which offer the same corners except for the Fancy option. In QuarkXPress, you create, or convert, a box to a variant that has one of these corner effects, while in InDesign, you apply the corner effect to a frame.

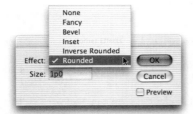

Figure 10-14: The Corner Effects dialog box lets you apply any of these five effects to frame corners.

To add a corner effect:

1. **Select either of the selection tools and click the shape to which you want to add a corner effect. Then choose Object ⇨ Corner Effects to display the Corner Effects dialog box.**

2. **Choose an option from the Effect pop-up menu.**

3. **Type a distance in the Size field.** The Size value determines the length that the effect extends from the corner.

4. **Click OK to close the dialog box and apply your changes.**

Select the Preview Option to view changes as you make them.

If you can't see a corner effect after applying one, make sure that a color is applied to the stroke or try making the object's stroke thicker. Increasing the Size value in the Corner Effects dialog box can also make a corner effect more visible.

Performing Other Transformations

Earlier in this chapter, I explained how to change the size of an item by clicking and dragging bounding box handles with the selection tools and by changing the values in the Control palette's or Transform pane's W(width) and H(height) fields. InDesign also provides some tools and several controls in the Control palette and Transform pane that let you perform more-dramatic effects on objects, such as rotation, mirroring, and *shearing* (which distorts a shape by applying a combination of rotation and slant). Keep in mind that if you press Option or Alt as you drag, you'll work on a copy of the object. To get finer control as you drag, click farther from the active object's point of origin.

How you use these special effects is up to you and is limited only by your imagination. As always, discretion is advised. Just because InDesign has some pretty cool features doesn't mean that you should use them in every publication you create.

If you drag immediately after clicking on an object, the object appears in its original location and the object's bounding box moves as you drag. If you click and then pause until the cross hair changes to an arrowhead, the object is displayed as you drag.

Using the Rotation tool

If you need to rotate an object, and you prefer to accomplish such tasks by clicking and dragging rather than by typing values in fields, you'll want to use the Rotation tool. Here's how:

1. **Select the Rotation tool.** If the Type tool isn't selected, you can also press R to select the Rotation tool.

2. **If it's not already selected, click the object you want to rotate.** If you want, you can click and drag the point of origin from its default location in the upper-left-hand corner of the bounding box to a different location. The object rotates around the point of origin. Figure 10-15 shows a text frame being rotated around the default point of origin (the upper-left corner).

3. **Move the pointer away from the point of origin, then click and drag with a circular motion, clockwise or counterclockwise.** Press and hold Shift as you drag to constrain rotation increments to the nearest 45-degree angle.

4. **Release the mouse button when the object is at the angle you want.**

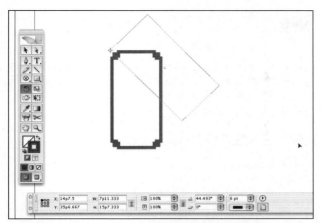

Figure 10-15: When you rotate an object with the Rotation tool, a moving bounding box appears along with the original object if you drag immediately after clicking, as in this example. If you pause before dragging, the moving object and its contents appear as you drag.

Using the Scale tool

The easiest way to scale an object is to click and drag a bounding box handle, as described earlier in this chapter.

To scale an object manually:

1. **Select the Scale tool.** If the Type tool isn't selected, you can also press S to select the Scale tool.

2. **If it's not already selected, click the object you want to scale.** If you want, you can click and drag the point of origin from its default location in the upper-left-hand corner of the bounding box to a different location. When the object grows or shrinks, the point of origin doesn't move.

3. **Move the pointer away from the point of origin, then click and drag.** Press and hold Shift and drag horizontally to apply only horizontal scale, vertically to apply only vertical scale, and diagonally to apply horizontal and vertical and keep the object's original proportions.

4. **Release the mouse button when the object is the size you want.** Figure 10-16 shows an object that's being scaled with the scale tool.

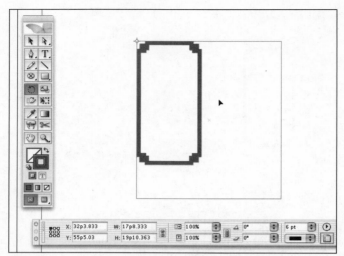

Figure 10-16: Clicking and dragging with the Scale tool enlarges or reduces a frame. In this example, the Scale tool is being used to enlarge a frame.

Caution   If you use the Scale tool on a text frame, the text within is scaled as well. However, if you use the Scale tool on a graphics frame, the picture is not scaled. You can prevent InDesign from scaling text in a scaled frame by deselecting the Adjust Text Attributes When Scaling option in the Type pane of the Preferences dialog box (choose InDesign ⇨ Preferences on the Mac or Edit ⇨ Preferences in Windows, or press ⌘+K or Ctrl+K).

Using the Shear tool

When you shear an object with the Shear tool, you actually perform two transformations at once: rotation and slant. Because the contents within text frames and graphics frames are distorted along with the frames when you shear an object, you'll probably use this tool only for special effects.

QuarkXPress User   The InDesign Shear tool is not the same as the QuarkXPress Skew tool—Shear both slants and rotates an object, while Skew just slants it. To simulate the QuarkXPress Skew tool, move the mouse horizontally when using the InDesign Shear tool—this ensures that there is no rotation. You can also use the Shear fields in the Control palette or Transform pane to only slant an object.

To shear an object manually:

1. **Select the Shear tool.** If the Type tool isn't selected, you can also press O to select the Shear tool.

2. **If not already selected, click the object you want to shear.** If you want, you can drag the point of origin from its default location in the upper-left-hand corner of the bounding box to a different location. When you shear an object, the point of origin doesn't move.

3. **Move the pointer away from the point of origin, then click and drag.** Hold the Shift key and drag to constrain rotation increments to multiples of 45 degrees. Figure 10-17 shows a frame being sheared.

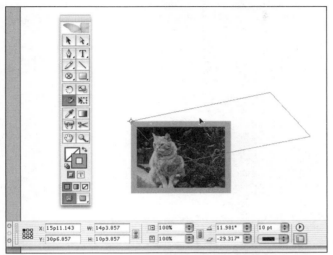

Figure 10-17: In this example, a frame is being sheared using the Shear tool.

Modifying objects using the Transform pane

If you prefer to modify objects by specifying values in fields rather than by clicking and dragging, you can use the Transform pane (Window ⇨ Object & Layout ⇨ Transform or F9). Some designers prefer the click-and-drag approach when modifying objects because it more closely mimics traditional paste-up techniques: You put objects onto a page, then you move them around until you're satisfied. Others prefer the precision that typing transformation values into fields offers. Chances are, you'll do a little of both.

For example, if you want to rotate a block of text exactly 45 degrees, typing a rotation value in the Transform pane is probably the quickest method. If you want to rotate a block of text to match the angle of a shape in an imported picture, you might decide that clicking and dragging is the best approach.

In the Transform pane, highlight the appropriate field in the Transform pane, type a new value, and then press Return or Enter. When an object is selected, you can also highlight fields in the pane by double-clicking on the corresponding transformation tools: Double-click the Rotation tool to highlight the Rotation field, the Scale tool to highlight the Horizontal scale field, or the Shear tool to highlight the Shear X angle field.

Tip　Press Shift+Return or Shift+Enter to apply changes without leaving the pane. Press Option+Return or Alt+Enter to apply a transformation value to a copy of the selected item.

The Transform pane contains separate fields for horizontal scale (Scale X Percentage) and vertical scale (Scale Y Percentage). You can distort an object by applying different scale values. Applying equal horizontal and vertical scale values maintains an object's original proportions. Use the Constrain Proportions for Scaling button (the chain icon) to have changes in one scale field be automatically applied to the other: If the chain is solid, the proportions will be constrained; if the chain is broken, they will change independently of each other.

Like almost all InDesign panes, the Transform pane includes a palette menu, shown in Figure 10-18, that contains additional commands for modifying objects. Before you try to apply any of the effects in the palette menu, make sure the object you want to change is selected.

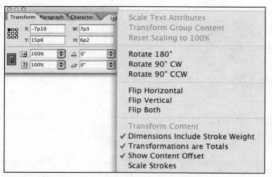

Figure 10-18: The Transform pane's palette menu provides several commands for modifying objects.

If you select a text or graphics frame with the Selection tool and then apply a transformation, both the contents and the frame are affected. If you select a frame with the Direct Selection tool and then apply a transformation, only the frame is affected.

Here's list of the commands and a brief description of what each one does:

✦ **Scale Text Attributes.** Select this option before changing a text frame's horizontal and/or vertical scale if you don't want to change the scale of the text within.

✦ **Transform Group Content.** If you've selected multiple objects, this option becomes available, and it works like Transform Content (described later in this list) does.

✦ **Reset Scaling to 100%.** If selected, this option resets the scaling to 100% anytime the object is resized.

✦ **Rotate 180°, Rotate 90° CW, and Rotate 90° CCW.** These commands provide an alternative to the Rotation field. You can rotate an object 180 degrees, 90 degrees clockwise, or 90 degrees counterclockwise.

✦ **Flip Horizontal, Flip Vertical, and Flip Both.** These commands let you create a mirror version of the original.

✦ **Transform Content.** If this option is selected, the frame's content (text or picture, plus fills and gradients) is transformed along with the frame. For example, if you rotate a frame, the text is rotated as well. If this option is not selected, the text would not be rotated along with the frame.

✦ **Dimensions Include Stroke Weight.** If this option is selected, the width of any stroke is added to the frame dimensions. This helps precise placement because frames extend beyond the frame, so adding a 6-point frame to a rectangle in effect increases its width and height by 12 points (6 points on each side). If this menu option is selected, the dimensions shown in the Control palette and Transform pane reflect the strokes' widths.

✦ **Transformations Are Totals.** When this option is selected, the angle of rotation of a nested object is calculated relative to the horizontal/vertical orientation of the page. If Transformations Are Totals is selected, the angle of a nested object is calculated relative to the angle of the frame that contains it. For example, if Transformations Are Totals is selected and you paste an unrotated item into a frame that's been rotated 30 degrees, the angle of rotation for the nested item is 0 degrees; if you then deselect Transformations Are Totals, the nested object's angle of rotation is –30 degrees.

✦ **Show Content Offset.** If selected, this option shows the position of the origin content (a picture) relative to the frame containing it in the X and Y fields in the Transform pane. If you move a picture within the frame, the offset will be positive as you move it to the right and/or down, and negative as you move it to the left and/or up. If deselected, the Transform pane instead shows the absolute position on the page of the current reference point.

✦ **Scale Strokes.** If selected, this option makes InDesign scale the frame's stroke (border) as the frame is resized. For example, a frame with a 1-point border will have its border scaled to 0.5 points if the frame is scaled to 50 percent. If this option is not selected, the stroke width is not affected when you scale the frame.

Modifying objects using the Control palette

I prefer using the Control palette rather the Transform pane because the Control palette gives you more control over selected objects (refer to Figure 10-4).

For the operations such as scaling, shearing, rotating, and flipping, the Control palette works like the Transform pane described in the previous section. Its palette menu is also the same, with the following exception: There are three options that control its placement — Dock at Top, Dock at Bottom, and the default Float.

But, as Figure 10-19 shows, the Control palette provides access to many options not available in the Transform pane for working with frames:

✦ You can set the frame stroke width and type, using the Stroke Styles menu option in the palette menu or the Stroke Type and Stroke Width pull-down menus.

✦ You can have content resized to fit the frame or have the frame resized to fit the content, as well as center the content in the frame, using the various fitting buttons.

✦ You can access the Select submenu options (covered earlier in this chapter), using the selection buttons.

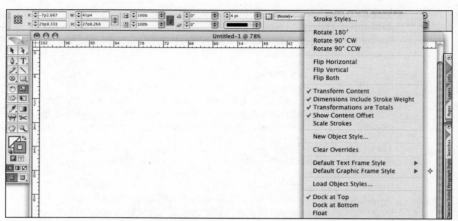

Figure 10-19: The Control pane's palette menu provides many commands for modifying objects.

✦ You can align objects when several are selected, using the alignment buttons.

✦ You can apply object styles to selected frames, using a pop-up menu. You can also remove an object's object style using the Break Link to Object Style button, as well as clear attributes not defined in an object style using the Clear Attributes Not Defined by Style menu option in the Object Styles pane's palette menue.

✦ For text frames, you can set the number of columns in the frame and control the vertical justification of paragraphs.

✦ For text in a frame or on a path, you can set many character and paragraph attributes, such as font, size, leading, kerning, tracking, style (boldface, italics, strikethrough, and so on), vertical and horizontal scaling, skew, baseline shift, character style, language, ligatures, underline and strikethrough options, paragraph alignment (horizontal justification), indents, drop caps, baseline grid alignment, hyphenation, paragraph rules, keep options, and paragraph styles.

Repeating transformations

Whatever transformations you use, you can apply them repeatedly. InDesign remembers the effects you apply to frames with the Control palette, Transform pane, and Transform tool. Choose Object ➪ Transform Again ➪ Transform Again (or press Option+⌘+3 or Ctrl+Alt+3) to repeat the last transformation on the selected object (it can be a different object than you last applied a transformation to). Or choose Object ➪ Transform Again ➪ Transform Sequence Again (or press Option+⌘+4 or Ctrl+Alt+4) to apply all recent transformations to a select object. That sequence of transactions stays in memory until you perform a new transformation, which then starts a new sequence, so you can apply the same transformation to multiple objects.

New Feature   InDesign CS2 now keeps a history of your transformations, so you can apply them again.

Not only can you apply transformations repeatedly, you can also save transformations, strokes, and other object attributes as styles, so they can be applied at any time. Chapter 11 covers this new feature in detail.

Modifying Lines

When you create a line with the Line tool, there's not much to it. It's plain, black, and 1 point wide. But, like a frame, you can modify the color, tint, and thickness of a line, and you can optionally apply a custom dashed style and endpoints. You can also apply and change object styles applied to a line. The process for modifying lines is the same as for modifying frames and for creating strokes in the first place, both of which are described earlier in this chapter.

Preventing Objects from Printing

InDesign lets you prevent an object from printing. To do so, select the object with the Selection or Direct Selection tool, open the Attributes pane (Window ⇨ Attributes), and then select the Nonprinting option. Figure 10-20 shows the pane. (The other settings in this pane duplicate stroke settings covered earlier in this chapter.)

You would use this feature for comments and other elements that should not print but that the designer needs to have visible on-screen. Another approach to nonprinting objects is to place them all on a layer and make the entire layer nonprinting.

Figure 10-20: The Attributes pane

 Chapter 6 covers layers.

Applying Lighting Effects

InDesign offers sophisticated built-in drop shadow and feathering that let you create dimensional effects based on simulated lighting. It also lets you apply transparency to objects, so you can make them fade away or overlap so that the underlying object is somewhat visible.

 QuarkXPress does not offer lighting-effects features, although there are third-party plug-ins to add these capabilities.

Using transparency

One of InDesign's most sophisticated tools is its set of transparency options that lets you make items partially transparent. You apply transparency with the Transparency pane (Window ➪ Transparency or Shift+F10). Figure 10-21 shows the pane as well as a brochure that uses transparency to create a vellum effect on a stripe that contains text that overprints a background photo. The artist, Shawn Busse, chose a transparency setting of 74 percent for the white frame's Opacity, as well as the Screen setting for transparency type.

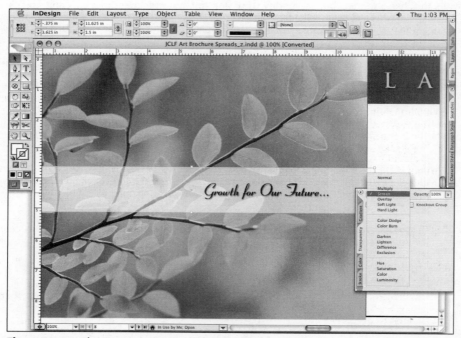

Figure 10-21: The Transparency pane and its palette menu, as well as an example of a transparent object overprinting the photograph

> **Note**
>
> You cannot apply transparency to text selections or to layers, nor can you apply different transparency settings to an object's fill and stroke. Also, if you remove an object from a group that had transparency applied (via cut and paste or copy and paste), that pasted object will not have the group's transparency settings applied to it.

There are 16 different transparency types — called *blending modes* — as shown in Figure 10-21. The differences among them can be subtle or extreme, depending on a variety of issues. (Photoshop and Illustrator users will recognize these options from those programs.) You should experiment with them to see what effect works best in each case. The 16 modes are:

✦ **Normal.** Colors the selection with the blend color, without interaction with the base color. This is the default mode.

✦ **Multiply.** Multiplies the base color by the blend color. The resulting color is always a darker color. Multiplying any color with black produces black. Multiplying any color with white leaves the color unchanged. The effect is similar to drawing on a page with multiple Magic markers.

✦ **Screen.** Multiplies the inverse of the blend and base colors. The resulting color is always a lighter color. Screening with black leaves the color unchanged. Screening with white produces white. The effect is similar to projecting multiple slide images on top of each other.

✦ **Overlay.** Multiplies or screens the colors, depending on the base color. Patterns or colors overlay the existing artwork, preserving the highlights and shadows of the base color while mixing in the blend color to reflect the lightness or darkness of the original color.

✦ **Soft Light.** Darkens or lightens the colors, depending on the blend color. The effect is similar to shining a diffused spotlight on the artwork. If the blend color (light source) is lighter than 50 percent gray, the artwork is lightened, as if it were dodged. If the blend color is darker than 50 percent gray, the artwork is darkened, as if it were burned in. Painting with pure black or white produces a distinctly darker or lighter area but does not result in pure black or white.

✦ **Hard Light.** Multiplies or screens the colors, depending on the blend color. The effect is similar to shining a harsh spotlight on the artwork. If the blend color (light source) is lighter than 50 percent gray, the artwork is lightened, as if it were screened. This is useful for adding highlights to artwork. If the blend color is darker than 50 percent gray, the artwork is darkened, as if it were multiplied. This is useful for adding shadows to artwork. Painting with pure black or white results in pure black or white.

✦ **Color Dodge.** Brightens the base color to reflect the blend color. Blending with black produces no change.

✦ **Color Burn.** Darkens the base color to reflect the blend color. Blending with white produces no change.

✦ **Darken.** Selects the base or blend color — whichever is darker — as the resulting color. Areas lighter than the blend color are replaced, and areas darker than the blend color do not change.

✦ **Lighten.** Selects the base or blend color — whichever is lighter — as the resulting color. Areas darker than the blend color are replaced, and areas lighter than the blend color do not change.

✦ **Difference.** Subtracts either the blend color from the base color or the base color from the blend color, depending on which has the greater brightness value. Blending with white inverts the base color values; blending with black produces no change.

✦ **Exclusion.** Creates an effect similar to, but lower in contrast than, the Difference mode. Blending with white inverts the base color components. Blending with black produces no change.

✦ **Hue.** Creates a color with the luminance and saturation of the base color and the hue of the blend color.

✦ **Saturation.** Creates a color with the luminance and hue of the base color and the saturation of the blend color. Using this mode in an area with no saturation (a gray) produces no change.

✦ **Color.** Creates a color with the luminance of the base color and the hue and saturation of the blend color. This preserves the gray levels in the artwork, and is useful for coloring monochrome artwork and for tinting color artwork.

✦ **Luminosity.** Creates a color with the hue and saturation of the base color and the luminance of the blend color. This mode produces the inverse of the Color mode.

Note The Difference, Exclusion, Hue, Saturation, Color, and Luminosity modes do not blend spot colors, just process colors.

Note InDesign's blending calculations differ based on whether the document is to be printed (usually in CMYK) or seen on-screen (as RGB). Be sure to choose the right blending space based on the intended output. To do so, choose Edit ➪ Transparency Blend Space ➪ Document CMYK or Edit ➪ Transparency Blend Space ➪ Document RGB, as appropriate.

Transparency Tips

The use of transparency can result in very cool effects in your layout, but it can also cause major problems when you print because transparency requires very complex calculations for the imagesetter to handle, calculations that can be tripped up by how source files and other settings are applied. To minimize such issues, keep these items in mind, based on advice from publishing consultant Training Resources:

✦ Don't mix RGB and CMYK objects in the same layout if you use transparency; convert your source images to the same color model in their originating programs, such as Illustrator and Photoshop. Convert spot colors to CMYK in those programs as well, except, of course, for those that print on their own plates.

✦ Keep transparent elements on their own layers, and if possible keep your text on its own layer above all the others. This helps the imagesetter's raster-image processors (RIPs) digest the print job in manageable chunks.

✦ If your source files have transparency, don't flatten them or save them in formats that flatten them. That means you should keep files with transparency in these formats: PDF 1.4 or later, Illustrator 10 or later, and Photoshop 6 and later. Note that Illustrator EPS files keep their transparent areas separate when worked on in Illustrator but not when used by separate programs, so don't use the Illustrator EPS format for transparent objects if you can avoid it.

✦ The use of Color, Saturation, Luminosity, and Difference blending modes can cause output problems when used with spot colors or gradients.

✦ Use the Overprint Preview (View ➪ Overprint Preview, or Option+Shift+⌘+Y or Ctrl+Alt+Shift+Y), Separations (Window ➪ Output ➪ Separations), and Transparency Flattener (Window ➪ Output ➪ Flattener) preview features in InDesign to check how transparent effects will likely print.

Chapter 30 covers these issues in more detail from an output perspective.

You have two other options in the Transparency pane:

✦ **Isolate Blending.** This option restricts the blending modes to the objects in a group, instead of also applying them to objects beneath the group. This can prevent unintended changes to those underlying objects.

✦ **Knockout Group.** This option obscures any objects below the selected group. But those objects beneath the knocked-out group are still affected by any blend mode settings applied to the group, unless the Isolate Blending option is also selected.

Drop shadows

The Drop Shadow dialog box, shown in Figure 10-22, is accessed by choosing Object ⇨ Drop Shadow or pressing Option+⌘+M or Ctrl+Alt+M. To apply a drop shadow to an object, you select it with a selection tool — you cannot apply the shadow to just highlighted characters. In the dialog box, you set the following options:

✦ Select the Drop Shadow option to turn on the drop shadow function.

✦ Select a lighting type (technically, a blend mode) by choosing one of the 16 options in the Mode pop-up menu. These are the same blending modes used in transparencies and covered earlier in this section.

✦ Specify the opacity by typing a value in the Opacity field — 0% is invisible, while 100% is completely solid.

✦ Specify the shadow's position relative to the object using the X Offset and Y Offset fields. A positive X Offset moves the shadow to the right, while a positive Y Offset moves the shadow down. Negative values go in the other direction.

✦ Specify the shadow's size by typing a value in the Blur field — this blurs a copy of the text used in the drop shadow to make it look like it was created by shining light on solid letters.

✦ Choose a color source — Swatches, RGB, CMYK, and LAB — from the Color pop-up menu, and then select a color from the sliders or swatches below. You'll get sliders for RGB, CMYK, and LAB with which to mix a color if you selected RGB, CMYK, or LAB in the Color pop-up menu, and a set of previously defined color swatches if you selected Swatches in the Color pop-up menu.

✦ To see the effects to your selected object as you experiment with various settings, select the Preview option.

Tip   Although traditionally associated with text, you can apply drop shadows to any objects, such as frames and shapes.

Figure 10-22: The Drop Shadow dialog box and an example drop shadow

Feathering

A similar option to drop shadows is feathering, which essentially softens the edges of objects. Like drop shadows, feathering can be applied only to objects, not individual text, paths, or strokes. To feather an object, first select it and then choose Object ➪ Feather. You'll get the dialog box shown in Figure 10-23.

To apply feathering, select the Feather option. You then type a value for the degree of feathering— smaller numbers have the least effect; larger numbers have the most effect. The featuring area starts at the outside edge of the object, so a larger number "eats into" the object, making it a wispier version of itself. The Corners pop-up menu gives you three options: Sharp, Rounded, and Diffused. The Sharp option retains the original corner shape as much as possible. The Rounded option rounds the corners of the object; it can distort the shape dramatically at larger Feather Width settings. The Diffused option creates a soft, almost smoky effect by making the object borders and corners more translucent.

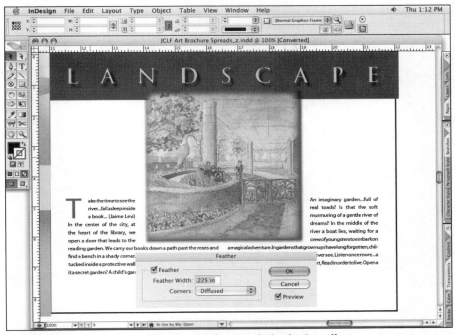

Figure 10-23: The Feather dialog box and a sample feathering effect

Summary

After you create an object, you can move, modify, or delete it. If the object is a frame, you also have the option of modifying the text or picture within. Before you can modify an object, you must select it. When an object is selected, commands and controls for changing its position and appearance become available. To select an object, you must first choose either the Selection tool or the Direct Selection tool.

If a frame is selected, you can add a stroke around its border, add a color to its background, or change its shape using the Rotate, Scale, or Shear tools or the corresponding fields in the Control palette or Transform pane. If a line is selected, you can change its width, color, and style. A new feature in InDesign lets you apply a sequence of transformations over and over again to one or more objects.

Finally, there are several special effects you can apply to objects, including transparency, drop shadows, and feathering.

✦　　✦　　✦

Orchestrating Objects

Text frames, graphics frames, shapes, and lines are the building blocks with which you construct InDesign pages. Becoming familiar with creating and modifying individual objects, which is the focus of Chapters 9 and 10, is a key step in learning how to create publications with InDesign. The next step is to learn how to use several features that let you manipulate multiple objects at once and quickly adjust the relationships among the various objects that make up a page. A good InDesign user can handle individual objects one at a time with ease; a virtuoso user can simultaneously juggle several objects with equal ease.

Think of it this way: As an InDesign user, you're much like an architect. You begin with a blueprint — perhaps a rough, felt-tip pen sketch; maybe just a picture in your mind's eye — open a new document, and start construction. The settings you establish in the New Document dialog box (File ➪ New ➪ Document, or ⌘+N or Ctrl+N) — the page size, margin placement, column arrangement, and number of pages — serve as the foundation as you begin adding objects to your pages. You must then construct your building — or rather, your publication — using four basic components: text frames, graphics frames, shapes, and lines. Each of those components can be tweaked and twisted in a nearly endless variety of ways while retaining basic properties. After all, a sheared (skewed) and mirrored text frame with a purple dashed stroke, a gradient background, and magenta text outlined in cyan is still just a text frame.

As a publication evolves, plans invariably change: An advertiser pulls out and a magazine article needs to be stretched an extra half-page by enlarging an InDesign-created illustration. A client loves his company's newsletter but wants the front-page picture cropped differently. A new product is added to a catalog and half the pages reflow. If you build your documents soundly from the ground up and use the features covered in this chapter, you'll be prepared to handle even the most challenging page building — and rebuilding — tasks.

Stacking Objects

Each time you begin work on a new page, you start with a clean slate (unless the page is based on a master page, in which case the master objects act as the page's background; see Chapter 7 for more on master pages). Every time you add an object to a page — either by using any of InDesign's object-creation tools or with the Place command (File ➪ Place, or ⌘+D or Ctrl+D) — the new object occupies a unique place in the page's object hierarchy, or *stacking order*.

The first object you place on a page is automatically positioned at the bottom of the stacking order; the next object is positioned one level higher than the first object (that is, on top of and in front of the backmost object); the next object is stacked one level higher; and so on for every object you add to the page. (It's not uncommon for a page to have several dozen or even several hundred objects.)

Tip

When building pages, always try to keep the number of objects to a minimum. For example, instead of putting a headline in one text frame and a subhead in a separate text frame directly below the one that contains the headline, use a single text frame. The leaner your pages, the leaner your documents. Lean documents save and print more quickly and are less problematic to modify than bloated documents.

Although each object occupies its own level, if the objects on a page don't overlap, then the stacking order is not an issue. But some of the most interesting graphic effects you can achieve with InDesign involve arranging several overlapping objects, so it's important to be aware of the three-dimensional nature of a page's stacking order.

Because objects are added in back-to-front order, it makes sense to build your pages from back to front. For example, if you want to use a lightly tinted version of a scanned image as the background for a page, you would first place the image on the page, and then add other objects on top of or in front of the graphics frame.

In an ideal world, the first object you place on a page would remain forever the backmost, the last object would be the frontmost, and every object in between — created in perfect order from back to front — would relate correctly with every other object. In this perfect world, you would never have to worry about moving objects backward or forward.

But the world is not perfect, and you may change your mind about what you want to achieve in your layout after you've already placed objects in it. To change an object's position in a page's stacking order, use the Arrange command (Object ➪ Arrange), which offers four choices:

✦ Bring to Front (Shift+⌘+] or Ctrl+Shift+])

✦ Bring Forward (⌘+] or Ctrl+])

✦ Send to Back (Shift+⌘+[or Ctrl+Shift+[)

✦ Send Backward (⌘+[or Ctrl+[)

For example, you might want to see how a piece of text looks in front of an illustration. But if you create the text frame before you create or place the illustration, you'll have to move the text frame forward (or the illustration backward) in the stacking order.

Cross-Reference

In addition to letting you change the stacking order of objects on a page, InDesign also lets you create document-wide layers. Each layer contains a separate collection of stacked objects. For more information about using layers, see Chapter 6.

To change the stacking order of objects:

1. **Use any of the object-creation tools to create four overlapping shapes, as shown in Figure 11-1.** The numbers in parentheses indicate the order in which you should create the shapes.

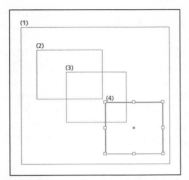

Figure 11-1: The first shape you create is the backmost, the second is one level above, and so on. In this example, the three smaller boxes partially overlap each other and they are all in front of the largest box.

2. **If it's not already displayed, open the Swatches pane by choosing Window ➪ Swatches or pressing F6.** You'll use this pane to change the shade of each object so you can easily tell them apart.

3. **Click the Selection tool, click the last object you created, and then use the color tools in the Tools palette or the Swatches pane to fill the object with a color.**

4. **Use the Swatches pane to fill each of the remaining boxes with a successively lighter tint of the color, as shown in Figure 11-2.** In the example, the remaining shapes are tinted at 25 percent, 50 percent, and 75 percent, respectively.

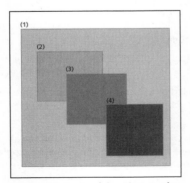

Figure 11-2: Applying tints to the shapes lets you see the stacking order of the four rectangles. Every InDesign object occupies one level in the stacking order.

Cross-Reference   See Chapter 10 for more information about applying strokes and fills to objects.

5. **Click the frontmost shape (the last one you created), and then choose Object ⇨ Arrange ⇨ Send Backward or press ⌘+[or Ctrl+[.** Notice that the Bring to Front and Bring Forward commands are not available. That's because you can't move the front-most object any farther forward in the stacking order.

6. **Click the backmost shape (the first one you created), and then choose Object ⇨ Arrange ⇨ Bring Forward or press ⌘+] or Ctrl+].**

   When you bring the object forward, one of the objects becomes obscured.

7. **Choose Object ⇨ Arrange ⇨ Bring to Front or press Shift+⌘+] or Ctrl+Shift+].** The smaller shapes are now obscured by the largest one.

8. **Choose Object ⇨ Arrange ⇨ Send to Back or press Shift+⌘+[or Ctrl+Shift+[.** The hidden objects are once again visible.

Tip   To select an object that's hidden behind one or more other objects, press and hold ⌘ or Ctrl, and then click anywhere within the area of the hidden object. The first click selects the top-most object; each successive click selects the next lowest object in the stacking order. When the bottom object is selected, the next click selects the top object. If you don't know where a hidden object is, you can simply click the object or objects in front of it, then send the object(s) to the back.

Combining Objects into a Group

InDesign lets you combine several objects into a group. A group of objects behaves like a single object, which means that you can cut, copy, move, or modify all the objects in a group in a single operation. Groups have many uses. For example, you might create a group to:

✦ Combine several objects that make up an illustration so that you can move, modify, copy, or scale all objects in a single operation.

✦ Keep a graphics frame and its accompanying caption (text) frame together so that if you change your mind about their placement, you can reposition both objects at once.

✦ Combine several vertical lines that are used to separate the columns of a table so that you can quickly change the stroke, color, length, and position of all lines.

Tip   If you want to manipulate a group, choose the Selection tool, and then click any object in the group. The group's bounding box appears. Any transformation you perform is applied to all objects in the group. If you want to manipulate a specific object in a group, choose the Direct Selection tool.

To create a group:

1. **Switch to the Selection or Direct Selection tool.**

2. **Select all the objects you want to include in your group.**

3. **Choose Object ➪ Group or press ⌘+G or Ctrl+G.**

Cross-Reference

See Chapter 10 for more information about selecting multiple objects.

That's all there is to it. When you create a group from objects that do not occupy successive levels in the stacking order, the objects are shuffled as necessary so that the grouped objects are stacked on adjacent layers directly below the topmost object. If you create a group from objects on different layers, all objects are moved to the top layer and stacked in succession beneath the topmost object.

Cross-Reference

See Chapter 6 for more about layers.

Note

You cannot create a group if some of the selected objects are locked and some are not locked. All selected objects must be locked or unlocked before you can group them. (Locking and unlocking objects is covered later in this chapter.)

Groups within groups

One nifty thing about groups is that you can include a group within a group. For example, all the objects in Figure 11-3 — five stars and two circles (a gray circle and a white circle form the moon) — have been grouped, making it easy to manipulate the whole illustration. But that's not all. The stars within the group are also a group. So are the two circles that make up the crescent moon. That is, first the stars were grouped together, then the two circles were grouped together, and finally then the group of stars was grouped with the circles that form the moon to create a larger group. Grouping the stars makes it easy to change all of them at once, as shown in Figure 11-4. And grouping the two circles that make up the crescent moon makes it easy to move the moon.

Note

A group can contain as many levels of subgroups, or *nested* groups, as you want, but it's best to keep things as simple as you can. The more levels of nested groups you have within a group, the more work it is to ungroup the objects.

Figure 11-3: The bounding box indicates that all the objects within have been grouped. What you can't tell from this illustration is that the five stars are a group within the larger group, which lets you move or modify all of them in a single operation, as shown in Figure 11-4.

Figure 11-4: The group selection tool (explained in the next section) lets you select a nested group. In this example, the nested group of stars was selected, and then a radial gradient was applied to all of them.

Selecting objects within groups

The main reason you create groups in the first place is so that you can delete, copy, move, or modify all the objects at once. But sometimes, you'll want to modify an object within a group. No problem. You don't have to ungroup objects to modify an individual object. InDesign offers several options for selecting objects — and nested groups — within groups. You can:

✦ Select an individual object by clicking it with the Direct Selection tool.

✦ Select the bounding box of an individual object by clicking it with the Direct Selection tool, then switching to the Selection tool.

✦ Select multiple objects within a group by Shift+clicking each object with the Direct Selection tool.

✦ Select the bounding box of multiple objects within a group by Shift+clicking each object with the Direct Selection tool, then switching to the Selection tool.

✦ Select a nested group by clicking any object within the nested group with the Direct Selection tool, then pressing and holding Option or Alt and clicking the object again. Pressing and holding Option or Alt in this situation temporarily accesses the Group Selection tool, indicated by a small plus sign (+) below and to the right of the arrow pointer.

Ungrouping

After creating a group, you may eventually decide that you want to return the objects to their original, ungrouped state. To do so, simply click any object in the group with the Selection tool, then choose Object ➪ Ungroup or press Shift+⌘+G or Ctrl+Shift+G. If you ungroup a group that contains a group, the contained group is not affected. To ungroup this subgroup, you must select it, and then choose Ungroup again.

Locking Objects

If you're certain that you want a particular object to remain where it is, you can use Object ➪ Lock Position, or ⌘+L or Ctrl+L, to prevent the object from being moved. Generally, you'll want to lock repeating elements such as headers, footers, folios, and page numbers so that they're not accidentally moved. (Such repeating elements are usually placed on a master page; you can lock objects on master pages, too.) A locked object can't be moved whether you click and drag it with the mouse or change the values in the X and Y fields in the Control palette or Transform pane. Not only can you *not* move a locked object, you can't delete one, either. However, you can change other attributes of a locked object, including its stroke and fill.

To unlock an object, use Object ⇨ Unlock Position, or Option+⌘+L or Ctrl+Alt+L.

Cross-Reference

You can also lock entire layers, as described in Chapter 6.

QuarkXPress User

QuarkXPress's lock feature is meant to prevent accidental repositioning or resizing by the mouse; it lets you modify the locked object through dialog boxes and the Measurements palette. By contrast, locking in InDesign is meant to truly lock the object from any changes, not just accidental ones.

Nesting Objects within Frames

Not only does InDesign let you combine several objects into a group, you can also place an object within the boundaries of a frame. Just as a group that's embedded within a larger group is said to be a *nested* group, an object that's been placed within another frame is said to be a *nested* object. When you place an object within a frame, the containing frame acts as the cropping shape for the object within.

One of the more common uses of nested frames is for cropping imported graphics. When you place a graphic onto a page, the graphic is automatically placed within a frame. (You can also place a graphic within an existing frame.) You can reveal and hide different areas of the graphic by resizing or reshaping the container frame. Figure 11-5 shows an imported picture that's been placed within a circular frame.

Figure 11-5: In this example, the rectangle displayed with handles indicates the border of a picture that's been placed into a round frame. Clicking the picture with the Direct Selection tool selects the picture rather than the round frame. To select the frame's bounding box instead of the picture, click the picture with the Direct Selection tool.

For more information about importing and modifying pictures, see Part V.

Nesting Frames within Other Frames

As you can with groups, you can place a frame within a frame within a frame and so on, to create as many nested levels as you want. The same caveat applies: Keep things as simple as possible to achieve the desired effect. To nest a frame within a frame:

1. **Use either the Selection tool or the Direct Selection tool to select the frame you want to nest within another frame.**

2. **Choose Edit ➪ Copy or press ⌘+C or Ctrl+C.**

3. **Select the frame into which you want to place the copied object, and then choose Edit ➪ Paste Into or press Option+⌘+V or Ctrl+Alt+V.** Figure 11-6 shows a before/after example of a squiggly line that's been pasted into a circular frame that serves as the masking shape for the line.

Tip   Selecting nested objects can be tricky. In general, the same selection techniques that work with groups also work with nested frames. If you need to modify text within a nested — or grouped — text frame, simply click within the frame with the Type tool.

QuarkXPress User   InDesign's nested frames are similar to QuarkXPress's constrained boxes, though the QuarkXPress constrained boxes don't let you mask objects as InDesign's nested frames do — the entire nested box must fit within the enclosing box in QuarkXPress.

Figure 11-6: The squiggly line (left) was created with the Pen tool. It was then copied and pasted into (Edit ➪ Paste Into) a circular frame (right). Selecting the line with the Direct Selection tool shows the visible portion of the line within the oval cropping frame, as well as the parts of the line that are cropped.

Creating Inline Frames

In most cases, you'll want the objects you place on your pages to remain precisely where you put them. But sometimes, you'll want to place objects relative to related text in such a way that the objects move when the text is edited. For example, if you're creating a product catalog that's essentially a continuous list of product descriptions and you want to include a picture with each description, you can paste pictures within the text to create inline graphics frames.

An inline frame is treated like a single character. If you insert or delete text that precedes an inline frame, the frame moves forward or backward along with the rest of the text that follows the inserted or deleted text. Although inline frames usually contain graphics, they can just as easily contain text or nothing at all.

There are two ways to create an inline frame: using the Paste command and using the Place command.

Caution Inline frames may interfere with line spacing in paragraphs with automatic leading. If the inline frame is larger than the point size in use, the automatic leading value for that line is calculated from the inline frame. This leads to inconsistent line spacing in the paragraph. To work around this, you can either apply a fixed amount of leading to all characters in the paragraph, adjust the size of inline frames, place inline frames at the beginning of a paragraph, or place inline frames in their own paragraphs.

QuarkXPress User InDesign's inline frames are similar to QuarkXPress's anchored boxes, with two important differences: First, if an inline frame is wider than the containing text frame, InDesign hangs the extra width of the inline frame outside of the width of the text frame instead of causing a text overflow as it does in QuarkXPress. Second, QuarkXPress does not offer the same level of positioning control as InDesign does.

There are three ways to create inline frames. The first two are the simplest, but the third gives you more control over the inline frame when you create it.

Note You can set text wraps on inline frames using the standard Text Wrap pane (Window ➪ Text Wrap, or Option+⌘+W or Ctrl+Alt+W), as described in Chapter 24. But note that such wraps affect only text that appears on the same line or below the inline frame, not text above the inline frame or text in other frames.

Creating an inline frame with the Paste command

If you want to create an inline frame from an object you've already created, all you have to do is copy — or cut — the object and then paste it into text as you would a piece of highlighted text. Here's how:

1. **Use the Selection tool to select the object you want to paste within text.** Any type of object can be used: a line, an empty shape, a text or graphics frame, even a group of objects.

2. **Choose Edit ➪ Copy or press ⌘+C or Ctrl+C.** If you don't need the original item, you can use the Cut command (Edit ➪ Cut; ⌘+X or Ctrl+X) instead of the Copy command. (An object that you cut or copy remains on the Clipboard until you cut or copy something else or you turn off your computer. If you intend to use the original object elsewhere, it's better to use the Copy command when creating an inline frame.)

3. **Select the Type tool (or press T), and then click within the text where you want to place the copied object.** Make sure the cursor is flashing where you intend to place the inline frame.

4. **Choose Edit ➪ Paste or press ⌘+V or Ctrl+V.** Figure 11-7 shows an example of an inline frame.

> **Tip** Inline frames often work best when placed at the beginning of a paragraph. If you place an inline frame within text to which automatic leading has been applied, the resulting line spacing can be inconsistent. To fix this problem, you can resize the inline frame.

To change the position of an inline frame, choose Object ➪ Anchored Object ➪ Options. The Anchored Object Options dialog box that appears is the same as the Insert Anchored Object dialog box covered later in this section and shown in Figure 11-8.

Creating an inline frame with the Place command

In addition to using the Paste command to create an inline frame from an existing object, you can use the Place command to create an inline graphics frame from an external picture file. (You can't use this technique for inline text frames.) Here's how:

1. **Select the Type tool (or press T), and then click within a text frame to establish the insertion point.**

2. **Choose File ➪ Place or press ⌘+D or Ctrl+D.**

3. **Locate and select the graphics file you want to place within the text, and then click Choose or Open.**

> **Tip** You can use the transformation tools (Rotate, Scale, and Shear) and the Control palette or Transform pane to modify an inline frame as you modify any other frame.

> **Tip** To delete an inline frame, you can select it, and then choose Edit ➪ Clear or Edit ➪ Cut, or you can position the cursor next to it and then press Delete or Backspace.

Figure 11-7: The YMCA logo in designer Branimir Zlamalik's brochure is placed in the text as an inline frame so that it moves up and down with the surrounding text.

Creating an inline frame using the Anchored Object command

You can also choose Object ⇨ Anchored Object ⇨ Insert to insert an inline frame. This option opens a dialog box, shown in Figure 11-8, that lets you control the positioning of the inline frame as you insert it.

New Feature   The Anchored Object command and related dialog boxes are new to InDesign CS2.

Note   This method inserts a new frame in your text, in which you paste or place a graphic or text. To create an inline frame using an existing frame, use the cut-and-paste method described earlier in this section.

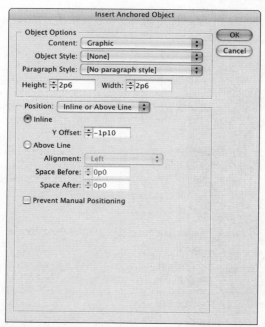

Figure 11-8: The Insert Anchored Object dialog box for inline frames

To create an inline frame with the Anchored Object command, follow these steps:

1. **Select the Type tool (or press T), and then click within a text frame to establish the insertion point.**

2. **Choose Object ➪ Anchored Object ➪ Insert.**

3. **Choose Inline or Above Line from the Position pop-up menu.** The Insert Anchored Object dialog box shown in Figure 11-8 appears.

4. **In the Object Options section, specify inline frame's settings.** You choose the type of frame (text, graphics, or unassigned) using the Content pop-up menu, apply an object style if desired using the Object Style pop-up menu, apply a paragraph style if desired

using the Paragraph Style pop-up menu, and set the inline frame's dimensions using the Height and Width fields.

Note that the Paragraph Style you choose, if any, applies to the inline frame, not to the paragraph in which the inline frame is embedded. Oddly, InDesign lets you apply a paragraph style to the inline frame even if it contains no text.

5. **In the lower part of the dialog box, set the desired position settings.** You have two basic choices for position:

   • The Inline option, if selected, places the frame at the text-insertion point, setting it in the same line as that insertion point. You can adjust the inline frame's vertical position on that line by typing a value in the Y Offset field, which works like shifting the baseline of any text.

   • The Above Line option, if selected, places the inline frame above the current line. Typically, you would use this when you want to place a frame above the first line of a paragraph. An example would be using pictures as the equivalent of headlines above specific paragraphs. You can adjust the alignment of the inline frame relative to the paragraph using the Alignment pop-up menu, as well as control how much space is above and below the inline frame using the Space Before and Space After fields.

   No matter which position you choose, selecting the Prevent Manual Positioning option ensures that the positions of individual frames can't be adjusted using InDesign's other text and frame controls (such as Baseline Shift). This forces users to use this dialog box to change the inline frame's position.

6. **Click OK to insert the inline frame.**

7. **Add any desired content to the inline frame as you would with any other frame.**

Anchored objects added by choosing Object ➪ Anchored Object ➪ Insert do not have text automatically wrapped around them. Use the Text Wrap pane (Window ➪ Text Wrap, or Option+⌘+W or Ctrl+Alt+W) to open this pane and set text wrap. Figure 11-9 shows an inline frame before and after text wrap has been applied.

But anchored objects created by pasting a graphic into text *do* automatically have text wrap around them.

Adjusting inline frames

After you create an inline frame, you can adjust its position vertically or horizontally. Again, there are several methods.

A quick-and-dirty method to move an inline frame vertically is as follows:

1. **Use the Type tool to highlight the inline frame as you would highlight an individual text character.** In the Character pane or Control palette, type a positive value in the Baseline Shift field to move the inline frame up; type a negative value to move the frame down.

2. **Use the Selection tool or Direct Selection tool to select the inline frame, and then drag the frame up or down.**

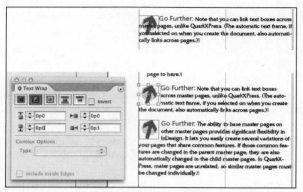

Figure 11-9: Choosing Object ➪ Anchored Object ➪ Insert does not make InDesign wrap text around the resulting frame (top). Use the Text Wrap pane to set text wrap for such objects (bottom).

A quick way to move an inline frame horizontally is as follows:

1. **With the Type tool selected, click between the inline frame and the character that precedes it.**

2. **Use the kerning controls in the Character pane or Control palette to enlarge or reduce the space between the inline frame and the preceding character.**

Note that these preceding methods work only if the Prevent Manual Positioning option remains unchecked in the Insert Anchored Object dialog box or Anchored Object Options dialog box. (This option is not selected by default.) You can also adjust the vertical (Y) position of an inline frame by choosing Object ➪ Anchored Object ➪ Options. The resulting Anchored Object Options dialog box is the same as the Insert Anchored Object dialog box covered previously in this section and shown in Figure 11-8, except the Anchored Object Options dialog box does not have the Object Options section.

Of course, you can also adjust its other attributes as needed, such as strokes, fills, dimensions, rotation, and skew using the Tools palette, Control palette, and other panes.

Deleting inline frames

It's easy to delete an inline frame: Select the frame with the Selection or Direct Selection tool and then choose Edit ➪ Clear or press Delete or Backspace. If you want to remove the object but keep it in the Clipboard for pasting elsewhere, choose Edit ➪ Cut, or press ⌘+X or Ctrl+X.

Setting Up "Follow Me" Anchored Frames

InDesign offers another way to associate frames to text, and this one can make it easier to have sidebars, pull-quotes, info boxes, and other elements that relate to a specific piece of text remain near that text even as it reflows. The difference between an inline frame and an anchored frame is that an anchored frame is not embedded in the text frame—it is simply leashed to it.

The ability to create "follow me" anchored frames is new to InDesign CS2.

InDesign CS2 also now retains anchored frames set up in Microsoft Word documents. It also preserves anchored frames when exporting as RTF.

Before I explain how to create anchored frames, it's important for you know when to use them. There are several caveats to consider:

✦ Because an anchored frame follows its text as it flows throughout a document, you need to ensure your layout retains clear paths for those anchored objects to follow. Otherwise, you could have anchored frames overlap other frames as those anchored frames move.

✦ Anchored frames should generally be small items and/or used sparingly. The more items you have anchored to text, the greater the chance that they will interfere with each other's placement. Likewise, large items can be moved only so far within a page, so the benefit of keeping them close to their related text goes away.

✦ Items such as pull-quotes are obvious candidates for use as anchored frames. But in many layouts you will want the pull-quotes to stay in specific locations on the page for good visual appearance. The InDesign anchored-frame function can accommodate that need for specific positioning on a page, but you need to be careful as you add or delete text so that you do not end up with some pages that have no pull-quotes at all because there is so much text between the pull-quotes' anchor points. Conversely, you need to make sure you don't have too many pull-quotes anchored close to each other, which could result in overlapping objects.

Typically, you would use anchored frames for small graphics or icons that you want to stay next to a specific paragraph. Another good use would be for cross-reference ("For More Information") text frames.

Figure 11-10 shows the Insert Anchored Object dialog box for an anchored object, while Figure 11-11 shows an example of an anchored frame in use.

Adding anchored frames

The process for adding an anchored frame is similar to that for inline frames (described in the previous section). But the controls over positioning are quite different.

Here are the steps:

1. **Select the Type tool (or press T), and then click within a text frame to establish the insertion point.**

2. **Choose Object ⇨ Anchored Object ⇨ Insert.**

3. **Choose Custom from the Position pop-up menu.** The Insert Anchored Object dialog box shown in Figure 11-10 appears.

4. **In the Object Options section, specify the inline frame's settings.** Choose the type of frame (text, graphics, or unassigned) using the Content pop-up menu; apply an object style, if desired, using the Object Style pop-up menu; apply a paragraph style, if desired, using the Paragraph Style pop-up menu; and set the inline frame's dimensions using the Height and Width fields.

Note that the Paragraph Style you choose, if any, applies to the inline frame, not to the paragraph in which the inline frame is embedded. Oddly, InDesign lets you apply a paragraph style to the inline frame even if it contains no text.

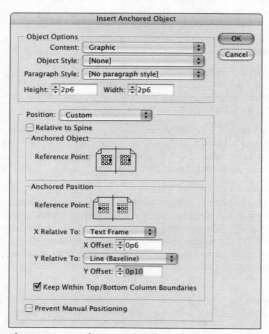

Figure 11-10: The Insert Anchored Object dialog box for anchored objects

5. **Decide whether to select the Relative to Spine option.** If this option is not selected, the anchored frame is placed on the same side of the text frame on all pages, whether left-facing or right-facing. If this option is selected, InDesign places the text frame on the outside of both pages or inside of both pages, depending on how the anchored position is set. In other words, if the anchored frame is set to be on the left of the reference text for a left-hand page, selecting this option puts the anchored frame to the right of the reference text on a right-hand page. If this option is not selected, InDesign places the anchored frame to the left of the text frame on both left-hand and right-hand pages.

6. **In the Anchored Object section of the dialog box, click one of the positioning squares to set up the text frame's relative position.** Note that you need to think about both the horizontal and vertical position you desire. For example, if you want the anchored frame to appear to the right of the text reference, click one of the right-hand squares. (Remember that selecting the Relative to Spine option overrides this, making the right-hand pages' positions mirror that of the left-hand pages, rather than be identical to them.) If you choose the topmost right-hand square, the anchored frame is placed to the right of the text reference and vertically appears at or below that text reference. But if you choose the bottommost right-hand square, you're telling InDesign you want the anchored frame to appear vertically above the text reference.

You'll need to experiment with your layout to see what works best in each case.

7. **In the Anchored Position section of the dialog box, click one of the positioning squares to set up the text reference's relative position.** Although there are nine squares shown, the only three that matter are those in the middle row. Typically, you'd have the text reference be on the opposite side of the anchored frame — if you want the anchored frame to be to the left, you thus would indicate that the text reference is to the right. (If you set the text reference to be on the same side as the anchored frame, InDesign places the anchored frame over the text.) The reason there are three squares (left, middle, and right) is to accommodate layouts where you want some anchored frames to appear to the left of the text and some to the right; in that case, choose the middle position here and select the right- or left-hand position in the Anchored Object section as appropriate to that object.

   I mentioned that you can ignore the top and bottom row of position squares in the Anchored Section. If you click any left-hand position box, InDesign sets the position as if you clicked the middle row's left-hand position box. If you click any right-hand position box, InDesign treats it as if you clicked the middle right-hand position box. The only reason the nine squares are there is for consistency with the Anchored Object section's icons.

8. **There are three options in the Anchored Position section that you may need to set that give InDesign more precise instructions on how to place the anchored frames:**

   - The X Relative To pop-up menu tells InDesign from where the horizontal location is calculated, using the following options: Anchor Marker, Column Edge, Text Frame, Page Margin, and Page Edge. The right option depends both on where you want the anchored frames placed and whether you have multicolumn text frames (in which case Text Frame and Column Edge result in different placement, while in a single-column text frame they do not).

     You can also specify a specific amount of space to place between the chosen X Relative To point and the anchored frame by typing a value in the X Offset field.

   - The Y Relative To pop-up menu tells InDesign from where the horizontal location is calculated, using the following options: Line (Baseline), Line (Cap-height), Line (Top of Leading), Column Edge, Text Frame, Page Margin, and Page Edge.

     As you would expect, you can also indicate a specific amount of space to place between the chosen Y Relative To point and the anchored frame by typing a value in the Y Offset field.

9. **No matter which position settings you apply, you can select the Prevent Manual Positioning option to ensure that the positions of individual frames can't be adjusted using InDesign's other frame-positioning controls (such as the Control palette's or Transform pane's X: and Y: fields).** This forces users to use this dialog box to change the anchored frame's position.

10. **Click OK to insert the anchored frame.**

Tip To see the results of various position options as you work in the Insert Anchored Object dialog box, select the Preview option. This greatly helps you to understand the results of various settings before you commit to them.

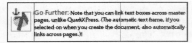

Go Further: Note that you can link text boxes across master pages, unlike QuarkXPress. (The automatic text frame, if you selected on when you create the document, also automatically links across pages.)!

Figure 11-11: Example of an anchored frame

Converting existing frames to anchored frames

Once you get the hang of when and how to use anchored frames, you'll likely want to convert some frames in existing documents to be anchored frames. There's no direct way to do that in InDesign, but there is a more circuitous path you can take:

1. **Use the Selection or Direct Selection tool to cut the existing frame you want to make into an anchored frame by choosing Edit ➪ Cut or pressing ⌘+X or Ctrl+X.** You can also copy an existing frame by choosing Edit ➪ Copy or pressing ⌘+C or Ctrl+C.

2. **Switch to the Type tool, and click in a text frame at the desired location to insert the text reference to the anchored frame.**

3. **Paste the cut or copied frame into that insertion point by choosing Edit ➪ Paste or pressing ⌘+V or Ctrl+V. You now have an inline frame.**

4. **Choose Object ➪ Anchored Object ➪ Options to display the Anchored Object Options dialog box (refer to Figure 11-10).**

5. **Using the Position pop-up menu, choose Custom. This converts the frame from an inline frame to an anchored frame.**

6. **Adjust the position for the newly minted anchored frame as described in the previous section.**

7. **Click OK when done.**

Adjusting anchored frames

After you create an anchored frame, you can adjust its position.

A quick-and-dirty method is simply to click and drag anchored frames or use the Control palette or Transform pane to adjust their position. If the text the frame is anchored to moves, however, InDesign, of course, overrides those changes. (You can't manually move an anchored frame if the Prevent Manual Positioning option is selected in the Insert Anchored Object dialog box or Anchored Object Options dialog box. This option is not selected by default.)

For the most control of an anchored frame's position, choose Object ➪ Anchored Object ➪ Options. The resulting Anchored Object Options dialog box is the same as the Insert Anchored Object dialog box covered previously in this section and shown in Figure 11-10, except that the Anchored Object Options dialog box does not have the Object Options section.

And, of course, you can adjust its other attributes as needed, such as strokes, fills, dimensions, rotation, and skew.

Releasing and deleting anchored frames

If you no longer want an anchored frame to be anchored to a text location, you can release the anchor. To do so, select the anchored frame with the Selection or Direct Selection tool and then choose Object ➪ Anchored Object ➪ Release.

It's also easy to delete an anchored frame: Select the frame with the Selection or Direct Selection tool and then choose Edit ➪ Clear or press Delete or Backspace. If you want to remove the object but keep it on the Clipboard for pasting elsewhere, choose Edit ➪ Cut, or press ⌘+X or Ctrl+X.

Defining and Applying Object Styles

For many years, desktop-publishing programs have let designers save textual styles for easy reuse and application to text throughout a document. But none of the main desktop publishing programs — PageMaker, QuarkXPress, and InDesign — lets you do the same for objects. That's no longer true. InDesign now lets you create object styles, so you can assure that multiple objects have the same attributes and that any changes to the style are made to all the objects using that style.

New Feature　　Object styles are new to InDesign CS2.

Designers will find the process of creating and applying object styles very familiar because the concept is the same as creating other types of styles, such as paragraph, character, and stroke styles.

Cross-Reference　　Paragraph and character styles are covered in Chapter 19. Stroke styles are covered in Chapter 10.

There are no hard-and-fast rules about how best to implement them. Like handwriting, you should develop your own style. How many styles you create, the names you use, and whether you apply them with keyboard shortcuts or through the Object Styles pane are all matters of personal taste. One thing is indisputable: You should use object styles whenever you're dealing with multiple objects that need to be formatted the same way.

Creating object styles

You create object styles using the Object Styles pane (Window ➪ Object Styles, or ⌘+F7 or Ctrl+F7), shown in Figure 11-12. You can also click the New Object Style button at the bottom of the pane.

Tip　　The simplest way is to apply various attributes to an object (text frame, graphics frame, unassigned frame, or line) is to select it with the Selection or Direct Selection tool, and then choose New Object Style from the Object Style pane's palette menu. InDesign records all those settings automatically, so they're in place for the new object style.

Whether you start with an existing object or create a new object style completely from scratch, you use the New Object Style menu option that opens the New Object Style dialog box shown in Figure 11-13.

At the left side of the dialog box is a list of types of attributes that are or can be set. The checked items are in use for this style — you can uncheck an item so InDesign doesn't apply its settings to objects using the style. For example, if Fill is unchecked, the object style won't apply any Fill settings to objects using that style.

To switch from one type of attribute to another, simply click the item name for the type of attributes on which you want to work, such as Stroke or Transparency.

Tip   Be sure to select the Preview option to see the results of object styles on the currently selected object. Of course, you'll need to make sure the object is visible on-screen to see those effects.

Deleted Selected Style

Clear Overrides

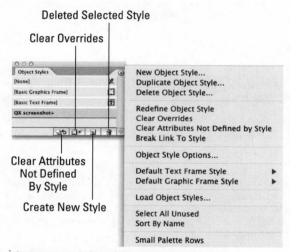

Clear Attributes
Not Defined
By Style

Create New Style

Figure 11-12: The Object Styles pane and its palette menu

The General pane

When you open the New Object Style dialog box, you'll see the General pane, which lets you create a style based on an existing object style (using the Based On pop-up menu), and which lets you assign a keyboard shortcut for fast application of this style (using the Shortcuts field).

You can use the Based On feature to create families of object styles. For example, you can create a styles called Photo/Base for the bulk of your placed photographs, and then create variations such as Photo/Sidebar and Photo/Author. The Photo/Base style might specify a hairline black stroke around the photo, while Photo/Sidebar might change that to be a white stroke. But if you later decide you want the stroke to be 1 point and change it in Photo/Base, Photo/Sidebar automatically gets the 1-point stroke while retaining the white color.

The General pane also lets you see the current style settings. Click any of the arrows in the Style Settings section to get more details on how they are set for this object style.

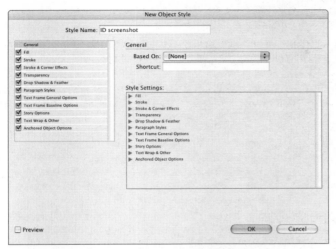

Figure 11-13: The New Object Style dialog box and its General pane

The Fill pane

Shown in Figure 11-14, the Fill pane of the New Object Style dialog box lets you set colors for fills using whatever colors are defined in the Swatches pane. You can also set the tint and, if you select a gradient fill, the angle for that gradient. Finally, you can choose to have the fill overprint the contents of the frame by selecting the Overprint Fill option.

Cross-Reference   Chapter 8 covers the definition and application of colors, gradients, and tints.

The other options are grayed out because they do not apply to fills.

Tip   If you click the Stroke icon in the pane, you are taken to the Stroke pane of the New Object Style dialog box. This emulates the behavior of the Stroke and Fill buttons in the Tools palette and the Swatches pane.

The Stroke pane

The Stroke pane in the New Object Style dialog box is identical to the Fill pane except that options specific to fills are grayed out and options available to strokes are made available. The color, tint, and gradient angle options are the same as for the Fill pane.

In the Stroke pane, you choose the type of stroke (solid line, dashed line, or dotted line) using the Type pop-up menu, and the thickness using the Weight field. You can also choose to overprint the stroke over underlying content by selecting the Overprint Stroke option. Finally, if your stroke is a dotted or dashed line, you can set the color, tint, and overprint for the gap in the Gap Color section.

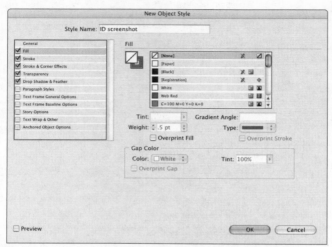

Figure 11-14: The Fill pane of the New Object Style dialog box

Tip   If you click the Fill icon in the pane, you are taken to the Fill pane of the New Object Style dialog box. This emulates the behavior of the Stroke and Fill buttons in the Tools palette and the Swatches pane.

Cross-Reference   Chapter 8 covers the definition and application of colors, gradients, and tints. Chapter 10 covers the use of strokes and settings such as gap.

The Stroke & Corner Effects pane

Shown in Figure 11-15, the Stroke & Corner Effects pane of the New Object Style dialog box lets you set stroke position and how corners and line ends are handled. It also lets you apply fancy corners to frames.

The Stroke Effects section is where you align the strokes to the frame edges, using the Stroke Alignment buttons. You also control how lines join at corners using the Join buttons. The End Cap buttons control how the lines end (such as immediately, or with a rounded or squared-off cap). You can also use the Miter Limit field to tell InDesign when a corner point should switch from *mitered* (squared off) to a beveled appearance, based on the sharpness of the corner's angle. Finally, you can select line endings such as arrowheads using the Line Start and Line End pop-up menus.

The Corner Effects section is where you select from five fancy corners, such as Bevel and Rounded, using the Effect pop-up menu and where you specify the radius, or reach, of the corner using the Size field.

Cross-Reference   Chapter 10 covers the use of strokes and settings such as alignment and line endings. Chapter 24 covers corner effects.

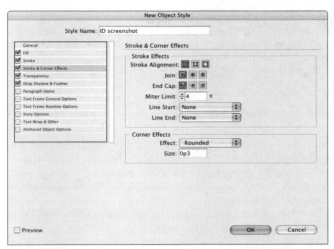

Figure 11-15: The Stroke & Corner Effects pane of the New Object Style dialog box

The Transparency pane

Shown in Figure 11-16, the Transparency pane of the New Object Style dialog box controls an object's opacity, with 0 percent being invisible and 100 percent being completely solid. The Mode pop-up menu lets you select the transparency effect. The Isolate Blending and Knockout Group options affect how transparency affects other objects in specific cases.

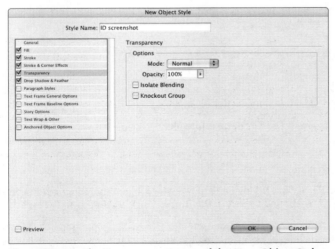

Figure 11-16: The Transparency pane of the New Object Style dialog box

Cross-Reference

Chapter 10 covers the transparency settings in detail.

The Drop Shadow & Feather pane

Shown in Figure 11-17, the Drop Shadow & Feather pane of the New Object Style dialog box controls two types of lighting effects for objects: drop shadows and feathering.

The Drop Shadow section lets you create drop shadow and specify the transparency mode and percentage for that shadow, the degree of blur over the width of the shadow, the shadow's size, and its position relative to the frame.

The Feather section lets you feather (blur) a frame's edges, determining the extent and type of the blur.

Chapter 10 covers the drop shadows and feathering settings in detail.

Chances are you won't use this setting except for frames that contain only consistent, very simple text, such as pull-quotes or bios.

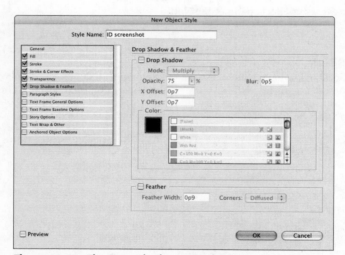

Figure 11-17: The Drop Shadow & Feather pane of the New Object Style dialog box

The Paragraph Styles pane

Shown in Figure 11-18, the Paragraph Styles pane of the New Object Style dialog box controls what paragraph style, if any, is applied to text in the frame. You choose the style from the Paragraph Style pop-up menu. If that style is set to invoke another style for the next paragraph, be sure to select the Apply Next Style option — otherwise, the object style will insist on making every paragraph use the style specified here.

Chapter 19 covers paragraph styles in detail.

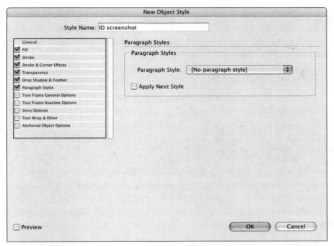

Figure 11-18: The Paragraph Styles pane of the New Object Style dialog box

The Text Frame General Options pane

Shown in Figure 11-19, the Text Frame General Options pane of the New Object Style dialog box controls how text is handled within a frame. This essentially replicates the controls in the General pane of the Text Box Options dialog box (Object ➪ Text Frame Options, or ⌘+B or Ctrl+B), including number of columns, column width, gutter settings, inset spacing (how far from the frame edge text is placed), vertical justification (how text is aligned vertically in the frame), and whether text wrap settings are ignored when this frame overlaps other frames.

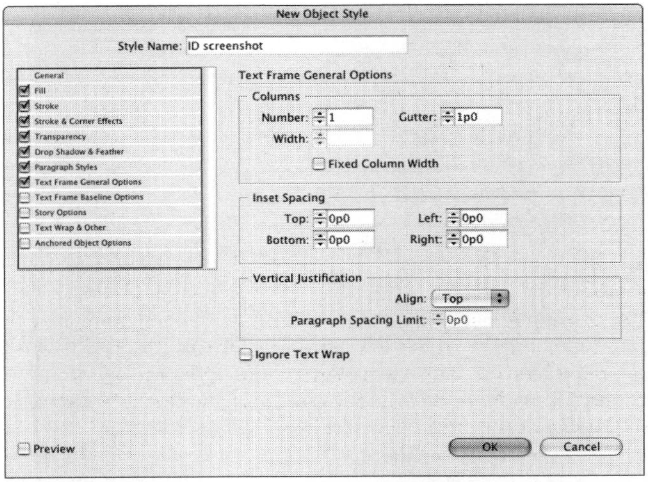

Figure 11-19: The Text Frame General Options pane of the New Object Style dialog box

Note You can set text frame options even if the current object is not a text frame. That's so you can have a consistent style for multiple kinds of objects, with the text attributes coming into play only for objects that actually are text frames.

Cross-Reference Chapter 14 covers text frame options in detail.

The Text Frame Baseline Options pane

Shown in Figure 11-20, the Text Frame Baseline Options pane of the New Object Style dialog box controls how text is handled within a frame. This essentially replicates the controls in the Baseline Options pane of the Text Box Options dialog box (Object ➪ Text Frame Options, or ⌘+B or Ctrl+B), including how the text baseline is calculated for the frame and whether the text frame gets its own baseline grid.

The Story Options pane

Shown in Figure 11-21, the Story Options pane of the New Objects Style dialog box lets you enable optical margin alignment — its controls are the same as the Story pane (Window ➪ Type & Tables ➪ Story). Optical margin alignment adjusts the placement of text along the left side of a frame so the text alignment is more visually pleasing.

Note You can set optical margin alignment even if the current object is not a text frame. That's so you can have a consistent style for multiple kinds of objects, with the text attributes coming into play only for objects that actually are text frames.

Cross-Reference Chapter 18 covers optical margin alignment in detail.

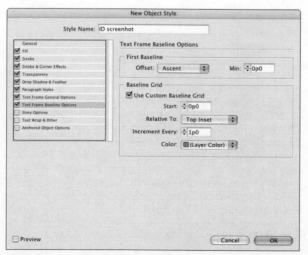

Figure 11-20: The Text Frame Baseline Options pane of the New Object dialog box

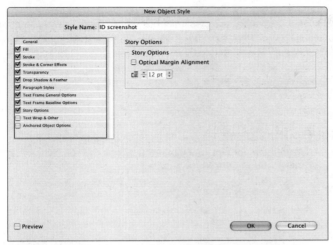

Figure 11-21: The Story Options pane of the New Object dialog box

The Text Wrap & Other pane

Shown in Figure 11-22, the Text Wrap & Other pane of the New Object Style dialog box lets you set text wrap—mirroring the features of the Text Wrap pane (Window ➪ Text Wrap, or Option+⌘+W or Ctrl+Alt+W), as well as make an object nonprinting (normally handled through the Attributes pane by choosing Window ➪ Attributes).

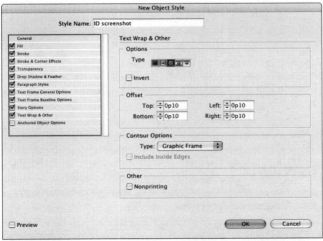

Figure 11-22: The Text Wrap & Other pane of the New Object dialog box

Note   You can set text wrap even if the current object is not a text frame. That's so you can have a consistent style for multiple kinds of objects, with the text attributes coming into play only for objects that actually are text frames.

Cross-Reference   Chapter 24 covers text wrap settings in detail. Chapter 10 covers nonprinting objects.

The Anchored Object Options pane

Shown in Figure 11-23, the Anchored Object Options pane of the New Object Style dialog box lets you set the attributes for inline and anchored frames.

Cross-Reference   Anchored objects are covered previously in this chapter.

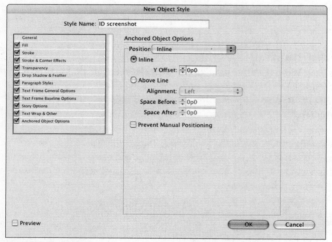

Figure 11-23: The Anchored Object Options pane of the New Object dialog box

Managing object styles

The Object Styles pane's palette menu of the New Object Style dialog box (refer to Figure 11-12) has several options for managing object styles:

✦ **Duplicate Object Style.** Click an object style's name, and then choose this menu option to create an exact copy. If you want to create an object style that's similar to one you've already created, you might want to choose New Object Style rather than Duplicate Object Style, and then use the Based On option to create a child of the original. If you choose Duplicate Object Style, the copy is identical to, but not based on, the original; if you modify the original, the copy is not affected. The pane also has an iconic button to create a new style.

✦ **Delete Object Style.** Choose this to delete selected object styles. To select multiple styles, press and hold ⌘ or Ctrl as you click their names. To select a range of styles, click the first one, and then press and hold Shift and click the last one. You can also delete styles by selecting them in the pane and then clicking the trash can icon at the bottom of the pane.

✦ **Redefine Object Style.** This option lets you modify an existing object style by first making changes to an object that already has an object style defined for it, and then clicking Redefine Style. The newly applied formats are applied to the object style.

✦ **Object Style Options.** This option lets you modify an existing object style. When a style is highlighted in the Object Styles pane, choosing Style Options displays the Object Style Options dialog box, which is identical to the New Object Style dialog box covered earlier.

✦ **Load Object Styles.** Choose this option if you want to import object styles from another InDesign document. You will get a dialog box listing the styles in the chosen document, so you can decide which ones to import.

If you import styles whose names match those in the current document, InDesign gives you a chance to let the imported style overwrite the current style or to leave the current style as is and give the imported style a new name. If there is an entry in the Conflict with Existing Style, you can click that entry for a pop-up menu that provides two choices: Auto-Rename and Use Incoming Style Definition. Figure 11-24 shows this Load Styles dialog box.

Note that at the bottom of the dialog box is the Incoming Style Definitions window, which lists the style definitions to help you decide which to import, as well as which to overwrite or rename.

New Feature The ability to select which styles to load from another InDesign document is new to InDesign CS2. The ability to choose how to handle style conflicts is also new to InDesign CS2 and puts it on par with QuarkXPress.

✦ **Select All Unused.** Select this option to highlight the names of all object styles that have not been applied to any objects. This is a handy way of identifying unused styles in preparation for deleting them (by choosing the Delete Object Style menu option).

✦ **Sort by Name.** This option alphabetizes your object styles for easier access. (InDesign adds styles to the Object Styles pane in the order in which they were created.)

✦ **Small Palette Rows.** Click this option to reduce the text size in the Object Styles pane. Although harder to read, a pane with this option selected lets you access more styles without having to scroll. To return the pane to its normal text size, deselect this option.

Note that InDesign comes with three predefined object styles — [Normal Text Frame], [Normal Graphics Frame], and [Normal Grid] — that you can modify as desired. Frankly, they're not necessary because it makes more sense for you to create object styles using your own naming conventions. Adobe's rationale is that there should be at least one style defined, so if you delete all other styles, there's still a style that can be applied to objects. While I don't buy that argument, it doesn't matter because you can easily ignore these default styles if you prefer.

Applying object styles

After you create an object style, applying it is easy. Just click an object, and then click the object style name in the Object Styles pane, or press its keyboard shortcut. (Windows users must make sure Num Lock is on when using shortcuts for styles.)

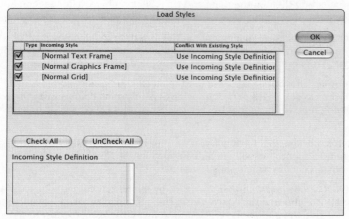

Figure 11-24: The Load Styles dialog box

 Tip   You can set which object styles are automatically used for new text and graphics frames: In the Object Styles pane's palette menu, choose Default Text Frame Style and then the desired style from the submenu to set a default text frame; choose Default Graphic Frame Style and then the desired style from the submenu to set a default graphics frame. To no longer have object styles automatically applied to new objects, choose [None] in the Default Text Frame and/or default Graphic Frame submenus.

The Quick Apply option

Another way to apply object styles is using the Quick Apply feature in InDesign. Quick Apply is a consolidated list of styles that you access by choosing Edit ⇨ Quick Apply or pressing ⌘+Return or Ctrl+Enter. If you select an object, the Quick Apply palette, shown in Figure 11-25, presents all paragraph, character, and object styles available. You can scroll down to the one you want or type the first few letters of the style name in the text field at the top to jump to styles beginning with those letters, and then navigate to the one you want and press Return or Enter, which brings you back to where you were working with your object and closes the Quick Apply palette.

 New Feature   Quick Apply is new to InDesign CS2.

It seems easier to stick with the Object Styles pane because you won't have to worry about wading through the character and paragraph styles at the same time. The Object Styles pane, however, doesn't let you quickly jump to styles by typing the first letter or two of their names as Quick Apply does.

But for users who are working on layouts from their keyboards — perhaps a layout artist who's working on a notebook while commuting — Quick Apply can be handy. You can switch to it, apply the style, and return to your object or text, all without touching the mouse.

Figure 11-25: The Quick Apply palette

How existing formatting is handled

When you apply an object style to selected objects, all local formats are retained. All other formats are replaced by those of the applied style. That is, unless you do one of the following:

✦ If you press and hold Option or Alt when clicking a name in the Object Styles pane, any local formatting that has been applied to the objects is removed. You can achieve the same effect by choosing Clear Attributes Not Defined by Style from the Object Styles pane's palette menu or by clicking the Clear Attributes Not Defined by Style button at the bottom of the Object Styles pane.

✦ If you want to override any local changes with the settings in the object style, choose Clear Overrides in the palette menu or click the Clear Overrides button at the bottom of the Object Styles pane. The difference is that Clear Attributes Not Defined by Style removes all attributes for which the object style contains no settings, while Clear Overrides imposes the object style's settings over conflicting attributes that you set manually.

Note   If a plus sign (+) appears to the right of an object style's name, it means that the object has local formats that differ from those of the applied object style. This can occur if you apply an object style to an object text to which you've done some manual formatting or if you modify formatting for an object after applying an object style to it. (For example, you may have changed the fill color; that is a local change to the object style and will cause the + to appear.)

Removing an object style from an object

To remove a style from an object, choose Break Link to Style from the Object Styles pane's palette menu. The object's current formatting won't be affected, but it will no longer be updated when the object style is changed.

Summary

Most InDesign pages are made up of several objects. Each object occupies a separate level in a page's stacking order. The first object you place on a page occupies the bottom later, and each new object you create or place occupies a new layer that's on top of all other layers. You can change a page's stacking order by moving individual items forward or backward in the stacking order. InDesign also provides several options for working with several objects at once. When multiple items are selected, you can combine them into a group that behaves like a single item. You can also place an object within a frame to create a nested object.

InDesign provides two ways to associate frames with text. One method lets you insert objects within a text thread to create inline frames that flow with the surrounding text. The other creates a link between a specific location in your text thread and an outside frame, so the frame moves along with that location as the text moves.

Finally, InDesign now lets you create object styles, named collections of attributes, that you can apply to objects to ensure consistent formatting and to easily update formatting across multiple objects, sort of the frame version of a paragraph style for text.

✦   ✦   ✦

Timesaving Techniques

In This Chapter

Creating copies of objects

Aligning multiple objects

Using grid lines and guidelines when positioning objects

One of the advantages of using a computer for publishing is that it can do a lot of the work for you. That's particularly true of detail-oriented or repetitive work. InDesign has several features that let you save time by handling such repetitive, exacting chores for you. For example, if you're creating a checkerboard pattern as a page background, there's no need to create, modify, and place 20 or more frames by hand. You might start with one or two, and then automatically duplicate and distribute the copies on your page.

Creating Copies of Objects

Once you create something — a simple, rectangular frame or a complicated graphic made up of several dozen objects — InDesign makes it easy to reuse the original.

Here are your options:

+ **Copy and Paste commands (Edit ➪ Copy, or ⌘+C or Ctrl+C; Edit ➪ Paste, or ⌘+V or Ctrl+V).** Using these commands is a good choice if you have to copy something from one page to another or from one document to another. But if you need a duplicate on the same page as the original, the Duplicate command is quicker. A great option is Paste in Place (Edit ➪ Paste in Place, or Option+Shift+⌘+V or Ctrl+Alt+Shift+V), which pastes an object in the same place as the original object. It's very handy when copying an element from one page to another because it places the copy in the same location on the new page, saving you the effort of having to move it. (When copying among documents, Paste in Place may not be able to copy the object to the exact same location because page dimensions may differ; in that case, Paste in Place uses the same X and Y coordinates as the original.)

+ **Duplicate command (Edit ➪ Duplicate, or Option+Shift+⌘+D or Ctrl+Alt+Shift+D).** When you duplicate an object, the copy is placed one pica below and to the right of the original.

+ **Manual cloning.** When you click and drag an object while pressing and holding Option or Alt, a copy of the selected object is created. If you're a click-and-dragger, you may prefer this manual method to the Duplicate command.

✦ **Cloning with the Transformation tools.** If you press and hold Option or Alt while using any of the Transformation tools (Rotate, Shear, and Scale), a copy of the selected object is transformed. The selected item remains unchanged.

✦ **Control palette and Transformation pane cloning.** If you press and hold Option or Alt when you exit the Control palette or Transform pane (by pressing Return or Enter or releasing the mouse after choosing an option from a menu), the transformation is applied to a copy of the selected item.

✦ **Step and Repeat command (Edit ⇨ Step and Repeat, or Shift+⌘+U or Ctrl+Shift+U).** Think of the Step and Repeat dialog box (shown in Figure 12-1) as the Duplicate command on steroids. It lets you create multiple duplicates of selected objects and specify the horizontal and vertical offset of the duplicates. This command is handy if you have to create, for example, a vertical and/or horizontal grid of lines on a page. Simply draw a horizontal line at the top of the page or a vertical line along the left edge of the page. With the line selected, use the Step and Repeat command to place—and evenly space—as many additional lines as you need.

New Feature The shortcut for Step and Repeat has changed in InDesign CS2 to Shift+⌘+U or Ctrl+Shift+U.

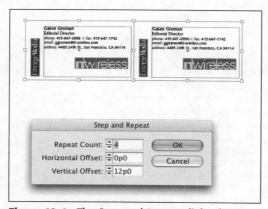

Figure 12-1: The Step and Repeat dialog box

Figure 12-2 shows a typical task that's easily handled with the Step and Repeat command. First, the top row was built by creating two copies of the original; the rest of the rows were created by step-and-repeating the four grouped objects in the top row.

Tip If you need to use an object or a group of objects repeatedly, storing them in a library is a good idea. For example, if you've used InDesign to create a logo or a house ad, copy the objects into a library. Once you place something in a library, you can drag-copy as many clones as you want into any document. For more information about using libraries, see Chapter 7.

Figure 12-2: These business cards were created with one trip to the Step and Repeat dialog box.

Cross-Reference

InDesign CS2 now lets you repeat transformation done to one object onto other objects repeatedly, which saves time in formatting objects. Chapter 10 covers the new repeat-transformation capabilities.

Copying Objects between Documents

Occasionally, you'll want to use something you've created in one InDesign document in another document. For example, maybe an ad that ran in last month's newsletter is needed again for this month's edition. Or perhaps you created a small illustration for an ad that you want to use in a companion brochure. InDesign offers several options for moving objects between documents. You can:

✦ Open the document that contains the objects you want to copy, select the objects, and then copy them to the clipboard with Edit ➪ Copy, or ⌘+C or Ctrl+C. Open the target document and use Edit ➪ Paste, or ⌘+V or Ctrl+V, to place the copied objects. You can also use Edit ➪ Paste in Place, or Option+Shift+⌘+V or Ctrl+Alt+Shift+V, to paste the object at the same X and Y coordinates as the original.

✦ If you need to use the objects in more than one document, you can copy them into a library, which lets you place as many copies as you want in any document.

✦ You can open the source document (the one that contains the objects) and the target document and drag-copy the objects from the source document to the target document. (Choose Window ➪ Arrange ➪ Tile to display both document windows side by side.)

For text, you can drag text from one object to another, from one document to another, from one window to another, from other applications into InDesign, from one Story Editor window to another, and even to the Find/Change dialog box. If you press and hold Option or Alt when dragging text, you drag a copy, and InDesign creates a new text frame if needed at the destination.

To enable drag-and-drop text movement in layouts, go to the Type pane of the Preferences dialog box (InDesign ➪ Preferences on the Mac or Edit ➪ Preferences in Windows, or ⌘+K or Ctrl+K). Be sure to select the Enable in Layout View option in the Drag and Drop Text Editing section. (The Enable in Story Editor option is selected by default; if you're unable to drag text in the Story Editor, make sure that option is selected here.)

New Feature   Drag-and-drop text movement and copying are new to InDesign CS2.

Aligning and Distributing Objects

InDesign lets you align and distribute objects, saving you the hassle of manually moving and placing each element, or figuring out the correct locations in the Control palette or Transform pane to do so. The Align pane is where InDesign offers these timesaving abilities.

Tip   You can create keyboard shortcuts for the Align and Distribute buttons. Although there are no default shortcuts, these buttons are listed in the Object Editing commands in the Keyboard Shortcuts dialog box (Edit ➪ Keyboard Shortcuts) so you can create shortcuts for them. Chapter 3 covers keyboard shortcuts in more detail.

The Align pane (Window ➪ Object & Layout ➪ Align or Shift+F7), shown in Figure 12-3, has several buttons that let you manipulate the relative position of multiple objects in two ways. (The buttons show the alignments they provide.) You can:

✦ **Line up objects along a horizontal or vertical axis.** For example, if you've randomly placed several small graphic frames onto a page, you can use the alignment buttons in the Align pane to align them neatly—either horizontally or vertically. Figure 12-4 shows a before-and-after example of objects aligned with the Align pane.

✦ **Distribute space evenly among objects along a horizontal or vertical axis.** Here's a typical problem that's easily solved by using this feature: You've carefully placed five small pictures on a page so that the top edges are aligned across the page and there is equal space between each picture. Then you find out one of the pictures needs to be cut. After deleting the unneeded picture, you could use the Align pane to redistribute the space among the remaining pictures so that they're again equally spaced. Figure 12-5 shows a before-and-after example of the Align pane's Distribute Spacing capability using a series of vertically arranged objects.

Note   The Align buttons don't work with objects that have been locked with the Lock Position command (Object ➪ Lock Position, or ⌘+L or Ctrl+L). If you need to align a locked object, you must first unlock it (Object ➪ Unlock Position, or Option+⌘+ L or Ctrl+Alt+L). If the objects are on a locked layer, you need to unlock the layer.

Tip   The six alignment buttons are also available in the Control palette if you've selected multiple objects with the Selection tool (see Chapter 10 for more on the Control palette).

When you click a button in the Align pane, selected objects are repositioned in the most logical manner. For example, if you click the Horizontal Align Left button, the selected objects are moved horizontally (to the left, in this case) so that the left edge of each object is aligned with the left edge of the leftmost object. Along the same lines, if you click the Vertical Distribute Center button, the selected objects are moved vertically so that there's an equal amount of space between the vertical center of each object.

Spacing can appear uneven if you click the Horizontal or Vertical Distribute buttons when objects of various sizes are selected. For objects of different sizes, you'll usually want to use the Distribute Spacing buttons (which make the space between objects even) rather than space objects based on their centers or sides (which is how the Distribute Object buttons work).

Note If the two Distribute Spacing button do not appear at the bottom of the palette and you want to distribute objects, choose Show Options from the palette menu.

Tip Sometimes the result of clicking a button in the Align pane isn't what you anticipate — or want. If this happens, simply choose Edit ➪ Undo or press ⌘+Z or Ctrl+Z and try another button.

Figure 12-3: The Align pane contains 14 buttons that let you control the alignment and space among selected objects. If the two Distribute Spacing buttons do not appear at the bottom of the palette, choose Show Options from the palette menu.

Figure 12-4: The rectangles on the left were aligned along the left edge of the leftmost object by clicking the Horizontal Align Left button in the Align pane. The result of the alignment operation is shown on the right.

Figure 12-5: The objects on the left are unequally spaced. Clicking the Vertical Distribute Space button in the Align pane repositions the objects so that the spaces between the objects are equal, as shown on the right.

Positioning Objects Precisely with Guides

Just as carpenters often use chalk lines to make sure things are straight when putting up the framework of a house, you can use guidelines and grid lines to help achieve precise object placement and alignment when building InDesign documents. InDesign lets you show or hide three kinds of guides: user-created vertical and horizontal guidelines, document grid lines, and baseline grid lines. You can tell InDesign to automatically snap object edges to guidelines and grid lines when you create, resize, or move an object within a user-specified distance.

Cross-Reference   For more about creating and using guidelines and grids, see Chapter 7.

You can create horizontal and vertical guidelines whenever you want by clicking on either the horizontal or vertical ruler and dragging the pointer onto the page or pasteboard. Choosing View ➪ Guides & Grids ➪ Show Guides or ⌘+; (semicolon) or Ctrl+; (semicolon), turns guides on. The menu option name then changes to Hide Guides, so you can toggle guides on and off using the same shortcut.

When guidelines are displayed and Snap to Guides (View ➪ Guides & Grids ➪ Snap to Guides, or Shift+⌘+; [semicolon] or Ctrl+Shift+; [semicolon]) is selected, an object edge snaps to a guideline when you create, resize, or move the object within the number of pixels specified in the Snap to Zone preference. (Choose InDesign ➪ Preferences on the Mac or Edit ➪ Preferences in Windows, or press ⌘+K or Ctrl+K, and then go to the Guides & Pasteboard pane.)

Note   When the Snap to Guides option is selected in the View menu, guidelines must be displayed (View ➪ Guides & Grids ➪ Show Guides, or ⌘+; [semicolon] or Ctrl+; [semicolon]) for objects to snap to them. However, when the Snap to Document Grid option is selected, objects snap to document grid lines and, when the Snap to Guides option is selected, objects snap to baseline grid lines), regardless of whether the document grid or the baseline grid is displayed.

All documents include a document-wide grid of vertical and horizontal lines that you can use for creating, resizing, and positioning objects. The View ➪ Guides & Grids ➪ Show Document Grid and Show ➪ Guides & Grids ➪ Hide Document Grid commands, or ⌘+' (apostrophe) or Ctrl+' (apostrophe), toggle the document grid display on and off. When displayed, the document grid looks much like graph paper. When guidelines are displayed and View ➪ Guides & Grids ➪ Snap to Document Grid, or Shift+⌘+' (apostrophe) or Ctrl+Shift+' (apostrophe), is selected, an object edge will snap to a document grid line when you create, resize, or move the object within the number of pixels specified in the Snap to Zone preference in the Preferences dialog box's Guides & Pasteboard pane.

Tip   If you want to align objects with text baselines and text baselines with the baseline grid, use the Grids pane preferences in the Preferences dialog box to specify the same vertical spacing for the Document Grid as for the Baseline Grid. For example, specify an Increment Every value of 1 pica in the Baseline Grid area, and specify a Subdivisions value of 6 in the Document Grid area.

In addition to the document grid, all documents have a built-in baseline grid that represents the leading increments of body text. The View ➪ Grids & Guides ➪ Show Baseline Grid and View ➪ Grids & Guides ➪ Hide Baseline Grid commands, or Option+⌘+' (apostrophe) or Ctrl+Alt+' (apostrophe), toggles the baseline grid display on and off. When the baseline grid is displayed and the Snap to Guides option is selected, an object edge will snap to a baseline grid line when you create, resize, or move the object within the number of pixels specified in the Snap to Zone preference in the Guides & Pasteboard pane of the Preferences dialog box. You can use the Align to Baseline Grid option in a paragraph style or through the Paragraph pane (Type ➪ Paragraph, or Option+⌘+T or Ctrl+Alt+T) to lock the baselines of text in selected paragraphs to baseline grid lines, and you can modify a document's baseline grid through the Grids pane in the Preferences dialog box.

Tip   In addition to aligning objects with guides, you can also use the arrow keys to nudge items when precise positioning is required. This method works well when you're positioning an object relative to another object rather than aligning the object with a grid line. Each press of an arrow key moves the selected objects 1 point. If you press and hold Shift when nudging, the increment is 10 points. You can set alternative nudge settings with the Cursor Key field in the Units & Increments pane of the Preferences dialog box. Pressing and holding Shift when nudging moves the selected objects 10 increments of whatever the Cursor Key is set to.

Summary

When it comes to working with the objects you've placed on a page, InDesign provides several timesaving features. You can create a single copy of any object using the Copy and Paste commands (Edit menu), using the Duplicate command (Edit menu), or by Option+dragging or Alt+dragging a clone of the original. The Step and Repeat command (Edit menu) lets you create multiple copies of objects and position the copies relative to the originals. The Paste in Place command pastes on object on a new page at the same X and Y coordinates as the original object.

The Align pane (Window ➪ Object & Layout ➪ Align or Shift+F7) lets you align multiple objects and control the amount of space between them, while vertical and horizontal ruler guides and snap-to-grid features help you accurately position and align items.

✦   ✦   ✦

Text Fundamentals

Preparing Text Files for Import

♦   ♦   ♦   ♦

In This Chapter

Determining which formatting tasks to do in InDesign

Working with files across platforms

Preparing files for import from word processors and spreadsheets

Working with special file formats

♦   ♦   ♦   ♦

You can import text into your InDesign documents in several ways. InDesign is particularly adept at importing documents created in popular Macintosh and Windows formats. And through the use of the Macintosh and Windows clipboards (copy and paste), you can import file formats — to a limited degree — that are not directly supported by InDesign.

Determining Where to Format Documents

InDesign import capabilities may tempt you to do a lot of your text formatting outside the program; however, it's not always wise to do so.

Because a word processor's formatting capabilities won't match all InDesign typographic features, it's often not worthwhile to do extensive formatting in your word processor. This is particularly true of layout-oriented formatting. Multiple columns and page numbers, for example, will be of a much higher standard in your final InDesign document than you could hope to create in a word processor. After all, even the sophisticated formatting features in today's word processors don't begin to approach those needed for true publishing.

It used to be true that more sophisticated formatting, such as tables, was ignored by layout programs during file import, but that is no longer true. So you can produce your tables, footnotes, and even paragraph styles in Microsoft Word. However, I would not spend much time on such formatting, because you'll want to use InDesign's more sophisticated tools. Use InDesign for your layout and complex text formatting (fonts, leading, and hyphenation), and use your word processor for basic table setup (leave the high-end formatting to InDesign), footnotes, basic text editing, paragraph style assignments (identifying headlines, body copy, and so forth), and basic character formatting (boldface, italics, and other meaning-oriented formatting).

Working with Files Across Platforms

It's very common for people in publishing to work in a cross-platform (Mac and Windows) environment. Even if you do all your InDesign work on one platform, chances are high that you'll receive files created on the other platform. (Most text editing is done on PCs, while most graphics and publishing work is done on the Mac, for example.)

Even with the improved compatibility between Mac and PC (mostly thanks to additions to the Mac OS that make it easier to share files with PCs), you may still encounter some trip-ups dealing with something as simple as filenames when sharing files across platforms.

Both Windows and the Mac OS use icons to show you (and tell programs) what format a file is in. Windows and Mac OS X (but not earlier versions of the Mac OS) use filename extensions (often hidden from user view) to identify the file type. InDesign uses the filename extension .indd to denote InDesign documents. Without this filename extension, you won't be able to double-click a file icon to open it, although you can still open the file from InDesign's Open dialog box (File ⇨ Open, or ⌘+O or Ctrl+O), as long as you select All Documents from the Enable pop-up menu (on the Mac) or All Files from the Files of Type pop-up menu (in Windows). Note that the Place dialog box for importing text and graphics does not have the Enable pop-up menu on the Mac; InDesign for Mac will show all files, even unsupported ones, in this dialog box.

If filename extensions are hidden in Windows, click Tools ⇨ Folder Options and then select the View tab to make the pane shown in the following figure appear. (You have to have a disk or folder open to have the View menu.) Deselect the Hide Extensions for Known File Types option, and then click OK.

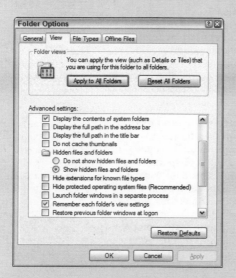

If filename extensions are hidden in Mac OS X, click Finder ⇨ Preferences, and then click the Always Show File Extensions option, as shown in the following figure, and close the dialog box. (You have to be using the Finder, not be in an application, to get this menu,

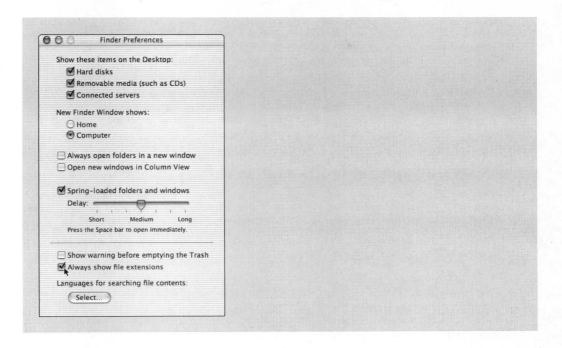

Importing Text Files

What preparation do you possibly need to do for your word processor files? They should just load into InDesign as is, right? Not necessarily, even if your word processor supports one of the InDesign text-import formats. Actually, the key to preparing text files is to not *over*prepare them.

Most of today's major word processors include basic graphics and layout features to help users format single-document publications. Avoid using these features in files you intend to bring into InDesign. Do your sophisticated formatting in InDesign — that's one of the reasons you invested in such a powerful tool. This approach also lets you do formatting in the context of your layout, rather than in a vacuum. Much of the graphics and layout formatting you do in a word processor is all for naught anyway because most such nontextual formatting does not import into InDesign — you're importing text, not documents. (Exceptions include footnotes and sidebars, which InDesign CS2 now supports from Word.)

Tip   Limit your word processor formatting to the type of formatting that enhances reader understanding or conveys meaning. Such formatting may include using italic and boldface to emphasize a word, for example, or using style sheets to set headlines and bylines in different sizes and typefaces. (See Chapter 19 for tips on using style sheets in word processor text.) Let your editors focus on the words; leave presentation tasks to your layout artists.

One type of file preparation you may need to do is to translate text files into formats supported by InDesign. InDesign supports just Microsoft Word, Rich Text Format (RTF), and text-only

(ASCII) formats. If you use Corel WordPerfect or AppleWorks, you'll need to save in one of those supported formats. Where possible, you should save in Microsoft Word format (up through the Office 11 version), because InDesign supports more Word formatting capabilities than it does RTF capabilities, and the text-only format preserves no formatting.

Note InDesign also imports InCopy files. InCopy is an Adobe text editor available only from publishing systems integrators who set up entire newsrooms, magazines, and other companies with large numbers of users to base their publication operations on InDesign. Appendix E covers InCopy in more detail.

Preserving special features in text files

Today's word processors let you do much more than type and edit text. You also can create special characters, tables, headers and footers, and other document elements. Some of these features work when imported into a publishing program, but others don't.

InDesign imports the following Word formatting (from Mac version 98 and later and from Windows version 97 and later):

✦ All caps

✦ Boldface

✦ Color

✦ Condense/expand

✦ Drop caps

✦ Font

✦ Footnotes and endnotes

✦ Indents

✦ Index and table-of-contents text

✦ Inline graphics (if in an InDesign-supported format)

✦ Italics

✦ Outline

✦ Page breaks

✦ Paragraph and character style sheets

✦ Point size

✦ Small caps

✦ Strikethrough

✦ Subscripts and superscripts

✦ Tables

✦ Text boxes, including any follow-me links to them

✦ Underlines

New Feature Newly supported text attributes in InDesign CS2 for importing include character style sheets and anchored text boxes, which also adds enhanced controls over style sheet import, as covered in Chapter 14.

The following formats are partially supported or are converted during import:

✦ Bulleted lists (bullets are retained but they are no longer automatic bullets)

✦ Double strikethrough (converted to single strikethrough)

✦ Double underline (converted to single underlines)

✦ Embossed text (made into paper color, usually white)

✦ Engraved text (made into paper color, usually white)

✦ Numbered lists (numbers are retained but they are no longer automatic numbers)

✦ Redlining/revisions (converted to underline for additions and to strikethrough for deletions)

✦ Word-only underline (converted to single underlines, including for spaces and punctuation)

The following format is not supported, and any text using it is imported as plain text:

✦ Shadow

The following formats are not supported, and any text using them is removed during import:

✦ Annotations and comments

✦ Hidden text

✦ Section breaks

✦ Subscribed/OLE items

Tables

Word processors have developed very capable table editors, letting you format tabular information quickly and easily — and often rivaling dedicated spreadsheet programs. InDesign is rare in the world of page-layout programs in that it can import tables created in Word or Excel, as well as tables in RTF documents.

QuarkXPress User InDesign does a good job of importing Word tables and Excel spreadsheets as tables, unlike QuarkXPress 6.0 and earlier. (Note that QuarkXPress 6.1 added support for importing such tables from Excel.)

Cross-Reference Chapter 20 covers tables in depth.

Headers and footers

Headers and footers are a layout issue, not a text issue, so there is no reason to include these elements in your word-processor document. Because page numbers will change based on your InDesign layout, there's no point in putting the headers and footers in your word processor document anyway. Note that if you do use them, they will not import into InDesign.

Chapter 5 explains how to add headers and footers to your layout.

Footnotes and endnotes

If you use a word processor's footnote or endnote feature and import the text file, the notes are placed at the end of the imported text. The superscripted numerals or characters in the notes usually translate properly.

InDesign CS2 now imports footnotes from Word and lets you control their layout and formatting in InDesign. Chapter 32 covers footnotes in depth.

Hyperlinks

Modern word processors, such as Word, let you include hyperlinks in their text, so when you export to HTML or PDF, the reader can click the link and jump to a Web page or to another PDF file. When you import text files with such hyperlinks, InDesign will retain their visual formatting — hyperlinks usually display as blue underlined text — as well as the actual link.

InDesign retains hyperlinks for documents that are exported as PDF files. Chapter 33 covers such documents in more detail.

Inline graphics and text boxes

Modern word processors typically support inline graphics, enabling you to import a picture into your word-processor document and embed it in text. Word, for example, lets you import graphics, and InDesign, in turn, can import the graphics with your text — as long as they are in formats supported by InDesign. But graphics embedded in your word-processor document through Mac OS 9's Publish and Subscribe or through OLE (Object Linking and Embedding, available in Windows and Mac OS) will *not* import into InDesign.

InDesign also will import text boxes from a Word file (these are usually used for sidebars, captions, and pull-quotes) as separate text frames. If those Word text boxes are tied to a specific piece of text, so they flow with that text, InDesign will honor those follow-me links and let you adjust them.

The support for follow-me links and for importing Word text boxes is new to InDesign CS2. Chapter 11 covers follow-me links and related anchoring features in more detail.

Using Special Characters

The Mac and Windows both have built-in support for special characters, such as symbols, accented characters, and non-English letters. There are several ways to access these characters:

✦ **On both platforms, using keyboard shortcuts (see Chapter 41).**

✦ **On the Mac, your options depend on the version of Mac OS X you are using:**

- **In Mac OS X 10.2 (Jaguar) and earlier, use Apple's Key Caps program, which is located in the Applications\Utilities folder.** The following figure shows the program. The two sets of special characters are found by pressing Option and Option+Shift (each results in a different set). Some fonts also have symbols accessible by pressing the Control key. Use the Fonts menu, as shown in the figure, to change fonts in Key Caps, in case a symbol you want is available in a font other than the one currently in use.

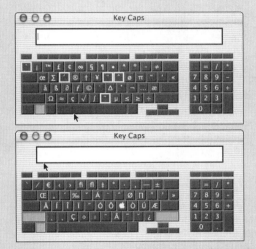

- **In Mac OS X 10.3 (Panther and later), use the Keyboard Viewer or Character Palette. Both are available under the Keyboard Input menu item.** Note that the Keyboard Input menu item may need to be turned on by choosing ⌘ ⇨ System Preferences, and then going to the International control panel's Input Menu pane. Select the Show Input Menu in Menu Bar option.

Continued

✦ **On both platforms, using a shareware utility like Günther Blaschek's PopChar control panel, which adds a quick-access icon to the Mac and Windows menu bars.** The following figure shows PopChar X, the Mac version. Notice how the keyboard shortcut for each special character is shown at the bottom right as a character is highlighted. (The companion Web site, www.InDesignCentral.com, has links to this and other utilities.)

✦ **On Windows, using the Character Map utility that comes with Windows.** The following figure shows the program. Character Map is usually installed in the Windows Start menu (Start ⇨ Programs ⇨ Accessories ⇨ System Tools ⇨ Character Map).

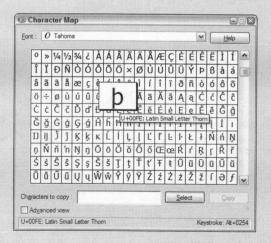

On both platforms, you can use a word processor's own feature for special character access. Microsoft Word, for example, has such an option (as the following figure shows) by clicking Insert ⇨ Symbol or through the toolbar (if you added this command to your toolbar, look for the button with the Ω character). WordPerfect has a similar dialog box accessed by clicking Insert ⇨ Symbols (Mac) or Insert ⇨ Character (Windows). (InDesign has its own dialog box like this for when you're adding symbols to your text from within your layout; access it by clicking Type ⇨ Glyphs.)

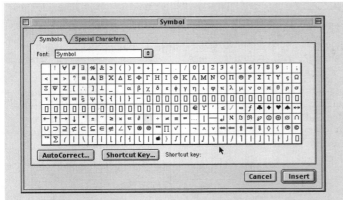

Some fonts may not have all special characters available. Typically, fonts from major type foundries like Adobe and Monotype have all the characters in each font, but custom-made fonts and those from other foundries may use different characters or have fewer. Also, fonts translated from Windows to the Mac, or vice versa, through a program like Pyrus FontLab, will likely have special characters in different locations than a native Mac or Windows font; Windows PostScript fonts generally have fewer special characters in the font than their Mac counterparts.

Avoiding text-file pitfalls

Sometimes, issues not related to the contents of a word-processor file can affect how files are imported into InDesign.

Fast save

Several programs (notably Microsoft Word) offer a fast-save feature, which adds information to the end of a word-processor document. The added information notes which text has been added and deleted and where the changes occurred. You can use this feature to save time because the program doesn't have to write the entire document to disk when you save the file. When you use the fast-save feature, however, text import into publishing programs — including InDesign — becomes problematic. I suggest that you turn off fast save, at least for files you import into InDesign. With today's speedy hard drives, the time you gain by using fast save is barely noticeable anyway. The vast majority of file corruption problems and bugs in Word are related to the fast-save feature and that its use makes file recovery in the event of a crash problematic at best. To disable fast save in word, click Tools ➪ Options, go to the Save pane, and deselect the Allow Fast Saves option.

Software versions

Pay attention to the version number of the word processor you use. This caution may seem obvious, but the issue still trips up a lot of people. Usually, old versions (two or more revisions old) or new versions (newer than the publishing or other importing program) cause import problems. The import filters either no longer recognize the old format (something has to go to make room for new formats) or were written before the new version of the word processor was released. InDesign supports Microsoft Word for Windows versions 97, 2000, XP, and 2003, and Microsoft Word for Mac versions 98, 2001, X, and 2004, as well as the same-numbered versions of Excel.

Fixing Microsoft Word's Bad Dashes

Most versions of Word have a default setting that converts two hyphens to an en dash (–) rather than an em dash (—), which is simply wrong typographically. (Word 98 for Mac and Word 2002/XP for Windows *don't* have this problem.)

To solve this problem, I recommend that you turn off Word's automatic conversion of two hyphens to a dash (choose Tools ⇨ AutoCorrect ⇨ AutoFormat as You Type). Instead, type two hyphens in the Replace box in the AutoCorrect dialog box's AutoCorrect pane and put an em dash (shortcut Option+Shift+– [hyphen] on the Mac or Alt+0151 in Windows) in the With box, and then click Add. This causes Word to substitute the correct dash when you type two consecutive hyphens.

Using Tagged Text

InDesign offers a file format of its own: Adobe InDesign Tagged Text. Tagged Text actually is ASCII (text-only) text that contains embedded codes to tell InDesign which formatting to apply. You embed these codes, which are similar to macros, as you create files in your word processor.

No matter what layout program they use, most people don't use the tagged-text option because the coding can be tortuous. Because you can't use tagged-text codes with your word processor's formatting, you must code everything with tagged text and save the document as an ASCII file. So why have Tagged Text at all? Because this format is the one format sure to support all the formatting you do in InDesign.

Working with exported Tagged Text files

The usefulness of Tagged Text is not in creating text for import, but in transferring files created in InDesign to another InDesign user (including someone working on another platform) or to a word processor for further work. You can export an InDesign story or piece of selected text in the Tagged Text format, and then transfer the exported file to another InDesign user or to a word processor for further editing.

Exporting a Tagged Text file into a word processor makes sense if you want to add or delete text without losing special formatting — such as fonts, kerning, or styles — that your word processor doesn't support. After you edit the text, you can save the altered file (make sure that it is saved as ASCII text) and reimport it into your InDesign layout.

The best way to understand the Tagged Text format is to export some of your own documents to it, and open the resulting file in a word processor to see how InDesign coded the file. A warning: The Tagged Text format can be complex, especially because most codes have two forms: a short (abbreviated) form and a long (verbose) form — you choose which InDesign exports from the Export dialog box in InDesign (File ⇨ Export, then choose InDesign Tagged Text as the file format). Note that a Tagged Text file is simply an ASCII text file, so it will have the filename extension .txt and use the standard text-only file icon in Windows and on the Mac.

Here's an example of verbose coding (because the code is so long, I had to add line breaks; slightly indented lines are actually part of the same code segment):

```
<ASCII-WIN>
<DefineParaStyle:Normal=<Nextstyle:Normal><cTypeface:Regular>
    <cSize:10.000000><pHyphenationLadderLimit:0><pHyphenation:0>
    <pHyphenationZone:18.000000><cFont:Times New Roman>
    <cColorTint:100.000000>>
<DefineCharStyle:Default Paragraph Font=<Nextstyle:Default Paragraph Font>>
<DefineCharStyle:Hyperlink=<BasedOn:Default Paragraph Font>
    <Nextstyle:Hyperlink><cColor:Blue><cTypeface:Regular>
    <cSize:10.000000><cHorizontalScale:1.000000><cBaselineShift:0.000000>
    <cCase:Normal><cStrokeColor:><cUnderline:1><cFont:Times New Roman>
    <cPosition:Normal><cStrikethru:0><cColorTint:100.000000>>
<ColorTable:=<Black:COLOR:CMYK:Process:0.000000,0.000000,0.000000,1.000000>
    <Blue:COLOR:RGB:Process:0.000000,0.000000,1.000000>>
<ParaStyle:Normal><pHyphenation:1><CharStyle:Default Paragraph Font>
    <CharStyle:><CharStyle:Hyperlink>www.adobe.com<CharStyle:>
    <CharStyle:Default Paragraph Font>. <CharStyle:><pHyphenation:>
```

Here is the same text with abbreviated tags:

```
<ASCII-WIN>
<dps:Normal=<Nextstyle:Normal><ct:Regular><cs:10.000000><phll:0><ph:0>
    <phz:18.000000><cf:Times New Roman><cct:100.000000>>
<dcs:Default Paragraph Font=<Nextstyle:Default Paragraph Font>>
<dcs:Hyperlink=<BasedOn:Default Paragraph Font><Nextstyle:Hyperlink>
    <cc:Blue><ct:Regular><cs:10.000000><chs:1.000000><cbs:0.000000>
    <ccase:Normal><csc:><cu:1><cf:Times New Roman><cp:Normal><cstrike:0>
    <cct:100.000000>>
<ctable:=<Black:COLOR:CMYK:Process:0.000000,0.000000,0.000000,1.000000>
    <Blue:COLOR:RGB:Process:0.000000,0.000000,1.000000>>
<pstyle:Normal><ph:1><cstyle:Default Paragraph Font> <cstyle:>
    <cstyle:Hyperlink>www.adobe.com<cstyle:><cstyle:Default Paragraph
    Font>. <cstyle:><ph:>
```

What does all that coding mean? Well, that's for a one-page document with one frame that has simply one line of text:

```
This is a hyperlink to www.adobe.com.
```

The text is black, except for the Web address, which is in blue underline.

As you can see, there's a lot to Tagged Text codes. InDesign comes with a complete list of codes in a PDF file called Tagged Text.pdf that you'll find in the Tagged Text folder within the Adobe Technical Info folder on the InDesign CD-ROM.

In practical terms, you may not mind editing Tagged Text slightly or leaving the tags in a file when you alter the files text. But you're not likely to forgo the friendly formatting available in your word processor and in InDesign to apply Tagged Text coding to everything in your text files.

Using Tagged Text for database publishing

Tagged Text format can be very handy as a start to database publishing. The codes in the preceding section define the formatting in a document. However, you don't need to go that far; you can simply *specify* paragraph tags using Tagged Text, so when text is imported into an

InDesign document, InDesign knows what styles to apply. (The styles, of course, need to be already defined in that document.) You would use this technique to import data gathered by, for example, a Web-based survey page or exported from a database. By placing the Tagged Text codes before each paragraph, you will save the effort of manually tagging every paragraph in InDesign.

For example, say you have a product directory that lists the company name, URL, and product description. You'd have a text file with entries that look something like this:

```
<ASCII-WIN>
<pstyle:Company>Name 1
<pstyle:URL>Web address 1
<pstyle:Description>Descriptive text 1 goes here.
<pstyle:Company>Name 2
<pstyle:URL>Web address 2
<pstyle:Description>Descriptive text 2 goes here.
```

The `<ASCII-WIN>` (or `<ASCII-MAC>` if the file was created on a Mac) code appears only at the top of the file. The code `<pstyle:style name>` specifies the paragraph style to apply (for character styles, the code is `<cstyle:style name>`)—be sure that the name is an exact match, including any capitalization; otherwise, InDesign won't recognize the style you want to use.

To use text coded this way, you open an existing document that is already set up with text frames and text styles, then place the text file into the document. The tagged text will take on the designated styles, making it easy, for example, to flow an updated catalog into a template. Figure 13-1 shows a document created this way.

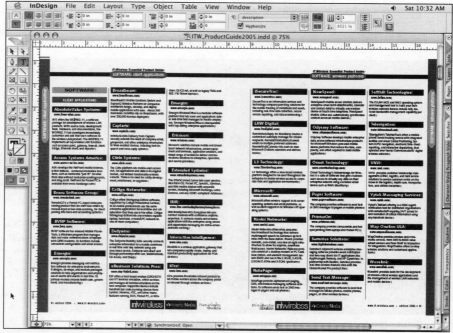

Figure 13-1: A catalog created by importing a Tagged Text file

Summary

Because today's word processors are so powerful, there's a temptation to do a lot of sophisticated, layout-oriented formatting in them before bringing the files into a layout program like InDesign. But don't. No word processor has the typographic or layout ability of InDesign, and doing a lot of work in your word processing file is simply a waste of time — you'd need to do it over again in InDesign in the context of your layout anyhow.

Focus on the meaning-oriented formatting in your word processor: use of style sheets to indicate headlines, bylines, quotation blocks, and so on, as well as local formatting like italics, superscripts, and font changes.

When you're done preparing your text, be sure to save it in a format compatible with InDesign. Even if your word processor format is not compatible with InDesign, chances are it can save in one that is.

Finally, consider using the Tagged Text format to specify sophisticated formatting, such as defining paragraph and character styles in InDesign, in your word processor. This requires a familiarity with programming or coding in formats like HTML but can be a powerful way to add formatting for highly predictable, structured documents in your word processor before importing the file into InDesign. Using it just to specify paragraph and style sheets is a great way to bring database-oriented data, such as catalogs, into an InDesign template.

✦   ✦   ✦

Working with Text

Although you can use InDesign as your primary word processor, doing so is a little like buying a Hummer for suburban errands — glamorous but unnecessary. In publishing, at least the first draft of text is generally written in Microsoft Word because this word processing program offers many editorial bells and whistles. Text is then imported into an InDesign publication.

But that doesn't mean you shouldn't do word-processor functions in InDesign. It makes a lot of sense to write captions, headlines, and other elements that need to fit a restricted area, as well as to do copy editing and minor revisions. InDesign lets you do such writing and editing in the actual layout, or in a built-in text editor that mimics the Mac's TextEdit or Windows' WordPad, except it does layout-specific things for you as well, such as tracking line counts for you.

Either way, you'll extensively use InDesign's editing, search and replace functions, and spell checker to refine your content.

Adding Text

No matter where your text originates — in your mind, in e-mail, on the Web, or in a word processor — you can add it to an InDesign publication easily. You can type text directly in InDesign, paste it, drag and drop it, or import it.

InDesign works with text inside *frames* — holders for the copy — that you can create in advance or let InDesign create for you when you import text.

Typing text

First, you can't do anything with text without the Type tool. Once the Type tool is selected, as shown in Figure 14-1, you can click in an existing block of text, or click and drag to create a new text frame. You can even click in any empty graphics frame or unassigned frame with the Type tool to convert it to a text frame.

Note   What you can't do is simply click in your document and begin typing, as you can in PageMaker. InDesign is like other page-layout programs in that the text must be in a frame. Fortunately, you can create that frame just by clicking and dragging with the Type tool.

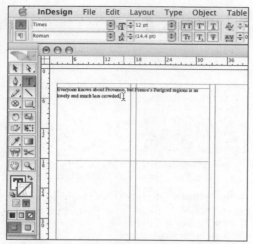

Figure 14-1: When the Type tool is selected, you can click in a text frame and start typing.

From this point, start typing to enter text.

Tip   You can't click in *master text frames* — text frames that are placed on the page by the master page in use — and simply start typing. To select a master text frame and add text to it, Shift+⌘+click or Ctrl+Shift+click it. (For more on master pages, see Chapter 7.)

When you type new text, it takes on whatever style attributes are set for [Basic Paragraph Style], a predefined style in InDesign. You can modify this predefined style as you can any style you create.

Cross-Reference   Chapter 19 covers styles in more detail.

Pasting text

When text is on the Mac or Windows Clipboard, you can paste it at the location of the cursor (text-insertion pointer) or replace highlighted text with it. If no text frame is active, InDesign creates a new rectangular text frame to contain the pasted text.

InDesign uses standard menu commands and keyboard commands for cutting and copying text to the Clipboard, and for pasting text. On the Mac, press ⌘+X to cut, ⌘+C to copy, and ⌘+V to paste. In Windows, press Ctrl+X to cut, Ctrl+C to copy, and Ctrl+V to paste.

Text that is cut or copied from InDesign normally retains its formatting, while text pasted from other programs normally loses its formatting. (Text pasted from other programs always retains its special characters such as curly quotes, em dashes, and accented characters.) In InDesign, you can specify while you are pasting text whether it retains its formatting. Choose Edit ➪ Paste without Formatting (Shift+⌘+V or Ctrl+Shift+V) to lose the formatting, so

Keep Characters to a Minimum

If you're new to professional publishing, you have a few things to learn about the difference between typing on a typewriter or into a word processor and entering text for a high-end publication:

- ✦ Remember that there's no need to type two spaces after a period or colon. In fact, it will cause awkward spacing and perhaps even text-flow issues.

- ✦ Don't enter extra paragraph returns for space between paragraphs and don't enter tabs to indent paragraphs — you'll accomplish both more consistently with paragraph attributes (Type ➪ Paragraph, or Option+⌘+T or Ctrl+Alt+T).

- ✦ When you need to align text in columns, don't enter extra tabs; place one tab between each column, and then align the tabs (Type ➪ Tabs, or Shift+⌘+T or Ctrl+Shift+T).

To see where you have tabs, paragraph breaks, spaces, and other such invisible characters, use the command Option+⌘+I or Ctrl+Alt+I, or choose Type ➪ Show Hidden Characters, as the following figure shows.

Program Change Highlights for Adobe Open Options 3.0¶

¶

- • NEW! SPECIAL DISCOUNT FOR HIGH-VOLUME ORDERS OF ADOBE ACROBAT® SOFTWARE¶
- • NEW! EXCLUSIVE AVAILABILITY OF ADOBE ACROBAT ELEMENTS SOFTWARE¶
- • DISCONTINUED! ADOBE ACROBAT SITE LICENSE PROGRAM¶

Q. What are the benefits of Adobe Open Options 3.0?¶

A. Adobe Open Options® 3.0 volume software licensing programs streamline the procurement of licenses for the Adobe Acrobat product family. The new Adobe Acrobat Elements software is exclusively available through the Transactional License Program (TLP) and the Contractual License Program (CLP). These programs are the only venue for acquiring licenses of this new, essential PDF-creation tool for corporations and business users who do not need full Acrobat functionality. A minimum initial order of 1,000 licenses of Acrobat Elements is required. For Acrobat users who need more than PDF creation, Adobe Acrobat 6.0 Standard and Acrobat 6.0 Professional software will also be available under the TLP and CLP.¶

Adobe will offer corporate customers special high-volume discounts on orders of 1,000 or more units of new licenses and maintenance of Acrobat 6.0 Professional, Acrobat 6.0 Standard, or Acrobat Elements, when ordered in a single transaction under the CLP. This offer replaces the former Adobe Acrobat Site License Program (SLP) previously available to corporations and government entities; however, the SLP remains available to education customers. The order must be for one of the products in the Acrobat product family, on one line item in the order; different product titles and Maintenance Program orders cannot be combined to meet the 1,000-unit order minimum.¶

Q. How do I qualify for the Acrobat high-volume discounts?¶

InDesign instead applies the formatting of the text at your insertion point, or choose the standard Edit ➪ Paste (⌘+V or Ctrl+V) to keep InDesign's default paste behavior.

New Feature   The Paste without Formatting option is new to InDesign CS2.

To change the default behavior of copying just plain text from other applications, go to the File Handling pane in the Preferences dialog box (choose InDesign ➪ Preferences on the Mac or Edit ➪ Preferences in Windows, or press ⌘+K or Ctrl+K) and select the All Information (Index Marker, Swatches, Styles, Etc.) option at the bottom of the pane.

New Feature   This All Information option replaces the Preserve Text Attributes When Pasting option that used to reside in the General pane.

Also, when you paste text, InDesign is smart enough to know to remove extra spaces or add them around the pasted text. You can disable this by deselecting the Adjust Spacing Automatically When Cutting and Pasting Words option in the Type pane of the Preferences dialog box.

New Feature   Automatic spacing adjustment is new to InDesign CS2.

Dragging and dropping text

If you're the kind of person who likes to juggle many open windows and applications, you can drag highlighted text from other programs — or even text files from the desktop or a folder — into an InDesign document. As with pasted text, text that you drag and drop is inserted at the location of the cursor, replaces highlighted text, or is placed in a new rectangular text frame.

Cross-Reference   Text files that are dragged in must be in a supported format: Microsoft Word 97/98 or later, Excel 97/98 or later, Rich Text Format (RTF), or text only. Chapter 13 covers this in detail.

When you drag and drop a text selection, its formatting is lost (that's because InDesign assumes you want it to take on the attributes of the text you're inserting it into). However, when you drag and drop a text file, the process is treated more like a text import: The text retains its formatting and it brings its style sheets with it. Unlike using the Place command (File ➪ Place, or ⌘+D or Ctrl+D) to import text, drag and drop does not give you the option to specify how some of the formatting and styles in the text file are handled.

Importing text

If the text for your InDesign publication was created in a word processor, you can import it, with many styles intact, into a publication if it's in Word 97/98 or later or in the Rich Text Format (RTF). You can also import ASCII text files and Tagged Text files. (See Chapter 13 for more details.)

When you import text using the Place dialog box, shown in Figure 14-2, it's placed according to your current selection:

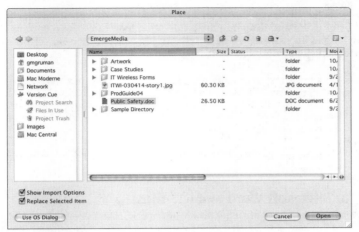

Figure 14-2: The Place dialog box

✦ If the text-insertion pointer is within text in a text frame, the text is inserted at that location.

✦ If a text frame is selected but you have not clicked within the frame's text, the text is imported into the frame, replacing any existing text. If two or more text frames are selected, a loaded-text icon appears instead.

✦ If no text frames are selected, a loaded-text icon (shown in Figure 14-3) lets you draw a rectangular text frame to contain the text or click in an existing empty frame or text frame.

Figure 14-3: The loaded-text icon (left). There are two variants — autoflow (center; press and hold Shift) and semiautoflow (right; press and hold Option or Alt) — that let text flow to other frames during import.

To place text:

1. **Choose File ➪ Place, or press ⌘+D or Ctrl+D.**

2. **Locate the text file you want to import.**

3. **If you want to specify how to handle current formatting in the file, select the Place dialog box's Show Import Options option, shown in Figure 14-2, and click Open.** This opens the appropriate Import Options dialog box for the text file's format. Then click OK to import the graphic. (I cover the Import Options dialog box a little later in this section.) If you don't select the Show Import Options option, clicking Open will import the graphic using default settings.

Tip

If you prefer memorizing keyboard commands to simply checking boxes, press Shift while you open the file to display the import options.

4. **If you had not selected a frame before starting the text import, specify where to place the text by clicking and dragging the loaded-text icon to create a rectangular text frame, clicking in an existing frame, or clicking in any empty frame.** To cancel the text import, just select a different tool.

Caution

If you click a frame that holds text or a graphic when importing text, the text will replace the existing text or graphic.

Cross-Reference

If all the text you import doesn't fit in the selected text frame, see the "Threading Text Frames" section in Chapter 15 for more information on how to make it flow to other text frames.

Import options for Microsoft Word and RTF files

InDesign offers a slew of options for controlling how Word and RTF files are imported. There are so many options that you can actually save your import preferences as a preset file for repeat use.

Figure 14-4 shows the Import Options dialog box for Microsoft Word. It has four groups of options. (The import options for RTF files are identical.)

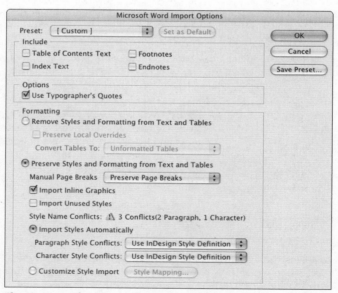

Figure 14-4: The Microsoft Word Import Options dialog box

At the top of the pane is the Preset pop-up menu, which lets you select from saved sets of import options. (If you change any options in this dialog box, the pop-up menu will show [Custom], so you know that any selected preset's settings have been altered for this specific file import. You can save settings by clicking Save Preset. And you can set a preset as the default import behavior by clicking Save as Default; these settings will be used for all Word file imports unless you choose a new default or make changes in this dialog box. This lets you avoid using the Import Options dialog box for your routine imports.

New Feature The ability to save import presets is new to InDesign CS2 and is available only for Word and RTF import.

The next section, Include, lets you strip out specific types of text from the Word file: Table of Contents Text, Index Text, Footnotes, and Endnotes. Any selected items will be imported. It's common *not* to import table-of-contents or index text because you typically create your TOCs and indexes in InDesign.

The third section, Options, has just one option: Use Typographer's Quotes. If selected, it converts keyboard quotes (' and ") to the curly typographer quotes (', ', ", and ").

QuarkXPress User Unlike other layout programs, InDesign does *not* translate two consecutive hyphens (--) into an em dash (—) when you import text, even if you select the Use Typographer's Quotes option. Fortunately, many modern word processors translate two hyphens to an em dash as you type, so the chances of having two consecutive hyphens from recently created documents are slim. (In Word, use Tools ⇨ AutoCorrect to enable this feature; in WordPerfect, use Tools ⇨ QuickCorrect. Chapter 13 covers this in more detail.)

The fourth section, Formatting, is fairly complex.

To remove text formatting during import, so you have fresh text to which you can apply your InDesign styles, select the Remove Styles and Formatting option from Formatting section. Two additional controls become available if you select this option:

✦ **Preserve Local Overrides.** Selecting this option retains local formatting such as italics and boldface while ignoring the paragraph style attributes. You'd usually want this selected so meaning-related formatting is retained.

✦ **Convert Tables To.** You can use this pop-up menu to choose how tables are unformatted during import. The Unformatted Tables menu item retains the table's cell structure but ignores text and cell formatting, while the Unformatted Tabbed Text menu item converts the table to tabbed text (with a tab separating what used to be cells and a paragraph return separating what used to be rows) and strips out any formatting. If you intend to keep tables as tables but format them in InDesign, choose Unformatted Tables.

New Feature The two controls for handling unformatting are new to InDesign CS2.

To retain text formatting during import, so the InDesign document at least starts out using the settings done in Word, select the Preserve Styles from Text and Tables option. There are two reasons to select this option. The most common reason is because you are using style sheets in Word with the same names as in InDesign. This saves your designers from having to manually apply the correct styles when working on layouts (the editors basically do it in Word when editing). The other reasons is your Word file is really a rough template of your eventual InDesign file, so you want to keep all that Word effort and use it as the basis for refinement in InDesign.

There are several controls for this option:

✦ **Manual Page Breaks.** This pop-up menu lets you retain page breaks entered in Word, convert them to column breaks, or strip them out. The break option you choose will depend on how your layout is structured compared to the Word file's layout.

✦ **Import Inline Graphics.** This option, if selected, will import graphics placed in the Word text. (Chapter 11 covers inline graphics in more detail.)

✦ **Import Unused Styles.** This option, if selected, loads all Word style sheets into InDesign, rather than just the ones you actually applied to text in the file. You normally would not want to import all of Word's styles because the program has dozens of predefined styles that will clog up your InDesign Paragraph Styles and Character Styles panes.

✦ **Style Name Conflicts:** If InDesign detects that the Word file has a style with the same name as your InDesign document, it will note how many to the right of the Style Name Conflicts label. (Note that word uses the term *style sheet* while InDesign uses the term *style;* they mean the same thing.) You then have two ways of handling these conflicts:

• If you select the Import Styles Automatically option you get three options for both paragraph and character styles, using the two separate pop-up menus (Paragraph Style Conflicts and Character Style Conflicts). The Use InDesign Style Definition menu item preserves the current InDesign styles and applies them to any text in Word that uses a style sheet of the same name. This is the most common option because it lets your editors indicate what styles to use in InDesign but relies on InDesign's more precise typographic settings. If you choose the Redefine InDesign Style menu item, the Word style sheet's formatting permanently replaces that of InDesign's style. If you choose the Auto Rename menu item, the Word file's style sheet will be renamed and added to the Paragraph Styles or Character Styles pane. This preserves your existing InDesign styles while also preserving the ones imported from the Word file.

• If you select the Customize Style Import option, you can decide which specific InDesign styles override same-name Word styles, which Word styles override same-name InDesign styles, and which Word styles are renamed during import to prevent any overriding. Click Style Mapping to open the Custom Style Mapping dialog box shown in Figure 14-5, where you make these decisions. You can also click Auto-Rename Conflicts in that dialog box to rename all conflicting Word styles to new names. (This is the same as choosing Auto Rename in the Import Styles Automatically pop-up menus.)

New Feature   All these options are new to InDesign CS2 except for the Manual Page Breaks pop-up menu.

Import options for text-only files

The options for text-only (ASCII) files are much simpler, as Figure 14-6 shows:

✦ **Character Set pop-up menu.** This lets you change the encoding type for the text file. There are 18 options, mainly for various languages and language groups such as Chinese, Central European, Greek, Baltic, and Japanese. In most cases, you leave the menu at its default of ANSI, which is what most North American PCs and Macs are set to. Choose another option only if you know the file is encoded in something else.

✦ **Platform pop-up menu.** This lets you choose between Macintosh and Windows. Choose whichever is appropriate for the source file. The biggest differences are in how paragraph returns are specified and in some supported special characters.

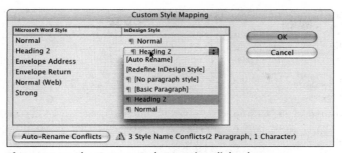

Figure 14-5: The Custom Style Mapping dialog box

✦ **Set Dictionary to pop-up menu.** This lets you assign the default spelling and hyphen-ation dictionary language. Unless you're publishing in multiple languages or regions (such as in English for use in the U.K., Canada, and the U.S.), you can leave this at the default setting, which is based on the language you selected when you installed InDesign.

✦ **Extra Carriage Returns.** In this section, you can control how carriage returns are handled. Select the Remove at End of Every Line option if the source file has a return at the end of each line (often the result of copying text from the Web or from a PDF file). Select the Remove Between Paragraphs option if the source file uses two hard returns to indicate new paragraphs. You can select neither, one, or both as appropriate to your source file.

✦ **Formatting.** In this section, you can select the Replace option to have several consecu-tive spaces converted to a tab (you specify the minimum number of spaces in the field that follows). You can also select the Use Typographer's Quotes option to convert key-board quotes (' and ") to the curly typographer quotes (', ', ", and "). This option is normally selected.

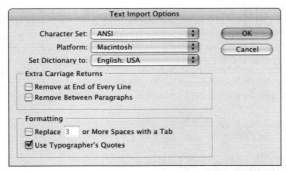

Figure 14-6: The Text Import Options dialog box for a text-only file

Import options for Microsoft Excel files

When importing Excel spreadsheets, you have several options, as Figure 14-7 shows.

In the Options section, you can control the following settings:

✦ **Sheet pop-up menu.** You can choose which sheet in an Excel workbook to import. The default is the first sheet, which is usually named Sheet1 unless you renamed it in Excel. (If you want to import several sheets, you need to import the same spreadsheet several times, choosing a different sheet each time.)

✦ **View pop-up menu.** You can import custom views you have defined in Excel for that spreadsheet. If the Excel document has custom views, you can ignore custom views by choosing [Ignore View] from the pop-up menu. If you have no custom views, this pop-up menu is grayed out.

✦ **Cell Range pop-up menu.** You can specify a range of cells using standard Excel notation *Sx:Ey*, where *S* is the first row, *x* the first column, *E* the last row, and *y* the last column, such as A1:G89. You can type a range directly in the pop-up menu, which also acts as a text-entry field, or you can choose a previously entered range from the pop-up menu.

✦ **Import Hidden Cells Not Saved in View.** By selecting this option, you import any hidden cells. Be careful when doing so because they're usually hidden for a reason (typically, they show noncritical data sources or interim calculations).

In the Formatting section, you can control the following settings:

✦ **Table pop-up menu.** You choose the Formatted Table menu item, which imports the spreadsheet as a table and retains text and cell formatting; the Unformatted Table menu item, which imports the spreadsheet as a table but does not preserve formatting; or the Unformatted Tabbed Text menu item, which imports the spreadsheet as tabbed text (tabs separate cells and paragraphs separate rows) with no formatting retained.

✦ **Cell Alignment pop-up menu.** You can tell InDesign how to align text within the cells. You can retain the spreadsheet's current alignment(s) by choosing Current Spreadsheet or override them by choosing Left, Right, or Center.

✦ **Include Inline Graphics.** If selected, this option allows you to import any graphics placed in the Excel cells. (Chapter 11 covers inline graphics in more detail.)

The ability to select whether inline graphics are imported from Excel files is new to InDesign CS2.

✦ **Number of Decimal Places to Include.** In this field, type how many decimal places to retain for numbers. For example, if you type 4 and have a cell that contains the value for π, InDesign imports the numeral 3.1415, even though the Excel spreadsheet displays 10 decimal places (3.1415926535). Note that InDesign does not import any formulas, just their numeric or textual results.

✦ **Use Typographer's Quotes.** Select this option to convert keyboard quotes (' and ") to the curly typographer quotes (', ', ", and "). This option is normally selected.

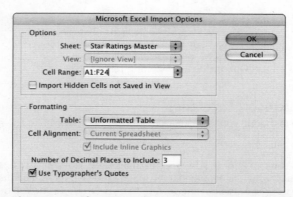

Figure 14-7: The Microsoft Excel Import Options dialog box

Exporting text

Unfortunately, you can't export text from InDesign into a word-processor format like Word; your options are RTF, InDesign Tagged Text, and text-only formats. (If you have the InCopy group editing tool covered in Appendix E, you can also export to the InCopy format.) The best option is RTF if you want to send the file to someone using a word processor, and it's Tagged Text if you want to send it to another InDesign user with all InDesign settings retained.

After you click in a text frame with the Type tool, you export text by choosing File ⇨ Export, which provides a dialog box very much like the Save As dialog box. Here, you choose the file format, filename, and file location. If you have selected text in a text frame, only that text is exported; otherwise, the entire story is exported.

Note   You can export only one story at a time. (A story is all text in linked text frames.)

Editing Text

When working in a layout, InDesign gives you the basic editing capabilities found in a word processor: cutting and pasting, deleting and inserting text, searching and replacing of text and text attributes, as well as help in spell checking.

Controlling text view

But before you begin to edit text, you need to see it. In many layout views, the text is too small to work with. Generally, you'll zoom in around the block of text using the Zoom tool. For quick access to the tool, press Z (except when the cursor is in a block of text! — in that case, you'll need to click the Zoom tool). Then click to zoom in. (To zoom out, press and hold Option or Alt when clicking.)

Another way to zoom in is to use the keyboard shortcut ⌘+= or Ctrl+=. Each time you use it, the magnification increases. (Zoom out by pressing ⌘+– [hyphen] or Ctrl+– [hyphen].)

Tip   It helps to think of the zoom-in shortcut as ⌘++ [plus] or Ctrl++ [plus], but if you do, remember that you don't also press the Shift key, which technically is what you would need to do to get a plus sign.

Tip   Choose the ⌘+= or Ctrl+= method when your text pointer is already on or near the text you want to zoom into — the pointer location is the center point for the zoom. Use the Zoom tool when your pointer is not near the text you want to magnify; then move the Zoom pointer to the area you want to magnify, and click once for each level of desired magnification.

In addition to seeing the text larger, it also helps to see the spaces, tabs, and paragraph returns that exist in the text. Choose Type ⇨ Show Hidden Characters or press Option+⌘+I or Ctrl+Alt+I (refer to Figure 14-1).

Navigating text

To work at a different text location, click in a different text frame or another location in the current text frame. You can also use the four arrow (cursor) keys on the keyboard to move one character to the right, one character to the left, one line up, or one line down. Add ⌘ or

Ctrl to the arrow keys to jump one word to the right or left, or one paragraph up or down. The Home and End keys let you jump to the beginning or end of a line; add ⌘ or Ctrl to jump to the beginning or end of a story. (A *story* is text within a text frame or that is linked across several text frames, as described in Chapter 15.) Note that if your story begins or ends in a text frame on another page, InDesign will bring you to that page.

Highlighting text

To highlight text, you can always use the old click-and-drag method. Or, you can add the Shift key to the navigation commands in the previous section. For example, while ⌘+right arrow or Ctrl+right arrow moves the cursor one word to the right, Shift+⌘+right arrow or Ctrl+Shift+right arrow highlights the next word to the right. Likewise, Shift+⌘+End or Ctrl+Shift+End highlights all the text to the end of the story.

For precise text selections, double-click to select a word and its trailing space (punctuation is not selected) and triple-click to select a paragraph. If you need the punctuation trailing a word, double-click, then press Shift+⌘+right arrow or Ctrl+Shift+right arrow to extend the selection. To select an entire story, choose Edit ➪ Select All, or press ⌘+A or Ctrl+A.

To deselect text, choose Edit ➪ Deselect All or press Shift+⌘+A or Ctrl+Shift+A. More simply, you can select another tool or click another area of the page.

Cutting, copying, and pasting text

After you've highlighted text, you can press ⌘+X or Ctrl+X to remove it from its story and place it on the Clipboard for later use. Use ⌘+C or Ctrl+C to leave the text in the story and place a copy on the Clipboard. Click anywhere else in text — within the same story, another story, or another publication — and press ⌘+V or Ctrl+V. If you're menu-driven, the Edit menu provides Cut, Copy, and Paste commands as well, plus the new Paste without Formatting command.

Deleting and replacing text

To remove text from a document, you can highlight it and choose Edit ➪ Clear or press Delete or Backspace on the keyboard. Or you can simply type over the highlighted text or paste new text on top of it.

QuarkXPress User   Don't use ⌘+K or Ctrl+K to clear text. While that works in QuarkXPress, this shortcut opens the Preferences dialog box in InDesign.

If text is not highlighted, you can delete text to the right or left of the cursor. On the Mac, press Delete to delete to the left and press Del (sometimes labeled Clear) to delete to the right. In Windows, press Backspace to delete to the left and Delete to delete to the right.

Tip   If you double-click a text frame with any tool other than a drawing or frame tool, InDesign automatically switches to the Type tool and places the insertion point where you double-clicked. (This also works for text paths and table cells.)

Tip   As with most text editors, you can't enter text below the existing text in a frame. You need to click directly after the last character in the frame to start typing again.

Undoing text edits

Remember to take advantage of InDesign's multiple undos while editing text. Choose Edit ⇨ Undo and Edit ⇨ Redo any time you change your mind about edits. The Undo and Redo keyboard commands are definitely worth remembering: ⌘+Z and Shift+⌘+Z or Ctrl+Z and Ctrl+Shift+Z.

Correcting mistakes on the fly

In our word processors, we've long taken it for granted that our text can be corrected as we type. Microsoft Word, for example, has a feature called AutoCorrect that lets you specify corrections to be made as you type, whether they are common typos or the expansion of abbreviations to their full words (such as having Word replace *tq* with *thank you*). This is also a handy way to convert two hyphens to an em dash or a keyboard sequence like *(r)* to the ® symbol.

Now, InDesign offers the same functionality, which it calls Autocorrect (with a lowercase *c*). You enable Autocorrect in the Autocorrect pane of the Preferences dialog box (InDesign ⇨ Preferences on the Mac or Edit ⇨ Preferences in Windows, or ⌘+K or Ctrl+K), as Figure 14-8 shows.

New Feature The Autocorrect feature is new to InDesign CS2.

Note Autocorrect works only for text typed in InDesign once Autocorrect is turned on; it will not correct imported or previously typed text.

It's easy to configure Autocorrect:

1. **Select the Enable Autocorrect option to turn on this feature.**

 Tip You can also enable Autocorrect by choosing Edit ⇨ Spelling ⇨ Autocorrect.

2. **If you want InDesign to automatically fix capitalization errors, select the Autocorrect Capitalization Errors option.** Typically, this finds typos involving capitalizing the second letter of a word in addition to the first. For example, InDesign would replace *FOrmat* with *Format*.

3. **Choose the dictionary whose spelling and capitalization rules you want InDesign to use from the Language pop-up menu.** The default will be based on the language you selected when you installed InDesign.

4. **To add your own custom corrections, click the Add button.** This opens the Add to Autocorrect List dialog box, also shown in Figure 14-8. Type the typo text or code you want InDesign to be alert for in the Misspelled Word field and the corrected or expanded text you want InDesign to substitute in the Correction field. Click OK or press Enter when done, or click Cancel or press Esc to close the dialog box without adding anything.

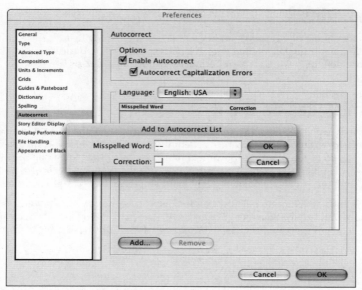

Figure 14-8: The Autocorrect pane of the Preferences dialog box, as well as its Add to Autocorrect List dialog box

Note   Oddly, you cannot use InDesign's symbol codes (such as ^+ for an em dash) in the Correction field. Instead, you'll need to know the Mac or Windows keyboard combination for special characters or have previously placed them into the Clipboard via a copy or cut operation so you can paste them into this field.

 5. **Click OK to close the Preferences dialog box when done.**

To remove an autocorrection, just select it in the Autocorrect pane's Misspelled Word list and click Remove.

Using the Story Editor

InDesign has a feature that has long been available in Adobe PageMaker: the Story Editor. This window, shown in Figure 14-9 for a workbook created by Ronald Lanham, lets you edit text without the distractions of your layout. It presents your text without line breaks or other nonessential formatting. You just see attributes like boldface and italics, and in a separate pane to the left, the names of the styles that have been applied are displayed. After clicking in a text frame, you open the Story Editor by choosing Edit ⇨ Edit in Story Editor or pressing ⌘+Y or Ctrl+Y.

The Importance of Capitalization in Autocorrection

The Misspelled Word and Correction fields are case-sensitive unless both entries are all lower-case. If you're not careful with how and when you capitalize text in these fields, you won't get the automated correction you expect.

The basic rule is this: Capitalize text in either field *only* if you are trying to fix capitalization errors. InDesign assumes you are fixing capitalization if you use any capital letters in these fields.

Thus, if you type *indesign* in the Misspelled Word field and *InDesign* in the Correction field, InDesign converts the *indesign, Indesign, inDesign*, and other miscapitalized variations to the properly capitalized *InDesign*. But if you type *Indesign* in the Misspelled Word field and *InDesign* in the Correction field, InDesign only corrects *Indesign*, not *indesign* and other miscapitalized variations.

Therefore, get in the habit of entering your text in lowercase in these fields. For example, type *portino* in the Misspelled Word field and *portion* in the Correction field, InDesign corrects *portino, Portino, POrtino*, and so on.

If you want to fix both spelling and capitalization errors at the same time, do it this way: Type the word in the Misspelled Word field in lowercase and the word in the Correction field as you want it capitalized. For example, type *indseign* in Misspelled Word and *InDesign* in Correction. This way, any instance of *indseign* — no matter how it is capitalized — will be replaced with the properly spelled and capitalized *InDesign*.

Cross-Reference

You set preferences for text size and font in the Story Editor Display pane of the Preferences dialog box (choose InDesign ➪ Preferences on the Mac or Edit ➪ Preferences in Windows, or press ⌘+K or Ctrl+K), as detailed in Chapter 3.

In the Story Editor, you use the same tools for selection, deletion, copying, pasting, and search and replace as you would in your layout. The Story Editor is not a separate word processor, simply a way to look at your text in a less distracting environment for those times your mental focus is on the meaning and words, not the text appearance.

The Story Editor also shows you the column depth for text, using a ruler along the left side of the text, just to the right of the list of currently applied paragraph styles. Overset text (text that goes beyond the text frame, or beyond the final text frame in a threaded story) is indicated by a depth measurement of *OV* and is furthermore noted with a red line to the right of the text.

New Feature

The display of column depth for text and the highlighting of overset text in the Story Editor are new to InDesign CS2.

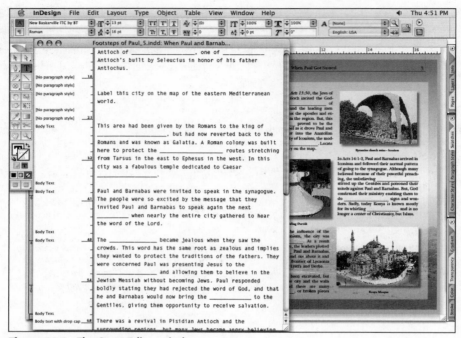

Figure 14-9: The Story Editor window

Searching and Replacing

InDesign's Find/Change dialog box (Edit ➪ Find/Change, or ⌘+F or Ctrl+F) lets you do everything from, for example, finding the next instance of *curry* in an article so you can insert *extra spicy* in red, to finding all instances of a deposed chef's name in six different documents. If you know how to use the search-and-replace feature in any word processor or page-layout application, you'll be comfortable with InDesign's Find/Change in no time.

Searching and replacing text

The Find/Change dialog box comes in two forms: reduced for finding and changing just text, and expanded for including attributes in a search. Click More Options to expand the dialog box to include formatting options for your search and replace, and Fewer Options to reduce it.

Before starting a Find/Change operation, determine the scope of your search:

✦ To search within a text selection, highlight it.

✦ To search from a certain location in a story to the end of it, click in that location using the Type tool to place the text cursor (also called the text-insertion point) there.

✦ To search an entire story, select any frame or click at any point in a frame containing the story.

✦ To search an entire document, simply have that document open.

✦ To search multiple documents, open all of them (and close any that you don't want to search).

To search for text:

1. **Determine the scope of your search, as just described, open the needed documents, and insert the text cursor at the appropriate location.**

2. **Choose Edit ➪ Find/Change or press ⌘+F or Ctrl+F.**

3. **Use the Search pop-up menu, as shown in Figure 14-10, to specify the scope of your search: Document, All Documents, Story, To End of Story, or Selection.** Which options are available are based on your current text selection in InDesign. Unavailable options are grayed out.

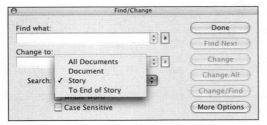

Figure 14-10: Use the Search pop-up menu in the Find/Change dialog box to specify the scope of the text to search.

Tip

As you're using the Find/Change dialog box to search and replace text, you can jump into a text frame (just click it with the Type pointer) and edit it as you please, and then return to Find/Change by clicking the Find/Change dialog box.

4. **Type or paste the text you want to find in the Find What field.** To search for special characters, type their codes (see Table 14-1) or use the pop-up list (the right-facing arrow icon) to select from a menu of special characters.

5. **Type or paste the replacement text into the Change To field.** To use special characters, type their codes (see Table 14-1) or use the pop-up list (the right-facing arrow icon) to select from a menu of special characters.

6. **Specify whether to find the word within other words (for example, *cafe* within *cafeteria* or just *cafe*) by selecting or deselecting the Whole Word option.** When selected, Find/Change locates only stand-alone instances of the Find What text.

7. **Specify whether to consider capitalization patterns in the Find/Change operation by selecting or deselecting the Case Sensitive option.** When selected, Find/Change follows the capitalization of the text in the Find What and Change To fields exactly.

8. **If you want to search for or replace with specific formatting, use the Format buttons.** These buttons are available only if you had clicked More Options. (These buttons are covered later in this chapter.)

9. **Click Find Next to start the search.** Thereafter, click Find Next to skip instances of the Find What text, and click Change, Change All, or Change/Find to replace the Find What text with the Change To text. (Change simply changes the found text, Change All changes every instance of that found text in your selection or story, and Change/Find changes the current found text and moves on to the next occurrence of it — it basically does in one click the actions of clicking Change and then Find Next.)

Note   If you use the Change All feature, InDesign reports how many changes were made. If the number looks extraordinarily high and you suspect the Find/Change operation wasn't quite what you wanted, remember you can use InDesign's undo function (Edit ➪ Undo, or ⌘+Z or Ctrl+Z) to cancel the search and replace, and try a different replace strategy.

10. **Click Done when you're finished.** Note that you can do several search-and-replace operations, which is why the dialog box stays open after completing a search.

Tip   InDesign records your last 15 entries in the Find What and Change To fields, so you can repeat previous Find/Change operations. That's why each field is a pop-up menu. Click the menu to open it, and use the down-arrow key to scroll through those recorded operations.

Finding special characters

You're not limited to finding and changing words and phrases. You can search and replace spaces, tabs, paragraph returns and other invisible characters along with special characters such as bullets, em dashes, and nonbreaking spaces. Searching and replacing these types of characters is often helpful for repair jobs such as fixing imported text that contains double spaces after periods, extra returns between paragraphs, and hyphens instead of em dashes.

To type invisible characters, special characters, or wild cards in the Find What or Change To fields, click the right-facing arrow buttons to the right of the fields. A menu appears that offers options such as Bullet Character, Hair Space, and Discretionary Hyphen, as shown in Figure 14-11. You can select any combination of these characters and combine them with other text and formatting attributes. Table 14-1 shows the text codes you can use in place of these menu items.

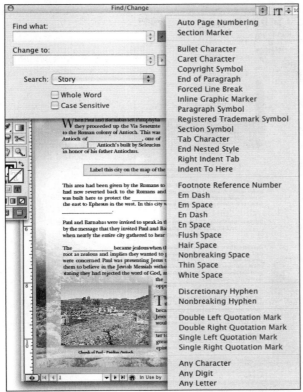

Figure 14-11: Click the right-facing arrow on the Find What and Change To fields to display a list of special characters.

Table 14-1: Text Codes for Search and Replace

Character	Code
Markers and Tabs	
Auto page numbering	^#
Section marker	^x
End of paragraph	^p
Forced line break	^n
Inline graphic marker*	^g
Tab	^t
Right-indent tab	^y
Indent to here	^l

Continued

Table 14-1 *(continued)*

Character	Code
Symbols	
Bullet (()	^8
Caret (^)	^^
Copyright (©) symbol	^2
Paragraph (¶) symbol	^7
Registered trademark (®) symbol	^r
Section (§) symbol	^6
Punctuation	
Double left quotation mark (")	^{
Double right quotation mark (")	^}
Single left quotation mark (')	^[
Single right quotation mark (')	^]
Em dash (—)	^_
En dash (–)	^=
Discretionary hyphen	^-
Nonbreaking hyphen	^~
Spaces	
Em space	^m
En space	^>
Flush space	^f
Hair space	^|
Nonbreaking space	^s
Thin space	^<
White space (any space or tab)*	^w
Wild Cards	
Any character*	^?
Any digit*	^9
Any letter*	^$

*Can be typed in the Find What field only

Note To search and replace regular spaces, type the number of spaces you want to find and change in the Find What and Change To fields — as if they were any other regular character.

If there are other characters not in InDesign's special-character menu that you want to search for or replace with, just type their keyboard codes (see Chapter 41) or paste them into the field. (You can paste them by first copying them to the Clipboard from your document text, or from a utility like PopChar X or Character Palette on the Mac or Character Map in Windows, as Chapter 13 explains.)

InDesign also provides three wild cards — Any Character, Any Digit, and Any Letter — that let you search for unspecified characters, numbers, or letters in other text. For example, if you want to change all the numbered steps in a document to bulleted lists, you might search for Any Digit and replace it with a bullet. Or you can search for variations of a word to find, say, *cafe* and *café* at the same time (in this case, you would type **caf** and then choose Any Letter).

Searching and replacing formatting

To find and change formatting or text with specific formatting, you can use the expanded Find/Change dialog box. For example, you might find all the blue words in 14-point Futura Extra Bold and change them to 12-point Mrs Eaves Bold. Or you might find all instances of the words *hot and spicy* in 15-point body text, and then resize the text to 12 point and apply the font Red Litterbox.

To replace text formatting, follow these steps:

1. **To add formats to a Find/Change operation for text, click More Options in the Find/Change dialog box (if it was not clicked earlier).** The dialog box expands to include the Find Format Settings and Change Format Settings areas, as shown in Figure 14-12.

2. **Use the Format buttons to display the Find Format Settings and Change Format Settings dialog boxes, which let you specify the formats you want to find.** The two dialog boxes are identical, except for their names; refer to Figure 14-12 for the Find Format Settings dialog box.

3. **Use the menu at the top to specify the type of formatting: Style Options (paragraph and character styles), Basic Character Formats, Advanced Character Formats, Indents and Spacing, Keep Options, Character Color, OpenType Features, Underline Options, Strikethrough Options, and Drop Caps and Other.** You can change multiple attributes at once by making selections from as many panes as needed.

Tip To search and replace formatting only — regardless of the text to which it is applied — leave the Find What and Change To fields blank.

Locating and specifying all the formatting you want to find and change requires you to dig deeper and deeper into the Find Format Settings and Change Format Settings dialog boxes. Unfortunately, you can't really get a picture of all the formats you're selecting at once, and you have to keep jumping from one pane to the next. Fortunately, when you're finished selecting formats, the selected options are summarized in the Find Style Settings and Change Style Settings areas.

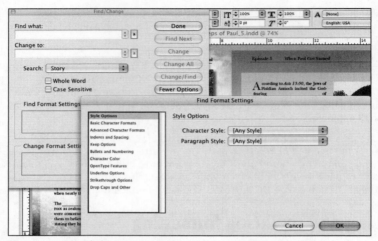

Figure 14-12: Clicking More Options in the Find/Change dialog box displays the Find Format Settings and Change Format Settings areas. Clicking Format opens either the Find Format Settings dialog box (shown here) or Change Format Settings dialog box, depending on whether you click Format in the Find Format Settings area or in the Change Format Settings area.

Changing fonts globally

Sometimes, you need to replace a font throughout your document. You can't use the Find/Change dialog box to do this because it requires that you specify specific text to find and replace. But you can choose Type ➪ Find Font and use the Find Font dialog box shown in Figure 14-13 to replace a specific font with another. The Fonts in Use section shows all fonts actually in use so you can select the one you want to replace. You then choose the new font and style using the Font Family and Font Style pop-up menus in the Replace With section.

Note

> The Find Font dialog box will *not* change fonts in your styles, only fonts actually applied to text. It will also show fonts used in graphics but it cannot replace those fonts (you need to do that in Illustrator or another illustration program).

Two other buttons in the Find Font dialog box help you understand what font you're replacing:

✦ **Reveal in Finder (Mac) or Reveal in Explorer (Windows).** This button opens the folder that contains the font, which is handy if you have the same font in multiple folders and want to know which one InDesign is using. (You control which fonts are used through your font manager, as covered in Chapter 38.)

✦ **More Info.** This button provides details on the selected font, such as any printing restrictions, font version, location, and PostScript font name.

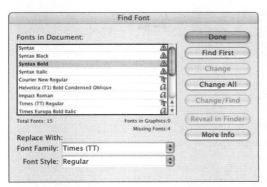

Figure 14-13: The Find Font dialog box

Checking Spelling

InDesign's Check Spelling feature flags three types of possible editorial problems: repeated words such as *an an,* words with odd capitalization such as the internal capitalization (called *intercaps*) in software and company names (like *InDesign*), and words not found in the spelling dictionary that may be spelled incorrectly. You can customize the spelling dictionary, and you can purchase other companies' spelling dictionaries to add words from disciplines like law and medicine, as well as for other languages.

Checking spelling as you type

You can have InDesign check your spelling as you type by simply choosing Edit ➪ Spelling ➪ Dynamic Spelling. (You can also choose Spelling ➪ Dynamic Spelling from the contextual menu if you are using the Type tool.) If that menu option is selected, InDesign checks the spelling as you type, as well as the spelling of any text already in the document. Suspected errors are highlighted with red squiggle underlining, so you can correct them as needed.

New Feature Dynamic spell checking is new to InDesign CS2.

There's no way to have InDesign help you correct misspellings with as-you-type spell checking; if you want InDesign to suggest proper spelling, you'll need to use the Check Spelling dialog box, which is covered in the next section.

Tip You can use the new Autocorrect feature, covered earlier in this chapter, to correct common misspellings that you've identified to InDesign. You turn it on (or off) by choosing Edit ➪ Spelling ➪ Autocorrect.

Using the Check Spelling dialog box

The other method to check spelling is to use the Check Spelling dialog box, which offers more control. First, it lets you choose what part of the document to spell check. Second, it provides suggestions on correct spelling and lets you add correctly spelled words that InDesign doesn't know about to its spelling dictionary. So even if you use the new dynamic spell-checking feature, you'll still want to do a final spell-checking pass in the Check Spelling dialog box.

As with Find/Change, specifying the text to check is a two-step process: First, set up the spell-check scope in the document; then specify the scope in the Search menu.

To set up the scope, highlight text, click in a story to check from the cursor forward, select a frame containing a story, or open multiple documents. Just as in search and replace, what you choose to open and select determines what scope options InDesign has for spell checking.

Then, open the Check Spelling dialog box (Edit ⇨ Spelling ⇨ Check Spelling, or ⌘+I or Ctrl+I) and choose an option from the Search pop-up menu: Document, All Documents, Story, To End of Story, and Selection. Figure 14-14 shows the dialog box. Depending on how you set up the scope, not all the options are available in the Search pop-up menu. For example, if you do not highlight text, the Selection option is not available. However, you can change the scope setup in the document while the Check Spelling dialog box is open. For example, you can open additional documents to check.

Tip To check the spelling of a single word, double-click to highlight it and then open the spell-checker—the Check Spelling dialog box's Search pop-up menu is automatically set to Selection.

Tip Control+click or right-click on a word, range of text, or a point in a text frame (using the Type tool) to get the contextual menu from which you choose Check Spelling.

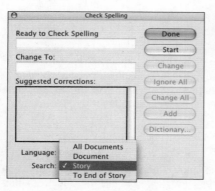

Figure 14-14: Use the Search pop-up menu in the Check Spelling dialog box to specify which text to spell check.

When you first open the Check Spelling dialog box, it displays "Ready to Check Spelling" at the top. To begin checking the text scope you specified in the Search pop-up menu, click Start. When the spell checker encounters a word without a match in the dictionary or a possible capitalization problem, the dialog box displays "Not in Dictionary" at the top and shows the word. When the spell checker encounters repetition such as *me me,* the dialog box displays "Duplicate Word" and shows the repeated words. Use the buttons along the right side of the dialog box to handle flagged words as follows:

✦ To leave the current instance of a Not in Dictionary word or Duplicate Word unchanged, click Ignore. To leave all instances of the same problem unchanged, click Ignore All.

✦ To change the spelling of a Not in Dictionary word, click a word in the Suggested Corrections list or edit the spelling or capitalization in the Change To field. To make the change, click Change.

✦ To correct an instance of a Duplicate Word, edit the text in the Change To field, and then click Change.

✦ To change all occurrences of a Not in Dictionary word or a Duplicate Word to the information in the Change To field, click Change All.

✦ To add a word flagged as incorrect — but that you know is correct — click Add to add the word to InDesign's spelling dictionary.

✦ To add a word flagged as incorrect to a specific dictionary, click Dictionary. The resulting Dictionary dialog box lets you choose which dictionary to add the word to, as well as what language to associate it with. You can also specify hyphenation settings. The options in this dialog box are covered in the "Customizing the Spelling and Hyphenation Dictionaries" section later in this chapter.

New Feature   The inclusion of the Dictionary button in the Check Spelling dialog box is new to InDesign CS2.

✦ To close the Check Spelling dialog box after checking all the specified text, click Done.

While you're using Check Spelling, you can jump between the dialog box and the document at any time. This lets you edit a possibly misspelled word in context or to edit surrounding text as a result of changed spelling. So if you find an instance of *a a* in front of *apple,* you can change the entire phrase to *an apple* rather than just replace the duplicate *a a* with *a* in the dialog box and have to remember to later change *a apple* to *an apple.*

Working with multiple languages

Each word in InDesign can have a distinct language assigned to it (English, French, Spanish, German, and so on). The word's language attribute tells InDesign which dictionary to consult when spell checking or hyphenating the word. For example, if you have the word *frères* in an English sentence, you can change the language of that word so it is no longer flagged by the English spell checker — the French spell checker is used and recognizes that the word is correctly spelled.

Note   Just because you have the ability to control language at the word level doesn't necessarily mean that you have to use it. In general, even when publishing to an international audience, full paragraphs or stories will be in the same language. For example, if you have the same packaging for a product sold in the United States and France, you might have one descriptive paragraph in English and the other in French. The English dictionary also contains many common words with foreign origins such as *jalapeño, mélange,* and *crêpe.*

To assign a language to text, highlight the text and choose an option from the Language pop-up menu on the expanded Character pane, as shown in Figure 14-15. You can also set the language as part of a character or paragraph style (see Chapters 16 and 17 for more details). In the Check Spelling dialog box, a field above the Search menu shows the language of each word as it's checked. Unfortunately, you can't change the language in that dialog box.

Note   There's a language option called [No Language]; selecting it prevents spell checking and hyphenation.

Figure 14-15: The Language menu on the Character pane lets you choose a different language for hyphenating and spell checking highlighted text.

Customizing the Spelling and Hyphenation Dictionaries

A spelling dictionary can never cover all the bases — you'll always have industry-specific words and proper nouns not found in the dictionary in use. In addition, copy editors tend to have their own preferences for how to hyphenate words. What they consider correct hyphenation may vary, and some word breaks are preferred over others. To solve both these problems, you can customize InDesign's dictionaries by adding words and specifying hyphenation. InDesign handles both spelling and hyphenation in one dictionary for each language, so you use the same controls to modify both spelling and hyphenation.

Changes made to a dictionary file are saved only in the dictionary file, not with an open document. So if you add words to the English: USA dictionary, the modified dictionary is used for spell checking and hyphenating all text in documents that use the English: USA dictionary.

Tip   If you're in a workgroup, be sure to share the edited dictionary file so everyone is using the same spelling and hyphenation settings. (The file is located in the Dictionaries folder inside the Plug-ins folder inside your InDesign folder.) You can copy it for other users, who must then restart InDesign or press Option+⌘+/ or Ctrl+Alt+/ to reflow the text according to the new dictionary's hyphenation.

Customizing the spelling dictionary

While spell checking, you often find words that don't match those in the dictionary. If you know the word is spelled correctly and likely to appear in your publications often, you can add it to the dictionary. In the future, this word will not be flagged and you won't have to click Ignore to skip it — and you can be sure that when it's used, it is spelled as it is in the dictionary.

When adding words to the dictionary, you can specify their capitalization. For example, InDesign's dictionary prefers *E-mail*. You can add *e-mail* if you prefer a lowercase *e* or *email* if you prefer to skip the hyphen. If you're adding a word that may have variations (such as *emailing*) be sure to add those variations separately.

To add words to the dictionary:

1. **Choose Edit ➪ Spelling ➪ Dictionary.** The Dictionary dialog box shown in Figure 14-16 appears.

New Feature

The menu sequence to open the Dictionary dialog box has changed in InDesign CS2. It is now accessed as a submenu to the Spelling menu rather than through its own menu option in the Edit menu.

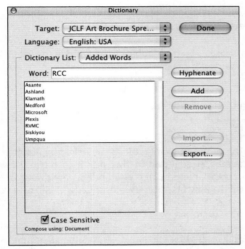

Figure 14-16: Type a new term in the Word field, and then click Add to include it in the spelling dictionary. Be sure to select the Case Sensitive option for proper names and acronyms.

2. **Choose whether the addition to the dictionary affects just this document or all documents.** To do so, use the Target pop-up menu, which lists the current document name as well as User Dictionary (to change the dictionary file). The advantage of making the spelling specific to the document is that all users, such as service bureaus, will have the same spellings; the disadvantage is that other documents won't share this spelling.

3. **Choose the dictionary that you want to edit from the Language menu.**

4. **Type or paste a word in the Word field.** The word can include special characters such as accents and hyphens, spaces, and a capitalization pattern to follow.

5. **If you want InDesign to accept only the added word with the capitalization typed in the Word field, select the Case Sensitive option.** This lets you add proper names, for example, but have them still flagged when typed in all lowercase or with extra capital letters. For example, if you type **Healdsburg** in the Word field and select Case Sensitive, InDesign won't flag *Healdsburg* but will flag *healdsburg* and *HEaldsburg*.

New Feature

Support for case-sensitive entries is new InDesign CS2.

6. **If you want to edit the hyphenation, click Hyphenate.** You can add, remove, or modify the number of tildes to change the hyphenation rules for the word, as covered in the next section.

7. **Click Add.**

8. **If you want to import a word list or export one for other users to import into their copies of InDesign, click Import or Export as appropriate.** You will then navigate to a folder and choose a filename in a dialog box similar to the Open a File or Save dialog boxes. Note that when you click Export, InDesign exports all *selected* words from the list. If no words are selected, it exports all the words in the list.

9. **Continue to add words, and when you're finished, click Done.**

Tip

When you're adding variations of words, you can double-click a word in the list to place it in the Word field as a starting place.

In addition to adding words through the Dictionary dialog box, you can click Add in the Check Spelling dialog box when InDesign flags a word that you know is correct, as covered earlier in this chapter.

To delete a word that you added to the dictionary, select it in the list and click Remove. To change the spelling of a word you added, delete it and then re-add it with the correct spelling. You can see all deleted words — just those deleted since you opened the dialog box — by selecting Removed Words from the Dictionary List pop-up menu, so you can add back any deleted by error.

Customizing hyphenation points

Industries and publications usually have internal styles on how words hyphenate — especially if the text is justified. For example, a bridal magazine that uses the term *newlywed* often may prefer that it breaks at the end of a line as *newly–wed*. But if that hyphenation would cause poor spacing, the publisher might let it break at *new–lywed* as well. InDesign lets you modify the hyphenation dictionary by specifying new, hierarchical hyphenation points.

Note

When you customize the hyphenation points, be sure to add variations of words (such as the plural form *newlyweds*). InDesign sees each word as wholly unrelated, and, thus, won't apply the hyphenation of, say, *newlywed* to *newlyweds*.

To specify hyphenation points:

1. **Choose Edit ➪ Spelling ➪ Dictionary.**

2. **Choose from the Language menu the dictionary that you want to edit.**

3. **Type or paste the word in the Word field; you can also double-click a word in the list.**

4. **If you want, click Hyphenate to see InDesign's suggestions for hyphenating the word.** You can then change the hyphenation according to Steps 5 and 6.

5. **Type a tilde (~, obtained by pressing Shift+`, the open single keyboard quote at the upper left of the keyboard) at your first preference for a hyphenation point.** If you don't want the word to hyphenate at all, type a tilde in front of it.

6. **Type tildes in other hyphenation points as well.** If you want to indicate a preference, use two tildes for your second choice, three tildes for your third choice, and so on. InDesign will first try to hyphenate your top preferences (single tildes), and then it will try your second choices if the first ones don't work out, and so on. Figure 14-17 shows an example.

7. **Click Add.**

8. **Continue to add words until you're finished, and then click Done.**

To revert a word to the default hyphenation, select it in the list and click Remove. To change the hyphenation, double-click a word in the list to enter it in the Word field, change the tildes, and then click Add. When you're adding variations of words, you can double-click a word in the list to place it in the Word field as a starting place.

Tip   If a word actually includes a freestanding tilde (not as an accent, as in ñ), type \~ to indicate the character is part of the word. These are rare and happen mostly in World Wide Web addresses.

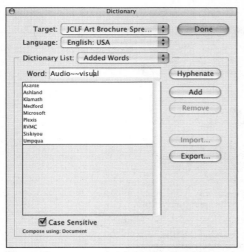

Figure 14-17: Type hyphenation preferences in the Word field, using tildes (~) to indicate hyphenation points; then click Add to include them in the spelling dictionary.

Setting spelling and hyphenation dictionary preferences

By default, when spell checking and hyphenating text, InDesign consults dictionaries created by a company called Proximity. Because spelling and hyphenation points vary from dictionary to dictionary, and you may prefer one dictionary over another, you can purchase and install other companies' dictionaries to use instead of Proximity's. However, it's very hard to find commercial alternatives to the Proximity dictionaries, so most users use the ones that come with InDesign and update them as needed.

The spelling and hyphenation in Proximity's dictionaries have the following origins: Catalan (Collins), Danish (IDE), Dutch (Van Dale), English: UK (Collins), English: USA (Franklin), English USA Legal (Merriam-Webster), English: USA Medical (Merriam-Webster), Finnish (IDE), French (Hachette), French: Canadian (Hachette), German: Traditional (Bertelsmann), German: Reformed (Bertelsmann), German: Swiss (Bertelsmann), Italian (Collins), Norwegian (IDE), Norwegian: Nynorsk (IDE), Portuguese (Collins), Portuguese: Brazilian (Collins), Spanish: Castilian (Collins), and Swedish (IDE).

To replace a dictionary:

1. **Place the dictionary file in the Dictionaries folder in the Plug-ins folder inside your InDesign folder.**

2. **Choose InDesign ⇨ Preferences on the Mac or Edit ⇨ Preferences in Windows, or press ⌘+K or Ctrl+K, and go to the Dictionary pane to get the dialog box shown in Figure 14-18.**

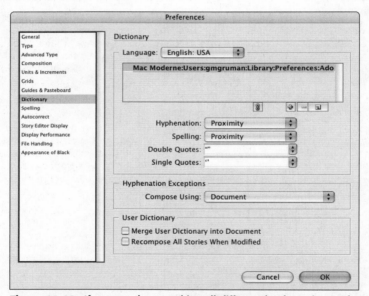

Figure 14-18: If you purchase and install different hyphenation and spelling dictionaries, you can select them in the Dictionary pane of the Preferences dialog box.

3. **In the Language pop-up menu, choose which language's dictionary you want to replace.** Dictionary files associated with that language appear in the list below the pop-up menu.

4. **Use the four buttons under the list of dictionary files to modify the dictionary files associated with the language.** They are, from left to right:

   • **Relocate:** This lets you select a replacement dictionary for the one selected in the list above. Navigate to the folder and dictionary file you want to use, and then click Open.

- **Add:** This lets you add a dictionary to the selected language. Thus, you can have multiple dictionaries per language, which is very useful for handling industry-specific terms or trademarked terms, for example.

- **Remove:** This removes a dictionary associated to a language. Note that there must be at least one dictionary per language, so this button is grayed out when only one dictionary remains in the list.

- **New:** This creates a new, empty dictionary file that you can then modify with the Dictionary dialog box covered earlier in this chapter.

New Feature   Support for multiple dictionaries per language is new to InDesign CS2.

5. **If you have multiple rules engines for hyphenation and spelling, choose the referred rules engine from the Hyphenation Vendor and/or Spelling pop-up menu.** Such rules engines are rare, so you typically have only the default choice of Proximity for these two pop-up menus.

6. **If you don't want to use the language's standard quotation characters, you can change them in the Double Quotes and Single Quotes pop-up menus.** You might change the default quotes if you are publishing in one language but have extensive phrases from other languages in them. For example, a French book that extensively uses English passages (perhaps a literary article) might want to apply French quotes to text tagged with one of the English languages.

7. **To regulate how hyphenation is handled, use the Compose Using pop-up menu.** Your choices are User Dictionary, which has InDesign ignore the hyphenation override settings that a user has made to this document (a great way to override someone's incorrect hyphenation changes); Document, which uses only the hyphenations specified in the document; and User Dictionary and Document, which uses hyphenation settings from the dictionary as well as any hyphenation specified in the document. This last setting is the default.

8. **To ensure consistent spelling and hyphenation, use the two options in the User Dictionary section:**

   - **Merge User Dictionary into Document:** If selected, this copies the user dictionary into the document, so if the file is used by someone else who doesn't have that user dictionary, the spelling and hyphenation rules are nonetheless retained.

   - **Recompose All Stories When Modified:** If selected, this rehyphenates and changes quote settings for all stories in the document, even those created before the user dictionary was modified or added.

9. **Click OK.**

Tip   If you change Dictionary Preferences with no documents open, the new dictionary becomes a program default and applies to all new documents. If a document is open, the change applies only to that document.

Adjusting Text Appearance in Text Frames

Although most adjustments to text frames — such as frame size, shape, and location — affect the layout, not the text, there are several text-frame attributes that *do* affect your text's appearance.

Setting text frame options

Most of these adjustments reside in the General pane of the Text Frame Options dialog box shown in Figure 14-19. You open the dialog box by selecting a frame and choosing Object ⟿ Text Frame Options, or pressing ⌘+B or Ctrl+B.

Cross-Reference   Chapter 9 covers the creation, modification, and deletion of text frames in more detail. Chapter 15 covers the Column settings in the Text Frame Options dialog box. The rest of Part IV covers formatting text.

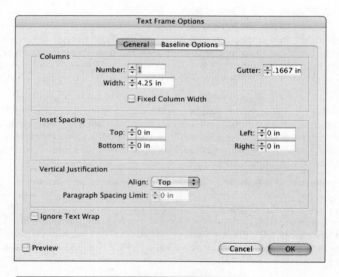

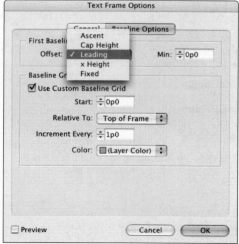

Figure 14-19: The General pane (top) and Baseline Options pane (bottom) of the Text Frame Options dialog box.

These four sections of the General pane of Text Frame Options dialog box provide the following controls:

✦ **Columns.** The section lets you specify the number of columns, column width, and gutter settings, as explained in Chapter 15.

✦ **Inset Spacing.** This section creates an internal margin in the frame, putting space between the frame edge and the text. You can set the Top, Bottom, Left, and Right settings separately.

✦ **Vertical Justification.** This section controls the placement of text vertically in a text frame, similar right-, center-, or left-aligning a paragraph horizontally. The Top, Center, and Bottom options move the text to the top, the center, or bottom of the text frame. The Justify option is a bit different: It permits variable spacing between paragraphs, so the text fits the full depth of the frame. If you choose Justify, the leading within paragraphs is unaffected, but InDesign adds as much space as needed between each paragraph — up to the value set in the Paragraph Spacing Limit field — to ensure that the last line of text in the frame is at the bottom of the frame. Because the default is 0p, text won't be vertically justified even if you choose Justify — you must also increase the Paragraph Spacing Limit value. Figure 14-20 shows some examples of this.

✦ **Ignore Text Wrap.** This option is in its own, untitled section. If selected, lets text in the text frame overprint another object, even if text wrap is set for that object. You would use this rarely. An example of when you might want to select this option is when you have a headline you want to overprint a graphic around which body text wraps.

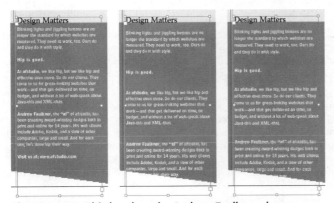

Figure 14-20: This brochure by Andrew Faulkner shows examples of vertical justification, showing how the spacing changes as the number of lines changes. (Normal, top-aligned text is at left.)

The Baseline Options pane provides controls for where text baselines begin relative to the frame's top:

✦ **First Baseline.** This section lets you determine where the baseline for the first line of text in the frame rests. (The baseline is the invisible line on which characters rest and through which descenders, such as the lower portions of letters like *p* and *g*, "poke through.") You have five options in the Offset pop-up menu. How you use each of them depends on your aesthetic goals:

- **Ascent.** This option puts the baseline as close to the top of the frame as possible, so the tops of characters graze the text frame's top (or the margin you set in the Inset Spacing section). This is the default.

- **Cap Height.** The Cap Height adjusts the baseline so that it is a cap height's distance from the frame top. The cap height is the height of a capital letter *C*, but some fonts have characters that extend above that location, and these fonts will have characters that rise above the top of the frame if you choose Cap Height here.

- **Leading.** This option places the baseline from the frame's top in the same amount as the text's leading. If leading is set to 13 points, for example, the baseline will be 13 points from the top of the frame, no matter if that makes characters rise above the frame top (such as if the text size is set at 15 points) or causes a gap (such as if the text size is set at 9 points).

- **x Height.** This adjusts the baseline so that it is an x height's distance from the frame top. The x height is the height of a lowercase letter *x*. Selecting x Height ensures that capital letters and letters with ascenders (such as *d* and *h*) will poke through the top of the frame.

- **Fixed.** This option uses the value in the Min. field to position the baseline. You use this if you want the baseline for all text frames to be the same no matter what the text size and appearance is. That's pretty rare. Standard practice is to have text positioned from the frame top relative to its size, which the other Offset options essentially do.

You can override any of the settings described here by specifying an amount in the Min. field. The Min. field tells InDesign that the first baseline must be at least a specific distance from the frame top. InDesign will first try to position the baseline based on the Offset amount, but if that is closer to the frame top than the Min. setting, the Min. setting will prevail.

✦ **Baseline Grid.** This section lets you set a baseline grid just for the selected text frame(s). The baseline grid provides a set of guidelines for your text, which helps ensure that columns stay aligned. Note that you can have your paragraphs snap to these guidelines if you enable baseline grid alignment in your paragraph formatting or paragraph styles. Also note that your document can have its own universal baseline grid, and selected text frames can have their own independent ones. You set the document baseline grid in the Grids & Guides pane of the Preferences dialog box and the text-frame-specific baseline grids here, by selecting the Use Custom Baseline Grid option.

Cross-Reference
The various baseline grid settings are covered in Chapter 3. Setting paragraphs to align to baseline grids is covered in Chapter 17.

Scaling text with the mouse

The other frame-oriented action you can take that affects text is resizing (scaling). Normally, when you resize a text frame, the text size is unaffected, and the text simply reflows in the new frame's dimensions. But you can also have the text resized along the same percentages as the frame itself. Here's how: Press and hold ⌘ or Ctrl when dragging a frame edge with the Selection tool. This resizes the text the same percentage horizontally or vertically as the frame is resized. (This also works for grouped text frames.)

Tip You can also resize text frames using the Type tool. To do so, press and hold ⌘ or Ctrl, select a text frame handle, and resize the frame by dragging the mouse. Likewise, you can move a text frame by pressing and holding ⌘ or Ctrl, clicking in the frame, and dragging the mouse. When you release the mouse, you'll revert to the Type tool and your cursor will still be at the previous text-insertion point so you can continue editing where you left off.

If you want to see how your text looks when you resize a text frame (whether you use the Type tool or not), hold the mouse button down for a second after selecting a handle; when you resize the frame, the text recomposes as you move the mouse.

Note Because these actions distort the text's appearance, you'll rarely use them. However, they can be useful when working on titles in creative materials such as ads where some distortion can result in an unusual but attractive look.

Summary

InDesign provides a variety of methods for getting text into your documents, including typing directly into a text frame, placing or dragging and dropping files generated in a word processor, and pasting text from other sources. You can also edit and type text in the Story Editor window.

You can export text from InDesign for use in a word processor or another InDesign user. Your options are RTF, InDesign Tagged Text, and text-only.

Once text is in InDesign, you can use the Find/Change feature to search and replace text and/or formatting in highlighted text, a whole story, a whole document, or a group of open documents. You have the same scope options when checking spelling. The new Autocorrect feature lets you make InDesign automatically replace specified abbreviations and misspellings as you type.

You can customize the spelling and hyphenation dictionary to include industry-specific words or proper nouns and to specify your preferences for how certain words are hyphenated. InDesign provides dictionaries for many languages to support international publishing, and it lets you create your own dictionaries.

The Text Frame Options dialog box lets you adjust the spacing of text within text frames. You can also resize text at the same percentages you resize its frame if you press and hold ⌘ or Ctrl when dragging a frame edge.

✦   ✦   ✦

Flowing Text through a Document

It doesn't take much experience with InDesign to discover that all your text doesn't fit into the finite space provided by individual frames. Consider these scenarios:

♦ If you're laying out a newsletter, you might receive an article in the form of a Microsoft Word document that you need to flow into several columns across a spread.

♦ A magazine might have an article that starts on page 20 and then continues on page 198, with the text originating in WordPerfect and saved as Rich Text Format (RTF) for import into InDesign.

♦ With catalogs, you might have a continuous file exported from a database that contains different product descriptions that are positioned below the items' pictures.

♦ In book publishing, each chapter may be imported as a separate word processing file and flowed continuously through many pages.

♦ The text of a simple advertisement, delivered by a client via e-mail, might flow through several text frames.

In all these cases, the benefits of frames — the ability to size, resize, reshape, and place them with precision — seem limiting. When the text doesn't fit in a frame, what are you supposed to do? Well, don't resort to cutting and pasting text into different frames. You need to keep the imported text together and link the frames that will contain the text. InDesign refers to the process of linking frames as *threading* and considers linked frames to be *threaded*. You can link frames on a single page, link frames from one page to another no matter how many pages are in between, and link frames automatically to quickly flow text while adding new pages with frames.

The text flowing through one or more threaded frames is considered a *story*. When you edit text in a story, the text reflows throughout the columns and threaded frames. You can also spell check and do search and replace for an entire story even though you have just one text frame active on-screen. Similarly, you can select all or some of the text in the story and change its formatting, copy it, or delete it.

Chapter 9 explains how to create frames, while Chapter 13 explains what kind of text can be imported. Chapter 12 explains how to select, spell check, and search and replace text. Chapters 16, 18, 19, and 20 explain how to format text. Chapter 27 explains how to make text follow a path such as a line or shape's boundary.

Working with Text Frames

On a simple layout such as a business card or advertisement, you might simply create text frames as you need them. In a newsletter, you might drag text frames for an article in from a library. But with a book or even a text-heavy magazine, text frames are usually placed on master pages — a template for document pages — so they automatically appear on document pages. Many publications will combine master frames, individual frames, and threaded frames, as shown in Figure 15-1.

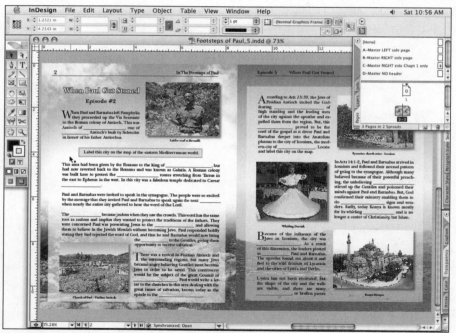

Figure 15-1: In this workbook spread by Ronald Lanham, a text frame on a document page contains the headline "The Noble Bereans" and a text frame placed by the master page contains the folios at top. The body of the article is in a master text frame, which is threaded to other master text frames containing the body of the article on other pages.

For detailed information about using libraries and master pages, see Chapters 5 and 7.

Creating text frames on master pages

Master pages — predesigned pages that you can apply to other pages to automate layout and ensure consistency — can contain several types of text frames. You can have the following:

✦ Text frames containing standing text such as a magazine's folio.

✦ Text frames containing placeholder text for elements such as figure captions or headlines.

✦ An automatically placed text frame for flowing text throughout pages. The automatically placed frame is called the *master text frame* and is created in the New Document dialog box (File ➪ New ➪ Document, or ⌘+N or Ctrl+N).

Creating a master text frame

A master text frame is an empty text frame on the default master page that lets you automatically flow text through a document. When you create a new document, you can create a master text frame, which will fit within the margins and contain the number of columns you specify. Here's how it works:

1. **Choose File ➪ New ➪ Document or press ⌘+N or Ctrl+N.**

2. **Select the Master Text Frame option at the top of the New Document dialog box as shown in Figure 15-2.**

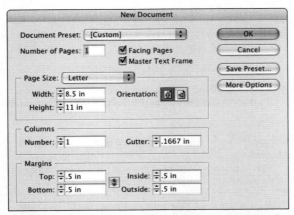

Figure 15-2: Selecting the Master Text Frame option in the New Document dialog box places a text frame on the default master page within the margins you specify.

3. **Use the Page Size area to set the size and orientation of the pages; select the Facing Pages option if your pages will have a different inside and outside margin (as a book would).**

4. **Specify the size and placement of the master text frame by typing values in the Top, Bottom, Inside, and Outside fields (or the Left and Right fields if Facing Pages is deselected).** InDesign places guides according to these values and places a text frame within the guides. The text frame fits within the boundaries of these values and the guides on the master page.

5. **Type a value in the Number field in the Columns area to specify the number of columns in the master text frame.** To specify the amount of space between the columns, type a value in the Gutter field. InDesign places guides on the page to indicate the columns.

6. **Click OK to create a new document containing a master text frame.**

After you create a document with a master text frame, you'll see guides on the first document page indicating the placement of the frame.

Modifying master text frames

Although you set up the master text frame in the New Document dialog box, you're not confined to those settings. As you design a publication, you may need to change the size, shape, and/or number of columns in the master text frame. To display the master page, choose Window ➪ Pages or press F12. In the Pages pane that appears, double-click the A-Master icon in the upper portion of the pane. Use the Selection tool to click the master text frame within the guides and modify it using the following options:

✦ The Control palette and Transform pane let you change the placement of a selected master text frame using the X and Y fields, the size using the W and H fields, the angle using the Rotation field, and the skew using the Shear field. You can also type values in the Scale fields to increase or decrease the width and height of the text frame by percentages. You can also use the mouse to resize and reposition the text frame.

✦ The General pane of the Text Frame Options dialog box (Object ➪ Text Frame Options, or ⌘+B or Ctrl+B), shown in Figure 15-3, lets you change the number of columns and the space between them, specify how far text is inset from each side of the frame, and specify the placement of the first baseline. If you don't want text within this frame to wrap around any items in front of it, select the Ignore Text Wrap option at the bottom of the dialog box.

Chapter 14 covers all the options in the Text Frame Options dialog box except for the Columns section. The Columns section is covered in the "Adjusting Columns" section later in this chapter.

✦ Paragraph styles, character styles, object styles, Story pane settings, and other text attributes are applied in the master text frame to the document text you flow into that frame. You can always override those attributes by applying other styles or formatting to the flowed text on your master text page.

You can't edit the text settings in a master text frame when working on a document page unless you Shift+⌘+click or Ctrl+Shift+click it, so most designers use the master text frame only as a guide for placing text frames on their document pages.

✦ The Direct Selection tool lets you drag anchor points on the frame to change its shape.

The InDesign master text frame is not the same as QuarkXPress's automatic text box on a master page. You cannot flow text into a QuarkXPress automatic text box while you're working on a master page — it is, instead, an empty text box that is placed on each of your layout pages for you automatically. Although you can have QuarkXPress flow text into automatic text boxes across pages as you add pages to your layout, you can also place text in these boxes individually, without them being linked. An InDesign master text frame is linked automatically from page to page and is not meant for holding text that does not flow from page to page.

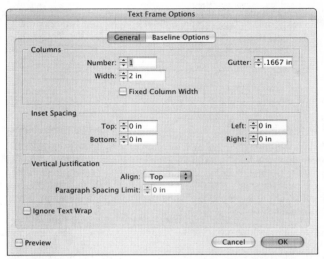

Figure 15-3: To change the properties of a master text frame, select it on the master page and use the General pane of the Text Frame Options dialog box.

Drawing additional text frames

The master text frame is helpful for containing body text that flows through a document. You're likely to need plenty of other text frames on both master pages and document pages. Generally, these are smaller text frames intended to hold headlines, captions, or short paragraphs of descriptive copy.

Creating text frames on master pages

If you're going to add text frames to a master page for repeating elements such as headers and footers, you need to display the master page. Choose Window ⇨ Pages or press F12 to display the Pages pane. Then double-click the A-Master icon in the upper portion of the pane, as shown in Figure 15-4. Any text frames you add to master pages will appear on document pages based on that master page. To switch back to the document and view the text frames, double-click a page icon in the upper portion of the Pages pane.

Creating rectangular and variable-shaped text frames

To create rectangular text frames on document pages or master pages, select the Type tool. Click and drag to create text frames, and use the Control palette or Transform pane to fine-tune the placement and dimensions. Figure 15-5 shows a rectangular text frame used for a magazine folio.

For variable-shaped text frames such as circles or Bézier shapes, use the Pen tool, Pencil tool, Ellipse tool, or Polygon tool to create an empty frame. Then convert the frame to a text frame by clicking it with the Type tool or a loaded-text icon or by choosing Object ⇨ Content ⇨ Text. (You get the loaded-text icon when you place a text file or when you flow text from an existing frame, which is described later in this chapter.)

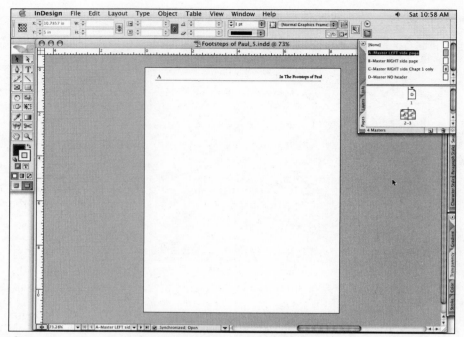

Figure 15-4: To access a master page so you can add or modify objects, double-click a master-page icon in the upper portion of the Pages pane.

Tip   If you're working on a document page and want to type in a text frame placed on the page by a master page, select the Type tool and Shift+⌘+click or Ctrl+Shift+click the frame.

Cross-Reference   You can also edit an existing rectangular text frame with the Direct Selection tool as if it were a free-form shape, as described in Chapters 10 and 26.

Figure 15-5: A rectangular text frame used on a master page for a folio

Getting the Text

Although you can type the text of a book or article directly into threaded text frames in InDesign, in most cases you will import text from a word processing program. Most writers and copy editors will not have page-layout software and will, therefore, provide the story in an importable form such as Microsoft Word. Depending on your production workflow, they may have applied style sheets to the text in the word processor to indicate how the text should be formatted in InDesign.

Importing text files

The process of importing text files — and otherwise adding text to a document — is explained in full in Chapters 13 and 14. When working with documents that require threaded text frames, text is generally imported according to a few simple steps:

1. **Using the Type tool, select the first text frame that will contain the imported story.** If you need to select a master text frame, Shift+⌘+click it or Ctrl+Shift+click it.

2. **Choose File ➪ Place, or press ⌘+D or Ctrl+D.**

3. **Use the controls at the top of the Place dialog box to locate the word processing file, and then click on it.**

4. **Check Show Import Options to open the Import Options dialog box, where you should ensure that the Use Typographer's Quotes option is selected to convert any straight quotes to curly, typesetter's quotes.** You can also control how style sheets and any special elements such as tables or footnotes are handled during import, as covered in Chapter 14. Click OK when done.

5. **Click Open to import the text into the selected text frame.** Text is likely to overflow the first frame, as shown in Figure 15-6.

Tip   You can see all the overset text two ways: One is to create a new text frame in the layout's pasteboard and thread the text to that new frame, which acts as an overflow container. The other is to switch to the Story Editor (Edit ➪ Edit in Story Editor, or ⌘+Y or Ctrl+Y) and scroll down to the overset text, which will be indicated by a red outline and have the code *OV* to the left of each overset line, as Chapter 14 explains.

Figure 15-6: The red plus sign in the lower-right corner of this text frame indicates there is more text (called *overset text*) than the frame can hold.

Other Text-Importing Techniques

As Chapter 14 explains, InDesign lets you place text in several ways, not just by using the Place command:

✦ If your word processor supports drag and drop, you can drag a text selection directly from your word processor into an InDesign page. This creates a new text frame with the dragged text.

✦ You can copy and paste text from a word processor to an InDesign frame.

✦ Finally, you can drag a text file's icon from the desktop or folder into an InDesign page. (The text file must be in a format supported by InDesign, such as text-only, RTF, or Word.) This results in a loaded-text icon that you then use either to click the text frame to which you want to add the text, or click and drag to draw a new text frame in which to place the text.

Handling word processor style sheets

Whether writers are working on a 1,000-word story or a 40-page chapter of a book, chances are they're using some sort of formatting or style sheets in their word processing files. This might be as little as bold on headlines and space between paragraphs, or as sophisticated as different style sheets for each level of heading and type of paragraph in the manuscript.

When you import a word processing file into InDesign, you can bring the formatting and style sheets with it.

Cross-Reference   See Chapter 13 for a complete list of formatting options that will import from Microsoft Word.

Isolated (local) formatting might be used to indicate which styles should be applied in InDesign — for example, the writer might apply bold to one-line paragraphs that should be formatted as a subhead. However, if the writer applies appropriate paragraph style sheets to text in his or her word processor, much of the formatting in InDesign can be automated by importing the style sheets.

New Feature   Microsoft Word character style sheets are now imported into InDesign CS2.

You can use these imported paragraph style sheets in two different ways, depending on whether styles with the same name already exist in the InDesign document.

Note   What most programs, including Microsoft Word and QuarkXPress, call *style sheets*, InDesign calls simply *styles*. Whatever your preference, they are saved groups of settings that can be applied to text.

Editing imported paragraph style sheets

If you import paragraph style sheets with text, you can simply use the style sheets specified in the word processor to format the text. This method works well for designs that do not follow a template — for example, brochures or feature stories. You might import the text, experiment with formatting it, and then edit the imported style sheets in InDesign to reflect your design.

For example, say you import a magazine feature article that is formatted with three paragraph style sheets (Headline, Byline, and Body Copy) into an InDesign document that does not contain styles with those names. The three style sheets are added to InDesign's Paragraph Styles list and have similar specifications to what they had in the word processor. However, because InDesign offers more formatting options, you might edit those imported styles to fine-tune the text formatting. To edit a paragraph style sheet, select it in the Paragraph Styles pane and choose Style Options from the palette menu, as shown in Figure 15-7.

Overriding imported paragraph style sheets

In documents that follow a template, you can provide writers with style sheet names that must be applied to their text. For example, say you're working on a tri-fold brochure that is part of an entire series of similar tri-folds. The writer might format the text with five paragraph style sheets that also exist in your InDesign document: Heads, Subheads, Body Copy, Bullets, and Quotes. The style sheet specifications in the word processor don't matter — only the name counts — because InDesign document styles override imported style sheets.

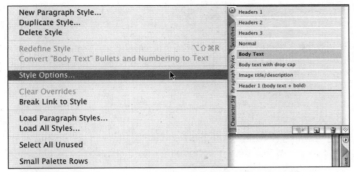

Figure 15-7: You can import simple style sheets from a word processor, and then edit them in InDesign using the Style Options command in the Paragraph Styles pane's palette menu.

For example, the writer's style sheets use standard fonts such as Times and Helvetica along with bold and italic type styles to distinguish the types of text. But, when the word processing file is imported into InDesign, the style sheets are overridden with InDesign styles that have the same name but specify the actual fonts used by the designer and the many formatting options available in InDesign.

You can supply writers either with actual style sheets or with only style-sheet names:

✦ To supply style sheets, export text from a similar story in RTF, which writers can open in their word processor; the word processor adds the style sheet names in the RTF file to its own style-sheet list. The writers can then save these style-sheet names to a template file and use that template for future documents. To export text from InDesign, use the Export dialog box (File ⇨ Export, or ⌘+E or Ctrl+E) and choose Rich Text Format from the Format pop-up menu.

✦ Or you can simply give writers a list of style sheet names that they can create themselves to their own specifications. In this case, it's particularly important that the style sheets created in the word processor have exactly the same names as those in the InDesign document.

Threading Text Frames

InDesign provides three options for *threading* (or linking) text frames: manual, semiautoflow, and autoflow. Each has its own icon, as shown in the sidebar "Threading Icons." The method you choose depends on how much text you're dealing with and the size and quantity of your text frames:

✦ You might use the manual method, in which you click the first text frame's out port and then on the second text frame, to link two text frames across several pages for an article continuation.

✦ The semiautoflow method lets you click on a series of text frames to flow text. It works well for linking a succession of text frames in something like a catalog layout.

✦ The autoflow method adds text frames and pages as you import text and is intended for flowing long text files such as a book chapter or annual report.

Text Frame Anatomy

Before you start threading text frames, you need to understand what a text frame is trying to tell you about its text. To get the message, you need to select the text frames with one of the selection tools; when the Type tool is selected, all you can see is overset text. The text frame provides the following indicators, as shown in the figure.

✦ **In port (empty):** A small white square on the upper-left corner of a text frame is the in port, indicating where a story enters the frame.

✦ **In port (with arrow):** Within a chain of threaded text frames, the in port might contain a right-facing arrow indicating that the story is continuing into this frame.

✦ **Out port (empty):** A small white square on the lower-right corner of a text frame is the out port, indicating that the story fits comfortably within the frame.

✦ **Out port (with arrow):** Within a chain of threaded text frames, the out port might contain a right-facing arrow indicating that the story is continuing into another frame.

✦ **Out port (with plus sign):** A small red plus sign in the out port indicates that more of the story exists than can fit in the text frame and that there is no subsequent text frame for the text to flow into.

✦ **Threads:** When you choose View ➪ Show Text Threads (or press Option+⌘+Y or Ctrl+Alt+Y), you can view threads, or lines, indicating the direction in which frames are threaded. (To see multiple text chains, Shift+click to select text frames from different threads.)

In the figure, the upper-right corner of the first text frame is empty, indicating that the text starts in this frame, rather than flow from another frame. The lower-right corner of the first text frame on the page displays an out port with an arrow, indicating that text is flowing to another frame (the text frame at right). A thread shows exactly where the text enters the next text frame at its in port, which contains another arrow. The lower-right corner of the text frame at right shows overset text (the red + symbol), indicating that all the text doesn't fit.

Threading frames manually

To thread text frames manually, you simply use a selection tool to link out ports to in ports. You can prethread existing text frames by linking empty text frames, and add text later, or you can create threads from a text frame that contains text.

Tip   Linking manually from out port to in port works well for continuing a magazine article from one page to the next.

Note   Oddly, you cannot thread frames while the Type tool is selected, so remember to switch to a selection tool.

To thread text frames:

1. **Create a series of frames or shapes through which you intend to flow text.** (Any empty non-text frames are converted to text frames as soon as you thread to them from a text frame. Thus, at least the first frame in this chain must be a text frame.) The frames do not need to be on the same page.

2. **Click either the Selection tool or the Direction Selection tool.**

3. **Click the out port of the first text frame in the thread.** The pointer becomes the loaded-text icon.

4. **Click the in port of the second text frame in the thread.** You can also click any empty frame or click and drag to draw a new text frame. How text flow behaves depends on the text frame's status:

   • If the first frame holds no text, when text is later placed or typed into it, any text that does not fit that first text frame flows into the second frame.

   • If the first frame holds text but is not already linked to another text frame, any overset text flows into the text frame you just selected.

   • If the first text frame is already linked to another text frame, the text is now redirected to the text frame you just selected.

5. **Use the Pages pane to add or switch pages as necessary while you continue clicking out ports and in ports until your chain of threaded text frames is complete.**

6. **When you finish threading text frames, select another object on the page or another tool.** When you import a story into any text frame in this chain, it starts in the upper-right corner of the first frame and flows through the frames in the same order as the threads.

 Tip   To see text threads easily while threading across pages, change the document view to 20 percent or so.

 Note   Text flows in the order in which you select frames. If you move a frame, its order in the text flow remains unchanged, so if you're not careful, you could, for example, accidentally have text flow from a frame at the top of the page to one at the bottom of a page, and then to one in the middle of a page.

Threading frames semiautomatically

InDesign's semiautoflow method of threading text frames varies only slightly from the manual method. Follow the same steps for threading text frames manually, except press and hold Option or Alt each time you click in the next text frame. This lets you bypass the in ports and out ports and simply click from text frame to text frame to establish links. Note that if a text frame contains overset text, the overset text flows through the additional frames as you create the thread.

 Tip   While first placing a word processing file, you can also Option+click or Alt+click in the first text frame to begin a semiautoflow process.

Note   Remember to Option+click or Alt+click each text frame, or you'll revert to manual threading.

Threading frames and adding pages automatically

The autoflow method for threading frames is what lets you flow a lengthy story quickly through a document. You can either autoflow text into the master text frame or into automatically created text frames that fit within the column guides. InDesign flows the text into any existing pages, and then adds new pages based on the current master page. You can initiate autoflow before or after placing a word processing file.

Placing text while autoflowing

If you haven't imported text yet, you can place a file and have it automatically flow through the document. This method works well for flowing text into pages that are all formatted the same way, such as a book. Here's how it works:

1. **Confirm that the master page in use has a master text frame or appropriate column guides.**

2. **With no text frames selected, choose File ⇨ Place or press ⌘+D or Ctrl+D.**

3. **Locate and select a word processing file, and then click Open.**

4. **When the loaded-text icon appears, Shift+click in the first column that will contain the text.** InDesign adds all the necessary text frames and pages, and flows in the entire story.

Autoflowing after placing text

If you've already placed a text file into a single text frame or even a threaded chain of text frames, you can still autoflow text from the last text frame. To do this, click the overset icon in the out port, and then Shift+click on any page to indicate where to start the autoflow.

Tip   You might use the autoflow after placing text method if you're placing the introduction to an article in a highly designed opener page, and then flowing the rest of the article into standard pages.

Breaking and rerouting threads

After text frames are threaded, you have three options for changing the threads: You can break threads to stop text from flowing, insert a text frame into an existing chain of threaded text frames, and remove text frames from a thread.

✦ To break the link between two text frames, double-click either an out port or an in port. The thread between the two text frames is removed and all text that had flowed from that point is sucked out of the subsequent text frames and stored as overset text.

✦ To insert a text frame after a specific text frame in a chain, click its out port. Then, click and drag the loaded-text icon to create a new text frame. That new frame is automatically threaded to the previous and next text frame.

✦ To reroute text threads — for example, to drop the middle text frame from a chain of three — click the text frame with the Selection tool and press Delete or Backspace. The text frame is deleted and the threads are rerouted. You can Shift+click to multiple-select text frames to remove as well. Note that you cannot reroute text threads without removing the text frames.

Threading Icons

While you're threading text, several icons provide visual cues as to the type of threading you're doing and what the results will be. (To view threads from a text frame selected with the Selection tool or Direct Selection tool, choose View ➪ Show Text Threads or press Option+⌘+Y or Ctrl+Alt+Y.) The figure shows, from left to right, the loaded-text icon, the loaded-text frame-flow icon, the thread icon, the semiautoflow loaded-text icon, and the autoflow loaded-text icon.

✦ The **loaded-text icon** contains text that needs to be placed or overset text that needs to be threaded into a new text frame.

✦ When the loaded-text icon is over a text frame, the icon changes so the icon appears in parentheses, becoming the **loaded-text frame-flow icon.** The same thing happens for the semiautoflow text-flow icon.

✦ The **thread icon,** which looks like two links in a chain, appears while you're threading text frames manually. Specifically, the loaded-text icon changes to this icon when it's over an empty text frame to which you can thread the current text frame.

✦ The **semiautoflow loaded-text icon** appears when you Option+click or Alt+click text frames while threading a series of text frames.

✦ The **autoflow loaded-text icon** appears when you Shift+click on a page to initiate the autoflow process, in which InDesign adds text frames and pages to contain the entire story.

Adjusting Columns

The placement of columns on the page and the amount of space between them has significant impact on readability. Column width, in general, works with type size and leading to create lines and rows of text that you can read easily. This means you're not getting lost from one line to the next, that you're not accidentally jumping across columns, and that you're not getting a headache while squinting at the page.

Tip As a rule of thumb: As columns get wider, the type size and leading increase. For example, you might see 9-point text and 15-point leading in 2½-inch columns, while 15-point text and 13-point leading might work better in 3½-inch columns.

InDesign lets you place columns on the page automatically, create any number of columns within a text frame, and change columns at any time.

Specifying columns in master frames

If you choose to create a *master text frame* — an automatically placed text frame within the margin guides — when you create a new document, you can specify the number of columns in it at the same time.

In the Columns area in the New Document dialog box shown in Figure 15-2, use the Number field to specify how many columns and the Gutter field to specify how much space to place between the columns. Whether or not you select the Master Text Frame option (which makes the frame appear on all pages), guides for these columns will still be placed on the page and can be used for placing text frames and other objects.

Adjusting columns in text frames

After you create a text frame and flow text into it, you can still change the number of columns in it. First, select the text frame with a selection tool or the Type tool (or Shift+click to select multiple text frames and change all their columns at once). Then choose Object ➪ Text Frame Options, or press ⌘+B or Ctrl+B. You can also use the Control palette to quickly change the number of columns (see Chapter 9).

Tip   Although programs like InDesign and QuarkXPress have long offered multiple-column text frames, many designers still draw each column as a separate frame (a holdover from PageMaker's approach). Don't do that—it makes it easy to have columns of slightly different widths and slightly different positions, so text doesn't align properly. Use the columns feature in your text frames so you won't have to worry about sloppy layouts. Plus, using this feature makes it easy to change the number of columns—no need to resize existing text frames or relink them.

Note that the options in the Columns area work differently depending on whether Fixed Column Width is selected or deselected:

✦ If it is not selected, InDesign subtracts from the text frame's width the space specified for the gutters, and then divides the remaining width by the number of columns to figure out how wide the columns can be. For example, a 10-inch-wide text frame with three columns and a gutter of ½ inch ends up with three 3-inch columns and two ½-inch gutters. The math is $(10–[2 \times 0.5]) \div 3$.

✦ If it is selected, InDesign resizes the text frame to fit the number of columns you selected at the indicated size, as well as the gutters between them. For example, if in a 10-inch-wide text frame you specify a column width of 5 inches and a gutter of ½ inch and you choose three columns, you'll end up with a 15-inch-wide text frame containing three 5-inch columns and two ½-inch gutters. The math is $(5 \times 3) + (2 \times 2)$.

Select the Preview option to see the effects of your changes before finalizing them.

Placing rules between columns

The use of vertical rules (thin lines) between columns—called intercolumn rules—is an effective way to separate columns with small gutters. (This is often done in newspapers, whose columns and gutters are usually thin.) It can also add visual interest and a sense of old-fashioned authority—it was a common technique for newspapers a century ago and is still used by the august *Wall Street Journal,* for example.

Unfortunately, InDesign does not provide an automatic method for creating intercolumn rules. To get around this lack, you need to draw lines on the page—in the center of the gutters—with the Line tool. Because you might resize text frames or change the number of columns while designing a document, you should add the vertical rules at the end of the process. In a document with a standard layout, such as a newspaper or magazine, you can place the rules between columns in text frames on the master page so they're automatically placed on every page. As always with such objects, you can modify them on individual document pages as needed (just be sure to Shift+⌘+click or Ctrl+Shift+click to select them when working in your document pages).

When drawing rules between columns, use the rulers to precisely position the lines. After you've drawn the lines, Shift+click to select all the lines and the text frames, and then choose Object ➪ Group, or ⌘+G or Ctrl+G. When the lines are grouped to the text frame, you can move them all as a unit. This also prevents someone from accidentally moving a vertical rule later.

Tip Keep the width of intercolumn rules thin: usually a hairline (¼ point) or ½ point. Larger than that is usually too thick and can be confused with the border of a sidebar or other boxed element.

Working with merged data

Word processing programs such as Microsoft Word have long let you create forms with mail merge, so you can send a letter to lots of people, letting Word automatically print a copy for all recipients and insert their names, addresses, and so forth into their copies. (Some programs have called this capability *variable text*.) PageMaker 7 added a similar capability called data merge, which uses the same principle to handle variable text for form letters, catalogs, and other documents where the layout is identical but specific pieces are customized. The $49 PageMaker Plug-In Pack for InDesign CS brought this functionality to InDesign, and now InDesign CS2 incorporates data merge.

New Feature Merged data is new to InDesign CS2, although it is based on an optional plug-in for InDesign CS.

Merged-data documents fall into two basic classes, as Figure 15-8 shows:

✦ Form letters, where one layout is printed multiple times, with each copy having personalized information.

✦ Labels, where layout components are repeated several times in the same layout, but with different information. There is usually just one copy that is printed.

What InDesign's data-merge feature cannot do is let you create catalogs in which you have different, variable-sized records on one page. You can use the data-merge feature for catalog-type documents if your layout is highly structured and each record will take exactly the same amount of space (like address labels).

Cross-Reference If you want to create catalogs or other documents with variable-sized records from databases or similar sources, use Adobe Tagged Text, as described in Chapter 13.

Figure 15-8: Two types of merged-data documents — a form letter (left) and a set of mailing labels

Regardless of which kind of merge documents you are creating, the setup is the same. Create a text file with the various data separated either by tabs or commas (use just one as your separator in the file, rather than mix the two). Start a new record by pressing Enter or Return (a new paragraph). The first row should contain the names of the fields. For example, for a local guidebook listing cafés, your data might look like this (I've put → characters to indicate the tabs):

```
name→address→phone
Martha & Bros.→3868 24th St.→(415) 641-4433
Martha & Bros.→1551 Church St.→(415) 648-1166
Martha & Bros.→745 Cortland St.→(415) 642-7585
Martha & Bros.→2800 California St.→(415) 931-2281
Diamond Corner Cafà→751 Diamond St.→(415) 282-9551
Farley's Coffeehouse→1315 18th St.→(415) 648-1545.
```

This simple file has three fields per entry: the café name, its address, and its phone number. The file uses tabs as the separators.

Note   Because the source file is a text-only file, it cannot contain any formatting such as boldface or italics.

Tip   To import graphics as inline graphics, precede the field name with @, such as @*photo*. The record fields will then need to provide the complete path to the graphic file, which must be in a supported format. For example, a file's complete path could be MacintoshHD:Images: myphoto.tiff on the Mac or C:\Images\myphoto.tif in Windows.

With the source file ready, create or go to the text frame in which you want to flow your data, selecting the insertion point with the Type tool. Now follow these steps:

1. **Open the Data Merge pane by choosing Window ➪ Automation ➪ Data Merge.**

2. **Choose Select Data Source from the Data Merge pane's palette menu, navigate to the desired file using the resulting dialog box, and click Open.** If your data file changes, you can import the most current version by choosing Update Data Source from the Data Merge pane's palette menu. Choose Remove Data Source to remove a data file from the pane.

3. **The Data Merge pane now lists the data file and the fields it contains, as Figure 15-9 shows.**

Figure 15-9: The Data Merge pane and its palette menu

4. **Click and drag the fields to the appropriate spots in your layout, or double-click a field name to insert it at the current text-insertion point.** For example, in a form letter, you might click and drag the Name field to a point right after the text *Dear* and before the comma in the salutation. The field names will be enclosed in French quotation marks (« »). In your layout, this would look like

```
Dear «Name»,
```

You can use a field more than once in the layout. The pane shows which page numbers each field is used in (to the right of the field name).

Tip

You can preview the data in your fields by selecting the Preview option in the Data Merge pane (or choosing preview from its palette menu). You can go through the actual data by using the arrow buttons to the right of the Preview option or by typing a record number in the preview field.

5. **Format the fields as desired.** They will take on any paragraph formatting applied to the paragraphs containing them. You can use character styles and/or other local formatting on the fields as desired.

6. **Click the Create Merged Document button at the bottom right of the pane or choose Create Merged Document from the palette menu to import the entire data file's contents into your layout.** The Create Merged Document dialog box shown in Figure 15-10 opens with the Records pane. In this pane, you have the following options:

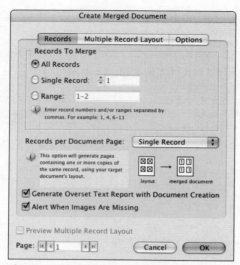

Figure 15-10: The Records pane of the Create Merged Document dialog box

- In the Records To Merge section, choose which record(s) to import. You can choose All, Single Record, or Range.

- In the Records per Document Page pop-up menu, choose Single Record if you want a new page output per record (such as in a form letter) or Multiple Records if you want to print multiple copies of the same record on a page (such as for business cards). Figure 15-11 shows a simple layout (of address labels) that is a typical example of where the Multiple Records option is used. You set up the placement of these records in the Multiple Record Layout pane, shown in Figure 15-12. Note that InDesign copies the entire text frame containing the data fields when you choose Multiple Records.

Caution

If you create multiple records on a page, be sure that you leave blank the space in which the labels' fields are copied—the Data Merge tool won't work around objects in the layout. Instead, it blindly follows the specs in the Multiple Record Layout pane, repeating fields until the page is full or until it runs out of fields.

Also don't copy the frames containing the Data Merge text in your layout to fill out your page— the Data Merge tool does that for you. Instead, there should just be one occurrence of your repeating record in your layout, placed at its topmost and leftmost position.

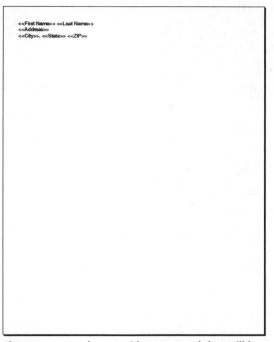

Figure 15-11: A layout with one record that will be copied multiple times on the page by using the Data Merge pane's Multiple Record Layout tool

7. **Go to the Options pane and verify the import options work for your document.** Figure 15-13 shows the Options pane, whose options are:

   - In the Image Placement section, choose how to fit any imported graphics by choosing an option in the Fitting pop-up menu. You'll typically pick Fit Images Proportionally, which is the default setting. You can also select the Center in Frame option to center the imported graphics, and the Link Images option to link to the source graphics files rather than embed the graphic into the InDesign layout.

   - In the lower section of the pane, you can have InDesign remove blank lines created by empty fields by selecting the Remove Blank Lines for Empty Fields option. This is handy, for example, if your layout permits two address lines per recipient. Anyone with a single address line will have no space between that address and the city name if this option is selected. You can also limit the number of pages in the merged document by selecting the Page Limit per Document option and typing a value in its field.

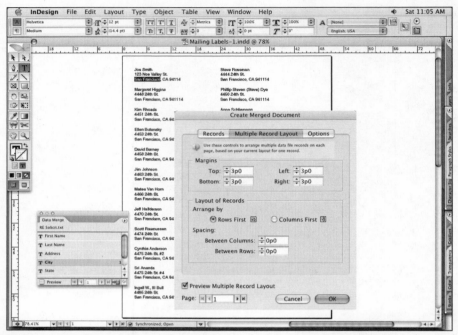

Figure 15-12: The Multiple Records pane of the Create Merged Document dialog box, along with the records previewed

8. **Click OK. InDesign creates a new document based on the original layout and merged data.** The merged text is now editable and is no longer linked to its source data, so to update the document you need to regenerate it from the document that contains the Data Merge records. (That's why InDesign creates a new document for the resulting data rather than replacing the source file.)

   There is a key exception: If you place the records on a master page, Data Merge creates document pages based on the imported data within the current document, rather than create an entirely new document. If you place the records on a master page, you can later update the records through the Data Merge pane and have the document pages updated as well.

Tip

There's a real benefit to putting your fields on master pages: You can then update the layout if the source data file changes (choose Update Data Fields from the Data Merge pane's palette menu). You cannot do this if you place the fields on a regular document page because InDesign would have created a new document containing the merged data.

New Feature

The ability to place fields on master pages and to update fields after data-merged document pages have been created is new to InDesign CS2, versus the capabilities of the PageMaker Plug-in Pack for InDesign CS.

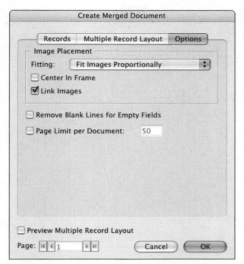

Figure 15-13: The Options pane of the Create Merged Document dialog box

Summary

When text doesn't fit within a single text frame—the case in almost any multipage publication—you need to link (or *thread*) the text frames. You can do this manually, threading one text frame to the next, or you can have InDesign automatically add pages containing threaded text frames. After frames are threaded, you can still reflow text by breaking text threads and rerouting the threads.

In addition to flowing text through the threaded frames, you can flow it through multiple columns within each frame. You can change the number of columns or their width within a frame at any time. To distinguish columns more visually, you can draw vertical lines between columns and group them with the text frames.

InDesign CS2 provides a new feature to produce data-merge documents. Such documents contain variable text, such as the address in a form letter or pricing and names in a catalog.

✦   ✦   ✦

Specifying Character Attributes

*T*ype is the visual representation of the spoken word. A *typographer* is a person who designs with type. As a user of InDesign, chances are you're going to be making lots of decisions about the appearance of the text in the publications you produce. You are, whether you consider yourself one or not, a typographer. And not only are InDesign users typographers, they're typographers who have an extensive arsenal of text formatting tools that let them tweak and polish their type in a nearly infinite variety of ways.

Of all the decisions an InDesign user makes when designing a publication, decisions about type are arguably the most important. Why? Because a publication can't be effective if the text is hard to read. The difference between good typography and bad typography is the same as the difference between clear speaking and mumbling. The intent of a clear speaker and a mumbler may be the same, but the effect on the listener is quite different. In publishing, the printed words are the containers in which the writer's message is transported to the reader. As the caretaker of those words, you hold great power. Whether or not the message is successfully transported depends largely on your typographic decisions.

As you learn to use InDesign's powerful type-formatting features, you should always remember the cardinal rule of typography: Type exists to honor content. By all means, you should take full advantage of the available tools, but sometimes knowing when not to use a fancy typographic feature is as important as knowing how to use the feature in the first place.

 Cross-Reference This chapter focuses on modifying character-level typographic formats; Chapter 17 focuses on modifying paragraph-level formats. Chapter 27 offers a broader look at using InDesign to design with type.

Working with Character Formats

Before you begin looking at InDesign's character-formatting features, you should be clear about a fundamental InDesign type-formatting concept: Using separate tools, InDesign lets you modify the appearance of highlighted characters *or* selected paragraphs:

✦ When characters are highlighted (or the text cursor is flashing), you can use the Character pane (Type ➪ Character, or ⌘+T or Ctrl+T) shown in Figure 16-1 to change their appearance in several ways. If you choose Hide Options from the palette menu, the Vertical Scale, Horizontal Scale, Baseline Shift, and Skew fields and the Language pop-up menu are not displayed.

✦ When paragraphs are selected, the Paragraph pane (Type ➪ Paragraph, or Option+⌘+T or Ctrl+Alt+T) lets you change how the paragraphs are constructed. (For more information about the Paragraph pane, see Chapter 17.)

The Character pane provides access to most of InDesign's character-formatting options. Three of the options — Font Family, Type Style, and Font Size — are also available in the Type menu, and several options have keyboard shortcuts. The Control palette offers all the formatting options of the Character pane plus others, as shown in Figure 16-2. (If the Control palette doesn't show the character formatting options shown in the figure, be sure to select text and click the A icon on the palette.)

Note   In InDesign (like most programs), you can select only contiguous text. So if you have, for example, several subheads to which you want to apply a font, you can't select them all and apply the formatting in one fell swoop. You have to do each text segment separately.

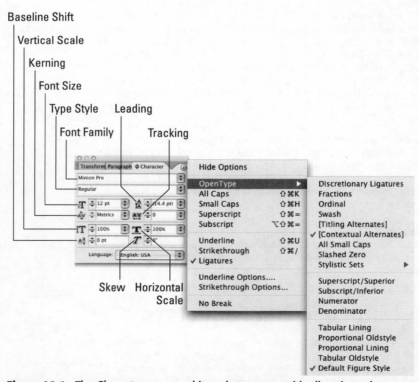

Figure 16-1: The Character pane and its palette menu with all options shown

Tip If the Type tool is selected and no objects are active, the controls in the Character pane are still available. In this situation, any changes you make in the Character pane become the default settings for the document and are automatically used when you create new text frames. If you change character formats when the cursor is flashing and no text is selected, your changes are applied at the insertion point. When you begin typing, you see the results of your changes.

InDesign lets you apply character formats to highlighted text in two ways: You can:

✦ Use the local controls in the Character pane, the Control palette, or the Type menu, or use the keyboard shortcuts

✦ Create and apply character-level styles

Either way, you can apply the same formatting. The difference is that a character style's settings are stored, so you can apply the exact same settings easily to other text. Plus, if you change a character style's settings, any text based on it is automatically changed to reflect the new settings.

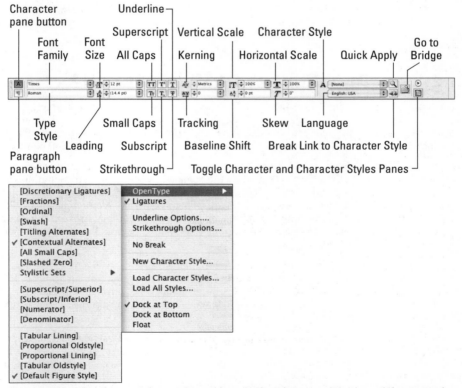

Figure 16-2: The character formatting options in the Character (A) pane of the Control palette and its palette menu

If you are working on a simple, one-page publication, such as a business card, a poster, or an ad, you'll probably use the Character pane to format the text elements. However, if you're producing a multipage publication — a newsletter, magazine, catalog, or newspaper, for example — you should take advantage of styles. Using them will save you time and make your job a whole lot easier.

Cross-Reference   For details about creating and applying character and paragraph styles, see Chapter 19.

Even if you do use styles for a particular publication, you'll probably also do some local formatting. For example, you would probably use the Character pane to format the type on the opening spread of a feature magazine article, and then use styles to quickly format the remainder of the article.

Cross-Reference   Some of the controls in the Transform pane let you change the appearance of all the text within a text frame. For more information about the Transform pane, see Chapter 10.

Tip   You can change the default character formats associated with the Type tool by making changes in the Character pane or Control palette when no text is selected or when the text-insertion cursor isn't flashing.

Changing Font Family, Type Style, and Size

These days, the terms *font, face, typeface, font family,* and *type style* are often used interchangeably. When you're talking with friends or colleagues about typography, it doesn't matter which term you use as long as you make yourself understood, but if you're going to be setting type with InDesign, you should be familiar with the font-related terms in the menus and panes.

The term *font,* or typeface, usually refers to a collection of characters — including letters, numbers, and special characters — that share the same overall appearance, including stroke width, weight, angle, and style. For example, Helvetica Plain, Arial Bold, Adobe Garamond Semibold Italic, and ITC New Baskerville Italic are well-known fonts. A *font family* is a collection of several fonts that share the same general appearance but differ in stroke width, weight, and/or stroke angle. Some examples of font families are Adobe Caslon, Berthold Baskerville, Times New Roman, and Tekton.

In InDesign, each of the fonts that make up a font family is referred to as a *type style*. For example, the Times Europa font family is made up of four type styles: Roman, Italic, Bold, and Bold Italic, as shown in Figure 16-3. When you choose a font family from the Character pane's Font Family menu, InDesign displays the family's type style variations in the accompanying Type Styles pop-up menu.

Unlike most word-processing and desktop-publishing programs, InDesign doesn't include built-in shadow and outline type styles. Most programs create these stylistic variations artificially by modifying plain characters. If you want to create outline text, you can use the Stroke pane (Window ➪ Stroke or F10) to apply a stroke. If you want to create a drop shadow for text, you can stack and offset two text frames or use the Drop Shadow feature.

Figure 16-3: The Times Europa font family includes four typestyles — Roman, Italic, Bold, and Bold Italic — as shown here.

Cross-Reference

For more on the Stroke pane and other text-as-art techniques, see Chapter 27. For more on creating special typographic effects, see Chapter 18.

Similarly, bold and italic variations are available only for font families that include these type styles. This prevents you from applying, for example, italic to Trajan, a font family that doesn't include an italic variation. (InDesign does let you create false italics by skewing text, which is covered later in this chapter. However, you should avoid such heavy-handed shape twisting unless it's absolutely necessary.)

When you change from one font to another in InDesign, you can choose a new font family and type style independently in the Character pane. For example, changing from Arial Bold to Times Bold or from Arial Regular to Berthold Baskerville Regular is a simple change of font family. However, if you switch from Bookman Light to Century Schoolbook Bold Italic, you're changing both family and type style.

Note

InDesign CS2 will sometimes display a font name multiple times in various panes and dialog boxes, such as the Character pane. This occurs if you have multiple versions of a font on your computer — say, both a TrueType and PostScript version of Helvetica. (Version 2 and earlier of InDesign would show only one of these fonts, making the others inaccessible.) You can tell which is which by the code that InDesign appends to the font name: (TT) for TrueType, (T1) for PostScript Type 1, and (OTF) for OpenType. You really shouldn't have multiple versions of a font on your computer because different versions can look and be spaced differently resulting in inconsistent appearance that's hard to fix. If you notice such multiple versions because InDesign calls them to your attention, delete or deactivate the unneeded fonts (typically, you would keep the PostScript version, or OpenType if supported by your service bureau).

New Feature

InDesign CS2 can display previews of fonts when you select fonts through the Control palette, various text-oriented panes, and the Type menu. You turn on this capability in the Type pane of the Preferences dialog box, as covered in Chapter 3. But it makes your menus so large that they may become unwieldy.

Selecting fonts

The Character pane and Control palette offer two methods for changing the font family applied to highlighted text. You can:

✦ Click the Font Family menu, and then choose a name from the list of available font families.

✦ Click in front of or highlight the font name displayed in the Font Family field, type the first few letters of the font family you want to apply, and then press Return or Enter. For example, typing **Ari** will select Arial (if it's available on your computer).

If you use the Font submenu in the Type menu, you can type the first letter of a font to skip to font names beginning with that letter once you have highlighted any font in the submenu.

You can select just the font family, as Figure 16-4 shows. When you change the font family applied to selected text, InDesign tries to maintain the applied type style. If, for example, you switch from Adobe Garamond Bold Italic to Adobe Caslon, InDesign automatically uses Adobe Caslon Bold Italic, which is one of several type styles that make up this font family. But if you switch from Arial Bold Italic to Avant Garde, which doesn't include a bold italic variation, Avant Garde Book is used instead.

Figure 16-4: To select a type style from the Control palette, you can first choose the font family from the Font Family pop-up menu, and then choose a typestyle from the Type Style pop-up menu, which shows only the type styles available for the selected font.

If a particular font family includes a submenu with type style variations, you can also choose a type style at the same time you choose a font family. If you choose only a font family when type styles are available in an accompanying submenu, no changes are applied to the selected text. Figure 16-5 shows an example of choosing both at the same time.

Note   InDesign sometimes uses the label Font Style in some palettes and in some documentation. It is the same as the label Type Style, just a different name for the same thing.

Changing type size

InDesign lets you specify type sizes from 0.1 point to 1,296 points (108 inches) in increments as fine as 0.001 point. Of course, even if it were possible to clearly print type as small as a thousandth of a point (that is, $\frac{1}{72,000}$ of an inch), which is beyond the capabilities of most printers, nobody could read it without a microscope anyway.

Use good judgment when choosing type sizes. For example, headlines should be larger than subheads, which in turn are larger than body text, which is larger than photo credits, and so on.

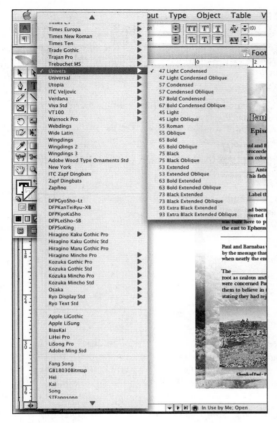

Figure 16-5: You can also select both the font family and the type style at the same time using the submenus in the Font Family menu in the Control palette, Character pane, or Character Styles pane, or in the Type menu's Font submenu.

InDesign offers several methods for changing the type size of highlighted text. You can:

✦ Use one of several techniques in the Character pane and Control palette:

- Choose one of the predefined sizes from the Size menu in the Character pane or Control palette.

- Highlight the currently applied type size displayed in the accompanying editable field, type a new size, and then press Return or Enter.

- Use the up and down cursor keys to increase or decrease the size in 1-point increments. Pressing and holding Shift multiplies the increment to 10.

✦ Choose Type ➪ Size, and then choose one of the predefined sizes listed in the Size submenu. If you choose Other from the submenu, the Size field is highlighted in the Character pane. Type a custom size, and then press Return or Enter.

✦ Control+click or right-click a text selection, and then choose a size from the Size submenu. If you choose Other from the submenu, the Font Size field is highlighted in the Character pane. Type a custom size, and then press Return or Enter.

✦ Use keyboard commands to adjust text size:

- Press Shift+⌘+. (period) or Ctrl+Shift+. (period) to enlarge highlighted text in 2-point increments. (You can set a different increment in the Units & Measurements pane in the Preferences dialog box, which is accessed by choosing InDesign ➪ Preferences on the Mac or Edit ➪ Preferences in Windows, or by pressing ⌘+K or Ctrl+K.)

- Press Shift+⌘+, (comma) or Ctrl+Shift+, (comma) to reduce highlighted text.

- Press Option+Shift+⌘+. (period) or Ctrl+Alt+Shift+. (period) to increase the text size in 10-point increments.

- Press Option+Shift+⌘+, (comma) or Ctrl+Alt+Shift+, (comma) to decrease the text size in 10-point increments.

Tip   It helps to think of these shortcuts as using the > and < characters rather than the period and comma, as mnemonics for *more* and *less*.

Note   If text is highlighted and the Size field is empty, it means that more than one type size is used in the selected text.

Applying Other Character Formats

Font family, type style, and type size are the most commonly modified character formats, but the Character pane and Control palette contain several other controls for managing the appearance of type. Some of these controls are displayed in the pane window; others are available in the pane's pop-up menu. The Control palette offers more formatting options than the Character pane.

In the Control palette, you can adjust all caps, small caps, superscript, subscript, underline, strikethrough, kerning, tracking, horizontal and vertical scale, baseline shift, skew, character style, and language. Through the palette menu, you can also set ligatures, modify underline and strikethrough settings, control whether text may break (be hyphenated), and select OpenType features. Figure 16-2 shows the palette menu for the Control palette's character formatting.

In the Character pane, you can adjust kerning, tracking, horizontal and vertical scale, baseline shift, skew, and language. Through its palette menu (refer to Figure 16-1), you can also set all caps, small caps, superscript, subscript, underline, strikethrough, ligatures, and underline and strikethrough settings, as well as control whether text may break (be hyphenated) and select OpenType features.

Note   You must choose Show Options from the Character pane's pop-up menu to display the Vertical Scale, Horizontal Scale, Baseline Shift, Skew, and Language options in the pane.

The Control palette has the same functions as the Character pane, except the all caps, small caps, superscript, subscript, underline, and strikethrough options are in the palette rather than in its palette menu.

Figure 16-6 shows the various effects in action.

You can do all sorts of *things with* text in InDesign

Figure 16-6: Various character-formatting options applied to text are illustrated here. Top row: *can* has been scaled horizontally, and *do* vertically, while *all* has had each letter's baseline shifted by a different amount. Compare that to the true superscript and subscript following the word *sorts.* Middle row: The word *things* has been skewed, while the word *with* is in real italics; notice how the letters *h, i,* and *t* differ between words.

Horizontal Scale and Vertical Scale

Some font families include condensed (that is, slightly squeezed) and/or expanded (slightly stretched) stylistic variations, but most don't. InDesign's Horizontal Scale option lets you create artificially condensed and expanded type by squeezing or stretching characters. Similarly, the Vertical Scale option lets you shrink or stretch type vertically.

Among typographers, there are two schools of thought about scaling type. One camp contends that such distortions of letterforms are taboo and should be avoided. The other side contends that a small amount of scaling doesn't adversely affect the original font and is acceptable. There's general agreement that overscaling should be avoided. For the most part, if you need to make text bigger or smaller, you should adjust font size; if you need to squeeze or stretch a range of text a bit, it's better to use InDesign's kerning and tracking controls (covered later in this chapter) because the letterforms are not affected. Only the space between letters changes when you kern or track text.

Unscaled text has a horizontal and vertical scale value of 100 percent. You can apply scaling values between 1 percent and 1,000 percent. If you apply equal horizontal and vertical scale values, you're making the original text proportionally larger or smaller. In this case, changing font size is a simpler solution. Keep in mind that when you scale text, you are not changing the font size. For example, 24-point type scaled vertically to 200 percent is 48 points tall, but its font size is still 24 points.

To change the scale of highlighted text, enter new values in the Horizontal and/or Vertical Scale fields in the Character pane or Control palette. If a value is highlighted in the Horizontal Scale or Vertical Scale field, you can also use the up and down cursor keys to increase and decrease the scaling in 1 percent increments; press and hold Shift to increase or decrease in 10 percent increments.

Baseline Shift

The *baseline* is an invisible horizontal line on which a line of characters rests. The bottom of each letter (except descenders, such as in *y, p, q, j,* and *g*) sits on the baseline. InDesign's Baseline Shift feature lets you move highlighted text above or below its baseline. This feature is useful for carefully placing such characters as trademark and copyright symbols and for creating custom fractions. (Unlike superscripts and subscripts, text whose baseline has shifted does not change size.)

To baseline-shift highlighted text, type new values in the Baseline Shift field in the Character pane or Control palette. You can also use the up and down cursor keys to increase the baseline shift in 1-point increments, or press and hold Shift when using the cursor keys to increase or decrease it in 10-point increments.

Skew (false italic)

For fonts that don't have an italic type style, InDesign provides the option to *skew,* or slant, text to create an artificial italic variation of any font. (You can also use it with fonts that have a natural italic; refer to Figure 16-6.) Like horizontal and vertical text scaling, skewing is a clunky way of creating italic-looking text. Use this feature to create special typographic effects, such as the shadow text shown in Figure 16-7, or in situations where a true italic style is not available.

Skewed shadow

Figure 16-7: Skewing and shading a copy of the black text creates this backlit shadow effect.

Note   Skewing as a form of italics typically works better for sans serif typefaces than for serif typefaces because the characters are simpler and have fewer embellishments that can get oddly distorted when skewed.

To skew highlighted text, you have two options:

✦ Type an angle value between –85 and 85 in the Skew field in the Character pane or Control palette. Positive values slant text to the left; negative values slant text to the right.

✦ Click the accompanying up or down cursors when the cursor is in the Skew field to skew text in 1-degree increments. Pressing and holding Shift while clicking the cursors changes the increment to 4 degrees.

Tip   You can also skew all the text in a text frame using the Shear tool or by changing the value in the Shear X Angle field in the Transform pane or Control palette after selecting the frame. Slanting text by shearing a text frame does not affect the skew angle of the text. You can specify a skew angle for highlighted text independently from the frame's shear angle.

Language

The ability to correctly hyphenate and check the spelling of text in several languages is one of InDesign's most powerful features. The program uses dictionaries to accomplish these tasks. These dictionaries, each of which contains several hundred thousand words, also let you specify a different language for text on a character-by-character basis, although chances are that a single word will be the smallest text unit to which you will apply a separate language.

For example, an article about Spanish cooking might include the word *albòndigas* (the Spanish term for meatballs). By applying the Spanish: Castilian language to this word, as shown in Figure 16-8, InDesign will not flag it when you check spelling. However, if you were to apply U.S. English to *albòndigas,* it would show up as a misspelled word (unless you add it to your dictionary).

To assign a different language to highlighted text, choose the appropriate language from the Language menu in the Control palette or from the Character pane's palette menu, as shown in Figure 16-8.

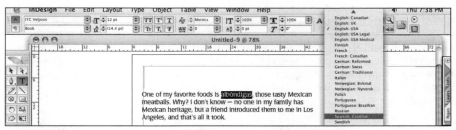

Figure 16-8: By applying the Spanish: Castilian language to *albòndigas,* as shown here, InDesign uses the associated dictionary when checking the spelling of this word.

Tip If you discover any correctly spelled words that are not included in a particular language dictionary, you can add the words to the dictionary. Choose Edit ➪ Spelling ➪ Dictionary and choose the appropriate dictionary in the Language pop-up menu to customize any dictionary.

QuarkXPress User The Passport edition of QuarkXPress has a similar feature to specify the hyphenation and spelling language. The standard version of QuarkXPress does not include this feature.

All Caps and Small Caps

When you choose All Caps, the uppercase version of all highlighted characters is used: Lowercase letters are converted to uppercase and uppercase letters remain unchanged.

Similarly, the Small Caps option affects just lowercase letters. When you choose Small Caps, InDesign automatically uses the Small Caps type style if one is available for the font family applied to the highlighted text (few font families include this type style). If a Small Caps type-style is not available, InDesign generates small caps from uppercase letters using the scale percentage specified in the Advanced Type pane of the Preferences dialog box (choose InDesign ➪ Preferences on the Mac or Edit ➪ Preferences in Windows, or press ⌘+K or Ctrl+K). The default scale value used to generate small caps text is 70 percent (of uppercase letters).

Tip You should avoid typing text in all capital letters, even if you think you want all caps. If you type lowercase letters, you can easily change them to uppercase by applying the All Caps format, but if you type uppercase letters, you can't change them to lowercase or to small caps without retyping them or having InDesign retype them for you. To have InDesign do the work, select the text and then choose Type ➪ Change Case ➪ Lowercase. You could also choose Title Case or Sentence Case (which capitalizes the first letter in each highlighted sentence) as appropriate to the text.

Superscript and Subscript

When you apply the Superscript and Subscript character formats to highlighted text, InDesign applies a baseline shift to the characters, lifting them above (for Superscript) or lowering them below (for Subscript) their baseline, *and* reduces their size.

The amount of baseline shift and scaling that's used for the Superscript and Subscript formats is determined by the Position and Size fields in the Advanced Type pane of the Preferences dialog box (choose InDesign ➪ Preferences on the Mac or Edit ➪ Preferences in Windows, or press ⌘+K or Ctrl+K). The default Position value for both formats is 33.3 percent, which means that characters are moved up or down by one-third of the applied leading value. The default Superscript and Subscript Size value is 58.3 percent, which means that superscripted and subscripted characters are reduced to 58.3 percent of the applied font size. The Advanced Type pane lets you specify separate default settings for Superscript and Subscript.

Tip

For most newspaper and magazine work, I prefer a size of 65 percent for superscripts and subscripts, as well as a position of 30 percent for subscripts and 35 percent for superscripts. These values work better than the InDesign defaults in the small text sizes and tight leading of such publications. If you change these settings when no document is open, they become the default for all future new documents.

You can use the Superscript and Subscript formats to create, for example, custom fractions or numbers for footnotes or to reposition special characters such as asterisks. To apply the Superscript or Subscript format to highlighted text, choose the appropriate option from the Character pane's pop-up menu. Figure 16-6 shows examples of text to which the default Superscript and Subscript settings have been applied.

QuarkXPress User

InDesign does not have an equivalent to QuarkXPress's superior format, which is like a superscript except that it aligns the top of the character to the text's cap height. This helps to ensure that the leading is not changed. Some OpenType fonts, however, have superior characters, as covered in the "OpenType Options" section later in this chapter.

Underline and Strikethrough

The Underline and Strikethrough formats are holdovers from the days of typewriters and are not typographically acceptable for indicating emphasis in text, which is better accomplished by using bold and/or italic type styles.

Underlines can be useful in kickers and other text above a headline, as well as in documents formatted to look as if they are typewritten. Strikethrough is rarely useful in a document, although in textbooks and other educational materials, you may want to use it to indicate incorrect answers, eliminated choices, or deleted text (when showing how to edit).

If you do use underlines and strikethrough, InDesign lets you specify exactly how they look through the Underline Options and Strikethrough Options dialog boxes available in the palette menus of the Character pane and Control palette.

Cross-Reference

Chapter 18 covers these custom underline and strikethrough settings in detail.

Note

If you don't set a specific size for underlines and strikethroughs, the weight of an underline or strikethrough line is relative to the type size.

Ligatures

A ligature is a special character that combines two letters. Most early typefaces included five ligatures: ff, ffi, fl, ffi, and ffl. These days, most fonts include just two ligatures: fi and fl. When you choose the Ligature option, InDesign automatically displays and prints a font's built-in ligatures — instead of the two component letters — if the font includes ligatures.

One nice thing about the Ligature option is that, even though a ligature looks like a single character on-screen, it's still fully editable. That is, you can click between the two-letter shapes and insert text if necessary. Also, a ligature created with the Ligatures option will not cause InDesign's spell checker to flag the word that contains it.

QuarkXPress User Unlike QuarkXPress for Windows, InDesign for Windows supports automatic ligatures in Windows fonts that have them.

To use ligatures within highlighted text, choose Ligatures from the Character pane's or Control palette's palette menu (Ligatures is set to On by default). Figure 16-9 shows a before-and-after example of text to which the Ligature option has been applied.

For most Mac fonts that include ligatures, pressing Option+Shift+5 inserts the fi ligature, while Option+Shift+6 inserts the fl ligature. In Windows, you'll have to use a program like Character Map that comes with Windows (usually available by choosing Start ➪ Accessories ➪ System Tools ➪ Character Map) to access the ligature characters in fonts that support them. Either way, if you type ligatures yourself, InDesign's spell checker will flag any words that contain them. For this reason, you may want to let the program handle the task of inserting ligatures.

finally, I
can float!

Figure 16-9: Ligatures are used in the top two lines but not in the bottom two. Notice the difference in space between the *fi* and *fl* letter pairs in *finally* and *float.*

finally, I
can float!

OpenType options

The OpenType font standard developed by Adobe and Microsoft supports many more character variations than the ones most publishers use. In OpenType, many variations of a character exist in the same font, and you specify which variant you want for highlighted text in the Character pane's or Control palette's palette menu.

Figure 16-10 shows examples of the two kinds of numerals supported in OpenType. The OpenType menu in the Control palette's and Character pane's palette menu has the following options:

1234567890

1234567890

Figure 16-10: The top row of numbers uses typical titling figures — all are the same height. The bottom row uses old-style numerals.

- ✦ **Discretionary ligatures.** This option creates ligatures whenever possible, rather than just for the standard fi, fl, ffi, and ffl combinations.

- ✦ **Fractions.** This option substitutes true fractions such as ½ for the text 1/2.

- ✦ **Ordinal.** This option raises the *st, nd,* and *th* portions of ordinal numbers such as *1st, 22nd,* and *345th*.

- ✦ **Swash.** This option adds embellishments in front of the first character or at the end of the last letter of a word.

- ✦ **Titling Alternates.** This option uses variants of a font for use in titles. These variants are usually a little clearer than the body-text version so they work better as titles where surrounding white space can make the normal variations within body text look strange.

- ✦ **Contextual Alternates.** This option uses variants for specific characters to improve legibility in some contexts. For example, a contextual alternate for *t* might drop the left-side bar in the *t* so it doesn't bump against an adjacent letter.

- ✦ **All Small Caps.** This option replaces all the text with true small caps, not the scaled-down version that the standard InDesign Small Caps feature uses. True small caps are usually a little thicker than their scaled-down version, so they have the same visual weight as lowercase letters.

- ✦ **Slashed Zero.** This option adds a slash over a 0 character for fonts that support it. The slashed zero is often used in European writing to differentiate from the letter *O*.

- ✦ **Superscript/Superior.** This option replaces scaled-down raised text that InDesign uses to create superscripts with thicker characters placed where the font designers think works best. As with true small caps, this results in superscripts that have more visual weight.

- ✦ **Subscript/Inferior.** This option replaces scaled-down lowered text that InDesign uses to create subscripts with thicker characters placed where the font designers think works best. As with true small caps, this results in subscripts that have more visual weight.

- ✦ **Numerator.** This option is used to build a fraction when the font does not have predefined ones, such as for $^{n\cdot}\!/_{5}$.

- ✦ **Denominator.** This option is used to build a fraction when the font does not have predefined ones, such as for $\!/_{n}$.

✦ **Stylistic Sets.** This option lets you choose which sets of variants within a font to use. A very few OpenType fonts, such as Poetica Std, use stylistic sets that provide multiple variations of the same characters, letting you choose which variants to use.

✦ **Tabular Lining.** This option uses standard numeric characters (which start on the baseline and have no descenders or ascenders) spaced evenly for proper alignment in tables.

✦ **Proportional Oldstyle.** This option uses old-fashioned numerals with ascenders and descenders that are spaced like any other characters, based on their width, shape, and visual weight.

✦ **Proportional Lining.** This option uses standard numerals spaced like any other characters, based on their width, shape, and visual weight.

✦ **Tabular Oldstyle.** This option uses old-fashioned numerals spaced evenly for natural alignment in tables.

✦ **Default Figure Style.** This option does whatever the font's designers want it to do by default (one of the previous four settings).

Cross-Reference
Chapter 41 covers OpenType in more detail, including examples of various effects.

For the vast majority of fonts in use today, applying an OpenType feature has no effect because most fonts in use are standard Type 1 PostScript or TrueType. Among OpenType fonts, there is wide variation in what variations they support; InDesign indicates unavailable options by enclosing them in brackets in the menu.

Note
There is a type of font called an *expert font* that includes old-style numerals, fractions, true small caps, and other special characters. It is used as an adjunct to the regular version of the font, letting you manually apply the special characters. For example, if you used Garamond as your font, you could apply Garamond Expert to the numerals to get old-style numerals. This is a lot of work, so most people don't bother except for typographically sophisticated — and short — documents, such as ads. Unfortunately, InDesign doesn't detect the availability of expert fonts (for when you don't have OpenType fonts) and use them to apply OpenType-like attributes such as old-style numerals, true small caps, and true fractions when they are available. Instead, you have to apply them manually — or buy and use OpenType fonts instead.

No Break

InDesign lets you prevent individual words from being hyphenated or a string of words from being broken at the end of a line. For example, you may decide that you don't want to hyphenate software names, such as InDesign, CorelDraw, or FreeHand. Or perhaps you don't want to separate the *J* and the *P* in *J. P. Morgan.* The No Break option was created for situations such as these.

To prevent a word or a text string from being broken, highlight it, and then choose No Break from the Character pane's or Control palette's palette menu.

Caution
If you apply the No Break option to a range of text that's longer than the width of the current column, InDesign will track the text so that it fits on a single line — squeezing it unacceptably.

Tip   You can also prevent a word from being hyphenated by placing a discretionary hyphen (Shift+⌘+− [hyphen] or Ctrl+Shift+− [hyphen]) in front of the first letter.

Leaving Space between Characters and Lines

Typographers often pay as much attention to the space between characters, words, and lines of text as they do to the appearance of the characters themselves. Their concern about space is well justified. The legibility of a block of text depends as much on the space around it — called *white space* — as it does on the readability of the font. InDesign offers two ways to adjust the space between characters:

✦ **Kerning.** This is the adjustment of space between a pair of characters. Most fonts include built-in kerning tables that control the space between pesky character pairs, such as *LA*, *Yo*, and *WA*, that otherwise could appear to have a space between them even when there isn't one. Particularly at small font sizes, it's safe to use a font's built-in kerning information to control the space between letter pairs. But for large font sizes, for example the front-page nameplate of a newsletter or a magazine headline, you may want to manually adjust the space between certain character pairs to achieve consistent spacing.

✦ **Tracking.** This is similar to kerning but applies to a range of highlighted text. Tracking is the process of adding or removing space among all letters in a range of text.

InDesign lets you apply kerning and/or tracking to highlighted text in $\frac{1}{1,000}$-em increments called *units*. An em is as wide as the height of the current font size (that is, an em for 12-point text is 12 points wide), which means that kerning and tracking increments are relative to the applied font size.

InDesign's Leading (rhymes with *sledding*, not with *deeding*) feature lets you control the vertical space between lines of type. It's traditionally an attribute of paragraphs, but InDesign lets you apply it on a character-by-character basis. (To override the character-oriented approach, ensuring that leading changes affect entire paragraphs, select the Apply Leading to Entire Paragraphs option in the Type pane of the Preferences dialog box (choose InDesign ➪ Preferences on the Mac or Edit ➪ Preferences in Windows, or press ⌘+K or Ctrl+K).

Cross-Reference   Chapter 17 explains how to control the spacing between words, which is part of paragraph formatting.

QuarkXPress User   InDesign users, especially QuarkXPress converts, may be surprised at the seemingly large kerning and tracking values produced by all the program's kerning and tracking methods. Keep in mind that InDesign lets you adjust space in 0.001-em units ($\frac{1}{1,000}$th of an em). In QuarkXPress, for example, the kerning unit is 0.005 em ($\frac{1}{200}$th of an em). So QuarkXPress users should not be surprised to see kerning and tracking values that are 10 to 20 times greater than you're used to — you're working with multiples of finer increments.

Kerning

The Kerning controls in the Character pane and Control palette provide three options for kerning letter pairs: Metrics kerning, Optical kerning, and manual kerning:

✦ **Metrics kerning** uses a font's built-in kerning pairs to control the space between character pairs in the highlighted text.

✦ **Optical kerning** has InDesign look at each letter pair in highlighted text and add or remove space between the letters based on the shapes of the characters.

✦ **Manual kerning** is adding or removing space between a specific letter pair in user-specified amounts.

The kerning method you use will depend on the circumstances. For example, some fonts include a large set of kerning pairs. Such fonts, especially at text font sizes (9 to 12 points) and lower, may look fine using the default Metrics kerning option, which uses built-in kerning pairs. On the other hand, if the font applied to highlighted text has few or no built-in kerning pairs or if several different fonts are mixed together, the text may benefit from the Optical kerning method. At display type sizes (36 points and larger) you may want to manually kern individual letter pairs to suit your taste.

When the flashing text cursor is between a pair of characters, the Kerning field displays the pair's kerning value. If Metrics or Optical kerning is applied, the kerning value is displayed in parentheses.

To apply Metrics or Optical kerning to highlighted text, choose the appropriate option from the Kerning pop-up menu. To apply manual kerning, click between a pair of letters, and then type a value in the Kerning field or choose one of the predefined values. Negative values tighten; positive values loosen.

Tip

You can also use a keyboard shortcut to apply manual kerning. Press Option+left arrow or Alt+left arrow to decrease the kerning value in increments of 20 units. Press Option+right arrow or Alt+right arrow to increase the kerning value in increments of 20 units. If you add the ⌘ or Ctrl keys to these keyboard shortcuts, the increment is increased to 100 units. If you use the up and down arrow keys in the Kerning field in the Character pane or Control palette, you change the kerning in increments of 10; while pressing and holding Shift the increments increase to 25.

Caution

A warning about kerning and tracking: InDesign happily lets you tighten or loosen text to the point of illegibility. If this is the effect you're after, go for it. But as a general rule, when letter shapes start to collide, you've tightened too far.

Tracking

If you understand kerning, you can think of tracking as uniform kerning applied to a range of text. You might use tracking to tighten character spacing for a font that you think is too spacey or loosen spacing for a font that's too tight. Or you could track a paragraph tighter or looser to eliminate a short last line or a *widow* (the last line of a paragraph that falls at the top of a page or column).

To apply tracking to highlighted text, type a value in the Character pane's Tracking field or choose one of the predefined values. Negative values tighten; positive values loosen (in 0.001-em increments). Use the same keyboard techniques as for kerning.

Leading

In the days of metal type, typesetters would insert thin strips of metal—specifically, lead—between rows of letters to aid legibility. In the world of digital typography, *leading* refers to the vertical space between lines of type as measured from baseline to baseline. Leading in InDesign is a character-level format, which means that you can apply different leading values within a single paragraph. InDesign looks separately at each line of text in a paragraph and uses the largest applied leading value within a line to determine the leading for that line.

QuarkXPress User   Leading as a character format is a carryover from PageMaker (and not necessarily a good one). QuarkXPress users may find InDesign's leading method to be odd at first because leading is a paragraph-level format in QuarkXPress. In most cases, you apply a single leading value to entire paragraphs, in which case leading behaves like a paragraph-level format.

By default, InDesign applies Auto Leading to text. When Auto Leading is applied, leading is equal to 120 percent of the type size. For example, if Auto Leading is applied to 10-point text, the leading value is 12 points; for 12-point text, Auto Leading is 14.4 points; and so on. As long as you don't change fonts or type sizes in a paragraph, Auto Leading works pretty well. But if you do change fonts or sizes, Auto Leading can result in inconsistent spacing between lines. For this reason, it's safer to specify an actual leading value.

Generally, it's a good idea to use a leading value that is slightly larger than the type size, which is why Auto Leading works in many cases. When the leading value equals the type size, text is said to be set *solid.* That's about as tight as you'll ever want to set leading unless you're trying to achieve a special typographic effect or working with very large text sizes in ad-copy headlines. As is the case with kerning and tracking, when tight leading causes letters to collide—ascenders and descenders are the first to overlap—you've gone too far.

Tip   You can change InDesign's preset Auto Leading value of 120 percent. To do so, choose Type ⇨ Paragraph, or Option+⌘+T or Ctrl+Alt+T, to display the Paragraph pane. Choose Justification in the palette menu, type a new value in the Auto Leading field, and then click OK. (What Auto Leading has to do with Justification is a mystery.)

QuarkXPress User   Another mystery is why you cannot specify Auto Leading amounts in anything other than percentages. This will cause many QuarkXPress documents imported into InDesign to flow incorrectly because QuarkXPress lets you set the Auto Leading to a specific value, such as +2 (which adds 2 points to the text size rather than use a percentage like 120 percent that results in awkward leading amounts like 14.4 points). Being able to specify a specific additive value like +2 makes sense for many kinds of layouts, so the inability to specify such values is an unfortunate continued omission in InDesign.

One thing QuarkXPress users can do to make InDesign work more like QuarkXPress's standard approach to leading is to ensure that the Apply Leading to Entire Paragraphs option is selected in the Type pane of the Preferences dialog box (InDesign ⇨ Preferences on the Mac or Edit ⇨ Preferences in Windows, or ⌘+K or Ctrl+K).

To modify the leading value applied to selected text, choose one of the predefined options from the Leading pop-up menu in the Character pane or Control palette, or type a leading value in the field. You can type values from 0 to 5,000 points in 0.001-point increments. You can also use the up and down cursor keys to change leading in 1-point increments.

Summary

As a user of InDesign, modifying the appearance of type is one of the more common tasks you'll perform. InDesign lets you modify the appearance of highlighted characters or selected paragraphs. When text is highlighted, you can use the controls in the Character pane or Control palette to change any of several character attributes: font family, size, type style, leading, kerning, tracking, vertical and horizontal scale, baseline shift, and skew. You can also set the hyphenation and spell-checking language, apply all caps or small caps, superscripts or subscripts, underline, strikethrough, ligatures, and OpenType variations. You also set line spacing (leading), something normally applied to entire paragraphs rather than InDesign's approach of applying it to selected text.

✦　　✦　　✦

Specifying Paragraph Attributes

In This Chapter

Understanding
paragraph
fundamentals

Changing basic and
advanced paragraph
formats

Applying automatic
bullets and numbering

Working with
hyphenation and
justification

Modifying other
paragraph formats

Much like an individual character, a paragraph in InDesign is a basic typographic unit. When you create a new text frame and begin typing, you create a paragraph each time you press Return or Enter. A paragraph can be as short as one character or word on a single line or many words strung out over many lines. When you press Return or Enter, the paragraph formats of the preceding paragraph are automatically used for the subsequent paragraph (unless you create styles that automatically change paragraph formats).

In general, paragraph formats control how the lines of text in the paragraph are constructed. Changing paragraph formats doesn't change the appearance of the individual characters within the paragraph. To do that, you must highlight the characters and modify character-level formats.

Cross-Reference This chapter focuses on modifying paragraph-level typographic formats; Chapter 16 focuses on modifying character-level formats. Chapter 19 covers the creation and use of styles for both characters and paragraphs.

Paragraph Basics

To select a paragraph, simply click within it. Any change you make to a paragraph-level format will be applied to all the lines in the paragraph. (Unlike character-level formats, you don't have to highlight all the text in a paragraph to modify a paragraph-level format.) If you need to change the paragraph formats of several consecutive paragraphs, you can highlight all the text in all the paragraphs, or you can click anywhere in the first paragraph, drag anywhere within the last paragraph, then release the mouse button.

Just as you can't apply two different colors to a single character, you can't apply conflicting paragraph formats within a single paragraph. For example, you can't specify for one line in a paragraph to be left-aligned and the rest right-aligned. All lines in a paragraph must share the same alignment, indents, tab settings, and all other paragraph-level formats.

As is the case with character formats, there are two ways to apply paragraph formats:

✦ Use the controls in the Paragraph pane or Control palette's Paragraph (¶) pane, shown in Figures 17-1 and 17-2, or their keyboard shortcuts.

✦ Create and apply paragraph-level styles.

A paragraph-level style is essentially a text-formatting macro that lets you apply several paragraph formats to selected paragraphs in a single operation. If you're working on a multipage publication such as a book, newspaper, magazine, or catalog that repeatedly uses the same basic text formats, you'll definitely want to use paragraph styles to handle the bulk of your formatting chores. But even if you use styles, you'll probably also use the Paragraph pane to do some manual paragraph formatting.

Cross-Reference   Tab settings are also a paragraph-level format. See Chapter 20 for a detailed explanation of InDesign's Tabs feature.

Figure 17-1 shows the Paragraph pane. It can have two appearances: If you choose Hide Options from the pop-up menu, the Space Before/After, Drop Cap, and Hyphenate controls are not displayed. You might want to combine the Character and Paragraph panes into a single text-formatting pane, as shown here. You can also use the Control palette's paragraph formatting options, shown in Figure 17-2. (Be sure to click ¶ to get the paragraph options.)

Tip   If the Type tool is selected and no objects are active, any changes you make in the Paragraph pane become the default settings for the document and are automatically used when you create new text frames.

The Paragraph pane (Window ⇨ Type ⇨ Paragraph, or Option+⌘+T or Ctrl+Alt+T) and Control palette provide access to most of InDesign's paragraph-formatting options. (To set tabs, you must open the Tabs pane by choosing Windows ⇨ Type & Tables ⇨ Tabs or by pressing Shift+⌘+T or Ctrl+Shift+T, as Chapter 20 covers.) Several of the options have keyboard shortcuts, as shown in the menus.

Leading

Leading, or the space between lines in a paragraph, is treated by InDesign as a character format through the Character pane or Control palette, even though it's traditionally an attribute of the paragraph. However, you can override InDesign's character-oriented approach so it works like all other layout programs. To ensure that leading changes affect entire paragraphs, select the Apply Leading to Entire Paragraphs option in the Type pane of the Preferences dialog box (choose InDesign ⇨ Preferences on the Mac or Edit ⇨ Preferences in Windows, or press ⌘+K or Ctrl+K).

Cross-Reference   For more details on how to apply leading, see Chapter 16.

Align Left

   Align Center

      Align Right

         Left Indent

           Left Justify

              Center Justify

                 Right Justify

                    Full Justify

                       Right Indent

                         Align Towards Spine

                           Align Away from Spine

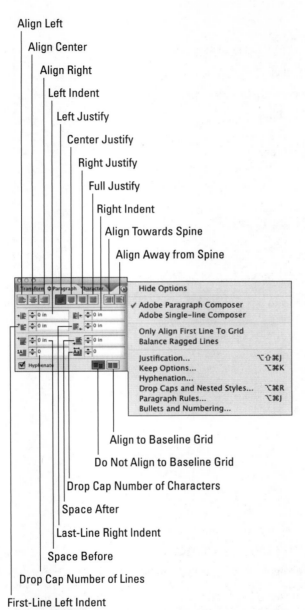

Align to Baseline Grid

Do Not Align to Baseline Grid

Drop Cap Number of Characters

Space After

Last-Line Right Indent

Space Before

Drop Cap Number of Lines

First-Line Left Indent

Figure 17-1: The Paragraph pane

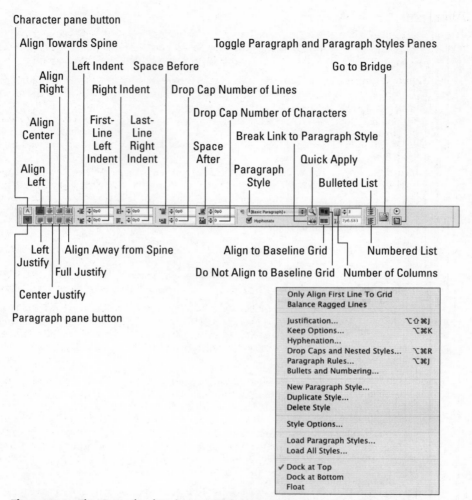

Figure 17-2: The Control palette's paragraph formatting options and palette menu

Controlling alignment and indents

The nine alignment icons at the top of the Paragraph pane and the four fields are always displayed; the four additional fields, two icons, and the Hyphenate option are also displayed when you choose Show Options from the palette menu. InDesign refers to the top set of options as Basic Paragraph Formats; the additional seven options are Advanced Paragraph Formats.

The top set lets you control a paragraph's alignment and indents (left, right, and first line) and lock text baselines to the document's baseline grid.

Alignment

The nine alignment icons at the top of the Paragraph pane control how line beginnings and endings in selected paragraphs are placed relative to the left and right margins. Here's a description of each alignment option (the icons do a pretty good job of showing what they do):

✦ **Align Left (Shift+⌘+L or Ctrl+Shift+L).** Places the left edge of every line at the left margin (the margin can be the frame edge, frame inset, left indent, or column edge) and fits as many words (or syllables, if hyphenation is turned on) on the line as possible. When a word (or syllable) won't fit at the end of a line, it's placed (flush left) on the next line. In left-aligned paragraphs, the right margin is said to be *ragged* because the leftover space at the right end of each line differs from line to line and produces a jagged edge.

Note Some designers prefer to use this alignment for columns of text because they like the irregular, somewhat organic shapes that result; others prefer to align both left and right edges by adding text as needed between characters (called *justification*), which produces a more rigid, vertical look. Similarly, left-aligned text is sometimes hyphenated, sometimes not. (You'll find more about hyphenation and justification later in this chapter.)

✦ **Align Center (Shift+⌘+C or Ctrl+Shift+C).** To create centered text, the leftover space of each line is divided in half. One-half of the leftover space is placed on the left end of the line; the other half is placed on the right end. The result is that both the left and right edges of the paragraphs are ragged, and the text is balanced along a vertical axis.

✦ **Align Right (Shift+⌘+R or Ctrl+Shift+R).** This is a mirror opposite of Align Left. The right edge is straight; the left edge is ragged. Columns of text are seldom set flush right because it's not as easy to read as flush left text. Right-aligned text is sometimes used for such things as captions placed to the left of a picture, blurbs on magazine covers, and advertising copy.

✦ **Left Justify (Shift+⌘+J or Ctrl+Shift+J).** In justified text, the left and right ends of each line are flush with the margins. The flush-left/flush-right results are produced either by sprinkling the spaces of each line among characters and/or words or by reducing space between characters and/or words to accommodate additional characters (more about justification later in this chapter). Justified text is nearly always hyphenated (if you don't hyphenate justified text, spacing between letters and words is very inconsistent). Aligning the last line flush left is the traditional way of ending a paragraph, which is why Left Justify is the justified-text style most often used on paragraphs.

✦ **Center Justify.** This is the same as Left Justify except that the last line is center-aligned.

✦ **Right Justify.** This is the same as Left Justify except that the last line is right-aligned.

✦ **Full Justify (Shift+⌘+F or Ctrl+Shift+F).** This is the same as Left Justify except that the last line is also forcibly justified. This option can produce very widely spaced last lines. The fewer the characters on the last line is, the greater the spacing.

Note These last three options are rarely used, and for good reason. People expect justified text to have the last line aligned left, and the space at the end of the line is a marker that the paragraph has ended. By changing the position of that last line, you can confuse your reader. So use Center Justify, Right Justify, and Full Justify options sparingly in special situations where the reader won't be confused — typically in brief copy like ads and pull-quotes.

✦ **Align Towards Spine.** This is similar to Left Justify or Right Justify except that InDesign automatically chooses a left or right alignment based on where the spine is in a facing-pages document. Essentially, this automatically creates right-aligned text on left-hand pages and left-aligned text on right-hand pages.

✦ **Align Away from Spine.** This is the same as Towards Spine, except that the alignment is reversed: text aligns to the left on left-hand pages and to the right on right-hand pages.

New Feature

The Align Towards Spine and Align Away from Spine options are new to InDesign CS2.

To apply a paragraph alignment to selected paragraphs, click on one of the icons. (The hand pointer appears when the pointer is over a pane button.) You can also use the keyboard shortcuts in the preceding list.

Note

Left-aligned and right-aligned paragraphs typically fit fewer characters per line than justified paragraphs. Most publications standardize on one of these two alignments for their body copy, and one factor in your decision may be how much copy you need to squeeze in.

Indents

You can move the edges of paragraphs away from the left and/or right margins and indent the first line using the indent controls in the Paragraph pane.

Left and right indents are often used for lengthy passages of quoted material within a column of text. Using indents is also handy way of drawing attention to pull quotes and moving text away from a nearby picture.

The options are:

✦ **Left Indent.** Type a value in this field to move the left edge of selected paragraphs away from the left margin. You can also use the up and down cursor keys. Each click increases the value by 1 point; pressing and holding Shift while clicking increases the increment to 1 pica.

✦ **Right Indent.** Type a value in this field to move the right edge of selected paragraphs away from the right margin. You can also use the up and down cursor keys.

✦ **First-Line Left Indent.** Type a value in this field to move the left edge of the first line of selected paragraphs away from the left margin. You can also press the up and down cursor keys. The value in the First-Line Indent field is added to any Left Indent value. For example, if you've specified a Left Indent value of 1 pica and you then specify a 1-pica First-Line Indent value, the first line of selected paragraphs will be indented 2 picas from the left margin. If you've specified a Left Indent value, you can specify a negative First-Line Left Indent value to create a *hanging indent* (also called an *outdent*). But you cannot specify a First-Line Left Indent value that would cause the first line to extend past the left edge of the text frame (that is, the First-Line Left Indent value can't exceed that of the Left Indent value).

Note

Using a tab or spaces to indent the first line of a paragraph, which is what was done in the age of typewriters, is usually not a good idea. You're better off specifying a First-Line Indent. Similarly, you can indent an entire paragraph by inserting a tab or multiple word spaces at the beginning of every line in the paragraph, but both are typographic no-nos. Use the indent controls instead.

✦ **Last-Line Right Indent.** Type a value in this field to move the right edge of the last line of selected paragraphs away from the right margin. You can also press the up and down cursor keys. This function otherwise works just like the First-Line Left Indent function, so the Last-Line Right Indent value cannot exceed that of the Right Indent value.

The ability to set last-line right indents is new to InDesign CS2.

Lock to Baseline Grid

Every document includes a grid of horizontal lines, called the *baseline grid,* which can be displayed or hidden (View ➪ Grids & Guides ➪ Show/Hide Baseline Grid, or ⌘+Option+' or Ctrl+Alt+') and used to help position objects and text baselines. A document's baseline grid is established in the Grids pane of the Preferences dialog box (choose InDesign ➪ Preferences on the Mac or Edit ➪ Preferences in Windows, or press ⌘+K or Ctrl+K, and then go to the Grids pane). Generally, a document's baseline grid interval is equal to the leading value applied to the body text.

You can ensure that lines of text align across columns and pages by locking their baselines to the baseline grid. To do so, click the Align to Baseline grid button in the Paragraph pane (the rightmost icon on the bottom). To prevent such locking to the baseline, click the Do Not Align to Baseline Grid button to its immediate left. These same buttons also exist on the right side of the Control palette's Paragraph (¶) pane.

InDesign CS2 lets you set baseline grids for text frames. You do so in the Baseline Options pane of the Text Frame Options dialog box (Object ➪ Text Frame Options, or ⌘+B or Ctrl+B). This is particularly handy for multicolumn text frames.

Chapter 7 covers how to set up baseline grids in more detail.

Although you can use InDesign's Lock to Baseline Grid feature to align text baselines across columns and pages (or within text frames), you can produce the same results by combining uniform body text leading with other paragraph formats (Space Before and Space After). Some designers like the certainty and simplicity of the Lock to Baseline Grid feature; others prefer to control text alignment across columns themselves. Whichever works best for you is fine.

Keep in mind that when paragraphs are aligned to the baseline grid, the applied leading values are ignored.

The Only Align First Line to Grid option in the Paragraph pane's and Control palette's palette menu, which aligns the first line of a paragraph to the baseline grid, is a handy way to align multiline subheads so the first line stays on the grid, but the extra lines can fall naturally. You can use this for any paragraph that you want to be the rest point if your text gets off the baseline grid, without forcing every line to align to the grid.

Another option, Balance Ragged Lines in the Paragraph pane's and Control palette's palette menus, ensures that the rag is balanced, that is to say where the lines alternate short and long (when possible), rather than fall in a seemingly random pattern. This is designed to make headlines and other large copy (such as in ads) more visually pleasing. You wouldn't use this for body text, where the small text size and need to have efficient spacing makes this feature irrelevant. Unfortunately, this setting also forces hyphenation to achieve the balanced rag, which may be contrary to your intent.

Adding Space between Paragraphs

When you choose Show Options from the Paragraph pane's palette menu, four additional fields appear, as shown earlier in Figure 17-1. They're also always in the Control palette. Two of these fields let you insert space before and/or after paragraphs.

When you need to format a lengthy chunk of text with multiple paragraphs, there are two ways to indicate a new paragraph. You can:

✦ Indent the paragraph's first line (by specifying a First-Line Left Indent value).

✦ Insert some extra space between the new paragraph and the preceding one.

Note   There's no rule that says you can't use both spacing methods, but generally you'll use one or the other. What you don't want to do is insert extra returns between a paragraph, which is what was done in the days of typewriters.

To insert space before selected paragraphs, type a value in the Space Before field in the Paragraph pane or Control palette. You can also use the up and down cursor keys; each click increases the value by 1 point, while pressing and holding Shift increases the increment to 1 pica.

The Space After field works the same as the Space Before field but inserts space below selected paragraphs. Generally, you'll use Space Before or Space After to separate paragraphs. Combining both can be confusing.

Adding Drop Caps

A drop cap is created by *notching* a paragraph's first letter — or letters — into the upper-left corner of the paragraph. Drop caps are often used to embellish the first paragraph of a story, to draw attention to paragraphs, and to interrupt the grayness in columns of text. In the Paragraph pane or Control palette, InDesign lets you specify the number of letters you want to include in a drop cap and the number of lines you want to notch them.

To add one or more drop caps to selected paragraphs, type a number in the Drop Cap Number field in the Paragraph pane or Control palette. That's how many characters will be made into drop caps. To specify the number of lines a drop cap will extend into a paragraph, type a value in the Drop Cap Depth field.

After you create a drop cap, you can modify it by highlighting it and then changing any of its character formats — font, size, color, and so on — using the Character pane or Control palette, as well as other panes (such as Stroke and Swatches). Figure 17-3 shows some examples of drop caps.

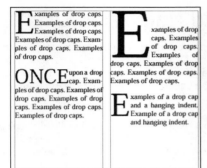

Figure 17-3: The drop cap in the top-left example has a one-character drop cap three lines deep. The bottom-left paragraph has a two-line, four-character drop cap. In the top-right example, the font size of a one-letter, four-line drop cap has been enlarged to raise it above the first line of text. In the bottom-right example, a Left Indent value combined with a negative First-Line Left Indent value produced the one-character, three-line drop cap's hanging indent.

A handy way to apply these settings is to use the Drop Cap & Nested Styles option in the Paragraph pane's or Control palette's palette menu. You can also use the shortcut Option+⌘+R or Ctrl+Alt+R. Figure 17-4 shows the dialog box.

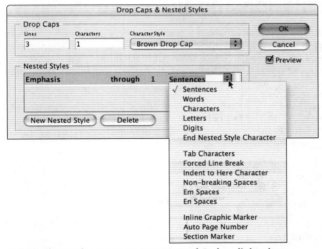

Figure 17-4: The Drop Caps & Nested Styles dialog box

With this dialog box, you can set a character style that is applied to the paragraph. You can also use it to apply another character style to other text in the paragraph. To do so, click New Nested Style, and then choose from the three (unnamed) pop-up menus to specify how the style is to be applied. The first pop-up menu lets you choose Through or Up To, the second the number of elements to apply the style through or up to, and the third pop-up menu lets you determine what elements you're using, as the figure shows.

Cross-Reference

Because this feature is most useful when coupled with a paragraph style (otherwise, it's easier to simply highlight some text in a paragraph and apply a character style to it), Chapter 19 covers drop caps and other nested styles in more detail.

Adding Automatic Bullets and Numbered Lists

Word processors have long been able to add automatic bullets and numbering to paragraphs. In the late 1980s, so could Ventura Publisher. Finally, InDesign can do it too. (QuarkXPress still cannot.) Automatic bullets and numbering are now available as a paragraph-level format, accessed in the Paragraph pane and Control palette's palette menus by choosing Bullets and Numbering Options.

Cross-Reference Chapter 18 covers the setup and application of bullets and numbering in more detail. Because this feature is most useful when coupled with a paragraph style (otherwise, you have to apply these settings for each selection of paragraphs you want to make into a list), Chapter 19 covers styles in more detail.

New Feature Automated bulleted and numbered lists are new to InDesign CS2, although a less capable version was available for InDesign CS as part of the $49 PageMaker Plug-in Pack.

Controlling Hyphenation and Justification

Hyphenation is the placement of hyphens between syllables in words that don't completely fit at the end of a line of text — a signal to the reader that the word continues on the next line. InDesign gives you the option to hyphenate or not hyphenate paragraphs, and if you choose to hyphenate, you can customize the settings that determine when and where hyphens are inserted.

As noted earlier, justification is the addition or removal of space between words and/or letters that produces the flush-left/flush-right appearance of justified paragraphs. InDesign's justification controls let you specify how space is added or removed when paragraphs are justified.

If your pages will contain columns of text, you'll have to decide whether to use left-aligned or justified paragraphs and whether you want to hyphenate words that don't entirely fit at the end of a line. As mentioned earlier, if you justify paragraphs, you'll almost certainly want to hyphenate them, too. If you opt for left-aligned paragraphs, whether to hyphenate is a personal choice.

InDesign offers two hyphenation methods: manual and automatic.

Manual hyphenation

If you want to break a particular word differently from the way InDesign would normally break the word, you can place a *discretionary hyphen* in the word. If the word falls at the end of a line in a hyphenated paragraph, InDesign will use the discretionary hyphen to split the word if the first syllable fits on the line. To insert a discretionary hyphen, use the shortcut Shift+⌘+– (hyphen) or Ctrl+Shift+– (hyphen) in the text where you want the hyphen to appear.

Tip If you place a discretionary hyphen in a word, InDesign breaks the word only at that point (or does not break it at all). But you can place multiple discretionary hyphens within a single word; InDesign uses the one that produces the best results.

Note InDesign uses discretionary hyphens only if you select the Hyphenate option in the Paragraph pane or in the Control palette. If Hyphenate is not selected, neither manual nor automatic hyphenation is applied.

Automatic hyphenation

To automatically hyphenate selected paragraphs, all you have to do is select the Hyphenate option in the Paragraph pane or Control palette. (The Hyphenate option appears only if you choose Show Options from the palette menu.)

If you choose to hyphenate paragraphs, you can control how hyphenation is accomplished through the Hyphenation option in the palette menu. When you choose Hyphenation, the Hyphenation Settings dialog box, shown in Figure 17-5, appears.

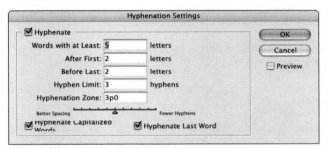

Figure 17-5: The Hyphenation Settings dialog box

Here's a brief description of each option:

✦ **Hyphenate option.** This is a duplicate of the Hyphenate option in the Paragraph pane and Control palette. If you didn't select it before opening the Hyphenation dialog box, you can select it here.

✦ **Words with at Least ___ Letters.** Here, you specify the number of letters in the shortest word you want to hyphenate. For example, if you specify four letters, *mama* can be hyphenated, but *any* can't be.

✦ **After First ___ Letters.** Here, you specify the minimum number of characters that can precede a hyphen. If you type **2**, for example, the word *atavistic* can be broken after *at*. If you specify **3**, *atavistic* cannot be broken until after *ata*.

✦ **Before Last ___ Letters.** This field is similar to After First ___ letters, but it determines the minimum number of characters that can follow a hyphen.

✦ **Hyphenation Limit ___ Hyphens.** Specify the number of consecutive lines that can be hyphenated in this field. Some designers limit the number of consecutive hyphens to two or three because they believe that too many consecutive hyphens produce an awkward, ladder-like look. If the Hyphenation Limit value you enter prevents hyphenation in a line that would otherwise be hyphenated, the line may appear more spaced out than surrounding lines.

✦ **Hyphenation Zone.** This field applies only to nonjustified text and only when the Adobe Single-Line Composer option is selected (in the Paragraph pane's palette menu). A hyphenation point must fall within the distance specified in this field to be used. Otherwise-acceptable hyphenation points that do not fall within the specified hyphenation zone are ignored. You can also click and drag the slider below the field to select a value rather than type a value in this field.

✦ **Hyphenate Capitalized Words.** Select this option to break capitalized words, such as proper names and the first word of sentences. If you don't check this box, a capitalized word that would otherwise be hyphenated will get bumped to the next line, possibly producing excessive spacing in the previous line.

✦ **Hyphenate Last Word.** Select this option to break the last word in a paragraph. Otherwise, InDesign moves the entire word to the last line and spaces the preceding text as necessary. Some typographers don't like having a word fragment as the last line, arguing that there's no need to break a word in two because there is clearly enough space to keep it together. I'm not so dogmatic.

New Feature   The Hyphenate Last Word option is new to InDesign CS2.

When you're done specifying hyphenation settings in the Hyphenation dialog box, click OK to close the dialog box and return to your document.

Tip   You can prevent a particular word from being hyphenated by highlighting it and choosing No Break from the palette menu of the Control palette (Window ➪ Control, or Option+⌘+6 or Ctrl+Alt+6) or from the palette menu of the Character pane (Window ➪ Type & Tables ➪ Character, or ⌘+T or Ctrl+T) or by placing a discretionary hyphen (Shift+⌘+– [hyphen] or Ctrl+Shift+– [hyphen]) in front of the first letter.

How Many Characters?

Consider changing the After First Letters hyphenation setting to 2 if you have narrow columns or large text. Although many typographers object to two-letter hyphenation—as in *ab-dicate* or *ra-dar*—it often looks better than text with large gaps caused by the reluctance to hyphenate such words. Hyphenation also makes sense for many words that use two-letter prefixes such as *in-*, *re-*, and *co-*.

Although I advocate two-letter hyphenation at the beginning of a word, I prefer three-letter hyphenation at the end (set through Before Last ___ Letters). Except for words ending in *-ed* and sometimes *-al*, most words don't lend themselves to two-letter hyphenation at the end of the word. Part of this is functional, as it's easy for readers to lose two letters beginning a line. I prefer two-letter hyphenations at the end of a word only when the alternative is awkward spacing. As with all typography, this ultimately is a personal or house style choice.

Regardless of the two- versus three-letter debate, words broken using minimum settings of 1 look awful. They also go against reader expectations because the norm is to have several letters after a hyphen. Never use a minimum setting of 1 for After First ___ Letters. If you do, you get hyphenations such as *A-sia*, *a-typical*, and *u-niform* that simply look terrible in print. They also don't provide enough context for the reader to anticipate the rest of the word. Likewise, never use a minimum of 1 for Before Last ___ Letters because you get hyphenations such as *radi-o*.

Justifications controls

InDesign provides three options for controlling how justification is achieved. You can:

✦ Condense or expand the width of spaces, or *spacebands,* between words.

✦ Add or remove space between letters.

✦ Condense or expand the width of characters, or *glyphs.*

The options in the Justification dialog box, shown in Figure 17-6, let you specify the degree to which InDesign will adjust normal word spaces, character spacing, and character width to achieve justification. You access this dialog box through the palette menu in the Control palette or in the Paragraph pane, or by pressing Option+Shift+⌘+J or Ctrl+Alt+Shift+J. Although you can use the Justification controls on selected paragraphs, in most cases you will specify Justification settings when you create styles, particularly your body-text styles.

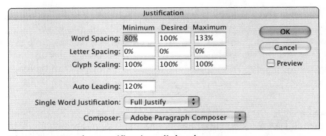

Figure 17-6: The Justification dialog box

Here's a brief description of each option:

✦ **Word Spacing.** Type the percentage of a spaceband character that you want to use whenever possible in the Desired field. (The default value is 100%, which uses a font's built-in width.) Type the minimum acceptable percentage in the Minimum field; type the maximum acceptable percentage in the Maximum field. The smallest value you can enter is 0%; the largest is 1000%. Some designers are adamant that only word spaces — not letter spaces — should be adjusted when justifying text. Others allow small adjustments to letter spacing as well.

✦ **Letter Spacing.** The default value of 0% in this set of three fields uses a font's built-in letter spacing. In the Desired field, type a positive value to add space (in increments of 1% of an en space) between all letter pairs; type a negative value to remove space. Type the minimum acceptable percentage in the Minimum field; type the maximum acceptable percentage in the Maximum field.

✦ **Glyph Scaling.** The default value of 100% uses a character's normal width. In the Desired field, type a positive value to expand all character widths; type a negative value to condense character widths. Type the minimum acceptable percentage in the Minimum field; type the maximum acceptable percentage in the Maximum field. Some designers adamantly contend that scaling characters is even more unacceptable than letter spacing, while others see no harm in scaling characters, as long as it's kept to a minimum. If you do apply glyph scaling, it's best to keep it to a range of 97 to 103 percent at most.

About Word Spacing

Word spacing — the space between words — is another important contributor to the aesthetics of a document. Think about it: If the words in a sentence are too close to one another, comprehension may be affected because of the difficulty in telling where one word ends and another begins. If the words are too far apart, the reader might have a difficult time following the thought that's being conveyed.

Here's a design rule I like to follow: The wider the column, the more space you can add between words. This is why books tend to have more word spacing than magazines. Like all other typographic issues, there's a subjective component to picking good word spacing. Experiment to see what works best in your documents.

Tip   I suggest 85 percent minimum, 100 percent optimum, and 150 percent maximum for word spacing; and −5 percent minimum, 0 percent optimum, and 10 percent maximum for letter spacing. I prefer minimum settings that are less than the optimum because they help text fit more easily in narrow columns. These settings work well for most newsletters and magazines output on an imagesetter. At the same time, I usually leave the maximum word spacing at 150 percent.

Note   When specifying values in the Justification dialog box, Minimum values must be smaller than Desired values, which in turn must be smaller than Maximum values.

The Auto Leading field in the Justification dialog box lets you specify a custom value for Auto Leading. In InDesign, this is a character-level format, even though it rightfully should be a paragraph format. Although it's great that InDesign also makes it available in this paragraph-oriented dialog box, it's a bit hidden here. Plus, it's too bad you can't specify an actual number of points (such as +**2** to indicate 2 points of leading more than the text size, which is how leading is traditionally calculated).

Cross-Reference   Leading is covered in detail in Chapter 16.

InDesign also lets you control what happens to words that end up taking a full line's width. In the Single Word Justification pop-up menu, you would normally keep the default Full Justification option, which spaces the word to fill the line. You could also choose Align Left, Align Center, or Align Right to avoid spacing out the word to fit. But that's a cure worse than the problem: Having a line of a different width than the others will look like either a new paragraph or a mistake, and both appearances are sure to confuse readers.

If you use the Adobe Paragraph Composer option (explained in the next section) for justified paragraphs, specifying a narrow range between minimum and maximum Word Spacing, Letter Spacing, and Glyph Scaling generally produces good-looking results. However, if you choose the Adobe Single-Line Composer option, a broader range between Minimum and Maximum gives the composer more leeway in spacing words and letters and hyphenating words and can produce better-looking results. The best way to find out what values work best for you is to experiment with several settings. Print hard copies and let your eyes decide which values produce the best results.

Note A paragraph's justification settings are applied whether the paragraph is justified or not. However, for nonjustified paragraphs, only the Desired values for Word Spacing, Letter Spacing, and Glyph Scaling are used.

Composing text

The Paragraph pane's palette menu — but not the Control palette's — offers two choices for implementing the hyphenation and justification settings you've established: the Adobe Single-Line Composer and the Adobe Paragraph Composer. (These are also available in the Justification dialog box covered in the previous section.)

Adobe Single-Line Composer

In the past, programs like QuarkXPress and PageMaker have used single-line composition methods to flow text. This method marches line by line through a paragraph and sets each line as well as possible using the applied hyphenation and justification settings. The effect of modifying the spacing of one line on the lines above and below is not considered in single-line composition. If adjusting the space within a line causes poor spacing on the next line, tough luck. When you use the Adobe Single-Line Composer, the following rules apply:

✦ Adjusting word spacing is preferred over hyphenation.

✦ Hyphenation is preferred over glyph scaling.

✦ If spacing must be adjusted, removing space is preferred over adding space.

Adobe Paragraph Composer

InDesign's Adobe Paragraph Composer (called the Multi-Line Composer in previous versions) is selected by default. It takes a broader approach to composition by looking at the entire paragraph at once. If a poorly spaced line can be fixed by adjusting the spacing of a previous line, the Paragraph Composer reflows the previous line. The Paragraph Composer is governed by the following principles:

✦ The evenness of letter spacing and word spacing is the highest priority. The desirability of possible breakpoints is determined by how much they cause word and letter spacing to vary from the Desired settings.

✦ Uneven spacing is preferred to hyphenation. A breakpoint that does not require hyphenation is preferred over one that does.

✦ All possible breakpoints are ranked, and good breakpoints are preferred over bad ones.

The paragraph composer is more sophisticated than the single-line option, offering generally better overall spacing because it sacrifices optimal spacing a bit on one line to prevent really bad spacing on another, something the single-line method does not do.

However, there is one frustration in dealing with the paragraph composer: When you try to edit text or play with tracking to get rid of an orphan or widow, the paragraph composer keeps adjusting the text across several lines, often counteracting your nips and tucks. The single-line composer doesn't do that.

Setting Other Paragraph Formats

The Paragraph pane's and Control palette's palette menu contains two additional paragraph-formatting options:

✦ **Keep Options.** This option lets you determine how and when paragraphs can be split when they fall at the bottom of a column or page.

✦ **Paragraph Rules.** This option lets you place a horizontal line in front of or after a paragraph. Lines placed using the Paragraph Rules feature become part of the text and move along with surrounding text when editing causes text reflow.

Keep Options

A widow is the last line of a paragraph that falls at the top of a column (the poor thing has been cut off from the rest of the family). An orphan is the first line of a paragraph that falls at the bottom of a column (it, too, has become separated from its family). InDesign's Keep Options feature lets you prevent widows and orphans; it also lets you keep paragraphs together when they would otherwise be broken at the bottom of a column.

When you choose Keep Options from the Paragraph pane's or Control palette's palette menu, the Keep Options dialog box, shown in Figure 17-7, appears.

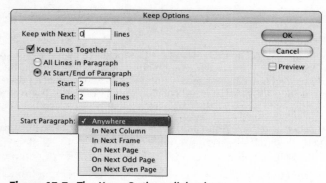

Figure 17-7: The Keep Options dialog box

The Keep Options dialog box provides several options for how paragraphs are managed as text breaks across columns and pages:

✦ **Keep with Next ___ Lines.** This option applies to two consecutive paragraphs. Specify the number of lines of the second paragraph that must stay with the first paragraph if a column or page break occurs within the second paragraph. This option is useful for preventing a subhead from being separated from the paragraph that follows.

✦ **Keep Lines Together.** Select this option to prevent paragraphs from breaking and to control widows and orphans. When this box is checked, the two options below it become available. (The radio buttons present an either/or choice. One must be selected; At Start/End of Paragraph is selected by default.)

✦ **All Lines in Paragraph.** Select this option to prevent a paragraph from being broken at the end of a column or page. When a column or page break occurs within a paragraph to which this setting has been applied, the entire paragraph moves to the next column or page.

✦ **At Start/End of Paragraph.** Select this option to control widows and orphans. When this option is selected, the two fields below it become available:

- **Start ___ Lines.** This field controls orphans. The value you type is the minimum number of lines at the beginning of a paragraph that must be placed at the bottom of a column when a paragraph is split by a column ending.

- **End ___ Lines.** This field controls widows. The value you type is the minimum number of lines at the end of a paragraph that must be placed at the top of a column when a paragraph is split by a column ending.

Caution   Keep in mind that when you eliminate an orphan or widow using Keep Options, the line that precedes the widow line is bumped to the next column or page, which can produce uneven column endings on multicolumn pages.

✦ **Start Paragraph.** From this pop-up menu, choose In Next Column to force a paragraph to begin in the next column; choose In Next Frame to force a paragraph to begin in the next frame; choose On Next Page to force a paragraph to begin on the next page (such as for chapter headings). Your other choices are similar: On Next Odd Page and On Next Even Page. Choose Anywhere to let the paragraph begin where it would fall naturally in the sequence of text (no forced break).

Paragraph Rules

Usually, the easiest way to create a horizontal line is to use the Line tool. But if you want to place a horizontal line within text so that the line moves with the text when editing causes the text to reflow, you need to create a paragraph rule. A paragraph rule looks much like a line created with the line tool but behaves like a text character. Paragraph rules have many uses. For example, you can place one above or below a subhead to make it more noticeable or to separate the subhead from the paragraph that precedes or follows it. Or you can place paragraph rules above and below a pull-quote so that the rules and the pull-quote text move if editing causes text reflow.

Here's how to place a paragraph rule:

1. **Select the paragraph(s) to which you want to apply a rule above and/or a rule below, and then choose Paragraph Rules from the Paragraph pane's or Control palette's palette menu, or use the shortcut Option+⌘+J or Ctrl+Alt+J.** You can also specify this as part of a paragraph style. The Paragraph Rules dialog box, shown in Figure 17-8, is displayed.

2. **Choose Rule Above or Rule Below, and then select the Rule On option.** You can add a rule above, below, or both. If you want to add rules above and below, you must select Rule On for both options and specify their settings separately. If you want to see the rule as you create it, select the Preview option.

3. **For Weight, choose a predefined thickness from the pop-up menu or type a value in the field.**

Figure 17-8: The Paragraph Rules dialog box

4. **Choose a rule type from the Type pop-up menu.** Typically, you'd use just a simple line, but InDesign offers 17 types of lines, including dashed, striped, dotted, and wavy.

5. **Choose a color from the Color pop-up menu, which lists the colors displayed in the Swatches pane (Window ⇨ Swatches or F5).** If you choose (Text Color), InDesign automatically uses the color applied to the first character in the paragraph. If your ruling line is not a plain line, you can also choose the Gap Color to determine what color goes between dashes, stripes, dots, and so on in your line. For both the Color and Gap Color options, you can specify a corresponding tint (shade) with the Tint and Gap Tint pop-up menus, respectively.

6. **From the Width pop-up menu, choose an option.** Choose Column if you want the rule to extend from the left edge of the column to the right edge of the column; choose Text if you want the rule to extend from the left edge of the frame or column to the line ending on the right.

7. **To indent the rule from the left and/or right edges, type values in the Left Indent and/or Right Indent fields.**

8. **To control the vertical position of the rule, type a value in the Offset field.** For a rule above, the offset value is measured upward from the baseline of the first line in a paragraph to the bottom of the rule; for a rule below, the offset is measured downward from the baseline of the last line in a paragraph to the top of the rule.

9. **Click the Overprint Stroke option if you want to print a rule on top of any underlying colors.** This ensures that any misregistration during printing will not result in white areas around the rule where the paper shows through. You typically use this for black or other dark colors. There's a similar Overprint Gap option for lines that have a Gap Color.

10. **Click OK to close the dialog box, implement your changes, and return to your document.**

To remove a paragraph rule, click in the paragraph to which the rule is applied, choose Paragraph Rules from the Paragraph pane's pop-up menu, deselect the Rule On option, and then click OK.

Tip   You can use the Paragraph Rules feature to place a band of color behind text by specifying a line thickness at least 2 points larger than the text size and offsetting the rule so it moves up behind the text.

Summary

Much like character formats, InDesign's paragraph formats let you control the appearance of selected paragraphs. For example, you can control a paragraph's alignment and specify left, right, and/or first-line indents, and you can use drop caps to add space between paragraphs. If you want to hyphenate a paragraph, you can add hyphenation points manually to individual words, or you can have InDesign automatically hyphenate words as appropriate.

If you choose to use InDesign's justification controls to specify how space is added or removed between characters and/or words to achieve justification, you also have two options for composing text (controlling the spacing approach): the full-paragraph composition method that looks at several lines of text at once, and the single-line method that looks at each line in isolation.

✦　　✦　　✦

Creating Special Text Formatting

◆ ◆ ◆ ◆

In This Chapter

Indenting text, adding bullets, and formatting lists

Adding initial caps and run-in heads

Creating reverse type, sidebars, and pull-quotes

Specifying hanging punctuation

Rotating and scaling text

◆ ◆ ◆ ◆

Once you learn the basics of typefaces, character formats, and paragraph formats, you can achieve just about any look with text. The trick is combining and applying the skills you've learned to produce special effects that not only look professional but also enhance the meaning of the text.

Glance at any professional publication — a national magazine, direct-mail catalog, cookbook, or product brochure — and you'll notice typographic techniques that set the publication apart from anything that can be easily produced in a word processor. (Even when word processors do offer a feature, they often lack the control necessary to really fine-tune an effect.) And skilled designers use these effects with a purpose — special bullet characters emphasize a theme, drop caps draw readers in, and pull-quotes tantalize.

Throughout this chapter, you learn how standard InDesign features can produce typographic special effects, and more important, when to use them.

Indenting Text

InDesign lets you indent paragraphs from the left side, right side, or both sides of the column or text frame. You can also indent the first line of a paragraph independently of the rest of the paragraph. To apply indents, you use either the Control palette or the Paragraph pane (Window ⇨ Type & Tables ⇨ Paragraph, or Option+⌘+T or Ctrl+Alt+T).

If Inset Spacing is selected in the General pane of the Text Frame Options dialog box (Object ⇨ Text Frame Options, or ⌘+B or Ctrl+B), text is indented from the frame's sides, in addition to any indentation set for the paragraphs.

Cross-Reference For more on indenting and other paragraph settings, see Chapter 17. When you have a setting that works for your layout, create a paragraph style using it, as explained in Chapter 19.

First-line indents

To indicate a new paragraph, you might indent the first line or put a noticeable amount of space between paragraphs. If you opt to indent the first line, don't do it the typewriter way with tabs. Select the paragraphs, and then type a value in the First Line Left Indent field in the Paragraph pane or Control palette, as shown in Figure 18-1. Press Shift+Return or Shift+Enter to see the results with the field still highlighted; press Return or Enter to get out of the pane and back into the document.

Left Indent

Right Indent

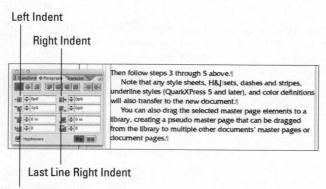

Last Line Right Indent

First Line Left Indent

Figure 18-1: In this book example, paragraphs have a first-line indent of 1p.

Hanging indents

In hanging indents, the first few characters of text (often a number or bullet) are aligned with the left margin while the remaining lines in the paragraph are indented. Notice the bulleted items in Figure 18-2; the text that makes up the rest of the paragraphs "hang" to the right of the bullets.

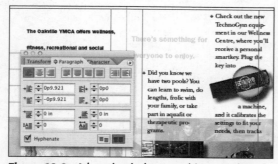

Figure 18-2: A hanging indent combines a tab and a left indent at the same value with a negative first-line indent.

Spacing Guidelines for Indents and Bullets

The easy part of creating first-line indents, hanging indents, bulleted lists, and numbered lists in InDesign is using the software. The hard part can be deciding how much space to use. How do you decide how deep to make a first-line indent? How much space goes between a bullet and the text following it? Amateur publishers or designers, who are likely to be thinking in inches rather than points or picas, are likely to use too much space. They're tempted to use 0.25", 0.125", or another nice dividend of an inch for spacing rather than a more appropriate value such as 6 points. When deciding on spacing, consider the following:

✦ First-line indents that indicate new paragraphs should generally be one or two em spaces wide. The width of an em space is equal to the point size in use — so 10-point text should have a 10- or 20-point first-line indents. Opt for less space in narrower columns to avoid awkward space and more space in wider columns so the spacing is evident.

✦ As you remember from grade-school outlines, indents help organize information, with deeper indents indicating more detail about a topic. Professional publications, though, have many organizational options — such as headlines, subheads, and run-in heads — so they rarely have a need for more than two levels of indents. You might use indents on lengthy quotes, bulleted lists, numbered lists, kickers, and bylines. If you do, stick to the same amount of indent for each so the readers' eyes don't wander.

✦ In bulleted lists, use a hanging indent for a succession of two- or three-line bulleted paragraphs in wider columns. If your bulleted items are five or more lines long, especially in narrow columns, it might work better to use run-in heads to break up the information.

✦ Generally, the amount of space between a bullet and its text is equal to half the point size of the text. So if you're working with 11-point text, place 5.5 points between the bullet and text.

✦ When it comes to numbered lists, you need to decide whether you're going to include a period or other punctuation after the number and whether you'll ever have two-digit numbers. Numerals in most typefaces are the width of an en space, and they should be followed by the same amount of space the numbers and their punctuation take up. If you have a two-digit numeral, the numbers take up one em space and so should be followed by one em space.

While these values give you a good starting point, you might need to modify them based on the typeface, font size, column width, design, and overall goals of the publication.

To create a hanging indent, first separate the textual items, bullets, or numbers from the text with a tab. Note the position of the tab, and then specify a left indent for the paragraphs at the same location. Use the Left Indent field in the Control palette or Paragraph pane, and then type the same value in the First Line Left Indent field — except make the value negative to pull the first line back. For example, if you have a tab at 1.75", use a left indent of 1.75", and a first-line indent of –1.75". Figure 18-2 shows the use of hanging indents for bullets in a brochure by Branimir Zlamalik, formatted with an indent hang of 9.921 pt.

Tip   Hanging indents often have awkward measurements because they depend on the width of the bullet or other lead-in character. That can involve lots of experimentation to get the hang right. A simpler way is to insert the Indent Here character (Type ⇨ Insert Special Character ⇨ Indent Here or ⌘+\ or Ctrl+\). InDesign will figure out the dimensions for you. Note that in this case, the Paragraph pane will not show any indent values. However, there is a risk with using Indent Here: You can have inconsistent hanging indents if the lead-in characters or space differ in your paragraphs, or if tracking or kerning of text before the indent-to-here characters varies from paragraph to paragraph.

Block indents

Publishers often offset quoted text that is longer than a few lines by indenting the paragraph from both sides of the text frame or column. To do this, use the Left Indent and Right Indent fields in the Paragraph pane or Control palette. In general, use the same values you use for first-line indents, and indent both sides the same amount.

Using Bullets and Formatting Lists

Automatic bullets and numbering are now available as a paragraph-level format in InDesign, accessed in the Paragraph pane and Control palette's palette menus by choosing Bullets and Numbering Options. Figure 18-3 shows the resulting dialog box.

New Feature   Automatic bulleted and numbered lists are new to InDesign CS2, although a less-capable version was available for InDesign CS as part of the $49 PageMaker Plug-in Pack.

The process for setting automatic bullets and numbered lists is almost identical; only the top part of the Bullets and Numbering dialog box differs, based on whether you select Bullets or Numbers from the List Type pop-up menu.

Follow these steps to set up a list (select the Preview option if you want to see the results of your choices before you finalize them):

1. **For bullets, choose a bullet character from the Bullet Character area.** The area shows bullet characters available for the current font; you can change the selection by changing the selected font or by clicking Add, which opens a dialog box similar to the Glyphs pane.

   For numbered lists, choose a numbering style in the Style pop-up menu, a separator character in the Separator pop-up menu, and a starting number in the Start At field. In the Style pop-up menu, your options are 1, 2, 3, 4 . . .; I, II, III, IV . . .; i, ii, iii, iv . . .; A, B, C, D . . .; and a, b, c, d . . .. In the Separator pop-up menu, your choices are None, Em Dash, En Dash, . (period), , (comma), : (colon),) (close parenthesis), and] (close bracket). In the Start At field, note that if multiple paragraphs are selected, the starting number will apply just to the first paragraph, and the others will be numbered consecutively from that start value.

2. **Set the font settings for the bullet or numbers using the Font Family, Font Style, Size, and Color pop-up menus.** The default settings are whatever formatting is currently applied to the selected paragraphs. Note that the look of the numerals is more of a design decision than an editorial decision. If numerals are in a different typeface and/or in a different color, a period following the numeral might just look cluttered.

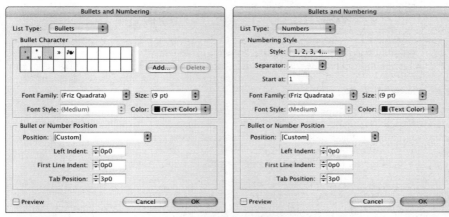

Figure 18-3: In the Bullets and Numbering dialog box, note the top part changes based on whether you are formatting bullets (left) or numbered lists (right).

3. **In the Bullet or Number Position section of the dialog box, set the indents for the list.**
   Using the Position pop-up menu, choose Hanging to have a hanging indent, where the bullet or number extends to the left of the text that follows, or choose Flush Left, where the bullet or number and the following text all align to the paragraph's left margin.

4. **Click OK when you are done with the settings.**

Note   The automatic numbered list feature in InDesign has a limitation that will annoy many designers: You can't place a tab before the numeral and follow it with a right-aligned tab. This is how many designers ensure that numbers line up when you have lists whose numbers include double-digit numerals like *10*. If you use the InDesign automatic numbered-list feature, you'll have to live with having just the single, left-aligned tab after the numbers — or manually number the list yourself and use the manual, two-tab approach.

But chances are, you're not writing the bulk of your text in InDesign. Instead, the text was delivered in the form of a word processing file, and the writer or editor made some decisions about bullets or numerals. A lot of times, writers simply type an asterisk followed by a space to indicate a bullet. Or maybe an editor typed a numeral followed by a parenthesis in front of each step. Other times, writers or editors use their word processor's automatic bullet or numbering feature. Here are the two most common scenarios for dealing with imported bulleted and numbered lists:

✦ **If the writer or editor typed numerals or used an automatic numbering feature, the numbers and their punctuation arrive in InDesign intact.** However, these won't use the InDesign automatic bullets and numbering feature, so new bullets and list numbers won't be automatically added or adjusted when you edit the copy in InDesign. You should override these imported paragraphs with an InDesign style that uses InDesign's bullets and numbering formatting capabilities. Furthermore, note that you'll need to delete the word processor–generated bullets and numbers from such imported text. That's because InDesign will simply add its own bullets and numbers to the existing text, not replace any existing bullets and numbers in that text. (You may be able to use the Find/Change dialog box (Edit ➪ Find/Change, or ⌘+F or Ctrl+F) to get rid of the now-extraneous bullet characters imported from the word processor.)

Bullet Character Options

Although you may not know what they're called, you're used to seeing en bullets, the small round bullet (•) included in most typefaces. But you're not limited to using this character. You can use any character in the body text font, or you can switch to a symbol or pi font and choose a more decorative character.

Zapf Dingbats and Wingdings are the most common symbol fonts, offering an array of boxes, arrows, crosses, stars, and check marks. These can be cute and effective, but cute isn't always a good thing. If you opt for a different bullet character, make sure you have a reason and that it works well with the rest of the design. Check-mark bullets in an election flyer might make sense; bulky square bullets in a to-do list for a wedding caterer might not make sense.

Note that you might want to reduce the size of the symbol slightly and that you might need to use different spacing values than you would use with an en bullet.

Don't limit yourself to these two common fonts either. You can purchase many different symbol fonts to support different content. For example, you might see leaf-shaped bullets in an herb article and paw-print bullets in a pet training article. To use your own drawing or a logotype as a bullet, convert the drawing to a font using a utility such as Pyrus FontLab (see the companion Web site `www.InDesignCentral.com` for links to this and other font utilities).

✦ **InDesign doesn't like word processors' automatic bullets and often converts them to characters in the current font, which will need to be changed to bullets.** Or, rather than using automatic bullets, the writer might have typed asterisks, hyphens, or another character to indicate bullets. Once you determine what characters indicate bullets in your text, use Find/Change to change it to the bullet character you want. For example, you can search for an asterisk and change it to an *n* in the Zapf Dingbats font, which looks like a square (■). If you use InDesign's automatic bullets feature, you would set the bullet to be a n in the Bullets and Numbering dialog box and instead use Find/Change to get rid of the now-extraneous bullet characters imported from the word processor.

Adding Initial Caps

Nothing sets off a professional publication from an amateur or word-processed document like the use of initial caps. Decorative characters at the beginning of paragraphs serve both editorial and design purposes, drawing readers into the content with their size and position, while emphasizing a theme with their style.

You'll see initial caps ranging from a single four-line drop cap in the same typeface as the paragraph in a financial publication's letter from the editor to a 140-point word in a script face kicking off a feature article in a bridal magazine. Initial caps often use more decorative typefaces — you can even purchase fonts that consist only of ornate capital letters. A children's book might use a graphic of a letter formed from an animal's body, and a cooking magazine might use the outlines of a letter filled with an image of related foods. You can achieve all these effects with the typographic and layout features in InDesign.

Note

Don't forget that text is for reading. Heavily designed initial caps can become unrecognizable as text, leaving the reader with a disjointed word or sentence in the first paragraph of a story. No matter how gorgeous a 192-point *S* looks flowing behind a paragraph in rose-colored Kuenstler Script, if the readers don't recognize the *S*, they're left trying to make sense of the word *ensitivity*. You would have been better off leaving *Sensitivity* to start the paragraph and drawing a nice curly shape behind the text.

Creating automatic drop caps

A *drop cap* is an enlarged capital letter at the beginning of a paragraph that drops down several lines into the text. In daily newspapers and weekly magazines, which are likely to have limited production time, the most common effect you'll see is a simple drop cap in the paragraph's font. Simple drop caps such as these can be created automatically in InDesign. Even though drop caps look like character formatting, they're actually created through a paragraph format. This ensures that drop-cap formatting remains in the paragraph even if you edit or delete the original first characters.

To create a drop cap:

1. **Select the Type tool and click in the paragraph to select it.**

2. **Make sure either the Control palette or Paragraph pane is open.**

3. **Specify how many lines down the characters should drop into the paragraph by typing a number between 2 and 25 in the Drop Cap Number of Lines field.** Generally, you'll drop the characters three to five lines.

4. **Specify how many characters in the first line should be enlarged as drop caps by typing a number between 1 and 150 in the Drop Cap One or More Characters field.** Generally, it looks best to drop the first character or the first word in the story. If the columns are wide enough, you can drop the first phrase.

5. **Press Return or Enter to see the drop caps.**

Once you create a drop cap with the InDesign feature, you can highlight the enlarged characters and change the font, color, or any other character formats. See Figure 18-4 for an example of a four-line drop in a different font and color.

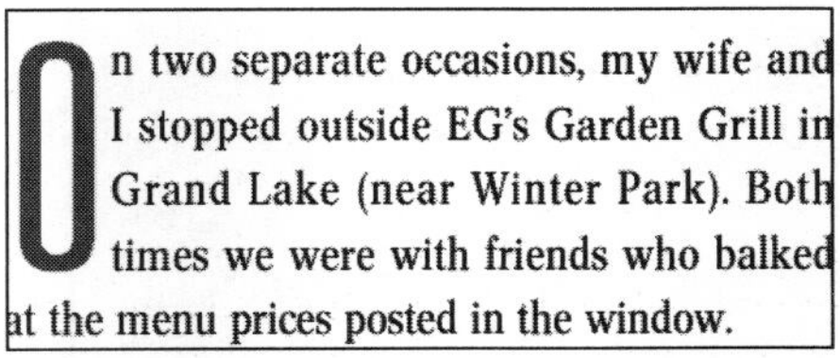

O n two separate occasions, my wife and I stopped outside EG's Garden Grill in Grand Lake (near Winter Park). Both times we were with friends who balked at the menu prices posted in the window.

Figure 18-4: This drop cap has an entry of 4 in the Drop Cap Number of Lines field and 1 in the Drop Cap One or More Characters field. The font has been changed to Univers Light Ultra Condensed and the color to brick red.

For different drop-cap effects, try the following:

✦ Tab after the drop cap, and then create a hanging indent so the text is aligned to the right of the characters.

✦ Kern between the drop cap and the paragraph text to tighten or expand the space.

✦ Baseline-shift the drop cap to move it up or down.

✦ Change the font size of the drop cap to enlarge it and raise it above the paragraph.

✦ Scale the drop cap to make it more dramatic.

Remember to save the drop cap's existence as a paragraph style, and any modifications to the drop cap as a character style.

Note   If you decide to drop the entire first word or phrase in a story, you have to count the number of characters and change the value in the Drop Cap One or More Characters field for each paragraph because each paragraph's initial word or phrase will have a different number of characters. This means you can't apply the formatting automatically with a paragraph style — you have to give each introductory paragraph individual attention.

Tip   If the first character in a paragraph is a quotation mark (" or '), it can look odd as a one-character drop cap. If you don't like this look, you have a couple of options: You can either delete the opening quotation mark, an acceptable but potentially confusing practice, or you can use the first two characters in the paragraph as drop caps instead. Some publications simply prefer not to start paragraphs with quotes, preventing the problem from the editorial side.

Creating raised initial caps

Raised caps are another form of initial caps, enlarging and raising the first few characters of the paragraph above the first line in the paragraph. Creating raised caps is simple — highlight the characters you want to raise with the Type tool and enlarge them using the Font Size field in the Character pane (Window ➪ Type & Tables ➪ Character, or ⌘+T or Ctrl+T) or in the Character pane of the Control palette (press the A button).

If you raise a word or phrase, you might need to track the raised words to tighten them. You also might need to kern between the raised text and the remainder of the line. Other options for raised caps include changing the font, color, and scale of the characters. See Figure 18-5 for an example of raised caps used in a subhead. If you plan to repeat the raised-cap formatting, save it as a character style.

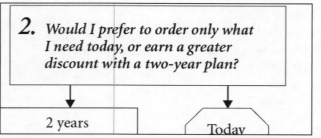

Figure 18-5: The first numeral *2* in this caption is an example of a raised cap — it has a larger size than the text that follows to call attention to it, in this case as a step.

Converting text to outlines for initial caps

You can convert drop caps, raised initial caps, or any character in any font to a frame. You can then resize, scale, shear, fill, and stroke the character-shaped frame. To do this, highlight the characters with the Type tool, and then choose Type ➪ Create Outlines, or press Shift+⌘+O or Ctrl+Shift+O. Frames are based on the size and outlines of the font in use and are automatically anchored in the paragraph so they flow with the text.

Note   When you convert text to outlines, the characters no longer exist as text. If you converted part of a word, the remaining portions of the word may be flagged during a spelling check. If you need to edit the converted text, you will need to delete the outlines, retype the word, and convert the characters again.

Using graphics as initial caps

Rather than using text for initial caps, you can use graphics. You can purchase clip art collections that consist of nothing but ornate capital letters to use as initial caps. To use a graphic as an initial cap, first delete the characters you will replace with graphics. Then, use the Place command (File ➪ Place, or ⌘+D or Ctrl+D) to import the graphic.

Size the graphic as appropriate, and then place it behind the paragraph, next to the paragraph, or anchored in the text of the paragraph. To anchor a graphic in text, select it with the Selection tool and choose Edit ➪ Cut, or press ⌘+X or Ctrl+X. Select the Type tool and click at the beginning of the paragraph; then choose Edit ➪ Paste, or press ⌘+V or Ctrl+V. The graphic is now anchored to the text, so if text reflows, the graphical drop cap flows with it.

In addition to importing graphics for use as initial caps, you can create your own graphics in InDesign. For example, you can place the initial cap character in its own text frame and create reverse type from it as discussed later in this chapter. Or you can shade the character and place it slightly behind the paragraph.

Labeling Paragraphs

Along with initial caps, changing the formatting of the first few words in a paragraph can indicate the beginning of a story or a new topic. This is commonly used for run-in heads, a short title usually in boldface or italic, and often in a contrasting font, that is on the same line as the rest of the paragraph.

The following descriptions show frequently used label formatting:

✦ **Boldface.** Bold speaks the loudest, and is generally used for subheads in magazines, newspapers, and reports. To apply boldface in InDesign, select the bold version of the typeface from the Type Style pop-up menu in the Character pane or in the Character pane of the Control palette.

Note   All character formatting options in the Control palette are in the Character pane; be sure the **A** button is selected to display them.

✦ *Italics.* If bold shouts, italics tends to whisper. It's a good choice for tertiary heads and to label bulleted items within a list. To apply italics in InDesign, select the oblique version of the typeface from the Type Style pop-up menu on the Character pane.

✦ Underlines. For a typewriter effect, you might underline the text of a label. Use the Underline command available from the menu on the Character pane—note that you have no control over the style, thickness, or placement of the line.

✦ SMALL CAPS. For a subtle, classic look that blends well with the rest of the document, use small caps on labels. However, don't use small caps if you're using labels as subheads that allow readers to skim through a document and read only relevant portions. You have two choices for applying small caps from the Character pane: Choose a small-caps variation of a typeface from the Type Style pop-up menu or choose the Small Caps command from the palette menu.

✦ **Typeface change.** Rather than relying on different variations of a font, you can use a different font altogether, such as Futura Medium as used on this paragraph, for a label. To contrast with serif body text, you might choose a sans serif typeface that complements the look of your publication. Often, this will be a variation of your headline font. To apply a typeface, use the Font Family pop-up menu in the Character pane or Control palette.

✦ Scaled text. Scaling text horizontally—up 10 or 20 percent—quietly differentiates it from the remainder of the paragraph. (More severe scaling distorts the typeface and could look unprofessional.) Unlike bold or underline, the text won't pop off the page at you, but it is visually distinct. Scaling text vertically, however, can be too subtle unless combined with boldface or another style. Use the Horizontal Scale and Vertical Scale fields in the Character pane or Control palette to scale text.

✦ Size change. Creating a label by simply bumping the size up a point or two is another subtle design choice. The labels blend well with the body text, but they don't announce their presence enough to be used as subheads for scanning. To change the size of type, use the Font Size field in the Character pane or Control palette.

The label technique—whether implemented with local character formatting, a character style, or a nested style—can be used for any amount of text, from a single bullet to one or more sentences. For example, the guidebook in Figure 18-6 styles the first sentence in the introductory paragraph as italic. In many magazines, the first paragraph of a story often starts with a single drop cap, followed by the entire first line in small caps.

The Nested Styles feature is flexible, letting you specify it to any number of characters, words, or sentences, as well as to specific locations such as the first tab. That lets you use it for numbered lists where the number of digits may change (such as a 15-item list that has both single-digit numbers like *9* and double-digit numbers like *10*)—you'd have the nested style apply the appropriate character style through the first tab, so any numerals before the tab take on that character style. (For example, you might want to boldface the numbers in a list and change the font to a sans serif one.) Figure 18-6 shows an example of this feature, where the intro paragraph uses a nested style to italicize the first sentence of the introductory paragraph. (The paragraph style also specifies the initial drop cap.)

Cross-
Reference

Chapter 19 covers nested styles in more detail.

To experiment with label formatting, use the attributes available through the Character pane or Control palette and their palette menus, such as font changes, horizontal scale, or small caps. Once you decide on the formatting for labels, you can apply it using character styles after paragraph styles are applied—and after the text is final. You may also be able to use the nested styles feature, if there is a consistent pattern to the label text, such as being a specific number of words or characters or being a sentence.

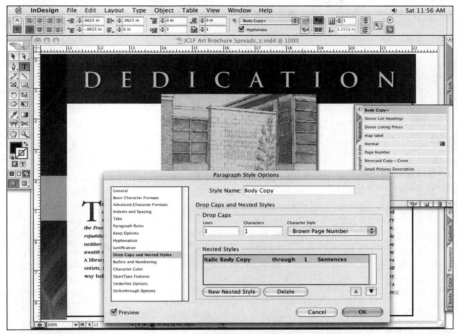

Figure 18-6: The use of nested styles in this paragraph automatically italicizes the first sentence in this intro paragraph.

Note Depending on the formatting, applying a label style might reflow the text, causing a need for copyfitting.

Tip To provide a little more space between the label and the text, you might want to use an en space rather than a normal space.

Adding Professional Touches

With today's word processors and low-end page-layout programs offering predesigned templates for birthday cards and reports, almost anyone can claim to be a designer. But a closer look reveals the difference—skilled graphic designers plan their typography and layout around the content, using typographic techniques to call attention to and refine content. The use of reverse type, sidebars, and pull-quotes helps break up pages and organize text, while careful formatting of fractions, hanging punctuation, and end-of-story markers adds a professional touch.

Reversing type out of its background

This is the reverse of what you usually see — white type on a black background rather than black type on a white background. Of course, reverse type doesn't have to be white on black, but any lighter color on a darker color. You'll often see reverse type in table headings, *kickers* (explanatory blurbs following headlines), and decorative elements. Reverse type, which brightens text and pulls readers in, works best with larger type sizes and bold typefaces so the text isn't swallowed by the background.

InDesign doesn't have a reverse type command or type style — but using this effect involves just a simple combination of basic InDesign skills. To lighten the text, highlight it with the Type tool, click the Fill button on the Tools palette, and choose a light color from the Swatches pane (Window ⇨ Swatches or F5). For a dark background, you have three options: filling the text frame with a darker color, making the text frame transparent and placing it on top of darker objects, or using a ruling line behind the text.

For the first two options, select the text frame with the Selection tool or the Direct Selection tool, and then click the Fill button on the Tools palette. To fill the text frame with a color, click a darker color on the Swatches pane. To make the text frame transparent, click the Apply None button on the Tools palette. Then place the text frame in front of a darker object or graphic.

For reverse-out type that is not in its own text frame, you use a ruling line of the appropriate width (at least a couple points larger than the text size) and move it into the text. If you use Rule Above, you move the line down behind the text; if you use Rule Below, you move it up. Figure 18-7 shows reversed-out type used as description headings, as well as the Paragraph Rules dialog box and the settings used to create the effect. (To access this dialog box, choose Paragraph Rules from the palette menu of the Control palette or Paragraph pane, or press Option+⌘+J or Ctrl+Alt+J.)

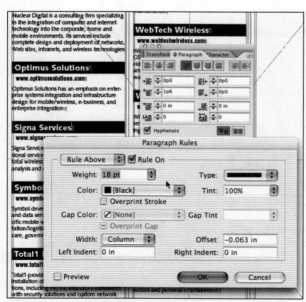

Figure 18-7: This product guide uses reversed-out text created with ruling lines for its description titles.

Tip

When designing elements with reverse type, make sure the point size of the text is large enough to print clearly on the darker background. Consider the thinnest part of characters, especially in serif typefaces, when judging the size and thickness of reverse type. You'll often want to use a semibold or bolder version of a font so the text maintains its visual integrity.

Note

All paragraph formatting options in the Control palette are in the paragraph pane; be sure the ¶ button is selected to display them.

Creating sidebars and pull-quotes

Pick up almost any publication, from *Newsweek* magazine to your neighborhood newsletter, and you're almost guaranteed to see sidebars and pull-quotes. So basic that you can even create them with a modern word processor, these treatments aren't really typographic treatments — they're just page-layout techniques involving text elements you create by applying simple InDesign skills.

A *sidebar* is supplemental text, formatted differently, and often placed within a shaded or outlined box. Sidebars help break up text-heavy pages and call attention to information that is often interesting but not essential to the main story. Even in technical publications, it's helpful to pull in-depth information or related text into sidebars to provide visual relief. To create a sidebar, you'll usually place the text in its own frame, and then stroke the frame and optionally fill it with a tint. To inset the text from the edges of the frame, use the Text Frame Options dialog box (Object ➪ Text Frame Options, or ⌘+B or Ctrl+B).

A *pull-quote* is a catchy one- or two-line excerpt from a publication that is enlarged and reformatted to achieve both editorial and design objectives. On the editorial side, pull-quotes draw readers into articles with excerpts that do everything from summarize the content to provide shock value. On the design side, pull-quotes break up staid columns and offer opportunities for typographic treatment that emphasize the content (such as colors and typefaces that reflect the mood of an article). Although the use of and length of pull-quotes are often dictated by design, an editorial person should select the text and indicate it on hard copy or within text files. To create a pull-quote, copy and paste the relevant text into its own text frame, and then reformat the text and frame as you want. Use the Text Wrap pane (Window ➪ Text Wrap, or Option+⌘+W or Ctrl+Alt+W) to control how text in columns wraps around the pull-quote.

Cross-Reference

InDesign CS2 now lets you anchor a sidebar, pull-quote, or other frame to a specific spot in the text so that it follows that text as the text reflows. Chapter 11 covers this new capability in detail.

Formatting fractions

If you're in a big hurry, it's fine to type *1/3 cup* and get on with your life. It looks like a fraction, but it's kind of big and ugly, and it calls a little too much attention to itself. Compare the first line in Figure 18-8, which is formatted appropriately for a fraction, to the last two lines, which are not. InDesign doesn't provide an automatic fraction maker, but you can use expert typefaces or character formats to achieve professional-looking fractions.

QuarkXPress User

InDesign has no equivalent to QuarkXPress's fraction-building tool, although the use of OpenType fonts that support automatic fractions can provide similar functionality.

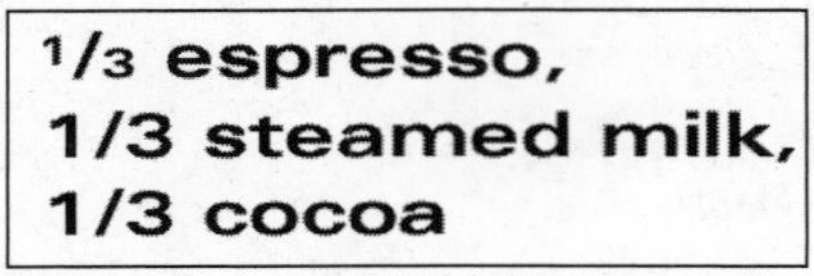

**1/3 espresso,
1/3 steamed milk,
1/3 cocoa**

Figure 18-8: In the first line of text here, the *1/3* text is formatted manually to look like a true fraction.

Applying a fraction typeface

Some expert typefaces include a variation, appropriately called fractions, that include a number of common fractions such as ½, ⅓, ¼, and ¾. Adobe has offered so-called Expert Collections for many of its popular fonts; these collections include true small caps, true fractions, and other typographic characters. Many OpenType fonts have these characters included as well. You can also use a symbol font, though the numerals may not exactly match the appearance of numerals in the rest of your text because symbol fonts typically use plain fonts like Helvetica as their basis.

To use a specific true fraction from an Expert Collection or OpenType font, or from a symbol font, choose Type ➪ Glyph, select the font and face from the pop-up menus at the bottom of the dialog box, and then select the fraction you want.

To use an automatic true fraction from an OpenType font that supports this feature, be sure the character or paragraph style enables fractions in the OpenType Features pane (select the Fractions option). Alternatively, you can highlight the text and choose OpenType ➪ Fractions from the Character pane's or Control palette's palette menu. InDesign will use the OpenType font's denominator and numerator characters, as well as the virgule character, to create a true fraction.

Note

If you're dealing with a wide range of fractions in something such as a cookbook, you probably won't find all the fractions you need in your Expert Collection font. Because it is difficult to format fractions such as ³⁄₁₆ exactly the same as an expert font's ¼, you might opt for formatting all the fractions manually or by replacing your non-OpenType fonts with OpenType equivalents that have all the necessary numerator and denominator characters to create any fraction.

Formatting fractions manually

You'll notice that expert fractions are approximately the same size as a single character in that font. That's your eventual goal in formatting a fraction. Usually, you achieve this by decreasing the size of the two numerals, raising the numerator (the first, or top, number in the fraction), and kerning on either side of the slash as necessary.

For example, see the fraction in the first line of Figure 18-9. The rest of the text is set at 9 points, but the denominator (the number after the slash in a fraction, or *3* here) has been set to 6 points using the Font Size field in the Character pane. The *1* is set as a superscript using the Character pane. The *1/* and the */3* pairs are both kerned by –50. (You can also use the Control palette to access these controls.) The font size and kerning that works for your font, size, and values will vary.

Macintosh fonts provide another option for refining fractions. It's a special kind of slash called a *virgule*, which is smaller and at more of an angle than a regular slash. Press Option+Shift+1 to enter a virgule, and then kern around it as you would a slash. (The fraction in the first line of Figure 18-8 uses a virgule rather than a regular slash.)

InDesign's default superscript and subscript size is 58.3 percent of the character's size (this odd value actually equals $\frac{7}{12}$, in keeping with typography's standard of using points, of which there are 12 in a pica, for text measurement). The numerator and denominator in a fraction should be the same size, so if you use InDesign's superscripts at its default settings, multiply the text's point size by 0.583 (just highlight the denominator text, go to the Size field in the Character pane or Control palette, and type ***0.583** in the Size field after the current point size). I recommend changing InDesign's superscript and subscript type styles to 65 percent to improve readability, especially at smaller sizes. You can change these default settings in the Advanced Type pane of the Preferences dialog box (choose InDesign ➪ Preferences on the Mac or Edit ➪ Preferences in Windows, or press ⌘+K or Ctrl+K).

Unless you're rarely confronted with fractions, by all means save your numerator and denominator formatting as character styles. You'll be able to apply the formats with a keystroke or use Find/Change (Edit ➪ Find/Change, or ⌘+F or Ctrl+F) to locate numbers and selectively apply the appropriate character style.

Hanging punctuation

When display type such as a pull-quote or a headline in ads is left-aligned or justified, the edges can look uneven due to the gaps above, below, or next to quotation marks, punctuation, and some capital letters, as shown in the text frame at right in Figure 18-9, which does not have hanging punctuation. To correct the unevenness, graphic designers use a technique called *hanging punctuation* in which they extend the punctuation slightly beyond the edges of the rest of the text as shown in the text frame at left in Figure 18-9.

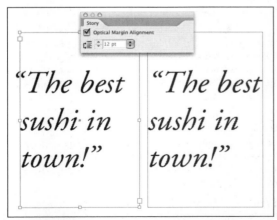

Figure 18-9: Notice the difference between the text frame at left with Optical Margin Alignment and the text frame at right with standard alignment.

Note   The *edge* of text is defined by the edges of the text frame or any Inset Spacing specified in the Text Frame Options dialog box (Object ⇨ Text Frame Options, or ⌘+B or Ctrl+B).

InDesign's Optical Margin Alignment feature automates hanging punctuation, extending punctuation and the edges of some glyphs (such as a capital *T*) slightly outside the edges of the text. (Adobe bills this feature as margin alignment rather than hanging punctuation because it also works with other characters.)

Unfortunately, you can't control how much the characters "hang" outside the text boundaries — InDesign decides that for you. And Optical Margin Alignment applies to all the text frames in a story, rather than to highlighted text. This means you need to isolate into its own story any text for which you want hanging punctuation.

To specify Optical Margin Alignment, select any text frame in a story and choose Window ⇨ Type & Tables ⇨ Story. Select the Optical Margin Alignment option, as shown in Figure 18-9.

Note   In general, Optical Margin Alignment improves the look of display type whether it's left-aligned, centered, justified, or even right-aligned. However, Optical Margin Alignment will actually cause columns of body text to look, at close inspection, slightly uneven (because they are).

Choosing and placing end-of-story markers

In magazines, newsletters, and other publications with multiple stories, the text often continues from one page to the next. In news magazines, a story might meander from page to page, interrupted by sidebars and ads. In a fashion magazine, stories generally open on a splashy spread, and then continue on text-heavy pages at the back of the magazine. In either case, readers can get confused about whether a story has ended. Designers solve this by placing a *dingbat* (a special character such as a square) at the end of each story.

You can use any dingbat character — in Zapf Dingbats, DF Organics, Woodtype, or Wingdings, for example — or an inline graphic to mark the end of a story. The end-of-story marker should reflect the overall design and feel of a publication or emphasize the content. You might see a square used in a financial publication, a heart in a teen magazine, or a leaf in a gardening magazine. A derivative of the company's logo might even be used to mark the end of a story — you can easily envision the Nike swoosh used in this way.

To place a dingbat, first decide on the character and create a character style for it. If you're using a graphic, you might consider converting it to a font with a utility such as Pyrus FontLab so you can insert and format it automatically. If you're using an inline graphic, you might store it in an InDesign library (see Chapter 7) so it's easily accessible. Make sure everyone working on the publication knows the keystroke for entering the dingbat or the location of the graphic.

Once you have the character established, you need to decide where to place it. Generally, the dingbat will be flush with the right margin or right after the final punctuation in the last line:

✦ To place the dingbat flush with the right margin, there are two ways to set a right-aligned tab:

   • One is to choose Type ⇨ Insert Special Character ⇨ Right Indent Tab or just press Shift+Tab.

   • The other way is to set a tab stop in the paragraph style you use for final paragraphs (see Chapter 20 for more details on setting tabs). Because InDesign offers an easier method to right-indent a dingbat, you should use this method only if you want to right-align the dingbat to a place in the column other than at the right margin — essentially, if you want to have it indented a little from the right margin.

✦ To place the dingbat after the final punctuation, separate the two with an en space by pressing Shift+⌘+N or Ctrl+Shift+N, or with an em space by pressing Shift+⌘+M or Ctrl+Shift+M.

Applying Color to Text

Just because you're printing on a four-color printing press or have a color printer doesn't mean you should get carried away with coloring text. You want to keep your content legible and unified, but that doesn't have to mean it's all black on white. You'll commonly see color in headlines, banners, subheads, and pull-quotes. However, you'll rarely see color applied to body text.

Colors applied to text are often derived from colors within related graphics or from a publication's traditional palette. In general, the smaller the type, the darker its color should be — with pastels reserved for large text, bright colors for bold text, and dark colors for body text. InDesign lets you make an entire character one color, or make the *fill* (inside) and *stroke* (outlines) of a character two different colors, as shown in Figure 18-10. You can even apply gradients to fills and strokes.

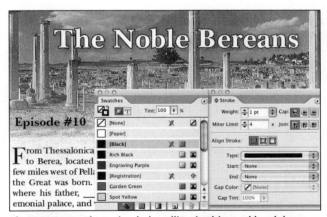

Figure 18-10: The episode headline in this workbook by Ronald Lanham has a 1-point black stroke and a fill color of white.

To color text:

1. **Click the Type tool in the Tools palette or press T.**

2. **Highlight the text you want to color.**

3. **Click the Fill button or the Stroke button on the Tools palette to specify whether you're coloring the character or its outlines.**

4. **If necessary, open the color Swatches pane by choosing Window ⇨ Swatches or pressing F5.**

5. **Click a color swatch to apply it to the stroke or fill.**

6. **To specify the thickness of the stroke, use the Strokes pane (Window ⇨ Stroke or F10), and to apply a gradient to the stroke or fill, use the Gradient pane (Window ⇨ Gradient).**

Cross-Reference

For information about creating color swatches or working with gradients, see Chapters 8 and 28.

Rotating Text

You've seen newsletters with nameplates running horizontally down the first page and catalogs with *sale* splashed diagonally across pages. You do this by placing the text you want to rotate in its own frame, and then rotating the entire frame. InDesign lets you rotate any object from 180 degrees to –180 degrees — basically, full circle. You can rotate in increments as small as 0.01 degree using the Rotate tool or as small as 0.001 degree using the Rotation Angle field on the Transform pane or Control palette (Figure 18-11 shows the icons).

    Figure 18-11: The Rotate tool (left) from the Tools palette and the Rotation Angle field from the Transform pane and Control palette

Using the Rotation Angle field

Use the Rotation Angle field on the Transform pane or Control palette if you know the angle you need. For example, to run text along the left side of a graphic like the photo credit in Figure 18-12, you rotate the frame 90 degrees. To use the Rotation Angle field, select the object with the Selection tool, and then choose an option from the pop-up menu, which offers 30-degree increments, or type a value in the field. Press Return or Enter to rotate the object.

Using the Rotate tool

Use the Rotate tool to experiment with different angles while designing. To rotate items freehand, select the Rotate tool by clicking it in the Tools palette or pressing R (unless the Type tool is selected). If the object you want to rotate isn't selected, ⌘+click it or Ctrl+click it. Drag in any direction to rotate the object. Release the mouse button as necessary to check the placement and any text wrap. To restrict the rotation to 45-degree increments, press Shift while you drag.

Tip

You can also double-click the Rotate tool to get a dialog box in which you enter a precise rotation value, as Figure 18-12 shows. Not only can you set the rotation amount, you can control whether the content rotates with the frame or whether the rotation will apply to a copy of the item.

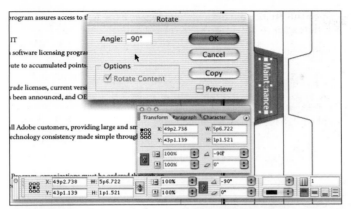

Figure 18-12: The Rotation Angle field on the Transform pane or on the Control palette lets you rotate selected objects with 0.001 degree of precision. Typing a value in the field is ideal for turning a tab-like section head 90 degrees to place it within a frame shaped like a binder tab. You can also double-click the Rotation tool to get the Rotate dialog box shown at top to enter a precise rotation amount.

Scaling Text

While you're roughing out a design, you'll probably find yourself changing type sizes, object placement, and colors as you go. Changing the size of text can get a little tedious — especially if the text is tucked into its own frame. You have to select the Type tool, highlight the text, enter a new size, and then often switch to the Selection tool to resize the frame so the text doesn't overflow. For a more interactive method of resizing text, you can use the Scale tool to resize the text and its frame at the same time.

To use the Scale tool, click it in the Tools palette or press S (if the Type tool is not selected). If the text frame is not already selected it, you need to ⌘+click or Ctrl+click. Then simply drag any frame edge or handle in any direction. To scale proportionally so the text is not distorted, press Shift while you drag. The amount of scaling is reported in the Scale X Percentage and Scale Y Percentage fields in the Transform pane or in the Control palette.

Caution   Be careful in scaling text frames and the text within them. If you modify multiple text frames that contain similar items (such as headlines), you end up with inconsistent text formatting for like items, which will look terrible. You should scale text only when it is a unique element, such as a headline in an ad, and thus not likely to create visual inconsistencies.

Underline and Strikethrough Options

InDesign lets you create custom underlines and strikethroughs. While you'll use these sparingly, they can be effective for design-oriented text presentation, such as shown in Figure 18-13.

The Character pane's and Control palette's palette menus provide the Underline Options and Strikethrough Options menu items to create customer versions. (You must have the Character pane of the Control palette selected to get these options; click the A button to display it.) The process for the two is similar:

1. **Highlight the text to which you want the custom underline or strikethrough.**

2. **Specify the thickness, type, color, and other settings for the line that makes up the underline or the strikethrough line.** Note that if you choose a line type that has gaps — such as dashed, dotted, or striped lines — you can also choose a gap color, such as was done for the top example in Figure 18-13. Figure 18-14 shows the Underline Options and Strikethrough Options dialog boxes.

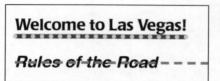

Figure 18-13: Examples of custom underlines and strikethroughs

3. **Apply the underline style through the Control palette or Character pane, or use the keyboard shortcut (Shift+⌘+U or Ctrl+Shift+U).** Apply the strikethrough style through the Control palette or Character pane, or use the keyboard shortcut (Shift+⌘+/ or Ctrl+Shift+/).

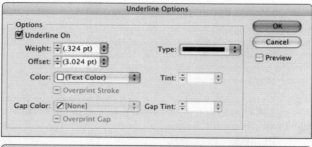

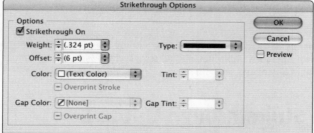

Figure 18-14: The Underline Options (top) and Strikethrough Options dialog boxes. In both, the Type pop-up menu at the right provides the list of line types available.

Note that a custom underline or strikethrough created and applied this way is in effect only for the first text to which an underline or strikethrough is applied. InDesign reverts to the standard settings the next time you apply an underline or strikethrough using the Character pane or Control palette or by using the shortcuts Shift+⌘+U or Ctrl+Shift+U for underlines and Shift+⌘+/ or Ctrl+Shift+/ for strikethroughs. If you want to use a custom underline or strikethrough setting repeatedly, you should define the setting as part of a character style, as described in Chapter 19.

QuarkXPress User   InDesign has no equivalent to QuarkXPress's Underline Styles. Instead, specify custom underlines and strikethroughs as part of a character style or by using the Underline Options or Strike through Options commands in the palette menu of the Control palette or Character pane. To add stripes and dashed lines, open the Strokes pane (Window ➪ Stroke or F10) and select the Stroke Styles option from the palette menu, as described in Chapter 10.

Drop Shadows and Feathering

InDesign offers built-in drop shadow and feathering that lets you create dimensional effects based on simulated lighting. These features cannot be applied to text selections, just to entire text (or other) frames.

Cross-Reference   Chapter 10 covers the use of drop shadows and feathering with frames.

Summary

InDesign gives you the power to embellish and manipulate text in almost infinite ways. It's your responsibility to format text in ways that clarify and reinforce the content rather than simply decorate it. Bulleted lists — often created with special character bullets, tabs, and hanging indents — help break out information. So do numbered lists. Initial caps and run-in heads call attention to the beginning of a story or to topic shifts within a story. You can pull readers into a story with sidebars and pull-quotes, which also break up text-heavy areas. For display type, InDesign provides an automatic method for hanging punctuation outside the margins, and it lets you rotate and scale text.

✦   ✦   ✦

Setting Up Styles

If you were assigned the task of making 500 star-shaped cookies, the first thing you'd do is find a star-shaped cookie cutter. Of course, you could shape each cookie by hand, but not only would this take considerably more time than using a cookie cutter, no two cookies would look exactly the same. Think of styles as cookie cutters for formatting text. They save you time and ensure consistency. If you'll be using InDesign to create long documents that require considerable text formatting, styles are indispensable.

InDesign lets you create two types of textual styles:

◆ A *character style* is a set of character-level formats you can apply to range of highlighted text in a single step.

◆ A *paragraph style* is a set of both character- *and* paragraph-level formats you can apply to selected paragraphs in a single step.

Note

InDesign calls these *styles*, not *style sheet* as other programs such as Microsoft Word and QuarkXPress do. I personally prefer *style sheet* because that term has a longer history in publishing terminology and because *style* is also used to indicate type styles such as boldface and italics. But in this book, I'm sticking with the InDesign term *style*.

Cross-Reference

InDesign CS2 also lets you create styles for objects such as frames and lines, as Chapter 11 explains.

In one respect, styles are far superior to cookie cutters. If you use a cookie cutter to create hundreds of cookies and then find out your cookies are the wrong shape, you're out of luck. But if you use a style to format hundreds of pieces of text and then decide you don't like the look of the styled text, you can simply modify the style sheet. Any text you've formatted with a style sheet is automatically updated if you modify the style.

Tip

When it comes to using styles, it's as important to know when *not* to use them as it is to know *when* to use them. For short documents — especially one-pagers such as business cards, ads, and posters — that contain relatively little text and don't use the same formats repeatedly, you're probably better off formatting the text by hand.

Tip

If you create multiple editions of a particular publication—for example, a form, a daily news-paper, a monthly magazine, or a corporate business card—you'll want to create a template. A template is a shell of a document that contains all the layout elements necessary to create the document—including styles if it's a multipage publication—but no content (except content that appears in every issue, such as copyright lines and mastheads). You use a template as the starting point each time you need to create a new version of a publication. For more information about templates, see Chapter 7.

Creating and Applying Styles

Before you can use a style to format text, you must create it. You can create styles whenever you want, but usually, creating styles is one of the first tasks you'll tackle when working on a long document. Also, you may want to create your paragraph styles first and then, if neces-sary, add character styles. In many cases, character styles are used to format text within paragraphs to which paragraph styles have already been applied.

Cross-Reference

See Chapter 16 for information about specifying character-level formats; see Chapter 17 for information about paragraph-level formats. Note that this chapter assumes you know how to use the character and paragraph formatting tools covered in those chapters.

Paragraph styles

Let's say you've been given the job of creating a newsletter. It will be several pages long and contain several stories. Each story will have the same text elements: a big headline, a smaller headline, an author byline, and body text. The stories will also include pictures, and each pic-ture requires a caption and a credit line. Before you begin laying out pages and formatting text, you should create styles for all these repetitive text elements. The Paragraph Styles pane (Window ➪ Type & Tables ➪ Paragraph Styles or F11), shown in Figure 19-1, is where you need to go for both creating and applying styles.

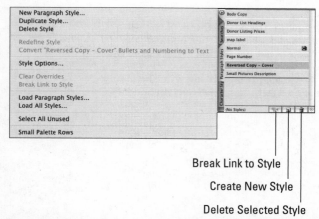

Break Link to Style
Create New Style
Delete Selected Style

Figure 19-1: The Paragraph Styles pane and its palette menu

Tip

You can combine the Character Styles and Paragraph Styles panes into a single palette by clicking and dragging the tab of one pane on top of the other pane and then releasing the mouse. Similarly, you can combine the Character (Window ➪ Type & Tables ➪ Character, or ⌘+T or Ctrl+T) and Paragraph panes (Window ➪ Type & Tables ➪ Paragraph, or Option+⌘+T or Ctrl+Alt+T). If you're really into combining panes, you can combine all four panes into a single text-formatting palette.

Creating paragraph styles

The easiest way to create a paragraph style is to manually apply character- and paragraph-level formats to a sample paragraph and then — with the sample paragraph selected — follow the next set of steps. If no text is selected when you create a style, you'll have to specify character- and paragraph-level formats as you create the style, which is more difficult than formatting a paragraph in advance. Here's how you create a paragraph style from a preformatted paragraph:

1. **If it's not displayed, show the Paragraph Style pane by choosing Window ➪ Type & Tables ➪ Paragraph Styles or pressing F11.**

2. **Make sure you highlight a paragraph that's been styled with all the character and paragraph formats you want to include in your style, and then choose New Style from the Paragraph Styles pane's palette menu, as shown in Figure 19-1.** The New Paragraph Style dialog box, shown in Figure 19-2, appears.

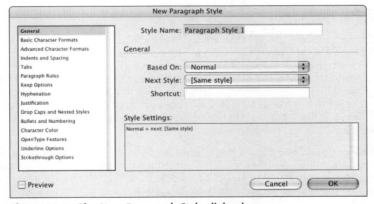

Figure 19-2: The New Paragraph Style dialog box

Tip

You can also create a new style by clicking the Create New Style button at the bottom of the Paragraph Styles pane. When you click this button, a new style with a default name (Paragraph Style 1, Paragraph Style 2, and so on) is added to the list. The formats applied to the selected paragraph are included in the new style; the New Paragraph Style dialog box is not displayed. If you want to modify any formats, double-click the new style name in the pane; the Modify Paragraph Style Options dialog box appears. This dialog box is identical to the New Paragraph Style dialog box.

3. **Type a name for the style in the Style Name field.**

Note

Assign your style names with care; be descriptive. Imagine that somebody else will be using the document, and assign a name that conveys the purpose of the style. For example, anybody will know what a style called Body Copy is used for, but a style called Really Cool Style won't mean anything to anybody but you.

Tip

You may want to consider using a naming scheme that displays families of related styles together in the Paragraph Styles pane. (Step 5 explains how to create a family of parent/children styles.) For example, you could use numbers (01, 02, 03, and so on) or letters (A. Body Copy/Base, A. Body Copy/Drop Cap, A. Body Copy/No Indent, and so on) in front of style names to group styles. For complex styles, use something like: 10.0 Title, 11.0 Subtitle, 20.0 Subhead, 30.0 Body First, 35.0 Body, 35.1 Body Last, 40.0 Bullet, 40.5 Bullet Last. This three-digit naming system allows for the addition of new styles in between existing styles as they are needed and also keeps similar styles grouped together.

4. **Change character- or paragraph-level formats.** The scroll list to the left of the dialog box shows 15 options, as shown in Figure 19-2. If you want to change any character- or paragraph-level formats, choose the appropriate option, and then make your changes.

5. **Use the Based On pop-up menu, which displays the names of other paragraph styles, to create families of styles.** For example, you could create a style called Body Copy/Base for the bulk of your body text, and then create variations such as Body Text/Drop Cap, Body Text/No Indent, and Body Text/Italic. If you use the Based On pop-up menu to base each of the variations on Body Text/Base and you then modify this parent style sheet, your changes are applied to all the variations.

6. **To automatically switch from the style you are creating to another style as you type text, choose a style from the Next Style pop-up menu.** If you specify a Next Style for a style, it's automatically applied to a new paragraph when you press Return or Enter. If you choose Same Style (the default), the style you're creating continues to be applied to new paragraphs when you press Return or Enter while typing. Typically, you'd use Next Style for things like headlines that are always followed by a specific kind of paragraph (like a byline). And you'd typically use Same Style for body text, where the next paragraph usually has the same formatting.

7. **Assign a keyboard shortcut.** If you want to (and you often should), you can assign a keyboard shortcut to a style (Windows users must make sure Num Lock is on). Press and hold any combination of ⌘, Option, and Shift, or Ctrl, Alt, and Shift, and press any number on the keypad. (Letters and non–keypad numbers cannot be used for keyboard shortcuts.)

8. **When you're done specifying the attributes of your style, click OK.**

Note

When you create a style based on highlighted text, the new style is automatically applied to the text.

QuarkXPress User

InDesign handles character formatting differently than QuarkXPress does in its style sheets. QuarkXPress lets paragraph style sheets get their character formatting from character style sheets. That lets character style sheets do double-duty: They can be the basis for character formatting in paragraph styles and also be used independently on text selections. InDesign does not work this way — you specify the character formatting in the paragraph style, and use character styles only for text selections. This can be frustrating if you have several styles that use the same character formatting; if that basic formatting needs to change, InDesign forces you to update each paragraph style separately. In QuarkXPress, you could just update the underlying character style sheet.

But the downside to QuarkXPress's approach is that if that underlying character style sheet changes, *all* paragraph styles sheets using it are affected. In InDesign instead would have you define a simple paragraph style with the character attributes and then have similar paragraph styles based on that first style sheet. The new styles could have different character settings, so if the parent paragraph style sheet's character attributes change, only the children styles' non-overridden attributes also change.

Applying paragraph styles

After you create a paragraph style, applying it is easy. Just click within a paragraph or highlight text in a range of paragraphs, and then click on the style name in the Paragraph Styles pane or press its keyboard shortcut. (Windows users must make sure Num Lock is on when using shortcuts for styles.)

If your selected paragraphs have more than one paragraph style applied within the group, the Paragraph Styles pane displays the text *(Mixed)* at the lower left.

When you apply a style to selected paragraphs, all local formats and applied character styles are retained. All other formats are replaced by those of the applied style.

If you press and hold Option or Alt when clicking on a name in the Paragraph Styles pane, any Character Styles that have been applied within selected paragraphs are retained, as are the following character formats: Superscript, Subscript, Underline, Strikethrough, Language, and Baseline Shift. If you press and hold Option+Shift or Alt+Shift when clicking a style name, all local formatting, including any Character Styles, within the selected paragraphs is removed.

If a plus sign (+) appears to the right of a style name, it means that some of the text within the selected paragraphs has local formats that differ from those of the applied style. This can occur if you apply a style to text to which you've done some manual formatting or if you modify text formatting in a paragraph after applying a style to it. (For example, you may have italicized the name of a book; that is a local change to the style and causes the + to appear.)

Another way to apply paragraph and character styles is using the Quick Apply feature in InDesign. Quick Apply is a consolidated list of styles that you access by choosing Edit ⇨ Quick Apply or pressing ⌘+Return or Ctrl+Enter. If you select text or the text-insertion point is active, the Quick Apply palette, shown in Figure 19-3, presents all paragraph, character, and object styles available. You can scroll down to the one you want or type the first few letters of the style name in the text field at top to jump to styles beginning with those letters, and then navigate to the one you want and press Return or Enter, which brings you back to where you were working with your text. Pressing ⌘+keypad Enter or Ctrl+Enter again closes the Quick Apply palette.

Quick Apply is new to InDesign CS2.

Frankly—unless you work only with a few styles — it seems easier to stick with the Paragraph Styles and Character Styles panes because you don't have to worry about wading through the character, paragraph, and object styles at the same time, although these panes don't let you quickly jump to styles by entering the first letter or two of their names as Quick Apply does.

But for users who are working on layouts from their keyboards — perhaps a layout artist who's working on a notebook while commuting — Quick Apply can be handy because you can switch to it, apply the style, and return to your text all without touching the mouse.

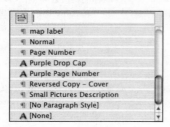

Figure 19-3: The Quick Apply palette

A few last words about paragraph styles. There are no hard-and-fast rules about how best to implement them. Like handwriting, you should develop your own style. How many styles you create, the names you use, whether you apply them with keyboard shortcuts or through the Paragraph Styles pane, and whether you use paragraph styles, character styles, or both are all matters of personal taste. One thing is indisputable: You should use styles whenever possible; they are a layout artist's best friend.

Managing paragraph styles

The Paragraph Style's pop-up menu, shown in Figure 19-1, displays 11 options for managing styles; three buttons at the bottom of the pane let you reapply, create, and delete paragraph styles. Here's a brief description of each option:

✦ **New Paragraph Style.** This option creates a new paragraph style. When you choose New Paragraph Style, the New Paragraph Style dialog box appears. The pane also has an iconic button to create a new style.

✦ **Duplicate Style.** Click on a style name, and then click this button to create an exact copy. If you want to create a style that's similar to one you've already created, you can choose New Paragraph Style rather than Duplicate, and then use the Based On option to create a child of the original. If you choose Duplicate, the copy is identical to but not based on the original; if you modify the original, the copy is not affected. The pane also has an iconic button to create a new style.

✦ **Delete Style.** Choose this option to delete highlighted styles. To select multiple styles, press and hold ⌘ or Ctrl as you click on their names. To select a range of styles, click the first one, and then press and hold Shift and click the last one.

New Feature

InDesign CS2 now gives you the option of replacing a deleted style with another style. You can also choose [No Paragraph Style] if you no longer want a style applied. In that case, select the Preserve Formatting option to convert the unapplied style's formatting to local formatting, or deselect it to make the text lose that formatting as well as its style.

✦ **Redefine Style (Option+Shift+⌘+R or Ctrl+Alt+Shift+R).** This option lets you modify an existing style. Highlight text to which the style you want to modify has been applied, change the formats as desired, and then click Redefine Style. The newly applied formats are applied to the style.

✦ **Convert *"current style name"* Bullets and Numbering to Text.** This option removes from selected paragraphs any automatic bullets or numbering defined through InDesign's bulleted and numbered lists feature (see Chapter 18). The paragraphs that this option is applied to will still have bullets and numbers, but they will no longer be updated if the style is changed or if paragraphs are added or deleted (this normally would add bullets and adjust numbering).

New Feature The capability to apply InDesign automatic bulleted and numbered lists to selected paragraphs is new to InDesign CS2.

✦ **Style Options.** This option lets you modify an existing style. When a style is highlighted in the Paragraph Styles pane, choosing Style Options displays the Modify Paragraph Style Options dialog box, which is identical to the New Paragraph Style dialog box.

✦ **Clear Overrides.** This option removes any local formatting such as boldface or small caps applied to the selected paragraphs. Note that the text within the paragraph that has the local overrides must be selected; you cannot simply just click anywhere in the paragraph. This is simply a more obvious alternative when clicking a style name to pressing and holding Option or Alt to remove local formatting (but retain any character styles applied) or to pressing and holding Option+Shift or Alt+Shift to remove both local formatting and applied character styles.

New Feature The Clear Overrides menu option is new to InDesign CS2.

✦ **Break Link to Style.** This option removes the style from the paragraph but leaves it with the formatting, now converted to local formatting. That way, the selected paragraph won't be changed if the paragraph style is later changed. Once you remove a style from a paragraph, InDesign displays (No Style) as at the bottom of the Paragraph Styles pane when the paragraph is selected.

New Feature The Break Link to Style replaces the [No Paragraph Style] option that InDesign CS and earlier had in the Paragraph Styles pane's list of styles.

✦ **Load Paragraph Styles.** Choose this option if you want to import styles from another InDesign document. (Importing styles is discussed in detail later in this chapter.)

✦ **Load All Styles.** This option lets you import both paragraph and character styles from another InDesign document. (Importing styles is discussed in detail later in this chapter.)

✦ **Select All Unused.** Select this option to highlight the names of all paragraph styles that have not been applied to any paragraphs. This is a handy way of identifying unused styles in preparation for deleting them (by choosing the Delete Style option).

✦ **Small Palette Rows.** Click this option to reduce the text size in the Paragraph Styles pane. Although harder to read, a pane with this option set lets you access more styles without having to scroll. To return the pane to its normal text size, select this option again.

Applying a Sequence of Styles All at Once

InDesign CS2 has a neat new capability that lets you apply multiple styles to selected text.

First, define the various styles, and be sure that each style has a different style selected in the Next Style pop-up menu in the Paragraph Style Options or New Paragraph Style dialog boxes. For example, if you have Headline, Byline, and Body Copy styles, make sure that Headline has Byline selected in Next Style and that Byline has Body Copy selected in Next Style.

Then highlight all the text that uses this sequence of styles. Now Control+click or right-click Headline and select Apply "Headline" + Next Style from the contextual menu. InDesign will apply Headline to the first paragraph, Byline to the second paragraph, and Body Copy to the rest.

New Feature   InDesign CS2 now comes with a built-in paragraph style called [Basic Paragraph]. You can edit this style like any other. It's the style that InDesign uses when you type new text or import text that has no style applied.

Character styles

Character styles are nearly identical in every respect to paragraph styles, but instead of using them to format selected paragraphs, you use character styles to apply character-level formats to a highlighted range of text. For example, you can use a character style to:

✦ Modify the appearance of the first several words in a paragraph. For example, some publications — particularly magazines — will use a type-style variation such as small caps as a lead-in for a paragraph. You can use a character style not only to switch the type style to small caps, but also to change size, color, font family, and so on.

✦ Apply different formatting to such text elements as Web site, e-mail, and FTP addresses within body text.

✦ Create other body text variations for such things as emphasis, book and movie titles, product and company names, and so on.

Creating and applying character styles

Using character styles is much the same as using paragraph styles. First you create them; then you apply them. And you use the Character Styles pane (Window ➪ Type & Tables ➪ Character Styles or Shift+F11), shown in Figure 19-4, to do both. As is the case with paragraph styles, the easiest way to create a character style is to apply the character-level formats you want to use in the style to some sample text, and then follow the steps in this section. You can create a character style from scratch (that is, without preformatting any text), but if you do, you'll have to set all the character formats when you create the style.

New Feature   If your selected text has more than one character style applied within the selection, the Character Styles pane will display the text *(Mixed)* at the lower left.

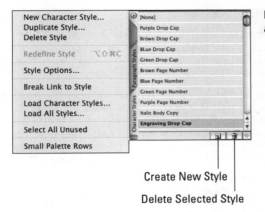

Figure 19-4: The Character Styles pane and its palette menu

Create New Style

Delete Selected Style

To create a character style from highlighted text:

1. **If it's not displayed, show the Character Style pane by choosing Type ➪ Character Styles or pressing Shift+F11.**

2. **Make sure you highlight text that's been styled with all the character formats you want to include in your style, and then choose New Style from the Character Styles pane's pop-up menu.** The New Character Style dialog box, shown in Figure 19-5, appears.

Tip

You can also create a new style by clicking the Create New Style button at the bottom of the pane. When you click this button, a new style with a default name (Character Style 1, Character Style 2, and so on) is added to the list. The formats applied to the selected text are included in the new style; the New Character Style dialog box is not displayed. If you want to modify any formats, double-click the new style name in the pane; the Modify Character Style, which is identical to the New Character Style dialog box, appears.

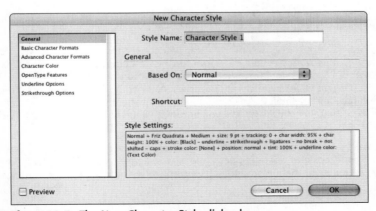

Figure 19-5: The New Character Style dialog box

3. **Type a name for the style in the Style Name field.**

4. **Choose the appropriate option from the scroll list to the left of the Style Name field if you want to change any character-level formats.** The list displays seven options: General, Basic Character Formats, Advanced Character Formats, Character Color, OpenType Features, Underline Options, and Strikethrough Options.

5. **Use the Based On pop-up menu to create families of styles.** This menu displays the names of other character styles. For example, you could create a style called Body Copy/Base Character that uses the same character attributes as your base Body Copy paragraph style and then create variations such as Body Text/Emphasis, Body Text/URLs, and so on. If you use the Based On pop-up menu to base each of the variations on Body Text/Base Character and you modify this parent style, your changes are applied to all the variations.

6. **If you want (and you should), you can assign a keyboard shortcut to a style (Windows users should make sure that Num Lock is on).** Press and hold any combination of ⌘, Option, and Shift, or Ctrl, Alt, and Shift, and press any number on the keypad. (Letters and nonkeypad numbers cannot be used for keyboard shortcuts.)

7. **When you're done specifying the attributes of your style, click OK.**

Managing character styles

The options displayed in the Character Styles pane's palette menu are the same as those for the Paragraph Styles palette menu, which are explained earlier in this chapter.

There is one set of interface differences, though, between paragraph styles and character styles: When you remove the link to a character style, the Character Styles pane displays [None] as the current style in its style list. When you remove the link to a paragraph style, the Paragraph Styles pane shows no style in the style list but instead displays (No Style) at the bottom of the pane.

A related interface difference is that there is no Clear Overrides button in the Character Styles pane (nor does the shortcut of Option+Shift+clicking or Alt+Shift+clicking perform this function). Instead, you apply the [None] style to clear a character style from text.

Working with Nested Styles

Often, you'll want to apply character formatting in a consistent manner to many paragraphs. For example, you may want to change the font for the first character in a bulleted list so that the correct symbol appears for the bullet. Or you might want to italicize the numerals in a numbered list. Or you might want the first four words of body text that appear after a head-line to be boldface and in small caps. Or you might want the first sentence in instructional paragraphs to be in italics. InDesign lets you automate such formatting through the Nested Styles feature.

Figure 19-6 shows an example of nested styles in use, along with the Paragraph Style Options dialog box's Drop Caps and Nested Styles pane in which you create them. Here, you can see that the first sentence of the introductory paragraph's text is set to appear in italics.

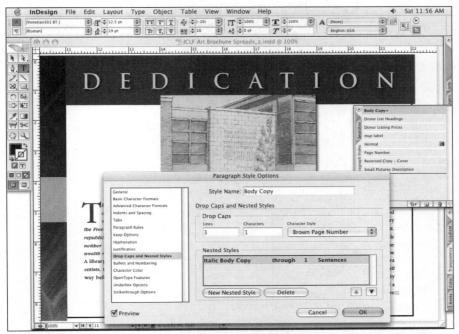

Figure 19-6: You can use a nested style to set the first sentence in the introductory paragraph in italics.

Here's how the nested styles work:

1. **Define any character styles that you'll apply to text through a nested style.** Even if all you're doing is making text italic, you need to define a character style to do so. The Nested Styles feature cannot apply any attributes other than those available in a character style.

2. **Go to the Paragraph Style Options dialog box (Window ➪ Type & Tables ➪ Paragraph Styles or F11) and select Drop Caps and Nested Styles.**

3. **Click New Nested Style.** An entry appears in the Nested Styles section of the dialog box. This is what will be applied to text.

4. **Click the style name in the Nested Styles section of the pane to choose from an existing character style.** When you click the style name, a list of other styles appears.

5. **Click in the second column to determine the scope end point.** Your choices are Through or Up To. For example, if you choose Through for a nested style that is set for four words, all four words will get the nested style. If you choose Up To, the first three words will get the style and the fourth will not.

6. **In the third column, specify how many items you want InDesign to count in determining the scope's endpoint.** For example, if you want to have the first seven characters have the style applied, choose 7. If you want to have the style applied up to the first tab, choose 1.

7. **Click the item in the fourth column to specify the scope of text to which you're applying the nested styles.** Figure 19-7 shows the options. They break into three groups: a number of items (characters, words, and so on), a specific character (tab, em space, and so on), and a specific marker character (inline graphic marker, auto page number, and section marker). Whatever you choose needs to be consistent in all your text because InDesign will follow these rules slavishly.

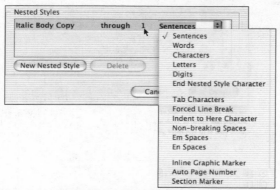

Figure 19-7: The scope options for a nested style determine what text receives the formatting.

8. **Create multiple nested styles in one paragraph with different rules for each.** Obviously, you may not need to do this, but the option exists. InDesign applies the styles in the order in which they appear in the dialog box, and each starts where the other ends. Use the up and down arrow buttons to change the order of nested styles.

A Wish for Nested Styles

About the only thing missing from the Nested Styles feature is, unfortunately, an effect favored by many designers: applying a format to the first line in a paragraph, usually a paragraph that follows a headline. The most common version of this has the first line formatted in all small caps, and then switching to normal capitalization for the rest of the paragraph.

InDesign's Nested Styles feature doesn't support this effect because it requires a specific stop point (number of characters, words, or sentences, or a specific character such as a tab, line break, indent-to-here, em space, en space, or the End Nested Style Character, which lets you set an arbitrary end). But there is no definite endpoint at the end of the line, as it depends on how InDesign flows and breaks the text, which will be different for each paragraph's first line.

The best you can do is highlight these manually and apply the small caps attribute yourself, or use the Nested Styles feature and manually insert the End Nested Style Character at the end of each line (choose Type ➪ Insert Special Character ➪ End Nested Style).

9. **Select the Preview option to preview the formatting if you selected sample text before opening the dialog box.**

10. **Click OK when you're done.**

Note The Nested Styles feature is included in the same dialog box as the Drop Caps feature. That's because a drop cap would be the first nested style in a paragraph and can never be anything but the first style. By combining the two into one dialog box, InDesign lets you treat a drop cap as part of a series of styles to be applied to a paragraph. If you want only a drop cap, you simply don't create a nested style.

Changing Styles

If you scratch your name into wet cement, you have only a few minutes to change your mind. After that, your formatting decisions are cast in stone, so to speak. Fortunately, styles are much more forgiving. Not only can you modify a style whenever you want, you're free to manually modify text to which styles have been applied.

Modifying styles

The most important thing to know about modifying a style is that all text to which a modified style has been applied is automatically updated. Additionally, if you modify a parent style, all children styles that were created by choosing Based On are also automatically updated.

There are two ways to modify an existing style. You can:

✦ **Click the style name in the Character Styles or Paragraph Styles pane, and then choose Style Options from the pane's palette menu.** The Modify Character Style Options or the Modify Paragraph Style Options dialog box appears. These dialog boxes are the same as the New Character Style and New Paragraph Style dialog boxes. Make whatever changes you want, and then click OK.

✦ **Double-click a style name to display the Modify Character Style Options or Modify Paragraph Style Options dialog box.** If text is highlighted, the style you double-click is applied to the text; if no text is selected, the style you double-click becomes the default style and is automatically applied when you type text in a newly created box. If you press and hold Shift+⌘ or Ctrl+Shift when you double-click on a style name, the style is not applied to text.

Modifying text that's been styled with a style

If you need to change the appearance of text that's been formatted using a style, all you have to do is highlight the text — characters or paragraphs — and then use the Control palette, Character pane (Window ➪ Type & Tables ➪ Character, or ⌘+T or Ctrl+T), or the Paragraph pane (Window ➪ Type & Tables ➪ Character, or Option+⌘+T or Ctrl+Alt+T) to change the formats.

When you change any formats in text to which a style has been applied, you are making local changes (to make global changes, you would modify the style). When you change formatting in style-formatted text, a plus sign (+) is displayed next to the style name in the Character Styles or Paragraph Styles pane, as shown in Figure 19-8.

Figure 19-8: The plus sign (+) next to the style name in the Paragraph Styles pane indicates that local formatting has been applied within a paragraph.

Unapplying styles

If you want, you can remove the link between style–formatted text and the assigned style. All you have to do is highlight the text — a range of characters if you want to disassociate them from the applied character style or one or more paragraphs if you want to disassociate it/them from the applied paragraph style — and then choose Break Link to Style from the Paragraph Styles or Character Styles pane's palette menu. Once you remove a style from text, InDesign displays (No Style) at the bottom of the Paragraph Styles pane and [None] in the Character Styles pane's list of styles, depending on what kind of style you unapplied.

When you break the link between text and its applied style, any local formatting is retained unless you press and hold Option or Alt when you click Break Link to Style. If you're working with paragraph styles, character styles are retained even if you press and hold Option or Alt. To remove both local formatting and character styles, press and hold Option+Shift or Alt+Shift when choosing Break Link to Styles.

New Feature

InDesign's Paragraph Styles pane no longer shows a style called [No Paragraph Style], which in earlier versions you used to remove any styles from selected text. You can still remove the style from a paragraph: Choose the Break Link to Style option in the palette menu. The Character Styles pane also no longer has a style [No Character Style], but it simply has been renamed [None] and works as it did in previous versions. You also have the option to choose Break Link to Style in the palette menu to remove the character style.

Along the same lines, if you delete a style that's been applied to text,. You'll get a dialog box that lets you choose a replacement style or choose [No Paragraph Style] or [No Character Style] to break the link to the style and leave the text formatting converted to local formatting

New Feature

InDesign CS2 now gives you the option of replacing a deleted style with another style.

Importing Styles

If you create a style, you never have to re-create it — assuming you save the document that contains the styles. InDesign lets you import character and paragraph stylefrom one document into another. Also, when you import text files from word processing programs that use style sheets, you can import the style sheets along with the text.

Importing styles from InDesign documents

The Paragraph Styles and Character Styles panes' palette menus contain commands that let you move styles between documents. The Paragraph Styles pane lets you import only paragraph styles or both paragraph and character styles; the Character Styles pane lets you import only character styles or both character and paragraph styles. Here's how you do it:

1. **If it's not displayed, show the Paragraph Styles pane by choosing Window ⇨ Type & Tables ⇨ Paragraph Styles or pressing F11, or show the Character Styles pane by choosing Window ⇨ Type & Tables ⇨ Character Styles or pressing Shift+F11.**

2. **Choose Load Styles from the Paragraph Styles pane's or Character Styles pane's palette menu if you want to import selected paragraph and/or character styles.** You can also choose Load All Styles from either pane's palette menu if you want to import all character and paragraph styles from that other document. Regardless of what kind of type(s) or styles you choose to import, the Open a File dialog box shown in Figure 19-9 appears.

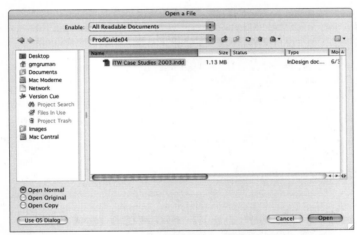

Figure 19-9: The Open a File dialog box when loading styles from other documents

3. **Use the controls in the Open a File dialog box to locate the InDesign document that contains the styles you want to import.**

4. **Double-click the document name or click the document name once and then click Open.** If you chose Load Styles, a dialog box appears listing the styles in the chosen document so you can decide which ones to import.

If you import styles whose names match those in the current document, InDesign gives you a chance to allow the imported style to overwrite the current style or to leave the current style as is and rename the imported style. If there is an entry in the Conflict with Existing Style, you can click that entry for a pop-up menu that provides two choices: Auto-Rename and Use Incoming Style Definition. Figure 19-10 shows this Load Styles dialog box.

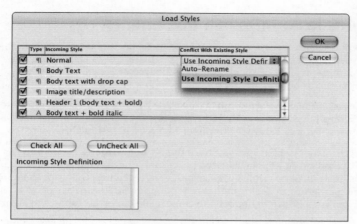

Figure 19-10: The Load Styles dialog box

Note that at the bottom of the dialog box there are two windows that list the style definitions to help you decide which to import, as well as which to overwrite or rename.

New Feature   The capability to select which styles to load from another InDesign document is new to InDesign CS2. The capability to choose how to handle style conflicts is also new to InDesign CS2 and puts it on par with QuarkXPress.

You can also use the Copy (Edit ➪ Copy, or ⌘+C or Ctrl+C) and Paste commands (Edit ➪ Paste, or ⌘+V or Ctrl+V) to move a style from one document to another. Simply copy some text in the source document to which the style you want to move has been applied. Then display the target document and use the Paste command to place the copied text into a text frame. The Character Styles and/or Paragraph Styles panes in the target document display the names of the new, "imported" styles.

Working with style sheets in imported text files

In most workgroup publishing environments, writers generate text using Microsoft Word, and InDesign users place the text in a layout and add other design elements — imported pictures, illustrations, lines, and so on — to create a finished publication. Whether writers are producing short magazine articles or lengthy book chapters, chances are they're doing some text formatting as they write — perhaps as little as applying occasional bold or italic styles or as much as using a complete set of style sheets, if their word processor supports them.

Note   I use the term *style sheet* to refer to the formatting capability in Microsoft Word, following Word's naming convention. And I use *style* when referring to the formatting capability in InDesign, per its naming convention. In the rest of this section, the use of the two terms should help you keep track of when I mean the style sheets from Word versus the styles in InDesign.

When you import a word processing file into InDesign, you can bring the formatting and style sheets along with the text.

See Chapter 13 for a complete list of formatting options that will import from Word.

Isolated formatting might be used to indicate which styles should be applied in InDesign — for example, the writer might apply bold to one-line paragraphs that should be formatted as a subhead. However, if the writer applies appropriate paragraph styles to text in her word processor, much of the formatting in InDesign can be automated by importing the style sheets. To import style sheets with a word processing file, select the Retain Format option in the Place dialog box (File ➪ Place, or ⌘+D or Ctrl+D). You can determine which style sheets import and how to handle any conflicts between style names if you select the Show Import Options option in the Place dialog box.

For more information about using the Place command to import text files and managing style-sheet import, see Chapter 15.

After you place a text file that contains style sheets, the Paragraph Styles pane and Character Styles pane display the names of all the imported styles, and any text to which style sheets have been applied in the word processor retain the imported style sheet's formats as well as a link to the style now available in InDesign.

InDesign CS2 now imports both paragraph and character style sheets from Microsoft Word and RTF files, not just paragraph style sheets.

Editing imported paragraph style sheets

If you import paragraph style sheets with text, you can simply use the style sheets specified in the word processor to format the text. This method works well for designs that do not follow a template — for example, brochures or feature stories. You might import the text, experiment with formatting it, and then edit the imported style sheets now available as styles in InDesign to reflect your design.

For example, say you import a magazine feature article that is formatted with three paragraph style sheets (Headline, Byline, and Body Copy) into an InDesign document that does not contain styles with those names. The three styles are added to InDesign's Paragraph Styles list and have similar specifications to what the same-named style sheets had in the word processor. However, because InDesign offers more formatting options, you might modify those styles to fine-tune the text formatting. To edit a paragraph style, select it in the Paragraph Styles pane, choose Style Options from the pane's palette menu, and then make your changes in the Modify Paragraph Style Options dialog box.

Overriding imported paragraph style sheets

In documents that follow a template, you can provide writers with style-sheet names that must be applied to their text. For example, say you're working on a tri-fold brochure that is part of an entire series of similar tri-folds. The writer might format the text with five paragraph style sheets that also exist as styles in your InDesign document: Heads, Subheads, Body Copy, Bullets, and Quotes. The style-sheet specifications in the word processor don't matter — only the name counts — because the styles in an InDesign document override same-name style sheets in imported text files.

For example, the writer's style sheets use standard fonts such as Times and Helvetica along with bold and italic typestyles to distinguish the types of text. But when the word processing file is imported into InDesign, the style sheets are overridden with InDesign styles that have the same name but specify the actual fonts used by the designer and the many formatting options available in InDesign.

You can supply writers either with actual style sheets or with only style-sheet names:

✦ To supply style sheets, export text in InDesign from a similar story as an Rich Text Format (RTF) file, which writers can open in their word processor; the word processor adds the style-sheet names in the RTF file to its own style-sheet list. The writers can then save these style-sheet names to a template file and use that template for future documents. To export text, use the Export dialog box (File ➪ Export, or ⌘+E or Ctrl+E) and choose Rich Text Format from the Formats pop-up menu.

✦ Or, you can simply give writers a list of style-sheet names that they can create themselves to their own specifications. In this case, it's particularly important that the style sheets created in the word processor have exactly the same names as those styles in the InDesign document.

Exporting styles

Although InDesign lets you export text (through the File ➪ Export command), only a few file formats are supported: Text-only (ASCII), RTF, and InDesign Tagged Text.

An exported RTF file keeps the style names but not the actual formatting, which can make further editing difficult in a word processor. An InDesign Tagged Text file retains the style definitions, but it does so as codes, so again it's hard to deal with in a word processor.

Summary

If you're working on a document that uses the same text formats repeatedly, you can save time and ensure consistency by using styles. A style is essentially a macro for formatting text. InDesign lets you create character-level styles and paragraph-level styles. Character styles let you apply several character attributes — such as font, size, leading, kerning, and tracking — to highlighted text at once. Similarly, you can use paragraph styles to apply several paragraph formats — alignment, indents, drop caps, space before or after, and so on — simultaneously to selected paragraphs. After you apply a style sheet to text, you can still manually modify the text by highlighting it and overriding the style's formats. If you're importing a text file from Microsoft Word, you can import any applied styles along with the text, making them available as InDesign styles.

✦   ✦   ✦

Setting Up Tabs and Tables

If you ever used a typewriter, you may remember pressing the tab key to indent each paragraph. And you may have pounded on it repeatedly to align columns of data. In InDesign, you use first-line indents to distinguish the first line of a new paragraph, and you reserve tabs for separating columns of data. Although InDesign has a built-in table editor, you can create simple tables using regular tabs quickly with the tabs feature. For more sophisticated tables, use the table editor.

In InDesign, tabs are part of paragraph formats — meaning that, when you set them, they apply to all the text in selected paragraphs rather than to selected characters within a paragraph. By default, when you start typing in a paragraph or you create a new paragraph style, there are invisible, automatic tab stops every half-inch. Regardless of the measurement system your rulers are set to use, when you press Tab you'll jump to the next 0.5-inch increment on the ruler.

As soon as you set a tab stop of your own, it overrides any of the automatic tab stops to its left. The automatic tab stops remain to the right until you override all of them.

Tip   Any tabs you set in the Tabs pane when no document is open are added to all future documents you create. Therefore, if tabs set at every quarter-inch are more useful to you, add them with no documents open.

InDesign provides four different types of tabs so you can:

   ✦ Left-align text to the left at a tab stop (the default setting, and the one you'll use most often)

   ✦ Center text on either side of the tab stop (very useful in column headers)

   ✦ Right-align text at a tab stop (useful for columns of integers)

   ✦ Align a specific character in the text with the tab stop (such as a comma or period in a number)

Figure 20-1 shows examples of tabs.

Item	»	»	Ingredient	»	Amount	»	Price¶
»	Trifle	»	lemon juice	»	3/4 cup	»	$.89/20 oz.¶
»	»	»	eggs	»	4	»	$1.99/dozen¶
»	»	»	sugar	»	1 1/2 cups	»	$1.79/pound¶
»	»	»	heavy cream	»	1 cup	»	$.99/quart¶
»	»	»	strawberries	»	1 1/2 cups	»	$2.09/pound¶
»	»	»	pound cake	»	1	»	$2.75 each¶
»Whip Cream	»	»	heavy cream	»	1 1/2 cups	»	$.99/quart¶
»	»	»	sugar	»	1/4 cup	»	$1.79/pound¶
¶							
Item	»	»	Ingredient	»	Amount	»	Price¶
»	Trifle	»	lemon juice	»	3/4 cup	»	$.89/20 oz.¶
»	»	»	eggs	»	4	»	$1.99/dozen¶
»	»	»	sugar	»	1 1/2 cups	»	$1.79/pound¶
»	»	»	heavy cream	»	1 cup	»	$.99/quart¶
»	»	»	strawberries	»	1 1/2 cups	»	$2.09/pound¶
»	»	»	pound cake	»	1	»	$2.75 each¶
»Whip Cream	»	»	heavy cream	»	1 1/2 cups	»	$.99/quart¶
»	»	»	sugar	»	1/4 cup	»	$1.79/pound¶

Figure 20-1: Under the Item column, Trifle and Whip Cream are positioned with right-aligned tabs. The three other column headings — Ingredient, Amount, and Price — are positioned with center tabs. In the chart, the ingredients are left aligned, the amounts are center aligned, and the prices are aligned on the dollar sign (top chart) and the decimal point (lower chart).

Preparing Text Files for Setting Tabs

When importing text, the most common problem a designer encounters is that writers try to line up the text on their screens by using multiple tabs between columns rather than setting appropriate tab stops in the first place and having one tab between each "cell." That's because word processors also have default tab stops of 0.5", and most users use those defaults rather than figure out how to set tabs themselves. When you import the file with these tabs, the chances of items lining up in InDesign as they do in the word processor are pretty close to zero. That means a lot of cleanup work for the designer.

Before you start setting tabs in InDesign, take a look at the tabs already entered in the text. You can check this out in your word processor or in text that has been placed in InDesign. To view tab characters in InDesign, choose Type ➪ Show Hidden Characters, or press Option+⌘+I or Ctrl+Alt+I. The light-blue double French closed quote quillemet symbols (») are tabs.

To set effective tabs for columns of data, each line or row of information should be its own paragraph, and each column of data should be separated by only one tab character. If there's only one tab between each column, you need to set only one tab stop per column and you can more carefully control a single tab stop rather than several.

Because the text is not in its final font or text frame, the current tab placement does not matter. But if necessary, the writer can change tab settings in Word to align the columns for proofreading or editing purposes.

As with multiple tabs stops, if there are extra paragraph returns between the rows or information, or if each line ends in a soft return or line break (Shift+Return or Shift+Enter) rather than a paragraph return (Return or Enter), you should fix these with search and replace in your word processor or Find/Change (Edit ➪ Find/Change, or ⌘+F or Ctrl+F) in InDesign.

It's best to insist that any word processor documents imported into InDesign be created so there is only one tab between each entry on a line, no matter how it looks in the word processor. Then you can set up the appropriate tab stops in InDesign.

Using the Tabs Pane

To set tabs in InDesign you use the Tabs pane, which floats above your text so that you can keep it open until you're finished experimenting with tabs. To open the Tabs pane, choose Window ⇨ Type & Tables ⇨ Tabs or press Shift+⌘+T or Ctrl+Shift+T. Figure 20-2 shows the Tabs pane along with a simple table created using one tab stop.

Bereaved Families of Ontario	905-318-0070
Big Brothers of Halton	905-637-9911
Big Sister of Oakville	905-338-0238
Child Support Guidelines	1-800-980-4962
Children's Aid	905-333-4441
Children's Information	905-815-2045
Halton Child & Youth Services	905-339-3525
Halton Autism Resource Team	905-339-3522
Halton Child Care Registry	905-875-0235
Halton Consumer Credit Counseling	905-842-1459
Halton Family Services	905-845-3811
Halton Preschool Speech & Language Program	905-815-1551
Halton Region	905-825-6000
Halton Trauma Centre	905-825-3242
Halton Women's Place (24-hour Crisis Line)	905-878-8555
Healthy Babies Healthy Children	905-693-4242
Kids Help Phone	416-586-0100

Figure 20-2: The Tabs pane and a simple table created with one tab stop. Note that I expanded the Tabs pane to be the width of the text that had tabs applied for better visibility.

Tip   If you find yourself adjusting tab settings and indents at the same time, you might want to combine the Tabs pane and the Paragraph pane. Simply drag the Tabs pane into the Paragraph pane or vice versa. Use the palette menu on the Paragraph pane to change its orientation to vertical so the palettes work together better. (By default, Adobe combines the Paragraph, Character, and Transform panes—I recommend you split the Paragraph and Character panes into separate palettes so you can see all your text formatting at once.)

Tab style buttons

Four buttons on the Tabs pane let you control how the text aligns with the tab you're creating:

✦ **Left.** The default tab stops are left-aligned, which means that the left side of the text touches the tab stop as if it were a left margin. Most tabs you create for text will be left-aligned.

✦ **Center.** Centered tab stops are like the centered paragraph alignment, with text balanced evenly on either side of the tab stop. Center tabs are often used for table headings.

✦ **Right.** When you set right-aligned tabs, the right edge of text touches the tab stop. This is commonly used for aligning numbers that do not include decimals or for the last column in a table.

✦ **Align On.** By default, the last tab style button is for decimal tabs, which means that a period in the text aligns on the tab stop. If there's no period in the text, InDesign pretends that there is one after the last character. Instead of aligning on a period, you can specify a different character — such as a comma or dollar sign — for an Align On tab, and text will align to that character. You do this using the Align On field, which is covered later in this section.

Tip   If you need a tab flush with the right margin, for example, to position a dingbat at the end of the story, click the Right Tab button and position it on the right side of the tab ruler. Then drag the right-aligned tab on top of the right indent arrow. (You can't actually click to place a tab on top of the arrow, but you can drag a tab on top of it.) An even faster way is to choose Type ➪ Special Characters ➪ Right Indent or press Shift+Tab.

X field

The X field of the Tabs pane lets you specify a position for a new tab stop. You can type a value in this field in 0.01-point increments, and then press Shift+Enter or Shift+Return to create a tab. InDesign positions tabs relative to the left edge of the text frame or column. Or you can just click the mouse on the ruler where you want the tab to be, as described later.

Tip   Why type numbers when you can just use the mouse? The reason is to get more accurate positioning than using the mouse usually allows, especially when you know exactly where the tab stop should be. Of course, you can add a tab by using the mouse, and then click the field and type a more precise value in the X field.

Note   If a text frame has Inset Spacing specified for its left edge in the General pane of the Text Frame Options dialog box (Object ➪ Text Frame Options, or ⌘+B or Ctrl+B), InDesign measures tabs from the text inset rather than from the frame.

As with other fields in InDesign, the X field can perform mathematical computations for you. So you can set a tab at half of 0.125" without figuring out that value, or you can move a tab by adding to or subtracting from its current value. It may seem unlikely that you would ever do this, but it's extremely handy for changing tab settings so they're, say, half as far apart as they used to be, or half as far apart plus 2 points to the right.

Note   The operands for performing math in fields are + (addition), − (subtraction), * (multiplication), and / (division). If you want to combine these operands — for example, add 5 then subtract 2 — you'll have to remember back to middle school and Algebra I to type the operands in the correct order: multiply, divide, add, and then subtract.

Leader field

A tab leader is a character or series of characters that fills the white space between tabs — like the periods you see between a table of contents entry and its page number. They got the name *leader* because they lead your eyes across the page. Figure 20-2 shows a dot leader in use between the donor's name and the donation amount.

InDesign lets you specify up to eight characters, including special characters that will repeat to fill any white space. When you set a leader for a tab stop, the leaders actually fill any space prior to that tab stop (between the previous text and the tab location).

To spread out the leader characters, type spaces between the characters you enter. Don't enter spaces before and after a single character though, as that will result in two spaces between the characters when the pattern repeats (unless that's the look you're going for). You can't enter special types of spaces — such as thin spaces or hair spaces — in the Leader field; you will always get em spaces.

Note

The reason to use tab leaders is to help the reader. Unless the design is more important than the content, you probably shouldn't use eight-character tab leaders even though you can. A cacophony of characters draws too much attention to itself and can be confusing. Because the pattern of leaders repeats, one space and a period are usually sufficient.

Note

To enter special characters in the Leader field, use keyboard commands, InDesign's Glyphs pane, or a utility such as PopChar, Mac OS X's Character Palette, or Window's Character Map. If you use InDesign's Insert Special Character command (Type ⇨ Insert Special Character) or the Glyphs pane (Type ⇨ Glyphs), you'll insert a character into your text, which you'll have to cut and paste into the Leader field. It won't be inserted directly in the Leader field as you would expect.

Align On field

The Align On tab style defaults to a period, but you can replace the period with any character, including special characters. When that character is found in tabbed text, it aligns on the tab stop. If that character is not found, InDesign pretends that it follows the last character in the tabbed string. The most common characters entered in the Align On field include a comma (,), dollar sign ($), cents symbol (¢), and opening or closing parentheses ((and)).

Tab ruler

Rather than typing values in the X field, you can position tabs by clicking on the ruler at the bottom of the Tabs pane. The Tab ruler has the following characteristics:

✦ **It displays in the same measurement system as the document, with 0 specifying the edges of the column.** If Inset Spacing is specified for the left edge of the text frame in the Text Frame Options dialog box (Object ⇨ Text Frame Options, or ⌘+B or Ctrl+B), the ruler starts after the text inset in the first column.

✦ **The ruler provides arrows for controlling and displaying the selected paragraph's first-line, left, and right indents.** Dragging the two left arrows changes both the paragraph's first-line and left indents, while dragging the top arrow changes only the first-line indent. Dragging the arrow at right changes the right indents. These arrows help you see indents in relation to tabs that you're setting.

✦ **Icons that match the tab styles display on the rulers to show you where and what type of tabs are already set.** You can drag these around to reposition existing tabs, and you can drag them off the ruler to delete tabs.

✦ **You can scroll through the ruler by clicking it and dragging to the left or right.** This lets you set tabs beyond the current column or text frame width, such as for text that flows into text boxes of different widths.

Magnet button

Under the right circumstances, clicking the Magnet button in the lower-right corner of the Tabs pane snaps the pane and the ruler to the selected text frame or column. The idea is to make it easier to see the tab stops in relation to an actual area of text.

For this to work, you need to make sure the top of the text frame is visible on-screen, the Type tool is selected, and you've placed the cursor in text or highlighted text. If you don't meet all these prerequisites, nothing happens.

Once you manage to get the Tabs pane positioned correctly, it's quite useful. You can add and adjust tabs in relation to the text (provided that the text is at the top of the text frame!) and you can always see from where the tabs are measured. Even better, if you move the cursor to another column in the text frame, you can click the Magnet again to position the Tabs pane over that column.

Tabs pane menu

In addition to setting tabs in the Tabs pane, InDesign provides two additional options through the palette menu: Clear All and Repeat Tab.

✦ The Clear All command deletes any tabs you've created, and any text positioned with tabs reverts to the position of the default tab stops. (You can delete an individual tab stop by dragging its icon off the ruler.)

✦ The Repeat Tab command lets you create a string of tabs across the ruler that are all the same distance apart. When you select a tab on the ruler and choose this command, InDesign measures the distance between the selected tab and the previous tab (or, if it's the first tab on the ruler, the distance between the selected tab and the left indent/ text inset). The program then uses this distance to place new tabs, with the same alignment, all the way across the ruler. InDesign repeats tabs only to the right of the selected tab, but it inserts tabs between other tab stops.

Creating Tables

Whether you're working on yesterday's box scores for the sports pages, an annual report, or a fun, little parenting magazine, you've got numbers — numbers with dollar signs, numbers with decimals, numbers intermixed with text. You have to line the columns up correctly, not only so the information looks good but also so it's easy to read. Then you often need to add ruling lines to separate the material visually for the reader.

You can do all this with tab stops, ruling lines, and other InDesign tools. Or you can make your life easier and use InDesign's table editor, which lets you specify almost any attribute imaginable in a table through the Table pane and the Table menu.

Cross-Reference   InDesign lets you import tables from Microsoft Word, RTF, and Microsoft Excel files, including some of their cell formatting. Likewise, you can convert their tables to tabbed text by using the options in the Import Options dialog box that is accessible when you place a file through the Place dialog box (File ➪ Place, or ⌘+D or Ctrl+D), as covered in Chapter 15.

Figure 20-3 shows the Table pane and Table menu, as well as a complex table created by Branimir Zlamalik that displays a YMCA activities schedule. You access the Table pane by choosing Window ➪ Type & Tables ➪ Table, or pressing Shift+F9.

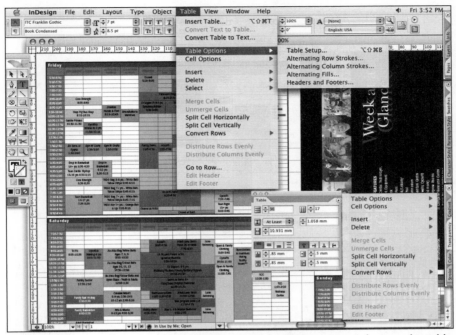

Figure 20-3: The Table pane and its palette menu, the Table menu, and a complex table created with them

QuarkXPress User

InDesign tables and QuarkXPress tables have several differences. Although both treat tables as collections of cells, InDesign offers more formatting options for cell strokes than QuarkXPress does. InDesign has more controls for text and row placement than QuarkXPress offers. InDesign also imports Word, Excel, and RTF tables, while QuarkXPress does not. But QuarkXPress offers more control over the flow of text among cells in a table. InDesign doesn't let you flow text from one cell to another, much less control the order of that flow.

Creating a table

To create a table in InDesign, you first create or select a text frame with the Type tool and then choose Table ⇨ Insert Table or press Option+Shift+⌘+T or Ctrl+Alt+Shift+T. That produces the Insert Table dialog box, where you type the number of body rows and columns and the number of header and footer rows. Click OK to have InDesign create the basic table, which will be set as wide as the text frame. The depth will be based on the number of rows, with each row defaulting to the height that will hold 12-point text.

With the basic table in place, you now format it using the Table pane and the Table menu. The pane contains cell formatting tools: You can increase or decrease the number of rows and columns, set the row and column height, set the text's vertical alignment within selected cells (top, middle, bottom, and justified), choose one of four text-rotation angles, and set the text margin within a cell separately for the top, bottom, left, and right. Note that all the Table pane's options affect only the currently selected cell(s), except for the Number of Rows and Number of Columns fields. Figure 20-4 shows the Table pane with its icons defined.

Vertical Alignment
Column Width
Number of Rows
Row Height
Rotate Text
Number of Columns

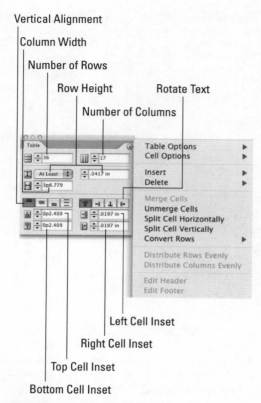

Left Cell Inset
Right Cell Inset
Top Cell Inset
Bottom Cell Inset

Figure 20-4: The Table pane

Note   You set cell text's horizontal alignment using the paragraph formatting controls covered in Chapter 17. You can apply other paragraph and character formatting to cell text as described in Chapters 16 through 19. You can also apply tabs within cells using the Tabs pane covered earlier in this chapter.

For more sophisticated table attributes, use the Table Options dialog box and its five panes, as shown in Figures 20-5 through 20-8. Access this dialog box using the Table Options menu item in the Table pane's palette menu or by choosing Table ➪ Table Options. In both menus, you can select a specific pane using a submenu from the Table Options menu item.

To add items to a table, you can type text in any cell, paste text or graphics into a cell, or place text or graphics into a cell by choosing File ➪ Place or pressing ⌘+D or Ctrl+D.

Table Setup pane

The Table Setup pane (which has the keyboard shortcut Option+Shift+⌘+B or Ctrl+Alt+Shift+B and is shown in Figure 20-5) lets you adjust the rows and columns, as you can do in the Table pane. It's also where you specify the table border's weight, line type, color, tint, gap color and tint (if you choose a dashed, dotted, or striped line for the border), the space before and after the table, and whether row lines (which InDesign calls *strokes*) are placed on top of column lines or vice versa. If your table has cells with different line settings that would be overridden by the table border, you can preserve those cell settings by selecting the Preserve Local Formatting option.

Table Options

| Table Setup | Row Strokes | Column Strokes | Fills | Headers and Footers |

Table Dimensions

Body Rows: 36   Columns: 17
Header Rows: 0   Footer Rows: 0

Table Border

Weight: 2 pt   Type: ▬▬▬▬▬
Color: ■ [Black]   Tint: 100%   ☐ Overprint
Gap Color: ☐ [Paper]   Gap Tint: 100%   ☐ Overprint
☐ Preserve Local Formatting

Table Spacing

Space Before: After: .0197 i

Best Joins
Row Strokes in Front
Column Strokes in Front
✓ InDesign 2.0 Compatibility

Stroke Drawing

Draw:

☐ Preview   (Cancel)   (OK)

Figure 20-5: The Table Setup pane

You also can set how strokes draw in the Draw pop-up menu at the bottom of the pane; note that InDesign 2.0 compatibility essentially places rows in front, but has them end inside the outside border, while the Row Strokes in Front has those strokes overprint the table border as well.

Tip You can open the Table Setup pane by pressing Option+Shift+⌘+B or Ctrl+Alt+Shift+B.

Row Strokes and Column Strokes panes

InDesign lets you have the lines between columns and rows alternate color, thickness, and even type. Figure 20-6 shows the Row Strokes pane; the Column Strokes pane is identical, except that it applies to column (vertical) strokes rather than to row (horizontal) strokes.

You can choose a predefined alternate pattern using the Alternating Pattern pop-up menu, or by simply typing a number in the First and Next fields. The First field at the left of the pane specifies how many row strokes (or column strokes) get the formatting specified on the left side of the pane, while the Next field at the right side specifies how many get the formatting specified at the right. InDesign applies the formatting at left to the number of rows specified in its First field, and then switches to the formatting at right for the number of rows specified in that First field. If there are still more rows, InDesign switches back to the left side's formatting, repeating the alternating pattern until it runs out of rows. The Column Strokes pane works the same way.

In addition to specifying the line attributes, you can also have InDesign skip a specified number of top and bottom rows (or columns) using the Skip First and Skip Last fields. You can specify these so header and footer rows are excluded from the pattern.

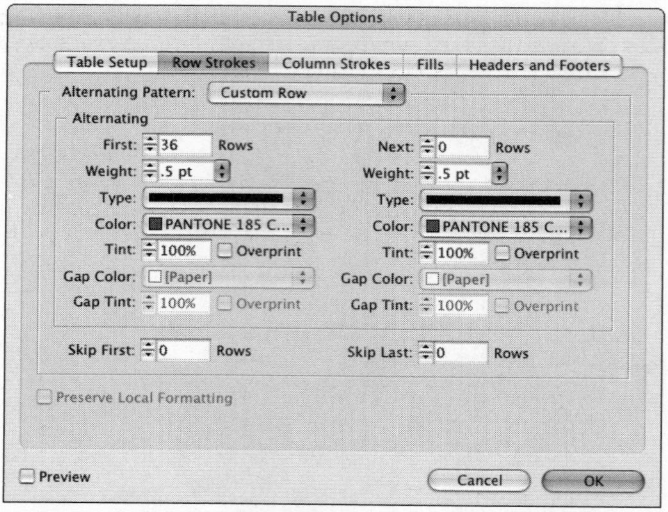

Figure 20-6: The Row Strokes pane, shown here, is identical to the Column Strokes pane.

Fills pane

The Fills pane, shown in Figure 20-7, is similar to the Row Strokes and Column Strokes panes. You set the color, tint, alternation pattern, and any skipped rows for fills you want applied to your table. The Alternating Pattern pop-up menu lets you pick from predefined numbers of columns or rows, depending on whether you want the fills to alternate from left to right or from top to bottom across the table.

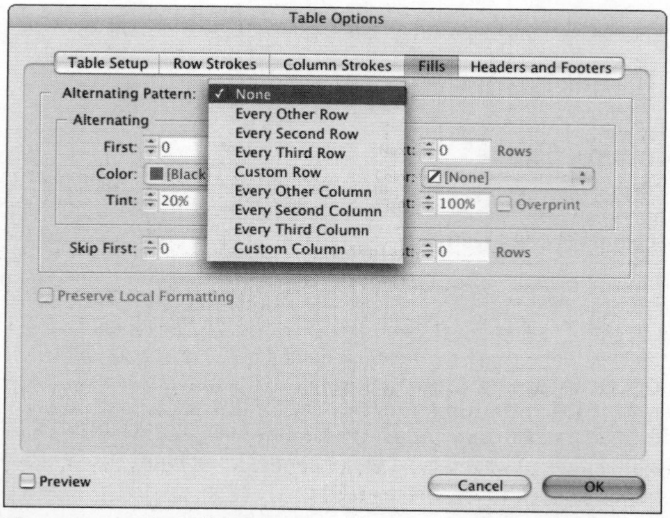

Figure 20-7: The Fills pane

If you choose Custom Row, InDesign uses the alternation settings in the Row Strokes pane; if you choose Custom Column, InDesign uses the alteration settings in the Column Strokes pane. That ensures the line color and other settings change with the fills.

Headers and Footers pane

The Headers and Footers pane, shown in Figure 20-8, lets you change the number of header and footer rows, as well as specify how often the header and footer repeats. (If your Word or RTF file's table uses a heading row, InDesign designates that as a header row.) Your options are Every Text Column, Once per Frame, and Once per Page. You'll usually use one of the latter options because it automatically repeats the header row for tables that break across text frames and/or pages.

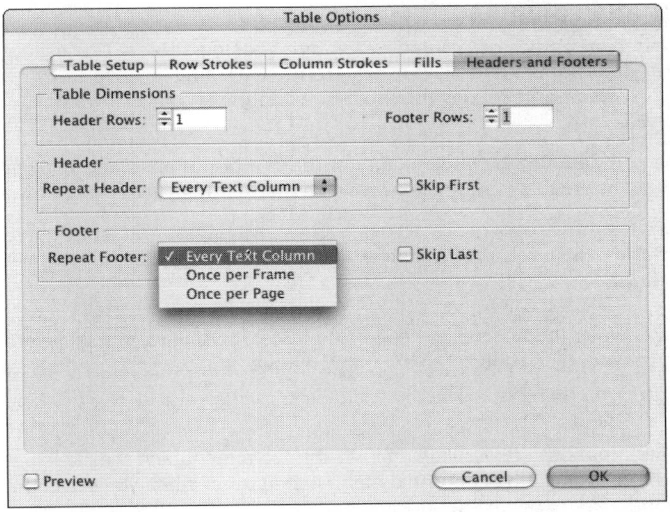

Figure 20-8: The Headers and Footers pane

Working with rows and columns

InDesign's table editing tools work very much like those in Microsoft Word. To select a row or column, click on an outside edge; you can also click in a cell with the Type tool and choose Table ➪ Select and then select Row (⌘+3 or Ctrl+3) or Column (Option+⌘+3 or Ctrl+Alt+3). The same submenu also lets you select all header rows, all footer rows, and all body (regular) rows.

To move to a specified row, you can choose Table ➪ Go to Row and type the row's number, but it's usually easier to use your mouse to move to the desired row. After all, how often do you know the row's number?

To quickly select header rows or footer rows, choose Table ➪ Edit Header or Table ➪ Edit Footer.

Note   Choose Table ➪ Select ➪ Table, or press Option+⌘+A or Ctrl+Alt+A, to select an entire table. Choose Table ➪ Delete ➪ Table to delete an entire table.

Adding and deleting

Insert or delete rows and columns using the Table menu or the Table pane's palette menu. Both have Insert and Delete menu options. Selected rows or columns are deleted, while new rows or columns are inserted before any selected row or column. You can also use the following shortcuts:

- ✦ **Delete Row.** ⌘+Backspace or Ctrl+Backspace
- ✦ **Delete Column.** Shift+Backspace
- ✦ **Insert Row.** ⌘+9 or Ctrl+9
- ✦ **Insert Column.** Option+⌘+9 or Ctrl+Alt+9

Manipulating rows and columns

You can make the space between rows or columns even by choosing Table ⇨ Distribute Rows Evenly, or Table ⇨ Distribute Columns Evenly. But be careful — merging several cells increases the perceived column or row size and causes InDesign to excessively space rows or columns based on those merged cells' size.

You can also resize rows and columns by clicking any of the cell boundaries and dragging them — similar to how you can resize columns and rows in Microsoft Word's table editor.

InDesign also lets you control how rows break across frames and pages, and whether rows must be kept together. But to do so requires a dialog box oriented to cell formatting, which is covered later in this chapter.

Tip   InDesign can convert regular (body) rows to header and footer rows, or vice versa. Select the row(s) you want to convert; then choose Table ⇨ Convert Rows; and then choose To Header, To Body, or To Footer as appropriate.

Note   All the row and column options are available in both the Table menu and the Table pane's palette menu, as well as through the contextual menu that appears when you select one or more cells and Control+click or right-click.

Working with cells

InDesign offers the Cell Options panes to manage the formatting of cells. It's accessible by choosing Cell Options from the Table menu or from the Table pane's palette menu. Four panes are available, as shown in Figures 20-9 through 20-12.

Text pane

The Text pane, which is accessible through the shortcut Option+⌘+B or Ctrl+Alt+B and shown in Figure 20-9, covers several options available in the Table pane covered earlier in this chapter, including the top, bottom, left, and right cell insets (margins), as well as vertical text alignment and text rotation. But it has several other options:

- ✦ **Paragraph Spacing Limit.** This option determines the maximum space between paragraphs in a cell when you choose Justify from the Align pop-up menu. This prevents there being too much space between paragraphs in a cell.

✦ **First Baseline.** This option determines how the text baseline is positioned from the top of a cell. The options are Ascent, Cap Height, Leading, x Height, and Fixed.

Vertical alignment and baseline positioning work the same as they do for text frames, as covered in Chapter 14.

✦ **Clipping Contents to Cell.** This option displays only the amount of text that fits in the cell's current size — it prevents the cell from expanding to accommodate the text.

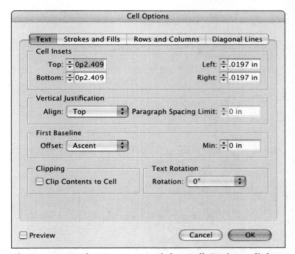

Figure 20-9: The Text pane of the Cell Options dialog box

Strokes and Fills pane

Shown in Figure 20-10, the Strokes and Fills pane lets you choose the weight, type, color, and tint of the strokes around a cell, as well as any gap color and tint (if you choose a striped, dashed, or dotted line as the stroke type).

At the top of the pane is the representation of the selected cell(s), depending on whether one or multiple cells are highlighted when opening this pane. Figure 20-10 shows the representation when multiple cells are selected across more than one row and more than one column. (If you select multiple cells in one row, you get two cells shown side by side; if you select multiple cells in one column, you get two cells, one on top of the other.)

Click on the cell boundary to which you want to apply the stroke formatting and then choose the formatting you want. You could have different formatting for each of the left, right, top, and bottom outside cell boundaries, as well as different formatting for the horizontal boundary between selected cells and for the vertical formatting for the vertical boundary between selected cells. Usually, you select all outside boundaries and apply stroke formatting to all of them simultaneously, and you may do the same for the interior boundaries as well.

Note InDesign does not show you the stroke formatting applied to the representation's segments, so you may not realize that different segments have different settings. Therefore, it's best to make sure the selected cells are visible and that you've checked the Preview option so you can see what you're actually applying to the cells.

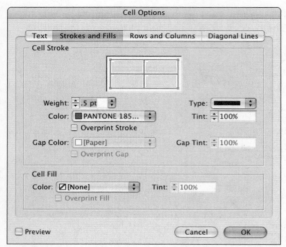

Figure 20-10: The Strokes and Fills pane of the Cell Options dialog box

In this pane, you can also select a fill color for the selected cells, based on existing color swatches, as well as a tint.

You can set both cell strokes and fills as Overprint, which means the color prints on top of any underlying color, rather than knocking out that color. Overprinting can change the color the reader sees because it essentially mixes inks. Overprinting a blue fill on a yellow background, for example, results in a green fill.

Rows and Columns pane

The Row and Columns pane (see Figure 20-11) sets row height and column width, as well as keeps options for rows:

✦ **Row Height pop-up menu.** Use this to specify the height as either Exactly or At Least the measurement to the right of the menu. This is the same as what you can specify in the Table pane.

✦ **Column Width field.** This field is also the same option you have in the Table pane to set the column width.

✦ **Keep Options.** Use the Start Row pop-up menu to determine where the selected row starts. You can choose Anywhere, which means after the previous row (space permitting in the text frame, of course); In Next Text Column; In Next Frame; On Next Page; On Next Odd Page; or On Next Even Page. Select the Keep with Next Row option to keep rows together.

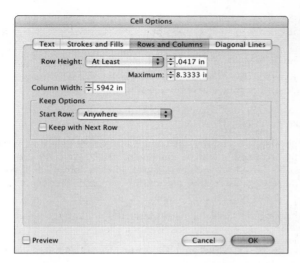

Figure 20-11: The Rows and Columns pane of the Cell Options dialog box

Diagonal Lines pane

A unique InDesign feature is the ability to place diagonal lines in table cells. Figure 20-12 shows the Diagonal Lines pane. It's similar to other panes involving strokes except for two specific options:

✦ You choose the type of diagonal line — top left to bottom right, bottom left to top right, or both — using the icons at the top of the pane.

✦ You determine whether the diagonal line appears on top of the cell contents or vice versa using the Draw pop-up menu.

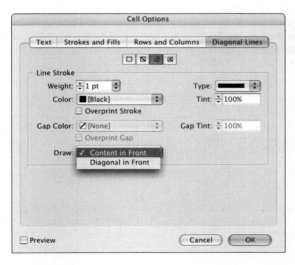

Figure 20-12: The Diagonal Lines pane of the Cell Options dialog box

Other cell options

Most of the work you'll do with cells will involve typing and editing text (or graphics), applying fills and strokes, and setting margins (as covered earlier in this chapter), as well as formatting text (as covered in Chapters 16 through 19) and formatting frames (as covered in Chapters 9 and 10). After all, a cell is essentially just a text or graphics frame that's contained in a table with other frames. But there are a few other things to know about working with cells:

✦ You can merge and unmerge cells by highlighting the cell(s) and choosing Table ⇨ Merge Cells or Table ⇨ Unmerge Cells.

✦ You can split cells by highlighting the cell(s) and choosing Table ⇨ Split Cell Horizontally or Table ⇨ Split Cell Vertically. To unsplit cells, you must merge them. (You can also choose Edit ⇨ Undo, or press ⌘+Z or Ctrl+Z, before taking another action.) Cells that are split take on the cell's current settings for text formatting, fill color, size, margins, and strokes.

✦ InDesign indicates text that does not fit in a cell with a large red dot in the cell, as Figure 20-13 shows.

Figure 20-13: InDesign indicates text that does not fit in a cell by displaying large red dots in the cell.

✦ You can apply colors and gradients to cells, as well as strokes, using the standard InDesign Swatches, Gradient, and Stroke panes (all accessible through the Window menu). These have the same effect as using the equivalent Table menu and Table pane options.

✦ The Control palette offers easy access to several cell and table features, as Figure 20-14 shows. (See Figure 20-4 for the meaning of most of the icons, which are the same in the Control palette as they are in the Tables pane. You'll also see some icons and controls that are the same as shown in Figure 20-10, for cell formatting.)

 Tip　You can apply strokes to cells through the Stroke pane (Window ⇨ Stroke or F10). Use its palette menu to select the Stroke Styles menu option, which provides a list of styles and the ability to create your own, as Chapter 10 explains.

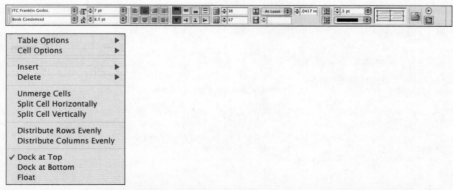

Figure 20-14: The Control palette and its palette menu when table cells are selected

Converting Tabs to Tables

Often, you'll have a table done using tabs — whether imported from a word processor or originally created in InDesign with tabs — that you want to convert to a real InDesign table. That's easy. Select the tabbed text you want to covert and choose Table ➪ Convert Text to Table. You get the Convert Text to Table dialog box shown in Figure 20-15.

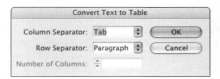

Figure 20-15: The Convert Text to Table dialog box

In the Convert Text to Table dialog box, you can choose a Column Separator (Tab, Comma, Paragraph, or a text string you type in the field) or a Row Separator (same options). Although most textual data uses tabs to separate columns and paragraphs to separate rows, you may encounter other data that uses something else. For example, spreadsheets and databases often save data so that commas separate columns rather than tabs. That's why InDesign lets you choose the separator characters before conversion.

During the conversion, InDesign formats the table using the standard settings, using the current text formatting and the default cell insets and stroke types. You can then adjust the table using the tools covered earlier in this chapter. Note that the conversion treats all rows as body rows.

You can also convert a table to text by selecting multiple cells or an entire table, as described earlier, and choosing Table ➪ Convert Table to Text. InDesign presents the same options as it does in the Convert Text to Table dialog box, so you can determine how the converted data appears.

QuarkXPress User

In one way, InDesign is savvier about text-to-table conversion than QuarkXPress because InDesign lets you choose any string as the column or row separator during conversion (just type that string in the appropriate field). But in another way, InDesign is less savvy: QuarkXPress lets you pivot data during conversion, so you can swap columns and rows for a better fit.

Summary

Unlike the typewriter days, creating tabs in a page-layout application provides various options for aligning text with a tab and creating tab leaders. The Tabs pane (Window ➪ Type & Tables ➪ Tabs, or ⌘+Shift+T or Ctrl+Shift+T) provides an interactive ruler for positioning tabs along with all the other controls you need. Your ultimate success with using the Tabs feature depends on how well you prepared the text in the first place — the key is to position one tab correctly rather than entering several tabs to achieve the correct placement.

To create tables in InDesign, you use the Table pane (Window ➪ Type & Tables ➪ Table or Shift+F9) to create the table outline, format cells, merge and split cells, apply colors and ruling lines, and do other complex table editing. You can also convert tabbed text into a table and vice versa.

✦   ✦   ✦

Graphics Fundamentals

✦   ✦   ✦   ✦

✦   ✦   ✦   ✦

Preparing Graphics for Import

You can import graphics into your InDesign documents in several ways. InDesign is particularly adept at importing documents created in popular Macintosh and Windows formats. And through the Mac and Windows Clipboards (copy and paste), you can import file formats — to a limited degree — that are not directly supported by InDesign.

Determining Where to Format Documents

Because InDesign has some built-in graphics features, as described in Chapters 25 through 27, you may be tempted to use InDesign as your graphics program. Don't. Its tools are fine for some work, such as creating shapes that text wraps around, borders, and gradations of color — but InDesign is not meant to be a professional graphics-creation tool. In fact, it's designed to work closely with such professional tools, especially Adobe's Illustrator and Photoshop.

Particularly for bitmap images such as scanned files and photographs, InDesign has few capabilities to apply special effects or otherwise manipulate the image's content, so you should do as much work as possible in your image editor before importing the file into InDesign. For example, you can resize, crop, rotate, and slant an imported image in InDesign, but you can't convert it from a full-color image into a duotone or change its line screen or brightness and contrast.

The bottom line is this: Use your graphics program for creating and editing original images and photos. Use InDesign's graphics features to embellish your layout, rather than create original artwork.

Tip InDesign lets you easily open a graphics program to edit placed images from within InDesign. Press and hold Option or Alt, and then double-click the image. InDesign launches the program that created the graphic; if you don't own that program, InDesign launches a compatible program if you have one. For example, if you Option+double-click or Alt+double-click an EPS file in your layout that was created in Adobe Illustrator, but you use Macromedia FreeHand instead, InDesign will launch FreeHand on your system.

Preparing Graphics Files

InDesign offers support for many major formats of graphics files. Some formats are more appropriate than others for certain kinds of tasks. The basic rules for creating your graphics files are as follows:

✦ **Save line art in a format such as EPS, PDF, Adobe Illustrator, Windows Metafile (WMF), Enhanced Metafile (EMF), or PICT.** (These object-oriented formats are called *vector* formats. Vector files are composed of instructions on how to draw various shapes.) InDesign works best with EPS, PDF, and Illustrator files.

✦ **Save bitmaps (photos and scans) in a format such as TIFF, Adobe Photoshop, PNG, JPEG, PCX, Windows Bitmap (BMP), GIF, Scitex Continuous Tone (SCT), or PICT.** (These pixel-oriented formats are called *raster* formats. Raster files are composed of a series of dots, or pixels, that make up the image.) InDesign works best with TIFF and Photoshop files.

Note PICT files can be in vector or bitmap format depending on the original image and the program in which it was created or exported from. If you enlarge a PICT image and it begins to look blocky, it's a bitmap. Similarly, EPS and PDF files can contain bitmap images as well as vector ones.

Tip Make EPS and TIFF formats your standards because these have become the standard graphics formats in publishing. If you and your service bureau work almost exclusively with Adobe software, you can add the PDF, Illustrator, and Photoshop formats to this mix. (The Illustrator and PDF formats are variants of EPS.) If you use transparency in your graphics, it's best to save them in Photoshop, Illustrator, or PDF formats because other formats (particularly EPS and TIFF) remove much of the transparency layering data that will help an imagesetter optimally reproduce those transparent files.

Graphics embedded in text files

Modern word processors typically support inline graphics, letting you import a graphic into your word-processor document and embed it in text. Word, for example, lets you import graphics, and InDesign, in turn, can import the graphics with your text. But graphics embedded in your word-processor document though Mac OS 8 and 9's Publish and Subscribe or Windows' OLE will not import into InDesign.

Inline graphics will import as their preview images, not as the original formats. This means that in most cases, you'll get a *much* lower-resolution version in your InDesign layout.

Tip Despite their limitations, the use of inline graphics in your word processor can be helpful when putting together an InDesign document: Use the inline graphics whose previews are imported into InDesign as placeholders so that the layout artist knows you have embedded graphics. The artist can then replace the previews with the better-quality originals. If you find yourself using several graphics as characters (such as a company icon used as a bullet), use a font-creation program like Pyrus FontLab to create a symbol typeface with those graphics. Then both your word processor and layout documents can use the same high-quality versions.

InDesign imports many file formats. If your graphics program's format is not one of the ones listed here, chances are it can save as or export to one. In the following list, the text in italics is the filename extension common for these files on PCs.

The file formats InDesign imports include:

✦ **BMP.** The native Windows bitmap format. (*.BMP, .DIB*)

✦ **EPS.** The Encapsulated PostScript vector format favored by professional publishers. A variant is called DCS, a color-separated variant whose full name is Desktop Color Separation. (*.EPS, .DCS*)

✦ **GIF.** The Graphics Interchange Format common in Web documents. (*.GIF*)

✦ **JPEG.** The Joint Photographic Expert Group compressed bitmap format often used on the Web. (*.JPG*)

✦ **Illustrator.** The native format in Adobe Illustrator 5.5 through CS2, is similar to EPS. (*.AI*)

✦ **PCX.** The PC Paintbrush format that was very popular in DOS programs and early version of Windows; it has now been largely supplanted by other formats. (*.PCX, .RLE*)

✦ **PDF.** The Portable Document Format that is a variant of EPS and is used for Web-, network-, and CD-based documents. InDesign CS2 supports PDF versions 1.3 through 1.6 (the formats used in Acrobat 4 through 7). (*.PDF*)

✦ **Photoshop.** The native format in Adobe Photoshop 5.0 through CS2. (*.PSD*)

✦ **PICT.** Short for *Picture,* the Mac's native graphics format until Mac OS X (it can be bitmap or vector) that is little used in professional documents and is becoming less common even for inexpensive clip art. (*.PCT*)

✦ **PNG.** The Portable Network Graphics format that Adobe introduced several years ago as a more capable alternative to GIF. (*.PNG*)

✦ **QuickTime movie.** For use in interactive documents, InDesign supports this Apple-created, cross-platform format. (*.MOV*)

✦ **Scitex CT.** The continuous-tone bitmap format used on Scitex prepress systems. (*.CT*)

✦ **TIFF.** The Tagged Image File Format that is the bitmap standard for professional image editors and publishers. (*.TIFF*)

✦ **Windows Metafile.** The format native to Windows but little used in professional documents. Since Office 2000, Microsoft applications create a new version called Enhanced Metafile. (*.WMF, .EMF*)

Note   Spot colors (called spot inks in Photoshop) are imported into InDesign when you place Photoshop, Illustrator, and PDF images into InDesign. They'll appear in the Swatches pane.

Tip   When importing any image, make sure Show Import Options is selected in the Place dialog box (File ⇨ Place, or ⌘+D or Ctrl+D). Even if you're happy with the default import options, it's good to see what the import options are so when a non-default option does make sense, you're aware you have access to it.

InDesign does not support a few somewhat popular formats: AutoCAD Document Exchange Format (DXF), Computer Graphics Metafile (CGM), CorelDraw, Eastman Kodak's Photo CD, and Scalable Vector Graphics (SVG). DXF and CGM are vector formats used mainly in engineering and architecture, while CorelDraw is the native format of the leading consumer-oriented Windows illustration program, and Photo CD is a bitmap format meant for electronically distributed photographs. SVG is a newer format that is a variant of XML; although InDesign CS can export SVG files, it cannot open or import them.

Issues with vector files

Vector images are complex because they can combine multiple elements — curves, lines, colors, fonts, bitmap images, and even other imported vector images. This means that you can unknowingly create a file that will cause problems when you try to output an InDesign layout file using it. Thus, when dealing with vector formats, there are several issues to keep in mind.

Embedded fonts

When you use fonts in text included in your graphics files, you usually have the option to convert the text to curves (graphics). This option ensures that your text will print on any printer.

Note   If you don't use this conversion, make sure that your printer or service bureau has the fonts used in the graphic. Otherwise, the text does not print in the correct font (you will likely get Courier or Helvetica instead).

If your graphic has a lot of text, don't convert the text to curves — the image could get very complex and slow down printing. In this case, make sure that the output device has the same fonts as in the graphic.

PostScript files: EPS, DCS, Illustrator, and PDF

PostScript-based files come in several varieties — EPS, DCS, Illustrator, and PDF — and because the format is a complex one, there are more issues to be aware of up front.

EPS

The usual hang-up with EPS (Encapsulated PostScript) files is the preview header. The preview is a displayable copy of the EPS file. Because EPS files are actually made up of a series of commands that tell the printer how to draw the image, what you see on-screen is not the actual graphic. Most programs create a preview image for EPS files, but many programs have trouble reading them, especially if the EPS file was generated on a different platform. In those cases, they display an X or a gray box in place of the image (the EPS file will print properly to a PostScript printer.) That's why InDesign creates its own preview image when you import EPS files, lessening the chances of your seeing just an X or a gray box in place of the EPS preview.

When importing EPS files, InDesign lets you control some settings if you check Show Import Options in the Place dialog box. You can apply Photoshop clipping paths in the file, choose the preview format, convert the PostScript vector information into a bitmap (a process called *rasterization*), or embed links to OPI high-resolution source images (see Chapter 30 for details on OPI). Figure 21-1 shows the EPS Import Options dialog box.

Tip　In CorelDraw 6.0 and later, and in Adobe Illustrator 6.0 and later, be sure to set the EPS creation options to have no preview header. This keeps your files smaller. (In CorelDraw, export to EPS. In Illustrator 6.0 and later, save as Illustrator EPS. Note that Illustrator 5.*x*'s native format is EPS, so don't look for an export or save-as option.)

Caution　If you use transparency in your graphics, it's best to leave the files in Adobe Illustrator format rather than save them to EPS. Chapter 10 explains the issues in more depth.

DCS

The Desktop Color Separation (DCS) variant of EPS is a set of five files: an EPS preview file that links together four separation files (one each for cyan, magenta, yellow, and black). Use of this format ensures correct color separation when you output negatives for use in commercial printing. These files are often preferred over standard EPS files by service bureaus that do color correction. One variation of the DCS file format, DCS 2.0, also supports spot color plates in addition to the standard plates for cyan, magenta, yellow, and black.

Note　You should not use DCS files if you intend to create composite proof files or in-RIP separations from InDesign — InDesign will ignore the DCS separation files and just use the preview file for output. Only use DCS files if you're outputting separations (but not in-RIP separations). Chapter 30 covers this in detail.

Illustrator

Adobe Illustrator files are very similar to EPS, except they don't have a preview header, and they better support transparency settings in graphics. There are no special concerns to Illustrator files; just be sure to note the font and color issues mentioned previously in this section.

New Feature　InDesign CS2 now can differentiate layers in an Illustrator image, letting you decide which one(s) to display in your layout, as Chapter 22 explains.

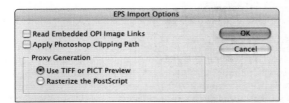

Figure 21-1: The EPS Import Options dialog box

PDF

InDesign imports PDF files similar to how it imports EPS and other graphics files (File ➪ Place, or ⌘+D or Ctrl+D). To select a specific page for import, select the Show Import Options check box in the Place dialog box; you'll then get a new dialog box called Place PDF that lets you select which page(s) to import, as Figure 21-2 shows. It also lets you determine how the file is cropped and whether InDesign places it on a transparent background (as opposed to the paper color).

When you import a PDF file, InDesign treats it as a graphic and can place one or more of the PDF file's pages (if it has more than one page) into your document as an uneditable graphic. You can crop, resize, and do other such manipulations common to any graphic, but you can't work with the text or other imported PDF file's components.

InDesign CS2 can now import multiple pages from a multi-page PDF file, as Chapter 22 explains. InDesign CS2 now can also differentiate layers in a PDF file, letting you decide which one(s) to display in your layout, as Chapter 22 also explains.

Special PDF features, like sounds, movies, hyperlinks, control buttons, and annotations, are ignored in the imported file. Also, PDF is a good format to use for graphics that contain transparency, as Chapter 10 explains.

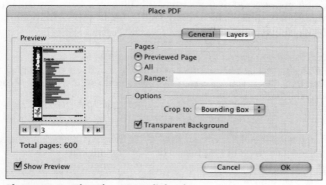

Figure 21-2: The Place PDF dialog box

Other vector formats

If you're outputting to negatives for professional printing, you should avoid non-PostScript vector formats. But they're fine for printing to inkjet and laser printers.

PICT

The standard Macintosh format for drawings, PICT (which stands for *Picture*) also supports bitmaps and is the standard format for Mac OS 8 and 9 screen-capture utilities. InDesign imports PICT files with no difficulty, but it cannot color-separate them for output to negatives. Because fonts in vector PICT graphics are automatically translated to curves, you need not worry about whether fonts used in your graphics are resident in your printer or available at your service bureau.

Windows Metafile

The standard Windows format for drawing, Windows Metafile is similar to PICT in that it can contain bitmap images as well as vector drawings. But InDesign will ignore bitmap information in Windows Metafiles, stripping it out during import. Microsoft Office 2000 introduced a new version of this format, called Enhanced Metafile, which InDesign also supports.

Issues with bitmap formats

Bitmap (also called *raster*) formats are simpler than vector formats because they're made up of rows of dots *(pixels)*, not instructions on how to draw various shapes. But that doesn't mean that all bitmaps are alike.

Professional-level bitmap formats

Although InDesign supports a wide variety of bitmap formats, there is usually just one to worry about if you're producing professional documents for output on a printing press: TIFF. (You may also use the Scitex CT format if you're using Scitex output equipment to produce your negatives.) I suggest you convert other formats to TIFF using your image editor (Corel Photo-Paint and Adobe Photoshop, the two top image editors, import and export most formats, as do other modern image-editing programs) or a conversion program like the Mac shareware program GraphicConverter, Equilibrium's DeBabelizer for Macintosh, or DataViz's Conversions Plus (for Windows) and MacLinkPlus (for Macintosh).

Cross-Reference

For links to graphics conversion tools, go to this book's companion Web site at www.InDesignCentral.com.

Photoshop

InDesign can import version 4.0 and later of this popular image editor's file format. When you place Photoshop files in InDesign, you can control how the alpha channel is imported — be sure to select Show Import Options in the Place dialog box to get this control. You also can apply any embedded clipping paths and import — or exclude — any embedded color profile.

Cross-Reference

The Photoshop format also supports transparency very well, which helps avoid later printing problems, as Chapters 10 and 30 explain.

New Feature

InDesign CS2 now can differentiate layers in a Photoshop image, letting you decide which one(s) to display in your layout during or after import, as Chapter 22 covers. For Photoshop images that have layers, the Image Import Options will offer a third pane, Layers, as covered in Chapter 22.

Scitex CT

The continuous-tone Scitex CT format is used with Scitex output high-resolution devices and is usually produced by Scitex scanners. If you're using this format, you should be outputting to a Scitex system. Otherwise, you're not going to get the advantage of its high resolution.

TIFF

The most popular bitmap format for publishers is TIFF, the *Tagged Image File Format* developed by Aldus (later bought by Adobe Systems) and Microsoft. TIFF supports color up to 24 bits (16.7 million colors) in both RGB and CMYK models, and every major photo-editing program supports TIFF on both the Macintosh and in Windows. TIFF also supports grayscale and black-and-white files.

The biggest advantage to using TIFF files rather than other formats that also support color, such as PICT, is that InDesign is designed to take advantage of TIFF. For example, in an image editor, you can set clipping paths in a TIFF file, which act as a mask for the image. InDesign sees that path and uses it as the image boundary, making the area outside of it invisible. That in turn lets you have nonrectangular bitmap images in your layout—the clipping path becomes the visible boundary for your TIFF image. InDesign also supports embedded alpha channels and color profiles in TIFF files. Figure 21-3 shows the two Image Import Options dialog box panes—Image and Color—that apply to TIFF images, as well as to Photoshop and other formats.

Caution TIFF files do not handle images with transparency well. Even though the files will look okay on-screen, they may not print well or may cause printer errors. It's best to stick with the Adobe Photoshop format if you use transparency.

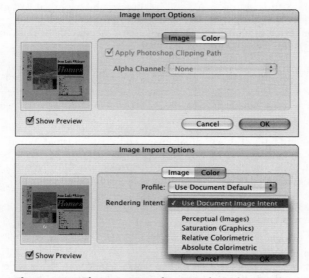

Figure 21-3: The two panes for TIFF, Photoshop, and most other bitmap images in the Image Import Options dialog box

TIFF files have several variations that are supported by InDesign. But because other programs aren't as forgiving, follow these guidelines to ensure smooth interaction:

✦ You should have no difficulty if you use uncompressed and LZW-compressed TIFF files supported by most Mac programs (and increasingly by most Windows programs). InDesign even supports the less-used Zip compression method for TIFF files. You should be safe using LZW-compressed TIFF files with any mainstream program, but if you do have difficulty, I recommend that you use uncompressed TIFF files. Also, always talk to your service bureau about LZW support before sending files for output. Many older imagesetters do not handle LZW compression and fail to output images that use it.

✦ Use the byte order for the platform for which the TIFF file is destined. Macs and PCs use the opposite byte order—basically, the Mac reads the eight characters that comprise a byte in one direction and the PC reads it in another. Although InDesign reads both byte orders, other programs may not, so why invite confusion? Of course, if your TIFF files will only be worked on by InDesign and Photoshop users, the byte order doesn't matter.

Web-oriented bitmap formats

In recent years, several formats have been developed for use on the Web in the Hypertext Markup Language (HTML) documents found there. These formats — GIF, JPEG, and PNG — achieve small size (for faster downloading and display on your browser) by limiting image and color detail and richness.

Although you can use any supported graphics format for documents you expect to export to the Web's HTML format (InDesign converts all images to GIF or JPEG when you export to the Adobe Go Live version of XML for further translation to HTML within Go Live), if you know your document is bound for the Web, you might as well use a Web graphics format from the start.

Because InDesign doesn't export layouts to the Web's HTML format, there's little reason to use Web-oriented graphics in your InDesign files. If you're using InDesign to create PDF files for access over the Web, or if you're using InDesign to create XML files that will be presented on the Web, you might want to use these Web-oriented formats because they are more compact. Otherwise, stick with the print-oriented ones to get their better image quality.

GIF

The Graphics Interchange Format (GIF) is the oldest Web format. To help keep file size down, it is limited to 256 colors. This reduces file size but also makes it unsuitable for photographs and graphics with color blends. But its compression approach doesn't lose any image detail, so it works well for sketches, cartoons, and other simple images with sharp details.

JPEG

The Joint Photographic Experts Group (JPEG) compressed color-image format is used for very large images and the individual images comprising an animation or movie. Images compressed in this format may lose detail, which is why publishers prefer TIFF files. JPEG can be used effectively even on documents output to an inkjet printer because you can set the level of loss to none during export. But in professional printing, don't use JPEG images. That's because JPEG images use the RGB color model, not the CMYK model of standard printing. While it is possible to create CMYK JPEG files with Photoshop, those CMYK JPEGs won't display in — and may even crash — other applications and Web browsers.

JPEG is more useful on the Web, where the limited resolution of a computer monitor makes most of JPEG's detail loss hard to spot and provides an acceptable trade-off of slightly blurry quality in return for a much smaller file size. It's particularly well suited for photographs because the lost detail is usually not noticeable because of all the other detail surrounding it.

If you do use JPEG for print work, note that you can provide a clipping path for it in programs like Photoshop. The clipping path lets the image have an irregular boundary (rendering the rest of its background transparent) so you can use InDesign effects such as text wrap.

PNG

A relatively new format, the Portable Network Graphics (PNG) format is meant to provide GIF's no-loss compression but support 24-bit color so it can be used for photography and subtly colored illustrations on the Web. The PNG format's other significant attribute is full transparency support with an embedded alpha channel. (That is why InDesign CS2 lets you replace the transparency with white or keep the background color in the Image Import Options dialog box.) The transparency also works in most current Web browsers.

Working with Files across Platforms

It's increasingly common for people in publishing to work in a cross-platform (Mac and Windows) environment. Even if you do all your InDesign work on one platform, chances are good that you'll receive files created on the other platform. (Most text editing is done on PCs, while most graphics and publishing work is done on the Mac, for example.)

Even with the improved compatibility between Mac and PC (mostly thanks to additions to the Mac OS, which makes it easier to share files with PCs), there are still some trip-ups that you may encounter when dealing with something as simple as filenames when sharing files across platforms.

Both Windows and the Mac use icons to show you (and tell programs) what format a file is in. Before Mac OS X, how those icons are created differ between the two platforms, and when you moved files from one platform to another, you could easily lose those icons. But Mac OS X, like Windows and Unix, relies on filename extensions — three or four letters after a period at the end of the filename — to identify the file type and thus display the correct icon. The default on both Windows and Mac OS X is to hide those filename extensions from display.

To see filename extensions in Windows, open any folder, choose Tools ➪ Folder Options, and then select the View tab to get the pane that appears in the following figure. (You must have a disk or folder open to have the View menu.) Deselect the Hide Extensions for Known File Types option, and then click OK. In Mac OS X, there's a similar control accessed from the Finder. Choose Finder ➪ Preferences, select the Advanced pane (in Mac OS X 10.3 [Jaguar] and later), select the Always Show File Extensions option, and close the dialog box.

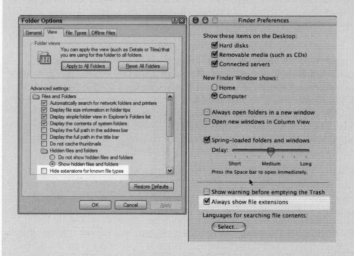

Note that even though most OS X–native programs such as InDesign automatically add filename extensions when you save, older programs — especially those running in Classic Mode — usually do not automatically add a filename extension. Be sure to add these extensions manually or configure the program to do so for you automatically if it has that option. (Microsoft Office 2001 applications do, for example, in the Save dialog boxes.)

When importing PNG files, you can choose whether to retain the background color defined in the file or to substitute white — just be sure that Show Import Options is selected in the Place dialog box so that choice is presented. Similarly, you can also adjust the gamma value during import. Gamma is a setting that describes the color range of a device, and to ensure most accurate reproduction, the gamma setting for the PNG file should be the same as that of your output device, such as a printer or monitor. Figure 21-4 shows the PNG Settings pane in the Image Import Options dialog box.

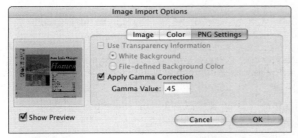

Figure 21-4: The PNG Settings pane of the Image Import Options dialog box

Other bitmap formats

The other supported formats are ones that you should avoid, unless you're printing to inkjet or laser printers. If you have images in one of these formats and want to use it for professionally output documents, convert them to TIFF before using them in InDesign.

✦ **BMP.** Like TIFF, the BMP Windows bitmap format supports color, grayscale, and black-and-white images.

✦ **PCX.** Like TIFF, PCX supports color, grayscale, and black-and-white images.

✦ **PICT.** PICT, the old standard Macintosh format for drawings, also supports bitmaps. InDesign imports PICT files with no difficulty.

Identifying Color Issues

It used to be that importing color from graphics files into publishing programs was an iffy proposition — colors would often not print properly even though they appeared correct on-screen. Those nightmares are largely a thing of the past, as modern page-layout software such as InDesign accurately detects color definitions in your source graphics, and modern illustration and image-editing programs are better at making that information accessible to page-layout programs. So, just note the following advice to ensure smooth color import.

If you create color images in an illustration or image-editing program, make sure that you create them using the CMYK color model or using a named spot color. If you use CMYK, the color is, in effect, preseparated. With InDesign, any spot colors defined in an EPS file are automatically added to the Swatches pane for your document and set as a spot color.

Cross-Reference   See Chapter 8 for more on creating and editing colors.

If your program follows Adobe's EPS specifications (Adobe Illustrator, CorelDraw, and Macromedia FreeHand all do), InDesign color-separates your EPS file, no matter whether it uses process or spot colors. Canvas automatically converts Pantone spot colors to process colors in your choice of RGB and CMYK models. For other programs, create your colors in the CMYK model to be sure they print as color separations from InDesign.

Color systems

There are several color systems, or models, in use, and InDesign supports the common ones, including CMYK (process), RGB, ANPA, Pantone, Focoltone, Dainippon Ink & Chemical (DIC), Toyo, Trumatch, and Web. A color system defines either a set of individual colors that have specially mixed inks (shown on swatchbooks, which have small samples of each color) or a range of colors that can be created by combining a limited number of inks (such as RGB for red, green, and blue and CMYK for cyan, magenta, yellow, and black).

Chapter 8 describes the various color models, but for file import, it's best to use just three — CMYK (process), RGB, and the Pantone Matching System — because they're universally used and tend to be the most reliable when passing information from one system to another.

Note

The advice on color systems applies to just vector images because bitmap programs use CMYK or RGB as their actual color models, even if they offer swatchbooks of other models' colors.

Tip

Most layout artists use Pantone to specify desired colors, so keep a Pantone swatchbook handy to see which CMYK values equal the desired Pantone color. (One of the available Pantone swatchbooks — *The Pantone Process Color Imaging Guide CMYK Edition* — shows each Pantone color next to the CMYK color build used to simulate it.) This book's companion Web site (www.InDesignCentral.com) provides links to Pantone and other color swatchbooks.

Of course, you can simply pick a Pantone color from the electronic swatchbook in InDesign, and InDesign converts it to CMYK if you specify it to be a process color (the default setting). Many high-end illustration programs, including Adobe Illustrator, support Pantone and can do this instant conversion as well. If available (as it is in InDesign), use the Pantone Process Coated color model because that is designed for output using CMYK printing presses. But remember: What you see on-screen won't match what you get on paper, so it's a good idea to have the printed Pantone swatchbook.

Calibrated color

With InDesign's Color Management System (CMS) feature enabled, the program calibrates the output colors (whether printed to a color printer or color-separated for traditional printing) based on the source device and the target output device in an attempt to ensure that what you see on-screen comes close to what you'll see on the printed page. Although color calibration is a tricky science that rarely results in exact color matches across all input and output devices, it can help minimize differences as the image travels along the creation and production path.

Today, most image-editing programs let you apply color profiles that conform with the International Color Committee (ICC) standards. If you use color calibration, it's best to apply these ICC profiles in the images when you create them.

If you can't — or forget to — apply an ICC profile when creating your image, don't worry. You can add a profile (if you're creating images in a program that doesn't support ICC profiles) or apply a different one from InDesign.

Cross-Reference   Chapter 28 covers color calibration in depth.

Summary

If you work with publishing-oriented graphics formats — EPS, PDF, Illustrator, TIFF, and Photoshop — created by mainstay programs like Adobe Photoshop, Adobe Illustrator, CorelDraw, Corel Photo-Paint, and Macromedia FreeHand, you'll likely have no difficulties importing graphics into or printing graphics from InDesign. But be sure to stick with common color models, particularly CMYK and Pantone.

And it's best to do any special effects in your graphics program — InDesign has limited abilities to manipulate graphics beyond layout-oriented functions like resizing, cropping, flipping, slanting, and text wrap. To ease access to your graphics programs, InDesign lets you open them from within InDesign.

✦   ✦   ✦

Importing Graphics

Although InDesign's shape-creation tools, type-formatting options, and object-manipulation features provide great flexibility when it comes to designing pages, you're probably going to want to use other graphics elements — particularly scanned images and computer-generated illustrations — in your publications. InDesign lets you import graphics files in a variety of formats (see Chapter 21 for details about supported graphics file formats), and once you've imported a graphic, you have several options for modifying its appearance (see Chapter 23 for information about modifying imported graphics).

Note   The terms *picture* and *graphic* are interchangeable, referring to any type of graphic. An *image* is a bitmap graphic, such as that produced by an image editor or a scanner, while an *illustration* or *drawing* is a vector file produced by an illustration program.

It's important to understand that when you import a graphic into a document, InDesign establishes a link between the graphics file and the document file and then sends the original graphics file to the printer when the document is output. (There is one exception to this scenario — when you copy and paste a graphic into an InDesign document, which is explained later in this chapter.) InDesign links to graphics because a graphics file, particularly a high-resolution scanned graphic, can be very large. If the entire graphics file were included in an InDesign document when you imported it, InDesign documents would quickly become prohibitively large. Instead, InDesign saves a low-resolution preview of an imported graphics file with the document, and it's this file that you see on-screen. InDesign remembers the location of the original file and uses this information when printing.

Note   If you place a graphic that's 48K or smaller, InDesign automatically embeds the full-resolution image rather than a low-resolution preview.

Cross-Reference   See Chapter 23 for more information about embedding graphics and about managing links to graphics files.

When it's time to import a graphic, you're responsible for knowing where the file is — whether it's stored on a floppy disk that your friend gave you, on your hard drive, on a networked file server, or on a local or networked CD-ROM.

In This Chapter

Using the Place command to import graphics

Specifying import options for various graphics formats

Figuring out other ways of importing graphics

♦ ♦ ♦ ♦

Note   If you import a graphics file that's stored on any kind of removable media, such as a floppy disk, Zip disk, or CD, the link between the document and the graphics file will be broken when the media is removed. Generally, it's best to copy graphics files to your hard drive or to a networked file server before importing them into an InDesign document.

Using the Place Command

Although there are several ways to add a graphics file to an InDesign document (all of which are explained in this chapter), the Place command (File ➪ Place, or ⌘+D or Ctrl+D) is the method you should use most often. When you use the Place command, InDesign offers import options for various graphics file formats that are not available if you use other import methods.

Here's how to use the Place command to import a graphic:

1. **Choose File ➪ Place or press ⌘+D or Ctrl+D.** If you want to import a graphic into an *existing frame*, select the target frame using either of the selection tools (either before you choose File ➪ Place or afterward). If you want InDesign to create a *new frame* when you import the graphic, make sure no object is selected when you choose Place. Either way, the Place dialog box shown in Figure 22-1 appears.

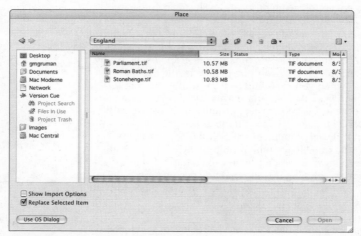

Figure 22-1: The Place dialog box

Note   You can import a graphic into any kind of frame or shape (including a curved line created with the Pen tool) except a straight line. Be careful: If the Type tool is selected when you use the Place command to import a graphic into a selected text frame, you'll create an inline graphic at the text-insertion point (see Chapter 11 for information about creating and managing inline graphics).

2. **Use the controls in the Place dialog box to locate and select the graphics file you want to import.**

3. **If you want to display import options that let you control how the selected graphics file is imported, either select Show Import Options, and then click Open; or press and hold Shift and double-click the filename, or Shift+click Open.** If you choose Show Import Options, the EPS Import Options, Place PDF, or Image Import Options dialog box — depending on what kind of graphic you are importing — appears.

4. **Specify the desired import options, if any are applicable, and then click OK.** (These options are covered later in this chapter.)

5. **You can place the graphic in an existing frame or in a new frame, as follows:**

   - If an empty frame is selected, the graphic is automatically placed in the frame. The upper-left corner of the graphic is placed in the upper-left corner of the frame, and the frame acts as the cropping shape for the graphic.

   - If a frame already holding a graphic is selected, InDesign replaces the existing graphic with the new one if you selected the Replace Selected Item option in the Place dialog box. Otherwise, InDesign assumes you want to put the new graphic in a new frame.

   - To place the graphic into a new frame, click the loaded-graphic icon (shown in Figure 22-2) on an empty portion of a page or on the pasteboard. The point where you click establishes the upper-left corner of the resulting graphics frame, which is the same size as the imported graphic and which acts as the graphic's cropping shape.

Figure 22-2: The loaded-graphic icons for PDF files (left) and all other graphics (right)

   - To place the graphic in an existing, unselected frame, click in the frame with the loaded-graphic icon. The upper-left corner of the graphic is placed in the upper-left corner of the frame, and the frame acts as a cropping shape.

After you place a graphic, it's displayed in the frame that contains it, and the frame is selected. If the Selection tool is selected, the eight handles of its bounding box are displayed; if the Direct Selection tool is selected, handles are displayed only in the corners. At this point, you can modify either the frame or the graphic within, or you can move on to another task.

Tip

If you can store all your graphics files in a single location — not necessarily in a single folder, but perhaps within a folder hierarchy on your hard drive or a file server — you can minimize link problems. If you move, rename, or delete the original file after importing a graphic, you'll break the link, which will cause printing problems. Keeping all graphics files in a single, safe place — a place that's backed up regularly — is a good idea.

New Feature

When importing JPEG files, InDesign CS2 now automatically scales the image to fit in the page. This helps deal with digital-camera graphics that tend to be very large and when imported end up taking much more than the width of a page. While you'll likely still need to scale the image to fit your layout, you can at least see the whole image before doing so.

Specifying Import Options

If you've ever used a graphics application—for example, an image-editing program such as Adobe Photoshop or an illustration program such as Adobe Illustrator or Macromedia FreeHand— you're probably aware that when you save a graphics file, you have several options that control such things as file format, image size, color depth, preview quality, and so on. When you save a graphics file, the settings you specify are determined by the way in which the image will be used. For example, you could use Photoshop to save a high-resolution TIFF version of a scanned graphic for use in a slick, four-color annual report or a low-resolution GIF version of the same graphic for use on the company's Web page. Or you could use Illustrator or FreeHand to create a corporate logo that you'll use in various sizes in many of your printed publications.

If you choose to specify custom import settings when you import a graphics file, the choices you make will depend on the nature of the publication. For example, if it's bound for the Web, there's no need to work with or save graphics using resolutions that exceed a computer monitor's 72 dpi. Along the same lines, if the publication will be printed, the image import settings you specify for a newspaper that will be printed on newsprint on a SWOP (Specifications for Web Offset Publications) press will be different than those you specify for a four-color magazine printed on coated paper using a sheet-fed press.

If you choose Show Import Options when you place a graphic, the options displayed in the resulting dialog boxes depend on the file format of the selected graphic. When you set options for a particular file, the options you specify remain in effect for that file format until you change them. If you don't choose Show Import Options when you place a graphic, the most recent settings for the file format of the selected graphic are used.

Import options for bitmap graphics

InDesign gives you two sets of import options for the following types of bitmap images: TIFF, GIF, JPEG, Scitex CT, BMP, and PCX. You get three options for PNG files, and a different set of three for Photoshop files. There are no import options for PICT or QuickTime movie files. Figure 22-3 shows the four possible panes for bitmap images.

QuarkXPress User

QuarkXPress lets you press and hold ⌘ or Ctrl when selecting a bitmap file to import; this makes QuarkXPress import a color bitmap as a grayscale image but not alter the source file— which can be handy in two-color publications such as newsletters and catalogs where you want all graphics to be grayscale but also print a separate color plate for a spot color. InDesign has no equivalent capability, so you'll need to convert any images to grayscale first in a program like Photoshop. Note that this is only an issue if you are working both with color images and spot colors; if your entire document will be printed as grayscale—with no color plates used at all—then you can import color images and let InDesign convert them to grayscale along with the rest of the document when you print.

Image pane

This pane lets you apply any embedded clipping path and/or alpha channel to the image to mask, or cut out, part of the image. Select the Apply Photoshop Clipping Path option to import the clipping path along with the image; select an alpha channel from the Alpha Channel pop-up menu to import the alpha channel along with the image.

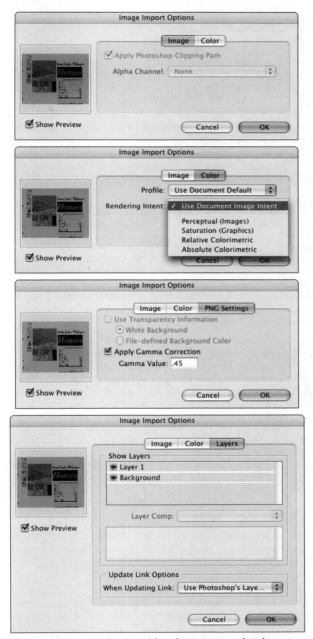

Figure 22-3: InDesign provides the Image and Color panes in the Image Import Options dialog box for most bitmap formats; PNG files have a third pane, PNG Settings; and Photoshop files also have a third pane, Layers.

Chapter 24 covers clipping paths in more detail.

Color pane

In the Color pane, you can turn on color management for the image and control how the image is displayed.

Select the Enable Color Management option to enable color management. Using the Profile pop-up menu, choose a color-source profile that matches the color *gamut* (range) of the device (scanner, digital camera, and so on) or software used to create the file. InDesign will try to translate the colors in the file to the colors that the output device is capable of producing. (These profiles are installed in your operating system by other applications, not InDesign.)

See Chapter 28 for more information about using InDesign's color-management features.

Use the Rendering Intent pop-up menu to determine how InDesign translates the color in the selected graphics file with the gamut of the output device. If the graphic is a scanned photograph, choose Perceptual (Images). The other options — Saturation (Graphics), Relative Colorimetric, and Absolute Colorimetric — are appropriate for images that contain mostly areas of solid color, such as Illustrator EPS files that have been opened in Photoshop and saved as TIFFs.

PNG Settings pane

Use this pane — available only if you place a PNG file — to use the transparency information in a PNG file, assuming it has a transparent background. You have two choices for controlling transparency handling: White Background and File-defined Background Color. The former forces the transparent portion to display as white in InDesign; the latter uses whatever background color is specified in the PNG file itself.

This pane also lets you adjust the gamma value during import — the gamma is a setting that describes a device's luminance, and to ensure most accurate reproduction, you want the gamma setting for the PNG file to be the same as that of your output device (a printer or monitor). It is meant to correct for the file being created on a specific type of monitor. However, to use this feature, you need to know the gamma setting for the final output device. Otherwise, leave it alone.

Layers pane

Use this pane — available only if you place a Photoshop image (or Illustrator or PDF vector file) — to select which layers you want imported into InDesign. You can then control which imported layers display in InDesign, though you cannot change their order (you'd need to go back to Photoshop and change the layer order there).

Although you can save an image file with layers as a TIFF, preserving those layers, InDesign CS2 does not give you the ability to manage which layers from a TIFF file import into InDesign.

There's also an option, in the When Updating Link pop-up menu, to control how changes to the file are handled in terms of layer management: If you choose Use Photoshop's Layer Visibility, InDesign makes all layers visible in Photoshop when you update the link to the graphic from InDesign. If you choose Keep Layer Visibility Overrides, InDesign imports only the layers chosen in this dialog box if you later update the graphic in Photoshop.

Linking and controlling layer visibility from within InDesign is covered in Chapter 23.

The capability to import layers from Photoshop files (as well as Illustrator and PDF files) is new to InDesign CS2.

Import options for vector file formats

If you're importing vector files, selecting the Import Options check box will result in one of several dialog boxes appearing, depending on what the vector file type is. If you import older-version Illustrator or EPS files, the EPS Import Options dialog box appears; if you import PDF and newer-version Illustrator files, the Place PDF dialog box, which has two panes, appears. (Both dialog boxes are shown in Figure 22-4.) There are no import options for Windows Metafile graphics.

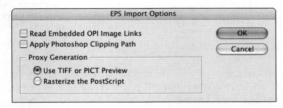

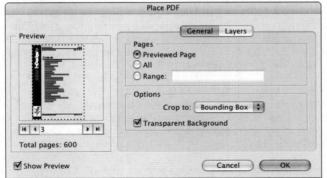

Figure 22-4: The EPS Import Options and Place PDF dialog boxes. The Place PDF dialog box has two panes: General and Layers. (The Layers pane for DPF files is almost identical to the Layers pane for Photoshop files shown in Figure 22-3.)

Note   Illustrator CS and CS2 use PDF as their native file format, even though the filename extension is .ai, so InDesign detects these as PDF files and provides the PDF options during import.
In earlier versions of Illustrator, the native format was actually a variant of EPS.

EPS Import Options dialog box

If you use an Open Prepress Interface-based proxy workflow — that is, if an OPI-based service
provider supplies you with low-resolution versions of graphics files that will eventually be
replaced by high-resolution files during output, select the Read Embedded OPI Image Links
option if you want InDesign, rather than your service provider, to perform image replacement
during output. You should also select this option if you import graphics files that contain OPI
comments for other imported graphics files; for example, an EPS file that contains OPI information for an embedded TIFF graphic. Don't select this option if you don't use an OPI-based
workflow or if you want your service provider to handle image replacement during output.
When the Read Embedded OPI Image Links option is not selected, InDesign retains OPI comments but doesn't use them. When you print (or export) the document, the proxy image and
the link information are sent.

Also use this pane to import any clipping paths embedded in images that are in the EPS file.
Select the Apply Photoshop Clipping Path option to enable this.

Finally, use this pane to control how the EPS file appears on-screen in InDesign. If you select
the Use TIFF or PICT Preview option, InDesign uses the low-resolution proxy image embedded
in the EPS file for display on-screen and prints the graphic using the embedded high-resolution
PostScript instructions. If you select the Rasterize the PostScript option, InDesign converts
the PostScript file into a bitmap image during import. There's rarely a reason to rasterize an
imported EPS file.

Place PDF dialog box

When you use the Place command to import a PDF file and you choose to Show Options, the
Place PDF file dialog box shown in Figure 22-4 appears. It provides several controls for specifying how the file is imported. In the General pane:

✦ In the Pages section, select Previewed Page, All, or Range to determine which page(s)
  you want to import. You can change the previewed page by using the arrow buttons
  under the preview image at left or typing a specific page number in the field below the
  preview image. If you want to import a range, use commas to separate pages and a
  hyphen to indicate range; for example, if you type **3, 5-9, 13**, pages 3, 5 through 9, and
  13 will be imported.

 Note   When you place the PDF in InDesign, you get a separate loaded-graphic icon for each page,
so as you place each page, a new loaded-graphic icon appears for the next page until there
are no more to place. You can tell you're placing multiple pages because the loaded-graphics
icon will have a plus sign in it.

✦ In the Options section, select one of the cropping options from the Crop To Pop-up
  menu. If you choose Bounding Box, the page's bounding box (or, if none is defined in
  the PDF file, a rectangle that encloses all items, including page marks), is used to build
  the graphics frame. Choosing Art places the area defined by the file's creator, if any, as
  placeable artwork. For example, the person who created the file might have designated
  a particular graphic as placeable artwork. Choosing Crop places the area displayed and

printed by Adobe Acrobat. Choosing Trim places the graphic in an area equal to the final, trimmed piece. Choosing Bleed places the page area plus any specified bleed area. Choosing Media places an area defined by the paper size specified for the PDF document, including page marks.

Also in the Options section, select the Transparent Background option if you want the white areas of the PDF page to be transparent. Deselect this option if you want to preserve the page's opaque white background.

New Feature The ability to import multiple pages from a PDF file is new to InDesign CS2.

Note Some PDF files are protected with passwords or have printing, text editing, and other content-access functions disabled. If a PDF file is password-protected, you'll be prompted to type the required password; do so and click OK. Note that some PDF files have a second password, called a permissions password, that you'll also need to open it.

If the selected file was saved with any security restrictions (no text editing, no printing, and so on), you can't place any pages of the file into InDesign. Ask the person who produced the file for an unrestricted copy.

In the Layers pane:

✦ You will see a list of image layers. Any that have the eye icon will import into InDesign, and you can select or deselect layers by clicking the box to the right of the layer name to make the eye icon appear or disappear. You can then control which imported layers display in InDesign, though you cannot change their order (you'd need to go back to Photoshop and change the layer order there).

✦ Use the When Updating Link pop-up menu, to control how changes to the file are handled in terms of layer management: If you choose Use PDF's Layer Visibility, InDesign makes all layers visible in Illustrator or Acrobat visible when you update the link to the graphic from InDesign. If you choose Keep Layer Visibility Overrides, InDesign imports only the layers chosen in this dialog box if you later update the graphic in Photoshop.

Cross-Reference Linking and controlling layer visibility from within InDesign is covered in Chapter 23.

New Feature The ability to import layers from Illustrator and PDF vector files (as well as Photoshop image files) is new to InDesign CS2.

Using Other Ways to Import Graphics

If you want to specify custom import options for an imported graphics file, you must use the Place command. However, if you don't need this level of control, InDesign offers three other options for importing graphics:

✦ You can use your computer's Copy (File ⇨ Copy, or ⌘+C or Ctrl+C) and Paste (File ⇨ Paste, or ⌘+V or Ctrl+V) commands to move a graphics file between two InDesign documents or from a document created with another program into an InDesign document.

✦ You can drag and drop graphics file icons from your computer's desktop into InDesign documents.

✦ For Illustrator files, you can drag or copy and paste objects directly from Illustrator into InDesign. Depending on your Clipboard preference, these objects may only be embedded PDFs, which are not editable in InDesign.

To set your preference for copying or dragging vector objects from Illustrator into InDesign, go to the File Handling pane of the Preferences dialog box (choose InDesign ⇨ Preferences on the Mac or Edit ⇨ Preferences in Windows, or press ⌘+K or Ctrl+K). If you want to place fully editable vector objects in InDesign, go to the Clipboard section of the File Handing pane, and deselect the Prefer PDF When Pasting option. Leave it selected if you prefer to copy or drag noneditable, embedded PDFs into InDesign instead.

Placing editable vector objects can be especially useful if you need to place a vector logo graphic into a template. An editable vector object entirely contained within InDesign reduces the need to jump between graphic applications to make changes such as to the logo's colors and to edit vector shapes.

If you use these methods to add a graphic to an InDesign document, some of the attributes of the original graphic may not survive the trip. The operating system, the file format, and the capabilities of the originating application may all play roles in determining which attributes are preserved. If you want to be safe, use the Place command or use the method described previously to move fully editable vector objects into InDesign.

Copy and Paste

If you copy an object in an InDesign document and then paste it into a different InDesign document, the copy retains all the attributes of the original. In the case of a copied and pasted graphic, all import settings, frame modifications, and graphic modifications are retained, as is the link to the original graphics file.

When you copy and paste a graphic into an InDesign document, a link between the original graphics file and the InDesign document is *not* established. The graphic becomes part of the InDesign document, as though you created it using InDesign tools. For vector images, such a pasted graphic is editable only if you deselect Prefer PDF When Pasting in the File Handling pane of the Preferences dialog box, as described in the previous section.

Cross-Reference   The Links pane (Window ⇨ Links, or Shift+⌘+D or Ctrl+Shift+D) helps you manage the links that are established between an InDesign document and a graphics file when you use the Place command. See Chapter 23 for more about managing links to graphics files.

Drag and Drop

When an InDesign document is open, you can import a graphics file in any supported file format by clicking and dragging the file's icon into the window of the InDesign document. When you drag and drop a graphics file into a document, a link between the original graphics file and the document is established, just as it would be if you had used the Place command.

Adobe Illustrator files

If you drag and drop an Illustrator file icon into an InDesign document window, the graphic behaves the same as it would if you had used the Place command. That is, individual elements within the graphic are not selectable or modifiable within InDesign. However, if you drag and drop Illustrator objects from an Illustrator document window into an InDesign document window, each object becomes a separate, editable InDesign object, as though you had created it in InDesign.

Note   For Illustrator objects to be editable in InDesign, be sure that Prefer PDF When Pasting is deselected in the File Handling pane of the Preferences dialog box, as described in the previous section.

This is a handy way of moving objects that you may want to modify between Illustrator and InDesign. For example, you can create text along a path in an Illustrator document, and then drag and drop the object into an InDesign document. Each character is converted into an editable shape, which you can stroke, fill, distort, and so on, using InDesign features. However, you cannot edit text along a path after you've dragged and dropped it into InDesign. (You have to go back to Illustrator, edit the original text, drag and drop it again, and then redo all your modifications.)

Using the Copy and Paste commands to add Illustrator objects to InDesign documents is the same as dragging and dropping objects between the programs. The copied objects behave the same as objects created in InDesign when you choose Paste, and no links are established.

Summary

InDesign lets you import graphics in any of several supported graphics file formats. The preferred method for importing graphics is the Place command (File ➪ Place, or ⌘+D or Ctrl+D) because it lets you customize various import settings that control how an imported graphic appears and prints.

You can also import graphics into an InDesign document by dragging and dropping graphics file icons into a document window or by copying and pasting objects between InDesign documents or between documents created with other programs and InDesign documents.

If you need to use Illustrator-generated objects or graphics files in your InDesign documents, several options are available: the Place command, the Copy and Paste commands, file drag and drop, and inter-application drag and drop. When using Copy and Paste or drag and drop from Illustrator, be sure to check InDesign's File Handling preferences first to choose between creating editable vectors or embedded PDFs in your document.

✦   ✦   ✦

Modifying Imported Graphics

Getting a graphic into your layout is one thing, but adjusting that graphic to make it really work in your layout is quite another. In almost every case, you'll want to manipulate the graphics you bring into your layout—change the size, crop out part of the image, wrap text around the image, and perhaps change the image color or distort its appearance.

The modifications you make will depend on your layout needs and the attributes of the graphics themselves. But no matter what modifications you end up making, you'll find yourself regularly using the techniques covered in this chapter.

Making Basic Graphic Modifications

After you import a graphic into an InDesign document, you can modify either the graphic or the frame that contains it. The following options are available for modifying imported graphics:

✦ You can crop graphics in a rectangular or free-form frame.

✦ You can use tools, the Control palette, or the Transform pane to rotate, scale, and/or shear graphics and/or their frames.

✦ You can flip graphics horizontally and/or vertically using commands in the Control palette's palette menu or in the Transform pane's palette menu.

✦ You can apply color and tint to imported grayscale and black-and-white bitmap graphics.

Cross-Reference

For information about modifying frames, see Chapter 10.

Whether you want to modify a graphic after importing it into a document or open the graphics file in its original program and modify it there is up to you.

InDesign lets you crop, rotate, scale, shear, and flip any imported graphic regardless of format. Generally, you're safe applying any of these transformations on vector-based formats such as Illustrator-native and Illustrator-, FreeHand-, and CorelDraw-generated EPS and PDF graphics — but not Photoshop EPS or PDF files, which are pixel-based images in an EPS shell. Applying these transformations to the DCS variant of EPS files is also safe. However, because EPS files are encased (thus, the term *encapsulated*) in a sort of protective shell, you can't select or modify any of the component pieces in InDesign — you must use a dedicated application to make such modifications.

For bitmapped images, such as TIFF, JPEG, GIF, and Photoshop-native files, all the aforementioned transformations except increasing horizontal and/or vertical scale are safe to perform in InDesign. But I recommend doing as much as possible in the original program, to minimize unexpected distortions in your final output. For example, if your imported images are more than twice as large as the size you need them to be in your layout, resize the images in an image editor, and then reimport the resized image in InDesign. This speeds printing and prevents moiré patterns that can result when InDesign takes the reduced pixels of the original image and creates new pixels for output — resizing the image in an image editor usually resizes the pixels in a way that outputs well. Similarly, enlarging an image in InDesign can cause a blocky look, while an image editor might let you resize it in a way that preserves image detail.

Cropping graphics

Remember, when you import a graphic using the Place command (File ➪ Place, or ⌘+D or Ctrl+D) or by clicking and dragging a graphics file into a document window, the graphic is contained in a graphics frame — either the frame that was selected when you placed the graphic or the frame that was automatically created if a frame wasn't selected. The upper-left corner of an imported graphic is automatically placed in the upper-left corner of its frame.

Resizing a graphic's frame

The easiest way to crop a graphic is to resize the frame that contains it. If you want to *mask out* (hide) portions of an imported graphic, you have the option of using an irregular shape as the frame, a graphic's built-in clipping path (if it has one), or a clipping path you generate in InDesign (by choosing Object ➪ Clipping Path or pressing Option+Shift+⌘+K or Ctrl+Alt+Shift+K).

Cross-Reference   Clipping paths are covered in Chapter 24.

To resize the frame, use the Selection tool to drag the frame's handles to reveal the portion of the graphic you want to print (and to conceal the portion you don't want to print). Press and hold Shift as you drag to maintain the proportions of the frame.

Moving a graphic in its frame

You can also click on a graphic with the Direct Selection tool and then drag the graphic in its frame to reveal and conceal different parts of the graphic. For example, you can crop the top and left edges of a graphic by clicking and dragging the graphic above and to the left of its original position (in the upper-left corner of the frame).

New Feature InDesign CS2 adds the Position tool, which in some cases works like the Direct Selection tool and in other cases works like the Selection tool. (For example, you could use the Position tool instead of the Direct Selection tool to drag a graphic within its frame.) The Position tool is designed for use by former PageMaker users, since it works much like PageMaker's Crop tool. See Chapter 2 and Appendix D for more details.

Of course, you can accomplish the same thing by selecting the frame with the Selection tool and dragging the upper-left corner down and to the right. The advantage of moving the image within the frame is that, when you've positioned the frame in the desired location in your layout, resizing the frame to crop the image then requires you to move the resized frame back to the desired location.

Using an irregular frame

If you want to use an irregular shape as the frame for a graphic that's currently cropped by a rectangular frame, here's what you do:

1. **Click the Direct Selection tool (or press A if the Type tool isn't selected).**

2. **Click the graphic you want to place in a free-form shape (don't click its frame), and then choose Edit ⇨ Copy or press ⌘+C or Ctrl+C.**

3. **Click the shape (or create one if you haven't already) you want to use as a cropping frame.** It can be any kind of object except a straight line.

4. **Choose Edit ⇨ Paste Into or press Shift+⌘+V or Ctrl+Shift+V.** Figure 23-1 shows an example.

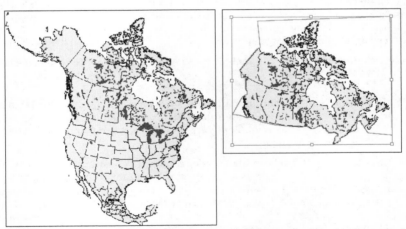

Figure 23-1: In this example, the map of North America (left) has been copied and pasted into a free-form frame that reveals only Canada (right). The free-form frame was created by using the Pen tool to trace the contour of Canada.

For more information about creating and modifying free-form shapes, see Chapters 25 and 26.

If you select a frame with the Direct Selection tool instead of the Selection tool, handles are displayed only at the frame corners rather than at the bounding-box corners and midpoints. When you select a frame with the Direct Selection tool, you can reshape the frame, and thus crop the graphic differently, by clicking and dragging corner points, adding and deleting points, and so on.

Of course, you could also create the irregular shape first, and then use the Place command to place the graphic file directly into the shape. (Or choose File ➪ Place Into, or press Option+⌘+V or Ctrl+Alt+V, to paste a cut or copied graphic inside the shape.) Using an irregular shape to crop a graphic is similar to using a clipping path except that you create the irregular shape yourself using InDesign's object-creation tools while a clipping path is either built into a graphics file or generated by InDesign (by choosing Object ➪ Clipping Path or pressing Option+Shift+⌘+K or Ctrl+Alt+Shift+K).

Rotating, scaling, and shearing graphics

InDesign provides two methods for rotating, scaling, and shearing graphics: You can click and drag a graphic using transformation tools, or you can use the Control palette or Transform pane, as explained in the next section, to type numerical values into fields or to choose a pre-set value from a pop-up menu.

The method you use is up to you. If you're into the hands-on-mouse approach to object manipulation and page building, you'll probably prefer the click-and-drag method of modifying graphics. Others prefer the pane approach. You'll probably end up using both methods. Regardless of the tool you use, the steps for transforming a graphic are pretty much the same:

1. **Click the Direct Selection tool (or press A if the Type tool isn't selected).**

2. **Click the graphic you want to modify.**

3. **If you want, you can click and drag the object's point of origin (by default it's in the upper-left corner of a graphics frame).** All transformations applied to an object are applied relative to the point of origin. For example, when you rotate an item, it rotates around its point of origin.

4. **Click and drag to perform the transformation.** To constrain transformation increments to preset values, press and hold Shift. For example, pressing and holding Shift while rotating a graphic limits rotation increments to multiples of 45 degrees. If you pause for a moment between clicking and dragging — long enough for the cross-hair pointer to change to the arrowhead pointer — the transformed graphic appears while you drag. If you don't pause, only the graphic boundary is displayed while you drag. If the Transform pane is open, the value in the field that's associated with the selected tool changes as you drag.

5. **Release the mouse button when the graphic looks the way you want it to look.**

If you press and hold Option or Alt while using a transformation tool, the modification is performed on a clone of the selected object.

Tip

If you double-click a transformation tool, a dialog box appears that lets you select the appropriate settings for that tool.

Each transformation tool has a few idiosyncrasies (Figure 23-2 shows the tool icons):

✦ **Rotate tool.** You can select this tool by pressing R if the Type tool isn't selected. Pressing and holding Shift while dragging limits rotation increments to multiples of 45 degrees.

✦ **Scale tool.** This tool shares a pop-up menu with the Shear tool. If you press and hold Shift while dragging with the Scale tool, only the horizontal scale of the selected graphic changes if you drag horizontally, only the vertical scale changes if you drag vertically, and the original proportions are maintained if you drag diagonally.

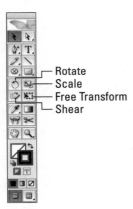

Figure 23-2: The buttons for the Rotate, Scale, Shear, and Free Transform tools in the Tools palette

— Rotate
— Scale
— Free Transform
— Shear

✦ **Shear tool.** This tool applies a combination of rotation and skew to a graphic. (The Transform pane includes separate Rotation Angle and Shear X Angle (skew) controls, but no Shear-specific controls. However, the Control palette has controls for all three.) Pressing and holding Shift constrains the selected graphic's rotation value to increments of 45 degrees.

✦ **Free Transform Tool.** Advanced users will like the Free Transform tool. When you select this tool, InDesign lets you scale, rotate, and resize — but not shear — selected objects. If you select within the frame, you can move the object by dragging it. If you select a frame handle (whether corner or midpoint), you can resize the object by dragging. Finally, if you move the mouse very close to a frame handle, you will see a curved arrow, which indicates you can rotate the object around that object's center point. Having a tool that does more than one thing can be confusing, but once you get the hang of it, it sure beats constantly changing tools!

Figure 23-3 shows the various dialog boxes that appear when you double-click the Rotate, Scale, and Shear tools. These provide numerical control over the operations, but also enable you to choose to copy the transformed item.

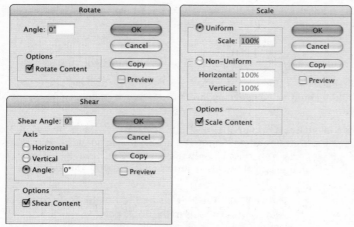

Figure 23-3: The Rotate, Scale, and Shear dialog boxes

Using the Control Palette and the Transform Pane

If you need more control than the Rotate, Shear, and Scale tools can provide, InDesign offers the Control palette (Window ➪ Control, or Option+⌘+6 or Ctrl+Alt+6) shown in Figure 23-5 and the Transform pane (Window ➪ Object & Layout ➪ Transform or F9) shown in Figure 23-4 to perform several other modifications on a selected graphic.

The Transform pane and Control palette have the following tools in common: Scale X Percentage, Scale Y Percentage, Rotation Angle, and Shear X Angle. Plus, both let you choose a selection point (such as for rotation or shearing) — also called the *point of origin* — and lock scaling to be proportional (making, for example, a 70 percent reduction in scale horizontally also reduces the graphic 70 percent vertically).

Note   If you change an object's scale using the Selection tool, the Control palette and Transform pane will likely report that scale as 100 percent because it is actually showing the change to the frame's stroke's size. Be sure to switch to the Direct Selection tool, which will then have the Control palette and Transform pane report on the current scale of the frame's contents (in other words, the graphic itself).

The palette menus are almost identical, with both letting you rotate objects in predefined increments (90° clockwise, 90° counterclockwise, and 180°) and flipping objects vertically and/or horizontally. Both also let you control the degree of precision in transformations, as described later. The Control palette's palette menu offers access to the Stroke Styles dialog box (see Chapter 27), while the Transform pane's palette menu lets you select whether scaling a text frame also scales the text within it, plus whether just the currently selected object or the entire group it belongs to is affected by the transformation.

The Control palette offers several additional controls: specifying the stroke width and type, selecting the object or contents (the same as using the Selection tool or the Direct Selection tool, respectively), fitting the content to the frame or fitting the frame to the content, centering the content, and selecting the previous or next object in a group.

Scale Y Percentage

Constrain Proportions for Scaling

Selection points (black is active point)

Size and position controls

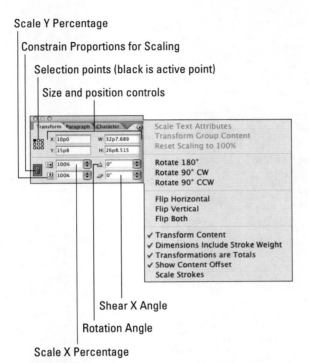

Shear X Angle

Rotation Angle

Scale X Percentage

Figure 23-4: The Transform pane and its palette menu.

Tip

If you press and hold Option or Alt when you press Return or Enter to apply a value you've typed into a field in the Control palette or Transform pane, the modification is applied to a clone of the selected object.

Cross-Reference

Chapter 10 covers the Control palette's selection options, such as Next Object in Group. Chapter 11 covers group creation and modification.

Changing an object's point of origin

The nine small, white squares at the top-left corner of the Transform pane and far left of the Control palette let you specify the point of origin for the selected object. An object's point of origin is used to determine the values in the X (horizontal distance from left edge of page) and Y (vertical distance from top of page) fields. When you apply a transformation, it's applied to the selected object relative to the fixed point of origin. By default, the point of origin of a graphics frame is the center point.

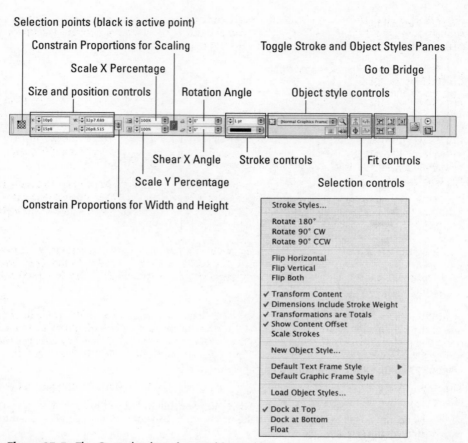

Figure 23-5: The Control palette for graphics and its palette menu. Note that the Transform pane offers a subset of the Control palette's functions.

A filled-in black square indicates the current point of origin. If no square is black, it means that a custom point of origin has been established by clicking and dragging the object's point of origin. In most cases, it's simplest to use the default point of origin, but you may want to click the middle square if, for example, you want to rotate a graphic around its center, or you may use a different corner or midpoint in certain situations. To change the point of origin for a selected object, click one of the small white squares.

Repositioning a graphic within its frame

You can reposition a graphic within its frame by changing the values in the Transform pane's or Control palette's X+ and/or Y+ fields. To see these fields, be sure that you have selected the graphic with the Direct Selection tool. If the Direct Selection tool is active, the values in these fields reflect the graphic's position relative to the frame's upper left corner. But if the Selection tool is active, the values in these fields indicate the distance between the upper-left corner of the page and the selected object's point of origin.

Scaling a graphic

You can scale a graphic by changing the value in the W and/or H fields or by changing the value in the Horizontal Scale and/or Vertical Scale fields. Most graphics designers are familiar with the concept of scaling an object by specifying a percentage value. If you're one of them, you'll probably use the Scale fields. After all, horizontally scaling a 4-inch-wide graphic to two-thirds of its original size by applying a Horizontal Scale value of 66.6 percent is easier than changing the graphic's width to 2.667 inches.

You can type scale values between 1 percent and 10,000 percent. If you want to maintain a graphic's original proportions, make sure the values in the Horizontal Scale and Vertical Scale fields are the same. If you want to return a graphic to the size it was when you first imported it, specify Horizontal Scale and Vertical Scale values of 100 percent.

Tip

You can use math to figure out scale entries. For example, if you want the scale to be 30 percent larger, you can type **+30%** rather than **130%**. Or you can type **/6** to make the object one-sixth of its current size. Other legitimate actions include subtraction (for example, **–29%**) and multiplication (for example, ***7**).

In addition to specifying a value in the Horizontal Scale or Vertical Scale field, you can choose one of the predefined values from the fields' pop-up menus, or you can highlight a value and press the up- or down-arrow keys on the keyboard. Each press of an arrow key changes the value by 1 percent. If you press and hold Shift while pressing an arrow, the increment of change is 10 percent.

The Fitting options (Object ➪ Fitting), which are explained later in this chapter, also let you change the scale of a graphic relative to the size of its frame.

Rotating a graphic

You can change the angle of a selected graphic by typing a different value in the Rotation Angle field, choosing one of the predefined angles from the field's pop-up menu, or by choosing any of the three rotation options—Rotate 180°, Rotate 90° CW, and Rotate 90° CCW—in the Transform pane's or Control palette's palette menu. If you choose one of these options, the current angle of the selected object is added to the applied angle. For example, if you choose Rotate 90° CCW (counterclockwise), an object that's currently rotated 12 degrees ends up with a rotation angle of 102 degrees. If you choose to type a value in the Rotation Angle field, positive values rotate the selected item counterclockwise; negative values rotate it clockwise.

Note

The Transformations Are Totals option in the Transform pane's and Control palette's palette menu relates to the angle of rotation of a nested object. If Transformations Are Totals is selected, the Rotation Angle displayed for a nested item is calculated by adding its angle to the angle of the containing frame. For example, if Transformations Are Totals is selected, a graphic that's been rotated 30 degrees that's in a frame that's been rotated 30 degrees will display a Rotation Angle value of 60°. If Transformations Are Totals is not selected, the Rotation Angle value is 30°.

Skewing a graphic

You can *skew*, or slant, a graphic in its frame by applying a Shear X Angle value in the Transform pane or Control palette, or by choosing a predefined value from the field's pop-up menu. Positive skew values slant an object to the right (that is, the top edge of the object is moved to the right), while negative values slant an object to the left (the bottom edge is moved to the right). You can type skew values between 1° and 89° (although values above 70° cause considerable distortion).

To unskew a graphic, type a Shear X Angle value of 0°. Figure 23-6 shows a graphic that's been skewed.

Note   When you use the Shear tool, you change the selected object's angle of rotation *and* skew angle simultaneously as you move the mouse.

Figure 23-6: The applied Skew X Angle value of 20° causes the graphic to lean to the right.

Flipping a graphic

The three flip commands — Flip Horizontal, Flip Vertical, and Flip Both — in the Transform pane's and Control palette's palette menu let you create a mirror image of a selected graphic. If you choose Flip Horizontal, the graphic is flipped along a vertical axis (that is, the right edge and left edge exchange places); if you choose Flip Vertical, the graphic is flipped upside down; and if you choose Flip Both, the graphic is flipped horizontally and vertically to produce an upside-down and backward version of the original.

Be careful when flipping graphics: Generally you'll want to flip both a graphic and its frame. To do so, make sure you select the frame using the Selection tool (rather than the Direct Selection tool, which selects only the graphic itself). If you flip a graphic that's been cropped in
a frame, you'll probably have to recrop the graphic.

Note   When you flip a graphic, the axis around which the graphic flips runs through the frame's point of origin.

Figuring Out the Fitting Commands

If you've placed a graphic in a frame that's either larger or smaller than the graphic, you can use the Fitting commands (Object ⇨ Fitting) to scale the graphic to fit the frame proportionately or disproportionately or to scale the frame to fit the graphic. Another option lets you center the graphic in the frame.

The Fitting commands for graphics are available only if you use the Selection tool to select a graphics frame. Here's a description of each of the five options:

Note All five of these commands are available through buttons in the Control palette.

✦ **Fit Content to Frame.** To resize a graphic to fill the selected frame, choose Object ➪ Fitting ➪ Fit Content to Frame or press Option+⌘+E or Ctrl+Alt+E. If the frame is larger than the graphic, the graphic is enlarged; if the frame is smaller, the graphic is reduced. If the graphic and the frame have different proportions, the graphic's proportions are changed so that the image completely fills the frame. Note that this can distort the graphic.

✦ **Fit Frame to Content.** To resize a frame so that it wraps snugly around a graphic, choose Fit Frame to Content or press Option+⌘+C or Ctrl+Alt+C. The frame is enlarged or reduced depending on the size of the graphic, and the frame's proportions change to match the proportions of the graphic.

✦ **Center Content.** To center a graphic in its frame, choose Center Content or press Shift+⌘+E or Ctrl+Shift+E. Neither the frame nor the graphic is resized when you center a graphic.

✦ **Fit Content Proportionally.** To resize a graphic to fit in the selected frame while maintaining the graphic's current proportions (preventing distortion), choose Object ➪ Fitting ➪ Fit Content Proportionally or press Option+Shift+⌘+E or Ctrl+Alt+Shift+E. If the frame is larger than the graphic, the graphic is enlarged; if the frame is smaller, the graphic is reduced. If the graphic and the frame have different proportions, a portion of the frame background appears above and below or to the left and right of the graphic. If you want, you can click and drag frame edges to make the frame shorter or narrower and eliminate any portions of the background that are visible.

✦ **Fill Frame Proportionally.** To resize a frame to fit the selected graphic, choose Object ➪ Fitting ➪ Fill Frame Proportionally or press Option+Shift+⌘+C or Ctrl+Alt+Shift+C. This guarantees that no space is left between the graphic and the frame. (The Fit Frame to Content option can result in such space at the bottom and/or right sides of a graphic.)

 New Feature The Fill Frame Proportionally option is new to InDesign CS2.

Note For frames with strokes, the Fitting options align the outer edge of a graphic with the center of the stroke. A stroke will obscure a strip along the graphic's edge that is half the width of the stroke. The wider the stroke, the more of the graphic that gets covered up.

Modifying Bitmap Graphics versus Vector Graphics

When it comes to working with bitmap and vector graphics in InDesign, there's not much difference. When you use the Place command, the import options for these two graphic formats are slightly different (see Chapter 22), but the transformation tools and the controls in the Control palette and Transform pane are available and work the same for all imported graphics, regardless of their file format.

When it comes to performing graphic modifications in InDesign, the only difference between bitmap graphics and vector-based graphics is that you can apply color and, optionally, tint to grayscale and black-and-white bitmaps. These options are not available for vector-based images and color bitmaps.

Applying color and tint to bitmap graphics

You can apply color and tint only to grayscale and black-and-white bitmap graphics. If you're unable to apply a color or tint to a bitmap graphic that you think should be modifiable, check the graphic's file type. To do so, open the Links pane (Window ➪ Links, or Shift+⌘+D or Ctrl+Shift+D), and then double-click the graphic's name or click once on its name and choose Show Link Information from the pane's pop-up menu. The graphic's color mode (CMYK, Grayscale, and so on) is displayed next to Color Space, and the graphic's file format is displayed next to File Type.

To apply color to a graphic:

1. **Click the Direct Selection tool (or press A if the Type tool isn't selected).**

2. **Click in the graphic's frame to select the graphic.**

3. **Make sure the Fill button is active in the Tools palette if you want to color the image's background.** Make sure the Stroke button is active if you want to color the frame's stroke (if any).

4. **If it's not displayed, show the Swatches pane by choosing Windows ➪ Swatches or pressing F5.**

5. **Click on a color in the scroll list.**

Cross-
Reference

See Chapter 8 for information about defining colors.

You can also apply color to a selected graphic's foreground by clicking and dragging a swatch from the Swatches pane and dropping it onto the graphic.

QuarkXPress
User

Although InDesign doesn't have Background, Frame, and Contents buttons in its Swatches pane to let you select where color is applied, as QuarkXPress does, InDesign lets you determine what component of the image gets the color based on how you apply the color, as described earlier. Furthermore, you can use the Control palette's Select Container and Select Contents buttons to choose whether the image background or contents, respectively, are colored when you click a swatch.

QuarkXPress User Note that InDesign does not have any options to change image contrast or line-screen element for grayscale and black-and-white images, as QuarkXPress does. You'll need to apply such effects in an image editor.

Applying a tint to a graphic

There are two ways to apply a *color tint* — that is, a shade or a percentage of the applied color — to a graphic. Either way, be sure the Fill button is active in the Tools palette.

The first way is to select a color swatch and type a tint value in the Tint field of the Swatches pane or choose a value from the Tint field's pop-up menu.

The second way takes more effort but lets you apply consistent tints to several graphics. You create a tint swatch in the Swatches pane that is then available to be applied like a color swatch. To create a tint swatch, click the base color in the Swatches pane and then choose New Tint Swatch from the Swatches pane's palette menu. Use the Tint controls in the New Swatch Tint dialog box to specify the percent of the color you want to use. After you create a tint, you apply it to a graphic following the same steps you would use if you were applying color.

Managing Links to Imported Graphics

As Chapter 22 explains, when you place a graphic into an InDesign document — either with the Place command (File ➪ Place, or ⌘+D or Ctrl+D) or by dragging and dropping a graphics file's icon directly into a document window — InDesign remembers the name and location of the original graphics file and uses this file when the document is printed.

If you always print your documents from your own computer, and your graphics never get modified, moved, renamed, or deleted, you won't have to worry much about managing the links between your InDesign documents and imported graphics files. But that scenario is the exception rather than the rule. Graphics files are often modified while the InDesign pages that contain them are under construction, and at many publishing sites, the computer used to create a document is seldom the computer from which it's printed.

Note If you import a graphics file that's 48K or smaller in size, the entire full-resolution image is automatically embedded in the InDesign document, while maintaining the link to the source file. The Links pane, explained later in this section, lets you manage links to imported graphics.

Tip If you'll be taking your documents to a service provider for output, be sure to include all imported graphics files. You can use InDesign's Preflight and Package features, which are covered in Chapter 29, to automatically collect graphics files in preparation for output.

The Links pane (Window ➪ Links, or Shift+⌘+D or Ctrl+Shift+D), shown in Figure 23-7, displays link-related information about all imported graphics files, and the pane's accompanying pop-up menu provides tools for managing links. The scroll list displays the name of each imported graphic. A Missing Link icon is displayed for graphics that have been moved, renamed, or deleted since they were imported into the document. A Modified Link icon is displayed for graphics that have been modified since being imported.

When you open a document that contains imported graphics files that have been modified, moved, renamed, or deleted since they were imported, the alert shown in Figure 23-8 appears. This alert tells you the number of files with *missing links* (that is, the original graphics file has been moved, renamed, or deleted) and with *modified links* (graphics files that have been opened and saved since they were imported). You don't have to update missing or modified links as soon as you open a document, but it's not a bad idea.

To fix missing or modified links, click Fix Links Automatically, which opens a Relink dialog box listing a missing link. Click Browse in the dialog box to find the missing file. As you relink each missing file, InDesign displays the next missing file until all are relinked. If you can't or don't want to relink a specific file, skip it by clicking Skip. When done, click OK.

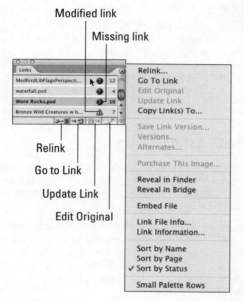

Modified link

Missing link

Relink

Go to Link

Update Link

Edit Original

Figure 23-7: The Links pane and its palette menu

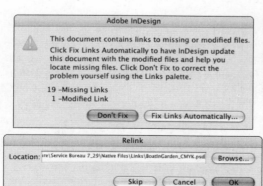

Figure 23-8: This alert appears when you open a document that contains imported graphics that have been modified, moved, renamed, or deleted. The Relink dialog box (bottom) appears if you click Fix Links Automatically.

If the status of a link to a particular graphics file changes while you're working on a document, a Missing Link or Modified Link icon appears in the Links pane. For example, if you import an illustration created with Illustrator or FreeHand into an InDesign document, then open, modify, and resave the illustration using its original program, the Links pane displays the Modified Link icon for that file.

Note Generally, you'll want to keep all links up to date. If you don't update the link for a modified graphic, it will still print correctly, but what you see on-screen may be quite different from what prints. Remember that when you import a graphics file, InDesign creates and saves a low-resolution screen preview for display. If the graphics file is then modified, InDesign continues to use the old screen preview for screen display until you update the link.

If you try to print a document that contains a missing graphics file, an alert appears letting you know that a graphic file is missing. At this point, you can click Cancel to abort the print job and then use the Links pane to update the link, or you can click OK to print anyway. If you print anyway, InDesign sends the low-resolution screen preview to the printer instead of sending the original graphics file.

Note If you import an EPS file that, in turn, contains OPI links to placed images in the file, the Links pane will display these links. You shouldn't change them. Doing so could cause printing problems.

The Links pane's palette menu has eight groups of commands that let you manage links, manage link versions in a Version Cue-enabled workflow, purchase a linked image, display the source graphic's location, embed the original graphics file of any imported graphic, display link information for individual graphics, control how filenames are displayed in the pane, and change the pane's view settings. If you want to update, relink, or view information about a specific file, click its name in the pane, and then choose a command from the palette menu or click a button at the bottom of the pane, all of which are explained in the following sections.

Cross-Reference For more on Version Cue–enabled workflow and version management, see Chapter 35.

Managing links and versions

The first eight commands in the Links pane's palette menu let you reestablish links to missing and modified graphics files, display an imported graphic in the document window, open the program used to create a graphics file, and work on copies and versions of the source graphics:

✦ **Relink.** This command, and the Relink button (the leftmost at the bottom of the pane), lets you reestablish a missing link or replace the original file you imported with a different file. When you choose Relink or click the button, the Relink dialog box appears and shows the original path name and filename. You can type a new path name and filename in the Location field, but it's easier to click Browse, which opens a standard Open a File dialog box. Use the controls to locate and select the original file or a different file, and then click OK. (You can also drag and drop a file icon from the Mac OS Finder or Windows Explorer directly into the Relink dialog box.) If you want to restore broken links to multiple files, highlight their filenames in the scroll list, and then choose Relink or click Update Link.

QuarkXPress User InDesign's relink function is not as smart as QuarkXPress's equivalent Picture Usage. If you have multiple broken links to the same file in an InDesign document, you must relink each one manually from the Links pane. (If the missing images are in the same folder, you can select all the images in the Links palette before clicking Relink, and then browse for the first missing image. InDesign *will* update all the selected missing images after you locate just that first one.) QuarkXPress will automatically fix all links to the same file as soon as you correct any link to it—there's no need to select the links to be fixed as in InDesign. That's another reason to use InDesign's automatic fix described earlier when you open a file with broken links.

✦ **Go To Link.** Choose this option, or click the Go to Link button (second from left) to display the highlighted graphics file in the document window. InDesign will, if necessary, navigate to the correct page and center the image in the document window. You can also display a particular graphic by double-clicking its name in the scroll list while pressing and holding Option or Alt.

✦ **Edit Original.** If you want to modify an imported graphic, choose Edit Original from the palette menu or click the Edit Original button (far right). InDesign will try to locate and open the program used to create the file. This may or may not be possible, depending on the original program, the file format, and the programs available on your computer.

✦ **Update Link.** Choose this option or click the Update Link button (third from the left) to update the link to a modified graphic. Highlight multiple filenames, and then choose Update Link or click the Update Link button to update all links at once.

To update multiple links at once, select all the links you want to modify in the Links palette (Shift+Click to select a range; ⌘+click or Ctrl+click to select noncontiguous files), and then choose Update Link from the palette menu.

When you update missing and modified graphics, any transformations—rotation, shear, scale, and so on—that you've applied to the graphics or their frames are maintained.

✦ **Copy Link To.** Choose this option to copy the source graphic to a new location and update the link so it refers to this new copy.

✦ **Save Link Version.** If you are working with Version Cue enabled and the source graphic is being edited, you can save a version of the graphic (with a new name and/or to a new location) and have the link changed to this new version of the graphic file by choosing Save Link Version.

✦ **Versions.** If you are working with Version Cue enabled, this option lets you choose from other versions of the source graphic.

✦ **Alternates.** If you are working with Version Cue enabled, this option lets you choose an alternate source graphic.

The Copy Link To, Versions, and Alternates menu options are new to InDesign CS2. (The version and alternates features of Version Cue are covered in more detail in Chapter 35.)

Purchasing imported graphics

The Links pane's Purchase This Image lets you buy images for which you have downloaded or otherwise acquired a trial version from the new Adobe Stock Photos service, which offers stock images from Comstock Images, DigitalVision, and Getty Images. Such trial images are typically low-resolution or have a watermark overlaying the image; when you buy usage rights to the image, you get the full version. You are free, of course, to purchase images from any provider of online or CD image libraries for your documents.

The Purchase This Image menu option is new to InDesign CS2.

Finding imported graphics

There are also two menu options to help you locate source files. The Reveal in Finder (Macintosh) and Reveal in Explorer (Windows) menu option opens a window displaying the contents of the folder that contains the source file, so you can perhaps move, copy, or rename it. Reveal in Bridge does the same thing, except that it opens the folder in the Adobe Bridge program that all Version Cue–enabled applications use as a central repository.

 The Reveal in Finder/Reveal in Explorer and Reveal in Bridge menu options are new to InDesign CS2.

Embedding imported graphics

The Links pane's Embed command lets you embed the complete file of any imported graphic. (Except for files that are 48K and smaller, you import only a low-resolution screen preview when you place a graphic.) If you want to ensure that the graphics file forever remains with a document, you can choose to embed it — however, embedding graphics produces larger document files, which means it will take you longer to open and save them.

To embed a graphic, click its name in the scroll list, and then choose Embed from the Links pane's palette menu. An alert appears and informs you about the increased document size that will result. Click Yes to embed the file.

 When you embed a file, the filename no longer appears in the Links pane, nor is an embedded file automatically updated if you modify the original. Generally, you should avoid embedding files, especially large ones, unless you're certain that they won't be modified.

Displaying link information

Choosing Link Information from the Links pane's palette menu displays the Link Information dialog box shown in Figure 23-9. This dialog box doesn't let you do much (the Previous and Next buttons let you display information about the previous and next files in the list, but that's about it), but it does display 11 sometimes-useful bits of information about the highlighted graphics file, including its name, status, creation date, file type, and location.

Sorting imported files in the Links pane

The next three commands in the Links pane's palette menu let you control how the files in the scroll list are arranged:

✦ **Sort by Status.** When this command is selected, files with missing links are listed first, followed by files that have been modified, and finally files whose status is OK.

✦ **Sort by Name.** Selecting this command lists all files in alphabetical order.

✦ **Sort by Page.** Selecting this command lists imported files on page 1 first, followed by imported files on page 2, and so on.

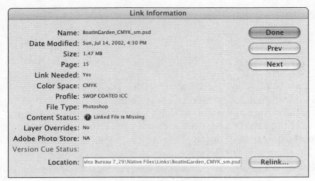

Figure 23-9: The Link Information dialog box

Tip   If you Option+double-click or Alt+double-click a graphic, InDesign opens the original in either the program that created it or, if you don't have that program, another program that can edit the graphic.

Changing the view

The Links pane's palette menu has an option called Small Palette Rows that lets you reduce the size of text in the pane and decrease the space between entries so you can see more entries at once. Of course, the reduced rows are also harder to read. To go back to the normal display size, simply select this option again.

Working with Imported Layers

As described in Chapter 22, InDesign lets you choose which layers in a Photoshop, Illustrator, or PDF file are imported into InDesign. Once such images are placed in InDesign, you can change which layers display, though you cannot change the order of layers.

Figure 23-10 shows the Layers pane of the Image Import Options dialog box that you can use when you import an image (File ➪ Place, or ⌘+D or Ctrl+D). At that time, you can select which layers of the imported graphic will display, or you can choose the layers once the image is in InDesign — either way, all layers are imported.

Once placed in your document, you can modify which layers display at any time. Select the object with the Selection or Direct Selection tool, and then choose Object ➪ Object Layer Options. You can also Control+click or right-click the graphic and choose Graphics ➪ Object Layer Options from the contextual menu. Either way, the Object Layer Options dialog box, shown in Figure 23-11, appears.

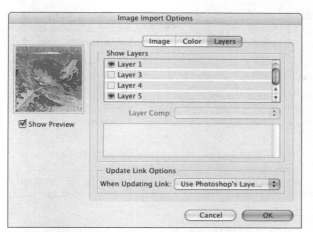

Figure 23-10: The Layers pane of the Image Import Options dialog box lets you choose which layers are visible after import.

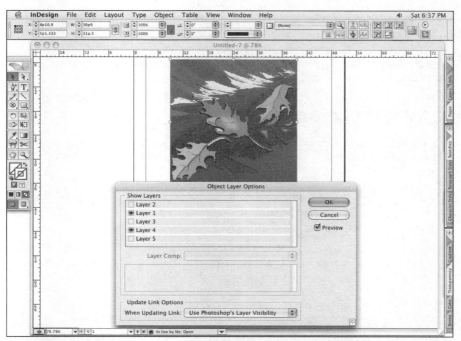

Figure 23-11: The Object Layer Options dialog box and an object with some layers made visible

In this dialog box, you click the check boxes to the left of the layer names that you want displayed — the eye icon indicates a visible layer. (Be sure to select the Preview option to see the effects of your layer-view changes.) Figures 23-11 through 23-13 show the same image with different layers made visible.

Your other options in the Object Layer Options dialog box are:

✦ **Layer Comp.** If your source file uses layer comps (a snapshot of the state of the Photoshop layers palette that essentially lets you group different layer visibility settings and save them for later application), you can choose those from the Layer Comps pop-up menu.

✦ **When Updating Link.** In the When Updating Link pop-up menu, you have two options that affect layer display if you update the link to the source graphic. Use Photoshop's Layer Visibility will use whatever layer views are set in Photoshop for the graphic, while Keep Layer Visibility Overrides will retain the InDesign layer settings when you relink the source graphic.

Note If the source graphic is an Illustrator or PDF file, the When Updating Link pop-up menu options replace *Photoshop* with *Illustrator* or *PDF*, as appropriate.

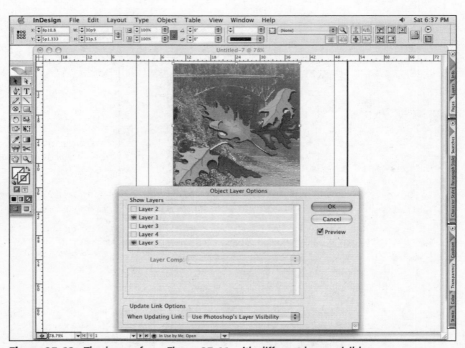

Figure 23-12: The image from Figure 23-11 with different layers visible

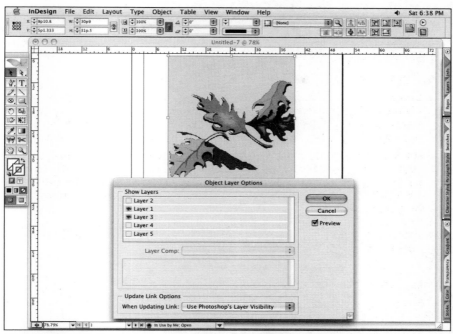

Figure 23-13: The image from Figure 23-11 with yet different layers visible

Summary

After you import a graphic into a document, you have many options for changing its appearance. You can crop it in a rectangular or free-form frame or manipulate it with three transformation tools — the Rotate, Scale, and Shear tools. The Transform pane and Control palette both let you perform the same modifications as the transformation tools and offer other choices for modifying graphics, including moving, scaling, skewing, and flipping. For grayscale and bitmap graphics only, you have the option to apply a color and a tint to the image.

The Fitting command (Object ➪ Fitting) provides four options for positioning and scaling a graphic relative to its frame, while the Links pane displays link-related information about imported graphics and lets you update links for graphics that are missing or have been modified. These commands are also available as buttons in the Control palette.

InDesign also lets you manage the visibility of layers in some imported graphics.

✦   ✦   ✦

Special Effects for Graphics

The options available through the transformation tools and the Control palette and Transform pane let you change the appearance of imported graphics in several ways, as covered in Chapter 23, but that's not all you can do with your graphics.

InDesign provides several other graphics-modification features that let you — among other things — wrap text around graphics, show and hide portions of graphics using clipping paths, place graphics within compound shapes, and place graphics within a text thread so that they move along with the surrounding text.

Wrapping Text around Graphics

In the days before personal computers and page-layout software, wrapping text around a graphic was a time-consuming and expensive task. Text wraps were rare, found only in the most expensively produced publications.

Not any more. Not only do all page-layout programs let you create text runarounds, most programs — including InDesign — provide several options for controlling how text relates to graphics and other objects that obstruct its flow.

When a graphics frame is positioned in front of a text frame, InDesign provides the following options. You can:

✦ Ignore the graphics frame and flow the text behind it

✦ Wrap the text around the frame's rectangular bounding box

✦ Wrap the text around the frame itself

✦ Jump the text around the frame (that is, jump the text from the top of the graphics frame to the bottom)

✦ Jump the text to the next column or page when the text reaches the top of graphics frame

✦ Specify the amount of distance between the text and the edge of the obstructing shape

✦ Flow text within the obstructing shape rather than outside it

Tip   InDesign lets you wrap text around frames on hidden layers — as well as remove text wrap for objects on hidden layers. This is handy when you want to hide images or other distracting items but preserve the layout.

Tip   If you want to wrap text around only a portion of a graphic — perhaps you need to isolate a face in a crowd — the best solution is to open the graphics file in its original program, create a clipping path around that portion, and then resave the file and import it and its clipping path into an InDesign document (clipping paths are explained in the next section). Another option is to use the Pen tool to create a free-form shape within InDesign and then use the shape as both a frame and a clipping path.

The Text Wrap pane

The controls in the Text Wrap pane (see Figure 24-1) let you specify how a selected object will affect the flow of text behind it. Remember, the flow of text around an obstructing object is determined by the text wrap settings applied to the obstructing object.

Tip   You can override the text-wrap settings of objects that are in front of a text frame by telling the text frame to ignore them. To do so, click a text frame, and then choose Object ➪ Text Frame Options or press ⌘+B or Ctrl+B. In the Text Frame Options dialog box's General pane, select Ignore Text Wrap, and then click OK. Text in the frame will now flow behind any obstructing items regardless of the text-wrap settings applied to them.

Note   The Text Wrap pane has only one option in its palette menu: Hide Options/Show Options, which hides or shows the Contour Options and Include Inside Edges sections of the pane. You can more easily hide/show these functions by double-clicking the double-arrow symbol to the right of the Text Wrap label in the pane's tab.

Here's how to apply text-wrap settings to a frame:

1. **If the Text Wrap pane is not displayed, choose Window ➪ Text Wrap or press Option+⌘+W or Ctrl+Alt+W.**

New Feature   InDesign CS2 moves the Text Wrap option back to the Window menu, where it had also resided in InDesign 2. (In InDesign CS, it was moved to be part of the Type & Tables submenu.)

2. **Click either of the selection tools.** If the Type tool isn't selected, you can press V to select the Selection tool or press A to select the Direct Selection tool.

3. **Click the graphics or text frame to which you want to apply text-wrap settings.** The frame can be anywhere, but you'll probably want to position it on top of a text frame that contains text so you can see the results of the settings you apply.

New Feature   In InDesign CS2, you can now set text wrap around inline frames, as well as for the newly supported anchored objects. Any wrap set for an inline frame affects text at the inline graphic's insertion point and below (not above the graphic). Chapter 11 covers inline frames and anchored objects in more detail.

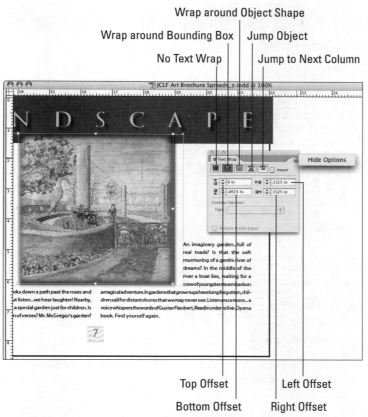

Wrap around Object Shape
Wrap around Bounding Box | Jump Object
No Text Wrap | Jump to Next Column

Top Offset | Left Offset
Bottom Offset | Right Offset

Figure 24-1: The Text Wrap pane and its palette menu. Also, note the preview frame for the wrap area outside the graphics frame's bounding box.

4. **Click one of the five text-wrap buttons at the top of the Text Wrap pane.** Figure 24-2 shows how each of these options affects a graphics frame, using layouts by designer Shawn Busse.

5. **If you want, adjust the space between the surrounding text and the obstructing shape by typing values in the Top Offset, Bottom Offset, Left Offset, and Right Offset fields.** (These fields are not available if you click the No Text Wrap button.) If the object is a rectangle, all four fields are available if you click the Wrap around Bounding Box button or Wrap around Object Shape. Only the Top Offset field is available if you click the Wrap around Object Shape button for an eliptical or free-form shape or if you click the Jump to Next Column button. The Top Offset and Bottom Offset fields are available if you click the Jump Object button.

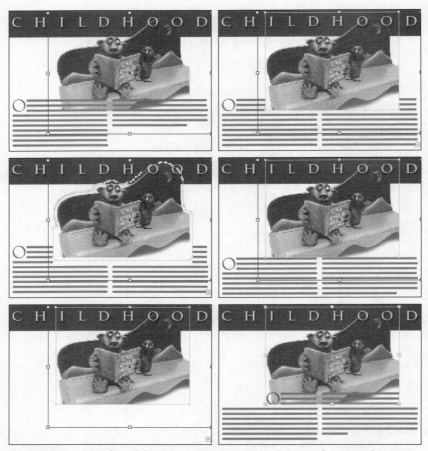

Figure 24-2: Examples of the five text-wrap options (left to right, top to bottom): No Text Wrap, Wrap around Bounding Box, Wrap around Object Shape, Jump Object, and Jump to Next Column, as well as the Invert option selected for the Wrap around Bounding Box option.

 Note A bounding box is the dimension of the graphic, whether or not it is wholly contained in its frame. You use a bounding box if you want to have the wrap follow the graphic's dimensions rather than that of the frame containing it.

6. **Select Invert if you want to flow the text in the obstructing shape.**

7. **If you choose the Wrap around Object Shape button, you can also select from the Contour Options's Type pop-up menu**. There are six options (Figure 24-3 shows examples of each):

    • Bounding Box is the same as clicking the Wrap around Bounding Box button.

    • Detect Edges tries to determine the graphic's outside boundary by ignoring white space — you would use this for bitmapped images that have a transparent or white background.

- Alpha Channel uses the image's alpha channel, if any, to create a wrapping boundary.

- Photoshop Path uses the image's clipping path, if any, to create a wrapping boundary.

- Graphic Frame uses the frame's boundary rather than the bounding box.

- Same as Clipping uses the clipping path for the graphic created in InDesign.

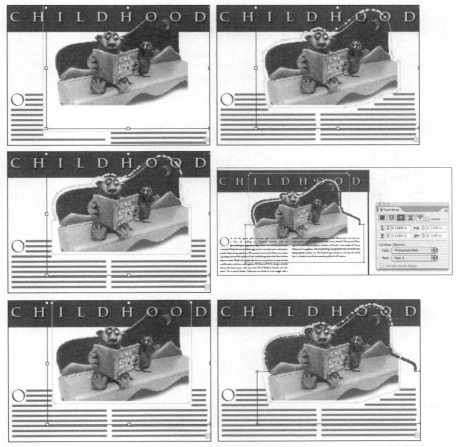

Figure 24-3: The six contour options for text-wrap options (left to right, top to bottom): Bounding Box, Detect Edges, Alpha Channel, Photoshop Path, Graphic Frame, and Same as Clipping

By selecting the Include Inside Edges option, InDesign enables text to appear inside any interior "holes" in the graphic. You'll rarely use this technique because in most cases it's hard for the reader to follow text that wraps around an image, flows inside it, and then continues to flow outside it. But if the interior is large enough and not too distant from the text that flows on the outside, this effect might be readable.

Tip   If you specify text-wrap settings when no objects are selected, the settings are automatically applied to all new objects.

Tip   To apply text-wrap settings to a master item on a document page, press and hold Shift+⌘ or Ctrl+Shift to select the item, and then use the controls in the Text Wrap pane as just described.

Setting text-wrap preferences

There are several global text-wrap options you should be aware of, all of which are accessed via the Composition pane of the Preferences dialog box (choose InDesign ➪ Preferences on the Mac or Edit ➪ Preferences in Windows, or press ⌘+K or Ctrl+K). Figure 24-4 shows the pane. Here are the options:

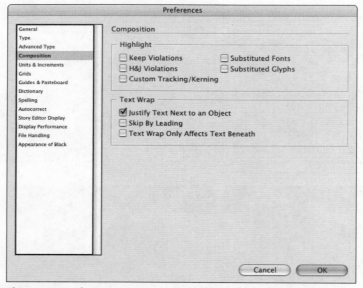

Figure 24-4: The text-wrap preferences in the Composition pane of the Preferences dialog box

✦ **Justify Text Next to an Object**. This option is useful when you have left-aligned text that wraps around an object at the right. (It also works if you have right-aligned text that wraps around an object at the left.) This can lead to an awkward wrap, however, because InDesign won't try to make the text align precisely to the wrap's contour (because the text isn't justified). Use this option to justify the text just around the wrap, and then continue using the text's specified non-justified alignment.

✦ **Skip by Leading.** This option makes text wrap below or above an object based on the text's leading, so there's at least a full line space between the text and the object, even if the object's text-wrap settings would allow less space.

Note

InDesign lets you select whether text wrap affects all text frames in a stack or just frames behind the text-wrap object.

✦ **Text Wrap Only Affects Text Beneath.** This option, if selected, prevents text frames placed on top of an object from wrapping, while those behind the graphic frame will still be allowed to wrap. This option allows some text to overlap the graphic and other text to wrap around it. Note this is a global setting, affecting all objects. To override wrap settings of individual text frames, choose Object ➪ Text Frame Options, or press ⌘+B or Ctrl+B, and select the Ignore Text Wrap option.

Changing the shape of a text wrap

When you specify text-wrap settings for an object, an editable shape is created. If the text-wrap shape is the same shape as the object, the text-wrap boundary is superimposed on the object. You can modify a text-wrap boundary by clicking it with the Direct Selection tool then moving, adding, deleting, and changing the direction of anchor points and by moving direction lines. Figure 24-5 shows a text wrap before and after being manually reshaped.

Cross-Reference

For more information about modifying freeform shapes, see Chapter 26.

Figure 24-5: The example on top shows a text wrap created by using the graphic's built-in alpha channel (Wrap around Object Shape). The text wrap was modified — by dragging anchor points — to create the variation on the bottom.

Working with Clipping Paths

Some graphics file formats — including TIFF, JPEG, Photoshop EPS, and Photoshop-native (PSD) files — let you embed a clipping path in the file. A clipping path is used to mask certain parts of a graphic and reveal other parts. For example, if you want to create a silhouette around a single person in a crowd of people, open the file in an image-editing program such as Photoshop, and then create and save a clipping path that isolates the shape of the person. (You can also erase everything except the person you want to silhouette; not only can this be time-consuming, but if you want to reveal other parts of the graphic later, you're out of luck.)

If you want to use a clipping path to mask parts of a graphic, InDesign offers three options. You can:

✦ Use a graphics file's built-in clipping path. (Be sure to select the Import Options in the Place dialog box when you import the image and select the Apply Photoshop Clipping Path option as described in Chapter 22.)

✦ Create a free-form shape that will act as your mask in InDesign and then place a graphic in the shape.

✦ Create a clipping path in InDesign by choosing Object ⇨ Clipping Path or pressing Option+Shift+⌘+K or Ctrl+Alt+Shift+K.

Regardless of the method you use to clip an imported graphic, you can modify a clipping path by moving, adding, deleting, and changing the direction of anchor points and by moving direction lines.

Creating Clipping Paths in Photoshop

Creating a clipping path in Photoshop is simple, once you get the hang of the process. A path is essentially a selection, which you can create with any of the Photoshop selection tools, including tracing your own selection to hand-drawing a path. Once you make the selection, here's how you make a path:

1. **Open the Paths pane by choosing Window ⇨ Paths.**

2. **Using the pane's palette menu, choose Make Work Path.** You'll be asked to choose a Tolerance setting in pixels — the smaller the number, the finer the path's shape.

3. **Click OK to accept your setting.** A work path appears in the Paths pane, showing in white the area contained by the path.

4. **Convert the work path into a named path by double-clicking the work path in the pane or by choosing Save Path in the palette menu.**

5. **Give the path a name, and then click OK.**

6. **Choose Clipping Path from the palette menu.** You'll be asked to choose which path to use as a clipping path (you can have multiple clipping paths in a Photoshop file), and then be asked to choose a Flatness setting. Like the earlier Tolerance setting, the smaller the number of pixels, the finer the path's contours.

7. **Click OK.**

That's it! The tricky part is creating the selection area to begin with.

See Chapter 24 for more information about modifying free-form shapes. See the *Photoshop Bible* series (Wiley Publishing) for more on creating clipping paths in Photoshop.

Using a free-form shape to clip a graphic

If you want to mask a portion of a graphic that doesn't include a built-in clipping path, it's no problem. The easiest way is to simply edit the text-wrap boundary. To do so, set the text wrap to Wrap around Object Shape, and then select the graphic with the Direct Selection tool. The text-wrap boundary appears as a blue line—you can make it easier to select by setting offsets in the Text Wrap pane, which moves the boundary away from the frame edge (see Figure 24-6). Now use InDesign's free-form editing tools, as covered in Chapter 26, to edit the text-wrap boundary.

Figure 24-6: To create a custom wrap, just edit the text-wrap boundary after selecting Wrap around Object Shape as if it were any other path. The boundary is the blue path that appears outside the frame; you can more easily see and work with the wrap boundary if you type offset amounts in the Text Wrap pane.

There are two other methods you can use as well:

✦ You can use the Pen tool to create the shape, and then use the Place command (File ⇨ Place, or ⌘+D or Ctrl+D) to place a graphic in the shape.

✦ You can import the graphic into a rectangular frame (by using the Place command with no object selected), use the Pen tool to create a free-form shape that surrounds the portion of the image you want to show, and then copy and paste the graphic into the free-form shape. In this case, you must use the Paste Into command (Edit ⇨ Paste Into, or Option+⌘+V or Ctrl+Alt+V) to place the copied graphic in the selected free-form shape. When you create the free-form shape, make sure that the default color for the Pen tool is set to None so that the shape you create is transparent. Otherwise, the colored area in the shape will obscure the graphic behind it.

You're more likely to use the second method than the first because it's difficult to mask a portion of a graphic without seeing it. Figure 24-5 shows a graphic in a rectangular frame next to a copy of the same graphic in a freeform shape.

The Pen tool lets you create one shape at a time. The Compound Paths command lets you combine multiple shapes to create more complex objects. For example, you can place a small circle on top of a larger circle, and then use the Compound Paths command to create a doughnut-shaped object. Figure 24-9, later in this chapter, shows a graphic in a compound path. (See Chapter 27 for more information about creating complex shapes with the Compound Paths command.)

Using InDesign's Clipping Path command

If you import a graphic that doesn't have a clipping path, you can use the Clipping Path command (Object ➪ Clipping Path, or Option+Shift+⌘+K or Ctrl+Alt+Shift+K) to generate one automatically in InDesign. The clipping paths that InDesign generates are based on a graphic's value. For this reason, the Clipping Path command works very well for images that have a white background but no clipping path. It's less useful for graphics whose backgrounds have not been erased and for graphics that contain a broad range of intermingling values.

Tip   If you use the Clipping Path command to generate a clipping path for a graphic that has a built-in clipping path, the one that InDesign generates replaces the built-in path.

To create a clipping path using the Clipping Path command:

1. **Select either the Selection tool or the Direct Selection tool, and then click the graphic to which you want to add a clipping path.** If the Type tool isn't selected, you can press V to select the Selection tool or press A to select the Direct Selection tool.

2. **Choose Object ➪ Clipping Path, or press Option+Shift+⌘+K or Ctrl+Alt+Shift+K to display the Clipping Path dialog box, shown in Figure 24-7.**

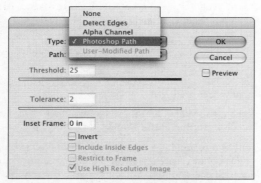

Figure 24-7: The Clipping Path dialog box

3. **To have InDesign detect the likely boundary of the image, as opposed to a white or other light background, choose Detect Edges from the Type pop-up menu.** You can use the other options to select Alpha Channel or Photoshop Path as the clipping path for graphics that have one or more of these. InDesign can only use one alpha channel or Photoshop path as the clipping path, so use the Path pop-up menu to choose the one you want.

4. **Type a value in the Threshold field or click and drag the field's slider to specify the value below which pixels will be placed outside the clipping path shape (that is, pixels that will become transparent).** Pixels darker than the Threshold value remain visible and thus are inside the clipping path shape. The lowest possible Threshold value (0) makes only white pixels transparent. As the value gets higher, less of the graphic remains visible. The lightest areas are removed first, then midtones, and so on. (Select the Preview option to see the results of your changes without closing the dialog box.)

5. **Type a value in the Tolerance field.** This value determines how closely InDesign looks at variations in adjacent pixels when building a clipping path. Higher values produce a

simpler, smoother path than lower values. Lower values create a more complicated, more exact path with more anchor points.

6. **If you want to enlarge or reduce the size of the clipping path produced by the Threshold and Tolerance values, type a value in the Inset Frame field.** Negative values enlarge the path; positive values shrink it. (The Inset Frame value is also applied to the path's bounding box.)

7. **Select the Invert option to switch the transparent and visible areas of the clipping path produced by the Threshold and Tolerance values.**

8. **If you want to include light areas in the perimeter shape InDesign generates based on the Threshold and Tolerance values, select the Include Inside Edges option.** For example, if you have a graphic of a doughnut and you want to make the hole transparent (as well as the area around the outside of the doughnut), click Include Inside Edges. If you don't click Include Inside Edges, InDesign builds a single shape (in the case of a doughnut, just the outside circle). The portion of the graphic in the shape remains visible; the rest of the graphic becomes transparent.

9. **Select the Restrict to Frame option if you want InDesign to generate a clipping path from just the portion of the graphic visible in the graphic frame, as opposed to the entire graphic (such as if you cropped the graphic).**

10. **Select the Use High Resolution Image option if you want InDesign to use the high-resolution information in the original file instead of using the low-resolution proxy image.** Even though using the high-resolution image takes longer, the resulting clipping path is more precise than it would be if you didn't check Use High Resolution Image.

11. **When you've finished specifying clipping path settings, click OK to close the dialog box and apply the settings to the selected graphic.**

Figure 24-8 shows a graphic before and after a clipping path was applied to it using the Clipping Path command.

Figure 24-8: At left is a graphic of coastal France with a graphic of a glider superimposed. At right is the same set of graphics, but with a clipping path applied to the glider so the outside area is masked out, making it transparent.

You can remove a clipping path by choosing None as the Type in the Clipping Path dialog box. You can also select a different path — Detect Edges, Alpha Channel, Photoshop Path, or User-Modified Path — than was selected previously if you decide to change the current clipping path.

New Feature You can convert a clipping path to a frame by choosing Convert Clipping Path to Frame for a selected object using the contextual menu (right-click or Control+click the object).

Trying Other Special Effects

When you combine your imagination with InDesign's graphic-modification, page-layout, and typographic features, the possibilities for manipulating imported graphics become endless. Here are a few of my favorite tricks for adding pizzazz to your graphics.

Using transparency, drop shadows, and feathering

One of InDesign's most sophisticated tools is its transparency options, which let you make items partially transparent. You apply transparency with the Transparency pane (Window ⇨ Transparency, or Shift+F10). Figure 24-9 shows the pane as well as a brochure that uses transparency to create a vellum effect on a stripe that contains text that overprints a background photo. The artist, Shawn Busse, chose a transparency setting of 74 percent for the white frame's Opacity, as well as the Screen setting for transparency type.

Figure 24-9: The Transparency pane, as well as an example of a transparent object overprinting the photograph

InDesign has two other special effects related to transparency, because they also involve lighting effects. One is customized drop shadows (Object ⇨ Drop Shadow, or Option+⌘+M or Ctrl+Alt+M), which lets you cast a shadow behind an object so that it appears to float. The other is feathering (Object ⇨ Feather), which lets you blur an object's edges.

Cross-Reference Chapter 10 covers transparency, drop shadows, and feathering in more detail.

Using text characters as graphics frames

InDesign's Pen tool lets you create any kind of shape for use as a graphics frame, but if you want to place a graphic in the shape of a text character or in several characters, there's a much easier way than drawing the characters yourself: You can use the Create Outlines command (Type ➪ Create Outlines, or Shift+⌘+O or Ctrl+Shift+O) to convert highlighted text into editable outlines, and then place a graphic in the character shapes. Here's how:

1. **Format and then highlight the text you want to use as a graphics frame.** You can use a single character or a range of text.

2. **Choose Type ➪ Create Outlines or press Shift+⌘+O or Ctrl+Shift+O.**

3. **Choose either of the selection tools, and then click on the highlighted text.**

4. **Choose File ➪ Place, or press ⌘+D or Ctrl+D, and then locate and select the graphics file you want to import.** You can also copy and paste a graphic you've already imported. In this case, when you're ready to paste the copied graphic, make sure you select the outlines and then choose Edit ➪ Paste Into, or press Option+⌘+V or Ctrl+Alt+V.

5. **Click OK or double-click the filename to place the graphic into the selected outlines.**

6. **Adjust the size and position of the imported graphic so that it's displayed the way you want it in the character shapes.**

You can modify character outlines created with the Create Outlines command the same as you modify any shape — by adding a stroke and/or fill, by using the transformation tools or Transform pane to apply rotation, scale, or shear, and so on.

When you convert text to outlines using the Create Outlines command, the outlines replace the highlighted text and are embedded in the text. One handy aspect of the Create Outlines command is that the text remains editable. If you want to remove the outlines from the text and place them elsewhere, select the outlines with either of the selection tools, copy them (Edit ➪ Copy, or ⌘+C or Ctrl+C), and then click on an empty portion of the page and choose Edit ➪ Paste or press ⌘+V or Ctrl+V. Figure 24-10 shows a graphic that's been placed in the outline of a converted word. (You can place or copy graphics into such frames, just as you can with any frame.)

Figure 24-10: Converting the word *France* into an outline with the Create Outlines command and then using the Paste Into command to copy a graphics file into the shape created this graphic-in-text effect.

Using compound shapes as graphics frames

The Object ➪ Compound Paths command lets you combine several paths into a single object. Once you create a multishape object, you can use the Place command or the Copy and Paste Into commands to put a graphic in. Figure 24-11 shows an example of a compound path.

Figure 24-11: Designer John Cruise created the picture with the hole in it (at right) by drawing a circular path (center) in front of a clone of the original picture frame (left), and then creating a compound path from the picture frame and the circular path. The background shape shows within the transparent circle.

Cross-Reference For more information about working with compound paths and reversing the direction of paths, see Chapter 26.

Applying corner effects

The Corner Effects command (Object ⇨ Corner Effects) lets you apply any of several graphic embellishments to a frame's corners. For example, you can use a corner effect to add pizzazz to the border of a coupon or a certificate. Generally, corner effects work best with rectangular shapes.

To apply a corner effect to a path:

1. **Use either of the selection tools to select the frame to which you want to apply corner effects.**

2. **Choose Object ⇨ Corner Effects.** The Corner Effects dialog box (see Figure 24-12) appears.

3. **Choose a Corner Effect from the Effect pop-up menu.** If you want to see the effect as you create it, select Preview option and, if necessary, move the dialog box out of the way so you can see the selected path.

4. **In the Size field, type the distance away from the corner point that the effect will extend.**

5. **After you finish specifying the appearance of the corner effect, click OK to close the dialog box.**

InDesign doesn't let you modify the built-in corner effects or add your own to the list of choices. Nor can you use the Direct Selection tool to modify the corner of a path to which a corner effect has been applied (anchor points are not displayed for the additional segments that are added when a corner effect is applied to a corner point). The only control you have over a corner effect is the value you specify in the Radius field of the Corner Effects dialog box.

Tip If you place an inline frame in text to which automatic leading has been applied, the resulting line spacing can be inconsistent. To fix this problem, you can resize the inline frame.

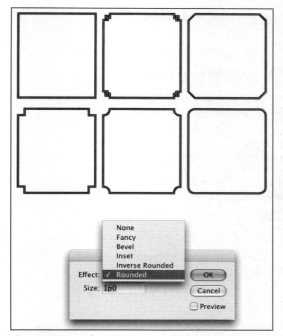

Figure 24-12: The Effect menu in the Corner Effects dialog box displays the names of five built-in corner effects. A standard corner plus the five effects are shown above the dialog box.

Creating inline frames

In most cases, you place a graphic into a graphics frame and then, if necessary, manually move the frame by clicking and dragging it with the Selection tool or by changing the frame's X or Y values in the Transform pane or Control palette. If you want to place a graphic relative to text in such a way that the graphic moves—and thus remains close to its associated text—when editing causes the text to reflow, you can create an inline frame out of the graphics frame. Inline frames are particularly useful for publications such as catalogs that contain lengthy text threads that, in turn, contain graphics that must flow with the text. An inline frame behaves much like a single character, yet it retains all the attributes of a frame, which means you can add a stroke or fill, transform it with the transformation tools, the Transform pane, or Control palette, and so on.

If you want to create an inline frame from an object you've already created, all you have to do is copy or cut the object, and then paste it into text as you would a piece of highlighted text.

In addition to using the Paste command to create an inline frame from an existing object, you can use the Place command to create an inline graphic from an external graphics file. The key is to use the Type tool to select an insertion point in your text before placing the graphic (using File ➪ Place, or ⌘+D or Ctrl+D); the graphic is placed in the text in an inline frame.

For more information about working with inline frames, see Chapter 11.

Slicing a graphic with the Scissors tool

The Scissors tool is the InDesign equivalent of a utility knife. It lets you slice objects into two parts. Figure 24-13 shows a graphic that's been cut into halves with the Scissors tool. To slice a graphic:

Figure 24-13: The Scissors tool was used to create the split image (right) from a clone of the original image (left).

1. **Select the Scissors tool.** If the Type tool isn't selected, you can press C to select the Scissors tool.

2. **Position the cross-hair pointer anywhere over a graphics frame, and then click.**

3. **Move the pointer to a different position along the frame edge, and then click again.**

4. **After you've clicked twice on the frame edge, you can switch to either of the selection tools and then click and drag either of the two graphic pieces that your scissors cut created.**

If you use the Scissors tool to split a frame to which a stroke has been applied, the resulting edges will not include the stroke.

Summary

After you import a graphic into an InDesign document, you can use the Text Wrap pane to control how text flows when the graphic is in front of a text frame. You can also use this to have one text frame wrap around another, although that is not common.

To mask out certain areas of a graphic, you can use a graphic's built-in clipping path (if it has one), edit the text-wrap boundary, place the graphic in a free-form shape created with the Pen tool, or use the Clipping Path command to have InDesign build a clipping path.

If you want to get even trickier with your imported graphics, you can place them in complex shapes created with the Compound Path command, apply corner effects to their frames, paste them into a text thread so that they move along with the surrounding text, or slice them into two pieces with the Scissors tool.

✦   ✦   ✦

Drawing Free-Form Shapes and Curved Paths

✦ ✦ ✦ ✦

In This Chapter

Understanding path basics

Drawing zigzag and wavy lines

Drawing closed shapes

Drawing free-form shapes

✦ ✦ ✦ ✦

InDesign's basic drawing tools let you create basic shapes, such as straight lines, rectangles and squares, circles and ellipses, and equilateral polygons. But what about when you need to create shapes that aren't so basic? An amoeba, perhaps, or a cursive version of your first name? That's where InDesign's Pen tool comes in. You can use the Pen tool to create any kind of line or closed shape. And anything you create with the Pen tool can be used as an independent graphic element or as a frame for text or a picture.

If you've ever used an illustration program such as Illustrator, FreeHand, or CorelDraw, or a page-layout program such as PageMaker or QuarkXPress, you may already be familiar with Bézier drawing tools. (Bézier tools are named after Pierre Bézier, a French engineer and mathematician, who developed a method of representing curved shapes on a computer in the 1970s.) If you aren't familiar with Bézier tools, you should know in advance that getting the hang of using them takes a little time and patience. Even if you're a virtuoso when drawing with a piece of charcoal or a Number 2 pencil, you'll need to practice with the Pen tool for awhile before your drawing skills kick in. The good news is that, once you get comfortable using the Pen tool, you can draw any shape you can imagine. (Of course, if you can't draw very well in the first place, using the Pen tool won't magically transform you into a master illustrator!) If this is new terrain for you, start simply and proceed slowly.

Tip　　If you intend to use InDesign extensively as a drawing tool, you might want to purchase a drawing tablet, which can make working with the Pen tool a bit easier than using a mouse or trackball. On both Macs and PCs, you can usually hook up multiple input devices, so you can switch from tablet to mouse or trackball and back as needed.

Finding Out All about Paths

Every object you create with InDesign's object-creation tools is a path. That includes:

✦ Straight lines created with the Line tool

✦ Lines and shapes created with the Pen tool or the Pencil tool

✦ Basic shapes created with the Ellipse, Rectangle, and Polygon tools

✦ Basic frames created with the Ellipse Frame, Rectangle Frame, and Polygon Frame tools

All of InDesign's object-manipulation features are available for all paths. This includes the transformation tools, the Control palette and the Transform pane, the Stroke and Color panes, and the option to place a text file or graphics file either on or within the path. (You can't place text within a straight line because there is not even a partial enclosure in which to create the bounds of a text frame.)

The properties of a path

Regardless of the tool you use to create a path, you can change its appearance by modifying any of four properties that all paths share: closure, stroke, fill, and contents.

Closure

A path is either *open* or *closed*. Straight lines created with the Line tool and curved and zigzag lines created with the Pen tool are examples of open paths. Basic shapes created with the Ellipse, Rectangle, and Polygon tools and free-form shapes created with the Pen and Pencil tools are examples of closed shapes. A closed free-form shape is an uninterrupted path with no endpoints. Figure 25-1 shows the difference between open and closed paths.

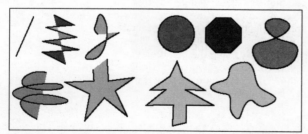

Figure 25-1: The five paths on the left are open; the five on the right are closed. A stroke and fill have been added to show how they affect open and closed paths.

Tip   You can use the Scissors tool to convert a closed path into two (or more) open paths, and you can use the Pen tool to create a closed path from an open path.

Cross-Reference   See Chapter 26 for more information about creating a closed path from an open path and vice versa.

Stroke

If you want to make a path visible, you can apply a *stroke* to it. (An unselected, unstroked path is not visible.) When you stroke a path, you can specify the stroke's width, color, tint, and style. Figure 25-2 shows a path before and after a stroke was added.

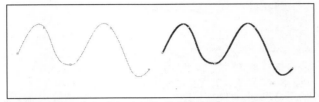

Figure 25-2: The original path (left) is selected. At right, a 2-point stroke was added to a clone of the original path.

Fill

A color, color tint, or gradient applied to the background of an open path or a closed path is called a *fill*. Figure 25-3 shows some examples of fills.

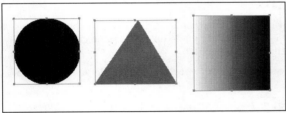

Figure 25-3: From left to right: a color fill (black), a color tint fill (50 percent black), and a gradient fill. The paths are selected and displayed in their bounding boxes.

Contents

You can place a text file or a graphics file in any path (with the exception of a straight line). When a path is used to hold text or a picture, the path functions as a *frame*. Although InDesign can place text in an open path, placing text and pictures in closed paths is far more common than placing them in open paths. Figure 25-4 shows several examples of pictures imported into paths.

QuarkXPress User

For QuarkXPress users, the idea of placing text and pictures in lines (that is, in open paths) may seem strange at first. (In QuarkXPress, lines cannot contain text or pictures, although line-like text paths can contain text.)

Figure 25-4: Top row: The same picture was imported into three different paths. (A stroke has been added to the paths to make them more visible.) Bottom row: Text has been placed in clones of the paths on the top row.

The anatomy of a path

No matter how simple (a short, straight line) or complicated (a free-form shape with several straight and curved edges) a path is, all paths are made up of the same components. Figures 25-5 through 25-7 show the parts that make up a path:

✦ A path contains one or more straight or curved *segments*, as shown in Figure 25-5.

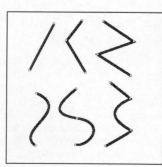

Figure 25-5: From left to right, each path contains one more segment than the previous path. (The top row shows straight segments and the bottom row shows curved segments.) The two rightmost paths each contain three segments.

✦ An anchor point is located at each end of every segment. The anchor points at the ends of a closed path are called *endpoints*. When you create a path of any kind, anchor points are automatically placed at the end of each segment. After you create a path, you can move, add, delete, and change the direction of corner points.

See Chapter 26 for more information about modifying paths.

Drawing Tools

InDesign uses the same drawing tools as Adobe Illustrator and Adobe Photoshop, so if you're familiar with those, you'll have no trouble using InDesign's tools. If not, it might help to get a refresher on the tools:

✦ **Pen tool:** This draws both segments and Bézier curves. It has several associated tools to add, delete, and convert corner points, which are the handles that you use to change direction and curvature of a curve or line segment.

✦ **Pencil tool:** This is a free-form drawing tool that simply draws out your mouse motions. The result is a Bézier curve. A Pencil tool is great if you have a steady, accurate drawing hand; the Pen tool is better if you want to control each segment and curve as you create it.

✦ **Shape tools:** The shape tools create closed objects that aren't intended to hold text or graphics—they're basically shapes you can color and/or stroke. There is a Rectangle, Polygon, and Ellipse version, as described in Chapter 10.

✦ **Frame tools:** The frame tools are the same as the shape tools, except they're meant to create shapes that will contain text or graphics, though they can also be empty.

✦ **Type and Type Path tools:** The Type and Type on a Path tools let you add text in an object and on an object's stroke, respectively. You cannot add text into a straight line, but you can add text to an open shape, as well as closed shapes and frames (You can edit the visual appearance, such as baseline alignment and dimensionality, of text following a line or frame by using the options in the Type on a Path Options dialog box, accessed by choosing Type ➪ Type on a Path ➪ Options.)

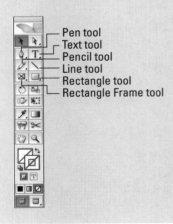

— Pen tool
— Text tool
— Pencil tool
— Line tool
— Rectangle tool
— Rectangle Frame tool

✦ There are two kinds of anchor points: *smooth points* and *corner points*. A smooth point connects two adjoining curved segments in a continuous, flowing curve. At a corner point, adjoining segments — straight or curved — meet at an angle. The corners of a rectangular path are the most common corner points. Figure 25-6 shows some examples of smooth and corner points.

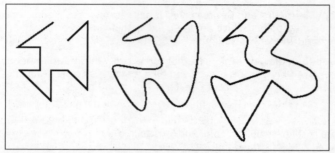

Figure 25-6: The path on the left has only corner anchor points; the path in the center has only smooth anchor points; and the path on the right has both kinds of anchor points.

✦ A *direction line* runs through each anchor point and has a handle at both ends. You can control the curve that passes through an anchor point by dragging a direction line's handles. Figure 25-7 shows how you can change the shape of a path by dragging a direction line handle.

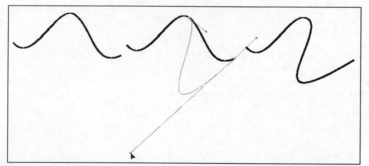

Figure 25-7: Cloning the original path on the left and then dragging the direction handle of the right endpoint created the path on the right.

Note   Anchor points and direction lines do not print.

Reading about riding a bike is one thing; riding a bike is another. If you've read Chapter 9, you already know how to ride with training wheels — you can create basic shapes with the basic object-creation tools. Now that you know more about what paths are made of, you're ready to tackle more-complex shapes. You're ready to wield the Pen tool.

Drawing Lines with the Pen Tool

The Pen tool is very versatile. With it you can create lines (open paths) and shapes (closed paths).

Straight and zigzag lines

The simplest kind of path is a straight line (that is, an open path) with a single segment, which you can create with either the Line tool or the Pen tool. But the Pen is much mightier than the Line because it lets you draw zigzag lines with multiple straight segments, curvy lines, and lines that contain straight and curved segments. You can't draw those kinds of shapes with the Line tool, or any of the other object-creation tools, for that matter.

Cross-
Reference

Chapter 9 covers the Line tool.

To draw lines with straight segments:

1. **Select the Pen tool or press P if the Type tool isn't selected.**

2. **Move the Pen pointer to where you want to place one of your line's endpoints, and then click and release the mouse button (make sure you don't drag before you release the mouse button).** When you click and release the mouse button while using the Pen tool, you create a corner point. A small, filled-in square indicates the anchor point, which is also an endpoint of the open shape you're creating.

3. **Move the Pen pointer to where you want to place the next anchor point, and then click and release the mouse button.** When you create the second point, a straight line connects it with the first point, the first anchor point changes to a hollow square, and the second anchor point is filled in. (If you want to create a line with a single segment, you can stop drawing at this point by choosing another tool.)

4. **For each additional anchor point, move the Pen pointer, and then click and release the mouse button.** If you hold down the Shift key as you click, the angles you create are limited to multiples of 45 degrees. To reposition an anchor point after you click the mouse button but before you release it, hold down the spacebar and drag.

Caution

If you drag before you press the spacebar, you'll create a smooth point and curved segments.

5. **To complete the path, press the ⌘ key or the Ctrl key and click on an empty portion of the page or choose another tool.** If you click on the page, the Pen tool remains selected and you can continue creating additional paths. Figure 25-8 shows a path in various stages of being drawn.

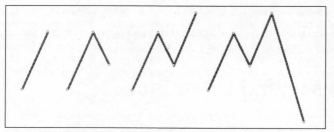

Figure 25-8: As each anchor point was created (from left to right), a new, straight segment was added to the path. The finished open path is a zigzag line that contains four straight segments produced by clicking and releasing the mouse a total of five times.

You can also complete the path by clicking on the first point you created, but if you do, you'll create a closed path (closed paths are covered in the next section).

Tip

As you create a path, you can move any anchor point, direction line handle, or the entire path by pressing the ⌘ or Ctrl key, and then clicking and dragging whatever element you want to move.

Curved lines

If all you ever need to create are zigzag lines with corner points and straight segments, the click-and-release method in the preceding section is all you need to know. But if you want to create curvy lines, you need to take the next step up the Bézier ladder and learn to add smooth points. Creating smooth points and curved segments is much like creating corner points and straight segments — with a twist. There are two ways of connecting curved segments when drawing a path: with smooth points and with corner points. Both methods are explained in the steps that follow.

Curved segments connected by smooth points

If you want to draw a continuously curvy path that contains no corner points and no straight segments, you should create only smooth points as you draw. Here's how:

1. **Select the Pen tool or press P if the Type tool isn't selected.**

2. **Move the Pen pointer to where you want to place one of your line's endpoints, and then click and hold down the mouse button.** The arrowhead pointer is displayed.

3. **Drag the mouse in the direction of the next point you intend to create.** (Adobe suggests dragging about one-third of the way to the next point). As you drag, the anchor point, its direction line, and the direction line's two handles are displayed, as shown in Figure 25-9. If you hold down the Shift key as you drag, the angle of the direction line is limited to increments of 45 degrees.

Figure 25-9: To create a smooth point when beginning a path, click and hold the mouse and drag in the direction of the next point. Here you see the direction line of a smooth endpoint created by clicking and dragging in the direction of the next anchor point.

4. **Release the mouse button.**

5. **Move the Pen pointer where you want to establish the next anchor point, which ends the first segment, and then drag the mouse.** If you drag in approximately the same direction as the direction line of the previous point, you'll create an S-shaped curve; if you drag in the opposite direction, you'll create a C-shaped curve. Figure 25-10 shows both kinds of curves.

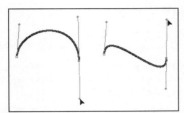

Figure 25-10: A C-shaped curved segment (left); an S-shaped curved segment (right)

6. **When the curve between the two anchor points looks how you want it to look, release the mouse button.**

7. **Continue moving the Pen pointer, clicking and dragging, and then releasing the mouse button to establish additional smooth points and curved segments.**

8. **To complete the path, hold down the ⌘ key or the Ctrl key and click on an empty portion of the page or choose another tool.** If you click on the page, the Pen tool remains selected and you can continue creating additional paths.

You can also complete the path by clicking on the first point you created, but if you do, you'll create a closed path (closed paths are covered in the next section). Figure 25-11 shows a finished line that contains several curved segments.

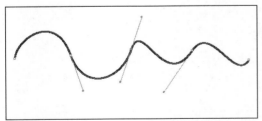

Figure 25-11: This line contains five anchor points — all smooth points — and four curved segments. The two segments on the left are both C-shaped curves; the two on the right are S-shaped.

Tip

The two segments that form a smooth point's direction line work together as a single, straight line. When you move a handle, the line acts like a teeter-totter; the opposite handle moves in the opposite direction. If you shorten one of the segments, the length of the other segment doesn't change. The angle and length of direction lines determine the shape of the segments with which they're associated.

Curved segments connected by corner points

Sometimes you may need to create a line with curvy segments that don't adjoin smoothly. Figure 25-12 shows an example of a line that's made up of several C-shaped curves that are connected with corner points. When adjoining segments — curved or straight — meet at a corner point, the transition is abrupt rather than smooth, as it is at a smooth point. To create this kind of shape, you need to be able to connect curved segments using corner points instead of smooth points. Here's how:

1. **Select the Pen tool or press P if the Type tool isn't selected.**

2. **Move the Pen pointer to where you want to place one of your line's endpoints, and then click and hold down the mouse button.** The arrowhead pointer is displayed.

3. **Drag the mouse in the direction of the next point you intend to create.** As you drag, the anchor point, its direction line, and the direction line's two handles are displayed. If you hold down the Shift key as you drag, the angle of the direction line is limited to increments of 45 degrees.

4. **Move the Pen pointer to where you want to establish the next anchor point, which ends the first segment, and then press Option or Alt and click and drag the mouse.** As you drag, the anchor point's handle moves and the direction line changes from a straight line to two independent segments. The angle of the direction line segment that you create when you drag the handle determines the slope of the next segment.

5. **Release the mouse button.**

6. **Continue moving the Pen pointer and repeat Step 4 and Step 5 to create additional segments joined by corner points.**

7. **To complete the path, hold down the ⌘ key or the Ctrl key and click on an empty portion of the page or choose another tool.** If you click on the page, the Pen tool remains selected and you can continue creating additional paths.

Figure 25-12 shows a line with several curved segments joined by corner points.

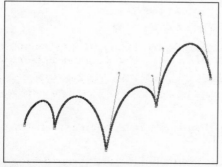

Figure 25-12: Here, three corner points join four curved segments. The direction handles of the two rightmost segments are visible. The direction handles of a corner point are joined like a hinge; moving one handle doesn't affect the other handle.

Note A corner point that connects two curved segments has two direction lines; a corner point that connects two straight segments has no direction lines; and a corner point that connects a straight and curved segment has one direction line. If you drag a corner point's direction line, the other direction line, if there is one, is not affected. The angle and length of direction lines determine the shape of the segments with which they're associated.

Combining straight and curved segments

By combining the techniques for drawing straight segments and curved segments, you can create lines that contain both. Figure 25-13 shows three lines made up of straight and curved segments, as well as curved segments joined by smooth points and curved segments joined by corner points.

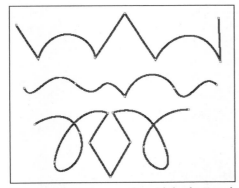

Figure 25-13: Three paths with both curved and straight segments, as well as corner points and smooth points

Here's how to draw a straight segment followed by a curved segment:

1. **While drawing a path, create a straight segment by clicking and releasing the mouse button, moving the Pen pointer, and then clicking and releasing the mouse button again.**

2. **Move the Pen pointer over the last anchor point you created in Step 1.** The Convert Point icon appears (it looks like the regular Pen icon except that a small triangle missing its base appears at the lower right).

3. **Click, drag, and then release the mouse button to create the direction line that determines the slope of the next segment.**

4. **Move the Pen pointer to where you want to establish the next anchor point, and then click and drag to complete the curved segment.**

Figure 25-14 shows a step-by-step sequence of a curved segment being added to a straight segment. You can also follow a straight segment with a curved segment by simply clicking and dragging to create a smooth point. However, if you don't use the method explained in the earlier steps, you'll be able to adjust the slope associated with only one of the curved segment's anchor points rather than both.

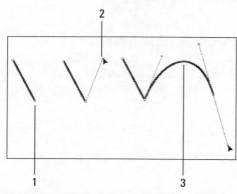

Figure 25-14: First, draw a straight segment, as shown at left. Second, click and drag to create a smooth anchor point. Third, move the pointer to the next desired anchor point location and then click and drag to create a curved segment.

Follow these steps to draw a curved segment followed by a straight segment:

1. **While drawing a path, create a curved segment by clicking, dragging, then releasing the mouse button, and then moving the Pen pointer, clicking, dragging, and releasing the mouse button again.**

2. **Move the Pen pointer over the last anchor point you created in Step 1.** The Convert Point icon appears.

3. **Click the anchor point to convert it from a smooth point to a corner point.**

4. **Move the Pen pointer to where you want to establish the next anchor point; then click and release the mouse button to complete the straight segment.**

Figure 25-15 shows a straight segment being added to a curved segment.

Tip   When creating paths, use as few anchor points as possible. As you become more comfortable creating free-form paths, you should find yourself using fewer anchor points to create paths.

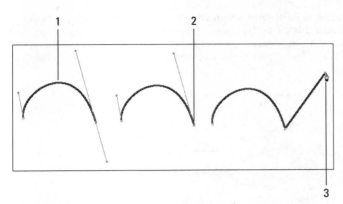

Figure 25-15: First, draw a curved segment, as shown at left. Second, move the pointer over the last anchor point and click on that anchor point. Third, move the pointer to the next desired anchor point location, and then click and release the mouse button to create a straight segment.

Drawing Free-Form Shapes

A closed path is an uninterrupted enclosure with no endpoints. When you apply a stroke to a closed path, there's no beginning or end. Generally, you'll create closed paths when you want to place text or pictures in free-form frames. Although you can place text or a picture in an open path, the result can look more than a little strange, especially if you add a stroke to the path. Then again, you can achieve some strange effects by using open paths as frames. If strange is your goal, go for it.

Tip

For an easy way to draw free-form shapes, use the Pencil tool. It simply traces the movement of your mouse (or pen tablet) as you move it, much like a pencil works on paper. Although not as exact as the Pen tool, the Pencil tool does create Bézier curves that you can later edit. Do note that the Pencil tool is not meant for creating straight lines — unless you can draw perfectly straight lines by hand, that is.

When it comes to creating closed paths with the Pen tool, the process is exactly the same as for creating open paths, as explained earlier in this chapter, with one difference at the end: If you click on the first endpoint you created, you create a closed path:

✦ To create a straight segment between the endpoint and the last anchor point you created, click and release the mouse button.

✦ To create a curved segment, click and drag the mouse in the direction of the last anchor point you created, and then release the mouse button.

Just like an open path, a closed path can contain straight and/or curved segments and smooth and/or corner points. All the techniques explained earlier in this chapter for drawing lines with curved and straight segments and smooth and corner points apply when you're drawing closed paths. Figure 25-16 shows several closed paths used as graphic shapes, text frames, and graphics frames.

Figure 25-16: Closed paths of various shapes

If you draw a path and it turns out to be a little (or a lot, for that matter) different than you intended, don't worry. You can always modify it by moving, adding, deleting, and converting anchor points and by adjusting direction lines. You can also use the transformation tools or the Transform pane to rotate, scale, shear, mirror, and change the position of the path.

See Chapter 26 for information about modifying lines and shapes. See Chapters 10 and 23 for more information about using InDesign's transformation features.

Summary

If you need to create free-form paths — zigzag or curvy lines or complex closed shapes — you must use the Pen tool. All paths are made up of one or more segments, which begin and end in anchor points. Direction lines control the behavior or anchor points, which in turn control the transition between adjoining segments. When you create an open or closed path using the Pen tool, you have the option of creating straight segments or curved segments, and corner points or smooth points.

✦ ✦ ✦

Modifying Shapes and Paths

No matter how skillful you become using InDesign's Pen and Pencil tools to create free-form paths, it's difficult to create exactly what you want on your first attempt. For example, after creating a path, you may want to add detail, smooth out a rough spot, or turn a straight segment into a curved one. No problem. InDesign lets you modify the paths you create in several ways. You can:

+ Add or delete anchor points

+ Move anchor points

+ Change corner points to smooth points and vice versa

+ Modify direction lines

+ Extend an open path

+ Erase parts of the path or cut paths into segments

+ Change a closed path to an open path and vice versa

Note The path-manipulation techniques explained in this chapter apply to all types of paths, including open and closed paths created with the Pen tool, the Pencil tool, and the object-creation tools; text and graphic frames (which are simply paths that act as containers); clipping paths created with the Clipping Path command (Object ➪ Clipping Path, or Option+Shift+⌘+K or Ctrl+Alt+Shift+K) or built into imported graphics; and text-wrap paths created with the Text Wrap pane (Window ➪ Text Wrap, or Option+⌘+W or Ctrl+Alt+W).

Generally, when you want to manipulate a path, you'll use one of the three variations of the Pen tool, all of which are displayed in a single pop-up menu in the Tools palette (shown in Figure 26-1):

+ Both the Add Anchor Point tool and the Delete Anchor Point tool let you add and delete anchor points.

+ The Convert Direction Point tool lets you change smooth points to corner points and vice versa.

Figure 26-1: The four
Pen tools in the Tools
palette

You can also use the Pen tool with keyboard shortcuts to perform all the functions of the Add Anchor Point, Delete Anchor Point, and Convert Direction Point tools.

Tip

If you find that you simply can't create a particular graphic effect within InDesign, you can always resort to your illustration program (assuming you have one). If you're an Adobe Illustrator user, you can easily drag and drop objects from Illustrator into InDesign documents.

Cross-Reference

See Chapter 22 for information about dragging and dropping Illustrator objects and files into InDesign documents.

Adding and Deleting Anchor Points

If you want to add detail to an existing path, you'll need to add anchor points that give you more precise control over a portion of the path. Perhaps you've drawn the profile of a face and you want to add detail to the lips. Or maybe you've written your name longhand and you need to add a flourish that your original attempt lacks. In both cases, you could add smooth or corner points and then manipulate the curves associated with those points by moving them or manipulating their direction lines. (The next section explains how to move anchor points and manipulate direction lines.)

On the other hand, maybe you've created a path that's more complicated than necessary. Perhaps you drew a hand with six fingers instead of five or a camel with one too many humps. In these instances, you need to simplify the path by removing anchor points. InDesign lets you add and delete as many anchor points as you want.

Tip

You should always try to use as few anchor points as possible in the paths you create. The fewer points a path has, the less likely it is to cause printing problems.

Note

When you want to modify the shape of a path, you should begin by selecting it with the Direct Selection tool rather than the Selection tool. If you select a path with the Selection tool, the path's bounding box is displayed with eight moveable handles. In this situation, you can modify the bounding box (thereby resizing the path), but you can't modify the path itself.

To add an anchor point:

1. **Select the path by clicking it with the Direct Selection tool.** You can also select multiple paths and then modify them one at a time.

2. **Select the Pen tool, the Add Anchor Point tool, or the Delete Anchor Point tool.** You can use any of these tools to add and delete anchor points. If the Type tool is not selected, you can select the Pen tool by pressing P, the Add Anchor Point tool by pressing =, and the Delete Anchor Point tool by pressing – (hyphen).

3. **Move the Pen pointer over the selected path at the point where you want to add an anchor point.**

4. **Click and release the mouse button.** A new anchor point is created where you click. If the Delete Anchor Point tool is selected, you must hold down the ⌘ or Ctrl key to add an anchor point. If you click on a straight segment between two corner points, a corner point is created. If you click on a curved segment between two smooth points or between a smooth point and a corner point, a smooth point is created. You can also click, drag, and then release the mouse button if you want to adjust the direction line of the point you create. Figure 26-2 shows a before and after example of a path to which a smooth anchor point is added.

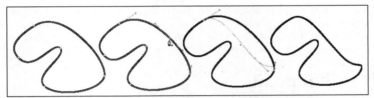

Figure 26-2: The original path (left) is modified by adding a smooth point (second from left). Dragging the smooth point (third from left) produced the final shape (right).

After you add an anchor point, you can hold down the ⌘ or Ctrl key or switch to the Direct Selection tool and drag it or either of its direction handles to adjust the adjoining segments.

Tip   Whenever you're working on a path, you can hold down the ⌘ or Ctrl key and then click and drag any element of the path — an anchor point, a direction line, or the entire path.

To delete an anchor point:

1. **Select the path by clicking it with the Direct Selection tool.** You can also select multiple paths and then modify them one at a time.

2. **Select the Pen tool, the Add Anchor Point tool, or the Delete Anchor Point tool.** You can use any of these tools to add and delete anchor points. If the Type tool is not selected, you can select the Pen tool by pressing P, the Add Anchor Point tool by pressing =, and the Delete Anchor Point tool by pressing – (hyphen) on the main keyboard or on the numeric keypad.

3. **Move the pointer over the anchor point that you want to delete, and then click.** If the Add Anchor Point tool is selected, you must hold down the ⌘ or Ctrl key to delete an anchor point. Figure 26-3 shows a before and after example of a path from which an anchor point has been deleted.

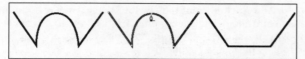

Figure 26-3: The curved segment of the original path (left) is removed by deleting the smooth anchor point (center) with the Delete Anchor Point tool. The resulting path is shown on the right.

Modifying Segments

In Chapter 25, you learned that a path is made up of one or more segments, and every segment is defined by a pair of anchor points. If you want to modify a segment, you can do so by dragging either or both of its anchor points, dragging the direction handles (if present) of the anchor points, or converting either of the anchor points from smooth to corner or vice versa. For example, you could drag an anchor point on a curvy path to increase or decrease the severity of a particular bump, or you could convert a straight-edged polygon into a curvy shape by converting all its corner points to smooth points.

Moving anchor points

When you select a path with the Direct Selection tool, its anchor points are displayed as small, hollow squares. When you click and drag an anchor point, the two adjoining segments change, but the direction handles, if present, are not affected. If you hold down the Shift key as you drag an anchor point, movement is restricted to increments of 45 degrees. Figure 26-4 shows how moving an anchor point affects adjoining curved and straight segments.

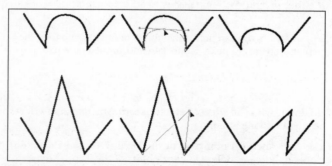

Figure 26-4: Top row: The arc of the curve is reduced (right) by clicking and dragging the smooth anchor point at the top of the curve (center). Bottom row: Dragging a corner (center) point changes the two adjoining segments (right).

Tip   If all you need to do is resize a path — particularly a simple rectangle — rather than change its shape, you should select it with the Selection tool rather than the Direct Selection tool, and then click and drag one of its bounding box handles.

Converting anchor points

If you want to change a wavy path that contains only curved segments to a zigzag path that contains only straight segments, you can do so by converting the smooth anchor points of the wavy path into corner points. Similarly, by converting corner points to smooth points, you can smooth out a path that contains straight segments. Figure 26-5 shows how straight and curved paths are affected by converting their anchor points.

Figure 26-5: Top row: The outer corner points of a straight-edged polygon path (left) were converted to smooth points to create the shape on the right. Bottom row: The zigzag path (right) was created by converting all the smooth points in the path on the left into corner points.

To convert an anchor point:

1. **Select the path by clicking it with the Direct Selection tool.**

2. **Choose the Convert Direction Point tool.** You can also perform the functions of this tool by holding down Option+⌘ or Ctrl+Alt when the Direct Selection tool is selected.

3. **Move the pointer over the anchor point you want to convert.** Depending on the point you want to convert, do one of the following:

   • To convert a corner point to a smooth point, click the corner point, and then drag (direction lines are created and displayed as you drag).

   • To convert a smooth point to a corner point without direction lines, click and release the mouse on the smooth point.

   • To convert a smooth point to a corner point with independent direction lines, click and drag either of the smooth point's direction handles.

   • To convert a corner point without direction lines to a corner point with direction lines, click and drag the corner point to create a smooth point, then release the mouse button. Then click and drag either of the direction lines.

Tip   When using the Convert Direction Point tool, you can temporarily switch to the most recently
used selection tool by pressing ⌘ or Ctrl.

**QuarkXPress
User**   QuarkXPress uses a very different approach to changing direction points from smooth to corner: It has iconic buttons in its Measurements palette that let you easily convert segment and
corner types. The InDesign approach is more efficient in that it uses one tool and relies on a
mouse-based tool (because you're likely using the mouse when you edit a shape), but it
does require a bit more getting used to initially.

Manipulating direction handles

In addition to dragging and converting anchor points, you can adjust the shape of a curved
segment by dragging any of the direction lines associated with the anchor points at either
end of the segment. Figure 26-6 shows how moving direction lines affects a curved segment.

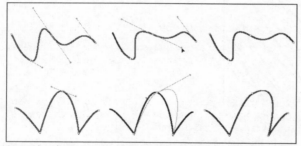

Figure 26-6: The top and bottom shapes on the right
were created by dragging a direction line of a smooth
point (center).

Note   Remember, corner points between straight segments don't have direction handles. If you
want to modify the segments associated with a corner point, simply click and drag the point.

To drag a curved segment's direction handle:

1. **Use the Direct Selection tool to select the path.**

2. **Click either of the two endpoints that define the curved segment.** Handles are displayed at the ends of the two lines that make up the selected point's direction line (and
the lines make up what appears to be a single, straight line). The direction lines of the
two adjoining segments (if present) also appear.

3. **Click and drag any available handle.** Press Shift as you drag to constrain movement
to multiples of 45 degrees. As you drag, the handle at the opposite end of the direction
line moves in the opposite direction like a teeter-totter. However, if you lengthen or
shorten one side of a direction line, the other side is not affected.

4. **Release the mouse button when the shape is the way you want it.**

Note   If you use the Convert Direction Point tool to click and drag a smooth point's direction-line handle, the opposite portion of the direction line remains unchanged. This lets you adjust the segment on one side of a smooth point without affecting the segment on the other side.

Working with Open and Closed Paths

If you've created an open path and subsequently decide that you want to extend the path at either or both ends, you can do so using the Pen tool. Along the same lines, you can use the Pen tool to connect two open paths and to close an open path. For example, if you've placed text or a graphic into an open path, you may decide that the path would work better in a closed frame. And if you want to get even trickier, you can use the Scissors tool to split an open or closed path into two separate paths.

Extending an open path and connecting open paths

The steps required to extend an open path and to connect two open paths are very similar. Here's how you extend an open path:

1. **Use the Direct Selection tool to select the path you want to extend.**

2. **Move the Pen pointer over one of the path's endpoints.** When the Pen pointer is over an endpoint, a small, angled line appears below and to the right of the Pen.

3. **Click and release the mouse button.**

4. **Move the pointer to where you want to place the next anchor point.** If you want to create a corner point, click and release the mouse button. If you want to create a smooth point, click and drag, and then release the mouse button.

5. **Continue adding smooth and corner points until you're done extending the path.**

6. **Finish the path by holding down ⌘ or Ctrl and clicking on an empty portion of the page or choosing another tool.**

To connect two open paths, follow Steps 1 through 3 in the preceding list, and then click on the endpoint of another path (the other path doesn't have to be selected). Figure 26-7 shows a path before and after being extended; Figure 26-8 shows an open path produced by connecting two open paths.

Figure 26-7: The original path (left) was cloned to create the path on the right. The cloned path was then extended by clicking its right endpoint with the Pen tool, and then clicking four more times to create four additional corner points.

Figure 26-8: Connecting the two open paths on the left with the Pen tool produced the single path on the right.

Tip

If you hold down the Shift key when you click an endpoint with the Pen tool, an endpoint for a new path is created (that is, the selected path remains unchanged). In this situation, a small *x* is displayed below and to the right of the Pen pointer. This is useful if you want to create two paths that touch at a particular point. For example, you could draw a path and apply a 4-point black stroke to it, and then create another path that shares an endpoint with the first path. By adding a different kind of stroke to the second path, the two paths look like a single path to which two kinds of stroke have been applied.

Closing an open path

Closing an open path is much the same as extending an open path. The only difference is that you *complete* the path — that is, you close it — by clicking on the other endpoint. For example, if you slice a graphics frame into two pieces using the Scissors tool (this is explained in the next section of this chapter), two open paths are created. If you add a stroke to these open frames, a portion of the graphic edge (the nonexistent segment between the endpoints) will not be stroked. If you close the path, the stroke completely encloses the graphic within. Figure 26-9 shows an open path that's been converted into a closed path.

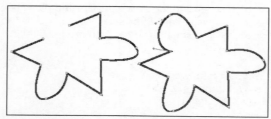

Figure 26-9: The closed path on the right was created from a clone of the open path on the left.

New
Feature

A quick way to close an open path is to select it and then choose Object ⇨ Paths ⇨ Close Path. You can also open a closed path by choosing Object ⇨ Paths ⇨ Open Path; this will separate the start point into a start point and endpoint, letting you move either point or the segments attached to them independently. These options are new to InDesign CS2.

Using the Scissors tool

The Scissors tool does precisely what its icon suggests: It lets you slice things. Specifically, it lets you split paths — open and closed — into two pieces. There are a few things you should know about using the Scissors tool:

✦ It takes only one click with the Scissors tool to split an open path, but it takes two clicks to completely split a closed path.

✦ You can split graphics frames, but you can't split text frames that contain text. If you want to split a text frame that contains text, you must first cut the text and paste it elsewhere.

✦ If you split a graphics frame, a copy of the graphic is placed within both frames.

✦ When you split a path, all stroke and fill attributes of the original path are inherited by the two offspring. After you split a path, it looks the same as before you split it until you move or modify one of the resulting paths.

To split an open path, use the Scissors tool and move the cross-hair pointer over a path, and then click and release the mouse button. You can click on an open portion of a segment (that is, between anchor points) or on an anchor point. In both cases, two anchor points — endpoints of the two resulting paths — are created.

To split a closed path, use the Scissors tool and move the cross-hair pointer over a path; then click and release the mouse button. You can click an open portion of a segment or an anchor point. In both cases, two anchor points — endpoints of the two resulting paths — are created. Move the cross-hair pointer to a different position along the same path, and then click and release the mouse button.

After you split a path, you can switch to either of the selection tools and then select, move, or modify either of the two resulting paths as you wish. If you've split a closed path, you may want to close the two open paths (as described in the previous section). Figure 26-10 shows a pair of open paths that were created using the Scissors tool on an open path. Figure 26-11 shows a closed graphics frame that's been split into two open frames.

Figure 26-10: The original path (left) was split into two pieces by clicking it with the Scissors tool (center). On the right, you see the two resulting paths after the one on the right has been moved.

Figure 26-11: The closed path (a graphics frame) on the left was cut twice with the Scissors tool (center). On the right, one of the resulting open paths has been moved with the Selection tool.

Working with Compound Paths

When more than one path is selected, you can use the Make (Compound Paths) command (Object ➪ Compound Paths ➪ Make, or ⌘+8 or Ctrl+8) to convert the paths into a single object. A compound path is similar to a group (Object ➪ Group, or Ctrl+G or ⌘+G), except that when you create a group out of several objects, each object in the group retains its original attributes, such as stroke color and width, fill color or gradient, and so on. By contrast, when you create a compound path, the attributes of the backmost path are applied to all the other paths (that is, the attributes of the backmost path replace the attributes of the other paths).

You can use a compound path to do such things as:

✦ **Create transparent areas within a path.** For example, by drawing a circular path in front of a graphic, you could then use the Make (Compound Paths) command to poke a hole in the graphic and reveal the objects or the empty page behind the graphic. Figure 26-12 shows a compound path used as a graphics frame.

Figure 26-12: Designer John Cruise created the graphic with the hole in it (right) by drawing a circular path (center) in front of a clone of the original graphics frame (left), and then creating a compound path from the graphics frame and the circular path. The background shape shows within the transparent hole.

✦ **Apply a single background color or place a single graphic within several shapes.** For example, you could use the Create Outlines command (Type ➪ Create Outlines, or Shift+⌘+O or Ctrl+Shift+O) to convert text characters into a compound path, and then place a blend behind the path so that it extends across all characters. (The Create Outlines command is explained in Chapter 27.) Figure 26-13 shows an example of this.

Figure 26-13: Designer John Cruise converted the text on the top into the editable outlines on the bottom. He then skewed the character outlines — which make up a compound path — by −30 degrees via the Shear X Angle field in the Transform pane or Control palette and applied a gradient fill.

✦ **Quickly create complex shapes that would be difficult to create with the Pen tool.** For example, you could create the complex shape in Figure 26-14 by drawing each of the shaded areas as a separate, closed path. Or you could simply create a square, place four circles in front of it so that they overlap the edges of the square, and then choose the Make (Compound Paths) command — a process that takes only a few seconds.

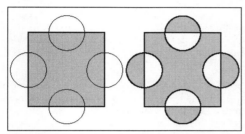

Figure 26-14: Designer John Cruise converted the five closed paths on the left into a compound path via the Make (Compound Paths) command to create the shape on the right. InDesign automatically applied the attributes of the original square path, which is the backmost path, to the resulting compound path. Notice that the four semicircular areas where the original shapes overlapped became holes after converting the shapes to a compound path.

That's only the beginning of what you can do with the Make (Compound Paths) command. Mix in a little bit of your imagination and InDesign's other path-, graphic-, and text-manipulation features, and the possibilities become endless.

Creating compound paths

You can create a compound path out of any kind of path, including open and closed paths as well as text and graphics frames. When you create a compound path, all the original paths become subpaths of the compound shape and inherit the stroke and fill settings of the path that's farthest back in the stacking order. After you create a compound path, you can modify or remove any of the subpaths.

Tip

If the results of choosing Make (Compound Paths) are not what you expected or want, you can undo the operation (Edit ➪ Undo, or ⌘+Z or Ctrl+Z). Try changing the stacking order, and then choose Make (Compound Paths) again.

Note

The direction of each subpath determines whether the subpath is filled or transparent. If a particular subpath is transparent instead of filled, or vice versa, you can use the Reverse Path command (Object ➪ Paths ➪ Reverse Path) to switch the behavior of a subpath.

If frames that contain text and/or graphics are selected when you choose Make (Compound Paths), the resulting compound path will retain the content of the frame that's closest to the bottom of the stacking order. If the bottommost frame doesn't have any content, the content — text or graphic — of the next highest nonempty frame is retained in the compound path. The content of all frames above the frame whose content is retained is removed.

Tip

To change an object's stacking order (to determine which path's attributes are used for the compound path), choose Object ➪ Arrange ➪ Send Backward, or ⌘+[or Ctrl+[, or choose Object ➪ Arrange ➪ Send Forward, or ⌘+] or Ctrl+].

Editing compound paths

After you create a compound path, you can change the shape of any of the subpaths by clicking one with the Direct Selection tool, and then clicking and dragging any of its anchor points or direction handles. The Pen, Add Anchor Point, Delete Anchor Point, and Convert Direction Point tools work the same for subpaths as for other paths, which means that you can reshape them however you want.

The Stroke pane (Window ➪ Stroke or F10), Swatches pane (Window ➪ Swatches or F5), and Color pane (Window ➪ Color or F6) — as well as the transformation tools, the Control palette (Window ➪ Control, or Option+⌘+6 or Ctrl+Alt+6), and the Transform pane (Window ➪ Object & Layout ➪ Transform or F9) — also let you change the appearance of a compound path. When you change the appearance of a compound path, the changes are applied uniformly to all subpaths.

Moving a subpath is a little tricky because you can't drag just that subpath. If you try, all the subpaths move. If you want to move an entire subpath, you must move each of the subpath's anchor points individually. In this case, it's probably easier to release the compound path, as described next, move the path as needed, and then re-create the compound path by choosing Make (Object ➪ Compound Paths ➪ Make, or ⌘+8 or Ctrl+8).

If you want to delete a subpath, you must use the Delete Anchor Point tool to delete all its anchor points. If you delete an anchor point of a closed subpath, it becomes an open subpath.

Note

If the Selection tool is active, you can't delete anchor points using the Cut command (Edit ➪ Cut, or ⌘+X or Ctrl+X), the Clear command (or Edit ➪ Clear, or Delete or Backspace), nor the Del or Delete key. All of these keyboard commands remove the entire path. To work on those individual points, be sure the Direct Selection tool is active.

Changing a path's direction

When you create a path, it has a built-in direction — clockwise or counterclockwise — that is generally not noticeable but affects a compound path. Generally, you can't determine the direction of a path by looking at it. However, you can tell if paths' directions differ by how subpaths in a compound path interact:

✦ If a subpath in a compound path has the same direction as the backmost path, the area within the subpath is transparent.

✦ Conversely, if a subpath's direction is different than the backmost path, the area within the subpath will be filled.

If a subpath is filled in and you want it to be transparent, or vice versa, click the compound path with the Direct Selection tool, and then click the compound path whose direction you want to change and choose Object ⇨ Compound Paths ⇨ Release, or Option+⌘+8 or Ctrl+Alt+8 to separate the subpaths. Figure 26-15 shows how changing the direction of a subpath changes it from filled to transparent.

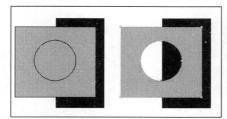

Figure 26-15: The gray square and circle on the left have been combined into a compound path, but the direction of the circular subpath causes it to be filled in instead of transparent. Changing the subpath's direction produced the results on the right: a transparent hole in the square shape.

Splitting a compound path

If you decide you want to deconstruct a compound path, you can do so by clicking anywhere within the compound path, and then choosing Object ⇨ Compound Paths ⇨ Release, or Option+⌘+8 or Ctrl+Alt+8. The resulting paths retain the attributes of the compound path.

Note   The Release command is not available if the selected compound path contains text or if it's nested within a frame.

Using the Pathfinder

Sometimes, you want to combine multiple paths. You could join them, as described earlier, or you could use the Pathfinder tool, accessed by selecting the objects, and then choosing Object ⇨ Pathfinder. You'll see five options in the resulting submenu: Add, Subtract, Intersect, Exclude Overlap, and Minus Back. Figure 26-16 shows how they affect a group of paths (two open and one closed).

New
Feature   InDesign CS2's Pathfinder tool now correctly handles path junctions that have had corner effects applied. Before, the Pathfinder tool didn't notice the corner effects, so joined paths could look odd. Now, it recognizes that there are corner effects and joins the paths appropriately so the corner effects are correctly applied to any new corners. (For more on corner effects, see the next section of this chapter.)

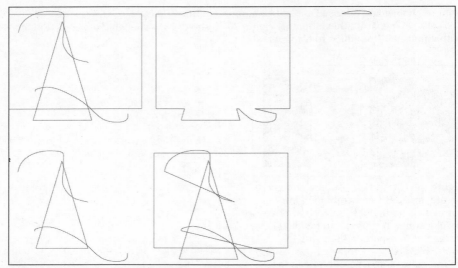

Figure 26-16: Three paths and the five Pathfinder options. Top row: The three original paths (left) and the same paths after applying Add and after applying Subtract. Bottom row: After applying Intersect, Exclude Overlap, and Minus Back.

Here's what they do:

✦ **Add** adds all objects' shapes together.

✦ **Subtract** subtracts all objects from the bottommost object in the stack.

✦ **Intersect** creates an object where objects overlap — this works only on closed paths.

✦ **Exclude Overlap** removes overlapping paths and keeps the nonoverlapping paths of all objects.

✦ **Minus Back** subtracts all objects from the top object in the stack.

 QuarkXPress User   The Pathfinder options are similar to QuarkXPress's Merge options.

Other Path Effects

InDesign provides several other functions to manipulate paths: shape conversion, the Erase tool, and corner effects.

Converting shapes

While you can edit a shape with the Bézier tools described earlier in this chapter, that can be a lot of work for what should be a simple operation. InDesign CS2 does give you an easy way to convert an object's shape: Choose Object ⇨ Convert Shape and then choose one of the submenu options: Rectangle, Rounded Rectangle, Beveled Rectangle, Inverse Rounded Rectangle, Ellipse, Triangle, Polygon, Line, and Orthogonal Line. These controls are also available as buttons in the Pathfinder pane (Window ➪ **Object & Layout** ➪ **Pathfinder**.

New Feature The Convert Shape menu is new to InDesign CS2.

QuarkXPress User The Convert Shape options are similar to those in QuarkXPress's Item ➪ Shape menu option, though their options differ. For example, there's no Bézier shape or line option in InDesign's Convert Shape menu; instead you need to edit the Bézier points manually. But InDesign offers the triangle and polygon shapes, which QuarkXPress does not.

The Erase tool

Just as there are tools to create paths, InDesign has a tool to delete them: the Erase tool, accessible via the Pencil tool's pop-up menu.

For straight lines, the tool works pretty much as you would expect; you drag the tool alongside the path segment to cut — be sure not to cross the path — and then release the mouse. The segment will be gone.

But for Bézier shapes, the tool takes some experimenting with. As Figure 26-17 shows, using the Erase tool will result in a different result depending on what side of a shape you use it. At top is the result of using the tool outside a closed shape's segment. At bottom is the result of using the tool inside the shape.

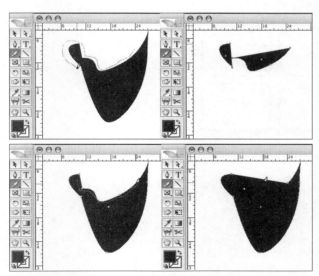

Figure 26-17: The Erase tool will delete path segments, which for a close shape can cause different results depending on whether you are erasing outside (above) or inside (below) the path segment.

Adding corner effects to paths

When a path is selected, the Corner Effects command (Object ⇨ Corner Effects) lets you apply any of several graphic embellishments to its corner points (if the path has any corner points). For example, you could use a corner effect to add pizzazz to the border of a coupon or a certificate. Generally, corner effects work best with rectangular shapes, but they can also produce interesting results when applied to free-form shapes, as shown in Figure 26-18.

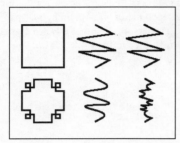

Figure 26-18: The original shapes are on the top row. The bottom row shows the same shapes after applying (from left to right) the Fancy, Rounded, and Inverse Rounded corner effects.

To apply a corner effect to a path:

1. **Use either of the selection tools to select the path to which you want to apply corner effects.**

2. **Choose Object Corner Effects. The Corner Effects dialog box, shown in Figure 26-19, appears.**

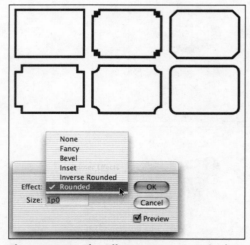

Figure 26-19: The Effect pop-up menu in the Corner Effects dialog box displays the names of five built-in corner effects. A standard corner plus the five effects are shown above the dialog box.

3. **Choose a Corner Effect from the Effect pop-up menu.** If you want to see the effect as you create it, select the Preview option and, if necessary, move the dialog box out of the way so you can see the selected path.

4. **In the Size field, type the distance away from the corner point that the effect will extend.**

5. **After you've finished specifying the appearance of the corner effect, click OK to close the dialog box.**

InDesign doesn't let you modify the built-in corner effects or add your own to the list of choices. Nor can you use the Direct Selection tool to modify the corner of a path to which a corner effect has been applied (anchor points are not displayed for the additional segments that are added when a corner effect is applied to a corner point). The only control you have over a corner effect is the value you specify in the Radius field of the Corner Effects dialog box.

Chapter 24 covers corner effects as applied to frames.

Summary

When it comes to drawing with the Pen or Pencil tool, close is plenty good enough. That's because InDesign lets you modify paths in many ways — by moving, adding, and deleting anchor points; by switching smooth points to corner points and vice versa; and by clicking and dragging direction lines. You also have the option to extend either or both ends of an open path and to close open paths.

If a path requires more drastic surgery, you can use the Scissors tool, which lets you split any kind of path into two pieces.

Because InDesign is primarily a page-layout program, it doesn't contain the breadth of illustration-specific features that you would find in a dedicated vector-based drawing program. Although you may decide that you need a dedicated illustration program to handle your industrial-strength drawing tasks, InDesign does have several features for creating complex shapes.

For example, the Compound Paths command lets you combine several paths into a single object. If you want to add a graphic flourish to the corners of a path, the Corner Effects command lets you apply any of several built-in corner styles and specify the size of the corner effect.

✦   ✦   ✦

Treating Text as Artwork

Text can be beautiful thanks to some of the innovative, engaging
letterforms that type designers have created. So it makes sense
to think of type as an art element, not just a medium with which to
convey information. For centuries designers have used type as a
design element, using beautiful letterforms to embellish the appearance of their layouts.

Desktop publishing quickly gave users much more control over
typography, blurring the distinction between type and art. On a computer, type is represented mathematically as a series of curves, just
as an illustration is. But it has taken almost 15 years for page-layout
programs to manipulate those curves, whether for type or illustrations. InDesign takes this to a whole new level.

Although InDesign will not replace programs such as Adobe
Illustrator, Macromedia FreeHand, and CorelDraw, it gives you many
tools to handle illustration (see Chapters 24 though 26). How does
this relate to type? You can use many of those tools to transform
letterforms — from their actual shapes to their use of color.

Applying Strokes to Type

Text is made up of a series of *outlines* — curves that form the shape —
as Figure 27-1 shows. When printed or displayed, those outlines are
filled in, giving the appearance of a solid shape. When you resize text,
programs like InDesign stretch those curves automatically, which is
how InDesign lets you use almost any size imaginable for your text.
Most programs keep those outlines hidden from you, using them only
for their internal calculations.

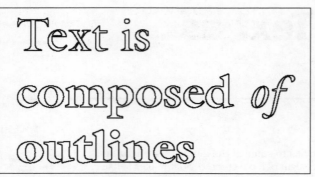

Figure 27-1: Text is made up of invisible outlines that InDesign can then manipulate to change size and create special effects.

But InDesign lets you work with those outlines to create special effects called *strokes*. A stroke is an outline of the character that is made visible and given a thickness (called a *weight*) and often a color. The thicker the stroke, the fatter the character will appear. Figure 27-2 shows some examples of what you can do with strokes.

 Note As you increase stroke size, the stroke grows outward from the letter. That can cause over-lapping into adjacent text, as you see in the *o* in Figure 27-2.

A 6-point light-colored stroke with a regular (black) character inside

A 1-point stroke using a gradient, with a colored character inside

A 1-point stroke the same color as text

A 2-point light-colored stroke with a colored character inside

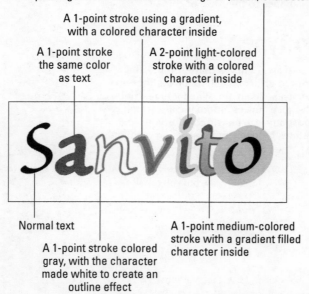

Normal text

A 1-point stroke colored gray, with the character made white to create an outline effect

A 1-point medium-colored stroke with a gradient filled character inside

Figure 27-2: Examples of how you can apply strokes—a process that makes the outlines visible and lets you change their size and coloration—to text

At first, using strokes with text can be a little confusing. There are several palettes and panes involved, and you'll also need to have defined the colors, tints, and gradient fills you want to use before you apply them. Figure 27-3 shows the palettes and panes involved.

Figure 27-3: The palettes and panes used to apply strokes to text. Note that all panes are showing all options (use the palette menu's Show Options menu option to display all options).

✦ **In the same floating palette are usually five panes related to strokes: Stroke, Swatches, Color, Gradient, and Attributes.** Use these to apply the stroke's attributes. Note that the Color and Gradient panes display only existing color, tint, and gradient definitions — you cannot create them from here.

Note — Because InDesign lets you move panes to new palettes or to other existing palettes, these panes may not appear together on your system, but you can always access them through the Window menu. Note that the Stroke pane also has the keyboard shortcut F10, the Swatches pane has the shortcut F5, and the Color pane has the shortcut F6.

Cross-Reference — Chapter 8 covers the Swatches and Color panes in detail, including how to define and apply color, tints, and gradients.

✦ **The Tools palette lets you switch between the stroke and the fill for text.** (By default, the stroke is the active control in this palette.) It also lets you apply the last-used color and gradient to either the stroke or fill, saving you the hassle of switching to the Swatches pane.

If question marks (?) appear on the Fill or Stroke buttons in either the Swatches pane or the Tools palette, that means there are several colors and/or gradients used in the selected text.

To create a stroke:

1. **Highlight the text to which you want to apply a stroke with the Type tool.** It can be as little as one character or as much as your entire story.

2. **Go to the Stroke pane (choose Window ➪ Stroke or press F10 if it is not on your screen).** I suggest you move the pane so the text to which you're applying the stroke remains visible on-screen and you can see the effects of your actions.

3. **Use the Weight pop-up menu to select a thickness for the stroke, or just type a value in increments as fine as 0.001 point.** Note that the other controls in this pane do not apply to strokes on text and are grayed out.

Once you've selected a weight, you can adjust it with the arrow buttons — up to increase and down to decrease — but you cannot use these buttons to increase the weight if the weight is empty or 0.

4. **Here's where you get choices that may initially be confusing. If you want to change the stroke color, you have several options:**

   • If you want to use the most recently used color, click the Stroke button on the bottom of the Tools palette and then click the Apply Color button (see Figure 27-3).

   • If you want to pick a different color, click the Stroke button on the bottom of the Tools palette and then click an existing color from, or create a new color in, the Swatches pane.

   • You can also click the Stroke button in either the Tools palette or Swatches pane, and then drag the color onto either location's Stroke button or directly onto selected text.

   • You can also use the Color pane. The small form of the pane shows just the None color and a range of *tints* (shades) for the last color used — select a tint by clicking on the tint range at the location of the tint you want. The full version of the pane shown here (use its palette menu and its Show Options menu option) lets you create colors by showing a range of colors (pick the color model — LAB, RGB, or CMYK — from the palette menu) and lets you define the color with sliders or by specifying exact percentages of each color. Click the Stroke button on the pane, and then select the color you want to apply.

The Color pane shows an additional item — the Last Color button, as shown in Figure 27-3 — only when the current stroke is set to either None or to a gradient. If you click the Last Color button, the last color selected (the button will be in this color) is applied to the stroke in place of None or of the gradient. You cannot use this to undo a color change — it works only if the stroke did not have a solid color applied to it.

Using the Color pane can introduce some problems during import, as Chapter 8 describes.

5. If you want to use a gradient fill, you also have some choices:

- If you want to use the most recently used gradient, click the Stroke button on the bottom of the Tools palette, and then click the Apply Gradient button (refer to Figure 27-3).

- Go to the Gradient pane and click the gradient — it will be the last-used color. (If there are no gradients defined in your document, you will need to create one via the Swatches pane.) When you click the gradient, you will see gradient controls (refer to Figure 27-3). The bottom ones (squares) display the colors used in the gradient, while the top ones (diamonds) show the gradation slope. You can slide the colors to change how the gradient looks. You can also add color controls by double-clicking in the gradient bar; the color at that point will appear as a control that you can then slide. You can also change the gradient slope — how quickly one color changes to the next by dragging the diamonds. Note that you cannot apply an angle to a gradient used on text.

- If you want to pick a different gradient, select the Stroke button on the bottom of the Tools palette and then click an existing gradient for, or create a new gradient in, the Swatches pane.

Note If you use the full Gradients pane (use the palette menu's Show Options item to display this, as shown in Figure 27-3), you can change the gradient type from radial (circular) to linear, or vice versa, as well as add exact percentages for the gradient controls (click a control and then change its location percentage; that percentage starts at 0 at the far left and ends at 100% at the far right of the gradient bar).

6. In the Attributes pane, decide whether to enable the Overprint Stroke option. Normally, this should not be selected. If checked, InDesign will have the stroke's color print on top of any object underneath them if you're making color separations for output to a printing press, which can make them appear wrong. For example, if you overprint blue on a yellow object, you get green where they overlap.

Tip You may want to overprint black strokes because doing so ensures that there are no registration issues in four-color printing; that is, no gap between the black stroke and the underlying color.

When you apply gradient to text, you'll find that InDesign makes some assumptions that you may not like. The gradient is centered in the text frame, so as your text moves, the gradient appears to move as well (see Figure 27-4 for examples). The same gradient is applied to any text, so you cannot have a gradient reset for each center. For example, if you use a radial gradient, you might want an effect where each letter appears to have a circular halo created from a gradient. You can't do that if you apply a gradient to the stroke, as the center of the radial gradient will be the center of the text frame, not of each character. You'll have to convert each letter to a graphic, as described later in this chapter, and apply the stroke to achieve this halo effect.

Tip You can also apply these settings in character and paragraph styles via the Character Color pane in the New Character Style dialog box when creating or editing a style.

Cross-Reference Chapters 16 and 17 cover style creation in depth.

Figure 27-4: InDesign keeps the gradient centrally located in your text frame, which affects how the gradient will appear in your text as the text moves within the frame. Here, you see three examples of how changes to the text frame's size — and thus to the text's relative position — affect the gradient for the 5-point strokes on this text.

The order in which you use the Swatches, Gradient, and Attributes panes doesn't matter, and you may find yourself jumping back and forth among those, the Stroke pane, and the Swatches pane as you experiment with various settings. In fact, expect to spend time experimenting — it's a crucial part of defining and applying special effects that enhance rather than disrupt.

Applying Color to Type

Applying color and gradients is almost exactly the same as applying color to strokes, except you choose the Fill button in the Tools palette or Swatches pane. Follow the steps for creating a stroke in the previous section, substituting *fill* for *stroke*. The same tips, notes, and caveats apply for fills as for strokes.

Note   If you want to color text consistently, such as having all subheads be green, do so using styles, as covered in Chapter 19.

Although I recommended earlier a case where it makes sense via the Attributes pane to overprint black strokes rather than have them print cleanly, that case doesn't apply for black fills. The only time you want to overprint black on a color is to get a richer, deeper black, but in that case, it makes more sense to not use the Overprint option and instead create a *superblack* (Also called *rich black*) color from 100 percent black and either 100 percent magenta or 100 percent cyan, and use that as the fill color.

Tip
For gray text, use a tint of black.

You can mix the use of colors and gradients for strokes and text to get some unusual typography. Figure 27-3 showed some examples; Figure 27-5 shows some more exotic ones, using 30-point text in all cases. Here are the techniques used:

Figure 27-5: Exotic examples of how you can apply strokes and fills to text

✦ The top text frame uses a linear gradient for the 6-point text stroke and the same gradient — with the colors in the opposite order — as the fill for the text frame.

✦ The first frame in the second row uses a light-gray fill with a radial gradient from white to black for the 2-point strokes. An optical illusion makes the gray fill appear to be a gradient as well because the progression of white to black next to gray makes the eye think the gray is changing as well.

✦ The second frame in the second row uses a 3-point gray stroke on just one letter to accentuate it.

✦ The first frame in the third row uses a 0.5-point, radial white-to-black gradient to soften the edges of the letters.

✦ The second frame in the third row uses a thicker gray stroke for each subsequent character, starting at 0.5 point and ending at 3.5 points.

Converting Text into Graphics

If you want to use the shape of a letter, or the combined shapes of several letters, as a frame for text or a graphic, you could test your skill with the Pen tool and create the letter shape(s) yourself. But getting hand-drawn characters to look just the way you want them can take lots of time. A quicker solution is to use the Create Outlines command (Type ➪ Create Outlines, or Shift+⌘+O or Ctrl+Shift+O) to convert text characters into editable outlines. The Create Outlines command is particularly useful if you want to hand-tweak the shapes of characters, particularly at display font sizes, or place text or a graphic within character shapes.

You can create outlines from TrueType, OpenType, and PostScript (Type 1) format fonts. When you create outlines of highlighted characters, any hinting information in the font is removed. (Hinting information is used to adjust the space between characters, especially at small font sizes.) Therefore, you should adjust the appearance of any characters before you choose Create Outlines.

Note The character shape information required to create outlines is not available in all fonts. If such information is not available when you choose Create Outlines, InDesign will alert you to this fact.

Tip If all you need to do is apply a stroke or fill to characters within text, you don't have to convert the characters into outlines. Instead, simply highlight the characters and use the Stroke pane (Window ⇨ Stroke or F10) and Swatches pane (Window ⇨ Swatches or F5) to change their appearance. This way you'll still be able to edit the text.

When you use the Create Outlines command, you have the choice of creating an inline compound path that replaces the original text or an independent compound path that's placed directly on top of the original letters. If you want the text outlines to flow with the surrounding text, create an inline compound path. If you want to use the outlines elsewhere, create an independent compound path.

To convert text into outlines:

1. **Use the Type tool to highlight the characters you want to convert into outlines.** Generally, this feature works best with large font sizes.

2. **Choose Type ⇨ Create Outlines, or press Shift+⌘+O or Ctrl+Shft+O.** If you hold down the Option or Alt key when you choose Create Outlines, or if you press Shift+Option+⌘+O or Ctrl+Alt+Shift+O, a compound path is created and placed in front of the text. In this case, you can use either of the selection tools to move the resulting compound path. If you don't hold down Option or Alt when you choose Create Outlines, an inline compound path is created. This object replaces the original text and flows with the surrounding text.

Tip If you hold the Option or Alt keys when creating text outlines, the text in the resulting inline compound path will be editable.

Figure 27-6 shows text outlines created with the Create Outlines command, and then modified using the Control palette.

Figure 27-6: Top: Designer John Cruise converted the highlighted characters into an independent compound path by holding down Option or Alt when applying the Make (Compound Path) command. Bottom: After moving the compound path with a selection tool, he placed the angled-line image in the path and added a 2-point stroke.

After you create text outlines, you can modify the paths the same as you can modify hand-drawn paths — by selecting them with the Direct Selection tool and then adding, deleting, or moving anchor points; clicking and dragging direction handles; and converting smooth points to corner points and vice versa. You can also use the transformation tools, the Control palette (Window ➪ Control, or Option+⌘+6 or Ctrl+Alt+6), and the Transform pane (Window ➪ Transform or F9) to change the appearance of text outlines. You cannot, however, edit text after converting it to outlines. (See Chapters 11 and 24 for more information about InDesign's transformation features.)

Additionally, you can use the Place command (File ➪ Place, or ⌘+D or Ctrl+D) to import text or a graphic into text outlines. Figure 27-7 shows character outlines used as text and graphics frames.

Figure 27-7: Both character shapes were created with the Create Outlines command. Designer John Cruise placed text into the shape on the left, and he placed a graphic with a clipping path into the shape on the right and then filled the path with a tint.

Tip

When you create outlines out of a range of highlighted characters, a compound path is created; and each of the characters becomes a subpath. You can use the Release (Compound Path) command (Object ➪ Compound Paths ➪ Release, or Option+⌘+8 or Ctrl+Alt+8) to turn each of the subpaths into independent paths.

Cross-
Reference

Chapter 26 covers editing paths and subpaths in more detail.

Making Text Follow a Path

InDesign lets you have text follow any open or closed path; simply select the line or shape with the Type on a Path tool, which is available from the Type's pop-up menu. Now start typing (or paste or place) your text.

Once you have entered the text and formatted it with font, size, color, and so forth, you can apply special effects to it using the Type on a Path Options dialog box, accessed by choosing Type ➪ Type on a Path ➪ Options, and then selection from its options. Figure 27-8 shows the dialog box and several examples of its formatting. In the dialog box:

✦ Use the Effect pop-up menu to choose an effect.

✦ Use the Align pop-up menu to choose what part of the text is aligned (baseline, center, ascender, or descender).

✦ Use the To Path pop-up menu to choose whether to align to the center, bottom, or top of the path.

✦ Flip the text by selecting the Flip option.

✦ Change the text's spacing by typing a value in the Spacing field (positive numbers space out the text, while negative numbers contract it).

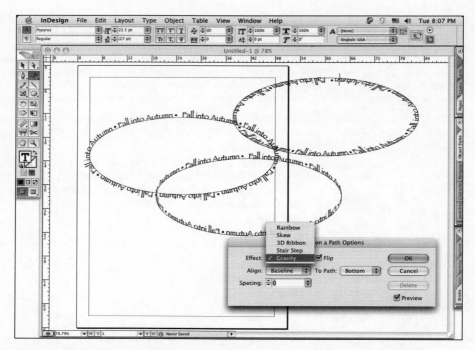

Figure 27-8: The Type on a Path Options dialog box lets you apply special effects, alignment, and flip to text following a path.

Summary

You can do more with text than adjust its font and size. In InDesign, you can color text and add *strokes* (outlines) that can also be colored. By using strokes and colors, you can create all sorts of text effects, from thickening the characters to creating a neon-glow effect.

You can convert text to a graphic, letting you import text or graphics into the frame, as well as apply colors, strokes, and other effects in InDesign.

✦   ✦   ✦

Output Fundamentals

◆ ◆ ◆ ◆

In This Part

◆ ◆ ◆ ◆

Preparing for Color Prepress

Since their invention in the mid-1980s, desktop-publishing programs have broadened their features to cover more and more color publishing needs. Many of the color-oriented features have caused consternation among professional color separators and printers who have seen amateurs make a tough job worse or ruin an acceptable piece of work. This situation is familiar to anyone in desktop publishing in the early years when the typographic profession looked on in horror at amateurs publishing documents without understanding tracking, hyphenation, and many other fundamental areas.

Some programs have added more and more high-end color prepress features. InDesign is one of those, offering two types of trapping engines, the ability to control trapping of individual objects and pages, the ability to apply color models to imported pictures to help the printer adjust the output to match the original picture's color intent, and support for composite workflow, which creates files that have a version for output on a proofing printer such as a color inkjet and a version for output on an imagesetter as film negatives or directly to plate.

The perfect scenario for InDesign color output is that you're using all Adobe software in their latest versions: Photoshop CS2 (9.0) or later, Illustrator CS2 (12.0) or later, and a PostScript Level 3 output device or PDF/X export file. But most people won't have that perfect scenario, especially the PostScript Level 3 part, because it's new and the output devices that commercial printers use are expensive and not replaced often. And not everyone uses Illustrator: Macromedia FreeHand is popular among professional artists, and CorelDraw has established a toe-hold among that group as well, especially among Windows users.

Having said that, don't panic if you're not using cutting-edge equipment and software. After years of user education and efforts by software developers like Adobe to build in some of the more basic color-handling assumptions into their programs, most desktop publishers now produce decent color output by simply using the default settings, perhaps augmented by a little tweaking in Photoshop or an illustration program. To really use the color-management and trapping tools in InDesign effectively, you should understand color printing. But if you don't, you can be assured that the default settings in InDesign will produce decent-quality color output.

Cross-
Reference Please note that the illustrations and figures in this chapter are in black and white. You'll need to look at your color monitor to see the effects of what's described here, or download the image files from the companion Web site (www.InDesignCentral.com). Also take a look at the full-color examples in this book's special eight-page insert "Color Techniques."

Calibrating Color

InDesign comes with several color management system (CMS) options. A CMS helps you ensure accurate printing of your colors, both those in imported images and those defined in InDesign. What a CMS does is track the colors in the source image, the colors displayable by your monitor, and the colors printable by your printer. If the monitor or printer does not support a color in your document, the CMS alters (recalibrates) the color to its closest possible equivalent.

New
Feature   In InDesign CS2, color management is always on, a change from previous versions.

You can set the CMS settings in InDesign by choosing Edit ➪ Color Settings to get the dialog box shown in Figure 28-1. (I'll get to these options a bit later in this chapter.)

If you're creating colors in a program and importing those colors into InDesign, it's important to calibrate them in the same way, or at least as closely as the different programs will allow. Other programs may have similar settings for calibrating their display against your type of monitor. Most of Adobe's Creative Suite 2 applications have the same dialog box as shown in Figure 28-1:

✦ **Photoshop CS2.** Access it by choosing Photoshop ➪ Color Settings on the Mac and Edit ➪ Color Settings in Windows, or pressing Shift+⌘+K or Ctrl+Shift+K.

✦ **Illustrator CS2.** Access it by choosing Illustrator ➪ Color Settings on the Mac and Edit ➪ Color Settings in Windows, or pressing Shift+⌘+K or Ctrl+Shift+K.

✦ **GoLive CS2.** Access it by choosing GoLive ➪ Color Settings on the Mac and Edit ➪ Color Settings in Windows. (There is no keyboard shortcut.)

✦ **Acrobat 7.** Access it by choosing Acrobat ➪ Preferences on the Mac and Edit ➪ Preferences in Windows, or pressing ⌘+K or Ctrl+K, and then going to the Color Management pane. Note that this pane's appearance differs from the appearance of other Creative Suite 2 applications' color-settings panes.

If you use Adobe Creative Suite 2, you can ensure that all CS2 programs use the same CMS, ensuring color consistency for elements that move among Photoshop, Illustrator, Acrobat, and InDesign. To select the CMS, open the Adobe Bridge application and choose Edit ➪ Creative Suite Color Settings; then select the desired CMS settings, and click Apply. I recommend you first select the Show Expanded List of Color Settings Files option before you click Apply. Figure 28-2 shows the dialog box.

Note   Don't confuse InDesign's CMS capabilities with color *matching*. It is impossible to match colors produced in an illustration or paint program, or through a scanner, with what a printer or other output device can produce. The underlying differences in color models (which actually determine how a color is defined) and the physics of the media (screen phosphors that emit light versus different types of papers with different types of inks that reflect light) make color matching impossible. But a calibration tool like a CMS can *minimize* differences.

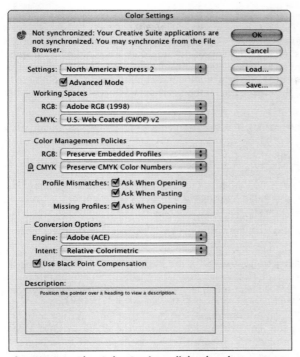

Figure 28-1: The Color Settings dialog box lets you set application color defaults.

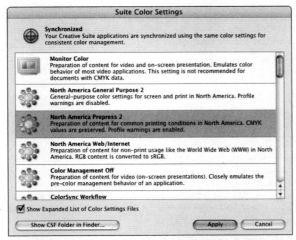

Figure 28-2: Set a consistent color management profile for all Creative Suite 2 programs using Adobe Bridge.

Setting up your system

To achieve the best reproduction of printed colors on-screen, you need a closely controlled environment for your computer. Most people don't bother, relying instead on their brain's ability to mentally substitute the print color for what they see on-screen after they've had experience seeing what happens in actual printed documents. But the more you do to control the color viewing environment, the closer the match between what you see on-screen and what you see on the page.

These tips on setting up your system are in order from simplest to most complex:

✦ **Dim the lights.** Most people turn the brightness of their monitors too high, which distorts colors by overdoing the blues and underdelivering on the reds. Adjust the brightness level of the monitor to between 60 and 75 percent maximum. To make sure you can still see the screen, lower the amount of light in your workspace by using lower-wattage bulbs, turning off overhead lighting right above your monitor, and/or using translucent shades in nearby windows.

✦ **Change the color temperature of your monitor to 7,200 degrees on the Kelvin scale.** Most monitors have on-screen controls to do so.

✦ **If your monitor has a color profile, use it.** On the Mac, the Displays system preferences panel has an option in the Color pane for setting color to a profile (stored in the System\Library\ColorSync\Profiles folder), or you can use the ColorSync system preferences panel to set profiles for several devices. In Windows, use the Display control panel; the Settings pane has an option called Advanced that will open a dialog box that has a Color Management pane. The profiles are stored in the Windows\System\Color folder. Some monitors or video cards come with their own color-setup software.

✦ **Use a calibration tool.** Tools such as X-Rite's Pulse or MonacoEZColor calibrate your monitor and create a color profile specifically for it. These calibrators cost $375 to $600, so they're typically purchased by graphics departments, not individual designers. Note that color calibration software without a hardware calibrator device is worthless — without being able to measure what colors actually come from your monitor, there's no way they can meaningfully adjust the colors in your display. Also note that monitors vary their color display over their lifetime (they get dimmer), so you should recalibrate every six months. For most users, the variances in monitor brightness, color balance, and contrast — coupled with the varying types of lighting used in their workspace — mean that true calibration is impossible for images created on-screen and displayed on-screen. Still, using the calibration feature will make the on-screen color closer to what you'll print, even if it's not an exact match.

✦ **Work in a color-controlled room.** In such a room, the lighting is at 5,000 degrees Kelvin, so the light reflecting off your color proofs matches that of a professional pre-press operation. Monitors should also be set with a white point of D65 (something done with calibration hardware and software). Also try to buy monitors with a neutral, light gray shade — or paint them that way — so your brain doesn't darken what you see on-screen to compensate for the off-white monitor frame right next to the screen image. Similarly, all furnishings should be neutral, preferably a light gray. Avoid having anything with a strong color in the room — even clothes.

Note   There's long been a standard, the latest version of which is called ISO 3664, which has set 5,000 degrees Kelvin as the industry standard for proofing color printing. Basically, 5,000 degrees is filtered daylight where the red, green, and blue components are equal. The International Prepress Association (www.ipa.org) has a lot of standards information and resources related to color accuracy.

Defining Color Models

Whether you define colors in InDesign or in your illustration or paint program, the method you use to define them is critical to ensuring the best possible output. Defining all colors in the same model as the target output device is best. Use the following guidelines:

✦ If your printer is RGB (this is rare), use the RGB model to define colors.

✦ If your printer is CMYK (such as an offset printer or most inkjets), use CMYK to define colors.

✦ If you're using Pantone colors for traditional offset printing, pick one of the Pantone solid models if using Pantone inks. Pick the Pantone Process Coated model if your printer is using inks from companies other than Pantone.

✦ If you're using Pantone colors for traditional offset printing, pick the Pantone Process Coated model if you will color-separate those colors into CMYK.

✦ Trumatch and Focoltone colors were designed to reproduce accurately whether they output as spot colors or are color-separated into CMYK. Other models (such as Toyo, ANPA, and DIC) may or may not separate accurately for all colors, so check with your printer or the ink manufacturer.

✦ If you're using any Pantone, Focoltone, Trumatch, Toyo, ANPA, or DIC color and outputting to a desktop color printer (whether RGB or CMYK), watch to ensure that the color definition doesn't lie outside the printer's gamut, as explained in the next section.

✦ Never rely on the screen display to gauge any non-RGB color. Even with the InDesign CMS's monitor calibration, RGB monitors simply cannot match most non-RGB colors. Use the on-screen colors only as a guide, and rely instead on a color swatchbook from your printer or the color ink's manufacturer.

✦ InDesign's CMS does *not* calibrate color in EPS or PDF files. If you use EPS, I strongly recommend that you use the DCS (preseparated CMYK) variant. If you use PDF files, embed the correct color profile in the application from which you create the PDF file or by using Adobe Acrobat Distiller's options to set color profiles.

Adjusting on-screen display

The following list shows how InDesign's CMS works in practice:

✦ To have color calibration in effect for a monitor, you must be displaying thousands of colors (16-bit color depth) or more colors (or a higher color depth, such as 24-bit). On the Mac, use the Displays system preferences pane to change your monitor's bit depth. In Windows, use the Display control panel.

✦ Select the monitor or color space in the RGB pop-up menu in the Working Spaces section of the Color Setting pane (refer to Figure 28-1). The monitor or color space that you select tells InDesign how to display imported images and colors defined within InDesign. The first four options — Adobe RGB (1998), Apple RGB, ColorMatch RGB, and sRGB IEC61966-2.1 — are all neutral color spaces, meaning that they aren't adjusted for specific monitors. Adobe programs typically save their images with the sRGB profile, which works well if you define colors based on swatches and use exact RGB settings or existing swatches. The other options are monitor-specific profiles, which make sense to use if you choose your colors based on what you see on-screen. Which ones you get depend on what profiles are installed on your computer by the operating system and/or the software that came with your monitor.

✦ Select the output devices in the CMYK pop-up menu in the Working Spaces section. This is only for the imaging device used at your prepress bureau to create the actual color separations (covered in more detail later in this chapter). If you output to PDF files for on-screen display, choose a neutral option in the RGB pop-up menu instead of a monitor-specific option.

✦ Set the color management of imported images in the Color Management Policies section of the dialog box. In the RGB and CMYK pop-up menus, you can select a color profile to apply to each imported or pasted picture — these will override any embedded profiles in the pictures. The default option for RGB is Preserve Embedded Profiles, which is the best option if your graphics sources have already had color models applied intentionally to help calibrate the output. For CMYK, the default option is Preserve CMYK Color Numbers, which ensures the actual CMYK values are preserved. If your pictures are not usually color-managed at the source, it's best to override the embedded profiles and choose either Convert to Working Space, which uses the color profiles selected in the Working Spaces section of the dialog box, or Off, which strips out any color profiles.

✦ There are also two options on when to notify you of profile mismatches (Ask When Opening and Ask When Pasting) and one to alert you to pictures without a profile (Ask When Opening). You should select all three; one exception is if you choose Convert to Working Space in the RGB and CMYK pop-up menus, you can deselect Ask When Opening for Missing Profiles because you won't be using any embedded profiles from the original picture.

✦ Use the Conversion Options section to control the display and printing of bitmapped images. (Make sure the Advanced Mode option is selected near the top of the Color Settings dialog box to display this section.) The Engine pop-up menu lets you choose the CMS technology to use, while the Intent field determines how colors are adjusted by the selected engine. You have four options in the Intent pop-up menu, as well as a related option:

In the Engine pop-up menu, the list of available CMSs depends on what platform you're using: The Adobe ACE CMS is available for all platforms, while the Apple ColorSync and Apple CMM CMSs are available just for Macintosh, and Microsoft ICM CMS is available just for Windows. Choose a CMS that is compatible with your output equipment; if in doubt, choose Adobe ACE.

• **Perceptual.** This selection tries to balance the colors in an image when translating from the original color range to the output device's color range under the assumption that it's a photograph and, thus, needs to look natural. This is appropriate for photographs.

• **Saturation.** This selection tries to create vivid colors when translating from the original color range to the output device's color range — even if doing so means some colors are printed inaccurately. This is appropriate for charts and other slide-like graphics whose colors are intended for impact rather than naturalness.

• **Relative Colorimetric.** This selection shifts all the colors to compensate for the white point of the monitor as set in the Monitor profile (essentially, adjusting the brightness of the output to compensate for any dimness or excess brightness in the monitor). It makes no other adjustments to the colors during output.

- **Absolute Colorimetric.** This selection makes no adjustments to the colors during output. So it allows, for example, an image that uses two similar colors to end up being output as the same color because of the printer's limited color range.

- **Black Point Compensation.** Select this option, which is located under the Intent pop-up menu, to adjust the color range for maximum range, which permits truer colors in most cases and a more natural look to converted photographs. Leave this option selected, unless you know your source image has a small range (such as being mostly midtones), in which case black-point compensation can distort shadows and subtle colors in an effect similar to a moiré pattern.

Tip

Depending on what kinds of documents you produce, you'll likely want Perceptual or Saturation as your setting.

QuarkXPress User

InDesign and QuarkXPress have comparable color-calibration features, but there are some differences: QuarkXPress does not let you apply black-point compensation. And InDesign lets you save your color-management preferences for use in other documents.

There are two related settings in the Appearance of Black pane of the Preferences dialog box (InDesign ➪ Preferences on the Mac or Edit ➪ Preferences in Windows, or ⌘+K or Ctrl+K) shown in Figure 28-3. Both the On Screen and Printing/Exporting pop-up menus offer the same two options:

✦ **Display All Blacks Accurately.** This does exactly what it says, which can lead to weaker-looking blacks in documents that are otherwise rich in color.

✦ **Display All Blacks as Rich Black.** This boosts the black output for better clarity, essentially by adding some magenta ink to make it appear darker. This helps black colors not look flat when surrounded by other rich colors.

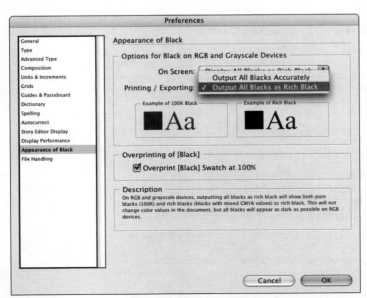

Figure 28-3: The Appearance of Black pane in the Preferences dialog box

Understanding Profiles

The mechanism that a color management system (CMS) uses to do its calibration is the profile that contains the information on color models and ranges supported by a particular creator (such as an illustration program or scanner), display, and printer. InDesign includes dozens of such pre-defined profiles.

A CMS uses a device-independent color space to match these profiles against each other. A color space is a mathematical way of describing the relationships among colors. By using a device-independent color model (the CIE XYZ standard defined by the Commission Internationale de l'Éclairage, the International Commission on Illumination), a CMS can compare gamuts from other device-dependent models (like RGB and the others). What this means is that a CMS can examine the colors in your imported images and defined colors, compare them against the capabilities of your monitor and printer, and adjust the colors for the closest possible display and printing.

By default, InDesign has both pop-up menus set to Display All Blacks as Rich Black.

Note   I'm not sure you should stick with this setting for output because you no longer get just black when you print. You can always use the [Registration] color swatch to get rich black and thus use that color when you want, rather than have all blacks automatically changed. While rich black helps blacks stand out when surrounded by other saturated colors, it can lead to overinking and bleedthrough in documents on thinner paper.

New Feature   The Appearance of Black pane and its functions are new to InDesign CS2.

Calibrating imported colors

When you load a bitmapped image into InDesign, the active CMS applies the default settings defined in the Color Settings dialog box (Edit ➪ Color Settings). If there is no embedded color profile in the document, the dialog box in Figure 28-4 appears when you open it. You might get one for RGB profile and/or one for CMYK profile, depending on what's embedded (if anything) in the document.

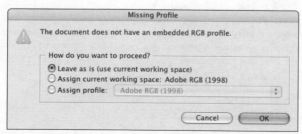

Figure 28-4: You can apply color profiles when importing pictures.

Whether or not there are embedded profiles for the document, you can change the color settings for specific images as follows:

✦ As you import each file, select Show Import Options when you place a graphic into InDesign in the Place dialog box (File ⇨ Place, or ⌘+D or Ctrl+D). In the resulting Image Import Options dialog box, go to the Color pane and select the appropriate profile from the Profile menu, as well as the appropriate rendering intent from the Rendering Intent pop-up menu. Figure 28-5 shows the Image Import Options dialog box.

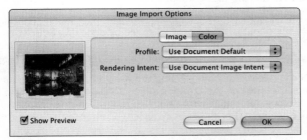

Figure 28-5: You can apply color profiles when importing pictures through the Image Import Options dialog box.

✦ Any time after you place an image, select it with a selection tool and choose Object ⇨ Image Color Settings to set a new profile and/or rendering intent. You can also choose Graphics ⇨ Image Color Settings from the contextual menu to open the Image Color Settings dialog box. Figure 28-6 shows the dialog box.

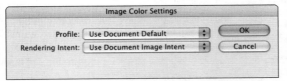

Figure 28-6: Using the Image Color Settings dialog box, you can apply color profiles to an object after it's placed in your document.

Only profiles appropriate for the image type will appear in these pop-up menus — for example, only CMYK profiles (generally, these are output devices) will appear for a CMYK TIFF file, even though the image may have been scanned using an RGB scanner and later converted to CMYK with Photoshop. This limitation exists because InDesign assumes that the image is designed for output to that specific printer and, thus, calibrates it with that target in mind. For RGB files, InDesign lets you apply monitor-oriented profiles and scanner-oriented profiles.

Saving color-management preferences

You can save and use color-management settings in other documents. The process is simple: Click Save in the Color Settings dialog box to save the current dialog box's settings to a file. If you want to use that saved color-settings information in another document, open that document and click Load in the Color Settings dialog box, and then browse for and select the color-settings file. That's it! This is a handy way to ensure consistency in a workgroup.

Changing document color settings

If you put together a document with specific color settings, as described earlier, but then decide you want to apply a new profile across your pictures or replace a specific profile globally in your document, you can.

Choose Edit Í Assign Profiles to replace the color management settings globally, as seen in Figure 28-7. You can set the RGB profile and CMYK profiles separately, as well as set the color intent for solid colors, bitmap images, and gradient blends using the Solid Color Intent, Default Image Intent, and After-Blending Intent pop-up menus.

Similarly, you can change the document's color workspace by choosing Edit ➪ Convert to Profile, which opens the Convert to Profile dialog box also shown in Figure 28-7. It also lets you change the CMS engine, rendering intent, and black-point compensation settings.

There's real overlap in these two dialog boxes. Using the Assign Profiles dialog box to replace the document profile does the same as the Convert to Profile dialog box when it comes to replacing the profiles. The only difference is that the Assign Profiles dialog box can also remove profiles from the document. Both dialog boxes let you change the rendering intents for colors, though the Assign Profiles dialog box gives you several levels of control not available in the Convert to Profile dialog box. But the Convert to Profile dialog box lets you change the black-point compensation and the CMS engine. These really could be combined into one dialog box.

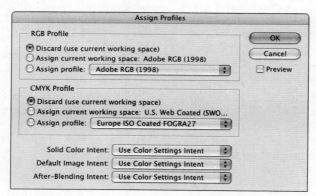

Figure 28-7: InDesign provides two dialog boxes—Assign Profiles (top) and Convert to Profile (bottom)—to change color-management preferences throughout a document. While their functions overlap, each has unique settings of its own.

Calibrating output

When you're ready to output your document to a printer or other device, you set the profile and rendering intent for that destination device in the Color Management pane of the Print dialog box (File➪Print, or ⌘+P or Ctrl+P), which has a Print Space section with a Profile pop-up menu and an Intent pop-up menu. Here you select the appropriate options for your output device.

Chapter 30 covers printing in more detail.

Working with Color Traps

Color trapping controls how colors overlap and abut when printed. InDesign offers moderate controls over trapping—enough to set the basics document-wide without getting into the expertise level of a commercial printer. It's also a feature that novice users can abuse terribly, which is one reason InDesign hides these options. If you don't know much about trapping, leave the features of the program at the default settings. Before you use InDesign trapping tools, study some books on color publishing, talk to your printer, and experiment with test files that you don't want to publish. If you're experienced with color trapping—or after you become experienced—you'll find InDesign trapping tools easy to use.

You'll still want to use the trapping tools within the illustration product with which you create your EPS and PDF graphics because these tools will help you to finely control the settings for each image's specific needs. Also, if you're using a service bureau that does high-resolution scanning for you and strips these files into your layout before output, check to make sure that the bureau is not also handling trapping for you with a Scitex or other high-end system. If it is, make sure you ask whether and when you should be doing trapping yourself.

If you print to a color laser, dye-sublimation, inkjet, or thermal wax printer, don't worry about trapping. You're not getting the kind of output resolution at which this level of image fine-tuning is relevant. But if you output to an imagesetter (particularly if you output to negatives) for eventual printing on a web-offset press or other printing press, read on.

Using choking versus spreading

So what is trapping, anyway? Trapping adjusts the boundaries of colored objects to prevent gaps between abutting colors. Gaps can occur because of misalignment of the negatives, plates, or printing press—all of which are impossible to avoid.

Colors are trapped by processes known as *choking* and *spreading*. Both make an object slightly larger—usually a fraction of a point—so that it overprints the abutting object slightly. The process is called choking when one object surrounds a second object, and the first object is enlarged to overlap the second. The process is known as spreading when you enlarge the surrounded object so that it leaks (bleeds) into the surrounding object.

The difference between choking and spreading is the relative position of the two objects. Think of choking as making the hole for the inside object smaller (which in effect makes the object on the outside larger), and think of spreading as making the object in the hole larger.

Tip   The object made larger depends on the image, but you generally bleed the color of a lighter object into a darker one. If you did the opposite, you'd make darker objects seem ungainly larger. Thus, choke a dark object inside a light one, and spread a light object inside a dark one. If the objects are adjacent, spread the light object.

Figure 28-8 shows the three types of trapping techniques. Spreading (upper right) makes the interior object's color bleed out; choking (lower left) makes the outside color bleed in, in effect making the area of the choked element smaller. The black lines show the size of the interior object; as you can see in the image at upper right, when you choke a darker object into a lighter one, the effect is to change its size (here, the interior object gets smaller). At upper left is an untrapped image whose negatives shifted slightly during printing, causing a gap.

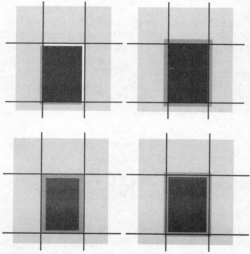

Figure 28-8: Three kinds of traps: spreading (upper right), choking (lower left), and centering (lower right), with an untrapped image in the upper left that was misregistered during printing.

There's a third type of trapping technique supported by InDesign: *Centering* both chokes and spreads, splitting the difference between the two objects. This makes traps look nicer (see the object in the lower right of Figure 28-8), especially between light and dark colors where regular choking and spreading can encroach on the light object.

Finally, InDesign offers a fourth trapping method — neutral density — that adjusts the trap as color hues and tints shift to minimize the possibility of darker lines where colors trap. But this can be dangerous — for a bitmap image, it will most likely create an uneven edge as the trapping changes from pixel to pixel.

In practice, trapping also involves controlling whether colors *knock out* or *overprint*. The default is to knock out — cut out — any overlap when one element is placed on top of another. If, for example, you place two rectangles on top of each other, they print like the two rectangles on the right side of Figure 28-9. If you set the darker rectangle in this figure to overprint, the rectangles print as shown on the left side of the figure. Setting colors to overprint results in mixed colors as shown on the left, while setting colors to knock out results in discrete colors as shown on the right.

In InDesign, you use the Attributes pane (Window ➪ Attributes) for individual objects — text, frames, shapes, and lines — to pick from the pane's four trapping options: Overprint Fill, Overprint Stroke, Overprint Gap, and Nonprinting. Most objects won't have all four settings available because not all objects have fills, gaps, and strokes, but all objects have Nonprinting available, which prevents the object from printing. All four options are normally deselected because you usually want objects' fills, gaps, and strokes to knock out (and you want the object to print). Figure 28-10 shows the pane.

Figure 28-9: The two kinds of untrapped options: overprint (left) and knockout

Figure 28-10: The Attributes pane lets you set whether objects overprint or knock out (the default, or deselected, status).

Specifying trapping presets

In InDesign, document-wide trapping settings are handled as part of the printing process (see Chapter 30). But you specify them like you do colors or other document attributes, through a pane. In this case, you use the Trap Presets pane (Window ➪ Output ➪ Trap Presets) that is shown in Figure 28-11. Choose New Preset from the pane's palette menu to create a new preset, or select an existing preset and choose Preset Options to modify it. (Figure 28-12 shows the New Trap Preset dialog box.) You can also delete and duplicate trap presets from the palette menu, as well as import them from other documents (through the Load Trap Presets option).

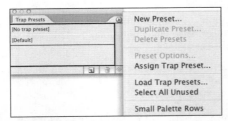

Figure 28-11: The Trap Presets pane

Note   Consult your service bureau or commercial printer before changing the default settings. It will know what setting you should used based on the paper, inks, printing press, and image types you're using.

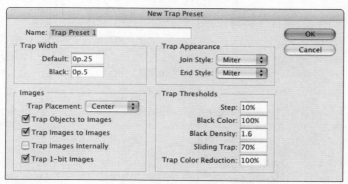

Figure 28-12: The New Trap Preset dialog box

Here are the settings you can change when creating or modifying a trap preset:

✦ **Name.** Type a name for the trap style in the Name field — make sure it's a meaningful name, such as Choke, rather than New Preset 1, so you'll know what it's for.

✦ **Trap Width.** Set your *trap width* (the amount of overlap you want between adjacent colors). The default is 0.25 point, a common setting. The Default field is for all colors except black and white. You set the trap width separately for black, using the Black field; this value is usually one and a half to two times as much as the regular trap settings because it controls how colors spread into black objects. The value is higher because you have more leeway with black — spreading a color into it won't change it from being black, while, for example, spreading yellow into blue makes a green, so you want to minimize that spreading.

✦ **Trap Appearance.** You can choose the type of joins and ends for traps, just as you do for strokes, with options of Miter, Round, and Bevel for both Join Style and End Style. In almost every case, you want to select Miter because this keeps the trap confined to the abutting images. If you choose another option, the choke or spread extends past the trapped objects a tad. If you think of the boundary of the trap as a line, then choosing Bevel or Round extends that line slightly past the objects. If the objects have white or a light color on either side, readers might notice that slight extension.

✦ **Images.** InDesign lets you use several options to control how trapping is applied: Trap Placement plus four picture-specific settings, Trap Objects to Images, Trap Images to Images, Trap Images Internally, and Trap 1-Bit Images.

  • **Image Trap Placement** determines how to handle trapping between an image and an abutting solid color. Your choices are Center, in which the trap straddles the edge between the image and the abutting color object; Choke, in which the abutting color object overprints the image by the Trap Width amount; Spread, in which the image overprints the abutting color object by the Trap Width amount; Neutral Density, which was defined earlier; and Normal, in which each pixel is trapped in the image individually and thus can result in an uneven edge between the image and the abutting object.

- **Trap Objects to Images** turns on trapping for images and any abutting objects such as text or graphics created in InDesign.

- **Trap Images to Images** turns on trapping for images and any abutting images.

- **Trap Images Internally** actually traps colors within the bitmap image. Use this only for high-contrast bitmaps, such as cartoons and computer screen shots, where the color has fewer gradations and more broad, consistent swaths.

- **Trap 1-Bit Images** traps black-and-white bitmaps to any abutting objects (including those underneath). This prevents the appearance of white ghost areas around black portions if there is any misregistration when printing.

✦ **Trap Thresholds.** These guide InDesign in how to apply your trapping settings:

- **Step** gives InDesign the color-difference threshold before trapping is implemented. The default is 10 percent, a value that traps most objects. A higher value traps fewer objects. The way this works is that the value represents the difference in color variance between adjacent objects, and you're telling InDesign not to worry about colors that are within the percentage difference. This is usually a low setting because that means you don't care if there are traps between similar colors because the human eye notices misregistration less between them because they are, in fact, similar. In most cases, keep this value between 8 percent and 20 percent.

- **Black Color** defines at what point InDesign should treat a dark gray as black for the trap width in Black Width. For coarse paper, which usually absorbs more ink, dark tints and grays often end up looking like a solid color — 85 percent black appears as 100 percent black. Use Black Color Limit in such cases so that an 85 percent black object traps as if were a 100 percent black object.

- **Black Density** is similar to Black Color Limit, except that it treats dark colors as black (like navy blue), based on their ink density. You can type a value of 0 to 10, with 1.6 being the default (0 is full black, while 10 is white).

- **Sliding Trap** adjusts the way a choke or spread works. The normal value is 70 percent. When the difference in ink density (a good measure of color saturation) is 70 percent or more, this tells InDesign not to move the darker color so much into the lighter color. The greater the contrast between two colors, the more the lighter object is distorted as the darker color encroaches on it. At 0 percent, all traps are adjusted to the centerline between the two objects, while at 100 percent, the choke or spread is done at the full trap width.

- **Trap Color Reduction** controls overinking that some traps can create. The default is 100 percent, which means that the overlapping colors in a trap are produced at 100 percent, which in some cases can cause the trap to be darker than the two colors being trapped, due to the colors mixing. Choosing a lower value in Trap Color Reduction lightens the overlapping colors to reduce this darkening. A value of 0 percent keeps the overlap no darker than the darker of the two colors being trapped.

Specifying trapping to pages

Once you create trapping presets, you apply them. To do so, choose the Assign Trap Presets option in the Trap Presets pane's palette menu. Figure 28-13 shows the dialog box.

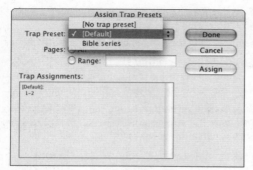

Figure 28-13: The Assign Trap Presets dialog box

Note   The [Default] preset, which you can modify, is applied to all pages by default.

The process is simple: Choose the desired trap preset from the Trap Preset pop-up menu, and then select the pages to which the preset will be applied. Make your selection in the Pages section (click All, or click Range; if you click Range, type the page numbers in the Range field). Click Assign to complete the application of the trap preset to the selected pages. You can set multiple presets in a document to different page ranges, so if you want, select another trap preset and assign it to the desired pages. InDesign will show you what pages have what trap presets applied at the bottom of the dialog box. When finished, click Done.

Note   If your document uses sections, you can type page numbers in the Range field using the section numbering style (such as **A–2, D-3, F–5–F–10**) or by using absolute page numbers (**+1, +5, +10–+15**).

Summary

Although it's often impossible to precisely match colors from an electronic image when printing, InDesign can help make the color fidelity as high as possible through its support of color profiles and color management. It can also help make what you see on-screen and print on proofing devices look close to the final output, to help you better gauge your actual colors.

If you use a compatible output device, InDesign also lets you control how adjacent colors print, in a process known as *trapping,* that minimizes the chances of gaps appearing between colored objects. Fortunately, most users won't need to worry about fine-tuning trapping settings because InDesign's default settings handle most objects well.

✦   ✦   ✦

Preparing for Printing

Once your document is created and all elements are perfectly in place, with the right colors, frame strokes, kerning, and so on, it's time to make tangible all that work you've done on-screen. You're ready to print the document.

Well, not quite. You may in fact be ready to just print your document, but if your document is at all complex or will be output at a service bureau or through your company's creative services group or print shop, you should take a few minutes and dot your *i*'s and cross your *t*'s. Little things can go wrong as you or your team work on a document — a font might deactivate, a picture might move or be renamed, or a new output device might be acquired.

That's where InDesign's Preflight and Package tools come into play. The Preflight tool checks your document to make sure that all elements are available, while the Package tool copies all required elements — from fonts to graphics — to a folder so you can give your service bureau all the pieces needed to print your document accurately.

Making Initial Preparations

Before you can do anything, you need to make sure your system is set up with the right printer driver and printer description files — without these, your output is not likely to match your needs or expectations. It's important to set these up before you use the Preflight tool because the Preflight tool checks your document against the printer settings you have active (such as color separations), and you can't have selected printer settings until the printer is set up.

The Mac and Windows platforms handle printing differently, so in this chapter I've divided all system-specific printing information, such as the coverage of drivers, into platform-specific sections.

Chapter 38 covers the different kinds of printers available.

Setting up Macintosh printers

Although you choose the printer type in the Setup pane of the InDesign Print dialog box, you still need to set up the printer on your Mac before you can use it.

The process varies based on the version of the Mac OS you have:

✦ In Mac OS X 10.3 (Panther) and later, use the Printer Setup Utility, which you access by clicking Print & Fax in System Preferences (⇨ System Preferences), and then clicking Set Up Printers in the resulting Print & Fax pane. You'll get the Printer List dialog box.

✦ In Mac OS X 10.2 (Jaguar), you use an application called the Print Center, which is in the Utilities folder in the Applications folder.

The Printer List dialog box or the Print Center will list any installed printers. Make sure the printer you want to set up is connected to your Mac (directly or through the network) and turned on. (If you're using a network printer, make sure the right network protocols, such as IP and AppleTalk, are turned on through the Network pane in the System Preferences dialog box, which you access by choosing ⇨ System Preferences.)

Either way, to install a printer, you typically run a program that comes with the printer. Such programs often add the printer to the Printer List. If not, click Add (in the Printer List) and locate the printer driver for your printer (again, usually found on a CD that accompanies the printer). Figure 29-1 shows the Printer List that appears when you open the Mac OS X 10.3 (Panther) Print & Fax pane and click Set Up Printers.

Configuring an installed printer varies based on the software provided with the printer. In some cases, a printer's configuration software is accessible when you add a printer through the Printer List dialog box. (In Mac OS X 10.3 [Panther], select the printer and click Show Info to get the Printer dialog box, which will have a pop-up menu that lets you move among the various setup panes. In earlier versions of Mac OS X, select the printer and click the Configure button.)

In other cases, you need to run a separate utility that comes with the printer or use controls on the printer itself.

Note   You may need to install a PostScript Printer Description (PPD) file that contains specific details on your printer; this file should come on a disk or CD with your printer and is often installed with the printer's setup program. Otherwise, download it from the printer manufacturer's Web site. These files should reside in the PPD's folder in the Mac's System\Library\Printers folder. Note that Mac OS X preinstalls some PPDs for you, particularly those for Apple-branded printers and some Hewlett-Packard printers.

If you're installing a printer not connected to your computer or network, such as the image-setter used by your service bureau, you'll need to install the PPD files so InDesign knows what its settings are. Installing the printer software isn't necessary.

Mac OS X supports multiple printers, but it also lets you define the default printer—the ones used unless changed through a button or pop-up menu in an application's Print dialog box.

(InDesign uses a pop-up menu called Printer to change the printer from the default setting.) In the Printer List dialog box, choose the printer you want to be the default, and then click Make Default.

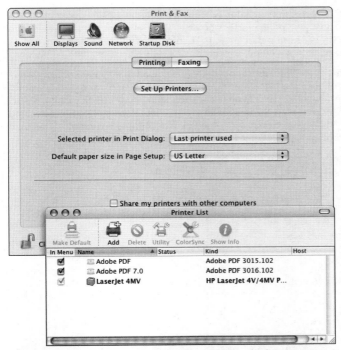

Figure 29-1: The Printer List dialog box shows which printers are installed and lets you add and configure them.

Setting up Windows printers

To set up a Windows 2000 or XP printer, choose Start ⇨ Settings ⇨ Printers and Faxes. (Some XP users will have to choose Start ⇨ Control Panel ⇨ Printers and Other Hardware.) You'll then see a window with a list of existing printers and an icon labeled Add New Printer. Double-click the printer to set up, or double-click Add New Printer (you'll likely need a disk that came with the printer, or the Windows CD-ROM, if you add a new printer because Windows needs information specific to that printer). Note that some printers have their own setup software that you should use instead of the Add Printer utility in Windows.

Note

If you're setting up a printer connected through the network, you usually should select the Local Printer option during installation. The Network Printer option is for printers connected to a print server, as opposed to printers connected to a hub or router. (A print server is a special kind of router, but it's typically used only for printers that don't have networking built in, such as many inkjet printers.) In some cases, even if your printer uses a print server, you'll still install the printer as a local printer, and then create a virtual port that maps to a network address (Hewlett-Packard uses this approach, for example, in Figure 29-2).

If you're installing a printer not connected to your computer or network, such as the image-setter used by your service bureau, you'll need to install the PPD files so InDesign knows what its settings are. You don't need to install the printer software.

When you open an existing printer, the dialog box shown in Figure 29-2 appears when you choose Printer ⇨ Properties. One pane matters greatly: The Device Settings pane is where you specify all the device settings, from paper trays to memory to how fonts are handled. For PostScript printers, this pane has several key options as follows:

✦ **Font Substitution Table.** This option opens a list of available fonts and lets you select how any TrueType fonts are translated to PostScript. The best (and default) setting is to have the printer translate TrueType fonts such as Arial to PostScript fonts such as Helvetica. (The Windows standards of Arial, Times New Roman, Courier New, and Symbol are set by default to translate to the PostScript fonts Helvetica, Times, Courier, and Symbol. PostScript fonts are set by default to Don't Substitute.)

✦ **Add Euro Currency Symbol to PostScript Fonts.** Be sure to select this option in this pane so the euro symbol (€) is available in all output.

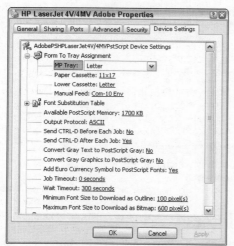

Figure 29-2: The Device Settings pane in Windows setup for PostScript devices is the key pane in the Properties dialog box for a Windows printer. (Not all panes appear for all printers, depending on the printer type chosen and the network protocols installed.)

Tip

I strongly recommend you use Adobe's PostScript driver rather than Microsoft's. The Microsoft driver often doesn't send fonts to the printer, and it often prints extra blank pages at the end of a job. The Adobe Universal PostScript driver doesn't have these issues. You can download the Adobe driver from www.adobe.com/support/downloads/main.html in the PostScript Printer Drivers section. When you install the driver, it gives you the option of converting your existing PostScript printers to the Adobe driver. You can also run this program again to install new printers using the Adobe driver—using the Add Printer wizard automatically installs the Microsoft driver for those new printers—or you can use the Drivers pop-up menu in the Advanced pane of the printer's Properties dialog box.

Note   You may need to install a PostScript Printer Description (PPD) file that contains specific details on your printer; this file should come on a disk or CD with your printer and is often installed with the printer's setup program. Otherwise, download it from the printer manufacturer's Web site. (Windows places PPD files in the Windows\System32\spool\drivers\w32x86 folder; note that the first folder may be named WinNT or WinXP instead of Windows.)

To set a printer as the default printer, right-click the printer in the Printers window (Start ➪ Settings ➪ Printers and Faxes), and select Set Default Printer from the contextual menu that appears. (Some Windows XP users will need to choose Start ➪ Control Panel ➪ Printers and Other Hardware.)

Preflighting Your Document

Now that your printers are set up, you can use InDesign's printing and preprinting checkup tools. The Preflight tool that's part of InDesign examines your document for any issues of concern and gives you a report on what may need to be fixed.

You might wonder why you need a preflight tool to check for things such as missing fonts and images when InDesign lists any missing fonts and graphics when you open a document. The answer is that sometimes fonts and graphics files are moved after you open a file, in which case you won't get the alerts from InDesign. This is more likely to happen if you work with files and fonts on a network drive, rather than with local fonts and graphics. Preflighting also checks for other problematic issues, such as the use of RGB files and TrueType fonts.

Before you run the Preflight tool, you may want to set up your printer output so the tool accurately checks your document's setup in anticipation of, for example, whether you plan to output color separations or spot colors. To do that, you need to go to the Print dialog box (File ➪ Print, or ⌘+P or Ctrl+P), set your output settings, click Save Preset, provide a name in the Save Preset dialog box, and click OK, and then click Cancel to put them into effect *without actually printing the document.*

Caution   Don't confuse InDesign's print setup with the operating system's printer setup. In InDesign's Print dialog box is a button called Printer on the Mac and Setup in Windows that lets you change print settings for all applications—it's essentially a shortcut to the operating-system controls described earlier in this section. You should only change these operating-system settings for output controls that InDesign's Print dialog box does not provide.

Cross-Reference   Selecting your output settings is covered in detail in Chapter 30.

Tip   If you're working with the InDesign Books feature (see Chapter 32), you can preflight the book's chapters from an open book's pane, using the Preflight Book option in its palette menu. (If one or more documents in the book are selected in the pane, the menu option changes to Preflight Selected Documents.) The options are the same as for preflighting individual documents.

Running the Preflight tool is easy. Choose File ➪ Preflight, or press Shift+Option+⌘+F or Ctrl+Alt+Shift+F. In a few seconds, a dialog box appears that shows the status of your document. Here's a walkthrough of what the six panes in the Preflight dialog box do:

✦ **Summary.** This pane (shown in Figure 29-3) shows you a summary of alerts. If your document has layers, you can select or deselect the Show Data For Hidden Document

Layers option. If selected, layers that won't print are analyzed for font, image, and other issues. Select this option only if the person receiving your document plans on printing hidden layers (for example, in a French-and-English document, you may have hidden the French layer for proofing but still want it checked because the service bureau is instructed to print the document twice — once with the English layer on and the French layer off, and once with the English layer off and the French layer on).

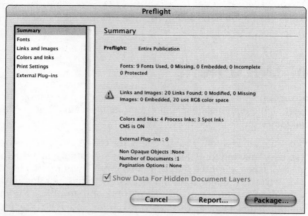

Figure 29-3: The Summary pane of the Preflight dialog box

✦ **Fonts.** This pane (shown in Figure 29-4) shows the type (Type 1 PostScript, OpenType, or TrueType) of each font, so you can spot any TrueType fonts before they go to your service bureau. (TrueType fonts usually don't print easily on imagesetters, so use a program like Pyrus FontLab to translate them to PostScript instead.) It will also show if any fonts are missing from your system. You can search for fonts by clicking Find Font.

You can also limit the list of fonts to those with problems by selecting the Show Problems Only option.

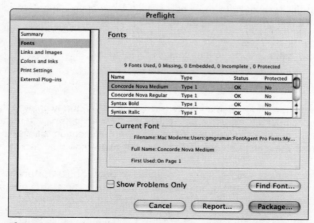

Figure 29-4: The Fonts pane of the Preflight dialog box

✦ **Links and Images.** This pane (shown in Figure 29-5) shows whether any graphics files are missing or if the original image has been modified since you placed it in your layout. You can click Update to correct any such bad links one at a time, or Repair All to have InDesign prompt you in turn for each missing or modified file. The pane also shows whether a color profile is embedded in your graphics in case files that should have them don't or in case a file that should not have an embedded profile does. It also alerts you if you use RGB images; although such images will print or color-separate, InDesign provides the warning because it's usually better to convert RGB images to CMYK in an image editor or illustration program so you can control the final appearance, rather than rely on InDesign or the output device to do the translation.

You can also limit the list of linked files to those with problems by selecting the Show Problems Only option.

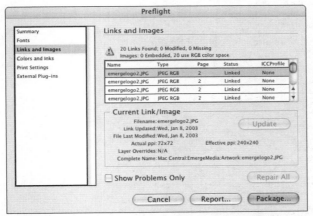

Figure 29-5: The Links and Images pane of the Preflight dialog box

✦ **Colors and Inks.** This pane (shown in Figure 29-6) shows the color of the inks that will be used in the output (if you are printing color separations, these correspond to the color plates that will eventually be used to print the document on a printing press). You can't modify anything here; it's simply for informational purposes.

In a complex document with lots of graphics and fonts, you may want to select the Show Problems Only option in the Fonts pane and in the Links and Images pane. If selected, this option displays only elements flagged by the preflight tool in that pane.

✦ **Print Settings.** This pane (shown in Figure 29-7) shows how the document is configured to print in the Print dialog box. That's why it's key to configure the output settings, as described earlier, before preflighting your document.

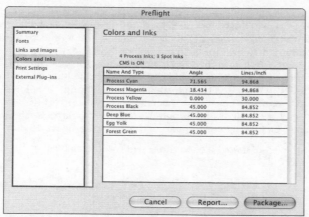

Figure 29-6: The Colors and Inks pane of the Preflight dialog box

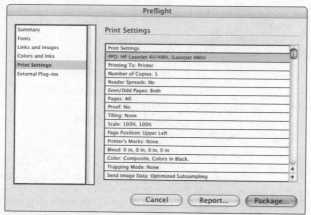

Figure 29-7: The Print Settings pane of the Preflight dialog box

✦ **External Plug-ins.** This pane (shown in Figure 29-8) shows any plug-in programs required to output the file. Some third-party plug-ins make changes to the InDesign document that require the same plug-in to be installed at each computer that opens the file. This dialog box alerts you if you have such a dependency.

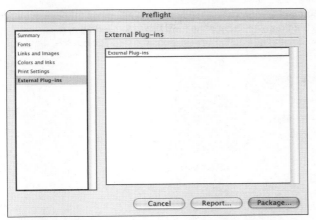

Figure 29-8: The External Plug-ins pane of the Preflight dialog box

You can create a report of the preflight information by clicking Report. It generates a text file containing the information from the Preflight dialog box's panes, which you can give to your service bureau to check its settings and files against.

You can also click Package to gather all related fonts and files into one folder for delivery to a service bureau or other outside printing agency. The next section describes this option in more detail.

Click Cancel to exit the Preflight dialog box and go back to your document.

Creating a Document Package

If you've ever had the experience of giving a page-layout document to a service bureau, only to be called several hours later by the person who is outputting your document because some of the files necessary to output it are missing, you'll love the Package feature in InDesign.

This command, which you access by choosing File ➪ Package, or Option+Shift+⌘+P or Ctrl+Alt+Shift+P, copies into a folder all the font, color-output, and picture files necessary to output your document. It also generates a report that contains all the information about your document that a service bureau is ever likely to need, including the document's fonts, dimensions, and trapping information. You can also create an instructions file that has your contact information and any particulars you want to say about the document.

When you run the Package command, InDesign preflights your document automatically and gives you the option of viewing any problems it encounters. If you elect to view that information, the Preflight dialog box appears (refer to Figures 29-3 through 29-8). You can continue to package your document from that dialog box by clicking Package once you've assured yourself none of the problems will affect the document's output.

Before you can actually package the document, you'll be asked to save the current document, and then fill in the Printing Instructions form shown in Figure 29-9. You can change the default filename from Instructions.txt to something more suitable, such as the name of your print job.

Caution If you *don't* want to create an instructions form, don't click Cancel—that cancels the entire package operation. Just click Continue, leaving the form blank. Similarly, you must click Save at the request to save the document; clicking Cancel stops the package operation as well.

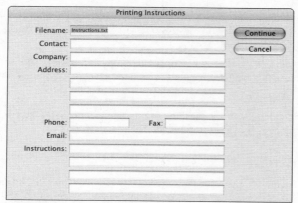

Figure 29-9: The Printing Instructions dialog box

The next step is to create the package folder. You do this in the dialog box that follows the Printing Instructions form, which on the Mac is called Create Package Folder and in Windows is called Package Publication. Figure 29-10 shows the Mac version, which except for the name at the top is the same as the Windows version.

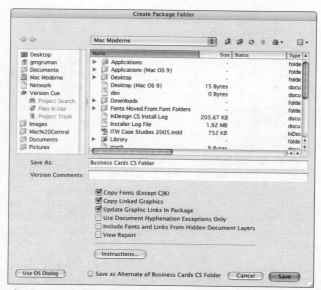

Figure 29-10: The Create Package Folder dialog box for Mac InDesign is called the Package Publication dialog box in Windows.

In the dialog box, you can select what is copied: the fonts, color-output profiles, and *linked graphics* (graphics pasted into an InDesign document rather than imported are automatically included). You can also have InDesign update the graphics links for those that were modified or moved; if this option is not selected, any missing or modified graphics files will not be copied with the document.

You can tell InDesign to include fonts and links from hidden layers (which you would do only if you want the service bureau to print those hidden layers or if you were giving the document's files to a colleague to do further work).

You also can specify whether the document should use only the hyphenation exceptions defined within it. This often makes sense because it ensures that the printer's hyphenation dictionary — which may differ from yours — doesn't cause text to flow differently.

Cross-Reference See Chapter 14 for more details on these dictionaries. The next section of this chapter explains which files you should send to others using your documents.

You can also modify the instructions text file by clicking Instructions.

Finally, you can choose to view the report after the package is created — on the Mac, InDesign launches TextEdit and displays the report file, while on Windows it launches Notepad and displays the report file.

Click Save (on the Mac) or Package (in Windows) when everything is ready to go. Your document is placed in the folder you specify, as is the instructions file (the report). There will also be a folder called Fonts that includes the fonts, a folder called Links that has the graphics files, and a folder called Output Profiles that has the color output profiles.

I strongly recommend using the Package feature. It ensures that your service bureau has all the necessary files and information to output your document correctly.

Dealing with Service Bureaus

Service bureaus are great: They keep and maintain all the equipment, know the ins and outs of both your software and your printing press requirements, and turn jobs around quickly — at least most of the time. Working with a service bureau involves commitment and communication between both parties. It needs your business; you need its expertise and equipment.

To ensure that you get what you want (fast, accurate service) and that the service bureau gets what it wants (no-hassle clients and printing jobs), make sure that you both understand your standards and needs. Keep in mind that the service bureau has many customers, all of whom do things differently. Service bureaus likewise must not impose unreasonable requirements just for the sake of consistency, because customers can have good reasons for doing things differently.

Paying attention to a few basic issues can help you establish a productive relationship with your service bureau.

Note When I say *service bureau*, I also mean your company's production or prepress department and your commercial printer — the people who actually convert your files into the final product.

Sending documents versus output files

Because you have the Package feature, do you give the service bureau your actual InDesign documents or do you send a PostScript or PDF output file?

Cross-Reference Chapter 31 shows you how to create output files.

Often, your service bureau will have its requirements and preferences as to what kinds of output files it wants and when it wants output files rather than native InDesign files. You usually should provide what the service bureau wants, but there are times that your goals or concerns will override the service bureau's. Among the issues that play into deciding what files to provide are the following:

✦ A document file, even if the graphics files are copied with it, takes less space than an output file created from your document, which means fewer disks or cartridges to sort through and less time copying files from your media to theirs.

✦ A document file can be changed accidentally, resulting in incorrect output. For example, a color might be changed accidentally when the service bureau checks your color definitions to make sure that spot colors are translated to process colors. Or document preferences might be lost, resulting in text reflow.

✦ The service bureau cannot always edit an output file. So the service bureau may not be able to come to your rescue if you make a mistake such as forgetting to print registration marks when creating the output file or specifying landscape printing mode for a portrait document.

Basically, the question is: Where should the control lie — with yourself or the service bureau? Only you can answer that question. But in either case, there are two things that you can do to help prevent miscommunication: Provide the report file to the service bureau, and also provide a proof copy of your document. The service bureau uses these tools to see if its output matches your expectations — regardless of whether you provide a document file or output file.

Determining output settings

A common area of miscommunication among designers, service bureaus, and printers is determining who sets controls over line screens, registration marks, and other output controls. (In some cases, when the printer is doing the film/plate output, it acts as both the service bureau and printer.) Whoever has the expertise to make the right choices should handle these options. And it should be clear to all parties who is responsible for what aspect of output controls — you don't want to use conflicting settings or accidentally override the desired settings:

✦ Assuming you're sending InDesign documents to the service bureau or printer, for output controls such as line screens and angles, the layout artist should determine these settings and specify them on the proof copy provided to the service bureau. That way the service bureau or printer can use its own PPD files rather than take the chance you had incorrect or outdated ones.

✦ If the publication has established production standards for special effects or special printing needs or if the job is unusual, I recommend that the layout artist determine the settings for such general printing controls as the registration marks and the printer resolution.

Cross-Reference   InDesign print-control setup is described in Chapter 30.

✦ For issues related to the service bureau's and/or printer's internal needs and standards, such as how much gap to have between pages and what trapping settings should be, I recommend that the service bureau and/or printer determine their own settings. If you're sending the service bureau or printer output files instead of InDesign documents, you'll have to type these settings in the Print dialog box pane before creating the file, so be sure to coordinate these issues with the service bureau and/or printer in advance.

✦ Coordinate issues related to the printing press (such as which side of the negative the emulsion should be on) with the printer and service bureau. Let the service bureau or printer determine this data unless you send output files.

In all cases, determine who is responsible for every aspect of output controls to ensure that someone does not specify a setting outside his or her area of responsibility without first checking with the other parties.

The preceding issues often take the form of a conversation among the printer, the service bureau, and the designer. This conversation should touch on the topics of traps, ink spread, registration, and so forth. Relying on only the service bureau to get all the details correct without that three-way conversation can result in a less-than-optimal final printed product. Also, including the printer (and service bureau) earlier in the design phase of complex jobs can help avoid printing and production issues. All three parties bring an area of expertise to the job and so can educate each other a little about the goals of the piece. A designer with some production skills who knows the limitations of output and a given press can avoid excessive costs and poor output.

Note   Smart service bureaus and printers do know how to edit an output file to change some settings, such as dpi and line screen, that are encoded in those files, but don't count on them doing that work for you except in emergencies. And then they should let you know what they did and why. And remember: not all output files can be edited (such as EPS and PostScript files created as binary files), or they can be edited only in a limited way (such as PDF files).

Ensuring correct bleeds

When you create an image that bleeds, it must actually print beyond the crop marks. There must be enough of the bleeding image that if the paper moves slightly in the press, the image still bleeds. (Most printers expect ⅛ inch, or about a pica, of *trim* area for a bleed.) In most cases, the document page is smaller than both the page size (specified in InDesign through the File ➪ Document Setup option) and the paper size, so that the margin between pages is sufficient to allow for a bleed. If your document page is the same size as your paper size, the paper size limits how much of your bleed actually prints: Any part of the bleed that extends beyond the paper size specified is cut off. (This problem derives from the way PostScript controls printing; it has nothing to do with InDesign.)

Note   This paper-size limit applies even if you set bleed and slug space in the Document Setup dialog box. These tell the printer how much of the material outside the page boundaries to output, so they're not cropped out automatically. But the paper, film negatives, or plates to which they are output must still be large enough to physically accommodate them.

Make sure that your service bureau knows that you're using bleeds and whether you specified a special paper or page size, because that may be a factor in the way the operator outputs your job.

Sending oversized pages

If you use a paper size larger than U.S. letter size (8½ × 11 inches), tell the service bureau in advance because the paper size might affect how the operator sends your job to the imagesetter. Many service bureaus use a utility program that automatically rotates pages to save film because pages rotated 90 degrees still fit along the width of typesetting paper and film rolls. But if you specify a larger paper size to make room for bleeds or because your document will be printed at tabloid size, this rotation might cause the tops and/or bottoms of your document pages to be cut off.

I've worked with service bureaus that forgot that they loaded this page-rotation utility, so the operator didn't think to unload it for our oversized pages. It took a while to figure out what was going on because my publication's layout staff was certain that it wasn't doing the rotation (the service bureau assumed our staff had), and the service bureau had forgotten that it was using the rotation utility.

Summary

After you install the printer drivers for the various printers you'll use — both those on-site for proofing and those at a service bureau or prepress house — you should turn your attention to setting global printing defaults, the ones that affect all printing jobs, such as the use of paper trays and the handling of TrueType fonts.

Before you actually print, InDesign checks your document for possible output problems using its preflight tools. You also have the chance to create a print package — which collects all graphics, fonts, and a copy of the document file — to send to your service bureau or other output service.

✦   ✦   ✦

Printing Techniques

Your document is done. Your printers and printer options are set up, and you've preflighted your document, as described in Chapter 29. You're ready to see all that effort become reality by printing a proof copy or an actual version on a high-resolution imagesetter or printer.

The good news is that your hard work is over. Printing from InDesign is straightforward once everything has been set up. Just choose File ⇨ Print, or ⌘+P or Ctrl+P, to go to the Print dialog box.

Selecting InDesign Printing Options

The Print dialog box has eight panes as well as several options common to all the panes. Change any options and choose Print, and InDesign sends your document to the printer. Figure 30-1 shows the dialog box.

Tip　　If you're working with the InDesign Books feature (see Chapter 32), you can print the book's chapters from an open book's pane using the Print Book option in its palette menu. (If one or more documents in the book are selected in the pane, the menu option changes to Print Selected Documents.) The setup options are the same as for printing individual documents.

General options

The general options available in the dialog box, no matter what pane is selected, are as follows:

- **Print Preset.** This pop-up menu lets you save a group of printer settings, which makes it easy to switch between, say, a proofing printer and a final output device.

- **Printer.** This pop-up menu lets you select the printer to use.

- **PPD.** This pop-up menu lets you select PostScript Printer Descriptions (PPD) files that contain configuration and feature information specific to a brand and model of printer. These are installed into your operating system using software that comes from your printer manufacturer. If it finds no compatible PPDs, InDesign uses generic options if there is no compatible PPD. If it finds just one compatible PPD, it uses that automatically; otherwise, it lets you select a PPD.

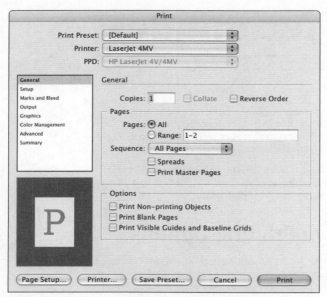

Figure 30-1: The default view for the Print dialog box

✦ **Save Preset.** Clicking this button saves any settings you change in the Print dialog box and lets you choose a name for those saved settings for reuse. If you change the dialog box's settings but don't save these changes as a print preset, InDesign changes the name of the current settings in the Print Preset pop-up menu to [Custom] to remind you the settings are changed and unsaved.

Tip

You can also create print presets by choosing File ➪ Print Presets ➪ Define, or edit an existing preset by choosing File ➪ Print Presets ➪ preset name. When you click New or Edit in the resulting dialog box, a dialog box identical to the Print dialog box appears, except that the Print button becomes the OK button.

✦ **Setup (Windows); Page Setup and Printer (Mac).** These buttons give you access to printer-specific controls. Figure 30-2 shows the three resulting dialog boxes. You use these dialog boxes to specify options such as printing to file, paper sources, and printer resolution. Note that if you add a printer, you may need to quit InDesign and restart it for it to see the new printer.

Windows and Mac OS X provide access to printer controls in different ways. In Windows, the Setup button gives you access to these, while on the Mac, you use both the Page Setup and Printer buttons to access these controls.

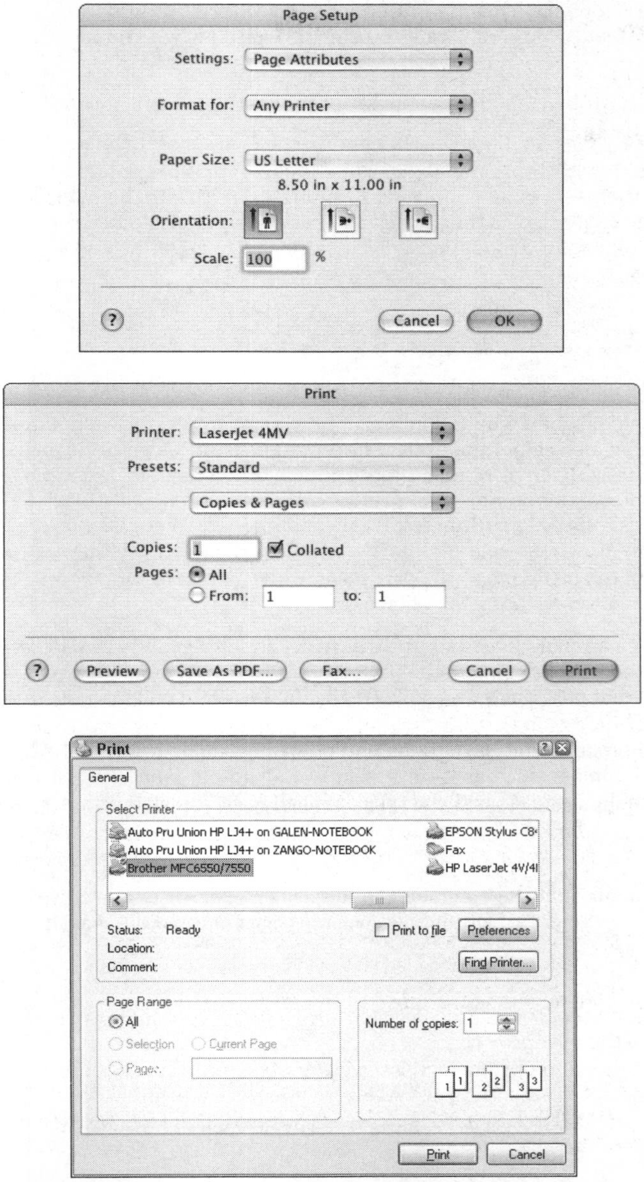

Figure 30-2: Mac OS X's Page Setup and Printer dialog boxes (top and middle) and Windows' Print dialog box (bottom).

✦ **Cancel.** Clicking this button closes the Print dialog box without printing. Use this if you've clicked Save Preset but don't want to print, as well as when you have any reason not to print.

✦ **Print.** Clicking this button prints the document based on the current settings.

✦ **Page preview panel.** This panel at lower left shows the current settings graphically. The page is indicated by the blue rectangle, while the direction of the large *P* indicates the printing orientation — in Figure 30-1's case, unrotated portrait. The panel shows that the paper is the same size as the page. If the page were larger than the paper, the overflow would be highlighted in light gray). This preview changes as you adjust settings in the dialog box.

The General pane

The General pane (refer to Figure 30-1) contains the basic settings for your print job:

✦ **Copies.** This text field is where you tell InDesign how many copies of the document you want to print. You can also select the Collate option to have InDesign print the pages in sequence. This is useful when printing multiple copies, so you get, for example, pages 1 through 16 printed in sequence, and then printed again in sequence if you're making two copies. Otherwise, InDesign prints two copies of page 1, two copies of page 2, and so on, forcing you to manually collate them. If you select the Reverse Order option, InDesign prints from the last page to the first page, which is meant for printers that stack pages face up rather than the usual face down.

✦ **Pages.** These options let you choose to print all pages or a range of pages, in which case you type a range in the Range field. When specifying a range of pages, you can type nonconsecutive ranges, such as **1-4, 7, 10-13, 15, 18, 20**.

Tip   If you want to print from a specific page to the end of the document, just type the hyphen after the initial page number, such as **4-**. InDesign will figure out what the last page is. Similarly, to start from the first page and end on a specified page, just start with the hyphen as in **-11**.

Tip   InDesign lets you type absolute page numbers in the Range field. For example, typing **+6-+12** would print the document's sixth through twelfth pages, no matter what their page numbers are.

✦ **Sequence.** The pop-up menu lets you choose from All Pages, Odd Pages Only, and Even Pages Only.

✦ **Spreads.** Selecting this option prints facing pages on the same sheet of paper — this is handy when showing clients comps, but make sure you have a printer that can handle that large paper size or that you scale the output down to fit (through the Setup pane, covered in the next section).

Tip   You may not want to use the Spreads option when outputting to an imagesetter if you have bleeds because there will be no bleed between the spreads. If you use traditional *perfect-binding* (square spines) or *saddle-stitching* (stapled spines) printing methods, in which facing pages are not printed contiguously, do not use this option.

✦ **Print Master Pages.** Select this option if you want to print your master pages. This is handy for making reference copies available to page designers.

✦ **Options section.** There are three options in this section that are self-explanatory: Print Non-Printing Objects, Print Blank Pages, and Print Visible Guides and Baseline Grids. Print Blank Pages is usually used for collation, such as when blank pages divide sections of a manual. The other two are used typically by page designers to display hidden designer notes or wrap objects, as well as to ensure that objects really do align to the standard grids.

The Setup pane

The Setup pane, shown in Figure 30-3, is where you tell InDesign how to work with the paper (or other media, such as film negatives) to which you're printing. The options are straightforward.

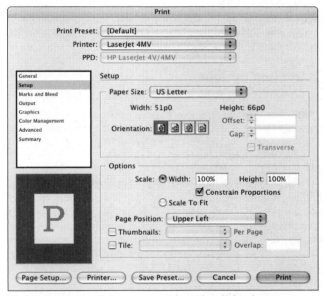

Figure 30-3: The Setup pane of the Print dialog box

Paper size and orientation

In the Paper Size section, choose the paper size using the Paper Size pop-up menu. You can also select page orientation by clicking any of the four buttons that rotate the image as follows from left to right: 0 degrees (standard portrait), –90 degrees, 180 degrees, and 90 degrees (standard landscape).

Choosing some printer models will in turn let you choose a Custom option in the Page Size pop-up menu, in which case you type the dimensions in the Width and Height fields, as well as position the output through the Offset and Gap fields. These latter two options are usually used when printing to a roll, such as in an imagesetter using photo paper (called *RC paper*, a resin-coated paper that keeps details extremely sharp), so you can make sure there is space between the left edge of the roll and the page boundary (the offset), as well as between pages (the gap). Most printers can't print right to the edge, thus the Offset setting; you also want a gap between pages for crop and registration marks, as well as to have room to physically cut the pages.

The Transverse option, if selected, rotates the output 90 degrees. This is done mainly for imagesetters whose paper and film negatives are usually about 12 inches wide. At that width, it's cheaper for the service bureau to rotate the pages 90 degrees in most cases (because most publications are usually no taller than 11 inches), packing more pages onto the RC paper or film.

Caution

Many service bureaus use a utility program that automatically rotates pages to save film, so check with your service bureau to make sure that selecting the Transverse option won't conflict with any rotation they might do. Also, if you specify a larger paper size to make room for bleeds or because your document will be printed at tabloid size, this rotation might cause the tops and/or bottoms of your document pages to be cut off. The basic rule: Discuss all output settings with your service bureau or prepress department first.

Scaling, positioning, and tiling options

The Setup pane also lets you set scaling, positioning, and tiling settings.

The Scale settings are straightforward. You can choose separate Width and Height scaling settings to reduce or enlarge the page image. If the Constrain Proportions option is selected, then a change in the Width field is applied to the Height field, and vice versa. To make a page fit the paper size, select the Scale to Fit option. InDesign will then display the actual percentage it will use. Note that Scale to Fit takes into account bleeds and crop marks, so even if the document page size is the same as the output device's paper size, Scale to Fit reduces it to make room for those elements.

The Page Position pop-up menu lets you choose how the page image is positioned on the paper to which you're printing. The default position is Centered, which centers the page image vertically and horizontally. You can also choose Center Horizontally, which aligns the top of the page image to the top of the paper and centers the page horizontally; Center Vertically, which aligns the left side of the page to the left side of the paper and centers the page vertically; and Upper Left, which places the page image's upper-left corner at the paper's upper-left corner.

QuarkXPress User

InDesign's Thumbnails option is more flexible than QuarkXPress's, letting you choose the number of thumbnails per page.

Potential Gotchas for Page Positioning

Which Page Position option—Upper Left, Center Horizontally, Center Vertically, and Centered—you choose in the Print dialog box's Setup pane will depend on what you are printing to. As a rule of thumb, use Centered for printing to paper. Use one of the other three choices for image-setters. Talk to your service bureau to find out which one is best.

Here's the potential problem: On a proofing devices such as an inkjet, thermal wax, or laser printer, the Upper Left, Center Horizontally, Center Vertically options run the risk of putting part of the page outside the printer's imaging margin (a space of a pica or so from the paper edge in which the printer cannot print). That's why it's best to use the Page Position setting of Centered when printing to paper. This option also makes room available on all sides where possible for crop marks and bleeds.

But when you print to an imagesetter or platesetter, Centered may not be the best option. That's because your service bureau or commercial printer may not want the pages centered because it may be spacing them or rotating them to minimize waste of paper or film negatives. Imagesetters output to rolls of paper or film, so the service bureau or commercial printer has some control over the page's size. Always check first.

A very nice option is InDesign's Thumbnails and its adjoining pop-up menu. Here, you can have InDesign print *thumbnails*—miniature versions of pages, several to a sheet—for use in presenting comps, seeing whole articles at a glance, and so on. If you select the Thumbnails option, you then select how many thumbnails you want per page from the adjoining pop-up menu. Your choices are 1×2, 2×2, 3×3, 4×4, 5×5, 6×6, and 7×7. InDesign sizes the pages based on what it takes to make them fit at the number of thumbnails chosen per page, the page size, and the paper size.

Use the Tile options to print oversized documents. InDesign will break the document into separate pages—called *tiles*—that you later can assemble together. To enable tiling, select the Tile option, and then choose the appropriate option from the adjoining pop-up menu:

✦ **Manual.** This lets you specify the tiles yourself. To specify a tile, you change the origin point on the document ruler, and that becomes the upper-left corner of the current tile. To print multiple tiles this way, you need to adjust the origin point and print, adjust the origin point to the next location and print, and so on, until you're done.

Chapter 2 covers the origin point-also called the zero point or ruler origin-in more detail.

✦ **Auto.** This lets InDesign figure out where to divide the pages into tiles. You can change the default amount of overlap between tiles of 1.5 inches using the Overlap field. The overlap lets you easily align tiles by having enough overlap for you to see where each should be placed relative to the others.

✦ **Auto Justified.** This is similar to Auto except that it makes each tile the same size, adjusting the overlap if needed to do that. (The Auto option, by contrast, simply starts at the origin point and then does as much of the page as will fit in the tile, which means the last tile may be a different width than the others. You can see the difference between the two by watching how the page preview window at left changes as you select each option.

The Marks and Bleeds pane

The Marks and Bleed pane, shown in Figure 30-4, lets you specify which printer marks are output with your pages, as well as areas to reserve for items that bleed off the page. The printer's marks are set in the Marks section, while the bleeds are set in the Bleed and Slug section.

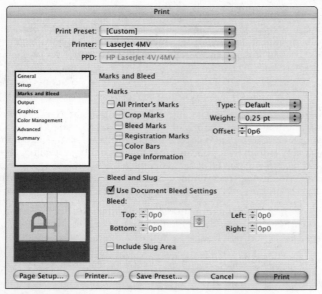

Figure 30-4: The Marks and Bleed pane of the Print dialog box

Printer's marks

In most cases, you'd select the All Printer's Marks option and have all print on each sheet or negative. But you can select which marks you want to print. Here's what each option means:

✦ **Crop Marks.** These are lines at the corners of the page that tell a commercial printer where the page boundaries are, and thus to where the paper will be trimmed.

✦ **Bleed Marks.** These add a very thin box around your page that shows the bleed area — where you expect items to print into, even though they're past the page boundary. (A *bleed* is an object that you want to be cut at the page boundary; the object needs to overshoot that boundary in case, during printing, the page is not trimmed exactly where it should be. Normally, 0p9, or 0.125 inches, is sufficient area for a bleed. You set the bleed area in the Marks and Bleeds pane, which is covered in the next section.

✦ **Registration Marks.** These are the cross-hair symbols that are used to ensure that the color negatives are properly aligned on top of each other when combined to create a color proof and to make sure that the colors are not misregistered on the final pages when they are lined up on a printing press.

✦ **Color Bars.** These print the CMYK colors and tints so a commercial printer can quickly check during printing whether ink is under- or oversaturated — the shades could be too light or dark. The CMYK colors also help a commercial printer know which color a particular negative is for (after all, negatives are produced using transparent film with black images).

✦ **Page Information.** This lists the filename and page number.

If a printer has options for printer's marks, they will display in the Type pop-up menu, but most will simply have one option: Default. You can also adjust the thickness of the printer's marks, using the Weight pop-up menu to 0.125, 0.25, and 0.5 points; the default is 0.25 points (a hairline rule). You can also control the offset of crop marks from the page corners by adjusting the Offset value; the default of 0.833 inches (6 points) usually suffices. For all of these, check with your service bureau.

Using any printer's marks automatically increases the page size in PDF files exported from InDesign to add room for the printer's marks. This is handy because when you output EPS or other PostScript files, the page size selected determines the page boundary, and printer's marks often get eliminated because they fall outside that boundary. One solution is to use a larger page size than your final output will be, so there's naturally enough room for printer's marks. The preview window on the right in the dialog box will show you if printer's marks fall outside the page's boundaries.

Bleeds and slugs

The Bleed and Slug area of the Marks and Bleed pane controls how materials print past the page boundary.

A bleed is used when you want a picture, color, or text to go right to the edge of the paper. Because there is slight variation on positioning when you print because the paper moves mechanically through rollers and might move slightly during transit, publishers have any to-the-edge materials actually print beyond the edge, so there are never any gaps. It's essentially a safety margin. A normal bleed margin would be 0p9 (⅛ inch), though you can make it larger if you want.

A *slug* is an area beyond the bleed area in which you want printer's marks to appear. The reader never sees this, but the staff at the commercial printer does and it helps them make sure they have the right pages, colors, and so on. Like the bleed, the slug area is trimmed off when the pages are bound into a magazine, newspaper, or whatever. (The word *slug* is an old newspaper term for this identifying information, based on the lead slug once used for this purpose on old printing presses.) The purpose is to ensure there is enough room for all the printer's marks to appear between the bleed area and the edges of the page. Otherwise, InDesign will do the best it can.

It's best to define your bleed and slug areas in your document itself when you create the document in the New Document dialog box (File ➪ New ➪ Document, or ⌘+N or Ctrl+N), as covered in Chapter 4. You can also use the Document Setup dialog box (File ➪ Document Setup, or Option+⌘+P or Ctrl+Alt+P). The two dialog boxes have the same options; if they don't show the Bleed and Slug section, click More Options to see them.

But if you didn't define your bleeds previously, you can do so in the Print dialog box's Marks and Bleed pane. You can also override those document settings here. To use the document settings, select the Use Document Bleed Settings option. Otherwise, type in a bleed area using the Top, Bottom, Left, and Right fields. If you want them to be the same, click the broken-chain button to the right of the Top field; it will become a solid chain, indicating that all four fields will have the same value if any is modified. Any bleed area is indicated in red in the preview pane at the bottom left.

If you want to set the slug area, select the Include Slug Area option. InDesign will then reserve any slug area defined in the New Document or Document Setup dialog box. You cannot set up the slug area in the Print dialog box.

The Output pane

The next pane is the Output pane, which controls the processing of colors and inks on imagesetters, platesetters, and commercial printing equipment. You'll definitely want to check these settings with your service bureau. For proof printing, such as to a laser printer or inkjet printer, the only option that you need to worry about is the Color pop-up menu, seen in Figure 30-5.

Caution   These options should be specified in coordination with your service bureau and commercial printer—they can really mess up your printing if set incorrectly.

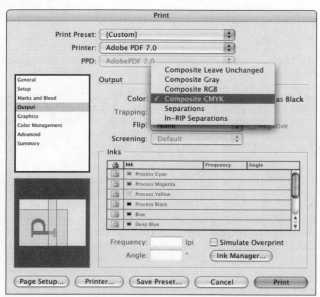

Figure 30-5: The Output pane of the Print dialog box

Here's what the options do:

✦ **Color.** Use this pop-up menu to choose how you want the document to print. Your options are Composite Leave Unchanged, Composite Gray, Composite RGB, Composite CMYK, Separations, and In-RIP Separations. (*RIP* stands for raster image processor, the device in a printer or imagesetter that converts lines, curves, colors, and pictures into the tiny dots that make up printed output.)

The Composite options are meant for proofing devices such as inkjets and laser printers. Most such printers are black-and-white or CMYK, so you'll usually pick Composite Gray or Composite CMYK. Pick Composite RGB for documents output to PDF format for display on screen. Composite Leave Unchanged is meant for proofing printers that support specialty ink swatches such as Pantone; very few do. (If your document uses colors like Pantone colors, you typically would pick Composite CMYK, and your printer will approximate the Pantone colors. Use Composite Leave Unchanged only if your proofing printer has actual Pantone inks.)

Select Separations if you're printing to an imagesetter to create film negatives or to a platesetter to create color plates. If your output device supports in-RIP separations — where the device creates the separate color plates, rather than having InDesign do it — choose In-RIP Separations. (Note that only a few printers' PPDs support this option.)

✦ **Trapping.** Use this pop-up menu to select how color trapping is handled. (This is grayed out if Separations or In-RIP Separations are not selected in the Color pop-up menu.) The choices are Off, Application Built-In (meaning, as set in InDesign), and Adobe In-RIP (available only for printers that have Adobe's in-RIP separations technology).

Note

Adobe would like the publishing world to standardize on its PostScript Level 3 printing language and its default trapping and color technologies, which is what the Adobe In-RIP option uses. Adobe may get its wish one day, but the reality is that most companies use a variety of technologies, so you'll likely use the standard Separations option that uses whatever settings you created in InDesign, or you'll select the Off option and let your service bureau manage trapping directly. Check with your service bureau.

✦ **Flip.** Use this pop-up menu and the associated Negative option to determine how the file prints to film negatives or plates. Commercial printers have different requirements based on the technology they use. They tend to use language such as *right reading, emulsion side up*, which can be hard to translate to InDesign's Flip settings. Type on the page is *right reading* when the photosensitive layer is facing you and you can read the text. Horizontally flipping the page makes it *wrong reading* (type is readable when the photosensitive layer is facing away from you). Check with your service bureau as to whether and how you should flip the output. Pages printed on film are often printed using the Horizontal & Vertical option in the Flip pop-up menu.

✦ **Text as Black.** If you select this option, text appears in pure black, rather than being converted to gray or printed in a color (even if you apply a color to the text). This can make text more readable in a proof copy.

✦ **Negative.** Selecting this option creates a photographic negative of the page, which some commercial printers may request. This option is available only if Composite Gray, Separations, or In-RIP Separations is selected in the Color pop-up menu.

✦ **Screening.** This pop-up menu works differently depending on whether you choose Composite Gray or one of the separations options in the Color pop-up menu:

- If you select Composite Gray in the Color pop-up menu, your Screen pop-up menu choices are Default and Custom. If you choose Custom, you can select the preferred line screen frequency and angle at the bottom of the pane using the Frequency and Angle fields.

- If you select Separations or In-RIP Separations in the Color pop-up menu, you get a series of options that vary based on the selected printer and PPD. But all will show an lpi setting and a dpi setting. (See the sidebar on lpi and dpi in this chapter for more on these.) And the Frequency and Angle fields at the bottom of the pane display very precise angles optimized for the selected output device based on the chosen lpi/dpi settings. Although you can change the Frequency and Angle fields, you shouldn't.

Note

The Inks section of the pane lets you see the frequency and angle settings for selected colors; you change a specific color plate's settings by first selecting the color and then altering the Frequency and Angle fields. You can also disable output of specific color plates by clicking the printer icons to the left of the colors—a red line is drawn through the icon for disabled plates—as well as control color plate output by clicking Ink Manager. Color output is covered in more detail later in this chapter.

✦ **Simulate Overprint.** Selecting this option at the bottom of the Output pane lets InDesign overprint colors for printers that normally don't support this. (You would set an object to overprint another by selecting one of the Overprint options in the Attributes pane.) This option is available only if the Color pop-up menu is set to Composite Gray, Composite CMYK, or Composite RGB.

QuarkXPress User

QuarkXPress lets you import color images as grayscale by pressing and holding ⌘ or Ctrl when importing them. That's very handy when you are working with a two-color document, where your images will print in grayscale, because it saves you the time of having to convert all your source images to grayscale in Photoshop. InDesign doesn't have a similar feature, and it also has no way in the Print dialog box's Output pane to convert the process (CMYK) colors to gray while letting spot-color plates print separately. This would let you work with color source images yet be able to work with two-color output as QuarkXPress can do through its import-as-grayscale option.

What lpi and dpi Mean

Lines per inch (lpi) and dots per inch (dpi) are not related because the spots in a line screen are variably sized, while dots in a laser printer or imagesetter often have a fixed size. (Because newer printers using techniques like Hewlett-Packard's Resolution Enhancement Technology or Apple Computer's FinePrint and PhotoGrade use variably sized dots, the distinction may disappear one day.)

Lines per inch specifies, in essence, the grid through which an image is filtered, not the size of the spots that make it up. Dots per inch specifies the number of ink dots per inch produced by the laser printer; these dots are typically the same size. A 100 lpi image with variably sized dots will, therefore, appear finer than a 100 dpi image. The figure shows an example, with a fixed-dot arrow at left and a variably sized-dot arrow at right.

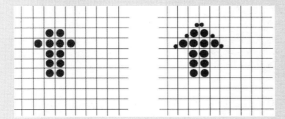

Depending upon the size of the line-screen spot, several of a printer's fixed-size dots may be required to simulate one line-screen spot. For this reason, a printer's or imagesetter's lpi is far less than its dpi. For example, a 300 dpi laser printer can achieve about 60 lpi resolution; a 1,270 dpi imagesetter can achieve about 120 lpi resolution; a 2,540 dpi imagesetter about 200 lpi resolution. Resolutions of less than 100 lpi are considered coarse, and resolutions of more than 120 lpi are considered fine.

But there's more to choosing an lpi setting than knowing your output device's top resolution. An often-overlooked issue is the type of paper the material is printed on. Smoother paper (such as *glossy-coated* or *super-calendared*) can handle finer halftone spots because the paper's coating (also called its *finish*) minimizes ink bleeding. Standard office paper, such as that used in photocopiers and laser printers, is rougher and has some bleed that is usually noticeable only if you write on it with markers. Newsprint is very rough and has a heavy bleed. Typically, newspaper images are printed at 85 to 90 lpi; newsletter images on standard office paper print at 100 to 110 lpi; magazine images are printed at 120 to 150 lpi; calendars and coffee-table art books are printed at 150 to 200 lpi.

Other factors affecting lpi include the type of printing press and the type of ink used. Your printer representative should advise you on preferred settings.

If you output your document from your computer directly to film negatives (rather than to photographic paper that is then shot to create negatives), inform your printer representative. Outputting to negatives allows a higher lpi than outputting to paper because negatives created photographically cannot accurately reproduce the fine resolution that negatives that output directly on an imagesetter have. (If, for example, you output to 120 lpi on paper and then create a photographic negative, even the slightest change in the camera's focus will make the fine dots blurry. Outputting straight to negatives avoids this problem.) Printer representatives often assume that you're outputting to paper and base their advised lpi settings on this assumption.

The Graphics pane

The Graphics pane, shown in Figure 30-6, controls how graphics are printed and how fonts are downloaded. The options here are meant for professional printing, such as to imagesetters, in situations where you're working with a service bureau or in-house printing department.

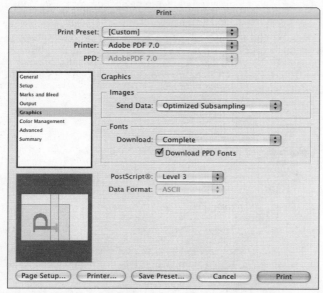

Figure 30-6: The Graphics pane of the Print dialog box

Your first option is the Send Data pop-up menu in the Images section. It has four options: All, Optimized Subsampling, Proxy (a low-resolution, 72 dpi version), and None. The Optimized Subsampling and Proxy options are meant to increase speed of proof prints, with Proxy being the fastest. The None option is handy for quick proofs meant to focus on the layout and the text.

The Fonts options require that you understand how your output device is configured to handle fonts. Be sure to ask your service bureau what options it prefers. Here are the options available:

✦ **Font Downloading.** Normally, when printing to a local printer, keep this option in the Download pop-up menu set to Subset, which sends font data to the printer as fonts are used. This means that if you use just one character of a font on a page, only that character is sent for that page, and if more characters are used on later pages, they are sent at that time. This is an efficient way to send font data to printers that don't have lots of memory or hard drive space to store complete font information for many typefaces.

✦ **Complete.** If you're printing to a device that has a lot of font memory — or if your document has many pages and uses a font in bits and pieces throughout — use this option from the Download pop-up menu. This sends the entire font to the printer's memory, where it resides for the entire print job. In cases such as those described, this is more efficient than the standard Subset method.

✦ **None.** Use this option from the Download pop-up menu if you're certain all the fonts you use reside in the printer's memory or on a hard drive attached to the printer. Many service bureaus load all the fonts for a job into the printer memory, and then print the job. They'll then clear out the printer memory for the next job and load just the fonts that job needs. This is efficient when a service bureau has lots of clients who use all sorts of fonts. Alternatively, some service bureaus attach a hard drive loaded with fonts to their imagesetters, saving the font-loading time for them and for InDesign.

✦ **Download PPD Fonts.** If selected, this option downloads any fonts specified as resident in the printer's PPD file. PPD files include lists of fonts that should reside in printer memory and thus don't need to be downloaded with each print job. Selecting this option overrides this, and downloads those fonts from your computer even if they should reside in the printer's memory. You'll rarely need to check this — it's more of a safety when creating output files for printing by someone else.

Finally, you can specify what PostScript language is used and how PostScript data is transmitted. Although you set these up in the Mac OS and Windows printer settings (refer to Figure 30-2), InDesign gives you the opportunity to override any defaults here, which can be handy when creating output files for printing elsewhere. From the PostScript pop-up menu, you can choose Level 2 or Level 3; use whichever the output device supports. (Most still use Level 2.) The Data Format pop-up menu is grayed out unless you chose PostScript File in the Printer pop-up menu; your choices are ASCII and Binary. If you choose ASCII, the PostScript file is more likely to be editable in programs like Adobe Illustrator, but the file will be larger. Ask your service bureau which it prefers.

The Color Management pane

The Color Management pane, shown in Figure 30-7, is where you manage color output (apply color calibration). The options are straightforward.

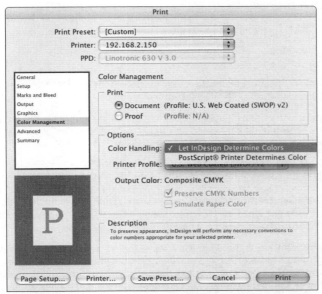

Figure 30-7: The Color Management pane of the Print dialog box

InDesign CS2 changes the options and layout of the Color Management pane. What had been called the Source Space section is now the Print section, while the previous Print Space section has been renamed the Options section and offers a different, simplified way to specify color output. Essentially, you no longer can specify an output intent or color reference dictionary (CRD) — these are now part of the profiles you assigned to your document and not individually changeable. But you also have new controls over CMYK number management and paper color simulation, as described later in this section.

Chapter 28 covers the techniques for and issues of applying color profiles and other color management settings that the profiles in the Color Management pane use.

✦ **Document or Proof.** In the Print section, select one of these options based on whether you want to use the document's profile or a different profile for proofing. The Proof option is available only if you choose an output device such as an imagesetter, for which you might make a proof locally using an inkjet or other printer and then use the imagesetter's profile (which you had embedded in your document, as explained in Chapter 28) when producing your final output.

✦ **Color Handling.** In the Options section, use this pop-up menu to choose between Let InDesign Determine Colors and PostScript Printer Determines Color. The first option uses the color-management options set in InDesign, while the latter lets the PostScript output device choose the color-management approach. This second option is not available unless you have chosen a color PostScript printer as the destination. (If you chose Composite Leave Unchanged in the Output pane's Color pop-up menu, you'll have the No Color Management option in the Color Handling pop-up menu.)

✦ **Printer Profile.** Use this pop-up menu to select the device to which the document will ultimately be printed. This is by default the same as the profile selected in the Edit Color Settings pane, which was covered in Chapter 28.

Depending on which Color Handling and Printing Profile options are selected, you may be able to use one or both of the following options:

✦ **Preserve CMYK Numbers.** This prevents the color management options from overriding the CMYK values in non-color-calibrated imported graphics.

✦ **Simulate Paper Color.** If you chose Proof of a Printing Condition as the Color Handling Method, selecting this option makes InDesign simulate the typical color of the paper you've chosen for proofing (through View ➪ Proof Setup).

The Advanced pane

The options in the Advanced pane, shown in Figure 30-8, control graphics file substitutions in an Open Prepress Interface (OPI) workflow and also set transparency flattening, which controls how transparent and semitransparent objects are handled during output.

If graphics files exist in high-resolution versions at your service bureau — typically, this occurs when the bureau scans in photographs at very high resolutions and sends you a lower-resolution version for layout placement — select the OPI Image Replacement option. This ensures that InDesign uses the high-resolution scans instead of the low-resolution layout versions.

The Omit for OPI section provides three additional related graphics file-handling options. You can have InDesign *not* send EPS, PDF, and bitmap images (such as TIFF files) by selecting the appropriate options. You would do so either to speed printing of proof copies, or when the service bureau will have such files in higher-resolution or color-corrected versions and will substitute their graphics for yours. InDesign keeps any OPI links, so the graphics at the service bureau will relink to your document during output.

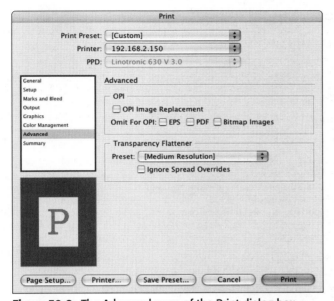

Figure 30-8: The Advanced pane of the Print dialog box

There are just two options in the Transparency Flattener section:

- ✦ **Preset.** This pop-up menu lets you select a transparency preset, or saved set of options. At the least, InDesign provides the three default options: [Low Resolution], [Medium Resolution], and [High Resolution].

- ✦ **Ignore Spread Overrides.** If this option is selected, any transparency settings you manually applied to document spreads are ignored and the selected preset in all cases is used instead.

Cross-
Reference

Transparency settings and setup are covered later in this chapter.

The Summary pane

The final Print dialog box pane is the Summary pane, shown in Figure 30-9. It simply lists your settings all in one place for easy review. The only option — Save Summary — saves the settings to a file so you can include it with your files when delivering them to a service bureau or for distribution to other staff members so they know the preferred settings.

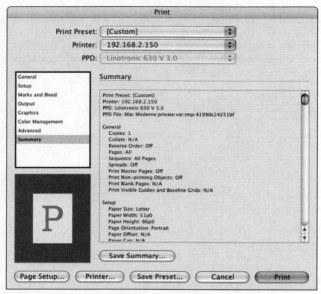

Figure 30-9: The Summary pane of the Print dialog box

Printing to File

You won't see an option to print to file in InDesign. If you choose PostScript File or Adobe PDF as your printers, InDesign creates a file in the chosen format. But if you want to print a document to file with specific printer settings embedded, you need to use the operating system's printer options. You access those by using the Printer and Page Setup buttons on Mac OS X and using the Setup button in Windows (see Figure 30-2).

 The process differs between Mac OS X and Windows.

In Windows, click Setup and then select the Print to File option in the resulting dialog box and click Print.

On the Mac, click Printer and choose the Output Options menu item from the pop-up menu in the resulting dialog box. Select the Save as File Option, choose the file format (PDF or PostScript) from the Format pop-up menu, and click Save.

 Note You should make all other Print dialog box changes in InDesign *before* taking this step because at this point you're actually creating the output file.

Working with Spot Colors and Separations

Accidentally using spot colors such as red and Pantone 111 (say, for picture and text box frames) in a document that contains four-color TIFF and EPS files is very easy. The result is that InDesign outputs as many as six plates: one each for the four process colors, plus one for red and one for Pantone 111. But, you can avoid these kinds of mistakes.

The Ink Manager dialog box

Accidentally using the wrong color type is exactly where the Ink Manager dialog box comes in. Accessed by clicking Ink Manager in the Output pane, this dialog box gives you finer controls over how color negatives output. Figure 30-10 shows the dialog box.

Most users will select the All Spots to Process option at the bottom of the dialog box. Selecting this option converts all colors to CMYK, reducing the print job to four plates (cyan, yellow, magenta, and black). Obviously, if you want to print a spot color on its own plate — perhaps a neon, metallic, or hard-to-simulate color like green or orange — you should not use this option. Instead, make sure that only the colors you do want to output to separate negatives are listed in the Ink Manager dialog box or in the Output pane.

If any colors should have been converted to process color but weren't, you have three choices:

✦ **Click the spot-color button.** You can override the spot color in the Ink Manager dialog box by clicking this button (a circle) to the left of the color's name. That converts it to a process color. (Clicking the process color button, a four-color box, converts a color back to a spot color.) This is the way to go for a quick fix.

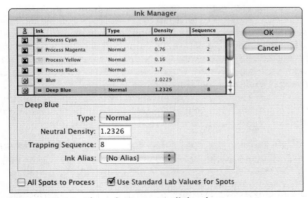

Figure 30-10: The Ink Manager dialog box

✦ **Make it a process color instead.** Do this by closing the Ink Manager and Print dialog boxes, and editing the color that was incorrectly set as a spot color in the Swatches pane (Window ➪ Swatches or F5) as covered in Chapter 8. This ensures that the color is permanently changed to a process color for future print jobs.

✦ **Convert all spot colors to CMYK process equivalents.** Do this by selecting the All Spots to Process option. This is the easiest method to make sure you don't accidentally print spot-color plates for a CMYK-only document.

The other Ink Manager options are for experts and should be changed only in consultation with your service bureau and commercial printer:

✦ **You can change the ink type in the Type pop-up menu.** Most inks — including the process inks — should be left at Normal. Use Transparent for varnishes and other finishes that let color through — you don't want InDesign to trap to such colors. If it did, no color would print under the varnish or finish. (A varnish is often used to highlight part of a page, such as making the text reflective in contrast to the rest of the page.) Use Opaque for metallics, pastels, and other thick colors; this setting lets adjacent colors trap to the edge of opaque objects, but it prevents trapping of underlying colors (because they will be totally covered over). Finally, use Opaque Ignore for inks that don't trap well with any other color — your service bureau or commercial printer will tell you when you need to do this.

✦ **You can change the neutral density for each ink.** This tells InDesign how to handle the trapping of differently saturated inks. For example, a dark color (highly saturated) needs to be trapped more conservatively against a light color to prevent excess intrusion. In coordination with your commercial printer, you might want to override the default neutral density settings if you find that the defaults don't properly handle some trapping combinations. It's possible that your commercial printer is using a different brand of ink than is assumed in the settings, for example, and that could require a density adjustment.

✦ **Arrange the order in which color negatives print.** Someone commercial printers permit you to do this. It affects the trapping, because InDesign presumes that the colors are printed in the standard order — cyan, then magenta, then yellow, then black, then any spot colors — and factors that into its trapping adjustments. In some cases, changing the printing order improves a publication's color balance, because it happens to favor a range of tones that the standard order might not treat properly. For example, if there's a lot of black in the background, you might want to print black first. Other colors overprint it, giving it a warmer feel than if black is printed on top of the other colors as is normal. To change the order of output used by InDesign's trapping calculations, select a color, and change its ink sequence number in the Trapping Sequence field; all other colors' sequences are automatically adjusted.

✦ **Apply a process color's settings to a spot color.** You can use the Ink Alias pop-up menu to do this, but I don't recommend you do this very often, as it makes the spot color print each dot over the dots of the selected process color, rather than be offset slightly so the color remains visible. You set an ink alias only if you are using a spot color in place of a standard process color — such as substituting a yolk color for standard yellow to create a special effect. In this case, the yolk color overprints the yellow color, replacing the yellow where both colors happened to be used.

✦ **Force one plate to be used for several versions of the same color.** Another case for using the Ink Alias feature is when your document has several color swatches that should be the same color. (Perhaps PDF files you placed used different names for the same color, such as PMS 175 and Pantone 175, so these multiple swatch names were all added to your document.) Ink Alias lets you have all these "colors" print on the same plate.

✦ **Force InDesign to substitute the basic CMYK process colors for the similar colors defined by the Pantone and HKS color models.** Do this by selecting the Use Standard Lab Values for Spots option. In most cases, the substitute colors are almost identical, so no one will notice, but check with your printer first because the type of paper you use or other factors may cause a different output than expected. Note that this option is selected by default.

New Feature The Use Standard Lab Values for Spots option is new to InDesign CS2.

Process colors

By default, each color defined in InDesign is set as a spot process color. And each spot color gets its own negative (plate), unless you specifically tell InDesign to translate the color into process colors. You do so when defining a new color by selecting the Process option in the Color Type pop-up menu in the Swatch Options dialog box that was described in Chapter 8, when you create or edit a color in the Swatches pane (Window ⇨ Swatches or F5). No matter whether a color is defined as a process or spot color, you can also select the All Spots to Process option in the Print dialog box's Output pane's Ink Manager dialog box when printing to convert all spot colors to process colors.

If you do primarily four-color work, edit the spot colors in the Swatches pane to make them process colors. If you make these changes with no document open, they become the defaults for all new documents.

If you do some spot-color work and some four-color work, duplicate the spot colors and translate the duplicates into process colors. Make sure that you use some clear color-naming convention, such as Blue P for the process-color version of blue (which is created by using 100 percent each of magenta and cyan).

The same is true when you use Pantone colors (and Trumatch, Focoltone, Toyo, ANPA, and DIC colors). If you do not select the Process option in the Swatch Options dialog box, these colors are output as spot colors. Again, you can define a Pantone color twice, making one of the copies a process color and giving it a name to indicate what it is. Then all you have to do is make sure that you pick the right color for the kind of output you want.

Tip You still can mix process and spot colors if you want. For example, if you want a gold border on your pages, you have to use Pantone ink because metallic colors cannot be produced through process colors. So use the appropriate Pantone color, and *don't* select the Process option when you define the color. When you make color separations, you get five negatives: one each for the four process colors and one for gold. That's fine because you specifically want the five negatives.

Color and separations preview

One thing to be careful of in computer-based layout is that colors interact differently on-screen than they do when printed. When inks overlap, the colors mix to produce a new color—cyan on yellow makes a green, for example. On-screen, cyan on yellow shows cyan where the two overlap. To compensate for that, InDesign can simulate color overprinting. To do so, choose View ⇨ Overprint Preview, or press Option+Shift+⌘+Y or Ctrl+Alt+Shift+Y. You should have this on as your default so what you see on-screen better represents what will print.

You can preview your color separations, as well as overprinting any other output by using the new Separations Preview pane (Window ⇨ Output ⇨ Separations or Shift+F6). Figure 30-11 shows the pane and its palette menu. By clicking each color and then the eye icon, you can turn on or off specific color plates; InDesign adjusts what appears on-screen accordingly.

To see just the CMYK plates, click the CMYK color (instead of turning on the cyan, yellow, magenta, and black plates individually). You can also hide all process colors the same way, so only spot colors are visible.

Figure 30-11: The Separations Preview pane

If you select Show Single Plates in Black in the palette menu and have the eye icon selected for only one plate, InDesign shows that plate in black on-screen. That's because it's often hard to see colors like magenta, yellow, and cyan clearly when they're by themselves.

And if color management is turned off, you can select the Desaturate Black option in the Separations Preview pane's palette menu. This converts any black objects overprinting other color objects to 80 percent black so the other objects are more visible during the preview.

The Separations Preview pane also lets you open the Ink Manager dialog box, which was covered earlier in this chapter.

QuarkXPress User   InDesign and QuarkXPress offer similar levels of color output controls, but InDesign does have several options QuarkXPress does not. One is setting ink density, another is automatic calculation of screen angles for spot colors, and a third is the ability to more accurately preview documents with overprinting colors.

Screen angles

Normally, you'd probably never worry about the screening angles for your color plates. After all, the service bureau makes those decisions, right? Maybe.

If you have your own imagesetter, or even if you're just using a proofing device, you should know how to change screen angles for the best output. If you're working with spot colors that have shades applied to them, you'll want to know what the screen angles are so that you can determine how to set the screening angles for those spot colors.

Screening angles determine how the dots comprising each of the four process colors — cyan, magenta, yellow, and black, or any spot colors — are aligned so they don't overprint each other. The rule of thumb is that dark colors should be at least 30 degrees apart, while lighter colors (for example, yellow) should be at least 15 degrees apart from other colors. That rule of thumb translates into a 15-degree angle for cyan, 75 degrees for magenta, 0 degrees for yellow, and 45 degrees for black.

But those defaults sometimes result in *moiré patterns*, which are distortions in the image's light and dark areas caused when the dots making up the colors don't arrange themselves evenly. With traditional color-separation technology, a service bureau would have to adjust the angles manually to avoid such moirés — an expensive and time-consuming process. With the advent of computer technology, modern output devices, such as imagesetters, can calculate angles based on the output's lpi settings to avoid most moiré patterns. (Each image's balance of colors can cause a different moiré, which is why there is no magic formula.) Every major imagesetter vendor uses its own proprietary algorithm to make these calculations.

InDesign automatically uses the printer's PPD values to calculate the recommended halftoning, lpi, and frequency settings shown in the Output pane of the Print dialog box. But for spot colors, it's basically a guess as to what screening angle a color should get. The traditional default is to give it the same angle as yellow, because if a spot color's dots overprint yellow dots, the effect is less noticeable than if it overprinted, say, black dots. But if you have multiple spot colors, that approach doesn't work. In that case, choose a screening angle for the color whose hue is closest to the spot colors. Fortunately, InDesign calculates a recommended angle for you, so you don't have to make any guesses. As always, don't forget to consult your service bureau or printing manager.

Working with Transparency

InDesign lets you import objects with transparent portions, as well as create transparent objects using the Color and Swatches panes. Using features such as the Drop Shadow and Feather options in the Object menu also might create transparency. But working with transparency can create unintended side effects in how overlapping objects actually appear when printed or viewed on-screen in a PDF file. To address that, InDesign offers the ability to both control transparency on selected objects and groups, as well as control how transparency is handled during output.

To apply transparency to objects in InDesign, you use the Transparency pane (Window ➪ Transparency or Shift+F10), as Chapter 10 explains. The more objects you have overlapping each other with transparency settings applied, the more complex the output calculations are to print those effects. This can prevent a document from printing because it can overwhelm the printer or other output device. That's where transparency *flattening* comes into play. This feature breaks up the overlapping areas into distinct graphics during output, creating a mosaic of pieces that produce the intended effect.

QuarkXPress User

QuarkXPress has no equivalent to InDesign's transparency settings. QuarkXPress users instead must rely on such settings in programs such as Adobe Photoshop and Illustrator for imported pictures and do without them for objects created in QuarkXPress.

InDesign comes with three transparency flattening settings — [Low Resolution], [Medium Resolution], and [High Resolution] — which you can edit in the Transparency Flattener Presets dialog box. To open this dialog box, shown in Figure 30-12, choose Edit ➪ Transparency Flattener Presets. The dialog box shows the settings for each preset as you select them. Use this dialog box to create, modify, delete, export (Save), and import (Load) presets. (You cannot modify or delete the three default presets.)

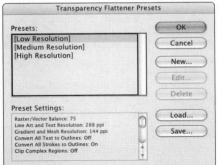

Figure 30-12: The Transparency Flattener Presets dialog box

Figure 30-13 shows the Transparency Flattener Preset Options dialog box, which appears when you create or modify a preset. There's a lot of trial and error in developing transparency flattener presets because the complexity of your documents and the capacity of your output devices will vary widely. But here are some guidelines:

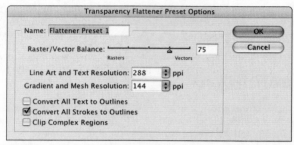

Figure 30-13: The Transparency Flattener Preset Options dialog box

✦ The most accurate transparency blends are achieved with a Raster/Vector Balance set to 100, which means use all vectors rather than convert blends to bitmap images. The [Low Resolution] preset is set at 75, which means that three-quarters of the blends are vectors and one-quarter is converted to bitmaps. The other options have higher vector proportions.

✦ Flattener resolution should be set to a value that corresponds with your output device's dpi. For Line Art and Text Resolution, 600 ppi or higher is fine, while 150 ppi is fine for gradients and meshes (overlapping transparencies). But the higher the output resolution of your output device, the higher you would make these values.

Note   InDesign uses pixels per inch, or ppi, rather than dpi in the Transparency Flattener Preset Options dialog box. They're equivalent measurements for computer-generated images. InDesign uses ppi for transparency because it's working with the pixels of your images rather than with the dots output by your printer.

✦ If you apply transparency to objects that overprint or underprint text, you likely will select the Convert All Text to Outlines option; otherwise, InDesign may make the text that interacts with transparent objects thicker than text that doesn't.

✦ Convert Strokes to Outlines has the same effect on lines and strokes for InDesign objects that overlap or underlap objects with transparency.

✦ The Clip Complex Regions options apply only if the Raster/Vector Balance is less than 100. It corrects for a phenomenon called *stitching,* in which a transparent area has both vectors and bitmaps that create a blocky feel. This option isolates those areas and forces them to be all-vector.

Note   You can apply transparency settings directly to a spread by selecting a spread in the Pages pane (Window ⇨ Pages or F12), and then choosing Spread Flattening ⇨ Custom from the palette menu. You'll get a dialog box like the Transparency Flattener Presets dialog box (refer to Figure 30-12), except that any settings created here are applied only to the selected spread and are not saved as a preset for use elsewhere.

Once set up, you can apply transparency presets to your document in the Advanced pane of the Print dialog box as described earlier in this chapter.

InDesign also lets you preview flattening settings, using the Flattener Preview pane. Shown in Figure 30-14, this pane lets you preview transparent objects and their flattening. To open the pane, choose Window ⇨ Output ⇨ Flattener Preview.

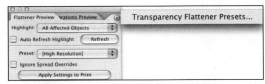

Figure 30-14: The Flattener Preview pane

In the pane, you can select what to preview in the Highlight pop-up menu. Your options are None, Rasterized Complex Regions, Transparent Objects, Affected Objects, Affected Graphics, Outlined Strokes, Outlined Text, Raster-Fill Text and Strokes, and All Rasterized Regions. (Note that the rasterized options display overlapping transparent objects that InDesign would need to convert to bitmaps during flattening—not simply any bitmap images in your document.) Select the area you're concerned may not output at sufficient quality. If you select the Auto Refresh Highlight option, InDesign updates the preview if you change any settings; if not, you can update the preview by clicking Refresh.

You can also check the flattening of different presets—just choose a preset from the Preset pop-up menu. Likewise, you can see what would happen to a spread that has a custom flattening applied if you were to override those custom settings—just select the Ignore Spread Overrides option.

If you like how the flattening looks, you can preapply them to the Print dialog box by clicking Apply Settings to Print.

Why Transparency Makes Printers Nervous

You should know that many printers dread transparency because these effects require very sophisticated calculations in their imagesetters, which can make output jobs slow to a crawl and often result in incorrect output. One reason is that Adobe PostScript Level 1 and 2, EPS, and Adobe PDF 1.3 do not support Adobe's transparency technology in its native state. Therefore, transparency information must be flattened—the overlapping elements in a stack of transparent objects are converted to a single, flat layer of opaque objects—for export to EPS or Adobe PDF 1.3 format, or for printing to PostScript desktop printers, PostScript Level 2 raster-image processors (RIPs), and some PostScript 3 RIPs. (Although newer Adobe applications and the PDF 1.4 format do, many printers use older imagesetters, whose high cost requires they be used for many years so the printer can recoup its investment.)

Flattening converts the objects that interact with transparency into a new set of discrete, abutting objects called *atomic regions*, each with its own blended color. The borders of the atomic regions follow the natural shapes and object boundaries whenever possible. Flattening retains the integrity of the original transparent objects whenever possible, so that vectors remain vectors and type remains type. However, depending on the complexity of a design and the flattener settings you select, the flattening process may rasterize type or vector objects, convert type or strokes to outlines, or expand patterns to flatten the objects while retaining the original appearance.

Ideally, your service bureau or printer will handle the flattening, so it can optimize the results for the equipment. If you send the printer native Creative Suite files or PDF 1.4 or later output, the printer should be able to work with the native transparency and do the flattening. Otherwise, it will have to live with the flattening results you create (be sure to test files in this case to identify any issues early).

Summary

In InDesign you have many options from which to choose to control exactly how your document prints. The right options will depend on the document's contents and the output device you're using.

Be sure to define your colors as process colors unless you want them to print on their own plates. Although InDesign will let you convert all colors to process colors when you print, there are times when you want some colors to print on their own plate (these are called *spot colors*) and others to be converted to process, and the only way to make that happen is to define colors as process or as spot in the first place.

InDesign's transparency options let you control how overlapping objects print, as well as how those overlapping areas are handled during output to ensure both quality reproduction and speedy processing.

✦   ✦   ✦

Creating Output Files

In this electronic age, there are many reasons not to print a document, at least not directly. You may want to deliver the document to readers in electronic format, such as in HTML or Adobe PDF. Or you may want to generate a file that your service bureau can output for you at an imagesetter — a file that you may send over a network, through the Internet, on a high-capacity disk, or even as an electronic-mail attachment to a device that could be down the hall or in another state.

Selecting the Best Output Option

InDesign has several options for creating output files:

✦ You can export to two variants of the PostScript printing language: Adobe Portable Document Format (PDF) or Encapsulated PostScript (EPS).

✦ You can print to file using all the settings described in Chapter 30 — either in EPS or plain PostScript format — rather than output directly to a printer, creating a file tuned specifically to the printer driver that you selected.

The option you pick has several advantages and consequences; let's look at each choice separately.

Exporting to PDF

This option creates a file that can be linked to a Web page, whether on the Internet or on a corporate intranet. It can also be accessed from a CD or other disk medium, as long as the recipient has the free Adobe Reader program (available for download from www.adobe.com/acrobat). Finally, a PDF file can be used by a commercial printer or service bureau as the master file from which to print your documents.

This file can include some or all of the fonts, or expect the ultimate output device to have them. You also have control over the resolution of the graphics, which lets you, for example, create a high-resolution file for output on an imagesetter or a low-resolution version for display on the Web.

The PDF file won't have information on the specific printer, so a service bureau or printing department could use it on any available output devices. But not all service bureaus and printing departments are geared to print from PDF files; while this is an increasingly popular option, it is by no means ubiquitous. To print a PDF file directly, the output device must be a PostScript Level 3 device; otherwise, the service bureau must print the PDF file from Adobe Acrobat or use a PDF-oriented workflow publishing system such as those offered by Creo (go to www.creo.com for more information on this product).

Exporting to EPS

This option creates a file that can be sent to many output devices or edited by a PostScript-savvy graphics program like Illustrator, FreeHand, or CorelDraw. With InDesign, you can add a margin for bleeds — but you can't include printer's marks.

Most service bureaus can print directly from EPS files. But note that each page or spread in your document is sent to a separate file, so a service bureau may prefer a prepress-oriented PostScript file or a PDF file that combines all pages into one file, which simplifies its output effort.

The lack of printer's marks might also bother your commercial printer because it needs them to properly combine film negatives. Using a system such as Creo's, the service bureau can add printer's marks and integrate high-resolution and color-corrected images — so EPS could remain a solid output option depending on your service bureau's capabilities.

Tip   Exported PDF or EPS files can be imported back into InDesign (or other programs, including QuarkXPress, PageMaker, FreeHand, Illustrator, CorelDraw, Photoshop, and Photo-Paint) as graphics. This is handy if you want, for example, to run a small version of the cover on your contents page to give the artist credit, or if you want to show a page from a previous issue in a letters section where readers are commenting on a story. If you're creating PDF files, be sure in these cases just to export the page or spread you want to use — even though only one page or spread displays when imported into a page-layout program, the file contains the data for all other pages, possibly and unnecessarily making its size unwieldy. (When exporting to EPS, a separate file is created for each page or spread, so this is not an issue.)

Exporting to PostScript prepress

If you know exactly what device your service bureau will use to output your document, and you know all the settings, you can create a PostScript prepress file. All your printer settings are embedded, making the file print reliably only by the target printer.

Note   Remember to work with your service bureau, commercial printer, or printing department — whoever will get the output file — to understand what their needs and expectations are. Although some output files are fully or partially editable, it's usually not easy to know what might be incorrect in a document until the expensive step of actually printing pages or negatives.

Creating PDF Files

Typically, you'll want to directly export your InDesign files as PDF files rather than create a PostScript file and translate to PDF using the separate Adobe Acrobat Distiller product. First, I'll show how to export, and then I'll explain how to print to PDF on those occasions when that's the better option.

Exporting PDF files

An easy way to create a PDF file from InDesign is to export it by choosing File ➪ Export, or pressing ⌘+E or Ctrl+E. The Export dialog box appears, which like any standard Save dialog box lets you name the file and determine what drive and folder the file is to be saved in. The key control in the Export dialog box is the Formats pop-up menu, where you choose the format (in this case, Adobe PDF).

Tip   The fastest way to create a PDF file is to choose File ➪ PDF Export Presets and then select a preset from the submenu. There are seven presets optimized for different output needs. You can also add your own, as explained a bit later in this chapter. When you select a preset from the submenu, you then see the Export dialog box. Choosing a preset defaults the Formats pop-up menu to Adobe PDF and preconfigures the PDF export settings covered in the following sections.

Tip   If you're working with the InDesign Books feature (see Chapter 32), you can export the book's chapters to PDF files from an open book's pane, using the Export Book to PDF option in its palette menu. (If one or more documents in the book are selected in the pane, the menu option will change to Export Selected Documents to PDF.) The setup options are the same as for exporting individual documents.

Understanding Imposition

Layout artists may work on single pages or spreads, but printing presses rarely do. Sure, for short-run jobs, your printer may actually work with one page at a time, but typically, it works with forms, also called *signatures*.

Forms are groups of pages aligned so that when they are folded, cut, and trimmed they end up in proper numerical sequence. This arrangement of pages on a form is called *imposition*.

One popular printing method takes a huge sheet that encompasses anywhere from four to 64 pages, folds it, cuts it into pages, and trims the pages. This results in a stack of pages in the right order — a process known as *perfect binding*. This technique is used for square-backed publications such as books, many magazines, and many catalogs.

The other popular printing method also uses forms, but alignment is completed in a different way. Here, the form is broken into two-page spreads that are cut and trimmed, and then stacked separately. A page from each stack is added to a pile, and the pile is then folded to create the right page sequence — this is called a *booklet*. These folded spreads are stapled in the center in a process known as *saddle stitching*. Many magazines and catalogs use this approach.

Continued

Continued

Both approaches usually use large sheets of paper, called a *web,* which is why such commercial printing is known as SWOP, or Specifications for Web Offset Publications. (*Offset* refers to the way the ink is delivered to the page, with the ink offset to an intermediate roller between the color plate and the paper. This ensures that just the right amount of ink is placed on each sheet, sort of how an ink stamp works.)

Understanding how forms are configured will show why what InDesign calls a *reader's spread* — the two adjacent pages that a reader sees when reading (and that a layout artist sees when designing on-screen) — is usually not how you want to output pages for use at a commercial printer. Printing reader's spreads makes more sense if you are, for example, wanting to show a client a mockup of the document, so you print spreads together on large paper (such as printing two 8½-x-11-inch pages on an 11-x-17-inch sheet of paper).

The figure shows how a perfect-bound publication form is numbered, as well as a saddle-stitched form. Note that a form can have a number of pages other than 16 but must be in multiples of four pages.

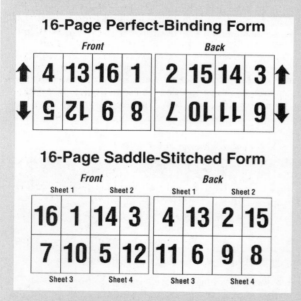

To figure out the page sequence for a perfect-bound form, take a sheet of paper, and fold it in half as often as needed to create the number of pages on the form. You now have a booklet. Number the pages (front and back) with a pencil, and then unfold the paper to see how the form is put together. The front sides are one form, and the back sides another.

To figure out the page sequence for a saddle-stitched form, you can take a sheet of paper for each spread, stack them, fold them once, and then number the pages (front and back) with a pencil, and then separate the sheets to see how the form is put together. The front sides are one form, and the back sides another. Another way to do it is to realize that the bottom sheet contains page 1 and the final page on the back, and page 2 and the next-to-final page on the front. The sheet on top would have pages 3 and FP–2 (where FP is the final page number) on the back and pages 4 and FP–3 on the back, and so on until the middle sheet.

After you select Adobe PDF in the Export dialog box's Formats pop-up menu and given the file a name and location, click Save to get the Export Adobe PDF dialog box shown in Figure 31-1. The dialog box has six panes; General is the one displayed when you open the dialog box. There are several options that are accessible from all six panes:

✦ **Adobe PDF Preset.** This pop-up menu lets you select from both predefined sets of PDF-export settings (similar to the printer presets covered in Chapter 30), as well as any presets you may have created.

✦ **Standard.** This pop-up menu lets you choose which PDF interchange (PDF/X) format to use. For prepress workflow, you might choose one of the PDF/X-1a or PDF/X-3 options in the Standard pop-up menu (the four-digit numbers at the end of the option names refer to the year that any revisions to the standard were added). PDF/X is a standard version of PDF, sanctioned by the International Standards Organization (ISO), meant to ensure consistent reproduction across a range of equipment. Irrelevant for on-screen viewing, PDF/X should be used if your service bureau is using compatible equipment. Otherwise, leave this pop-up menu at the default setting of None.

✦ **Compatibility.** This pop-up menu lets you choose which PDF file version to save the file as. Your options are Acrobat 4 (PDF 1.3), Acrobat 5 (PDF 1.4), Acrobat 6 (PDF 1.5), and Acrobat 7 (PDF 1.6). Choosing Acrobat 4 (PDF 1.3) is the best option for documents to be distributed on CD or over the Web because it ensures the broadest number of people will be able to view the file. Choose a later version only if you're certain your intended recipients use that version of Acrobat or Acrobat Reader. For example, if your company has standardized on Acrobat 5 and the document will be used only internally, it's fine to pick the Acrobat 5 (PDF 1.4) option. Likewise, if you're sending the PDF file to a service bureau, use the version of Acrobat it uses because later versions of Acrobat support more features, especially for commercial printing. (Versions 1.5 and later, for example, support native transparency.)

New Feature Support for Acrobat 7's PDF 1.6 format is new to InDesign CS2.

✦ **Save Preset.** Click this to save any settings made in the Export Adobe PDF dialog box as a new preset. (You can also define new PDF presets by choosing File ⇨ PDF Export Presets.)

✦ **Cancel.** Click this to cancel PDF export.

✦ **Export.** Click this to create the PDF file based on the settings selected in the various panes.

The General pane

Use the General pane to determine what is exported. The pane has four sections: Description, Pages, Options, and Include. The Description pane just says what the PDF export does.

In the Pages section, you can set the following options:

✦ **Description.** Type the description in this field that appears in the PDF file's Description pane of the Document Properties dialog box if opened in Adobe Acrobat (File ⇨ Document Properties, or ⌘+D or Ctrl+D).

✦ **Pages.** You can select from among these options to print all pages or a range of pages, in which case you type a range in the Range field. When specifying a range of pages, you can type nonconsecutive ranges, such as **1-4, 7, 10-13, 15, 18, 20**.

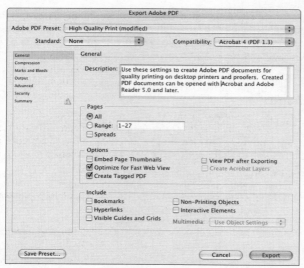

Figure 31-1: The General pane of the Export Adobe PDF dialog box

Tip

If you want to print from a specific page to the end of the document, just type the hyphen after the initial page number, such as **4-**. InDesign figures out what the last page is. Similarly, to start from the first page to a specified page, just start with the hyphen as in **-11**.

Tip

InDesign lets you type absolute page numbers in the Range field. For example, typing **+6-+12** prints the document's sixth through twelfth pages, no matter what their page numbers are.

✦ **Spreads.** When this option is selected the document prints facing pages on the same sheet of paper, which is handy when showing clients comps, but make sure you have a printer that can handle that large paper size.

Tip

You may not want to use the Spreads option when outputting a PDF file for eventual printing on an imagesetter if you have bleeds, because there will be no bleed between the spreads. If you use traditional *perfect-binding* (square spines) or *saddle-stitching* (stapled spines) printing methods in which facing pages are not printed contiguously, do not use this option.

In the Options section, you can select the following options:

✦ **Embed Page Thumbnails.** Select this option if you're creating a PDF file to be viewed on-screen — these thumbnails help people using the Adobe Reader program navigate your document more easily. But if the PDF files are being sent to a service bureau or commercial printer for printing, there's no need to generate the thumbnails.

✦ **Optimize for Fast Web View.** Always select this option — this minimizes file size without compromising the output.

✦ **Create Tagged PDF.** Select this option to embed XML tag information into the PDF file. This is useful for XML-based workflows and Adobe eBooks.

New Feature

The Create Tagged PDF option had been labeled eBooks Tags in InDesign CS and was located in the Include section.

✦ **View PDF after Exporting.** Select this option if you want to see the results of the PDF export as soon as the export is complete, Typically, however, you should not select this option because you likely will have other things you want to do before launching Adobe Reader (or the full Adobe Acrobat program, if you own it) to proof your files.

✦ **Create Acrobat Layers.** If you selected Acrobat 6 (PDF 1.5) or Acrobat 7 (PDF 1.6) in the Compatibility pop-up menu, you can select this option, which outputs any InDesign layers to separate layers in Acrobat. (Acrobat 6 was the first version of Acrobat to support layers.) If you choose a different Compatibility option, Create Acrobat Layers is grayed out.

In the Include section, you can select the following options:

✦ **Bookmarks.** This takes InDesign table-of-contents (TOC) information and preserves it as bookmarks in the exported PDF file.

✦ **Hyperlinks.** This preserves any hyperlinks added in InDesign. Otherwise, the hyperlinks are converted to standard text.

✦ **Visible Guides and Grids.** This includes the on-screen guides and grids in the output version — an option you'd use only when creating PDF files meant to be used as designer examples, not for readers or for prepress.

✦ **Non-Printing Objects.** This includes any objects marked as Nonprinting through the Attributes pane (Window ➪ Attributes).

✦ **Interactive Elements.** This preserves interactive objects such as buttons rather than convert them to static graphics.

✦ **Multimedia.** This pop-up menu lets you control how embedded sound and video are handled. This option is available only if you choose Acrobat 6 (PDF 1.5) or Acrobat 7 (PDF 1.6) in the Compatibility pop-up menu. The options are Use Object Settings, Link All, or Embed All. In InDesign, you can embed a sound or movie file, or link to one. This option lets you override the individual settings and make all such objects embedded or linked.

Cross-Reference

Chapter 33 covers interactive documents and eBooks, including the use of buttons and multimedia elements.

The Compression pane

All the options in this pane, shown in Figure 31-2, compress your document's graphics. For documents you're intending to print professionally, make sure that for Color, Grayscale, and Monochrome image types, the No Sampling Change option is selected (Figure 31-2 shows the option set to Bicubic Downsampling to), and that Compression is set to None. You don't want to do anything that affects the resolution or quality of your bitmap images if you're outputting to a high-resolution device.

But it's fine to select the Crop Image Data to Frames option because this discards portions of pictures not visible on-screen, reducing file size and reducing processing time during output (imagesetters and other devices usually have to process the entire image, even if only part of it is actually printed).

It's also fine to select the Compress Text and Line Art option. It compresses vector graphics (both imported and those created in InDesign) as well as text, but does so without affecting output quality.

The compression settings are more appropriate for documents meant to be viewed online, as explained in the sidebar "Settings for On-Screen Usage" later in this chapter. You usually leave the image downsampling at 150 pixels per inch (ppi) for color and grayscale images, and at 300 ppi for black-and-white images. Even though a computer monitor's resolution is 72 ppi, you want enough resolution so when a reader zooms in that the images are still clear. A good rule of thumb for documents to be printed is that the downsampling or subsampling ppi for color and grayscale images should be at least double the printer's lpi.

For the Image Quality setting for images, Medium quality is fine for on-screen documents, but not for documents you intend to let readers print or that will be output at a service bureau. A rule of thumb is to choose High if the documents will be printed on an inkjet or laser printer, and Maximum if they will be printed at an imagesetter or other high-end output device.

Note that JPEG compression is *lossy,* meaning it discards data to save space. That's why its Image Quality settings are characterized with subjective terms like Low, Medium, and High. Zip compression is lossless, so no image detail data is discarded. Instead, you limit the color depth by choosing between 4-bit (16 colors) and 8-bit (256 colors).

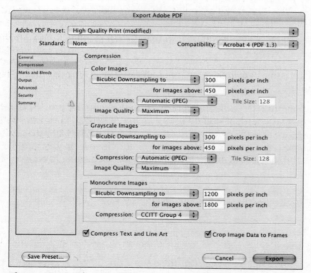

Figure 31-2: The Compression pane of the Export Adobe PDF dialog box

When Compatibility is set to Acrobat 6 or later (format version 1.5 or later) and Compression is set to Automatic (JPEG 2000), a Tile Size field is available and determines the size of the tiles for progressive display. For large images, this option will show subsequent pieces, or tiles, of the image, until the full image has been displayed, so the reader has a visual indication that the page is in fact loading. You can change the size of the tile from the default of 256 pixels.

Understanding Compression Methods

The act of choosing a compression method for the color, grayscale, and monochrome images in a PDF is simple—you just pick something from a menu in the Compression pane of the Export Adobe PDF dialog box. The challenge is in knowing what to pick. Take a look at the type of images the compression for which the methods work best, and then choose the one that represents the bulk of the images in your layout.

✦ Zip compression is appropriate for black-and-white or color images with repeating patterns (usually screen shots or simple images created in paint programs).

✦ JPEG compression works well for continuous-tone photographs in grayscale or color. JPEG results in smaller files than Zip compression, because it throws out some image data, possibly reducing image accuracy.

✦ Use CCITT compression for black-and-white images or 1-bit images. Group 4 works well for most monochrome images, while Group 3 is good for PDFs that will be faxed electronically.

Downsampling and subsampling accomplish similar goals, but use different mathematic techniques to do so. When you reduce the dpi, you're essentially throwing away image data to make it smaller—for example, replacing a 100-×-100-pixel image with a 25-×-25-pixel version reduces the file size to ¹⁄₁₆ of its original size. Downsampling averages adjacent pixels' colors and replaces the cluster of adjacent pixels with one averaged pixel as it reduces the image size. (There are two methods for downsampling: bicubic and average. Bicubic usually, but not always, results in a truer image. Average downsampling tends to work better in nonphotographic images, with less minute detail.) Subsampling does no averaging; it simply throws away pixels in between the ones it retains. Downsampling looks better for photographic images with lots of detail and color; subsampling looks better for images with clear color differences and few intricate details.

For prepress purposes, the resolution should be one and a half to two times the line screen ruling used to print the file. For on-screen purposes, keep in mind that higher resolutions are better when users need to increase the view scale in the PDF (for example, if they need to see detail in a map). In the Acrobat support section of www.adobe.com, you can find more details about specific image resolutions that work well with printer resolutions.

Marks and Bleeds pane

Use this pane, shown in Figure 31-3, to set the page bleed and printer's marks.

You typically set printer's marks only for files meant to be output on an imagesetter or other prepress device. Typically, you should select All Page Marks. Your Offset amount should be the same as or more than the bleed amount—if your Offset is less than the bleed, it's possible the marks could appear in your page's margins.

If you have elements bleeding off the page, you'll want a Bleed setting of at least 0p9 (⅛ inch)—that builds in enough forgiveness so that when the pages are folded and trimmed, any elements that bleed off the page will, in fact, do so even if there's a slip in the page alignment.

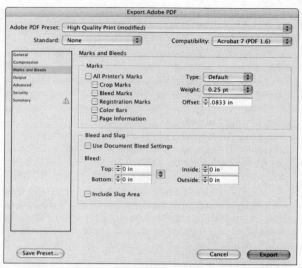

Figure 31-3: The Marks and Bleeds pane of the Export Adobe PDF dialog box

If you specified a slug area (which specifies space for the printing of printer's marks) in the New Document (File ➪ New ➪ Document, or ⌘+N or Ctrl+N) or Document Setup (File ➪ Document Setup, or Option+⌘+P or Ctrl+Alt+P) dialog boxes, select the Include Slug Area option to reserve that space in your PDF file.

Likewise, if you specified bleed settings in the New Document or Document Setup dialog boxes, you can have InDesign use those settings by selecting the Use Document Bleed Settings option.

Cross-Reference
These marks, bleed, and slug options are the same as for direct printing and are covered in detail in Chapter 30.

The Output pane

The Output pane, shown in Figure 31-4, has two sections — Color and PDF/X — where you control color calibration.

New Feature
The Output pane is new to InDesign CS2, though its features existed in the Advanced pane in InDesign CS. Several of the options have been changed to reflect InDesign CS2's new color-management settings.

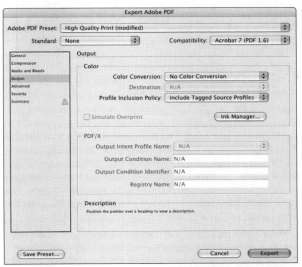

Figure 31-4: The Output pane of the Export Adobe PDF dialog box

In the Color section, you have the following options:

✦ **Color Conversion.** This pop-up menu lets you choose from among No Color Conversion, which keeps the colors in whatever model in which they were defined; Convert to Destination, which converts them to the printer's color space (typically CMYK); and Repurpose, which converts only colors in objects that have color profiles assigned to them.

✦ **Destination.** This pop-up menu lets you choose the target output device.

✦ **Profile Inclusion Policy.** This pop-up menu lets you embed the color profile for the destination device in the PDF file or exclude it. You can choose from Don't Include Profiles, Include All Profiles, Include Tagged Source Profiles, and Include All RGB and Tagged Source CMYK Profiles. (A tagged profile is one that is set in InDesign, as opposed to an object imported with no profile. In other words, any images without profiles will not get the default profile assigned to them.)

✦ **Simulate Overprint.** Select this option if you're exporting to Acrobat 4 (PDF 1.3) format and have objects overprinting each other (through the Attributes pane). This option is grayed out if you're exporting to Acrobat 5 or later format, because these formats support actual overprinting.

✦ **Ink Manager.** Click this button to change which color plates print, adjust ink density, and alter trapping sequence. (See Chapter 30 for more on this option, which is also offered when printing.)

✦ **Output Intent Profile Name.** If you're exporting with PDF/X compatibility, you can choose which output device or standard to be compatible with through this pop-up menu in the PDF/X section. (Note that whatever you choose here will change Destination popup menu's setting as well.) Depending on the output device or standard you select, you may be able to add device-specific comments in the Output Condition, Output Condition Identifier, and/or Registry name fields; consult with your service bureau.

See Chapter 28 for more on color calibration, rendering intent, and color trapping settings. See Chapter 30 for more on working with color plates, the Ink Manager, and ink density.

The Advanced pane

Use the Advanced pane, shown in Figure 31-5, to manage font embedding, Open Prepress Interface (OPI) image substitution, and transparency flattening.

The Fonts section lets you control which fonts are included in the PDF file. Including fonts increases the file size but ensures that the document displays or prints correctly, no matter if the recipient has the same fonts the document uses. The Subset Fonts When Percent of Characters Used Is Less Than field tells InDesign how to embed fonts in the exported PDF file. The default value of 100% tells it to include the entire font for each typeface used. This is the best option because it ensures that if your service bureau needs to edit the file later, the file will include all font information. If you choose a lower value and the service bureau changes some text, there's a chance that some characters used in the editing won't be in the file.

The value is a threshold, telling InDesign that if the file uses less than that percentage of the font's characters, to embed just the characters used; or, if the file uses more than that percentage, to embed them all. If your document uses many fonts but just a few characters in each, you might want to pick a value like 35%, because chances are less that you have typos in such documents (they tend to be ads and posters that are heavily proofed beforehand).

You can use a lower threshold for documents to be viewed solely on-screen because you don't expect readers to edit the files. In fact, you may lock the file to prevent such modification.

Note Some fonts can be locked, preventing their inclusion in PDF files. To avoid that problem, simply don't use them.

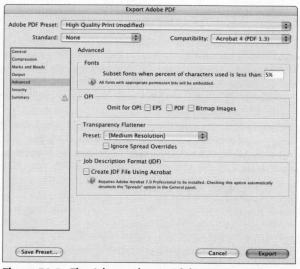

Figure 31-5: The Advanced pane of the Export Adobe PDF dialog box

In the OPI section, use the three options in the Omit For section to strip out EPS, PDF, and/or bitmap images — you would use this only if you had high-resolution or color-corrected versions of these files at a service bureau and wanted the bureau to substitute those files for the lower-resolution placeholder files you used during layout.

In the Transparency Flattener section, if you are exporting to Acrobat 4 (PDF 1.3) format, you can select a transparency preset, as well as override any transparency settings applied to individual spreads. Transparency flattening reduces the complexity of documents that have lots of transparent and semitransparent objects overlapping each other, which can dramatically increase output time and even prevent printing. If you are exporting to later versions of Acrobat, InDesign's flattening settings are passed on unchanged.

See Chapter 30 for more on OPI and transparency flattening.

Finally, the Create JDF File Using Acrobat option essentially passes on the instructions for the PDF creation onto Adobe Acrobat Professional 7 (which must be installed on your system) and has it actually implement them. This gives the service bureau (or whoever is producing the final file) the job instructions separate from the underlying data, so the instructions can be changed as needed. Otherwise, the PDF file produced in InDesign cannot be changed unless you regenerate it in InDesign. Note that JDF files work only with the new Acrobat Professional 7 software, so this option is useless for organizations using earlier versions of Acrobat.

Security pane

The Security pane, shown in Figure 31-6, has no relevance to documents intended to be output at a service bureau or commercial printer, so make sure the Require a Password to Open the Document and the Use a Password to Restrict Printing, Editing, and Other Tasks options are not selected in that case.

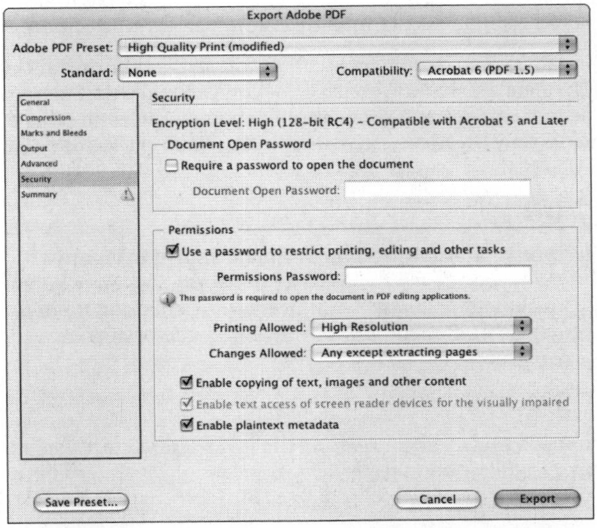

![Export Adobe PDF dialog box showing the Security pane]

Figure 31-6: The Security pane of the Export Adobe PDF dialog box

These settings *are* useful if you're publishing the document electronically, because they control who can access the document and what they can do with the document once it's open. Here's how they work:

✦ **Encryption Level.** This section's options depend on the option set in the Compatibility pop-up menu; Acrobat 5 (PDF 1.4) or higher use High (128-Bit RC4) encryption, while earlier versions use 40-bit RC4.

✦ **Document Open Password.** In this section of the Security pane, you can require a password to open the exported PDF file by selecting this option and typing a password in the associated text field. If no password is typed here, you'll be forced to type one in a dialog box that appears later. To access protected content, recipients must use the Security pane in Acrobat (File ➪ Document Properties, or ⌘+D or Ctrl+D).

✦ **Permissions.** You can restrict recipients' actions by selecting the Use a Password to Restrict Printing, Editing, and Other Tasks option in this section, and then specifying permissible actions using the Printing Allowed and Changes Allowed pop-up menus, as well as selecting from among the options that follow (the number of options displayed varies based on the preset chosen). You can also require a password to allow editing of the file in another application. Your management options include the following:

  • **Printing Allowed.** You can select None, Low-Resolution (150 dpi), and High Resolution.

  • **Changes Allowed.** You can select None; Inserting, Deleting and Rotating Pages; Filling in Form Fields and Signing; Commenting, Filling in Forms Fields, and Signing; and Any Except Extract Pages. (*Signing* means using digital signatures to verify sender and recipient identities.)

  • **Enable Copying of Text, Images, and Other Content.** If it's okay for recipients to use the PDF file's objects, select this option.

  • **Enable Text Access of Screen Reader Devices for the Visually Impaired.** If you are exporting to Acrobat 5 (PDF 1.4) or later and if you want the file to be accessible to visually impaired recipients that read text aloud, select this option.

  • **Enable Plaintext Metadata.** For documents with *metadata* — authoring information associated with XML documents and Web pages — you can make that metadata visible to Web-based search engines and similar applications by selecting this option. This option is available only if you are exporting to Acrobat 6 (PDF 1.5) or later.

Using the Summary pane

The final Export Adobe PDF dialog box pane is the Summary pane shown in Figure 31-7. It simply lists your settings all in one place for easy review. The only option — Save Summary — saves the settings to a file so you can include it with your files when delivering them to a service bureau, or for distribution to other staff members so they know the preferred settings.

Using Distiller job options

In addition to setting up PDF export presets as described in the last section, InDesign lets you import such settings from Acrobat Distiller job-options files. You can load such job-option files by clicking Load in the Adobe PDF Presets dialog box (choose File ➪ PDF Export Presets ➪ Define).

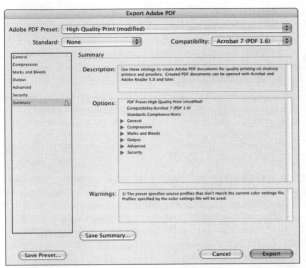

Figure 31-7: The Summary pane of the Export Adobe PDF dialog box

You can also create and edit these job-option files in this dialog box for sharing with Acrobat Distiller and other Creative Suite 2 users; click Save to save them for use by others. Figure 31-8 shows the dialog box. When creating or editing these PDF presets, you'll get the same options described in the previous section for the Export PDF dialog box.

New Feature

The ability to import and save Acrobat Distiller job-option files (called Adobe PDF settings in Acrobat Distiller 6 and later) is new to InDesign CS2.

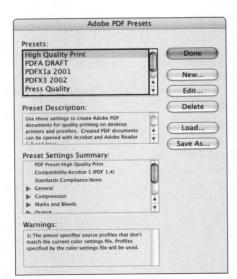

Figure 31-8: The Adobe PDF Presets dialog box

Settings for On-Screen Usage

If your output is destined for use on a monitor—such as from CD, on the Web, or in a corporate intranet—the settings you choose will differ from the print-oriented ones described in the "Exporting PDF files" section. Here's what you need to do:

✦ In the General pane, select the Embed Page Thumbnails and Optimize for Fast Web View options. If your document is designed as facing pages that you'd like the reader to see as a single unit, select the Spreads option.

✦ In the Output pane, select Convert to Destination in the Color Conversion pop-up menu, and then choose Document RGB–Adobe RGB (1998) in the Destination pop-up menu.

✦ In the Compression page, choose Bicubic Downsampling To or Subsampling To in all three images types' sections. The dpi value should be either 72 (if you intend people just to view the images on-screen) or 300 or 600 (if you expect people to print the documents to a local inkjet or laser printer—pick the dpi value that best matches most users' printers' capabilities). For the Compression pop-up menus, choose Automatic for the color and grayscale for bitmaps, and CCITT Group 3 (the standard method for fax compression) for black-and-white bitmaps. Set Image Quality to Maximum for color and grayscale bitmaps. Finally, select the Compress Text and Line Art option.

✦ In the Marks and Bleeds pane, make sure no printer's marks are selected.

✦ In the Security pane, select Use a Password to Restrict Printing, Editing and Other Tasks option, and then choose the options for which you want to add security. Use the Printing Allowed and Changes Allowed pop-up menus' options to prevent readers from copying and pasting your content, or to prevent printing—this is particularly aimed at Web-based readers or publicly distributed documents.

Printing to PDF files

Sometimes, you may want to create a PDF file when printing, such as to save printer-specific options in the file. Note that, using this method, you'll need the $449 Adobe Acrobat Professional software to create a PDF file for prepress output, or the $299 Acrobat Standard for documents meant for display on-screen and printing on inkjet, laser, and other medium-resolution printers. Both include the Acrobat Distiller program that creates PDF files. (The free Adobe Reader is only for viewing PDF files and, in version 7, for making comments viewable only by other version 7 users.)

Set up your Print dialog box settings as described in Chapter 30, but don't click Print. Instead, follow these steps:

1. **Whether you use a Macintosh or a Windows PC, open the Acrobat Distiller program.** In Acrobat Distiller 4 and 5, choose Settings ➪ Job Options to set the output options. In Acrobat Distiller 6 and 7, choose a setting from the Default Settings pop-up menu in the Acrobat Distiller dialog box. Then go back to the InDesign Print dialog box.

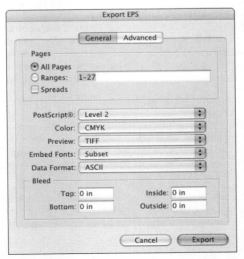

2. **On the Mac, click the Printer button, choose the Output Options menu item from the pop-up menu in the resulting dialog box, and then select the Save as File option, choose the file format (PDF) from the Format pop-up menu, and click Save.** The Save to File dialog box appears.

   In Windows, select Acrobat Distiller from the Printer pop-up menu, and click Print. In a few seconds, a new window appears asking for a filename and file location.

3. **Choose the filename and location, and then click Save to save the file.**

Note

You can also create PDF files by exporting to an EPS or PostScript file, and then using the Acrobat Distiller program to convert the file to PDF. There's no need to do this if you have InDesign unless you happen to have EPS or PostScript files you've previously generated that you'd rather convert to PDF through Distiller than find the InDesign originals and export PDFs from InDesign. You can, of course, use Distiller to create PDFs from any PostScript or EPS file, no matter what program created it.

Creating EPS Files

To create an Encapsulated PostScript (EPS) file from InDesign, choose File ⇨ Export, or press ⌘+E or Ctrl+E. The Export dialog box appears, which like any standard Save dialog box lets you name the file and determine on what drive and in what folder the file is to be saved in. The key control in the Export dialog box is the Formats pop-up menu, where you choose the format (EPS, in this case).

After you've selected EPS in the Export dialog box's Formats pop-up menu, and given the file a name and location, click Save to get the Export EPS dialog box, shown in Figure 31-9. The dialog box has two panes; the General pane is displayed when you open the dialog box.

The General pane

Most export options are in the General pane.

Figure 31-9: The General pane of the Export EPS dialog box

In the Pages section, you can set the following options:

✦ **All Pages.** Select this option to print all pages in a document.

✦ **Ranges.** Select this option when specifying a range of pages that you want to print. You can type nonconsecutive ranges, such as **1-4, 7, 10-13, 15, 18, 20**.

Tip

If you want to print from a specific page to the end of the document, just type the hyphen after the initial page number, such as **4-**. InDesign will figure out what the last page is. Similarly, to start from the first page to a specified page, just start with the hyphen as in **-11**.

Tip

InDesign lets you type absolute page numbers in the Range field. For example, typing **+6-+12** prints the document's sixth through twelfth pages, no matter what their page numbers are.

✦ **Spreads.** Select this option to print facing pages on the same sheet of paper — this is handy when showing clients comps, but make sure you have a printer that can handle that large paper size.

Tip

You may not want to use the Spreads option when outputting an EPS file for eventual printing on an imagesetter if you have bleeds because there will be no bleed between the spreads. If you use traditional *perfect-binding* (square spines) or *saddle-stitching* (stapled spines) printing methods in which facing pages are not printed contiguously, do not use this option.

The unnamed, middle section of the pane controls the handling of fundamental elements: PostScript version, graphics, and fonts. Here are the options:

✦ **PostScript.** Use this pop-up menu to choose the version of the PostScript language to use in creating the EPS file: The Level 2 option works on a PostScript Level 2 or later printer (the majority in professional environments), while Level 3 works only on the newer PostScript 3 devices, which can include built-in color calibration, color separation, and trapping. Be sure to ask whomever is outputting your files which version to use.

✦ **Color.** Use this pop-up menu to determine what happens to colors; your options are CMYK (for commercial printing), RGB (for online display), Gray (for black-and-white printing), or PostScript Color Management (which lets the output device figure out what to do with the colors based on the PostScript settings in the EPS file). For commercial printing, choose either CMYK or PostScript Color Management, depending on your service bureau's recommendations and the capabilities of its output devices. If your file uses spot colors, you'll want to use PostScript Color Management so they aren't converted to process colors, but the service bureau will need to have a printer that can handle that format.

✦ **Preview.** This pop-up menu lets you choose the format for the EPS file's on-screen preview, which is what you see on-screen when you place an EPS file in a program like InDesign, Adobe Illustrator, QuarkXPress, or Macromedia FreeHand. Your options are None, TIFF, and — on the Mac only — PICT. TIFF is a safe option if you use recent versions of image editing, desktop publishing, and illustration programs. Older Mac programs may require you to select PICT.

✦ **Embed Fonts.** Use this pop-up menu to determine whether all fonts, no fonts, or just the characters used will be embedded into the documents; the corresponding menu options are Complete, None, and Subset. Complete is the best option because it ensures that if your service bureau needs to edit the file later, the file will include all font information. If you choose Subset and the service bureau changes some text when editing the EPS file (such as to fix a typo), there's a chance that some characters used in the editing won't be in the file. Use None only if the service bureau has all the fonts you use and knows to load them into the printer before outputting this file.

✦ **Data Format.** Use this pop-up menu to select ASCII or Binary. The ASCII option creates a larger file but can be edited by someone who understands the PostScript language; the Binary option creates a smaller file that is not editable. The one you choose depends on whether you want or expect your service bureau or commercial printer to try to fix any problems in your file encountered during output. Be sure to talk to those people up front, so you and they agree on whether such efforts should be made.

In the Bleed section, you can set the bleed area for the Top, Bottom, Left, and Right sides of the page. If you have elements bleeding off the page, you'll want a bleed setting of at least 0p9 (⅛ inch) — that builds in enough forgiveness so that, when the pages are folded and trimmed, any elements that bleed off the page will in fact do so, even if there's a slip in the page alignment.

Note   The Export EPS option does not let you use any bleed settings you may have set in the New Document (File ➪ New ➪ Document, or ⌘+N or Ctrl+N) or Document Setup (File ➪ Document Setup, or Option+⌘+P or Ctrl+Alt+P) dialog boxes. That's odd, because the Export PDF (File ➪ Export, or ⌘+E or Ctrl+E) and Print (File ➪ Print, or ⌘+P or Ctrl+P) dialog boxes *do* let you use those document settings. Nor can you have all four bleeds automatically use the same settings, as you can in those other dialog boxes.

The Advanced pane

The Advanced pane contains specialty settings affecting image substitution, transparency flattening, and color plates. Figure 31-10 shows the pane.

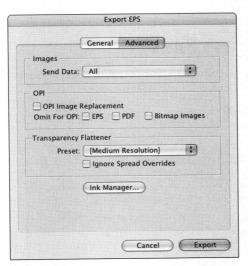

Figure 31-10: The Advanced pane of the Export EPS dialog box

The options are:

✦ **Send Data.** In the Images section's Send Data pop-up menu, you can select either All or Proxy. Use the All option (the default) for all documents that will be printed, even if you're publishing the file electronically (on a CD or through the Web). Use Proxy (which sends a low-resolution, on-screen preview version of the document's images) only for documents that will be viewed on-screen and won't be printed (or where you don't care that the printouts will have low-quality graphics).

✦ **OPI Image Replacement.** In the OPI section, select the OPI Image Replacement option if you're using Open Prepress Interface (OPI) image substitution, in which the high-resolution files are stored elsewhere and the layout uses for-position-only versions to save drive space and save screen redraw time. You can also use the three options in the Omit for OPI section to specify which images should be stripped out: EPS, PDF, and/or Bitmap Images. You would use this only if you have high-resolution or color-corrected versions of these files at a service bureau and want it to substitute those files for the lower-resolution placeholder files you used during layout. By omitting these graphics files from the EPS file, you make the EPS file much smaller.

✦ **Preset.** In the Transparency Flattener section, you can select a transparency preset as well as override any transparency settings applied to individual spreads. Transparency flattening reduces the complexity of documents that have lots of transparent and semi-transparent objects overlapping each other, which can dramatically increase output time and even prevent printing. Select the Ignore Spread Overrides option to tell InDesign to ignore any transparency flattener overrides you may have made to specific spreads in the Pages pane (Window ⇨ Pages or F12).

✦ **Ink Manager.** At the bottom of the pane, click Ink Manager to change which color plates print, adjust ink density, and alter trapping sequence.

See Chapter 30 for more on OPI and transparency flattening. See Chapter 28 for more on overprint simulation and the Ink Manager.

Creating PostScript Prepress Files

You'll use this option the least because it generates a file that is almost always sent directly to a printer. In most cases, generating an EPS or PDF file is a better option; because it gives the service bureau or commercial printer a more structured document it can usually troubleshoot or print more easily. But sometimes, this option is what the service bureau wants, based on its equipment and expertise.

To create a PostScript prepress file, you have two options. The simplest is to choose PostScript File from the Printer pop-up menu in the Print dialog box, as well as the appropriate PostScript Printer Description using the PPD pop-up menu (this should be the PPD for the ultimate output device). Then set the various options in the Print dialog's panes and click Save when done (the Print button becomes Save when you choose PostScript File in the Printer pop-up menu).

The other method is to print to file. *After* setting all the appropriate attributes in the Print dialog box (File ⇨ Print, or ⌘+P or Ctrl+P), do the following, as appropriate for your platform:

✦ On the Mac, click Printer, choose the Output Options menu item from the pop-up menu in the resulting dialog box, then select the Save as File Option, choose the file format (PostScript, in this case) from the Format pop-up menu, and click Save.

✦ In Windows, click Setup and then select the Print to File option in the resulting dialog box and click Print.

Creating JPEG and SVG Files

In some cases, you may want to create a JPEG or Scalable Vector Graphic (SVG) version of your document — perhaps for use as a Web graphic. InDesign lets you export pages in JPEG format through the Export dialog box (File ➪ Export, or ⌘+E or Ctrl+E). Choose JPEG, SVG, or Zipped SVG (for whichever format you want), navigate to the desired folder in which to save the file, and then click Save.

New Feature

InDesign CS2 now lets you export multiple pages to the JPEG format; each page is saved into its own file. You choose which pages to save in the Export JPEG dialog box that appears after you click Save in the Export dialog box.

Support for the SVG format is also new to InDesign CS2; this fairly new format is meant to become a sort of EPS for the Web, though it's not yet widely supported. As with JPEG export, you will get a dialog box letting you select which pages to export once you click Save in the Export dialog box.

Summary

In many cases, you'll want to generate an output file that ensures that your service bureau prints your document exactly as you want it, with no chance to accidentally make a change to your InDesign document. The service bureau's equipment dictates in most cases the format of these output files: EPS, PostScript, or PDF. Each option has pros and cons, and varying levels of controls, so be sure to use the option that gives you the most control and works with your service bureau's equipment.

✦   ✦   ✦

Specialty Publishing Techniques

Book and Long-Document Publishing

When you're working on any type of longer document — a saddle-stitched booklet, a magazine, a perfect-bound textbook — you can easily spend more time on tracking project files, communicating with your workgroup, and manually creating tables of contents and indexes than you spend designing the publication. Longer projects such as these generally consist of multiple InDesign documents, which lets multiple users work on the project and creates smaller, more manageable documents. If you're working on this type of document, by yourself or in a workgroup, InDesign provides the Book feature for managing the document files, updating page numbers across documents, and ensuring consistency in the book.

For longer projects, InDesign also provides its Table of Contents feature, which lets you create and update automatically formatted tables of contents (TOCs). These TOCs are compiled from text formatted with specific paragraph styles (heads, subheads, and so on). If your publication needs an index, you can tag words throughout your text, and then generate an automatically formatted index using the Index feature. The Table of Contents and Index features both work in single documents and for an entire book (and they both transfer to documents exported in PDF form).

And if you need to work with footnotes — whether for a book, journal, or other type of publication — InDesign lets you work with these much as you are used to doing in a word processor.

Managing Multiple Documents with Books

In InDesign, a *book* is a special type of file that you create to track multiple documents for yourself or for a workgroup. A book file displays as a palette, and it lists each InDesign document — let's call them *chapters* to distinguish them from stand-alone documents — that you add to the book. Using the book palette, you can add, open and edit, rearrange, and print chapters of the book. Although the

Book feature is intended for workgroups—and indeed, multiple users can open the same book and access chapters—it also works well in a single-user environment. See the sidebar "The Pros and Cons of Books" for more information.

The Pros and Cons of Books

Although designed for workgroups, the implementation of the Book feature in InDesign has some flaws that may discourage you from using it that way. The problem is with how multiple users access book chapters:

✦ For a workgroup to access a book, the book itself must be stored on a shared server. Users can then open the book across the network and leave it open while they're working. To work on a document in the book, the user opens the document across the network as well. Not only can opening and saving the file be slow, but it leaves documents vulnerable to any instability in your network. (While you're working on the document, there is no local copy of it—*unless* you are using the Version Cue workgroup publishing tools described in Chapter 35.)

✦ If multiple users are working on a book or its constituent documents, they might end up saving different versions, overwriting each other, because there is no built-in document-management system for multiuser access. Or they might end up with multiple versions of the various elements. Using Version Cue can prevent people from overwriting each other's files, but you still could end up with multiple versions that someone will need to reconcile. However, InDesign indicates in the book pane whether someone else has a document open, so you can at least monitor usage before saving changes.

Despite these drawbacks, the Book feature does provide advantages in a workgroup situation that may outweigh any concerns you have. These include the abilities to:

✦ See who is working on each chapter and when.

✦ Update character styles, paragraph styles, object styles, color swatches, and TOC styles across documents for consistency.

✦ Update page numbers across multiple documents.

✦ Create a table of contents and an index for multiple documents. (In fact, using a book is the only way to generate a TOC and index for multiple documents.)

✦ Easily print all the chapters of a book with the same settings.

If you need some of the benefits of using a book (such as a table of contents for multiple documents), but you can't live with one of the drawbacks, you can start out with separate documents. Then, once the documents are close to their final form, you can combine them into a book on one computer and finish the project in book form.

None of this is meant to discourage the single user from managing longer projects through the Book feature. If you're producing a book by yourself, and it consists of multiple InDesign documents, by all means take advantage of the Book feature. The only consideration is whether your output provider can handle the book file or will require you to combine the documents into a single document (or, more easily, export it to one production-quality PDF file).

Planning your book

If you decide that the Book feature is appropriate and useful for a project, you'll want to do some planning before you even create a book. Use the following guidelines before you begin building your book in InDesign:

✦ Organize your chapters in advance by deciding on the number, names, and order of the chapters. You can make changes to a chapter's number, name, and order at any time, but figuring out these basics ahead of time will save you time in the long run.

✦ Make decisions about the format of the book (styles, swatches, pagination style, and so on) at the chapter level, beginning with the first chapter.

✦ Pay attention to formatting. Formatting is important because if your chapters use different color swatch names, style names, and so on, synchronizing the formatting across the chapters will be difficult.

✦ Use templates and styles to format the chapters uniformly.

✦ Decide where to store the book file itself (this must be a shared server for a workgroup); store the documents in this folder as well. Set up the appropriate sharing through your operating system.

✦ Make sure members of the workgroup have access to any templates, libraries, graphics, fonts, plug-ins, and so on, that are necessary to work on the project.

Cross-Reference

If you decide to use the Book feature in a workgroup, be sure to review Chapter 36 for information about implementing standard preferences, templates, and more.

Creating and opening books

To create a new book, choose File ➪ New ➪ Book. The New Book dialog box, shown in Figure 32-1, lets you specify a location for the book and give it a name. If you're on a Mac and creating a book that may be used in Windows, you'll notice that InDesign automatically adds the .indb extension to the filename. Click OK to create and open the book.

To open an existing book, use the File ➪ Open command (⌘+O or Ctrl+O). The book appears in its own pane in the palette (the palette has no title and appears automatically if you open a book when no other books are open). If you're opening a book from a shared server, make sure to mount the server on your desktop first. You can also double-click a book's icon, which also shows the open book's pane. To close a book's pane, and any book documents that are in it, simply click its Close box.

Caution

If more than one book is open, closing any book closes all the books. That's because they are placed together in one palette, so you're really closing the palette when you close a book. You can prevent that by placing each book in its own palette — just drag each book pane by its tab out of the current palette; InDesign will create a new palette for each dragged-out pane.

Tip

Multiple users on the same platform (Mac or PC) — but not users from multiple platforms — can open the same book pane at the same time. If another user makes changes to the book, those changes appear in your copy of the book when you click on the pane.

Note   If you have multiple books open at the same time, each appears in its own pane in the book pane.

Figure 32-1: To create a new book, choose File ➪ New ➪ Book.

Adding chapters to books

New book panes are empty — you need to add your carefully prepared documents to them. To do this, click the Add Document button, the + button on the bottom right of your book's pane (see Figure 32-2), or use the Add Document option in the book pane's palette menu. Either way, use the resulting Add Documents dialog box to locate and select the first chapter you want to add. Click the Open button to make this the first chapter in the book. Repeat this process to add to the book all the chapters you have ready (you can also add more later).

Opening and editing chapters

To work on a chapter (document) in a book, first open the book. Then double-click the chapter name in the book's pane. The chapter will open in InDesign just like any other InDesign document opens. Note that to open a chapter, it must be available, as discussed in the next section. When you finish editing a chapter, save and close it as usual. (Any open chapter documents will remain open in InDesign even if you close the book's pane.)

Note   If you need to take a chapter home and work on it, you can edit a chapter outside the book. To do this, first move the chapter's file to a different folder so the chapter displays as Missing in the book pane. This keeps other users from editing it while you have it. When you finish editing the file, place the edited file back in its original folder. The book pane will show this chapter as Modified.

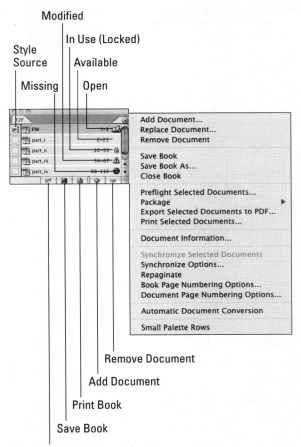

Figure 32-2: A book pane and its palette menu. The icon to the left of a chapter's filename indicates the style source. The status column shows which chapters are open on your computer, which are in use by others, which are available to be opened, and which are missing.

You can replace an existing chapter with another document by selecting the chapter in the book pane, and then choosing Replace Document from the palette menu. Navigate to a new document, select it, and click the Open button. InDesign replaces the selected chapter with the new document.

You can delete chapters from a book by choosing Remove Document from the palette menu or by clicking the Remove Document button (the – icon) from the bottom of the pane.

Finally, there are three other menu options in the palette menu that come in handy for managing the book: You can save books by choosing Save Book, save to a new name by choosing Save Book As, and close the book by choosing Close Book (any changes to the book are not saved, though you will get a warning box giving you the chance to save any unsaved books).

Note   Saving a book is separate from saving a document in a book. Any changes made to an open document are saved only if you save that document. But any changes you make through the book pane's palette menu, such as synchronizing styles (covered next), are automatically saved in the affected documents.

Tip   If the Auto Convert Documents menu option is selected in the book pane's palette menu, InDesign converts all chapters created in earlier versions of InDesign to the InDesign CS2 format. Otherwise, it saves any previous-version chapters to new InDesign CS2-format files with new names, leaving the originals untouched (the book pane will list the InDesign CS2-format files).

Understanding book pane status reports

If you're using the book palette in a workgroup, it provides helpful status reports about each chapter, as shown in Figure 32-2. The statuses include:

✦ **Available.** The chapter can be opened, edited, or printed. Only one user at a time can open a chapter.

✦ **Open.** You have the chapter open and can edit it or print it. Nobody else can open the chapter at this time.

✦ **In Use.** Another user has the chapter open. In this case, you cannot edit or open the chapter.

✦ **Modified.** The chapter has been changed since the last time you opened the book palette. Simply click on the book pane to update it.

✦ **Missing.** The chapter's file has been moved, renamed, or deleted since it was added to the book. Double-click the chapter name to open a Find File dialog box and locate it.

There's also the Document Information menu option in the book pane's palette menu. When you select a chapter and choose this option, InDesign shows you the file's modification date, location, and page range, as well as lets you replace it with a different document.

Working with style sources

The first chapter you add to the book is, by default, the style source, as indicated by the icon to the left of its filename. If the chapters of your book don't share common formatting, you don't need to worry about this feature. But with a book, that's rarely the case — usually you want the text formatting, object styles, colors, and so on to remain the same. The style source in an InDesign book defines the styles and swatches that are common to all the chapters in the book. When you use the Synchronize feature, discussed in the next section, InDesign makes sure that the paragraph styles, character styles, object styles, trap presents, TOC styles, and swatches in each chapter in the book match those in the style source.

If you decide to make a different chapter the style source, all you need to do is click in the column to the left of that chapter's filename. This moves the icon indicating the style source to that chapter (see Figure 32-2).

Synchronizing chapter formatting

To help you make sure that common formatting remains consistent across the document, the book pane provides a Synchronize button, as well as a Synchronize Selected Documents or Synchronize Book menu item in the palette menu. Follow these steps to synchronize:

1. **Be sure you're satisfied with the styles in the style source and that all chapters are available for editing.**

2. **Choose the style source (the document whose styles you want to be used everywhere) by clicking the box to the left of the source chapter so that the style-source icon appears.**

3. **Choose Synchronize Options from the book pane's palette menu, which opens the dialog box shown in Figure 32-3.** Make sure every type of item you want synchronized — Object Styles, TOC Style, Character Styles, Paragraph Styles, Trap Resets, and Swatches — is selected. You can select All Styles to ensure that all are synchronized across a book's chapters.

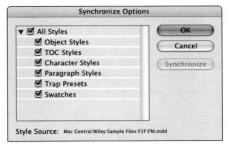

Figure 32-3: The Synchronize Options dialog box

4. **Select the chapters you want to synchronize and click Synchronize or choose Synchronize Selected Documents from the palette menu.** If no chapters are selected, InDesign assumes you want to synchronize all chapters; you'll see the menu option Synchronize Book in the palette menu rather than Synchronize Selected Documents in that case.

5. **Now compare the styles (character, paragraph, object, and TOC), swatches (color, tint, and gradient), and trap styles in the style source to those in each chapter.** If anything is different, the information in each chapter is updated to match the style source. This means that if someone changes the typeface in a style in a chapter, it reverts to the typeface specified in the style source. If anything is missing from a chapter — for example, if you just added a swatch to the style source but not to other chapters — that information is added to each chapter.

By using the Synchronize feature, each chapter will have the same basic set of styles and swatches as the style source. I say "basic set" because you can still add more of these specifications to each chapter. When using the Synchronize feature, you need to keep in mind the following:

✦ Synchronizing will *not* move additional paragraph styles, character styles, object styles, TOC styles, swatches, and trap presets with different names in chapters. Therefore, you can implement different formatting needs in a chapter by creating additional styles in that chapter.

✦ Synchronizing *cannot* solve any problems related to using the template or styles incorrectly, or change any local formatting applied to text (such as font changes or italics) or local changes to master page items.

Clearly, synchronizing is no cure-all for the renegade formatting that often occurs when multiple users work on the same project. Be sure everyone knows what the standards are for the design, how to implement the standards properly, and how to make local changes appropriately.

Printing chapters and books

If you want to print multiple chapters in the book with the same settings, you can print through the book pane. You can print any chapters with the status of Available or Open. Here's how:

1. **To print the entire book, make sure no chapters are selected.** To print a continuous range of chapters, Shift+click them. To print noncontiguous chapters, ⌘+click or Ctrl+click the chapters to select them.

2. **Click the Print Book button or choose Print Book or Print Selected Documents in the book pane's palette menu (the option will depend on whether chapters are selected in the book pane).** The standard InDesign Print dialog box opens. Note that the option to choose all pages or a range of pages is grayed out — you must print all chapters in the selected chapters.

3. **Make any adjustments in the Print dialog box.**

4. **Click Print to print the chapters.**

A related set of features includes the ability to output a book to PDF, using the Export Book to PDF or Export Selected Documents to PDF menu items in the palette menu. They work like their equivalent Print menus. You can also preflight a book or selected chapters and package a book or selected chapters for either a service bureau or for use in GoLive. The Preflight Book/Preflight Selected Documents and Package menu options in the book pane work like their equivalent menu options in the File menu.

For more on preflighting, packaging, printing, and output settings, see Chapters 29 through 31.

Handling chapters with sections

When working with books, you have two choices for numbering pages: You can let the book palette number pages consecutively from one chapter to the next, or you can add sections of page numbers, which carry through the book until you start a new section. In long documents, section page numbering is common because it lets you have page numbering such as 2.1–2.14 in, say, Chapter 2. (Plus, creating a section start is the only way to start a document on a left-facing page, which is often necessary in magazines.)

Numbering pages consecutively

If the chapters you add to a book have no sections in them, you end up with consecutive page numbering: The first page number of each chapter follows the last page number of the previous chapter (so if one chapter ends on page 16, the next chapter starts on page 17). If you open the Section dialog box (choose Numbering & Section Options in the Pages pane's palette menu), you'll see that Automatic Page Numbering is selected by default.

The consecutive page numbering works as follows:

✦ Whenever you add a chapter with no sections to a book, InDesign numbers pages consecutively throughout the book.

✦ As you add and delete pages from chapters, the page numbers are also updated.

✦ You can force repagination by choosing Repaginate from the book pane's palette menu.

✦ In facing-page documents, chapters always start on a right-facing page with an odd page number (even if the previous chapter ends on a right-facing page). In this case, InDesign "skips" the even page number (so one chapter might end on page 15 and the next chapter will start on page 17, leaving you to add a blank page 16 to the previous chapter for proper pagination).

Tip

InDesign lists chapters alphabetically by filename in a book pane, so if your chapters don't have section starts, the automatic page numbering may not follow your desired chapter order. To fix this, click and drag the chapters within the book pane to the desired location in the pane, so the first chapter is in the top position, the next chapter is in the second position, and so on.

Numbering pages with sections

If any chapters you add to books already contain sections of page numbers (implemented through the Section dialog box, which you access via the Numbering & Section Options menu option in the Pages pane's palette menu), the section page numbering overrides the book's consecutive page numbering. The section page numbering carries through chapters of the book until InDesign encounters a new section start. So if one chapter ends on page *iv,* the next page starts on page *v* unless you start a new section. Note that it's fairly typical in magazines to assign the page number in each article's document file because there are usually ads between articles that are inserted later in the printing process.

Cross-Reference

Using the options in the Section dialog box is covered in Chapter 5.

Creating Tables of Contents

Long documents such as books and catalogs lend themselves to tables of contents to give the reader a summary of the content and the locations for each section. In InDesign, a table of contents is simply a list of paragraphs that are formatted with the same styles. After you create a book (or even a single document), InDesign can build a table of contents by scanning the chapters for the paragraph styles you specify. For example, if you create a book, you might have paragraph styles named Chapter Title, Section, and Subsection that you apply to chapter titles, chapter sections, and chapter subsections. Using the Table of Contents feature, InDesign can generate a table of contents that has all three levels.

Note   If you want to use the Table of Contents feature, you have to use styles. Not only do styles guarantee consistent formatting, but they tell InDesign what text you want to include in your table of contents (TOC). The other thing to keep in mind for TOCs: They are linear, either listing from top to bottom the text in the order it appears in a document or in alphabetical order.

Cross-Reference   Tables of contents rely on paragraph styles. For more on styles, see Chapters 16 and 17.

Planning a TOC

Before you start whipping up a TOC in InDesign, decide what the content of your TOC will be: Is all the text tagged with Head and Subhead paragraph styles? (Be sure styles are applied consistently to generate an accurate TOC, so if you're not sure about that, look through the chapter documents.)

You'll also need to create paragraph styles for the TOC itself—it's easy to forget that because TOCs usually have several levels themselves (a title, as well as formatting specific to each level of listing), and each level should usually have its own paragraph style. You'll likely also need some character styles for your TOC—for example, you might want the page numbers to be bold, in which case you'd need a character style that applies boldface to them.

Tip   After you decide what will be in your TOC, use a little bit of dummy text to format a sample TOC *before* you create the styles to be used to format the TOC itself. Your formatting should include any indents for different levels in your list and it should include tabs and fill characters as necessary. When you're satisfied with the formatting of your sample TOC, create the TOC paragraph and character styles from it. Be sure to use clear names such as TOC-Level 1.

QuarkXPress User   Unlike QuarkXPress, InDesign can generate TOCs only based on paragraph styles, not on character styles. This means you can't create other kinds of lists, such as a list of companies in a magazine article or research report, based on the use of character styles. InDesign doesn't have a flexible Lists feature as QuarkXPress does, just the Table of Contents feature that is essentially a subset of QuarkXPress's Lists feature. However, as described in the sidebar "Creating Other Lists," you can use the InDesign Table of Contents feature to create some lists in addition to TOCs.

Defining a TOC

InDesign uses TOC styles to manage the formatting of TOCs. A TOC style defines the text you want in a table of contents, in what order it appears, how page numbers are added, and how the various TOC elements are formatted. To create a TOC style, you choose the Layout ⇨ Table of Contents Styles, which opens the dialog box shown in Figure 32-4.

In the Table of Contents Styles dialog box, click New to create a new TOC style. You can also edit an existing style by clicking Edit, delete one by clicking Delete, and import one from another InDesign document by clicking Load.

Here's how to create a TOC style after clicking New and getting the dialog box shown in Figure 32-5:

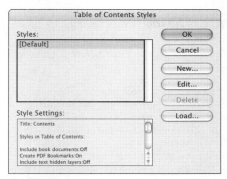

Figure 32-4: The Table of Contents Styles dialog box

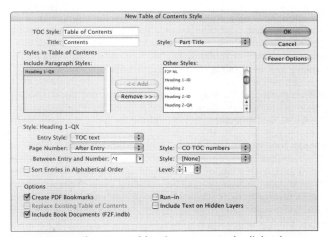

Figure 32-5: The New Table of Contents Style dialog box

1. **Type a name for the TOC style in the TOC Style field.** The default is TOC Style 1.

2. **In the Title field, type a heading for the TOC.** This is the actual text that will appear in your table of contents.

3. **Use the Style pop-up menu to its right to choose the paragraph style that this title will have.** If you don't want a title, leave the Title field blank, but note that you'll still get an empty paragraph at the top of your TOC for this title. You can always delete that paragraph.

4. **In the Styles in Table of Contents section of the dialog box, click a paragraph style from the Other Styles list on the right that you want to appear in your TOC.** For example, you might click Chapter Title in a book. Click <<Add to add it to the Include Paragraph Styles list at left. (Click Remove>> to remove any paragraph styles you don't want to be used in the TOC generation.)

5. **Now choose the formatting for the TOC entries that come from the selected para-graph style, using the Style section of the dialog box.** Here's where you apply the formatting to the text that appears in the TOC:

   - Use the Entry Style pop-up menu to select the paragraph style for the current TOC level.

   - Use the Page Number pop-up menu to determine how page numbers are handled: After Entry, Before Entry, and No Page Number (you might use this last option for alphabetically arranged categories in a catalog, where you want to list page numbers only for product classes and specific products). If you want the page numbers to have a character style applied, choose that style from the Style pop-up menu to the right of the Page Number pop-up menu. Use the Between Entry and Number field and pop-up menu to choose what appears between the TOC text and the page number. You can type any characters you want, as well as have multiple characters; use the pop-up menu to select special characters such as bullets and tabs. In most cases, you would select a tab; the paragraph style selected earlier for the TOC entry would include leader information, such as having a series of periods between the text and the number. You can also apply a character style to the characters between the text and the page numbers through the Style pop-up menu at right.

Note   If the Entry Style, Page Number, and other options don't appear, click More Options to see them.

   - If you want the entries at this level to be sorted alphabetically, such as for a list of companies in a magazine article, select the Sort Entries in Alphabetical Order option.

   - If you want to change the level of the current TOC entry, use the Level pop-up menu. Note that you do not have to manually rearrange the order of items in the Include Paragraph Styles list by clicking and dragging them if you change the level of entries — InDesign correctly sorts them when it creates the TOC, even if the levels seem out of order in the Include Paragraph Styles list.

   - Choose the appropriate options from the Options section of the dialog box. Select the Create PDF Bookmarks option if you're exporting the document as a PDF file and want the file to have *bookmarks* (which is essentially a clickable set of TOC links). Select the Run-in option if you want all entries at the same level to be in one paragraph; this is not common for TOCs but is used in indexes and lists of figures. Select the Replace Existing Table of Contents option if you want InDesign to automatically replace an existing TOC if the TOC style is changed. Select the Include Text on Hidden Layers option if you want text on hidden layers to be included in the TOC. Finally, select the Include Book Documents option if you have a book open and want InDesign to generate a TOC based on all chapters in that book. (InDesign will show the current open book's name.)

6. **Continue this process for each paragraph style whose text should be in the TOC, such as Section and Subsection in a book.** Note that the order in which you add these styles determines the initial levels: The first paragraph style added is level 1, the second is level 2, and so on. But you can change the order by changing the Level setting, as described earlier.

QuarkXPress User

The level of formatting you can achieve over TOC entries in InDesign is greater than in QuarkXPress.

After you define a TOC style, you can go to the Edit TOC Style dialog box — it's identical to the New Table of Contents Styles dialog box — and make any changes. Just choose Layout ➪ Table of Contents Styles, select the TOC style to edit, and click Edit.

With a TOC style in place and your document properly formatted with the paragraph styles that the TOC style will look for when generating a TOC, you're ready to have InDesign create the actual TOC for you. But before you do this, make sure you've saved space in the document for the TOC. This could consist of a single text frame or a series of linked text frames, or simply an empty page or set of pages (depending on how long your TOC will be). When you're creating a table of contents for a book, it might be useful to flow the table of contents into its own chapter.

Tip

You might need to generate a TOC just to see how long it really is, and then make the necessary space available in your document. It's imperative that you do this before generating a final TOC, because if you have to add or delete pages based on the TOC length, the TOC will have the old page numbers, not the current ones. If you do need to update page numbering after flowing a TOC, simply rebuild the TOC by selecting the text frame holding the TOC and then choosing Layout ➪ Update Table of Contents. Note that if you applied local formatting to the TOC after it was generated, you may need to reapply that local formatting to the updated TOC.

To generate a TOC, choose Layout ➪ Table of Contents. A dialog box appears that is identical to the New Table of Contents Style dialog box shown in Figure 32-5. If desired, you can make changes to the TOC style settings (if you want to save those changes for future TOCs generated by the TOC style, be sure to click Save Style). Then click OK to have InDesign generate the TOC. You may also get a dialog box asking if you want to include items in *overset text* (text that didn't fit in your document after you placed it); click Yes or No as appropriate. It may take a minute or two for the program to generate the TOC.

If you've selected a text frame (with or without text in it), InDesign places the TOC text in it. If no text frame is selected, InDesign displays the familiar loaded-text icon (the paragraph pointer) that it displays when you place a text file — either click a text frame to insert the TOC text in that frame or click on your document to have InDesign create a text frame in which to flow the TOC text.

Figure 32-6 shows a TOC generated by InDesign, in this case for a book.

Tip

To replace an existing TOC with an updated version, you can skip the Table of Contents dialog box altogether. Just select the current TOC's text frame and choose Layout ➪ Update Table of Contents.

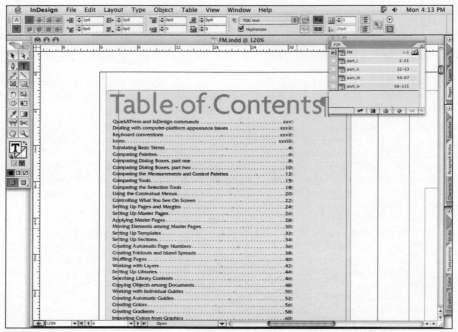

Figure 32-6: A sample TOC generated by InDesign

Creating Other Lists

Although InDesign calls its list-generation feature the Table of Contents feature, you can use it for other kinds of lists. Basically, anything that is tagged with a paragraph style can be used to create a list. For example, if your captions all have titles that use their own paragraph style, you can generate a list of figures by creating a TOC style that includes just, say, the Caption Title paragraph style. An InDesign document can have more than one TOC, so you can have multiple lists in your document.

What InDesign cannot do is create a list based on *character* styles, so you can't create a list based on, say, names in a gossip column where the names use a character style to make them bold and perhaps change font as well. Nor can you create a list based on caption titles that are part of a paragraph also containing the caption (you'd have a Caption Title character style to format the title within the complete paragraph)—and if you choose the Caption paragraph style to create a figures list in such a situation, your list would include the complete text of the captions as well as the embedded title. While that is awkward, you can still use the TOC feature to gather all those captions into a TOC-built list, and then remove all the text that you don't need. That'll still save you time and give you a better shot at having a complete list than entering all that text manually.

Indexing Documents and Books

If you've ever been unable to find information in a book that you knew was there, you can appreciate how important a good index can be. Short, simple documents can get by fine without indexes. But long books almost always need indexes to help the reader locate specific information. Indexing used to be a laborious process, involving lots of index cards. InDesign makes indexing much easier, while still relying on you to make key decisions about how the index will be formatted. The following sections show you how to do your part.

Cross-Reference

After reading this chapter, you may find that you need a more sophisticated indexing tool than InDesign provides. Check out Sonar Bookends InDex Pro by Virginia Systems, to which I have a link on the companion Web site (www.InDesignCentral.com). In addition, the company offers Sonar Bookends InXref for creating cross-references in text that update automatically.

Choosing an indexing style

Your approach to developing an index depends on the indexing style you want to use. Large publishers usually have their own house style guides for indexes. If you don't have a style guide for indexes, I recommend that you read through the indexing guidelines in *The Chicago Manual of Style.* Another option is to use an index you like as a model and then take the steps necessary in InDesign to achieve that index style. Before you begin indexing your document, ask yourself the following questions:

✦ Do you want to capitalize all levels of all entries, or do you just want sentence-style caps?

✦ Should headings appear in boldface?

✦ What type of punctuation will you use in your index?

✦ Should the index be nested or run-in style (see the sidebar "Nested or Run-In Index?")?

Once you make these decisions, it's a good idea to make a small dummy of your index. From the dummy, create a master page for index pages, paragraph styles for letter headings (A, B, C, and so on in the index), paragraph styles for each level of the index (including indents as appropriate), and character styles for any special formatting you want on page numbers or cross-reference text. InDesign doesn't do any of this for you — if you don't set up styles for your index, your multilevel index will simply look linear when it's built.

Using the Index pane

When a chapter or document is ready to be indexed, open the Index pane (Window ➪ Type & Tables ➪ Index or Shift+F8). You use this pane to add words to the index in up to four indent levels, edit or delete index entries, or create cross-references. The Index pane appears in Figure 32-7.

Understanding Reference and Topic modes

The Index pane has two modes, indicated by the radio buttons at the top: Reference and Topic. Reference mode is the mode you should be in when adding and editing entries from selected text. If you're creating an index in a book, be sure to select the Book option as well in the Index pane.

Nested or Run-In Index?

There is no right way to index, but common sense should be a guide. Determine which index format you use by the number of levels in the index's hierarchy. If the index has only two levels, a run-in format works well, but an index with three or more levels requires a nested format for the sake of clarity.

Nested indexes look like this:

Kitchen Hardware

Buying, 191

Cost estimates, 242–248

Design guidelines 92–94, 96, 99–101

Hiring contractors, 275–284

Installation, 180–195

Sizing, 91–99

Standards, 24–28, 98, 133

Tools, 199–203, 224, 282–283

Run-in indexes look like this:

Kitchen Hardware: Buying, 191; Cost estimates, 242–248; Design guidelines 92–94, 96, 99–101; Hiring contractors, 275–284; Installation, 180–195; Sizing, 91–99; Standards, 24–28, 98, 133; Tools, 199–203, 224, 282–283

Although InDesign doesn't force you to make this decision until you actually build the index, you really need to make it before you get started. If you tag words for a four-level nested index, but then build a run-in index, your index will have some logic problems.

The Topic mode is meant to give you a clean environment in which to enter the topic names and levels that you want your index to have. Then, when an indexer adds an index entry, she can use the topics that appear in the bottom of the New Page Reference and double-click the topic to use that topic definition rather than whatever she might enter herself in the dialog box. You don't have to use Topic mode if you don't want to — all index entries create *topics* (InDesign-speak for the entry text). Although a well-intentioned feature meant to help standardize index entries, the Topic mode's use is not intuitive, and most indexers will simply ignore it, adding entries manually from selected text or by typing phrases into the Index pane when in Reference mode.

Note that only topics that have actual references (where text occurs on actual pages, not in the pasteboard, on a master page, or in overset text) or cross-references. So don't worry about unused topic text appearing in your index.

The Index pane has the Book option. Select this option if you are creating an index for multiple chapters in a book. You must have a book open for this option to be available. If you do have a book open and do not select it, the index is saved with the current document, and not opened with any chapter of the book. If it is selected, you can see all topics indexed across a book if you select the Topic radio button.

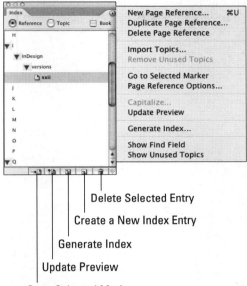

Delete Selected Entry

Create a New Index Entry

Generate Index

Update Preview

Go to Selected Marker

Figure 32-7: The Index pane

Entering index items via the Index pane

To add entries to your index, first select the text (or just click the Type tool inside a text frame or in a text path), then choose New Page Reference from the Index pane's palette menu, or press ⌘+U or Ctrl+U, to get the dialog box shown in Figure 32-8. (If no text is selected, you will see the New Cross-Reference menu option instead.) Here's how the controls work:

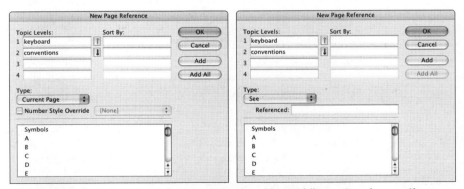

Figure 32-8: The New Page Reference dialog box. The middle portion changes if you select one of the cross-reference options such as See in the Type pop-up menu, as shown in the right-hand dialog box.

✦ If you selected text first in your document, the text is entered automatically into Topic Level 1. Otherwise, type the text that you want to add to the index. The text is added to the Topic list and, if it is in the document, also to the list of index entries.

✦ You can type text that controls how the entry is sorted in the Sort By column. For example, if the highlighted text is *The Zango Group,* but you wanted it sorted as if it were *Zango Group, The* (so it appears with the *Z* entries in the index), type *Zango Group, The* in the Sorted By column. Similarly, you might have the movie title *2001: A Space Odyssey* sorted as *Two Thousand and One: A Space Odyssey* so the listing appears properly with the *T* entries in the index.

✦ More complex indexes will take advantage of the four possible entry levels. You may want an index entry to appear under a higher-level topic. For example, you may want *2001: A Space Odyssey* to appear in the index under *Classic Science Fiction,* in which case you would enter *Classic Science Fiction* in the Topic Level 1 field and *2001: A Space Odyssey* in the Topic Level 2 field.

✦ Use the Type pop-up menu to determine the page entries for the index entry. The pop-up menu has two basic sections, shown in Figure 32-9.

  • One section covers the entry's range — typically, you just want the current page number on which the text appears, but in some cases, you might want to indicate that a topic spans a number of pages, a document section, all text with a specific style, or one of the other options. For example, if you have a section about France in a world history book, you might want the main entry to indicate the whole section — such as *France, 167-203,* while leaving references in other sections (such as references in a section on Germany) to be for just the page on which it appears. If you choose For Next # of Pages or For Next # of Paragraphs, the dialog box displays the Number field for you to enter how many paragraphs or pages you want the index entry's range to span. Note that you can apply a character style to the page number generated in the index by selecting the Number Style Override option and choosing a character style in the pop-up menu to its right.

  • The other section covers cross-references, letting you choose from several types. The dialog box changes slightly, as shown in Figure 32-8, if you choose a cross-reference entry. It adds the Reference text field for you to type the text that the index contains after the cross-reference. You can create your own custom cross-references by choosing [Custom Cross-reference]; InDesign displays the Custom text field and pop-up menu in which you type (or select from previously typed) text that you want InDesign to use. For example, you might want the cross-reference to say *Go to* rather than one of the defaults like *See.*

Note Use *See* to point readers to the appropriate index entry; use *See Also* to point the readers to additional useful information elsewhere in the index; use *See Herein* to point readers to a subentry for this index entry; and use *See Also Herein* to point readers to additional useful information in a subentry to this index entry.

✦ To add text within the range specified, click Add. (If the text entered is not in the specified range, the text will be added to the Topic list, but no index entry will appear for the text.) To add all occurrences of the text in the document (or book), click Add All.

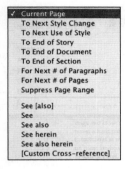

Figure 32-9: The Type pop-up menu's options in the New Page Reference dialog box

✦ To change previously defined index entries, choose Page Reference Options in the Index pane's palette menu.

New Feature InDesign CS2 changes how multiparagraph text selections are indexed. InDesign CS2 indexes each paragraph in that selection. The idea is that you can create lists this way.

Note At the bottom of the New Page Reference dialog box is a list of letters as well as the entry Symbols. You can scroll through this list of headings to see what is already in the index under each letter. Although you might think clicking a letter forces the current index entry to appear in that letter's section of the index, it does not.

To see which text in your document is indexed, choose Type ➪ Show Hidden Characters, or press Option+⌘+I or Ctrl+Alt+I. Index entries will have a wide blue caret symbol before them, as Figure 32-10 shows.

> Keyboard conventions¶
> This book provides both the Macintosh and Windows shortcuts th
> Mac shortcut first. In most cases, the Mac and Windows shortcut
> for the names of the keys, as follows:¶
>
> • The Mac's Command key (⌘) is the most-used shortcut key. Its
>   is Ctrl.¶

Figure 32-10: If hidden characters are displayed, you can identify index entries by the light blue caret in front of the indexed text (here, in front of *keyboard*).

Entering index items using keyboard shortcuts

To quickly add a word or text selection to an index, highlight the text and press ⌘+U or Ctrl+U to add the text to the New Page Reference dialog box (refer to Figure 32-8).

To index a word without opening that dialog box, just press Option+Shift+⌘+[or Ctrl+Alt+Shift+[. This adds the text to the index using its default settings. (You can always edit them later, as described in the next section.) And to enter an index entry in reverse order as a proper name (last name, first name), use the shortcut Option+Shift+⌘+] or Ctrl+Alt+Shift+].

New Feature The shortcuts to generate index entries without opening the New Page Reference dialog box have changed in InDesign CS2.

Working with the index

The Index pane's palette menu has several options useful in fine-tuning and generating the index:

✦ **Duplicate Topic.** This option lets you duplicate a topic entry so you use the settings in one entry without having to reselect them all.

✦ **Delete Topic.** This option removes a topic (and any associated entries) from the index.

✦ **Import Topics.** This option lets you import topic lists from other InDesign documents.

✦ **Go to Selected Marker.** This option causes InDesign to jump to the text that contains the selected index entry in the Index pane. This is a handy way of seeing if the reference in the text truly merits being listed in the index.

✦ **Topic Options.** This lets you edit the Level and Sort By settings for topic entries; these affect all index entries that use them.

✦ **Capitalize.** This option lets you standardize the capitalization of topic entries — you can choose Selected Topic, Selected Topic and All Subtopics, All Level 1 Topics, and All Topics.

✦ **Update Preview.** This option updates the index entries in the Index pane to reflect page-number changes, new occurrences of index text occurrences, and deleted occurrences of indexed text. It does not change the actual index.

✦ **Generate Index.** This creates the actual index in your document, via the dialog box shown in Figure 32-11. Here, you specify the title for the index, the paragraph style for that title, whether a selected index is replaced with the new one, whether an entire book is indexed, whether layers on hidden layers are indexed, whether the index is nested or run-in (see the sidebar "Nested or Run-In Index?" earlier in the chapter), whether empty index headings and sections are included, what paragraph styles are applied to each level of index entry and what character styles are applied to different portions of index entries, and finally, the characters used as separators within index entries. (Click More Options to see the nested/run-in and later options.) After you generate an index, you get the standard InDesign text-insertion pointer (the paragraph symbol); click an existing text frame into which you want to flow the index, or click anywhere in a document to have InDesign create the text frame for you and flow the index text into it.

Tip Each time you edit text in a document or book chapter, it's a good idea to rebuild the index so the page numbers in it are updated. There is no dynamic link between a flowed and formatted index and the index markers in text.

✦ **Show Find Field.** This lets you find text within the entries and topics in the Index pane—it adds a Find field and ↓ (Search Forward) and ↑ (Search Backward) buttons to the Index pane.

✦ **Show Unused Topics.** This highlights topics for which there are no index entries, so you can easily delete them.

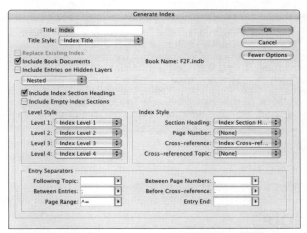

Figure 32-11: The Generate Index dialog box, with all options displayed

QuarkXPress User

The InDesign index features are similar to those in QuarkXPress, though the InDesign Index pane and QuarkXPress Index palette are organized differently. (Furthermore, InDesign puts all its controls in the Index pane; there are no preferences to set in the Preferences dialog box as there are in QuarkXPress.)

Among the differences in functionality: QuarkXPress lets you automatically reverse the text in the Text field as you add it to the index. (For example, you can change *Classic Science Fiction* to *Science Fiction, Classic.*) InDesign does not have this feature, nor does it have a shortcut command for quick index-entry additions as QuarkXPress does.

But InDesign has the ability to generate custom cross-reference text and to specify the capitalization for topics. InDesign can also show index entries for all chapters in a book, not just for the current chapter. (Although QuarkXPress can index an entire book, its Index palette can show entries for the current chapter only, which may lead to different index formatting and word choices from chapter to chapter.) InDesign also has more formatting options for index-entry text elements and separators.

Incorporating Indexing into a Workflow

If you're working on a document by yourself, or you're creating a fairly simple index in a workgroup, you can pretty much index as you go. Or you can plan some time at the end of the editorial cycle to go through a document or chapters to index them. But if your publication requires professional indexing — as would be the case for the multilevel index of a long book such as this one — deciding when to send your original InDesign files out for indexing is difficult. You might do it one chapter at a time, right after editorial approval and right before the file goes to production. Or you might send each chapter out for indexing before the last round of edits. What you can't do is continue working on one copy of your InDesign documents while another copy is being indexed — there is no way to move the index tags to another file.

On a tight schedule, you may be tempted to move your InDesign documents into production while another copy of your files is indexed. You then generate the index, send that file to production, and then send the whole thing to print. The index is trapped in InDesign documents that aren't final — unfortunate, because the next time you edit the document, you would like to have the index tags in it. If you have to work this way, you'll need to decide whether to reindex the publication or redo the production work.

Working with Footnotes

Many kinds of document use footnotes — academic articles and journals, books, manuals, and even some magazines. So it makes sense for InDesign to support them as well.

New Feature Support for footnotes is new to InDesign CS2.

InDesign imports footnotes from Microsoft Word files (see Chapter 13), as well as lets you add footnotes directly in InDesign. The process is simple: Choose Type ➪ Insert Footnote, and InDesign adds a footnote to the bottom of the column that contains the footnote entry, as Figure 32-12 shows. InDesign handles the footnote numbering as you add and delete footnotes; you have to type the footnote text.

But footnotes are more complicated than that, so InDesign lets you control much of the appearance of footnotes by choosing Type ➪ Document Footnote Options to open the Footnote Options dialog box, whose two panes are shown in Figure 32-13.

Note You cannot insert footnotes into tables. Instead, you will have to handle them the old, manual way: inserting a footnote character as needed and typing your footnotes below the table, and updating the footnote as needed manually.

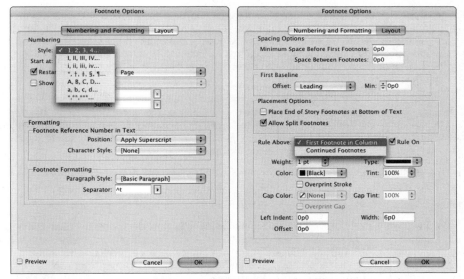

istration of your Adobe software. Volume licensing offers value, both in terms of unit cost and
total cost of ownership (TCO).[1]

And Adobe Open Options is the only source
for the new Adobe Acrobat Elements soft-

_____
1 Based on conmbination of volume discounts and eased administration savings
within purchasing and IT departments.

It contributes to the po
Adobe Open Options p
discounts available to y

The Maintenance Prog
insurance, which ensur
the latest technology to
ity. This program lets o

Figure 32-12: A two-column text box with a footnote in the
first column

Figure 32-13: The Footnote Options dialog box's two panes: Numbering and
Formatting (left) and Layout

Numbering and Formatting pane

Use the Numbering and Formatting pane to control the formatting of the footnote text and
footnote character in the current InDesign document. (To change these settings for future
documents, open the dialog box with no document open and set your new defaults.)

You have these options in the Numbering section:

✦ **Style.** Choose the numbering style through the Style pop-up menu, which gives you six
numbering options:

- a, b, c, d, . . .

- A, B, C, D, . . .

- *, †, ‡, §, ¶ . . .

- *, **, *** . . .
- i, ii, iii, iv . . .
- I, II, III, IV . . .
- 1, 2, 3, 4 . . .

✦ **Start At.** Choose the starting number by typing a value in the Start At field (the default is 1).

✦ **Restart Numbering Every.** If you want the numbering to restart on each page, spread, or section, select the Restart Numbering Every option and then choose Page, Spread, or Section from its pop-up menu.

✦ **Show Prefix/Suffix in.** If you want a prefix and/or suffix with the footnote number, select the Show Prefix/Suffix in option. Then choose where the prefix and/or suffix should be displayed with the adjoining pop-up menu. Its choices are Footnote Reference (that's the footnote in the text), Footnote Text (the actual footnote at the bottom of the column), and Both Reference and Text (at both locations).

Type your prefix character(s) in the Prefix field and your suffix character(s) in the Suffix field. Use the pop-up menu to the right of the Prefix field to insert any of several special characters into the Prefix field: (, [, a hair space, and a thin space. All characters in the Prefix field will precede the footnote character. Likewise, with the pop-up menu to the right of the Suffix field, you can insert a) or] in the Suffix field. All characters in the Suffix field will follow the footnote character.

In the Formatting section, there are two subsections: Footnote Reference Number in Text and Footnote Formatting.

In the Footnote Reference Number in Text subsection, you have two options:

✦ **Position.** Using the Position pop-up menu, specify how the footnote character is formatted; your options are Apply Superscript, Apply Subscript, and Apply Normal. Most documents use superscripts and don't have any suffixes or prefixes. But some documents enclose their footnotes in parentheses or brackets rather than superscript them; if that is your style, you would choose Apply Normal and type [in the Prefix field and] in the Suffix field in the Numbering section above.

✦ **Character Style.** If you want to apply a character style to the footnote character in text, select the Apply Character Style option and then choose the style in the adjoining pop-up menu.

In the Footnote Formatting subsection, you have these options:

✦ **Paragraph Style.** You can apply a specific paragraph style to the footnote text by choosing a style in the Paragraph Style pop-up menu. You typically should have a specific style for your footnotes.

✦ **Separator.** Type in the Separator field the character(s) you want to separate the footnote number and its text. (This will follow any text you typed in the Suffix field.) These are often various spaces, but they could also be a period or colon followed by a space. The pop-up menu below the field lets you choose several kinds of spaces (tab, em space, and en space).

You can use the codes for various space characters in the Prefix, Suffix, and Separator fields. Common ones are **^t** for a tab, **^m** for an em space, **^>** for an en space, **^<** for a thin space, and **^** for a hair space.

Layout pane

Use the Layout pane to control the placement of the footnote relative to the rest of the document.

In the Spacing Options section, you have these options:

✦ **Minimum Space Before First Footnote.** Set the space between the bottom of the column and the first footnote by typing a value in the Minimum Space Before First Footnote field.

✦ **Space Between Footnotes.** Set the space between footnotes by typing a value in the Space Between Footnotes field. You typically will not add a value here because you can better control spacing with your paragraph style used by the footnote text.

In the First Baseline section, you have these options:

✦ **Offset.** Set how the footnote's baseline should be determined; your options are Ascent, Cap Height, x Height, and Fixed.

✦ **Min.** You also can set the minimum distance from that location to the baseline by entering a value in the Min. field.

See Chapters 3 and 14 for more on setting baselines.

In the Placement Options section, you have these options:

✦ **Place End of Story Footnotes at Bottom of Text.** Select the Place End of Story Footnotes at Bottom of Text option to override end-of-story footnotes generated in Microsoft Word so they appear at the bottom of text columns in InDesign.

✦ **Allow Split Footnotes.** If you don't want footnotes to break across columns, deselect the Allow Split Footnotes option.

In the Rule Above section, you have these options:

✦ **Rule On.** Select the Rule On option to place a ruling line above the footnotes. In the Rule Above popup menu to its left, choose First Footnote in Column or Continued Footnotes to determine which footnotes get the ruling line above them.

✦ **Weight, Color, Type, Tint, Overprint Stroke, Gap Color, Gap Tint, and Overprint Gap.** Use these controls to format the stroke that is used as the ruling line. (Chapter 10 covers these settings in detail.)

✦ **Left Indent, Width, and Offset.** Use these fields to control how the line is positioned relative to the text frame.

Summary

The book, TOC, and indexing features of InDesign can significantly streamline longer projects, especially those consisting of multiple documents. Although the Book feature can be used in a workgroup, it's also ideal for a single user to combine multiple documents into a single publication. In fact, when working on projects divided into multiple documents, the only way to create a table of contents (or other list) or an index is to combine the documents into a book.

The TOC feature makes it easy to generate tables of contents, and it can also be used for some other kinds of lists, as long as the source text is tagged with consistent paragraph styles. The indexing feature, on the other hand, can be considered easy only by people with knowledge of the indexing process. Although most users can make use of the simpler features — such as adding a First Level entry that consists of text highlighted in the document — the more complicated your index, the more you may need a professional indexer. If you do need a professional, be sure your schedule allows time for the indexer to take possession of your InDesign files.

InDesign now supports footnotes — both those imported from Microsoft Word and those created in InDesign. You have several options to control the formatting of the footnote text and its placement in your document.

✦   ✦   ✦

Interactive Document Setup

In most respects, a document is a document is a document. But in today's electronic world, documents have evolved to include more than text and graphics that for centuries have comprised documents. Not only can you print documents the traditional way, you can deliver them electronically as Adobe Portable Document Format (PDF) files. And that electronic delivery format permits a degree of interactivity never possible in printed documents, including hyperlinks, automated page actions, and the use of audio and video objects.

You create interactive documents just as you create a print document. InDesign's interactive functions work with those traditional capabilities — there's no special "interactive" mode to work under.

Cross-Reference Chapter 31 covers how to export InDesign documents to PDF files.

Using Hyperlinks in PDF and eBook Files

The most common attribute you'll add to a print document to make it more useful when distributed electronically is the inclusion of hyperlinks. Just like Web pages, PDF files can include these hot spots that, when clicked, direct a browser to open a new file or page. It's a whole new way to deliver related contents through an active cross-reference.

InDesign uses its Hyperlinks pane (Window ➪ Interactive ➪ Hyperlinks) to add, edit, and delete hyperlinks. In a sense, a hyperlink is a character attribute — it's applied to selected text. Figure 33-1 shows the Hyperlinks pane and its palette menu.

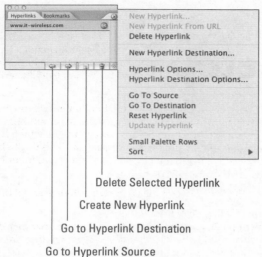

Delete Selected Hyperlink

Create New Hyperlink

Go to Hyperlink Destination

Go to Hyperlink Source

Figure 33-1: The Hyperlinks pane

InDesign and the Web

InDesign does not let you export documents to HTML format, the standard format for the Web. (This may be because Adobe has a separate product meant to create Web pages.) While you can create an XML version of your InDesign document for use only by Adobe GoLive CS2, GoLive is not a widely used Web development program.

That's too bad for publishers who want to convert their print layouts to a Web format, but because few publishers actually create their Web content directly from their print files, it will have limited effect. Instead, most publishers will do what they've long done — export or copy text from the final print document, and then import that text and associated graphics (converted from print standards such as TIFF and EPS to Web standards such as GIF and JPEG) into a Web-creation program like Macromedia Dreamweaver or Adobe GoLive, using Web-specific templates and formatting.

Publishers typically haven't directly converted their print documents to Web formats, even in programs like QuarkXPress that have the ability to do so, because the horizontally oriented, single-column, typographically plain Web page didn't allow for easy adaptation of print publications' vertically oriented, multicolumn, typographically sophisticated content. For many publishers, it was easier to start the Web layout from scratch than convert from print layouts.

Creating hyperlinks

Although the process is straightforward, InDesign's terminology can make it a bit confusing on how to start. You first create a hyperlink destination—the place a hyperlinks goes to, or its *target*—by choosing New Hyperlink Destination from the Hyperlinks pane's palette menu. Figure 33-2 shows the dialog box. You give the destination a name in the Name field and then choose from one of the three options in the Type menu:

✦ **Page.** This option lets you specify a specific page in a selected document. If you select this option, InDesign provides a Page field in which you specify the page number to open in the selected document, as well as the Zoom Setting pop-up menu, which lets you select how the page is displayed. (Options are Fixed, meaning at the default size in Adobe Reader; Fit View; Fit in Window; Fit Width; Fit Height; Fit Visible; and Inherit Zoom, which uses the current zoom setting in Adobe Reader.)

✦ **Text Anchor.** This option lets you specify a specific piece of text in the selected document. This would be the selected text.

✦ **URL.** This is a Web page address (the official name is Uniform Resource Locator), as shown in the New Hyperlink dialog box in Figure 33-2. If you select this option, InDesign displays the URL field in which you type the Web address.

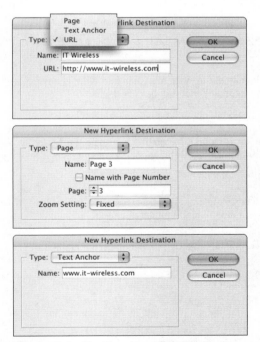

Figure 33-2: The New Hyperlink Destination dialog box's three variants are (from top to bottom) URL, Page, and Text Anchor.

Links to Other Documents

The process for linking to other documents depends on whether those documents are on the Web or on a CD or internal server.

If you want to create a hyperlink to another document, such as on a CD or server, you must do so in the New Hyperlink Destination dialog box, using the Page option. You cannot create a destination hyperlink until that file exists. Also, unintuitively, you must browse for the actual InDesign file to which you want to link. But the link will be to the PDF version of that file, which means you must be sure to create the PDF of that other document and use the same filename, except for the filename extension. For example, if you link to ITWForm.indd, the link will actually be to ITWForm.pdf. This approach requires that you have all the target files in InDesign format—you cannot link to a specific PDF file created in another program or by someone whose source files you don't have access to.

By contrast, Web links can link to any object available on a Web server, including PDFs, so you would simply use a hyperlink to a Web address, such as `http://www.it-wireless.com/ITWForm.pdf`, in the New Hyperlink dialog box. Note that such Web links cannot be made to a specific pages inside a PDF file, as InDesign allows when making links from one document to another as described in the previous paragraph.

With the destinations defined, you can now create the hyperlinks to them (the hyperlink *sources*).

Note To create a hyperlink to another PDF file, you can't use the New Hyperlink Destination method. You must use the New Hyperlink method described next.

To create a hyperlink source:

1. **Select the text or frame you want to be a hyperlink's source, and then choose New Hyperlink from the Hyperlinks pane's palette menu.** That opens the New Hyperlink dialog box, as shown in Figure 33-3.

Figure 33-3: The New Hyperlink dialog box

2. **Type a name for the hyperlink source.** This lets you apply the same link to more than one location in your document—sort of a character style for hyperlinks. If the name already exists, an error message appears when you click OK—there's no way to know ahead of time if the name has already been used in the document.

3. **If the hyperlink is to another InDesign document, you can select that document by choosing Browse from the Document pop-up menu.**

4. **Use the Type pop-up menu to determine what you're hyperlinking to.** You have the same three options as in the New Hyperlink Destination dialog box's Type menu—Page, Text Anchor, and URL—as well as All Types, which, if chosen, displays previously defined hyperlinks in the document.

5. **Use the Name pop-up menu to select a previously defined hyperlink destination (target) or an anchor.** You can also create a hyperlink to an Unnamed destination by leaving the Name pop-up menu set to [None].

Caution

I advise against the method described in Step 5 because that hyperlink destination won't appear in the menu for future hyperlink sources, making it hard to modify later.

6. **In the Appearance section, you can control how the hyperlink appears on-screen:**

   • Use the Type pop-up menu to choose Invisible Rectangle or Visible Rectangle. The Invisible Rectangle option gives no visual indication that the text contains a hyperlink, except that the mouse pointer becomes a hand icon when the reader maneuvers through the document. (You would typically pick this option when you've used blue underline as a character attribute for the hyperlink text to mirror the standard Web way of indicating a hyperlink.) The Visible Rectangle option puts a box around the text using the four settings below (they are grayed out if Invisible Rectangle is selected).

   • The Highlight pop-up menu lets you choose how the source text or frame is highlighted: None, Invert (reserve the foreground and background colors), Outline (places a line around the source), and Inset (places a line around the source, but inside any frame stroke; for text, it's the same as Outline).

   • The Color pop-up menu displays Web-safe colors, as well as any colors you defined in the document.

   • The Width pop-up menu lets you choose the thickness of the line used in the Outline and Inset options from the Highlight pop-up menu. The choices are Thin, Medium, and Thick.

   • You can choose the type of line in the Style pop-up menu: Solid or Dashed.

Tip

If your text includes a valid hyperlink, such as www.InDesignCentral.com, you can select it and create a URL hyperlink automatically by choosing New Hyperlink from URL in the Hyperlinks pane's palette menu.

Once your hyperlink sources are defined, you can easily apply them by selecting text and clicking an existing hyperlink source from the Hyperlinks pane. You can also jump to the source or destination by selecting the desired hyperlink in the Hyperlinks pane and choosing either Go to Source or Go to Destination from the palette menu, or click the Go to Hyperlink Source or Go to Hyperlink Destination buttons at the bottom of the pane. These make a handy way to verify the links are correct.

What Are eBooks?

InDesign lets you create eBook files. An eBook is a form of PDF meant for digital book readers, electronic devices to which you can download book files and read on-screen. Think of it as a read-only computer, or as a browser that only displays PDF files.

The big difference between a PDF file and an eBook file is that an eBook file includes a bunch of tags to help the reader device display it properly no matter what the screen dimensions are. These tags are added automatically by InDesign when you export to a PDF file, as long as you select the Create Tagged PDF option in the General pane of the Export PDF dialog box. Chapter 31 covers PDF export in detail.

Modifying and deleting hyperlinks

It's also easy to modify hyperlinks: Choose Hyperlink Options from the Hyperlinks pane's palette menu to open the Hyperlink Options dialog box, which has the same options as the New Hyperlinks dialog box, shown in Figure 33-3, to modify the source. Similarly, to modify hyperlink destinations, choose Hyperlink Destination Options from the palette menu to open the Hyperlink Destination Options dialog box, and then select the target from the Name pop-up menu. The Hyperlink Destination Options dialog box's options are the same as the New Hyperlink Destination dialog box shown in Figure 33-2.

You can change the source text or frame by selecting it, then clicking the hyperlink name in the Hyperlinks pane, and finally choosing Reset Hyperlink from the pane's palette menu. To change the target for a hyperlink to an InDesign document, choose Update Hyperlink from the palette menu (press and hold Option or Alt to select a file that is not open).

To delete a hyperlink target, choose it in the Hyperlink Destination Options dialog box, and then click Delete. (Click Delete All to delete all targets defined in the document.)

To delete a hypertext source, select it in the Hyperlinks pane and then choose Delete Hyperlink from the palette menu or click Delete Selected Hyperlinks at the bottom of the pane.

Note   When you export your InDesign files to PDF files (as described in Chapter 31), be sure to select the Hyperlinks option in the Include section of the General pane in the Export PDF dialog box (File ⇨ Export, or ⌘+E or Ctrl+E), and then choose Adobe PDF in the Format pop-up menu.

Creating Bookmarks

Bookmarks are an indexing mechanism used in Adobe PDF files. They typically act like tables of contents, letting you view the organization of a document through a set of clickable headings. Figure 33-4 shows an example file viewed in Adobe Reader.

InDesign has two ways to create bookmark entries. One is simply to create a table of contents using the standard InDesign Table of Contents tool. (Be sure that the Create PDF Bookmarks option is selected in the Table of Contents dialog box.) The other is to specify bookmarks to specific pages, objects, and/or text using the Bookmarks pane. Figure 33-5 shows the Bookmarks pane (Window ⇨ Interactive ⇨ Bookmarks) and its palette menu.

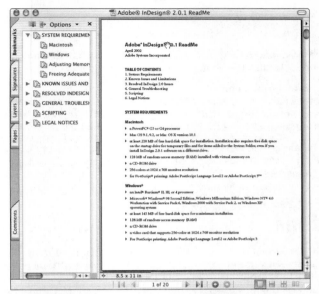

Figure 33-4: An example PDF document with bookmarks (at left)

Figure 33-5: The Bookmarks pane

Cross-Reference

Chapter 32 covers the Table of Contents feature.

To create your own bookmark entries — either instead of or in addition to having InDesign use the table of contents — choose what you want the bookmark to refer to (what will appear on-screen in the PDF file when a user clicks the bookmark in Acrobat or Adobe Reader). This can be a text selection or an object (frame or line), and then choose New Bookmark from the Bookmarks pane's palette menu. If nothing is selected, the bookmark will be to the current page. After you create the bookmark, use the Rename Bookmark menu option to give it a name — this is the name that appears in the Bookmarks pane in Acrobat.

Tip

If you want a bookmark to be a subentry of another bookmark — the equivalent to a second-level or third-level headline in a table of contents — make sure that, before you create the bookmark, you select a bookmark in the Bookmarks pane. Any new bookmark is made a child of the selected bookmark.

The other Bookmarks palette options are straightforward:

✦ Choose Delete Bookmark to delete any bookmarks selected in the pane.

✦ Choose Go to Selected Bookmark to jump to that page in your InDesign document. An easier way is to simply double-click the bookmark entry in the pane.

✦ Choose Sort Benchmarks to sort benchmark subentries — this alphabetizes second-level, third-level, and other page-based subentries, and it sorts in order of appearance on the page any text- and/or object-based entries. It will not sort the top-level bookmarks, which appear in sequential order from the beginning of the document.

However you create your bookmarks, you can have InDesign place them into your PDF file during PDF export. In the General pane of the PDF Export dialog box (choose File ➪ Export, or press ⌘+E or Ctrl+E, and choose Adobe PDF in the Format pop-up menu), make sure the Bookmarks section is checked in the pane's Include section.

Creating Page Actions

One underused feature of the PDF format is the ability to set page actions. Most people simply create PDF files that are on-screen versions of the print document — static representations — but PDF files can include forms, buttons, and other interactive elements. One reason for the under use of page actions is that few tools let you create the placeholder items for them and adding them in Acrobat Standard or Acrobat Professional is awkward — they really work best when created in the program that creates the whole document. InDesign addresses this reality with its support for interactive features.

In InDesign, you use the States pane to create buttons and other objects that have actions associated with them.

The first thing you do is draw a button using the Button tool. A button is essentially a rectangular frame. Once created, you can resize it like any other object, though you cannot create nonrectangular shapes.

Tip   You can convert an existing frame to a button by choosing Object ➪ Interactive ➪ Convert to Button.

After you create the button shape, you should immediately choose its appearance, using the Appearance pop-up menu in the States pane (Windows ➪ Interactive ➪ States). It's imperative that you choose the appearance now, because if you later change the appearance, any actions you associate to the button are wiped out. If you want a transparent button (perhaps to make part of an existing graphic a hot spot), choose None from the pop-up menu. The other options are Drop Shadow, Glow, Bevel, and Custom. Figure 33-6 shows the States pane, the three standard states (Up, Rollover, and Down), and an example button (the selected logos at the top).

Then you create the states for the button by choosing New State from the States pane's palette menu. You always have an Up state when you create a button. You'll get a Rollover state the first time you choose New States and a Down state the second time. You can have only these three states for any button.

The states correspond to mouse actions:

✦ Up is what is displayed and occurs when the mouse is not over the button, or when the mouse button has been released after pressing the button — the default appearance and action.

✦ Rollover is what displays and occurs when the mouse passes over the button but the mouse is not clicked onto the button.

✦ Down is what displays and occurs when the mouse clicks the button.

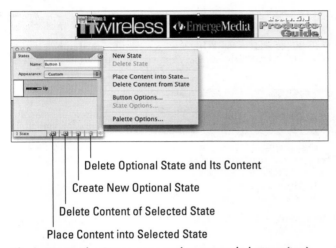

Delete Optional State and Its Content

Create New Optional State

Delete Content of Selected State

Place Content into Selected State

Figure 33-6: The States pane and an example button (top)

You can disable or enable any state by deselecting or selecting the option to its left in the pane. You can also select a state in the pane and choose State Options from the palette menu to disable or enable the state.

If you want to create a custom appearance for any state, select the state and choose Place Content into State from the palette menu or by clicking the button at the bottom of the pane. You will then be provided a Place dialog box from which to choose a picture file. You can crop, resize, and otherwise manipulate the picture as you would any picture in a frame. (Note how the Appearance pop-up menu changes to Custom when you do this.) To remove placed content, choose Delete Content from State.

Now comes the fun part: associating the action with the button. To do so, choose Button Options from the palette menu. You'll get the Button Options dialog box, which defaults to the General pane. In this pane, you provide a name for the button and set the button's visibility in the PDF file you'll later export. The options are self-explanatory: Visible, Hidden, Visible But Doesn't Print, and Hidden But Printable. (You can also open the Button Options dialog box for a selected object by choosing Object ➪ Interactive ➪ Button Options.)

The real action association happens in the Behaviors pane, shown in Figure 33-7. Here, you first select the event that triggers the action, using the Events pop-up menu:

✦ Mouse Up is when you release the mouse after clicking the button.

✦ Mouse Down is when you click the mouse button.

✦ Mouse Enter is when you move the mouse pointer over the button.

✦ Mouse Exit is when you move the mouse pointer away from the button after first passing over it.

✦ On Focus is when you tab into a form field (because a form field is simply a button, this is similar to Mouse Enter except that it detects keyboard access to the button).

✦ On Blur is when you tab out of a form field (because a form field is simply a button, this is similar to Mouse Exit except that it detects keyboard departure from the button).

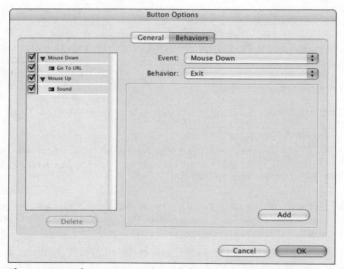

Figure 33-7: The Button Options dialog box and its Behaviors pane

Note   You may wonder what happens if you select a specific state before opening the Button Options dialog box. Nothing. It doesn't matter which state is selected in the pane — these are simply previews of the button's appearance based on the mouse status — because the behaviors selected in the Button Options menu affect the button as a whole.

You then choose the action in the Behavior pop-up menu. Most are self-explanatory: Close, Exit, Go to First Page, Go to Last Page, Go to Next Page, Go to Preview Page, Go to Preview View, Go to Anchor, Go to URL, Move, Open File, Sound, and View Zoom. Some of these — Go to Anchor, Go to URL, Movie, Sound, Open File, and View Zoom cause other pop-up menus and fields to appear in the palette to select a file to open or a hyperlink or anchor to jump to.

The Show/Hide Fields option is meant for Acrobat forms. InDesign considers every button to be a form field and provides a list of all buttons if you select this option. You can then decide which buttons (form entry fields in this case) display on the mouse action—you would have only those display that you want to be used as form-entry fields. (To specify the order in which a reader tabs through form fields [buttons], select the fields in the form, and then choose Object ➪ Interactive ➪ Set Tab Order, which opens a dialog box in which you can sort the buttons in the order that you want the reader to move through as he or she presses Tab.)

Click Add to add a behavior to this state. You can add multiple behaviors to each state. And each Event can have multiple behaviors—just select a new Behavior, and then click Add for each one.

Playing Movies and Sound

In addition to having a button that opens a movie or sound, you can simply place a movie or sound file in your InDesign document. (Once placed, you can size a movie file like any other placed graphic.)

Note InDesign can open QuickTime and Microsoft AVI movies only, so be sure to have a version in one of those formats. It also supports Macromedia Flash animations, though it can export those only to PDF files compatible with Acrobat 6 and later. For sounds, it supports the Apple AIFF and Microsoft WAV formats.

To control how a movie behaves and what control the reader has, choose Object ➪ Interactive ➪ Movie Options, as seen in Figure 33-8.

Tip A faster way to set movie and sound settings is to double-click the frame containing the movie or sound; the Movie Options dialog box or Sound Options dialog box appears, as appropriate.

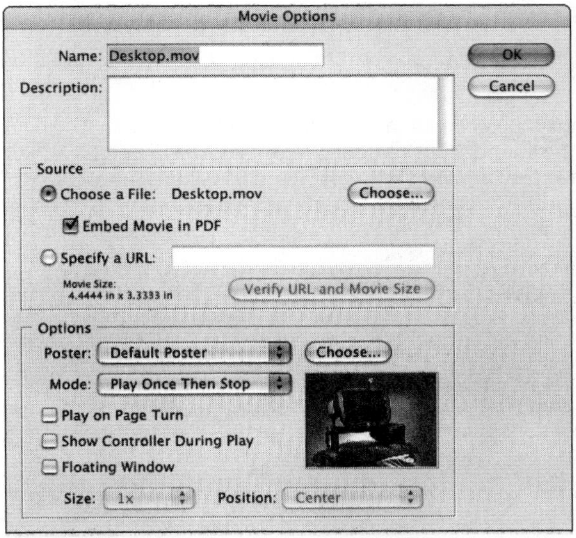

Figure 33-8: The Movie Options dialog box

Movie Options

The options in the Movie Options dialog box are straightforward:

✦ In the Source section, select whether the movie file is copied into your document or simply linked to a URL on the Web or on a CD. If you're embedding the movie file and plan to export the InDesign document as a PDF file, be sure to select the Embed Movie in PDF option — otherwise the PDF file won't have the movie available.

✦ In the Options section, you can change the Poster — the on-screen image inside the frame containing the movie. The default, Default Poster, lets Acrobat choose what displays (usually, it's the first frame of the movie). You can also select None (for a blank frame), Standard (for the Adobe logo), Choose Image as Poster (in which case you select an image using the Browse button, such as perhaps the QuickTime logo), or Frame from Movie (to select a specific frame from the movie; not all movies will let you select this option).

✦ You also set the Mode — Play Once Then Stop, Play Once Stay Open, and Repeat Play — to determine the movie's playback action. Note that the Play Once Stay Open option lets the user choose to play the movie again.

✦ The Play on Page Turn option, if selected, plays the movie when a reader moves to the page containing it (as opposed to going directly to the page through a hyperlink).

✦ The Show Controller During Play option displays the QuickTime or AVI movie controller to adjust sound volume; pause and resume play; and rewind and fast-forward the movie.

✦ The Floating Window option puts the movie in a window that the reader can move. If selected, the dialog box also makes two pop-up menus accessible: Size, which determines the size of the window relative to the movie frame size, and Position, which places the floating window on the page.

Sound Options

The options in the Sound Options dialog box (shown in Figure 33-9) are also straightforward:

✦ You can change the sound by clicking Choose to the right of the filename and then selecting a new sound.

✦ Using the Poster pop-up menu, you can change the placeholder image that appears on the page where you place the sound. Your options are None to have no placeholder image, Standard to have the speaker icon shown in Figure 33-9, and Choose Image as Poster to use an image of your own choice (click Choose to the right of the Poster pop-up menu to select the image file).

✦ If selected, the Play on Page Turn option automatically plays the sound when someone moves to this page in the exported PDF file.

✦ If selected, the Do Not Print Poster option hides the poster icon when someone prints the PDF page containing the sound.

✦ If selected, the Embed Sound in PDF option ensures that the PDF file exported from the InDesign document includes the sound file.

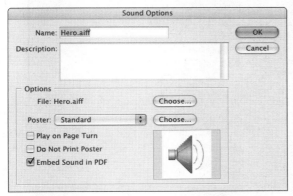

Figure 33-9: The Sound Options dialog box

Summary

InDesign lets you create hyperlinks and anchors within your documents — to Web addresses, pages, and text in your InDesign document, and to pages and text in other InDesign documents — that are then clickable from a PDF file created from your InDesign file.

You can also create buttons that have associated actions — such as opening a movie file, closing a page, changing the zoom level, or moving to a new page — when exported as a PDF file. InDesign also lets you import movie and sound files that likewise play in exported PDF files.

✦   ✦   ✦

Working with XML

One of the most complex features in InDesign is its set of XML features. XML is a structured language that essentially treats document components as data, so you can manage them through a database. The XML tools in InDesign let you treat InDesign documents as sources for XML databases, which are then linked into Web pages, PDF files, CD-ROMs, and so forth. They also let you create InDesign templates into which you flow data from XML files, all formatted and in the proper frames.

The key to XML is the fact that it's extensible. You create the tags, or labels, for various kinds of content (these are called *data type descriptions,* or DTDs) based on what makes sense for your content. Then you specify what happens to each of the types of labeled content in terms of what's published, how it's presented, and so forth. Compare that to the more rigid HTML and PDF systems, where there are only certain tags available that cannot be changed, and the presentation is fixed based on the label chosen.

XML code is similar to HTML in the sense that there are tags surrounded by angle brackets (< and >) and that commands and labels are turned on and off (such as <standardHeader> at the beginning of a header item and </standardHeader> at the end of it. Comments begin with <!-- and end with >, while custom commands and declarations (called *processing instructions*) begin with <? and end with ?>. You don't have to understand this level of detail — just keep in mind that there are different codes to look for in examining XML code, if the need arises.

Note A DTD may define several types of content that have their own subcontent types and rules. These are called *branches.* For example, there could be an AuthorInformation branch and a CustomerList branch that both contain tags named Name. You'll need to know which branch text tagged Name should go into, because XML won't know the context.

Note The use of XML will likely involve assistance from a Web master, content engineer, or other programming-savvy person. Page designers might also want to read *XML For Dummies,* 3rd Edition, by Ed Tittel (Wiley Publishing). The *Adobe InDesign CS2 Bible* limits itself to an overview of InDesign XML functions and is no substitute for a thorough understanding of XML.

Importing and Creating XML Tags

Chances are that most of the time, you'll be exporting InDesign documents for use in XML databases, such as converting a publication's articles into a structured format used by a Web site's content management system. To export content properly, you need to apply tags to it. In InDesign, you can do that directly or by having InDesign translate style tags into XML tags. You'll use both methods, because some content (such as images) wouldn't have style tags associated to it but needs XML tags for proper processing in an XML database.

Those tags come from two sources: They're imported from a file provided by the Web site's content engineer, or they're created in InDesign by the page designer. Most of the time, you should use tags created by the content engineer, because that engineer is creating a standard set of tags for multiple page designers (both print- and Web-based). You might create your own tags when helping develop the initial tags in concert with that content engineer — or if you also are the content engineer, as well as page designer.

New Feature   InDesign CS2's XML functionality supports table elements such as table cells, cell content, and table structure during import and export.

It also supports the definition of style attributes (for example, `<Title: paragraphpstyle="ChapterStyle"/>` to define and apply the style ChapterStyle to the element names Title) in an imported XML file and will import and apply those attributes to imported content.

Importing tags

There are two places where you import tags: the Tags pane (Window ⇨ Tags) and the Import XML dialog box (File ⇨ Import XML). In the Tags pane, shown in Figure 34-1, you use the Load Tags option in the pane's palette menu to import tags from an XML file or an InDesign document that has tags defined in it. All tags are imported when you choose Load Tags.

New Tag

Auto Tag   Delete Tag

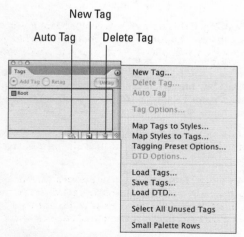

Figure 34-1: The Tags pane

The other way to import XML tags is to choose File ⇨ Import XML, which imports not only XML tags but also XML content from an XML file. This process works two ways, depending on how your document is set up:

✦ If your document has no content, importing an XML file adds the XML tags to the Tags pane and into the document's Structure window (covered later in this chapter). It also adds the content to the Structure pane, where you can click and drag it into InDesign frames in your layout.

✦ If your document has content, importing an XML file brings in the content to your document and places it in frames in your document that have the same tags already applied. This is a way to automatically populate a layout in InDesign.

 Caution The order of the tags in the XML file's tags definitions is important. If the XML file has three tags — defined in the order of Body, Head, and Caption — but the Structure pane in InDesign lists them in the order Head, Body, and Caption, InDesign imports only Body and Caption content. That's because it imports Body first and then looks for the first occurrence of the Body tag in the InDesign file. It then begins matching style tags at that point. Because Head is listed in InDesign before Body, Head is ignored. (All the tags will be in the Structure pane, so you can manually place the imported Head content.)

When importing XML documents, you can control some of the import operations by ensuring that Show XML Import Options is selected in the Import XML dialog box. When you choose an XML document, and then click Open, you will get a dialog box with the following import options:

✦ **Placement.** This pop-up menu gives you the options of merging the content into your InDesign document or appending it. Merge Content is the default and will match up content by tags during the import, overwriting content based on other options chosen in this dialog box.

✦ **Create Link When Importing XML File.** If this option is selected, it adds a link to the XML file in the Links pane.

✦ **Repeated Text Elements Inherit Formatting.** If this option is selected, the styles in the current InDesign document are preserved when importing content in the XML file that uses the same element names. In other words, it applies existing styles to new elements that use the same tags as existing elements.

✦ **Delete InDesign Namespace Attributes After Import.** If this option is selected, tags using InDesign XML naming are removed because they are not needed in InDesign and simply increase file complexity.

✦ **Only Import Elements That Match Existing Structure.** If this option is selected, elements in the imported file that vary from or are not defined by the existing InDesign document are stripped out.

✦ **Do Not Import Contents of Whitespace-Only Elements.** If this option is selected, elements that consist of nothing but spaces are ignored, so these blank elements do not overwrite same-name elements in InDesign. It also eliminates extraneous spaces where one will do, such as in documents that have two spaces at the end of each sentence.

✦ **Delete Elements, Frames, and Content That Do Not Match Imported XML.** If this option is selected, any elements and items in the InDesign document that are not defined in the XML document are removed. In other words, this makes the imported XML document overwrite the InDesign document.

The are several new options in the Import XML dialog box: Delete Elements, Frames, and Content That Do Not Match Imported XML; Only Import Elements That Match Existing Structure; Repeated Text Elements Inherit Formatting; and Do Not Import Contents of Whitespace-Only Elements. To access these controls, Show XML Import Options must be selected in the Import XML dialog box.

Creating tags

You also create XML tags in the Tags pane using the New Tag palette menu. A tag simply consists of the tag name and the tag color — its formatting is defined in the XML database or in a DTD file.

Mapping tags and styles

In the Tags pane's palette menu, you can also map style tags to XML tags and vice versa using the Map Tags to Styles menu option and the Map Styles to Tags menu option, respectively. (They're also available in the Structure pane's palette menu.) Figure 34-2 shows the Map Styles to Tags dialog box; the Map Tags to Styles dialog box is nearly identical, except the two columns are switched. Here's what they do:

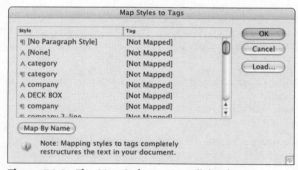

Figure 34-2: The Map Styles to Tags dialog box

✦ Map Tags to Styles tells InDesign what XML tag to substitute for a specified character or paragraph style during XML export. The text retains its original InDesign style tags.

✦ Map Styles to Tags tells InDesign to immediately replace the specified styles with the XML tags. You'll see colored brackets around each string of text (paragraphs for paragraph styles and text selections for character styles) to indicate the text has an XML tag applied to it. The color corresponds to the tag color in the Tags pane. (You can change tag colors, as well as the tag name, using the Tag Options menu in the pane's palette menu or simply by double-clicking the tag name in the pane.)

Note InDesign checks to make sure that you include valid XML tag names according to XML standards. If you include a space or an illegal character in the tag name, an alert message appears when you click OK.

Applying Tags

It's easy to apply tags to text: Simply select the text and click the tag name in the Tags pane. If you want to replace the tag for selected text, be sure to select the Retag option in the Tags pane — otherwise, the original tag will remain and the new tag applied as well. Unless they're style tags, multiple XML tags can be applied to the same object or text. If you choose View ➪ Structure ➪ View Tag Markers, tagged text will display brackets around it in the color of the tag in the Tags pane. Similarly, if you choose View ➪ Structure ➪ Show Tagged Frames, tagged frames and lines will also show a color indicator.

You can remove a tag by selecting the tagged text or object and then clicking Untag in the Tags pane.

It gets slightly more complex if you're using the Structure pane to place tagged content imported from an XML file into InDesign objects. Figure 34-3 shows the Structure pane, which opens automatically as you begin using XML tags. (You can hide this pane by choosing View ➪ Structure ➪ Hide Structure, or pressing Option+⌘+1 or Ctrl+Alt+1.) The pane shows the document's tagged content, as well as the tags associated with it. The content appears in a hierarchy, reflecting any nesting in the tags (similar to how a character style can be thought of as a subset of a paragraph tag, because it applies to a component of a paragraph).

To apply XML content to a frame, simply click and drag the appropriate content (indicated with the Text Content icon) onto a frame. As you apply tags from the Tags pane to selected objects, you'll see icons for text and objects appear along with the name of the applied tags.

You can reorder the tags in the Structure pane to reflect the hierarchy of elements. Do this in coordination with your content engineer because the hierarchy in the InDesign file needs to match the hierarchy expectations in the XML database or content system.

Validate Structure

Add an Attribute

Add an Element

Remove Selected Elements

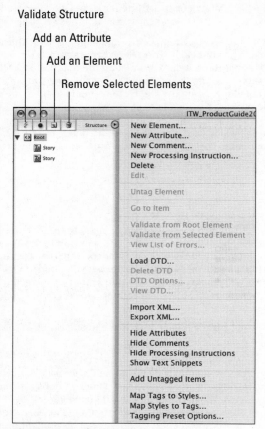

Figure 34-3: The Structure pane

Taking Advantage of Other XML Options

For the more XML-savvy, InDesign offers several controls in the Structure pane and its palette menu.

In the pane, you have these options:

✦ **Validate Structure.** This button checks the current XML structure in the Structure pane and compares it against the DTD file imported with the XML data or imported later using the Import DTD option in the pane's palette menu. There's a copy of the button at the bottom of the pane, along with the View Errors List button that shows any errors found.

✦ **Add an Attribute.** This button lets you add an XML attribute, which is essentially a comment such as the revision date. It has no effect on the flow of information or the appearance or role of an element.

✦ **Add an Element.** This button lets you add an XML element, which is a tag applied to text or an object.

✦ **Remove Selected Elements.** This button removes any selected elements.

In the palette menu, you have these options:

✦ The New Element, New Attribute, New Comment, and New Processing Instruction menu items let you add those items.

✦ Delete deletes items.

✦ Edit edits items.

✦ Untag Element removes an elements XML tag.

✦ Validate from Root Element verifies the structure starting at the *root* (topmost) object against the DTD information.

✦ Validate from Selected Element starts the validation at the selected item.

✦ View List of Errors shows a dialog box with any validation errors found.

✦ Import DTD imports a data type description file, which defines the "role" of tags (such as indicating that the Head tag begins a section of a story).

✦ Delete DTD removes the DTD file from the InDesign document but leaves the structure untouched.

✦ View DTD shows a dialog box with the actual DTD information (similar to a code preview in an HTML editor).

✦ The Hide Attributes, Hide Comments, and Hide Processing Instructions menu options remove these noncontent markers from view in the Structure pane so you can concentrate on just the elements.

✦ Show/Hide Text Snippets shows or hides the first few words of text for each Text Content icon in the pane. Seeing these snippets is very helpful in knowing what each element actually contains.

✦ Add Untagged Items adds to the Structure pane all objects in the InDesign document that aren't already tagged with an XML tag. This helps ensure that you don't miss any object when reviewing the document structure.

✦ The Map Tags to Styles and Map Styles to Tags menu options match InDesign styles to XML tags, as covered earlier in this chapter.

Exporting XML Files

When the InDesign document has the proper elements properly tagged to the document's content, you're ready to export it to an XML file for use by a Web site's content-management system or other XML database. Choose File ➪ Export, or press ⌘+E or Ctrl+E, to open the Export dialog box. In this dialog box, give the XML file a name in the Save As field (InDesign automatically adds the filename extension .xml), select a folder in which to place the file, and — most important — choose XML from the Format pop-up menu. Then click Save.

The Export XML dialog box appears, which opens with the General pane. This pane is simple:

✦ Select the Include DTD Declaration option to include the DTD information in the exported file. Otherwise, the XML database will need to import the DTD file separately.

✦ Select the View XML Using option and select a Web browser or Web-supporting application in the adjacent pop-up menu to preview the XML file in that browser or program.

✦ If an element is selected in the Structure pane, the Export from Selected Element option will be available; it exports the XML file only from that element on.

✦ Use the Encoding pop-up menu to choose the text encoding mechanism — a way of representing international characters across different computer systems. Your content engineer or Web master will tell you whether to select UTF-8, UTF-16, or Shift-JIS.

In the Graphics pane, you tell InDesign how to handle the output of any tagged pictures. Figure 34-4 shows the pane. Your options are:

✦ **In the Image Options section**, indicate which images to copy to the Images subfolder that InDesign will create. Your choices are Original Images, Optimized Original Images, and Optimized Formatted Images. You can select any or all of these. The optimized images are converted to GIF or JPEG for use on the Web unless you specify GIF or JPEG in the Image Conversion pop-up menu rather than leave the default setting of Automatic; the formatted images crop the images to reduce file size.

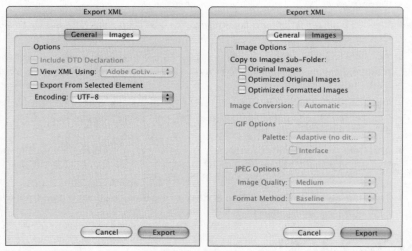

Figure 34-4: The Export XML dialog box and its General (at left) and Images panes

✦ **In the GIF Options section**, you can choose the color palette in the Palette pop-up menu, with choices of Adaptive (No Dither), Web, System (Mac), and System (Win). Ask your Web master what to use; usually, you select Adaptive (No Dither). For very large images, interlacing can make on-screen display over the Web seem faster (by building the image line by line rather than waiting until the whole image has been transferred to the browser before anything is displayed); if you want to have such interlaced display of GIF files, select the Interlace option.

✦ **In the JPEG Options section**, there are similar options for JPEG files. In the Image Quality pop-up menu, choose the desired image quality (Low, Medium, High, and Maximum). In the Format Method, choose Progressive to have the file displayed progressively (similar to the interlace option for GIF files) or Baseline to display it all at once. Unless your images are very large, keep the default Baseline.

When you export an XML file with pictures, InDesign automatically embeds XMP media management properties with the pictures' tags. You can view those properties by choosing File ⇨ File Info and then choosing the Advanced pane. This information may be of interest to your content engineer but has no real meaning for the page designer. However, the content engineer may want to fill out the information in the File Info dialog box's other panes — Description and Origin — into which you can add comments, creator information and contact details, copyright information, credit and source information, keywords, and copyright URLs.

InDesign provides another way to generate XML files: Choose File ⇨ Package For GoLive. This option creates an XML file preformatted for Adobe GoLive CS2 or later. You'll make adjustments to the XML file and choose image settings such as those in the Export XML dialog box in GoLive rather than in InDesign.

Creating XML Snippets

You can also export components in your InDesign document as XML snippets by choosing InDesign Snippets in the Export dialog box's Format pop-up menu. InDesign will export to a snippet file any selected objects. You can place those objects in an InDesign layout by placing them (File ⇨ Place, or ⌘+D or Ctrl+D) as you would any graphic or text file. (If no objects are selected, InDesign Snippet will not appear as a choice in the Format pop-up menu.) Note that InDesign Snippet files are given the filename extension .inds.

A faster way to create a snippet is to simply click and drag the item to the Macintosh or Windows desktop (or to a folder); InDesign creates a name for the snippet file that you can later rename if you choose to by using the Mac OS X or Windows file-management controls (usually just clicking the icon, which highlights the name, and then typing a new name).

Be aware that the snippet file contains the page location of the objects, so placing a snippet file of object or objects into a document with a different page dimensions than the original document can have unexpected results.

XML snippets are new to InDesign CS2.

Summary

InDesign lets you tag content within documents with XML tags, transferring that content to an XML database or Web content engine from which it can be used in a variety of media, formatted as appropriate for each. You can also import XML content into InDesign, automatically placing content into the appropriate frames if you've created an appropriate template and tagged it with the right XML tags. But InDesign's XML tools are only the beginning — you'll need an XML database and content-creation and content-presentation tools to use the XML data derived from InDesign documents.

You can also export XML files from InDesign, either entire documents or snippets composed of selected objects.

✦   ✦   ✦

Working with Others

Publishing is rarely a one-person enterprise. Chances are that the creators of your text and graphics are not the same people who do your layout. And in many environments, the chances are high that many people are involved in layout and production.

By its very nature, publishing is a group activity, so publishing programs must support workgroups. Yet a Mac or a PC is a *personal* computer, so it's easy to work on a Mac or PC without worrying about how your setup and work style might affect others. InDesign lets you create your own balance between the individual and the workgroup.

The key to working effectively in a workgroup environment is to establish standards and make sure they're easy to stick to. A basic way to accomplish this task is to place all common elements in one place so that people always know where to get the standard elements. This practice also makes it easy to maintain (add, modify, and delete) these elements over time, which is essential because no environment is static. How you do this depends on your computing environment:

 ✦ If you don't use a network, keep a master set of disks and copy elements from the master set in a folder with the same name on each person's computer. Update these folders every time a standard element changes on the master disk.

 ✦ If you do use a network, keep a master set of disks (networks do go down, so you'll want your files accessible when that happens) and create a folder for your standard elements on a network drive accessible to all users. Update this folder whenever a standard element changes on the master disk.

Sharing Elements with Other Users

Some standard elements can be accessed easily from a common folder because InDesign can import certain elements that are stored outside InDesign documents. These elements include graphics files, libraries, keyboard shortcut sets, and spelling dictionaries.

Other elements reside within documents and templates and cannot be saved in separate files. These elements include styles and master pages. But styles can be exported or imported from one document to another.

Caution   In several cases, multiple users can share the same preferences or other file using the Mac's alias feature or the Windows shortcut feature. (These are noted where I cover specific features that permit this.) But note that, as with all over-the-network alias/shortcut solutions, there are some risks. For example, it is easier to corrupt the file. Also, the network and the host machine must be available at all times. Finally, if two users save changes to the file at the same time, only one user's changes will get through.

Where InDesign stores what

The Presets folder in the InDesign application folder contains folders for several kinds of preference-related elements: InDesign Shortcut Sets, InDesign Workspaces, Scripts, and Swatch Libraries. The Presets folder also includes any document preset files.

The spelling and hyphenation exception dictionaries that come with InDesign are stored in the Plug-ins\Dictionaries\Proximity folder inside the InDesign application folder. But the exception dictionaries you create when adding words and hyphenation breakpoints in InDesign's spell checker and dictionary tools are stored elsewhere: On the Mac, they're stored in the path Users*user name*\Library\Preferences\Adobe InDesign\Version 4.0\Dictionaries\Proximity. In Windows, they're stored in Documents and Settings\user name\Application Data\Adobe\InDesign\Version n4.0\Dictionaries\Proximity.

Note   The Application Data folder in Windows is hidden by default. To see it, open any folder in Windows, and then choose Tools ➪ Folder Options to open the Folder Options dialog box. Go to the View pane and select the Show Hidden Files and Folders option. Click OK.

Plug-ins — both those that come with InDesign and those you buy from other companies — are stored in the Plug-ins folder, often in subfolders within it.

The actual InDesign preferences file — called InDesign Defaults — is stored in a different location on the Mac and in Windows. On the Mac, InDesign Defaults is stored in Users\ *user name*\Library\Preferences\Adobe InDesign\Version 4.0. In Windows, it is stored in Documents and Settings*user name*\Application Data\Adobe\InDesign\Version 4.0.

Preference files

When no document is open and you change the preferences, add swatches and styles, modify tool settings (such as change the number of sides on the Polygon or Polygon Frame tool by double-clicking it), and modify the default settings of some dialog boxes (such as Text Wrap and Text Frame Options), these changes are saved in the InDesign Defaults file.

Tip   You can use the Mac's alias feature or the Windows shortcut feature to use an InDesign Defaults file stored in a folder other than the one in which InDesign resides. On a network, being able to use this technique means that everyone can share the same InDesign Defaults file. You can also set keyboard shortcuts sets, spelling and hyphenation dictionaries, libraries, and swatch libraries to be shared this way. Note that if you're sharing these across platform, you'll need to create a Windows shortcut from Windows to these files as well as a Mac alias from the Mac.

The InDesign Defaults file cannot be shared across platforms, so if you want to have a master copy on a network server, you'll need to maintain two masters — one for Macintosh and one for Windows. Because the files have the same name on both platforms (there is no filename extension for this file in Windows), you'll need to store them in separate directories or add something to the name such as "Mac" and "Windows." If you do change the name, note that the alias on shortcut on each user's system must simply be named InDesign Defaults.

Color definitions

Wanting to keep color, tint, and gradient definitions consistent across documents isn't unusual. This consistency helps you ensure, for example, that corporate identity colors, if you have them, are used instead of someone's approximations.

You can import swatches created in other documents (and templates) by having both documents open, and then clicking and dragging the swatch from the source document's Swatches pane (Window ⇨ Swatches or F5) to anywhere in the other document's window. By creating a file that contains nothing but swatches, you can, in effect, create a color library for users.

You can't add swatches to a library, but any swatch used in a library element will be copied to a document along with that element. So you could use a library that has a series of rectangles each with a different swatch applied as another way of creating a color library.

InDesign also lets you share swatch libraries, even across platform (just be sure the ColorBook swatch library file has the filename extension .ase if you're transferring a swatch library from the Mac to Windows).

 See Chapter 8 for more on creating swatches.

 On the Mac, color profiles are stored in the path Users*user name*\Library\ColorSync\Profiles. In Windows, they're stored in the System32\Color folder inside the folder that contains Windows (usually called Windows or WinNT).

Paragraph, character, and object styles

The Character Styles pane (Window ⇨ Type & Tables ⇨ Character Styles or Shift+F11) and the Paragraph Styles pane (Window ⇨ Type & Tables ⇨ Paragraph Styles or F11) include an option in the palette menu to import styles from other InDesign documents and templates. Choose Load Character Styles or Load Paragraph Styles from the palette menu to import just character or paragraph styles, respectively; use Load All Styles to load both from a document or template.

The Object Styles pane (Window ⇨ Object Styles, or ⌘+F7 or Ctrl+F7) also includes an option to import object styles from other InDesign documents and templates. Choose Load Object Styles from the palette menu to import object styles.

Note that the Load dialog boxes accessed through the Character Styles, Paragraph Styles, and Object Styles dialog boxes let you select which styles to load, as well as let you decide how to handle the import of styles that have the same names in the two documents.

By importing styles with no document open, you copy all new styles into your global defaults (those stored in the InDesign Defaults file covered earlier). This technique is a handy way of bringing new styles into your default settings without affecting existing styles.

See Chapter 19 for more on paragraph and character styles and Chapter 11 for more on object styles.

Spelling dictionaries

InDesign saves any spelling or hyphenation exceptions you add through Edit ⇨ Dictionary or when spell-checking through Edit ⇨ Check Spelling, or ⌘+I or Ctrl+I. These exception dictionaries can be copied from one computer to another (regardless of platform), or you can use an alias or shortcut from each computer to a central location on a server.

On both Mac and Windows, hyphenation exception files have the filename extension .not, while the spelling exception dictionaries have the extension .udc. The files will have the same name as the language dictionaries (but different filename extensions) to which they are associated, such as FREN.not for French hyphenation exceptions and USA.udc for U.S. English spelling exceptions.

See Chapter 14 for more on hyphenation and spelling dictionaries.

Graphics and text files

Perhaps the most obvious elements to standardize are the *source elements* — the text and graphics that you use in your documents — especially if you have common elements, such as logos that are used in multiple documents.

The simplest method of ensuring that the latest versions of these common elements are used is to keep them all in a standard folder (either on each computer or on a network drive). This method works well when you first use a text or graphic element, but it does not ensure that these elements are updated in InDesign documents if the elements are changed after being imported.

For text and graphics files, using InDesign's links feature — when you keep common elements in a common location — can ensure consistency across documents. You can also use libraries and snippets to store commonly used graphics and text blocks (including any formatting for the text and its frame).

See Chapter 23 for more on graphics links and Chapter 13 for more on text links.

Libraries

InDesign libraries are a great aid to keeping documents consistent. Because libraries are stored in their own files, common libraries can be put in common folders. You can even access them across the network. If you want, you can keep an alias to a library elsewhere on the network on your computer's local drive.

For many people, libraries offer more flexibility than just linking to graphics files because all attributes applied to graphics and their graphics frames are also stored in the library.

Libraries can be shared across platform, and although Windows InDesign libraries have the filename extension .indl, that extension is not required for Windows InDesign to open and use Mac libraries.

 See Chapter 7 for more information on libraries.

Snippets

You can also share elements through the use of XML snippets, which contain InDesign objects. Snippet files have the filename extension .inds and can be placed in an InDesign document like any graphic or text. They retain all their attributes, much like libraries, except that each snippet is stored in its own file. Unlike library items, snippets retain their object coordinates, which can create some minor issues when a snippet made from a larger document is placed into a second, smaller document. The objects will not fall off the pasteboard, but it may take some effort to find it.

 See Chapter 34 for more information on XML snippets.

Templates

In the course of creating documents, you're likely to evolve templates (called *stationery* by earlier versions of the Mac OS) that you want to use over and over. InDesign can save a document as a template. The only difference between a template and a document is that a template forces you to use Save As rather than Save in the File menu so that you don't overwrite the template but instead create new documents based on it.

Although the optimum approach is to design a template before creating actual documents, the truth is that no one can foresee all possibilities. Even if you create a template (and you should) with styles, swatches, and master pages intended for use in all new documents, you can expect to modify your template because working on real documents brings up the need for modifications and additions.

Whether or not you use templates, you'll still need to transfer basic layout elements like styles and master pages from one document to another, as described earlier in this chapter.

Templates can be shared across platforms, and although Windows InDesign templates have the filename extension .indt, that extension is not required for Windows InDesign to open and use Mac templates. (I still recommend that you always use the filename extensions, so the correct icons appear in your folders.)

See Chapter 4 for more on templates.

Master pages

Moving master pages between documents is tricky because InDesign offers no feature that explicitly performs this task. But this technique works well to accomplish this goal:

1. **Open both documents (choose File ➪ Open or press ⌘+O or Ctrl+O).**

2. **Drag the master page from the source document's Pages pane (Window ➪ Pages or F12.) into the target document's window.**

Tip

Choose Window ➪ Arrange ➪ Cascade or Window ➪ Arrange ➪ Tile to manage how documents display if you have several open. Tile creates nonoverlapping windows — either side by side or one at the top and one at the bottom, if you have two documents open — while Cascade overlaps the windows. The names of all open documents also appear in the Window menu so that you can switch among them. You can also resize windows manually by clicking and holding the mouse on the window's resize box on the Mac, or by clicking and holding any of its sides or corners in Windows.

Cross-Reference

See Chapter 7 for more on master pages.

InDesign documents

An easy way to share InDesign documents with others is to use the Package feature (File ➪ Package, or Option+Shift+⌘+P or Ctrl+Alt+Shift+P), which copies all files needed to one folder. This lets you place a complete package for others to work on in one location, whether on a network folder or on a removable medium such as a CD-RW.

Cross-Reference

Chapter 29 covers the package feature.

If you're working on a network, the Version Cue file-version management software that comes with Adobe Creative Suite 2 applications, including InDesign CS2, can also help. It lets you create shared folders across the network that you save your files to once you're ready for others to work on them. Version Cue also retains earlier versions, so there is a history of changes that you can use to undo design directions that don't work out. A related tool is the InCopy CS2 software that Adobe sells separately; this software lets development editors and copy editors work on an InDesign document's text while the designer is working on the layout.

Cross-Reference

Version Cue is covered in the next section of this chapter, while Appendix E provides an introduction to InCopy.

Managing Shared Projects and File Versions

A challenge in any workgroup is managing files. Such management boils down to two issues:

✦ When an individual is working on a project, should he or she keep copies of significant versions of the file as it evolves?

✦ When files are shared with others, where should they reside and how do you ensure that only one person is working on the current file at a time?

Typically, organizations develop their own procedures, such as having layout artists add version numbers or dates to layout iterations and creating shared network folders such as *Ready for Copy Edit* and *Ready for Production* through which files move as they progress through the production cycle. Very large organizations may use a workflow tool such as those from Managing Editor. And QuarkXPress-based publishers may have used the Quark Publishing System, which offers some file-management features in addition to the copy-editing modules that Adobe InCopy provides.

Fundamentally, Version Cue does two things:

✦ It adds an alternative set of folders to the standard Mac and Windows folder hierarchy called Workspaces — almost as if they are a virtual hard drive that everyone has access to. These shared folders can reside anywhere on the network, but users don't have to have to navigate through the network to find them. (They are automatically made available to all Version Cue users and present everyone the same folder hierarchy, so users don't get confused as to what folder is which.)

✦ It lets you save versions of your files, so you (or others) can go back to earlier versions if you don't like how the layout has evolved. Version Cue handles the naming of these versions and keeps track of when each was created, so you don't have to.

Version Cue also works the same way across platforms, which can be helpful in cross-platform organizations.

Adobe introduced Version Cue with the first Adobe Creative Suite. But that version of Version Cue was hard to figure out, so many users simply used the Mac OS's or Windows' native shared-folder features instead. Adding to Version Cue's adoption woes, it came only with the Adobe Creative Suite, not with individual copies of InDesign CS.

InDesign, like other Adobe Creative Suite 2 programs, comes with a revised version of Version Cue, and you no longer have to buy the full suite to get it. The revised Version Cue is easier to use, though it is still a bit complex.

The Version Cue interface

The shared folders created with Version Cue appear in the Workspaces sections of the Open a File, Save, Export, and Place dialog boxes. If Version Cue is enabled (which it is by default) and you have chosen the Version Cue folder view (by clicking the Use Adobe Dialog button in the various dialog boxes), you will see both the Workspace folders and your computer's regular folders. This lets you work on both shared projects and local projects from one set of dialog boxes.

Emulating Mac OS X's and Windows XP's quick-access sidebar, InDesign's Version Cue–enabled dialog boxes also have a sidebar that gives you quick access to the local Desktop folder, the local Documents folder (Mac) or My Documents folder (Windows), and the Version Cue folder.

(In Windows, you also get access to the My Pictures and My Network Places folders.) You also get quick access to the Project Search, Project Trash, and Files in Use functions, the latter two being virtual folders and the first being a search function that works with Version Cue's folders. Finally, you also get access to user-chosen favorites at the bottom of the pane; you add them by selecting a folder and then choosing Add to Favorites from the Project Tools drop-down menu (covered later in this section).

You set the Version Cue defaults using the Adobe Bridge application, which manages Creative Suite 2–wide settings. Choose Bridge ➪ Preferences or ⌘+K on the Mac or Edit ➪ Preferences or Ctrl+K in Windows. Figure 35-1 shows the dialog box. At the bottom of the General pane, you set the default folders to display in Version Cue dialog boxes' Favorites sidebar section.

The Version Cue–enabled dialog boxes also have several buttons, as labeled in Figure 35-2. The functions of the first four — Up One Folder, New Folder, Refresh, and Trash — are self-explanatory. The fifth, Project Tools, is a drop-down menu that contains the functions to create projects (shared folders), connect to existing projects, manage sharing and versions, manage project items, synchronize items, and revert to the standard dialog boxes (by choosing the Show OS Dialog menu option). The sixth icon, at far right, is the View drop-down menu that offers file view choices of Details, Icons, Thumbnails, and Tiles.

To switch back to the standard Mac or Windows dialog boxes, click Use OS Dialog or choose Use OS Dialog from the Project Tools drop-down menu. To get the Version Cue–enabled dialog boxes back, click Use Adobe Dialog, which appears at the bottom of the regular Mac and Windows dialog boxes.

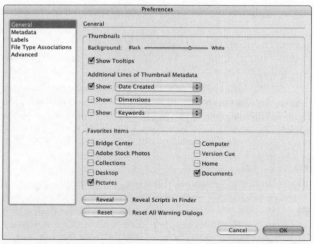

Figure 35-1: The General pane of the Preferences dialog box in Adobe Bridge. The Favorites Items section manages Version Cue's default folder display.

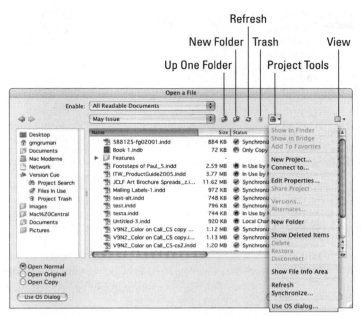

Figure 35-2: With Version Cue enabled, the Open, Save, Export, and Place dialog boxes gain several new features for managing shared projects and controlling file versions, as well as a modified appearance for navigating through both Version Cue and normal folder hierarchies. An Open a File dialog box is shown here.

Because all local folders — those on your computer or mounted through your computer's network connections — display in the Version Cue–enabled dialog boxes, even if you never use shared workspaces, you still have access to all your local files, as well as to any files accessible over the network. That means you can leave Version Cue turned on even if you never use it, without losing any functionality. However, there are reasons that you might want to turn off Version Cue if you end up not using it:

✦ Version Cue takes a lot of RAM — about 128MB.

✦ You want to use the standard Mac and Window dialog boxes, so InDesign will work like other programs you use.

✦ Version Cue–enabled dialog boxes tend to display more slowly than the standard dialog boxes.

✦ The default Version Cue dialog boxes don't show previews of selected documents or graphics, making it harder to use to choose the right elements. However, if you switch to the Icons, Thumbnails, or Tiles view, you can see previews of some images.

In a nutshell, the trick to using Version Cue is to know whether files are stored in a Version Cue workspace folder or in a regular folder, and then navigate accordingly.

Enabling and disabling Version Cue

InDesign turns Version Cue on by default. There are two ways to turn it off (or back on):

✦ **Permanently.** Deselect the Version Cue option in the File Handling pane of the Preferences dialog box (InDesign ⇨ Preferences on the Mac or Edit ⇨ Preferences in Windows, or ⌘+K or Ctrl+K). Make sure it is selected if you want to turn Version Cue back on.

✦ **Temporarily.** Using the Project Tools drop-down menu in the Version Cue–enabled dialog boxes, choose Show OS Dialog to revert to the standard dialog box for as long as that particular dialog box is open. Click Use Adobe Dialog at the lower left of the dialog box to get the Version Cue–enabled view back.

Note   Although Version Cue should automatically find shared workspaces for and from any PC or Mac that has Version Cue enabled, you might not find all such workspaces in your copy of InDesign. That typically has to do with network access and connection settings, so be sure to involve your network administrator if you use Version Cue.

Working with versions

When you open a file through Version Cue, you are actually working on a copy of the master file. Depending on how you save the file, you'll get different results:

✦ **Save** (File ⇨ Save, or ⌘+S or Ctrl+S). All changes are saved locally, and the master version in the project folder is not modified. You can add version comments in the Save dialog box.

✦ **Save As** (File ⇨ Save As, or Shift+⌘+S or Ctrl+Shift+S). If you save in a local folder, all changes are saved locally to a new file (with a different, user-defined name), and the master version in the project folder is not modified. Otherwise, it saves the file into the project folder as a new version of the original file, leaving the original file unchanged. Either way, you can add version comments in the Save As dialog box.

✦ **Save a Copy** (File ⇨ Save a Copy, or Option+⌘+S or Ctrl+Alt+S). All changes are saved locally to a new file (with a new name chosen by InDesign — the word "copy" is added to the end), and the master version in the project folder is not modified. You can add version comments in the Save a Copy dialog box.

✦ **Save a Version** (File ⇨ Save a Version). All changes are saved both locally and to the master project folder, replacing the master file. The file name remains the same as when you opened it. You can add version comments in the Save a Version dialog box; InDesign automatically increments the version number each time you save a version (so if the file was version 4 when you opened it, it will be version 5 when you save a version).

If a second person opens a document, that person gets a message saying that someone else is working on the file. Both people can work on local copies, but their respective changes will not be integrated back to the master file, even if one or both later tries to save a version. Instead, there will be two new files with different changes, plus the original master, in the project folder. But if the first user locks a file, the other person can only work on a copy of the original file — the original user's changes will be made to the master file once he or she saves a version.

Caution Version Cue works with files from both CS and C2 programs. Because you can open CS files with a CS2 application, you could end up with, for example, a file that started in InDesign CS format that is now in InDesign CS2 format, making it inaccessible to InDesign CS users.

Working with Version Cue tools

If you want to take advantage of the Version Cue project management and versioning tools, you'll use the Project Tools drop-down menu extensively (refer to Figure 35-2).

Managing file access

Here's a run-through of the Version Cue features for managing shared projects:

✦ **Reveal in Finder (Mac) or Reveal in Explorer (Windows).** Opens a new window with the folder containing the selected file.

✦ **Reveal in Bridge.** Opens the Bridge program that Adobe provides to manage project preferences across the Creative Suite and shows the selected file's status there.

✦ **Add to Favorites.** Adds the selected file to the Favorites (Macs) or My Favorites (Windows) list in the Version Cue–enabled dialog boxes.

✦ **New Project.** Lets you create a new project.

✦ **Connect To.** Lets you connect to another computer or server on which Version Cue projects might reside; you need to know the IP address.

✦ **Edit Properties.** Lets you set basic project settings, such as folder location within the workspace hierarchy and whether a project is shared.

✦ **Share Project.** Shares the project so others can work on it.

✦ **New Folder.** Creates a new folder at the current location.

✦ **Show Deleted Items.** Shows items deleted through the Version Cue and Bridge tools.

✦ **Delete.** Deletes a file from a Version Cue project without removing it from the computer. The file is in the Project Trash folder, accessible at the left side of the Version Cue–enabled dialog boxes.

✦ **Restore.** Restores a deleted file to the project.

✦ **Disconnect.** Removes a file from the project list without deleting it from the project.

✦ **Show File Info Area.** Adds a pane to the right of the filename list that provides information on the selected file, such as date modified and size.

✦ **Refresh.** Updates the Workspace and project information to reflect any deletions, additions, and changes.

✦ **Synchronize.** Synchronizes project status information between the master project and your locally stored files.

Working with versions

There are also two menu options in the Project Tools drop-down list that manage document versions.

✦ **Versions.** Displays the version comments for a selected file, as well as lets you view any of the versions. It also lets you promote an earlier version so it becomes the current version — this is a handy way to keep layout experiments that you reject and make an earlier version the new starting point for further explorations. Figure 35-3 shows this Versions dialog box.

✦ **Alternates.** Similar to versions, an alternate is a variation of a file that starts a new version "chain." This option shows you the alternates for the selected file, letting you designate one as the primary alternate (your working "master"). The dialog box is similar to the Versions dialog box shown in Figure 35-3.

When you save a file, you can choose File ➪ Save a Version to get the dialog box shown in Figure 35-4, where you can add your own comments. You can also choose File ➪ Save As (Shift+⌘+S or Ctrl+Shift+S), and then click Save Version when InDesign asks if you want to save the file as a new document or as a version of the existing document. However, you won't get the dialog box shown in Figure 35-4 to add comments.

To save a file as an alternate, check Save as Alternate in the Save As or Save a Copy dialog box.

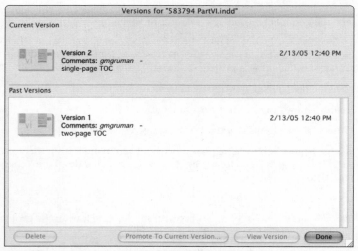

Figure 35-3: The Versions dialog box lets you view previous versions of a document as well as promote a previous version to be the new current master version.

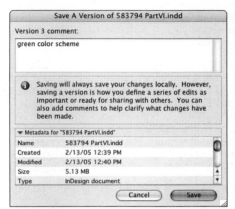

Figure 35-4: The Save Version dialog box lets you add comments to the current version of your file.

Mixing Mac/Windows Environments

As a cross-platform application, InDesign appeals strongly to all sorts of users who find that they must deal with "the other side." This includes corporate users whose various divisions have standardized on different platforms, service bureaus whose clients use different machines, and independent publishers or layout artists who deal with a range of clients.

InDesign differences

InDesign can read document files from either platform. However, the Windows version may not recognize a Mac-generated file as an InDesign file unless you do one of two things:

✦ **Filename extension.** Add .indd for documents or .indt for templates to the Mac-generated file's name. InDesign does this automatically, so unless a Mac user removed the filename extension, most files will have it.

✦ **All Documents.** Select this in the Enable pop-up menu (Mac) or in the Files of Type pop-up menu (Windows) in the Open dialog box (File ➪ Open, or Ctrl+O) for cases when the document does not have its identifying filename extension.

On the Mac, you'll typically not be able to double-click a PC-generated InDesign document (it'll have the PC icon rather than the InDesign icon); instead, you'll need to open it from the InDesign Open dialog box (File ➪ Open, or ⌘+O).

Which elements transfer

The following elements may be transferred across platforms, with any limits noted:

✦ **Color, tint, and gradient swatches.** These are retained and may also be imported across platforms. For Adobe Swatch Exchange swatch libraries copied from the Mac to Windows, be sure to add the filename extension .ase.

✦ **Color profile files.** Although these cannot be exchanged across the two platforms, both the Mac and Windows InDesign versions retain color-profile information from the other platform's files. And if both platforms have color profiles for the same device (monitor, scanner, printer, and so on), InDesign applies the correct color profiles. If a color profile is not available on the new platform, you can apply a new profile or ignore the issue. (If you ignore this issue, the correct profile will be in place when you bring the document back to the original platform.) If you print with a missing profile, InDesign substitutes the default profile based on the type of color model used (RGB or CMYK).

✦ **Paragraph, character, and object styles.** These are retained and may also be imported across platforms.

✦ **Hyphenation and spelling exceptions.** These are retained. The files use a filename extension on both the Mac and in Windows: .not for hyphenation additions, .udc for spelling additions.

✦ **Document preferences.** These are retained, but the InDesign Defaults file cannot be shared across platforms.

✦ **Plug-ins.** These files are not interchangeable across platforms. Plug-ins must be present on both platforms if you move documents that use the features of specific plug-ins. You'll need versions specific to each platform because these are essentially miniprograms that must be written to work on the Mac or Windows.

Which elements don't transfer

Adobe has removed most barriers between Mac and Windows in InDesign. Only the following elements cannot be moved across platforms:

✦ Shortcut sets

✦ Color profiles

✦ The InDesign Defaults preferences file

✦ Scripts other than those using JavaScript

Platform differences

There are also some general differences between Windows and Macintosh themselves that will add a few bumps along the road to cross-platform exchange.

Filenames

The most noticeable difference between Windows and Macintosh is the file-naming convention, and that difference is no longer so great since the advent of Mac OS X.

Macintosh files follow these rules:

✦ Names are limited to 255 characters (to 31 characters for Mac OS 9 applications).

Note Although the Mac OS X supports filenames longer than 31 characters, you may have trouble copying Windows files to the Mac if the Windows filenames exceed 31 characters and you use the AppleTalk protocol to connect your Macs and PCs. That's because of limits in some of the software to make these cross-platform connections, which enforce pre–Mac OS X filename conventions on all files.

✦ Any character may be used except for colons (:). Colons are used by the Macintosh system software internally to separate the folder name (which is not visible on-screen) from the filename. Also, a slash (/) may cause problems in some programs.

✦ Filenames typically have a file extension of up to four characters, which is often added by newer programs such as InDesign CS2 to identify the file type. A period separates the filename from the extension: Filename.ext. Mac OS X hides these filename extensions from view, unless you select the Always Show File Extensions option in the Finder Preferences pane (choose Finder ➪ Preferences) to make Mac OS X display them. Mac OS 9 files typically did not have file extensions, so documents, graphics, and other materials created under Mac OS 9 programs usually won't have file extensions.

✦ Case does not matter. FILE, file, and File are all considered to be the same name. If you have a file named FILE and create or copy a file named file, FILE will be overwritten.

Windows files follow these rules:

✦ Names are limited to 250 characters.

✦ Names must also have a file extension of up to four characters, which is almost always added automatically by programs to identify the file type. A period separates the filename from the extension: Filename.ext. Windows hides these filename extensions from view, unless you use the View pane accessed by choosing Tool ➪ Folder Options in a drive or folder window to make Windows display them (Deselect the Hide Extensions for Known File Types options.).

✦ Names may use any characters except for most punctuation. Pipes (|), colons (:), periods (.), asterisks (*), double quotes ("), less-than symbols (<), greater-than symbols (>), question marks (?), slashes (/), and backslashes (\) are all used by Windows to separate parts of paths (file locations, such as drives and folders) or to structure commands. A period may be used as the separator between a filename and an extension.

✦ Case does not matter. TEXT, text, and Text are all considered to be the same name. If you have a file named TEXT and create or copy a file named text, TEXT will be overwritten.

When you bring Mac InDesign files and any associated graphics to Windows, you'll have to translate the Mac names into names that are legal on Windows. Similarly, you'll need to make Windows filenames Mac-legal when going the other direction. This rule applies not only to the InDesign document but also to any associated files, such as graphics.

If you rename these files, either before transferring or while transferring, you'll find that, within the InDesign document itself, the original names are still used. When InDesign tries to open these files, it looks for them by their original names.

The simplest way to assure that you won't have problems with transferred files looking for incompatible names is to use a naming convention that satisfies both Windows and Mac standards. That means you should:

✦ Keep file names to 250 characters.

✦ Always include the file extension. Use .indd for documents, .indt for templates, .indl for libraries, /ase for Adobe Swatch Exchange swatch libraries, .not for hyphenation exceptions, and .udc for spelling exceptions. Typical extensions for cross-platform graphics are .tif or .tiff for TIFF, .jpg or .jpeg for JPEG, .eps for Encapsulated PostScript, .ai for Adobe Illustrator, .pct for PICT, .pcx for PC Paintbrush, .bmp and .rle for Microsoft bitmap, .pdf for Adobe Portable Document Format, .gif for Graphics Interchange Format, .wmf for Windows metafile, .emf for Enhanced Windows metafile, and .psd for Adobe Photoshop. Microsoft Word files typically have the file extensions .doc, Rich Text Format files use the extension .rtf, text-only (ASCII) files use the extension .txt, and Microsoft Excel files use the extension .xls.

✦ Don't use the pipe (|), colon (:), period (.), asterisk (*), double quote ("), less-than symbol (<), greater-than symbol (>), question mark (?), slash (/), or backslash (\) characters.

Font differences

Although the major typeface vendors like Adobe Systems, Linotype, and Bitstream offer their typefaces for both Windows and Macintosh users, these typefaces are not always the same on both platforms. Cross-platform differences are especially common among typefaces created a few years ago, when multiplatform compatibility was not a goal for most users or vendors.

Differences occur in four areas:

✦ **Internal font name.** The name used by the printer and type scalers (such as Extensis Suitcase, Extensis FontReserve, and Adobe Type Manager) is not quite the same for the Mac and Windows version of a typeface. This discrepancy will result in an alert box listing the fonts used in the document that are not on your computer. The solution is to use the Find Font dialog box or the Find/Replace dialog box (both covered in Chapter 14) to replace all instances of the unrecognized font name with the correct one for the current platform.

✦ **Tracking, kerning, and character-width.** These may vary between the two platforms even if typefaces use the same internal names, which could possibly result in text reflow. The solution is to check the ends of all your stories to make sure text did not get shorter or longer.

✦ **Symbols.** Even when created by the same vendors, the character maps for each font file differ across platforms because Windows and the Macintosh use different character maps. This problem is complicated by the fact that some vendors didn't stick to the standard character maps for any platform or didn't implement all symbols in all their typefaces. The solution is to proofread your documents, note the symbols that are incorrect, and then use the Find/Change dialog box to replace them with the correct symbol. (Highlight the incorrect symbol, and use the copy and paste commands to put it in the Text field of the Find/Change dialog box rather than trying to figure out the right keypad code in Windows or the right keyboard shortcut on the Mac.) If you use OpenType fonts, you'll find far fewer issues with symbol translation than with PostScript Type 1 and TrueType fonts.

✦ **Ligatures.** These are supported only on the Mac (Windows doesn't support ligatures at all). Windows InDesign will use just the regular fi, fl, ffi, and ffl letter combinations, and Mac InDesign will substitute the ligatures (fi, fl, ffi, and ffl) if you bring the file back to the Mac.

To minimize font problems, use a program like Pyrus FontLab to translate your TrueType and PostScript files from Mac to Windows format or vice versa. (FontLab is available in both Mac and Windows versions.) This ensures that the internal font names, width information, and symbols are the same on both platforms. The companion Web site (www.InDesign Central.com) includes links to these and other utilities.

See Chapters 38 and 40 for more information on fonts, and Chapter 41 for more information on special characters.

Transfer methods

Moving files between Macs and Windows PCs is easier now than ever before, thanks to built-in support of Windows formats and networking in Mac OS X, the use of TCP/IP networking by both the Mac and Windows, and a selection of products on both platforms that let each machine read the other's disks (floppies, removable disks like Zip disks, and even hard drives).

Chapter 38 covers these disk-reading products in detail.

Summary

When working with other users, you can share preferences by copying or making aliases to just one InDesign Defaults file, ensuring that all users have the same preferences. But the InDesign Defaults file is not cross-platform–compatible, so Windows users cannot use a Mac user's file or vice versa.

InDesign lets you work on shared projects and manage versions using Adobe's Version Cue feature. This feature alters the Save, Open, Export, and Place dialog boxes and requires that everyone on the project use it to ensure correct management.

Except for shortcut sets, color profiles, the InDesign Defaults preferences file, plug-ins, and scripts, cross-platform users can share InDesign support documents. Otherwise, sharing files between PC and Mac users is very simple, thanks to a variety of disk- and network-based utilities now available for both platforms.

✦   ✦   ✦

Using Plug-Ins

In This Chapter

Using the default plug-ins

Purchasing special-purpose plug-ins

How plug-ins work within InDesign

Setting plug-in preferences

The InDesign team engineered the software to be *extensible* — meaning you can extend its capabilities by adding more software. To do this, you use *plug-ins,* which are small software modules often developed by third parties. If you're a Photoshop user, you might be familiar with plug-ins such as Alien Skin's Eye Candy; or if you're a QuarkXPress user, you're probably familiar with the concept of add-on software through XTensions. Even if you're new to publishing, you may have purchased add-on software for your operating system, such as a custom screen saver or virus-protection software.

Extensible programs solve the one-size-fits-all nature of most software, letting you customize your tools to your workflow. If InDesign doesn't meet a need of yours — such as indexing, table editing, or imposition — you can look for a plug-in that does.

Using the Default Plug-Ins

Many core features in InDesign are actually implemented through plug-ins. When you launch the application, you may notice the words *Caching plug-ins* on the InDesign startup screen — this is when the plug-ins load. Structuring the software this way lets Adobe update or modify a finite area of the software, and then distribute a new plug-in, instead of updating and distributing the entire application. Go to the Adobe Web site (www.adobe.com) periodically to look for both fixes and new plug-ins. There's also a directory of plug-ins at this book's companion Web site (www.InDesignCentral.com).

The default plug-ins are stored in a folder called Plug-Ins inside your InDesign application folder. If you open the Plug-Ins folder, as shown in Figure 36-1, you'll notice the plug-ins have been consolidated into special-purpose folders such as Filters and Text. You should leave the default plug-ins alone, for the most part.

QuarkXPress User

QuarkXPress users might be accustomed to removing XTensions to reduce launch time and consume less RAM. Don't use this technique with InDesign. Many core features of the application — such as the text handling — are implemented through plug-ins, and the program may not work at all if you remove required plug-ins.

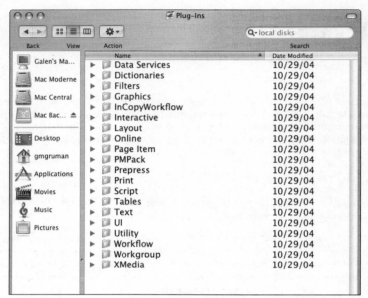

Figure 36-1: The InDesign Plug-Ins folder stores the default plug-ins, as well as additional plug-ins you may install.

Purchasing Special-Purpose Plug-ins

With the backing of a software and publishing giant like Adobe, InDesign has enticed a variety of proven developers to create special-purpose plug-ins.

Many plug-in developers provide a free evaluation copy so you can try before you buy. This is important because you can figure out if the plug-in really solves your problem, whether everyone in your workgroup will need it, and whether your service bureau will need it as well.

Note   To quickly find available InDesign plug-ins, go to the Plug-Ins page of this book's companion Web site (www.InDesignCentral.com).

How Plug-Ins Work within InDesign

To use a new plug-in, the first thing you need to do is install it. Many plug-ins include their own installers that search out your copy of InDesign and plant themselves in the Plug-Ins folder. If a plug-in doesn't include an installer or installation instructions, try clicking and dragging it into the Plug-Ins folder. Once a plug-in is in the correct location, you need to restart InDesign so the plug-in is recognized and its code is loaded. You cannot install a new plug-in while InDesign is running—you should always quit the application before changing anything in the Plug-Ins folder and then restarting.

If a plug-in cannot load with InDesign, an alert appears while the application is starting up. Usually, loading errors result from incompatible versions of InDesign and the plug-in. Check the plug-in's ReadMe file or contact the developer for assistance. To remove a plug-in, simply click and drag it out of the subfolder of the Plug-Ins folder and store it someplace else. (You might create a folder called Disabled Plug-Ins in which to store plug-ins that you're not using — just be sure it's not stored in the Plug-Ins folder!)

When a plug-in is loaded with InDesign, new controls appear in the interface. You might see entire menus, menu commands, dialog boxes, panes, palettes, and tools added to the application by a plug-in. No matter the combination of interface elements, when you're using the features of a plug-in, it should look and feel as if you're using InDesign. Some plug-ins meet this criteria; others will not.

For example, the MultiDocs plug-in from 65-Bit Software adds two menu options — Undo Multiple and Redo Multiple — to the Edit menu, permitting multiple levels of undo and redo from which the user can choose. Otherwise, InDesign's interface is unaffected. Other plug-ins might add panes or change other menus.

Caution   In some cases, plug-ins may add objects or information to documents that can be recognized only when the plug-in is loaded. If the plug-in is missing, you may not be able to open the document, or the document may look differently. If it turns out that a plug-in is required to open a document or preserve information, you'll need to ensure that each member of a workgroup and your service bureau owns the same plug-in.

Note   Plug-ins are designed for specific platforms (Macintosh or Windows) as well as for specific versions of InDesign (2, CS, or CS2), so you will need to get new versions of your plug-ins if you change platforms or upgrade to a new version of InDesign.

Setting Plug-In Preferences

After acquiring several plug-ins, you may have trouble managing all the features in InDesign because you'll have new panes, toolbars, and menu options throughout the program. Fortunately, InDesign has a tool to let you manage your plug-ins, so you can turn them on and off as needed, as well as save sets of plug-ins so you can turn on and off related plug-ins simultaneously.

To manage plug-ins, use the Configure Plug-ins dialog box shown in Figure 36-2. To open this dialog box, choose InDesign ➪ Configure Plug-Ins on the Mac and Help ➪ Configure Plug-Ins in Windows.

The default list of plug-ins will be very long because so many basic InDesign features are implemented through plug-ins. To help manage the display, you have six options at the bottom of the dialog box that filter what appears: Enabled, Adobe, Required, Disabled, Third Party, and Optional. Deselecting any of these options does *not* disable the plug-ins themselves; it simply removes them from the dialog box's list.

To manage plug-ins, you'll want to enable Third Party to see non-Adobe plug-ins and Optional to see plug-ins that can be turned off safely. Be sure that Enabled is also selected to see what is enabled or that Disabled is selected to see what plug-ins have been previously turned off. If neither Enabled nor Disabled is selected, you won't see any plug-ins in the list — you have to use these options in combination with each other. For example, selecting Enabled, Adobe, and Required shows only required Adobe plug-ins that are enabled.

Note   Required plug-ins will have a lock icon to their left, while other plug-ins will have a check mark to their left if enabled and nothing if disabled.

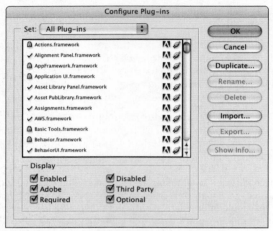

Figure 36-2: The Configure Plug-ins dialog box

To enable and disable plug-ins, simply click to the left of the plug-in name—if checked, a plug-in will be enabled when you relaunch InDesign. If unchecked, it will be disabled. If you're not sure what a plug-in does, you can get more information (the name of the developer, the version, and a brief description) by clicking the plug-in name and then clicking Show Info.

When you first disable plug-ins, InDesign forces you to create a new *set* of plug-ins—sets are essentially a list of which plug-ins should be enabled and which should be disabled. You can copy, edit the name of, and delete sets using the Duplicate, Rename, and Delete buttons. You choose a set of plug-ins to put in use by using the Set pop-up menu at the top of the dialog box. You can also import and export plug-in sets by clicking Import and Export. Click OK when done or Cancel to leave the plug-ins as they were when you first opened the Configure Plug-ins dialog box.

Note   You must quit and relaunch InDesign for any changes to plug-ins to take effect.

Summary

Plug-ins are software modules that serve two purposes in InDesign: incorporating core features into the application and adding special functions. Plug-ins are stored in the Plug-Ins folder within the InDesign application folder. Many established developers of QuarkXPress XTensions and Photoshop plug-ins have developed InDesign plug-ins to provide additional features such as mathematical typesetting and page imposition. When purchasing and using plug-ins, consider whether other users of your workgroup and your service bureau will need the plug-in as well. Finally, you can manage which plug-ins are in use through the Configure Plug-ins dialog box.

✦   ✦   ✦

Using Scripts

Scripting automates many features in InDesign — it's essentially a way to program InDesign to do specific actions. Because InDesign uses standard script languages, you can also run scripts that work with multiple programs in concert, including InDesign. (All the applications must support the same scripting language, of course.) For example, you might use scripts to automate database publishing, such as to run a database search, export data to a text file, import that file into InDesign, and then apply the appropriate formatting.

InDesign supports three scripting languages:

  ✦ JavaScript on both Mac and Windows

  ✦ AppleScript on the Mac only

  ✦ Visual Basic for Applications (VBA), on Windows only

Because only JavaScript is supported by both platforms, I recommend you use it wherever possible, so your scripts can work in cross-platform environments. InDesign doesn't force you to choose just one scripting language, so you could keep using old AppleScript or VBA scripts created for previous versions of InDesign, as well as new scripts written in JavaScript.

As you become comfortable with scriptwriting, you're also likely to discover that virtually everything you do with InDesign is a repetitive task. The more you can free yourself of this kind of work by using scripts, the more time you have to be creative. The possibilities are endless. But before you get too excited, remember that scripting *is* programming, so most layout artists stay clear, using scripts only if they have a programmer available to write them.

Using Scripts

Accessing scripts is easy — they show up in the Scripts pane (Window ➪ Automation ➪ Scripts) if you've placed scripts in the Scripts folder inside the Presets folder inside the folder that contains the InDesign application, as shown in Figure 37-1. Scripts don't have to be in the Scripts folder — they can be anywhere on your computer — but to use a script outside this folder means you have to double-click the script from your desktop rather than access it from within InDesign.

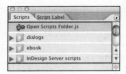

Figure 37-1: The Scripts pane in InDesign

No matter what scripting language you use, there are several basic principles to observe. These fall into four basic categories:

✦ **Grammar.** All languages — including programming languages such as Pascal and C++, as well as scripting languages — include grammatical components that are used in standardized sequences. In English, we combine nouns, verbs, adjectives, adverbs, and so on to create sentences. Everybody knows the meaning of "The weather is especially nice today," because it uses common words in a sequence that makes sense. The sentence "Nice is the especially today weather," has the right components, but it's arranged in the wrong sequence, so the meaning is lost.

✦ **Statements and syntax rules.** In JavaScript, AppleScript, and VBA, verbs, nouns, adjectives, and prepositions are combined to create statements; statements are combined to form scripts. Verbs are also called *commands* and *methods;* nouns are called *objects;* and adjectives are called *properties.* Syntax rules specify how statements and scripts must be constructed so that a computer can understand them.

✦ **Object hierarchy.** All three scripting languages use a structural element called an *object hierarchy.* It's a fancy term for a simple concept. An object hierarchy works like a set of boxes within boxes. A large box contains a smaller box, which contains a smaller box, which contains a smaller box, and so on, until you reach the smallest box, which contains nothing and is the final level in the hierarchy of boxes.

✦ **InDesign hierarchy.** InDesign contains its own hierarchy, which lends itself nicely to scripting. A document contains pages, pages contain frames, and frames contain text and pictures. You can create scripts that perform actions at any of these levels. In other words, with scripts you can create documents, add pages, add items to pages, and modify the contents of frames — right down to a particular character in a text frame. You can think of this hierarchy in InDesign as a chain of command. You can't talk directly to an item that's at the bottom of the chain. Rather, you must first address the top level, then the next, and so on, until you've reached the item at the bottom of the chain. This is analogous to the way you use InDesign: You create new documents, add pages, place text and graphics on the pages, and, finally, modify the contents of the frames containing those items.

If you're thinking about dabbling with any of the scripting languages supported by InDesign, the following words of both caution and encouragement are in order. First the encouragement: You don't necessarily need programming experience, scripting experience, or a pocket protector to begin creating scripts. A bit of curiosity and a touch of patience will suffice. Now the caution: Scripting is essentially a euphemism for programming (that is, figuring out the right commands and then typing them for the application to execute). Writing scripts isn't a matter of choosing commands from menus, clicking and dragging, or entering values into fields; nor is it like writing a limerick. If you're starting from scratch, know in advance that you'll have to learn some new skills.

Learning to create scripts is like learning to swim: You can read books, documentation, and articles until your head spins, but eventually you have to get a little wet. The best way to learn about scripting is to write a script. So put on your swimsuit and dive in.

Be forewarned: There's something almost narcotic about creating scripts, and it's not uncommon for novice scriptwriters to get hooked. Don't be surprised if what starts out to be a 15-minute look-see turns into a multihour, late-night programming episode.

Note   Because scripting languages differ, you can't always duplicate the functionality of a specific script in one language into a script written in a different language.

Note   Adobe has a nearly 2,000-page scripting guide available as a PDF file. It comes with your InDesign or Creative Suite software, residing on the installation CD. You can also download it from www.InDesignCentral.com.

Exploring JavaScript

JavaScript is a scripting language developed by Netscape Communications, based on Sun Microsystems' Java language that was meant to let Web browsers manage resources on far-flung servers by running scripts to control the servers from a desktop. JavaScript soon became a popular scripting language because, like Java, it runs on so many types of computers, including Windows, Macintosh, and Unix. Because it is based largely on the object-oriented approach taken by professional computer languages such as C and C++, it can be difficult for nonprogrammers to use.

Tip   There are lots of JavaScript editor programs available. Most of these are developed by individuals and small firms, so the list is always changing. I recommend you use the Google search engine (www.google.com) and search for *JavaScript editor* to find the most current programs. A great script-editing program for Mac users is Bare Bones Software's venerable BBEdit; you can get more information at www.barebones.com.

Learning the language

JavaScript is a very complex language based on object-oriented programming, which abstracts items and attributes as objects that are then grouped, changed, or otherwise manipulated. This means that JavaScript is less "Englishlike" than other scripting languages because it requires a fair amount of setup of the objects before they can be manipulated.

```
myObject.strokeTint = newValue;
```

This example shows that there is a current object named strokeTint that is being set to a new value; the actual value for newValue is set earlier in the script.

What you need to write and run scripts

You'll need a program that can display, edit, and test your JavaScript — there is no bundled JavaScript editor in Windows or Mac OS X. Such editors typically format the JavaScript code for you, indenting it automatically, graying out comments, and highlighting certain keywords.

You can use a word processor or text editor to write and edit scripts, but such programs can't check the syntax or automatically format the script text to help show nested loops, conditional branches, and so forth. Also, you can usually use an HTML editor such as Macromedia Dreamweaver or Adobe GoLive in which to edit JavaScripts, though they also typically don't provide any debugging tools to help you track and fix coding (syntax) errors. (Figure 37-2 shows a JavaScript script being edited in Dreamweaver.) In this case, you will need to open the error window in your browser as you test the code and see if it identifies the error location to help you find it in your HTML editor.

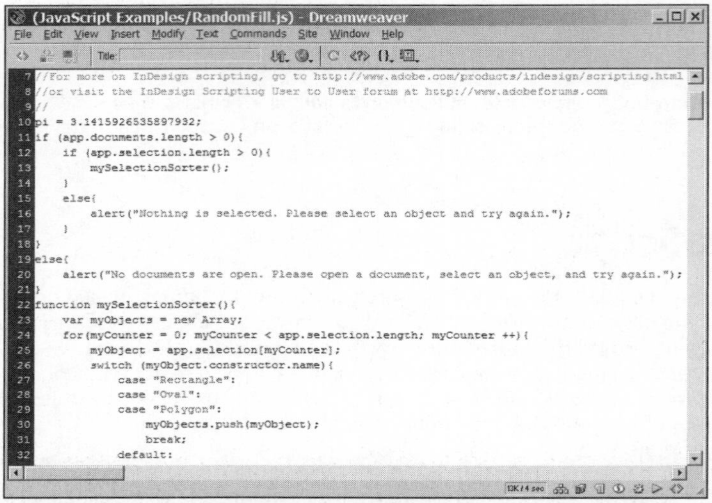

Figure 37-2: A JavaScript program viewed in Macromedia's Dreamweaver

When you're finished writing and testing a script, save it in the Scripts folder inside the InDesign Presets folder (usually Applications\Adobe InDesign CS2\Presets\Scripts on the Mac and C:\Program Files\Adobe\InDesign CS2\Presets\Scripts in Windows) so it will show up in the Scripts menu (if it doesn't show up immediately, quit and reopen InDesign).

Getting More Information on JavaScript

Before you venture too far into scripting, you should review the JavaScript-related information provided with InDesign:

✦ **JavaScript documentation and tools.** Sun places the very technical JavaScript documentation on its Web site at http://devedge.netscape.com/central/javascript/. A good independent source is the scripting section of the O'Reilly & Associates Web site's scripting section (http://scripting.oreilly.com).

✦ **InDesign scripting documentation.** The InDesign installation CD contains a 2,000-plus-page PDF file that explains scripting for InDesign. This document, although a bit on the technical side, is a valuable resource. It includes an overview of JavaScript scripting and the object model, as well as a list of InDesign-specific scripting terms and scripting examples.

If you want still more information about JavaScript, several books are available, including *Beginning JavaScript, 2nd Edition,* by Paul Wilton and *JavaScript Bible, 4th edition,* by Danny Goodman (Wiley Publishing).

Exploring AppleScript

AppleScript is a scripting language developed by Apple and initially released with System 7.5 that can be used to control Macs, networks, and scriptable applications, including InDesign. The AppleScript language was designed to be as close to normal English as possible so that average Mac users — specifically, those who aren't familiar with programming languages — can understand and use it.

Note   InDesign can run text-only AppleScripts in addition to compiled (binary) ones.

Learning the language

Many of the actions specified in AppleScripts read like sentences you might use in everyday conversation, such as:

```
set color of myFrame to "Black"
```

or

```
set applied font of myCharacterStyle to "Times"
```

Getting More Information on AppleScript

Before you venture too far into scripting, you should review the AppleScript-related information provided with the Mac OS and with InDesign:

✦ **Mac scripting documentation and tools.** Apple places the AppleScript documentation on its Web site at `www.apple.com/applescript`. In your hard drive's Applications folder, you should have a folder called AppleScript that contains the Script Editor program, along with a folder of example scripts and the AppleScript Script Menu that adds the Script menu to the Finder. Apple also offers a professional AppleScript editor called AppleScript Studio for download at its developer Web site, `http://www.apple.com/macosx/features/xcode/`. Recently, Apple made AppleScript Studio part of its Xcode scripting tool, so you need to get Xcode to get AppleScript Studio.

✦ **InDesign scripting documentation.** The InDesign CD contains a 2,000-plus-page PDF file that explains scripting, including AppleScript programming, for InDesign. This document, although a bit on the technical side, is a valuable resource. It includes an overview of Apple events scripting and the object model, as well as a list of InDesign-specific scripting terms and scripting examples.

If you want still more information about AppleScript, several books are available, including *AppleScript For Dummies, 2nd Edition*, by Tom Trinko and *Beginning AppleScript* by Stephen G. Kochan (both available from Wiley Publishing).

What you need to write and run scripts

The Script Editor provided with the Mac OS lets you write scripts. You'll find the Script Editor inside the AppleScript folder inside your Applications folder (at the root level of your hard drive). An uncompiled script is essentially a text file, so you can actually write scripts with any word processor. The Script Editor, however, was created for writing AppleScripts and includes several handy features for scriptwriters.

Checking for syntax errors

The next step is to determine if the statements are correctly constructed. Click the Check Syntax button. If the Script Editor encounters a syntax error, it alerts you and highlights the cause of the error. If the script's syntax is correct, all statements except the first and last are indented, and a number of words are displayed in bold, as illustrated in Figure 37-3. Your script has been compiled and is ready to test.

Figure 37-3: This Script Editor window contains sample AppleScript text. When you check the syntax of a script, the Script Editor applies formatting and indents.

Running your script

Click the Run button, and then sit back and watch. If you've done everything correctly, you'll see InDesign become the active program, and then the actions you put in your script will take place. Voilà—and congratulations! You can now call yourself a scripter without blushing. That's all there is to creating and running a script.

If you have trouble getting a script to run, double-check the name that InDesign uses for itself. It might use InDesign® CS2 or simply InDesign® (yes, the name may include the registered trademark symbol). If you run a script from AppleScript (rather than just double-clicking it) and AppleScript can't find InDesign, it will give you a dialog box with which you find the InDesign program. When you've found and selected the InDesign application, AppleScript will find out what InDesign's filename is and use that in your script.

Saving your script

When you're finished writing and testing a script, choose Save from the Script Editor's File menu. Name your script, choose its storage location, and choose Compiled Script from the Format pop-up menu. It's best to save the script in the Scripts folder inside the InDesign Presets folder (usually Applications\Adobe InDesign CS2\Presets\Scripts) so it will show up in the Scripts menu (you may need to quit and reopen InDesign).

Note

If you save the script in Application format and want to edit your script later, you must open it by dragging and dropping it on the Script Editor application. This is because Application-format scripts are designed to immediately run when double-clicked. You would choose the Application format when creating scripts for use by others because chances are you don't want them to open the script in Script Editor but instead simply want them to use the script by double-clicking it like any other application. (It doesn't matter whether the script is in Application format if you run it from InDesign's Scripts pane.)

Locating more AppleScript tools

A few software utilities are also available for AppleScripters. The most widely used is Script Debugger, from Late Night Software ($189, www.latenightsw.com); it's an interface development tool to quickly create AppleScript-based applications that have the standard Mac look and feel. Apple also offers its AppleScript Studio as a free download to developers who register at the Apple site (www.apple.com/macosx/features/xcode); this is more capable than the basic Script Editor that comes with Mac OS X. Recently, Apple made AppleScript Studio part of its Xcode scripting tool, so you need to get Xcode to get AppleScript Studio.

Exploring VBA

VBA, and its subset version VBScript, is Microsoft's technology for writing your own programs, both those that run in other programs (scripts) and those that run by themselves (custom applications). InDesign works with both VBA and VBScript. The Visual Basic language that underlies both VBA and VBScript is not meant for everyday computer users — knowledge of programming is very useful in taking advantage of this technology. Although based on the Basic language developed in the 1970s to help new users write their own programs, it has evolved a lot since then and is no longer so simple.

Learning the language

Many of the actions specified in VBA have some degree of English, such as:

```
set myTextFrame = InDesign.Documents.Item(1).Spreads.Item(1).
TextFrames.Add
```

or

```
mySelection.RotationAngle = 30
```

But as you can see, VBA has moved far from English. The first code segment, for example, means to add a text frame to the first spread in the first document. The second means to rotate the selected object by 30 degrees.

Getting More Information on VBA

Before you venture too far into scripting, you should review the VBA-related information provided by Microsoft and with InDesign:

✦ **Microsoft scripting documentation and tools.** Microsoft has a lot of information on VBA, Visual Basic, and VBScript on its Web site. Unfortunately, it's not well organized and is hard to find and understand. There's no tutorial that simply explains how a new scripter needs to get started. However, you can search on the Microsoft site for VBA, Visual Basic, and VBScript to get links to documents that may prove useful.

✦ **InDesign scripting documentation.** The InDesign CD contains a 2,000-plus-page PDF file that explains scripting in InDesign, including VBA programming. This document, although a bit on the technical side, is a valuable resource. It includes an overview of VBA scripting and the object model, as well as a list of InDesign-specific scripting terms and scripting examples.

If you want still more information about VBA and its two "sister" technologies, several books are available, including *Visual Basic 6 For Dummies,* by Wallace Wang, and *Visual Basic 6 Bible* by Eric A. Smith, Valor Whisler, and Hank Marquis (both available from Wiley Publishing).

What you need to write and run scripts

To use InDesign scripting in Windows, you'll need Microsoft Visual Basic or an application that contains Visual Basic for Applications (VBA); these include Microsoft Office, Microsoft Visio, and AutoCAD. In Microsoft Office, you can run the Microsoft Script Editor by choosing Tools ➪ Macros ➪ Microsoft Script Editor, which lets you create scripts, edit them, test your code, and fix errors. Figure 37-4 shows the editor with a sample script.

You can also write scripts in VBScript, a VBA subset, in a text editor such as WordPad. You'll need Microsoft's free Windows Scripting Host (WSCRIPT.EXE), which is usually installed with Windows and can be downloaded from Microsoft's Web site.

There's a third choice for your scriptwriting: You can also use the full Microsoft Visual Basic product from Microsoft.

Note   To use InDesign scripting in Windows, your user profile must have Administrator privileges.

Running your script

To run a VBA, Visual Basic, or VBScript program, simply double-click the script. You can also run the script directly from the application in which you created a VBA or Visual Basic script, such as the Microsoft Script Editor. (For VBScripts, you can run them from the Scripting Host application.) If you've done everything correctly, you'll see InDesign become the active program, and then the actions you put in your script will take place. Voilà — and congratulations! You can now call yourself a scripter without blushing. That's all there is to creating and running a script.

Figure 37-4: The Microsoft Script Editor window contains sample VBA text. When you work on a script, the Microsoft Script Editor applies indents automatically.

Saving your script

When you're finished writing and testing a script, choose Save from the script editor's File menu. Name your script and choose its storage location. It's best to save the script in the Scripts folder inside the InDesign Presets folder (usually C:\Program Files\Adobe\InDesign CS2\Presets\Scripts), so it will show up in the Scripts menu (you may need to quit and reopen InDesign).

Creating and Running Scripts

At this point, I'm assuming that the appropriate scripting software is installed on your computer. If this is the case, you're ready to begin. For your first trick, you're going to make InDesign roll over — sort of. Actually, you're going to rotate an EPS graphic. First, you'll prepare InDesign for its role. Launch the program, and then create a new document (do not check Automatic Text Frame). In the middle of the first page, place an EPS graphic. Make sure that it remains active after you place it.

Writing simple scripts

The following three scripts, taken from Adobe's InDesign script examples, do the same thing in JavaScript, AppleScript, and VBA — they rotate an EPS graphic and its frame.

Cross-Reference

All of the scripts in this chapter are available for download at www.InDesignCentral.com. Just cut and paste them from the text files into the appropriate scripting editor. Adobe's user forums are also a good place to go for scripting help.

Type the lines that follow this paragraph exactly as they're written for the scripting language you've chosen. Type a return character at the end of each line. Note also the use of straight quotation marks instead of curly typesetter's quotes (the script editor does this for you). Be very careful when you type the text: Typos are script killers.

 Note   In the code samples below, the ¬ symbol indicates where a line of code is broken to fit the page width; in the actual script, there would be no ¬ character and the line that follows would be combined with the line that now ends in ¬.

JavaScript

```
var myLink, myEPs, myFrame;
if(app.documents.length != 0){
   if(app.activeDocument.links.length != 0){
      for(var myLinkCounter = 0; myLinkCounter < ¬
      app.activeDocument.links.length; myLinkCounter ++){
         myLink = app.activeDocument.links.item(myLinkCounter);
         if(myLink.linkType == "EPS"){
            myEPS = myLink.parent;
            myFrame = myEPS.parent;
            myFrame.rotationAngle = 30;
         }
      }
   }
}
```

This script first searches through all the items on the page and checks if any are EPS; if so, it sets the rotation of the item to 30. (Thanks to Adobe's InDesign scripting guru, Olav Martin Kvern, for developing the JavaScript code example.) Note the sequence of actions: First you verify that there is a nonempty document open, and then you check the content type of objects. For those objects that are of the EPS type, you activate the frame and then apply the rotation to that frame. JavaScripts require you to set your own variables (the `var` statements) that define what the object is (here, `myLink` is used for each object, `myEPS` is the object that contains the EPS attribute, and `myFrame` is the parent frame containing the EPS graphic. You work with those variables to see what their attributes are and then change those attributes

If you're in an adventurous mood, try substituting the statement `myFrame.rotationAngle = 30;` in the preceding script with each of the following statements:

```
myFrame.shearAngle = 30;
myFrame.verticalScale = 200;
```

If you want to get really fancy, combine all the `myFrame.` statements into a single script, so you can use the script to make all the changes at once.

AppleScript

```
tell application "Adobe InDesign CS2"
   activate
   set myPageItems to {EPS, oval, rectangle, polygon}
   set mySelection to selection
   if class of item 1 of mySelection is in myPageItems ¬
   and (count mySelection) > 0 then
      if class of item 1 of mySelection is EPS then
         set myFrame to parent of mySelection
```

```
         else
            set myFrame to item 1 of mySelection
         end if
         set rotation angle of myFrame to 30
      end if
   end tell
```

Note   Be sure a document is open and that you have selected at least one frame of any type before starting the script. Also in the script itself, make sure to type the name of your InDesign program exactly as it appears in the Finder. Because you're free to rename your program, the name may not match the name in the first line of the script.

If you're in an adventurous mood, try substituting the statement `set rotation angle of myFrame to 30` in the preceding script with each of the following statements:

```
set shear angle of myFrame to 30
set vertical scale of myFrame to 200
```

If you want to get really fancy, combine all the `set` statements into a single script, so you can use the script to make all the changes at once.

VBA

```
Dim myInDesign As InDesign.Application
Set myInDesign = CreateObject("InDesign.Application.CS2")
Set mySelection = myInDesign.Selection
If TypeName(mySelection.Item(1)) = "EPS" Then
   mySelection.Parent.RotationAngle = 30
Else
   mySelection.RotationAngle = 30
End If
```

If you're in an adventurous mood, try substituting the statement `mySelection.RotationAngle = 30` in the preceding script with each of the following statements:

```
set the color of the current box to "Blue"
set the shade of the current box to 50
set the width of the frame of the current box to 10
set the box shape of the current box to ovular
```

If you want to get really fancy, combine all the `set` statements into a single script so you can use the script to make all the changes at once.

Tip   Perhaps you noticed the chain of command used in the preceding scripts. First, the script addresses InDesign, then the active document (layout), and finally the active frame. If you understand this concept, you'll be scripting like a pro in no time.

Labeling items

As you can see from the examples in the previous section, scripts often refer to items by their type and location in the document. But there's another way to refer to objects that makes sure you can select an item precisely: You can label, or name, an item. You do so in the Script Label pane (Window ➪ Automation ➪ Script Label). The process is easy: Select the object, and then type a name in the pane. That's it!

When writing scripts, you refer to the labeled object as follows. In these examples, the label is *TargetFrame,* and don't worry that the samples seem to do different things — they in fact are unrelated examples, not variations of the same command.

JavaScript

```
with(app.documents.item(0).pages.item(0)){
  myTargetFrame = textFrames.item("myTargetFrame");
}
```

AppleScript

```
select (page item 1 of page 1 of myTargetDocument whose  ¬
label is "TargetFrame")
```

VBA

```
Set myAsset = myLibrary.Assets.Item("TargetFrame")
```

Writing conditional scripts

Some scripts simply automate a set of tasks in documents whose content is predictable. But more often than not, documents differ, and so you need conditional statements to evaluate certain things to see if they are true before applying a script's actions. Otherwise, you'll get an error message when something turns out not to be true. As a simple example, a script that does a search and replace needs to have a document open and a frame selected. If no frame is selected, the script won't know what to search, and the user will get an error message.

The same issue arises for repeated series of actions, where you want the script to do something for all occurrences. The script needs to know what to do when it can't find any more such occurrences. As an example, look at the following script, which counts all open documents. For it to work, at least one document has to be open, so the script checks first to see if in fact any documents are open, and delivers an error message that the user can understand if none is open. The rotate-EPS-graphic script earlier also used a conditional to make sure there was an EPS graphic in the document. Notice that in all three scripting languages, it is the command If that you use to set up such conditionals.

JavaScript

```
if(app.documents.length==0){
  alert("No InDesign documents are open!");
}
```

 Note   JavaScript uses == for comparing values (as in the example above) and = for assigning values. Visual Basic and AppleScript use = for both purposes.

AppleScript

```
tell application "Adobe InDesign CS2"
  activate
  set myNumberOfDocuments to (count documents)
  if myNumberOfDocuments = 0 then
    display dialog "No InDesign publications are open!"
  end if
end tell
```

VBA

```
Dim myInDesign as InDesign.Application
  Set myInDesign = CreateObject ("InDesign.Application.CS")
  If myInDesign.Documents.Count
    MsgBox "No InDesign publications are open!"
  End If
End Sub
```

Another form of conditional is what's called a *control loop,* in which an action occurs either for a specified number of iterations or until a condition is met. The following scripts show an example of each for each language. Note the use of comments in the scripts — a handy way to document what you're doing for later reference. In JavaScript, a single-line comment begins with //, while a multiline comment begins with /* and ends with */. In AppleScript, a comment begins with -- and continues until you press Enter or Return. In VBA, it begins with Rem followed by a space, and it continues until you press Enter or Return.

JavaScript

```
for(var myCounter = 0; myCounter < 20; myCounter++){
  //do something
}
while (myStop == false){
  /* do something, at some point setting myStop to true  ¬
  to leave the loop. */
}
```

AppleScript

```
repeat with counter from 1 to 20
  --do something
end repeat

set myStop to false
repeat while myStop = false
  --do something, at some point setting myStop to true to  ¬
  leave the loop.
end repeat
```

VBA

```
For counter = 1 to 20
  Rem do something
Next counter

Do While myStop = false
  Rem do something, at some point setting myStop to true  ¬
  to leave the loop.
loop
```

Summary

If your workflow goes beyond original designs for each client and reaches into repetitive production, scripting is for you. Scripts are ideal for automating repetitive tasks — from importing pictures to creating and formatting entire documents. You can even link InDesign to other scriptable applications.

Because InDesign supports JavaScript on the Mac and Windows, as well as AppleScript on the Mac only and VBA on Windows only, you can choose the script language you're most familiar with and/or that is compatible with your other applications. Even better, you can use more than one scripting language with InDesign (though any individual script can use only one language).

✦   ✦   ✦

Introduction to Publishing

The Publishing Environment

InDesign by itself doesn't do anything. You need to work with it in the context of a computer, add-on hardware, other software, and, of course, the operating system of your Mac or PC. And once you have the equipment and platform that's right for you, you need to learn to make the most of it. This chapter gives you the basic information you need to get the right equipment and to get started on your platform of choice. However, I do recommend that you pick up more detailed books on Mac OS or Windows; the publisher of this book, Wiley Publishing, has many good books for beginners (the *For Dummies* series) and for more experienced users (the *Bible* series).

Choosing the Right Hardware

You don't need the fastest computer available to use InDesign, but factors such as processor (CPU) speed, RAM, hard drives, removable media, connectivity, and input/output devices can make a difference. The following sections take you on a tour of what works best in a full spectrum of publishing situations.

The computer

Adobe provides system requirements for InDesign, but this is just the bare minimum you need to run the software. Adobe is not concerned about whether you can run InDesign and, say, Photoshop at the same time or whether your font manager will run on the operating system it supports. But because you need to be concerned about your entire publishing system — not just InDesign — let me provide a realistic minimum system for Mac OS and Windows. Then I'll give you a wish list for the ideal publishing system.

The minimum system

For Adobe's official system requirements, see Appendix A. But for best results, I recommend the following minimum publishing system:

✦ **Mac OS:** A G4 or newer processor running Mac OS X 10.3 (Panther) or higher, with a minimum of 512MB of RAM and a 60GB hard drive. Note that InDesign CS 2 will not run on Mac OS 8 or 9.

✦ **Windows:** An Intel Pentium 4, AMD Athlon, or newer processor running at least at 2GHz, running Windows 2000 or Windows XP, with 512MB of RAM, a 60GB hard drive, and a video card with 128MB of RAM. Note that InDesign CS 2 will not run on Windows 95, 98, Millennium (Me), NT 3, or NT 4.

The ideal system

In any kind of graphic-arts environment, you typically need to run at least Adobe InDesign, Photoshop, and Illustrator — not to mention an e-mail program and a Web browser — at the same time. And chances are you'll be using Microsoft Word and Adobe Acrobat often as well. Photoshop, in particular, runs faster and more reliably with plenty of RAM. Plus, images, EPS files, and the like eat up disk space fast. As a rule, buy as much RAM and the largest hard drive you can afford. If you're just getting started or have just come into some money, set yourself up right with the following system:

✦ **Mac OS:** A 1.8GHz or faster Power Mac G5 running Mac OS X 10.4 (Tiger) with 1GB of memory (online sources such as `www.ramseeker.com` have Mac memory available at very affordable prices), a 100GB or greater hard drive, and a CD-RW (read/write) or DVD-RW drive.

✦ **Windows:** A 2.4GHz or faster AMD Athlon 64 or 3.4GHz or faster Intel Pentium 4 computer running Windows 2000 or XP with 1GB of RAM (online sources such as `www.newegg.com` have PC memory available at very affordable prices), a 100GB or greater hard drive, a video card with 128MB of RAM, and a CD-RW or DVD-RW drive. Note that although Windows typically requires less operational overhead than Mac OS; the RAM requirement for applications is usually the same.

Computer Acronyms Explained

If you're not a techie, here are the acronyms explained:

✦ **MHz, or megahertz,** is the speed of the chip, in millions of processor cycles, that does all the calculation in a computer. Only older computers still run at megahertz speeds.

✦ **GHz, or gigahertz,** is the speed of the chip, in billions of processor cycles, that does all the calculation in a computer. Most computers since 2003 run at 1GHz speed or faster.

✦ **MB, or megabyte,** is a unit of storage capacity equal to 1,024 kilobytes, or about 1 million characters. (A kilobyte is 1,024 bytes, and a byte is essentially one character.)

✦ **GB, or gigabyte,** is a unit of storage capacity equal to 1,024MB, or about 1 billion characters.

✦ **bps, or bits per second,** is the speed at which data travels over a wired or wireless connection. These speeds are typically shown as Kbps (1 Kbps equals 1,024 bits per second) and Mbps (1 Mbps equals 1,024 Kbps). There are 8 bits in a byte, so to calculate transmission time, multiply the number of bytes of file size by 8 to get the number of seconds of transmission time. For example, a 2MB file transmitted at 1 Mbps will take 16 seconds: $2,048 \div 1024 \times 8 = 16$.

Storage capacity

Today, computers usually come with plenty of RAM (memory) and storage capacity (hard-drive space). But if you have an older computer, or you're taxing your current system, upgrading RAM and storage can speed up your work significantly. Here are my recommendations for storage:

✦ **RAM.** Adding RAM lets the computer work more efficiently, and you'll want 128MB as a bare minimum, which you can get by with if you work with just one program at a time. Better for publishers is 256MB to 1GB, and more than that if you're doing complex work on large files in Adobe Photoshop as well (512MB is typical for such users). Be sure to check the maximum amount of RAM your system can accommodate before making an upgrade purchase.

✦ **Hard drives.** Programs and files eat through disk space, so these days, a 10GB to 20GB drive (which holds about 10 to 20 billion characters) is considered small. Look for 60GB to 100GB — or higher. And remember that you can usually add hard drives to your Mac or PC. You don't have to replace your existing one in most cases. Be sure to check the largest capacity of hard drive that your system can fully use. Because of upper limitations of the internal ATA hard connection, many Mac and PC systems more than a few years old can only use hard drives of 120GB or less. Buying a drive larger than 120GB may just be a waste of money, because an older Mac or PC will be able to use only the first 128GB of the drive. External FireWire and USB hard drives are generally not subject to this 128GB limitation.

✦ **CD-RW or DVD RW.** Using a read/write CD or DVD drive (also called a *CD burner* or *DVD burner*) as part of your storage solutions is your best choice for long-term archiving. CDs and DVDs also work well for delivering large projects — including documents, graphics, and fonts — to service bureaus and printers. CD-RW drives are cheap ($50 to $200) depending on the speed and whether they are internal or external, and the CD-R discs themselves are very inexpensive. (You can also use the more expensive CD-RW discs, which let you erase and modify the CD's contents, but for delivering, say, an issue of a magazine to a printer, there's no reason to use such a rewritable disc because you're not expecting the CD back. CD-RWs are great, though, for storing templates that might be adapted over time and as a backup device.) Be aware that CD-RW media can only be rewritten a relatively few number of times, depending on the quality of the media. Each CD can hold 650MB of data and it's easy to store, permanent, and universal. DVD-RW drives cost more — the drives and media cost about double what CD-RW drives and media do — but they hold seven times as much per disc. Early competition between formats is winding down, as are the compatibility issues this competition introduced, but do note that older DVD, DVD-R, and DVD-RW drives may not be able to read all DVD-RW discs.

✦ **Zip drives.** If your computer didn't come with a Zip drive, don't worry. While this had been a standard way to exchange files in the mid-1990s, the 100MB and 250MB Zip drives have fallen into disuse because CD and DVD drives and media offer much more storage capacity at cheaper prices for the media. And the new 750MB drives didn't really take off, either, likely because almost any computer can read a CD and most can read a DVD, so Zip is just not needed.

✦ **Tape drives.** If you don't have a CD-RW, DVD-RW, or external hard drive and don't work on a network that automatically backs up files to a server, you can use a tape drive for backups. Prices range from $100 to $1,000 depending on the capacity, with the majority under $400.

✦ **Extra hard drives.** An increasingly popular alternative to tape, which can be slow and subject to physical damage, are second hard drives — internal or external — on which you make mirror copies of your data and from which you can easily start up in case of failure. Note that you'll want to get backup software that works with the hard drive, so it's best to buy drives that come with such software. A consistent backup method using a second hard drive, tape drive, CD-R, or DVD-R can mean the difference between tearing every last hair out or staying sane even under the tightest of deadlines. You'll appreciate the nearly incalculable value of a complete daily or weekly backup the first time you lose everything on a 100GB hard drive in your Mac or PC. I promise.

Connectivity

Another essential component in workgroup environments is a network. At the very least, you want peer-to-peer networks, in which your Macs and PCs are connected to one another so they can share files. Both the Mac OS and Windows have this capability built in.

The Mac/PC connection

The following list describes programs that Macs and PCs use to connect to each other and read each other's disks:

✦ Mac OS X includes both Apple and Windows file-sharing support, so you can connect a Mac OS X system out of the box to Windows PCs. It also lets Windows computers connect to it without additional software.

✦ Computer Associates' PC MacLAN lets PCs join Mac-based networks, whether AppleTalk- or IP-based. It provides better control over what items are accessed and shared than Mac OS X does, and unlike Mac OS X, it allows PCs to use Mac-connected printers. It costs about $200 per person but needs to be installed only on PCs. (This software used to be owned by Miramar Systems, which sold it to CA in 2004.)

✦ DataViz's MacOpener and Media4's MacDrive let PCs read Mac disks (floppies, CDs, Zips, SyQuests, external hard drives, and so on). They cost about $50 per user. Access Systems' TransMac does the same for about $65.

✦ DataViz's MacLinkPlus lets Macs read PC disks and also offers file translation. Most people don't need file-translation capability because most programs now use the same file format on Mac and Windows, but if you tend to use older or specialty programs, MacLinkPlus is a necessity. It costs about $100 per person. Apple's Mac OS X supports PC disks natively as well, although with less control than MacLinkPlus allows.

The network connection

Ethernet has become the standard means of networking computers together. Ethernet is a kind of wiring that lots of different transmission protocols, like TCP/IP or AppleTalk, can run and it's pretty fast yet inexpensive. All Macs built since late 1998 have Ethernet connectors built in, and so do most PCs. For those that don't, the cost is $10 to $50 per computer for the needed card or adapter box.

Older Macs have both AppleTalk and Ethernet, so you need to tell the Mac which you want to use; you can switch back and forth. However, I recommend you stick with Ethernet, using AppleTalk only if you have a printer that is not Ethernet-compatible (such as an older color inkjet printer). Similarly, on a PC, getting an Ethernet version of your printers is better than relying on the slow, single-user parallel port or USB connection. Of course, if you're a one-person design firm, that's not a big issue.

Finally, consider wireless networks in small offices. The 802.11g wireless standard supports wireless connections of up to 54 Mbps (more typically, 20 Mbps to 24 Mbps), as well as the previous 802.11b 11 Mbps technology, and costs about $50. (Note that an 802.11b client device running over an 802.11g network will force all 802.11g client devices to run at the slower 802.11b speed.) 802.11a is a third 54 Mbps wireless technology that has been slow to catch on because it suffers from a smaller typical coverage area and is not compatible with the widely installed 802.11b devices, such as the Apple AirPort wireless networking products. Although 802.11a suffers less from radio interference than 802.11b/g does, most hardware and networks run 802.11b, so at the least you would want a trimode client device [802.11a/b/g] so you can connect both at your local wireless network and at public hot spots.) But don't waste money on nonstandard technologies such as "preN"or "108 Mbps" — those require that all equipment on the wireless network come from the same company to achieve their stated performance.

At the center of a wireless network is a wireless access point, which contains a radio transmitter and can serve a half-dozen connected systems and printers in a typical 150- to 300-foot radius, depending on whether there are major obstructions and interference from other wireless devices such as cordless phones and microwave ovens. (No matter which kind of wireless networking you use, there is a significant gap between the advertised rate and the real rate that your data can move. The wireless network's bandwidth must accommodate the overhead of interference and its transmission protocol. For example, 802.11b is commonly rated at 11 Mbps but rarely achieves a real-world data-transfer rate of more than 6 Mbps.

If your Mac or PC doesn't have wireless networking built in, an internal PCI card or external USB box costs typically about $50 to $75. Just be sure to turn on encryption if you use wireless networks so no one can snoop into your network. There are several encryption methods available, and 802.11i and WPA-2 are much more secure than the more commonly used WEP.

You should be aware that even using the built-in encryption methods will not keep determined snoops out of your wireless network. There are alternative methods for improving the security of a wireless network, but they typically require a corporate network be in place, so are not really an option for small businesses and individual users. The surest way to secure a wireless network is to place the access point or wireless router so its transmission range does not extend beyond the walls, floor, and ceiling of the space that you can physically control access to. If someone can get physical access to your space, then the security of your wireless network is a fairly minor concern by comparison.

The Internet connection

Even if you're working just on print projects, you'll need to be on the Internet. You need to be able to send and receive files (from e-mail to text files to entire InDesign documents and graphics) download program updates, and use your computer as a fax. Basically, you should get the fastest Internet connection available to you. Unfortunately, availability is often limited by the phone lines and other factors in your area.

If you can get a cable, ISDN, or DSL connection from your cable or phone company, that's ideal. Cable modems and DSL are quickly becoming the connections of choice based on cost, availability, and ease of use. They let you access and download data at 384 Kbps or higher — often at speeds of more than 1 Mbps. Most often, the provider will send you the equipment you need or tell you what to buy. Make sure you carefully research all the types of cable modem and DSL services available in your area. Price, speed, and flexibility vary a lot from company to company. Cable modem service tends to be faster and pricier than DSL, but not always — it depends on the provider's deployment.

The best service is one that is not shared — where that 384 Kbps or whatever is yours alone. Some companies offer dedicated DSL service, while others offer shared DSL high-speed Internet. By contrast, all cable-modem lines are shared with other users in your neighborhood, but because cable modem service tends to be faster, you often end up with better performance than DSL even with that sharing.

Caution   Note that in any shared service — DSL, cable modem, or wireless — someone else on the connection could access your computers unless you have enabled the Mac OS X or Windows security software and, better, are using a hardware firewall on your router or gateway.

If you're stuck with a dial-up account because DSL or other services are not available where you live, you need some type of modem. Most new computers, such as iMacs or any PC, have an internal 56 Kbps modem, so all you do is plug a phone line into the computer. If you need an external modem, be sure to buy one that supports speeds of 56 Kbps.

Input and output devices

The following sections cover some of the things you'll need to consider in the input/output realm: printers, scanners, digital cameras, CD-ROM drives, multibutton mice, trackballs, and pen-based tablets.

Printers

Invest in a good printer. You'll want a black-and-white laser printer capable of 600 dots per inch (dpi) output or better. Older printers support 300 dpi output, which is acceptable but not as sharp when it comes to printing text and images. Get a printer with PostScript language built in because you'll get better output, more functionality, and a more accurate preview of what you'll get on your imagesetter (these are PostScript-based). That pretty much means a pricier Hewlett-Packard printer because most other manufacturers don't provide PostScript options. But another good option is a PostScript or PostScript-compatible printer from Brother International (even the PostScript emulation on its lower-end printers is very good).

Fast network printers

If you work in an office and need only black-and-white or gray-scale output, you can buy one or two fast network printers (16 to 25 pages per minute [ppm] or faster) and share them. Such printers — such as the Hewlett-Packard 2300n or 4200n series — cost between $1,100 and $2,400 each. They typically have PostScript, the printing language standard for desktop publishing, already installed and can hold lots of paper, often in several sizes.

Personal laser printers

If you work alone and need only black-and-white or gray-scale output, you can consider an affordable laser printer such as the HP 1300 or 2300 series. Look for one that prints between 9 and 15 ppm. Consider getting a refurbished printer, especially if it has Ethernet built in (Ethernet is an expensive option for personal laser printers). A better choice for personal printing is one of the newer color inkjets.

PostScript printers

If you're producing final output, as opposed to proofs, you'll want a PostScript-capable printer because that's the language that all professional output devices, such as imagesetters, use. Printers aimed at Mac owners almost always have PostScript, while printers aimed at PC owners usually do not. Mac-oriented printers almost always work with PCs, so PC owners will find it easier to get PostScript by looking at Mac-oriented printers than by looking at PC-oriented printers. You can have Macs and PCs plugged into them and use them simultaneously.

Note If you use Windows 2000 or XP, be sure to go to Adobe's Web site (www.adobe.com) and download its free PostScript printer driver rather than use the one that comes with Windows because the Windows PostScript driver is less capable and can result in output errors. On a Mac, the Apple PostScript driver that comes with the Mac OS is fine, though Adobe also offers its own version.

Color inkjet printers

For graphic arts applications, the inexpensive color inkjet printers, such as an Epson Color Stylus or Canon S series, are a great choice. These printers are essential if you're doing color work and want to get color proofs occasionally. And for low-volume color printing, they're a great deal and very convenient. Color inkjets cost between $100 and $500. Although they're slower than most laser printers, they provide glorious color and gray-scale output. The biggest issue with inkjets is the cost of ink. Many use small, expensive ink cartridges, so be sure to check the cartridges' capacities before you buy. (HP's newest printers are notorious for their high ink costs.) Ideally, each color will have its own cartridge, so you don't throw away unused ink just because one color is depleted.

While most of these do not support PostScript, you can purchase Strydent Software's PowerPrint PostScript rendering software for many models for about $100 (for serial and USB printers) or $250 (for network printers); just be sure it works with your inkjet printer. Epson also sells PostScript software ($145 to $200, depending on the model) for many of its inkjet printers.

Multifunction printers

Multifunction printers — which include copy and scanner functions — from Brother, Canon, Epson, and Hewlett-Packard can be great printers for simple proofing. They come in both color inkjet and black-and-white laser models, but they almost never include PostScript support. (Brother does offer quite-capable PostScript emulation in some models.)

Color scanners

One device that has recently become very affordable is a color scanner. Epson, Umax Technologies, Agfa, and Canon are all excellent and inexpensive ($150 to $500), yet have color quality that approaches that of a professional scanner costing several thousand dollars. (Other brands tend to rate unevenly in reviews, but because manufacturers' quality changes over time, be sure to check out reviews at places such as *Macworld, MacAddict, PC World, PC Magazine,* and Cnet to see who's got the best current models.) These scanners work with both Macs and PCs, feature USB connectivity, and at these low prices and great quality, are almost a requirement to own. They also can double as copy machines or fax machines. You scan in a paper document and then print it to your printer or fax it from your Internet connection.

Digital cameras

These are becoming popular, and their image quality is presentable; however, you'll need to spend $600 or more for the 4- to 5-megapixel versions. This resolution is adequate for print publishing if your final output is under 8×10 inches and you're doing super-high-quality printing. The less-expensive 3- to 4-megapixel cameras, which cost $200 to $600, are fine for images that are printed at no larger than 5×7 inches.

The biggest problem with using a digital camera for print publishing is that most of the cameras use JPEG image compression, so you're not necessarily dealing with optimum quality no matter how high the resolution of the camera is. The best solution is to experiment — some image subjects work better than others. For Web publishing, however, digital cameras are fine, and using them is more convenient than having your 35mm film processed and scanned.

Mice, trackballs, and tablets

I strongly suggest that you get a multibutton mouse, since InDesign heavily uses the contextual menus that having a right mouse button will make easier to access. The extra buttons can save you strain on your hands and arms if you use them for common operations such as dragging and double-clicking. I advise both Mac and Windows users to get a three- or four-button mouse (or trackball, if that's your fancy); Kensington Microware and Logitech offer good models for both platforms. A pen-based tablet makes sense if you're also doing illustration work, but consider that a secondary input device, not a primary one. However many buttons you get on your mouse, I strongly recommend the optical mice, which don't require a mousepad, don't get gunk in their gears that can interfere with scrolling, and generally are easier to operate on most surfaces. You may find a mouse pad is necessary for use with an optical mouse if your desk or work surface is highly reflective or made of glass (optical mice work best when there is a slight variation in the texture of the surface they're placed on).

Tip   If your optical mouse skips or jumps, try taping a piece of plain copier paper on the work surface for use as a mouse pad.

Getting the Essential Software

A flurry of utility programs, specialized software, fonts, and plug-ins can help you complete your specific publishing environment. The following items detail some of the more outstanding ones:

✦ **An image editor.** Almost all publishers need an image editor, and the standard is really Adobe Photoshop (for both Macintosh and Windows). Even if you're more of an editor, you'll be surprised at how often you'll need to open a graphic file in Photoshop to simply crop or edit a photograph. For professional work, get the full version. If you really just need to resize and crop photos and other images, you can get buy with the much cheaper LE version. You can also buy InDesign as part of the Creative Suite, which makes the price for Photoshop and Illustrator quite low.

✦ **An illustration program.** If you draw or you need to edit EPS files you need an illustration program such as CorelDraw, Adobe Illustrator, or Macromedia FreeHand. They're all good cross-platform programs, so try them out first to see what feels best to you. All three companies let you download demo versions from their Web sites.

Cross-Reference   Go to www.InDesignCentral.com for easy links to these and other software demos.

✦ **A word processor.** A word processing program is a must. Microsoft Word is the standard, but a few people still use WordPerfect — it's up to you. If you use WordPerfect, save your InDesign-destined files in Word or RTF format because InDesign does not import the WordPerfect format directly.

✦ **A font manager.** See the section "Working with Fonts" for more information.

✦ **A compression utility.** Files are always too big, so compression utilities are a must. Here are two of the more common ones:

- **StuffIt Deluxe.** On the Mac, there's no substitute for Allume Systems' StuffIt Deluxe, a $50 utility package that reads both Mac SIT files and PC ZIP files, as well as several Internet compression formats. Allume (formerly Aladdin Systems) also has a Windows version of StuffIt.

- **WinZip.** On Windows, the equivalent program to StuffIt Deluxe is the $30 shareware program WinZip from Niko Mac Computing.

✦ **Plug-ins.** You'll probably want add-on programs, known as *plug-ins,* for InDesign that extend its capabilities.

Cross-Reference See Chapter 36 and this book's companion Web site, `www.InDesignCentral.com`, for comprehensive coverage of plug-ins.

Working with Fonts

Fonts, traditionally known as *typefaces,* are a collection of characters that share a similar look. Fonts usually include several variations such as bold and italic. The electronic files that make up fonts are managed by your operating system or other utilities, not by InDesign. InDesign doesn't come with fonts and it doesn't manage fonts. So when you're talking about fonts, you're talking about *foundries* (companies that design and distribute fonts), Mac OS and Windows features, and third-party utilities and applications that manage fonts.

Procuring fonts

No matter what type of design or publishing you're doing, you'll need — or you'll eventually acquire — lots of fonts. You can never have enough, and there are so many interesting yet useful ones. There are five ways to get fonts: You can create your own, get them free with applications, acquire them through colleagues, purchase them, or translate them from one platform to another.

✦ **Created fonts.** The FontLab program for Windows and Macs lets you create fonts in all popular font formats for both Windows and Mac users.

✦ **Free fonts.** More and more programs come with free fonts (all the image-editing and illustration programs mentioned earlier do, for example). In addition, you can download free fonts from many Web sites. We list some popular sources at `www.InDesignCentral.com`. Or just type **free fonts** into a search engine such as Google (`www.google.com`) and it's a free-for-all. Although this is an inexpensive way to build a font collection, it may not provide all the fonts you need. The quality can vary, and service bureaus may balk at using some of these fonts because they don't come from a source they know. For a variety of technical and aesthetic reasons, it is generally prudent to avoid substituting free fonts for their similar-looking, more costly, and usually more carefully created cousins from Adobe, Bitstream, or Agfa Monotype and the like. Your files may have bad reflow or even fail to output at all.

✦ **Acquired fonts.** Often, people will e-mail fonts with a file they want you to edit. And most people will send you fonts upon request, because the files are small and easily portable. In most cases, this is in violation of the font's license agreement, so it isn't a good way to build a font library. Providing fonts to a service bureau for one-time output is usually okay, but acquiring fonts in this way is generally a poor — even illegal — way to build a font collection.

✦ **Purchased fonts.** Although you can go into a computer store and purchase font CDs, the most convenient method is to buy them online. You can do everything from purchasing base collections of fonts to get you started to buying a single font you need to work on a client's document. Good sites include www.adobe.com, www.fonts.com, www.fontsite.com, www.itcfonts.com, and www.myfonts.com. All five sites are worth visiting to learn about and explore typography.

✦ **Translated fonts.** Although major font houses offer Mac and Windows versions of their fonts, many free and low-price fonts come only in one version of the other. Cross-platform publishers need to have the same fonts on both platforms, and to do so, Acute Systems offers the $45 CrossFont, a Windows program that translates TrueType and PostScript fonts bidirectionally between Mac and Windows. FontLab offers TransType, a $97 Mac program that converts fonts across platforms, as well as from TrueType to PostScript or vice versa. And UniDoc Systems offers the $50 Truekeys to convert East Asian TrueType fonts between Mac and Windows.

Tip

A book such as the *Adobe Type Library Reference Book,* available from www.adobe.com, shows printed samples of hundreds of typefaces. You can use this kind of book to select a typeface for a specific job, and then you can purchase the font. This can save you hours in sifting through your fonts and poring over Web pages to find the typeface you want to use.

Cross-Reference

Go to www.InDesignCentral.com for quick links to font sources and other font resources.

Installing fonts through the operating system

When you get a font on your computer, you need to install it so applications such as InDesign can recognize it — and let you use it. The procedures are different depending on your operating system and whether you're using a font manager.

Macintosh fonts

In Mac OS X, fonts can exist in several places:

✦ **Fonts folder in the Library folder (/Library/Fonts/).** This is where you should place fonts that you want all users to have access to. Just drag them in, whether PostScript, TrueType, or Open Type.

✦ **Fonts folder in the user's Home folder's Library folder (/Users/*user name*/Library/Fonts/).** Any fonts dragged here will be available only to that user.

✦ **Fonts folder in the System folder's Library folder (/System/Library/Fonts/).** This is where Apple places the default fonts for Mac OS X applications. You can add fonts here as well by dragging them, but I recommend you leave this folder alone — you can create a horrible mess on your system if you place your own font files here.

TrueType, OpenType, or PostScript?

The most basic question about fonts usually is whether you should use TrueType, OpenType, or PostScript fonts. The answer depends on the work you do. If you produce newsletters, magazines, ads, or brochures that you output on a typesetter or imagesetter, use PostScript because PostScript is the standard format on these devices. If your final output is to a laser or inkjet printer, TrueType is probably the better bet because it prints faster in most cases, especially if you print to a non-PostScript printer. However, you don't have to use one font format exclusively: OpenType is increasingly popular because it is a merger of PostScript and TrueType. But make sure your service bureau can work with OpenType fonts before using them. Follow these guidelines when choosing which font formats to use:

✦ If you see a TrueType typeface that you want to use in your typeset document, use it. The Mac and Windows operating systems automatically convert TrueType fonts into PostScript format when printing to a PostScript device (or to a file designated for use by a PostScript device). The drawback is that this conversion process may make your files larger because the computer must download the converted TrueType font file into your document.

✦ But if you're sending files to a service bureau for output, don't use TrueType fonts. Stay all-PostScript. Similarly, if you're outputting to the Acrobat Portable Document Format (PDF), either for prepress or electronic distribution, avoid using TrueType fonts. You cannot reliably embed TrueType fonts in PDF files.

✦ Conversely, if you have PostScript typefaces, there's no reason to give them up if you switch to TrueType. On a PostScript printer, you can use both formats. On other printers, all you need is a program such as the free Adobe Type Manager Light for Windows to make the outlines of the letters appear smooth when they print. Mac OS X does this conversion automatically.

Don't base decisions about whether to use TrueType or PostScript fonts on assumptions about quality. Both technologies provide excellent results, so any quality differences are due to the font manufacturer's standards. If you purchase typefaces from recognized companies, you don't need to worry. (Many smaller companies produce high-quality fonts as well.)

There's a new format slowly coming into use called OpenType, which essentially is a merger of the TrueType and PostScript standards. Before using these fonts, make sure your service bureau or imagesetter can handle them. Mac OS X, Windows 2000, and Windows XP all support them, as do current versions of font managers. In a few years, they'll be normal and supported by newer equipment, but it generally takes several years for new technologies to be widely deployed, so check first. InDesign supports these fonts, including their special capabilities such as access to more special characters and international characters.

Any fonts installed in the Mac OS X folders will not be available to Mac OS 9 applications. You need to also maintain fonts in the System Folder's Fonts folder — note that the Mac OS 9 folder name is System Folder while the Mac OS X folder name is simply System — or use a Mac OS 9 font manager such as Adobe Type Manager.

If you use a third-party font manager such as Extensis's Font Reserve or Suitcase, your fonts can be installed anywhere as long as you have told the font manager where they are stored. These programs can autoactivate fonts as needed for both Mac OS X and Mac OS 9 applications, and I strongly recommend you invest in one. (Note that Adobe has no plans to release a Mac OS X version of Adobe Type Manager or Adobe Type Reunion.)

Another source of confusion for new Mac OS X users is its nonsupport of Multiple Masters PostScript fonts. The Multiple Masters format lets programs modify fonts on the fly, such as creating a semibold version from a bold typeface. But the format never got widespread adoption. So Mac OS X has essentially killed off the format. That means that Mac OS 9 applications running under Mac OS X can use Multiple Masters fonts, but native Mac OS X applications like InDesign CS2 cannot. That can cause problems when opening older InDesign documents with Multiple Masters fonts in InDesign CS2. So, you'll need to replace the Multiple Masters fonts with PostScript or OpenType fonts. If you created instances of Multiple Masters fonts — such as a semibold — don't worry: When those instances are saved or exported as their own font files, they're no longer Multiple Masters fonts and should work just fine under Mac OS X.

Note When you install Mac fonts, make sure you install both the screen fonts and the printer fonts for each PostScript font. You may have a *font suitcase* — a special font file — with several screen fonts for your PostScript font, or you may have separate files for each screen font, depending on which option the company decided to use. OpenType and TrueType fonts don't come in several files — all variants are in one suitcase. Also, the same single OpenType suitcase file will work for both Mac OS X and Windows 2000 and XP, so there is no need to purchase separate Mac and PC versions of an OpenType font.

Windows fonts

You can add TrueType and OpenType fonts to Windows through the Fonts control panel. PostScript fonts, however, require a font manager such as Extensis Font Reserve, Adobe ATM Light or Deluxe, or Extensis Suitcase; follow the installation instructions from their documentation.

To add TrueType and OpenType fonts to Windows:

1. **Choose Start ⇨ Settings ⇨ Control Panel to open the Control Panel folder, and then double-click the Fonts folder.**

2. **Choose File ⇨ Install New Font to get the Add Fonts dialog box shown in Figure 38-1.**

3. **Navigate the dialog box using the Folders and Drives scroll lists to get to the folder or disk that has the TrueType or OpenType fonts you want to install.** A list of fonts will appear in the dialog box.

4. **Select the fonts to install and click OK.**

Using a font manager and font utilities

Although you can manage fonts to a certain extent through the operating system, I highly recommend that you use a font manager. With a font manager, you can control precisely which fonts are active at any one time. This is important because many different versions and kinds (PostScript, TrueType, and OpenType) of fonts exist with the same name; simply using any font with the same name is not okay. For example, if you use TrueType Helvetica instead of PostScript Helvetica, the text in the document may reflow, altering the design and even cutting off text. In addition to a font manager, most Windows users will need the free Adobe ATM Light for viewing PostScript fonts on-screen and most Mac users will want a font menu manager.

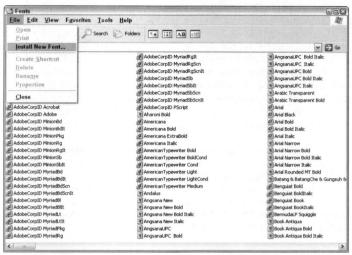

Figure 38-1: The Fonts window for adding TrueType fonts in Windows

Using font managers

With a font manager such as Extensis Font Reserve, Extensis Suitcase, or Adobe ATM Deluxe (Windows only), you can see more information about fonts and activate fonts on the fly without restarting programs. On the Mac, the drag-and-drop interface makes it easy to install and export fonts; on Windows, you can easily create a library of all the TrueType, PostScript, and OpenType fonts on your system. On both platforms, Font Reserve and Suitcase provide features such as on-screen previews, sample printing, character maps, and sets for grouping fonts for projects (see Figure 38-2, which displays the Font Reserve program).

Using ATM Light in Windows

Although ATM Deluxe incorporates ATM Light, you don't need it—and in fact, you can't use it—if you're using another font manager or are installing fonts through the operating system. If you're using Suitcase or Font Reserve, you can't simply disable the Deluxe features of ATM Deluxe. To prevent conflicts, you need to remove ATM Deluxe and replace it with ATM Light.

A potentially confusing issue with Windows font managers is that a necessary control panel—ATM Light—often masquerades as the font manager ATM Deluxe. That's not a problem if you're using ATM Deluxe in Windows, but it is if you use another font manager. The reason is that no matter what font manager you use, you need the ATM Light control panel to render PostScript fonts on-screen for Windows. ATM Light comes with many programs and is available from www.adobe.com.

Figure 38-2: Like Extensis Suitcase, Extensis Font Reserve provides an intuitive interface for installing fonts, activating fonts on the fly, previewing fonts, and creating font sets.

Summary

Modern computers are typically well equipped for publishers. Boosting memory and hard drive size are typically the only changes users need to make.

Publishers will want several peripherals, either attached to their computer or available on the network, including a PostScript printer for high-volume output, a low-cost inkjet printer for basic color proofing, and a scanner for image capture — as well as a fast Internet connection.

Font management software is a must for Mac and Windows users. Both Extensis Suitcase and Extensis Font Reserve can do the job. On Windows, Adobe Type Manager also fits the need.

✦   ✦   ✦

Layout Theory and Practice

✦ ✦ ✦ ✦

In This Chapter

Understanding layout terms

Knowing the seven basic rules of good design

Getting started

Imitating and creating good designs

✦ ✦ ✦ ✦

Many InDesign users are not trained graphic designers — they're administrators, hobbyists, entrepreneurs, or volunteers who have something to say. Armed with the best layout and typography tool in the world, they sometimes forget that they're not, in fact, armed with the training (and sometimes the talent) that producing clear, interesting publications requires. That's okay. A quick review of standard layout terminology and design rules helps any user get started in the right direction. Then, by dissecting other people's designs and messages, you can learn to plan and create publications that clarify and reinforce your message. Armed with this background in layout and design, you can step into the world of InDesign and have at it.

Layout Terms

Document layout — the placement of text, images, and other items on a page — involves many elements. To communicate effectively with your peers and service providers, it helps to understand layout terminology, much of which is rooted in printing and production history. A brief primer on layout terms follows.

Layout tools

When a graphic designer creates a layout, he or she uses the following tools — either on paper or through software such as InDesign:

- ✦ **Grid.** The basic layout design of a publication. It includes standard positions of folios, text, graphics, bylines, and headlines as shown in Figure 39-1. A layout artist modifies the grid when necessary. Grids also are called *templates*.

- ✦ **Dummy.** A rough sketch of the layout of a particular story.

- ✦ **Guidelines.** Lines that show the standard placement of columns and margins in the grid. In most layout programs, guidelines are nonprinting lines that you can use to ensure that elements align.

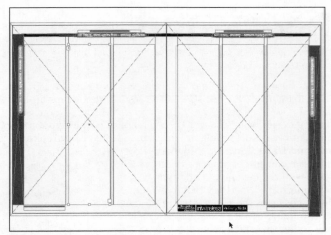

Figure 39-1: This master-page template contains placeholders for the logos, headlines, and artwork for the pages of a product catalog.

✦ **Overlay.** A piece of transparent paper or film laid over a layout board. On the overlay, the artist can indicate screens in a different color or overprinted material such as text or graphics. InDesign has the electronic equivalents of overlays: layers (Window ⇨ Layers or F7).

✦ **Knockout.** When one element cuts out the part of another element that it overlaps, a designer would say that one element *knocks out* the other or that one element is *knocked out of* the other. In either phrasing, it means the first element covers up the part of the other element under it. This differs from overlaying the other element, because in an overlay, both elements are visible (as in a superimposed image).

✦ **Galleys.** Single columns of type that are not laid out in any sort of printed-page format. In the past, publishers used galleys to check for proper hyphenation and to proof for errors. Galleys also were sent to authors for proofreading so that corrections could be made before the text was laid out. Galleys have all but disappeared from publishing because most people now proofread on the first draft of page layouts instead of making the intermediate step of proofreading on galleys.

Design elements

Most publications, regardless of size and style, consist of the same basic design elements: columns, margins, frames, and so on. Take a look at what you'll be dealing with:

✦ **Column.** A block of text.

✦ **Gutter.** The space between columns that are placed side by side. (In newspapers and magazines, gutter space is usually 1 or 2 picas.)

✦ **Margin.** The space between the edge of a page and the nearest standard block of text. Some designers allow text or graphics to intrude into the margin for visual effect.

✦ **Bleed.** An image, graphic element, or block of color that, in the final printed version, extends to the trimmed edge of the final printed page. To achieve a bleed, the items on the layout must extend a specified distance beyond the page's trimmed edge, so even if there are slight variations of where pages are cut during the final binding, the item never stops short of the trimmed edge.

✦ **Wrap.** When text follows the contours of an obstructing element such as a graphic or other text. The column margins are altered so that the column text wraps around the intruding graphic or text instead of being overprinted by the intruding element. Depending on what the text wraps around and the capabilities of the layout program, a wrap can be rectangular, polygonal, curved, or irregular. InDesign can wrap text around any shape, including a picture's clipping path, as shown in Figure 39-2.

Figure 39-2: InDesign lets you easily wrap text around the contours of images.

✦ **Folio.** The page number and identifying material (such as the publication name or month) that appears at the bottom or top of every page.

✦ **White space.** The part of the page left empty to create contrast with the text and graphics. White space provides visual relief and emphasizes the text and graphics.

✦ **Frames.** The boxes or containers that hold layout elements (text, graphics, and blocks of color) on a page. Using a mouse, you can delete, copy, resize, reshape, or otherwise manipulate frames in your layout.

✦ **Strokes.** The ruling lines around frames that hold layout elements.

✦ **Template.** By filling a project with empty frames and defining style tags in advance, you can use the resulting template repeatedly to create projects that use the same frames and styles.

Image manipulation

Page-layout programs make it easy for you to decide which parts of an image to display and at what size. Although InDesign doesn't provide the power of a dedicated illustration program such as Adobe Illustrator, you can perform some special effects as well:

✦ **Cropping.** Selecting a part of an image for use on the page.

✦ **Sizing (scaling).** Determining how much to reduce or enlarge the image (or part of the image). With layout programs, you often can distort an image by sizing it differently horizontally and vertically, which creates special effects such as compressing or stretching an image.

✦ **Reversing.** Also called *inverting* in some programs, reversing exchanges the black and white portions of an image. This effect is similar to creating a photographic negative.

✦ **Special effects.** *Flipping* (mirroring) and *skewing* (slanting) are other popular design effects. InDesign even lets you apply color to some types of grayscale images, plus apply drop shadows, transparency, and feathering effects.

Seven Basic Rules of Good Design

Think about it: Many documents are off-putting. What makes them that way, and how do you build a layout that is inviting? Figure 39-3 shows two pages that contain the same information but use different layouts. The page on the left has body text set close to the headline. The leading is tight, and except for a spot around the illustration, the white space is in short supply. Notice how the page on the right has a lighter, more vibrant look. Also note the variety of sizes, the use of generous margins, and a few strategic elements that don't quite align with the others (providing something for the eye to follow). Which page are you more inclined to read?

Figure 39-3: The page on the left is clean but dull — even the image adds little visual interest. The page on the right uses different typefaces, alignment, color, and text wraps to create interest and reinforce the subject matter without getting too busy.

If you're a trained graphic designer, you already know the basics. You can immediately put InDesign to use, creating effective layouts. But if you're new to the field of graphic design, try keeping the following seven basic rules in mind as you begin learning about layout.

Rule #1: Keep an idea file

As you read magazines, books, newspapers, annual reports, ads, and brochures, save page layouts you like and dislike. Keep these layouts — good and bad — in a file, along with notes to yourself about which aspects of the layout work well and which work poorly. As you build your layout file, you educate yourself about layout basics.

Rule #2: Plan your document

It sounds corny, but it's true: Laying out a document is a lot like taking a journey. If you know where you're headed, it's much easier to find your way. Because InDesign makes it easy to experiment as you design a document, it's also easy to end up with a messy conglomeration of text and images. You can avoid this pitfall by knowing ahead of time what you're trying to accomplish with the document's layout. Don't be afraid of those old low-tech tools — pencil and paper.

Rule #3: Keep it simple

When it comes to page layout, simple is better. Even the most experienced, trained graphic designers can tell you that this rule applies at least 99 percent of the time. If you're just beginning to learn how to lay out pages, you'll make far fewer design mistakes if you follow this rule. Regardless of the application, simple layouts are appealing in their crispness, their readability, and their straightforward, no-gimmicks approach.

Rule #4: Leave some white space

Pages that are crammed full of text and pictures tend to be unappealing — meaning that the average, busy reader is likely to skip them. Keep some space between text columns and headlines and between page edges and layout elements. This white space is refreshing and encourages the reader to spend some time on the page. Regardless of the particular document type, readers always appreciate having a place on every page to rest their eyes, a place that offers an oasis in a sea of ink.

Rule #5: Don't use every bell and whistle

InDesign is powerful, yes, but that doesn't mean that it's necessarily a good idea to push the program to its limits at all times. You can, for example, lay out a page with 30 columns of text, but would you want to try reading such a page? With InDesign, you can achieve an amazing number of special effects:

- ✦ Stretch, condense, and scale type
- ✦ Create frames of almost any shape, and then fill and frame them
- ✦ Add graphics and lines (with custom dash or stripe patterns)
- ✦ Bleed photos and artwork off the edge of the page
- ✦ Flow text along a path; wrap text around all sides of any shape
- ✦ Add colors and create a variety of vignettes (called *blends* and *gradients*)

✦ Make objects fade, for ghosting or merge effects

✦ Apply drop shadows and feathering, which adds lighting and shadow effects to objects

✦ Rotate and skew text and graphics

Using all these effects at once, however, can overwhelm readers and cause them to miss any message you're trying to convey. Conveying a message with words and images is usually the most important task of the design and typography. A good rule: Use no more than three special typographic or design effects per two-page spread.

Rule #6: Make it look like what it is

Lay out the document so that someone looking at it can get an idea of what it is. This sounds like a common-sense rule, but you'd be surprised at how often this rule is broken. If you're laying out an ad for a product, make sure the layout *looks* like an ad, not like a technical brochure. See Figure 39-4 for a sidebar that ended up looking like an ad.

Figure 39-4: There's nothing wrong with this design — except that it's supposed to be a sidebar, not an ad. Placed on a crowded page, its intent was lost on readers.

Rule #7: Don't break Rule #6

Creativity is okay — and InDesign helps you express your layout ideas creatively — but unless you know what you're doing, don't get carried away. If you *are* laying out a technical brochure, for example, don't make it look like a display ad unless you understand that this may confuse readers, and you're doing it for a compelling reason.

Getting Started

After you come up with a design, expect it to evolve over time. Styles change, and so does your content. So don't be afraid to try different techniques over the months and years — just make sure that you're not making changes willy-nilly, for change's sake.

The key to a successful layout is planning, a rule that matches the InDesign approach to design. You don't just start doing a layout in InDesign. Instead, you start building the foundation of your document — the page size and columns, the paragraph and character styles, the standard elements such as page numbers and logos — to serve as a receptacle for the content. The idea is that most content you create is a variation on a theme. For example, if you produce a magazine, each issue is different, but the basic design structure is the same from month to month. Rather than start each month from scratch, you start with a template and modify it each month as necessary. The same approach works for newspapers, catalogs, brochures, newsletters, and books.

Visualizing your layout

Even before you build your basic structure, you need a mental image of what your document will be. Have no fear — nothing is cast in stone. If you change your mind as you work on your first document, you can modify your structure. Having an initial structure in mind before starting, however, helps immensely.

Sketching your layout on paper

How do you start to develop a layout plan? If you're still thinking about what the pages should look like, you can develop some more-specific ideas by spending a few minutes sketching out the layout before you sit down to produce the document on the computer.

Using the dummy approach

Let's say you want to create an eight-page newsletter that has standard, 8½-×-11-inch pages. One way to do this is to create a dummy document, a valuable layout-planning aid. Figure 39-5 shows a sample dummy — the cover and the first two pages.

Here's how to create a dummy:

1. **Take two sheets of blank, 8½-×-11-inch paper, aligning one on top of the other, and folding them in half across the width of the paper.** This technique gives you a miniature version of your eight-page newsletter.

2. **Use a pencil to sketch the dummy's masthead, the cover art and/or stories, and the running headers or footers for each page.**

3. **Form an idea about how wide you want the top, side, and bottom margins to be, and mark them on the pages.**

4. **Indicate which pictures and stories go on each page.** Of course, because you will be using InDesign to format the document, you can make changes right up to the point when you produce camera-ready pages.

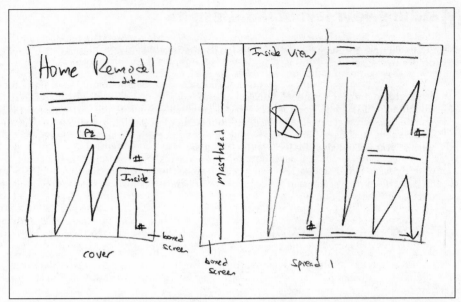

Figure 39-5: A pencil-sketch dummy lets you think through the basic structure quickly and easily.

Here are some conventions to remember as you make your sketches:

✦ A down arrow means the story continues on another page, while a # symbol means the story ends.

✦ Horizontal lines usually indicate titles, bylines, and other such specific text elements, while vertical lines indicate a column of text.

✦ A frame with an *X* through it indicates a picture or photo.

✦ The abbreviation *pq* means a pull-quote — text that is taken from the article and put in a frame or other shape to draw attention, similar to a photo.

✦ A *screen* is a background of color or gray ink.

You can see from Figure 39-5 that the basic layout structure is three columns, with a self-contained front page that has a small table of contents and interior pages that put the *masthead* (the list of staff) and a viewpoint column on the second page. The third page has two stories, which of course may not start exactly where indicated on the sketch. The point is, merely, that multiple stories can appear on a page.

Taking the next step

You should find all this planning — which actually doesn't take that much time in relation to the other publishing tasks involved — to be time well spent. The process of sketching out the layout helps clarify your thoughts about the basic layout of your document. You can make preliminary decisions about such things as where to put each illustration and section of text on a page, how many columns of text to use, and whether to use any repeating elements (such as headers and footers).

Sketching your layout in InDesign

If you're already comfortable using InDesign, you may decide to forgo the paper-and-pencil sketching of a new document and use InDesign to do the rough design instead. The obvious advantages to this approach are as follows:

✦ **You can experiment with different approaches.** When a document has a set number of text and graphic elements, you can use InDesign to make a series of sketches of the document. If you like, you can save each sketch as a separate file with a distinct file-name. In each sketch, you can use different element positioning, type styles, masthead placement, and so on. Then you can print a copy of each file and use the copies to assist you in finalizing the look of the layout.

✦ **You can print thumbnail views.** If you're considering many different layout possibilities, you can develop them quickly in InDesign and then print the series in *thumbnail* (miniature) size (choose File ⇨ Print, and then click the Thumbnails check box in the Setup pane's Options section, as shown in Figure 39-6). You can also set the number of thumbnails per page using the Per Page pop-up menu. Seeing the pages in thumbnail view makes it easier to evaluate the overall balance between page elements because you aren't distracted by the text or the graphics in such a reduced view.

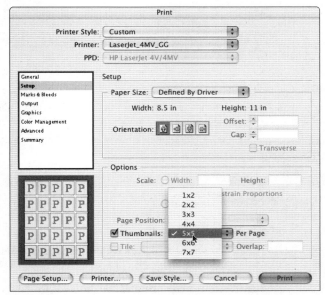

Figure 39-6: Selecting Thumbnails in the Setup pane of the Print dialog box lets you print miniature versions of your pages.

✦ **You can get your client's approval.** Printed InDesign copies of rough sketches have a cleaner look, which is especially helpful if you're designing a layout for a client. The advantage to presenting rough sketches that look more final is that it tends to make the client approval process go more smoothly, and it can make it easier for you to sell the client on your design. At the same time, slick-looking rough drafts do have a disadvantage: They make it more difficult for clients to understand that what they're seeing is just a rough draft and not a final copy.

Imitating and Creating Good Designs

Imitation is the sincerest form of flattery, and as long as you don't cross the line into blatant copying, go ahead and flatter as many people as you can. Go to the newsstand and thumb through a bunch of magazines. (But buy just the ones you really like.) Get a couple of colleagues — or just consult the other coffee lovers in line with you — and look through designs together. Talk about what you like, what you don't like, and — most important — *why* you react the way you do.

You can call this flower-power consciousness-raising. Or you can call it being a copycat. The point is, it's the best way to learn good design. As with any good design ideas, the ones used as good examples in this chapter are based on years of experience and, of course, honest-to-goodness pilfering of other people's good work.

Avoiding formulas

Although I say to borrow ideas and follow the rules, I don't mean for you to flat-out copy other designs, making yours look *exactly* like someone else's. Your designs should elucidate *your* message — not somebody else's.

Stealing from great artists

A couple more clichés to drive home the point: Good writers read good writers. (I'm sure someone has said, "Good designers study good designers," but this hasn't gotten enough buzz to become a cliché yet.) Good artists imitate; great artists steal.

Avoiding design recipes

Don't confuse examples of good design with recipes. I don't pretend to be Picasso or even Haring. My designs (and my colleagues' designs) might make no sense for your documents. After all, you need to make sure the designs you produce meet several needs:

✦ Your sense of aesthetics.

✦ The requirements of the content being presented.

✦ The image you or your organization wants to convey.

✦ The financial limitations you're working under. (We'd all love to do everything in full, glorious color, but until money comes out of printers without resulting in jail terms, most people do have some concerns about costs.)

The design of the ad mockup in Figure 39-7 works well because the simple black-and-white graphic communicates a 3-D stage. Plus, the company can rotate out the center text each month to sell whatever is hot that month. But if a new drugstore came to town and asked a designer to adapt the design of this ad for its grand opening, the designer would have to refuse — it's just the wrong approach for a grand opening.

Learning to improvise

Use design samples as starting points, and don't confuse the techniques and fundamental principles they illustrate with the implementation I happened to choose for this particular example. You could use those same techniques and fundamental principles and come up with completely different designs for your projects. Great artists may steal, but they also improvise.

Laying out ads and circulars

The elements of ads, circulars (fliers), and other such sales- and marketing-oriented materials are a critical type of publication because they must work the first time. You may be willing to put up with a design you don't care for in a newsletter that contains information you find valuable. But an ad has the burden of needing to attract your attention, holding you long enough to deliver its message, and letting you go with a favorable impression. In the following sections, I show you three ads to identify the techniques they use to accomplish these goals. Whether it's an ad, a report cover, a prospectus, a pamphlet, or another such publication, these techniques apply.

Figure 39-7: The design of this ad works well for its original content, but it is not likely to adapt well to another type of business.

An airline ad mockup

Figure 39-8 shows an ad mockup for a fictitious airline. Notice the following about its design:

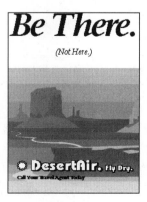

Figure 39-8: A simple ad with a simple message deserves a simple treatment to attract attention. But notice that simple does not mean simplistic — every element has a character of its own.

✦ **The large type.** This is kerned so that the spacing between each pair of characters is the same — just at the point of touching.

✦ **The small type.** This forces the eye to take a look, because of the contrast with the big type above and all the space on either side. This use of contrast is a good way to get attention. Never underestimate the power of type. It is as important as graphics in garnering attention and conveying both the substance and the nuances of the message.

✦ **The airline logo.** This uses reverse-video and shadow effects on a fairly common font (Bauhaus). Notice the sun symbol to the logo's left: That's a symbol in the Zapf Dingbats font. The use of symbols really helps establish a logo as a logo, rather than just a bunch of letters. Also notice the use of a catchphrase (also called a *tag line*) in the same font as the logo. You would do this for a catchphrase that you plan to use in several places. It becomes an extension of the logo. (The desert tableau is a color image, and in color the text is very striking against the colors; in black-and-white, it loses a little of that zing.)

✦ **White space.** Blank areas provide a visually calm port in a storm of images and text. Be sure to provide these resting spots in all your work.

A restaurant ad mockup

The ad mockup for a seafood restaurant shown in Figure 39-9, presents a tighter interplay of text and graphics. It also shows, although not at first glance, the power of InDesign's graphics manipulation tools. Here's what to look for:

Figure 39-9: The interplay between the text and graphics in this ad reinforces the message.

✦ **The schools of fish.** They're in glorious color, although you can't see that in black and white, and there are really only three fish in the ad. I used the copy function in InDesign to create the schools. And to make sure that they didn't look like clones, I used the rotate and skew tools to make each cloned fish slightly different from the others. I used only a very slight skew, less than 5 percent; the rotation accounts for most of the difference in the fishes' appearance. The lesson: Don't forget to use basic tools such as rotation and copying.

✦ **The descriptive text.** The text describing all the sumptuous seafood options (Atlantic cod. Alaska salmon.) wraps around the pictures of fish, using InDesign's Bézier picture frame to hold the pictures, combined with the ability to have text wrap around both sides of an image.

✦ **The headlines.** Can you tell what this ad is selling? Why, fresh fish, of course! The repetitive use of the text reinforces the message. Placing the repeating text in different positions among the fish makes sure it doesn't look repetitive. (Predictability is a major reason that repetition is boring, so this design finds a way to repeat without being boring.)

✦ **The tag line.** This added repetition of the words *Fresh Fish* reinforces the primary message. In the case of this ad, there's no large text identifying the restaurant (it's in the body text), but this tag line is one the restaurant uses a lot, so the ad can get away with the low-key treatment of the restaurant's name—just as if an ad said only "Have it your way," you'd probably think of Burger King, while "Just do it!" would evoke thoughts of Nike.

✦ **Italics.** All the text here, except the list of locations at the bottom, is in italics, which is unusual. But the fluidity of italics works well with the fish theme (underwater, get it?), and by making the text large enough and the layout uncluttered, it works.

✦ **Going beyond the margins.** The fish swim past the margins on the page, which makes the page feel less boxed-in. Overstepping margins to provide a feeling of flexibility and give the eye something unusual to notice is often a good idea.

A public service announcement

Let's take a look at one more ad. This one is not a full page. It's the kind of ad you'd probably run in an in-house publication; it's what magazines call a PSA (short for *public service announcement*). It's the type of thing you can easily put together using clip art and basic typefaces when you have a hole to fill or need to make an announcement or advertisement for your organization (see Figure 39-10). Notice the following:

Figure 39-10: A public service announcement designed for black-and-white reproduction

✦ **The simple graphic.** This simple graphic works well in black and white. Photos can be very effective in catching attention—they scream "real!" The simple composition is also pleasing. You'll find many such images in clip-art libraries.

✦ **The message.** Simple text with a simple message that ties into the image—that's the ticket.

✦ **The headline.** A loud, bold title would have competed with the photo. This one's easy to read, but it doesn't fight for attention. If you see the photo and stop, you'll see the headline, and that's all that's required. The centering makes sure that it's clear the headline goes with the text below. It also follows the centered shape of the chair.

✦ **The alignment.** The more ways things line up, the more distracting a layout can be, so try to use only one or two alignments. A left alignment might have worked here, but then the symmetry of the chair would not have been picked up in the rest of the ad — and such reuse of basic visual themes is a hallmark of pleasing design. People just get all warm and fuzzy with such continuity.

✦ **The justified text.** The text is short, readable, and justified. Although having justified text may seem to violate the minimal-alignment rule, the fact is that centered text is rarely easy to read if there are more than a few lines of it. Having the text justified keeps the symmetry of the centered text because the right and left margins in justified text are symmetrical.

✦ **The dashed lines.** We all know what a dashed line means. The ad practically screams, "Cut me out!" To get a dashed box, just use one of InDesign's frame tools and change the frame style to a dashed one. To reinforce the "Cut me out!" message, you could add a pair of scissors (from a symbols font or from clip art) along a top corner of the dashed box.

✦ **The coupon.** In the box is the coupon you're hoping people will fill out. The font here is different (a condensed sans serif, compared to the text's normal serif). The font reinforces that it is a separate element. You want the readers to think of the coupon as separate, so they know that it's okay to remove it from the rest of the ad. The use of a condensed font also gives you more room for the information you want people to fill in. The underlines are right-aligned tabs using an underline leader. That's the simplest way to create fill-in-the-blank lines.

Creating newsletters

Quintessentially, publishing newsletters and magazines represents the focus of page-layout programs, even though InDesign is also great for a whole range of documents, including ads, reports, and catalogs. But when you think publishing, you are more likely to think newsletters and magazines. So, let's spend a little time going over ways of making top-notch newsletters and magazines, without hiring a huge crew of designers.

Intentional evolution

Newsletters and magazines generally redesign themselves every couple years. The redesign might be subtle, or it might be extreme. But it happens. Why? Because the new art director or publisher wants to put his or her imprint on the publication, you might say.

Well, that's partially true, but the real reason is more basic: If you don't revisit your look every once in a while, you appear stale, and people will think you're lazy or don't care about them. People do it for their personal appearance, too. (Want proof? Take a look at a snapshot of yourself from five years ago.)

The opposite can also happen: The content changes over time but the design and image goals do not. When the content changes but the image goals don't, the situation is a little trickier because you need to update the design to accommodate the new content (such as increased use of profiles, short stories, gossip and rumors, question-and-answer interviews, and so on) while still reflecting the feel of the old design. For examples of what I mean, take a look at current issues of *The New York Times*, *The Wall Street Journal*, *Business Week*, *Time*, or *Newsweek*. Then compare them with issues from five years ago. You'll find a different look and mix of content, but the same overall feel.

Understanding newsletter basics

A newsletter's main goal is to provide information. So, the focus should be on text: how to make it readable, how to call attention to it, and how to make sure the reader knows where all relevant content is. Here are some basic newsletter design issues to consider:

✦ **Column width.** Most newsletters are two or three columns wide. A three-column format gives you more flexibility, because you can have graphics of three different sizes (one, two, and three columns wide), plus you can add sidebars and separate stories fairly easily to a page, because again there are multiple sizes to choose from. A two-column format is more straightforward, but it gives you fewer options. It's best for newsletters that are essentially sequential — without multiple stories and sidebars on a page or spread.

✦ **Page numbers and folios.** As always, make sure you add page numbers and an identifier of the publication (called a *folio*). Some include a corporate symbol after the page number, to add visual interest and reinforce the identity.

✦ **Body text.** The body text should use a very readable, straightforward font; examples include Caslon, Cheltenham, Concorde, Garamond, Janson Text, Minion, New Baskerville, and Stone Serif. Avoid Times and Times New Roman, because they're so overused (consider instead variations such as Times Ten and Times Europa). A typical size for newsletters and magazines is 10 points with 13 points of leading. Generally speaking, point size should range from 9 to 10 points (you can use half-point sizes), and leading from 10.5 to 13 points, with the most typical being 2 points more than the font size. Justified text is often used for an authoritative look and left-aligned text for a friendlier look.

✦ **Drop caps.** Using a drop cap is an effective way to alert the reader to the beginning of a new story — you can also use it for the beginning of the conclusion — as well as to provide a visual contrast on the page. Often, drop caps are in a different typeface (sometimes picking up the headline font) and color from the body text. Generally, you should boldface the drop cap to make it more readable. (Otherwise, the drop cap looks wimpy, which is not what you want for such a big element.)

✦ **Headlines, kickers, and bylines.** The headline, the *kicker* (the type above it, also called a *slug line* for reasons that have nothing to do with gardening), and the byline are usually related. For example, the headline may reflect the body text (Minion Condensed Bold and Minion, respectively) and the kicker and byline may be from the same typeface (Helvetica Condensed Medium and Helvetica Light, respectively). The use of related typefaces provides consistency while still producing a subtle difference from the rest of the text.

Caution

Be careful when combining multiple fonts. If they don't work together, it can be a disaster. A rule of thumb is to restrict the number of fonts (not including variants such as boldface and small caps) to two per page. You can break this rule occasionally by using a font that has similarities to one of the other two.

✦ **Dingbats.** A nice touch is to end a story with a *dingbat* (publishing speak for a symbol). The dingbat might be as simple as a single character or the corporate logo — anything that reinforces the identity. Inserting a dingbat is easy: Just add the symbol after the last paragraph either by putting a tab before it (and defining the tab in your text style to be flush right against the right margin, or pressing Shift+Tab to create a right-aligned tab) or an em space (Shift+⌘+M or Ctrl+Shift+M). Either way is fine for justified text. Pick a method based on your preferences. But use only the em space if your text is not justified.

✦ **Sidebars.** You can make a sidebar or a separate, minor story distinct by putting a shaded background behind it. Make sure you have a margin between the edge of the background and the text. You can also box a sidebar, with or without the background, using frames. Or you could just put a line above and below the background. Making sidebars have a different number of columns from the main text — for example, a two-column sidebar that is the width of one column of main text — also helps make the sidebar distinct from the surrounding text. (Obviously, you don't want column widths that are too narrow for easy readability, so if your sidebar column widths need to be the same as the main text's column widths, so be it.)

✦ **Pull-quotes.** A pull-quote is a great way to call out some interesting material in a story to attract readers' attention. Often, the style reflects the sidebars, including a shaded background or lines above and below. Any embellishments, such as dingbats, should help the text stand out while still providing continuity with the overall design. Pull-quotes also help to break up long passages of text when you don't have an image to do so.

Working with magazines

Magazines are very similar to newsletters, except that they generally have color images, more graphics, a cover that has no stories on it, and a full-page (or larger) table of contents. Note that magazines usually are highly designed, so they often look very different from one another.

Creating tables of contents

Let's look first at a sample contents page from a magazine. So take the following techniques as starting points:

✦ **The logo.** This should be distinct and readable. Typically, the name is large and clear.

✦ **The banner.** The issue date and number is called a *banner*. There should usually be a generous amount of space so it isn't lost. Also, when you use a banner, make sure the text is bold; otherwise, it is can be hard to read.

✦ **Feature and column entries.** Magazines generally have *features* (longer articles that appear only once), along with *columns* (regular, short articles that appear in each issue, usually covering a certain topic). Label the content accordingly (for example, the columns might be called *Departments*).

✦ **Page numbers.** The use of large page numbers for the features reinforces that this is a table of contents. You might even use a different font for these page numbers. For departments, the page numbers might use the same font as the story titles, or use the same font that feature page numbers do if you use a different font for them. Either way, set them off from the text with an em space or by making them two-line drop caps.

✦ **Photo and graphic listings.** Putting a page number near any photo or graphic you have in your contents page is a good idea. If people are interested in the photo, they should be able to know where to find the associated article.

Formatting feature articles

An eye-catching design is critical to entice readers to sample a publication's contents. Most publications use a variety of tools — for example, InDesign, Adobe Illustrator, Macromedia FreeHand, and Adobe Photoshop, among others — to create visually rich pages. Feature articles showcase a magazine's many design approaches, because articles of that length give the designers the opportunity to use multiple techniques within the overall design framework.

Working with flexible grids

The magazine's design offers a flexible grid that allows different numbers of columns and column widths from feature to feature. By having a standard grid, the magazine's design director can be assured that the entire package will be cohesive. By allowing individual designers options within that structure, appropriate creative flexibility is available to keep the reader engaged. Every standard element — body text, sidebars, screen images, diagrams, tables, and captions — must take up an integral number of columns, but the number per element is up to the designer.

You can also mix grids on a page. For example, the main text might follow a two-column grid. But the sidebar on the left-facing page might span all the columns in the grid, allowing for wider columns. Staying within the geometry of the grid, the designer can easily connect sidebars and graphics to related text while creating enough visual distinction. That's the beauty of having multiple grids to use in a layout.

Working with gatefolds

Every once in a while, you see a magazine that has an article with a fold-out page. Called a *gatefold,* this kind of page requires some special work in your layout. To create a gatefold, you just add a page to the right of an existing right-hand page, making sure to add an extra page to the left of the next spread's existing left-hand page. (Chapter 5 covers how to use the Pages pane to create gatefolds.) That's the easy part. But there are three possible hazards:

✦ Although it appears on-screen as if the three pages are one long sheet of paper, in the actual magazine the far-left page is a separate sheet of paper, while the two right pages are indeed one sheet of paper (folded where the line numbers are).

Tip   Be sure to leave sufficient space between the two sheets so text and images don't get swallowed up in the gutter.

✦ The folded-over page in a gatefold needs to be a bit narrower than the other pages. That's so when it's folded, it doesn't actually get so far into the gutter that it's bound shut into the magazine. Typically, keep an extra pica (⅙") on the outside edge of a gatefold's folded page.

✦ A gatefold must be at the beginning or end of a *form* or *signature* (the sequence of pages printed and bound at a time on a printing press). That's because the extra-wide sheet must be the first or last sheet in the stack. (Magazines are composed of multiple forms, usually of 8, 16, 24, or 32 pages in length.)

Note   Check with your printer before using a gatefold. Also tell your service bureau you're outputting a gatefold, so the staff can ensure that the extra width doesn't inadvertently get cut off during output to film.

Doing other cool stuff

By combining various techniques, you can create some cool-looking stuff for any of a variety of documents. Figure 39-11 shows some examples, which are described as they appear from top to bottom, left to right:

Figure 39-11: Various special effects

✦ **Embossed text.** You can create various embossed text effects by duplicating a text frame and making one slightly overlap the other. Then make the one on top white (or the paper color).

✦ **Textual graphics.** By duplicating a text frame several times and rotating each copy at a different angle, then applying different shades of gray to each, you can create a textual graphic. Here, each subsequent copy (moving from the bottom to the top of the arc) is rotated 10 degrees more than the previous and is 10 percent darker.

✦ **Stretched text.** Each letter in the word *Stretch* is set 10 percent wider than the previous letter, which gives it the effect of being stretched.

✦ **Spaced-out text.** By increasing the space between letters, you can space out text — an effect lots of designers use. You could put spaces (whether regular spaces, en spaces, or em spaces) between the letters, but by using the intercharacter spacing controls (tracking), you ensure that the text is treated as one word and you make it easy to change your spacing settings. (It's easier to adjust the tracking than, say, to replace em spaces with en spaces between every character.)

✦ **Combining skew and shadow.** By combining the skew feature with the shadow feature for text, you can alter how a font looks to create logos. Here, I went a step further and mirrored the text block and changed its color to a shade of gray (by defining a tint of 39 percent black).

✦ **Tinting grayscale images.** For grayscale images, you can apply a color or tint to make them ghostly or subtle. It's a great way to mute a photo enough so that you can place text over it.

✦ **Cameo effects.** By using an oval or Bézier frame (with a very thick frame), you can create a cameo effect. It's a way to create a different type of shape or frame.

✦ **Altered opening-page text.** In some publications, the text on the opening page has a radically different style from the rest of the pages. Often, there is little text on the opening page, because the title and graphics usually take up much of the space. The text that's on the page is also treated graphically. One method is to have no paragraph breaks but to use a symbol instead to indicate paragraph breaks.

✦ **Embedded graphics.** Although drop caps are popular, you can also use an embedded graphic to accomplish the same purpose, or if you want the graphic to be dropped down into the text, you can place the graphic at the appropriate location and turn text wrap on.

✦ **Copying and flipping graphics.** By making a copy of the Skew! graphic and flipping it vertically, I made the text feel even more like a graphic.

Looking at common threads

Creative design means taking some risks, trying out new ideas. Because you can easily use InDesign to try out ideas — and to abandon those that just don't cut it — you should set aside some time in every project to play around with your design. Save a copy of your original, of course, and then see if you can discover some new approach that adds that special edge. While you're doing that, keep the following principles in mind:

✦ **Look intentional.** A former boss gave me some advice I'll never forget: Make sure you look intentional. Everything in your design should look like you wanted it to be there. If something looks odd, it should look as it were meant to look odd. If it looks intentional — whether or not it actually was! — the reader will think you put a lot of care and attention into your work, which enhances your credibility.

✦ **Have enough white space.** People need a visual resting place as they thumb through a publication. Give it to them. If you don't, they'll start to fall asleep, and they'll stop reading. If it's too *gray* (where everything looks like everything else) or too *busy* (where there are so many things to look at that readers don't know where to start), people will stop making the effort.

✦ **Make the text readable.** Remember that the basic point of publishing is to convey information. So don't make it difficult for the reader to get the information you're providing. Make sure the text is readable. Captions and headlines should be both informative and interesting. Make sure people can tell where a story continues and which stories are related to each other.

✦ **Use type creatively.** Fonts are neat and fun. Invest in several fonts, and use them creatively by applying effects such as small caps, colors, banner backgrounds, rotation, skewing, and mixed sizes (but not all at once, of course).

✦ **Use graphics effectively.** They should be fairly large — lots of small images are hard to look at — and should complement the rest of the layout.

✦ **Use visual themes.** Use a core set of fonts. If you use lines in one place, they may be effective in another. If you use frames to separate some elements, don't use colored backgrounds to separate others. Instead, pick one approach and stick with it. There can be variances within the approaches, but by picking up variations of the same core approach, you keep your reader from getting distracted by visual chaos — yet you can still be creative.

✦ **Use color judiciously.** Color is expensive and can overwhelm the content. Used well, grays can provide as much visual interest as color. In fact, in something laden with color, a gray image will stand out as distinct and gain more attention than the surrounding color images.

Summary

As much as you might love the hands-on approach — getting in the software and creating those neat-looking columns and boldface type — you need to do your homework first. You need to understand the terminology and the tenets of good design, and then you need to think through a project before you jump in and start laying it out. The more you know about design, the more quickly you can produce them with InDesign.

Sketches or rough proofs produced in InDesign help designers get buy-in on their approach. Whether you're showing ideas to a client, a board of directors, or a supervisor — or even reviewing them yourself — getting your different ideas on paper helps you decide on a direction. Then, when you get into InDesign, you can focus on perfecting the final look that speaks to *your* content — not someone else's.

✦   ✦   ✦

Typography Theory and Practice

Desktop publishing has changed typography forever. In the old, old days, typefaces were available in a limited number, and those were available only in a limited number of sizes. You couldn't condense or expand them. And you certainly couldn't add drop shadows or make them print as outlines without hours of work in a darkroom. Desktop publishing has changed all that. By rendering type into a series of mathematical equations — curves and lines and angles — and manipulating that math with today's fast computers, type can be almost anything. In the early days of desktop publishing, that led to experimentation, often without the understanding of several hundred years of typographic traditions and that led to a lot of bad results. That was more than a decade ago, however, and good taste has prevailed. InDesign has very good typographic tools that can dramatically reduce typographic awkwardness. This chapter is your guide to typographic good taste.

While typography can be decorative, at its core it is the art of *not* calling attention to the typeface, but to the content itself, letting the shapes of the letters on a page serve as a carefully constructed, yet transparent guide for the reader's eye to follow.

Identifying Terms

Typography terms include words that describe the appearance of text in a document or on a computer screen. These terms refer to such aspects of typography as the size and style of the typeface used and the amount of space between lines, characters, and paragraphs.

Characters

+ **Font.** This is a set of characters of a certain size, weight, and style (for example, 10-point Palatino Bold). This term is used often as a synonym for *typeface,* which is a set of characters of a certain style in all sizes, weights, and stylings (for example, Palatino).

+ **Face.** A face is a combination of a weight and styling in all sizes of a font (for example, Palatino Bold Italic).

✦ **Font family.** This is a group of related typefaces (for example, the Franklin family includes Franklin Gothic, Franklin Heavy, and Franklin Compressed).

✦ **Weight.** This describes typeface thickness. Typical weights, from thinnest to thickest, are ultralight, light, book, medium, demibold, bold, heavy, ultrabold, and ultraheavy.

✦ **Style, type style, font style.** Type can have one of three basic stylings: Roman type is upright type; oblique type is the Roman type that has been mathematically slanted to give the appearance of italic type; and italic type is both slanted and curved (to appear more like calligraphy than Roman type). Type also may be expanded (widened), condensed (narrowed), or compressed (severely narrowed). See Figure 40-1 for examples of some of these stylings. Many programs call these attributes *styles*, while InDesign calls them *type styles* and, occasionally, *font styles*.

Syntax Medium

Syntax Medium Italic

Syntax Bold

Syntax Bold Italic

Syntax Black

Syntax Black Italic

Syntax Ultrablack

Syntax Ultrablack Italic

Figure 40-1: A sample sans serif typeface with different stylings

Tip

Keep in mind that some of these type-style variations are created mathematically, while other fonts are created to appear a certain way. For example, you can compress a Roman font, but it won't be the same as the official, compressed version of the face and will most likely appear squished rather than compressed.

✦ **x-height.** This refers to the height of the average lowercase letter (this is based on the letter x). The greater the height, the bigger the letter looks when compared to letters in other typefaces that are the same point size but have a smaller x-height (see Figure 40-2).

✦ **Cap height.** Cap height is similar to x-height. It refers to the height dimension of the average uppercase letter (based on the letter C). (Refer to Figure 40-2.)

✦ **Descender.** In a letter such as q, the part of the letter that drops below the baseline is called a *descender*. (Refer to Figure 40-2.)

✦ **Ascender.** The part of a letter that extends above the x-height (as in the letter b) is called an ascender. (Refer to Figure 40-2.)

Figure 40-2: The elements of a typeface

✦ **Serif.** This is a horizontal stroke used to give letters visual character. The strokes on the upper left and bottom of the letter *p* in a typeface such as Times are serifs. The serif is usually designed to improve the horizontal flow of letters and words, making serif typefaces easier to read at small sizes and in long paragraphs. (Refer to Figure 40-2.)

✦ **Sans serif.** This means that a typeface does not use serifs. Helvetica is an example of a sans serif typeface.

✦ **Ligature.** A ligature is a set of joined characters, such as fi, fl, ffi, or ffl. The characters are joined because the characters' shapes almost blend together by default, so typographers of yore decided to make them blend together naturally.

Note   Automatic ligatures are available only for fonts that support them. OpenType fonts do, as do most PostScript and TrueType fonts created by professional type foundries. For InDesign to set ligatures for such fonts, make sure that Ligatures is selected in the Character pane's palette menu or that it is selected in the Basic Character Formats pane of the New Character Styles or Character Styles Options dialog boxes.

Typographic measurement units

✦ **Pica.** A pica is a measurement unit that specifies the width and depth of columns and pages. A pica is just a little less than ⅙ of an inch (most people round it up to an even ⅙ inch). All major desktop publishing applications — including QuarkXPress and InDesign — use the 6-picas-per-inch conversion ratio.

✦ **Point.** A point is a measurement used to specify type size and the space between lines. There are 12 points in a pica, so there are about 72.27 points to an inch. Although this is the historically accurate measurement, desktop publishing software generally drops the extra $^{27}/_{100}$ of a point per inch. As with picas, the conversion ratio of points to inches is simplified so that there are only 72 points per inch in all major desktop-publishing applications, including InDesign. However, InDesign does let you choose the traditional method if you prefer, using the Preferences dialog box.

✦ **Cicero.** A cicero is a unit of measure used in many parts of Europe. One inch equals about 5.62 ciceros.

✦ **Agate.** An agate is used for measuring vertical column length in classified ads. One agate equals about 5.5 points. An agate inch is one column wide and ⅟₁₄ of an inch deep.

✦ **Em, en, and punctuation spaces.** The terms em, en, and punctuation space (also called a thin space) are units of measurement that reflect, respectively, the horizontal space taken up by a capital *M*, capital *N*, and lowercase *t*.

Note

Typically, an em space is the same width as the current point size; an en space is ½ of the current point size, and a punctuation (thin) space is ¼ of the current point size. In other words, for 12-point type, an em is 12 points wide, an en space is 6 points wide, and a punctuation or thin space is 3 points wide.

✦ **Figure space.** This refers to the width of a numeral, which usually is the same as an en. (In most typefaces, all numerals are the same width so that tables align naturally.)

Spacing

✦ **Leading.** This term, also called line spacing, refers to the space from the base of one line (the baseline) to another. (Leading is named after the pieces of lead once used to space out lines.) See Figure 40-3 for examples of leading.

> This is 14-point type set to +1 point of leading in the QuarkXPress Measurements palette. As you can see, the lines are simply too close to each other. See how the text almost overlaps between the first two lines?
>
> This is 14-point type with the leading set to Auto in the QuarkXPress Measurements palette—the normal setting for leading. Notice how the space in between lines is more than enough to avoid text overrunning other text, but not so much that there are large gaps between lines. Note that Auto sets the leading to be 20 percent more than the point size, which usually results in the correct 1.5 to 3 points of extra space between lines (for 14-point text, that means leading of 16.8 points, or 2.8 points extra space). As text gets larger than about 18 points, you'll want to avoid Auto and use a specific leading amount (usually 2 points more than the text size). You can specify your own Auto value in the Document Preferences dialog box's Paragraph pane (⌘+Y).
>
> This is 14-point type with the leading set to 20 points in the QuarkXPress Measurements palette—the normal setting for leading. Notice how the space in between lines is far more than enough to avoid text overrunning other text,; in fact, it's an unusually large amount that probably looks a little strange. You might find such large leading in a kid's book, since young children need help distinguishing characters and the extra space does that. It also makes sense in very wide columns, so people can keep the long lines separated visually. You'll also find it in some layouts for parts of an introduction or other special elements that you want to call attention to. But you rarely find this amount of leading in regular body text.

Figure 40-3: The same type with different leading has a very different appearance.

✦ **Tracking.** *Tracking* determines the overall space between letters within a word.

✦ **Word spacing.** This defines the preferred, minimum, and maximum spacing between words.

✦ **Letter spacing.** Letter spacing (sometimes called character spacing) defines the preferred, minimum, and maximum spacing between letters.

Note   InDesign uses your preferred spacing specifications unless you justify the text or apply manual spacing adjustments; if you justify text, the program spaces letters and words within the limits you set for maximum and minimum spacing.

✦ **Kerning.** This refers to an adjustment of the space between two letters. You kern letters to accommodate their specific shapes. For example, you probably would use tighter kerning in the letter pair *to* than in *oo* because *to* looks better if the *o* fits partly under the cross of the *t*.

✦ **Pair kerning.** This is a table of characters, built into the font itself, that indicates the letter pairs you want the publishing program to kern automatically. InDesign lets you adjust the kerning on a case-by-case basis or for all highlighted text. Kerning is used most frequently in headlines where the letter spacing is more noticeable. See Figure 40-4 for an example of kerning.

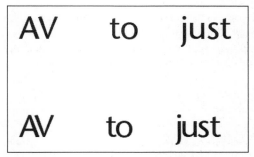

Figure 40-4: An example of unkerned (top) and kerned letter pairs

✦ **Justification.** Justification adds space between words (and sometimes between letters) so that each line of text aligns at both the left and right margin of a column or page. Justification also is used to refer to the type of spacing used for optimum letter and word spacing: justified, ragged right, centered, or ragged left (see the following definitions).

• **Ragged right and flush left.** Both these terms refer to text that aligns with a column's left margin but not its right margin.

• **Ragged left and flush right.** This refers to text that aligns with the right margin but not the left margin.

• **Centered.** This refers to text that aligns so that there is equal space on both margins.

• **Vertical justification.** This adds space between paragraphs (and sometimes between lines) so that the tops and bottoms of each column on a page align. (This term is often confused with column balancing, which ensures that each column has the same number of lines.)

• **Carding.** Carding is a vertical-justification method that adds space between paragraphs in one-line increments.

• **Feathering.** This is another vertical-justification method that uses fractional-line spaces between paragraphs.

Paragraphs

✦ **Indent.** You typically indicate a new paragraph with an indent, which inserts a space (often an em space in newspapers and magazines) in front of the paragraph's first letter.

✦ **First-line indent.** An indent that affects just the first line of the paragraph, typically used to show the start of a new paragraph. InDesign CS2 also has a similar feature to apply a righthand indent to only the last line of a paragraph.

✦ **Outdent, exdent.** An outdent (also called an exdent) shifts the first characters past the left margin and places the other lines at the left margin. This paragraph alignment is typically used in lists.

✦ **Block indent.** A block indent, a style often used for long quotes, moves an entire paragraph in from the left margin.

✦ **Hanging indent.** A hanging indent is like an outdent except that the first line begins at the left margin and all subsequent lines are indented.

✦ **Bullet.** This is a character (often a filled circle) used to indicate that a paragraph is one element in a list of elements. Bullets can be indented, outdented, or kept at the left margin.

✦ **Drop cap.** A drop cap is a large capital letter that extends down several lines into the surrounding text (the rest of the text wraps around it). Drop caps are used at the beginning of a section or story.

✦ **Raised cap.** A raised cap is the same as a drop cap except that it does not extend down into the text. Instead, it rests on the baseline of the first line and extends several lines above the baseline.

✦ **Style sheets, styles.** These contain named sets of such attributes as spacing, typeface, indent, leading, and justification. In Microsoft Word and QuarkXPress, each set of specifications is called a *style sheet*, while in InDesign, each set is called simply a *style*. Only those of us who remember the days before desktop publishing still think that *style sheet* means a collection of such sets.

Note   Essentially, styles are formatting macros. You *tag* each paragraph or character with the name of the style that you want to apply. Any formatting changes made to one paragraph or character are automatically reflected in all other paragraphs or characters tagged with the same style.

Hyphenation

✦ **Hyphen.** A hyphen is used to indicate the division of a word at the end of a line and to join words that combine to modify another word.

✦ **Hyphenation.** This determines where to place the hyphen in words that need to be split.

✦ **Consecutive hyphenation.** This determines how many lines in a row can end with a hyphen (more than three hyphens in a row is considered bad typographic practice).

✦ **Hyphenation zone.** The hyphenation zone determines how far from the right margin a hyphen can be inserted to split a word.

✦ **Exception dictionary.** An exception dictionary lists words with nonstandard hyphenations. You can add words that the publishing program's default dictionary does not recognize and override the default hyphenations for a word such as *project,* which is hyphenated one way as a noun (*proj-ect*) and another as a verb (*pro-ject*).

✦ **Discretionary hyphen.** Placing a discretionary hyphen (also called a *soft hyphen*) in a word tells the program to hyphenate the word at that place if the word must be split. A discretionary hyphen affects only the word in which it is placed.

Using Typographic Color and Typefaces

Throughout the history of publishing, professional typographers have enhanced the look of documents by selecting from a variety of fonts to produce a desired look, and by increasing or decreasing character spacing. When done correctly, character spacing gives a finished look. Words set in characters that are surrounded by generous amounts of space have a light, airy feel; words set in characters that are close together feel heavier and more serious.

Typographic color

As a group, four aspects (kerning, tracking, scale, and hyphenation) determine what typographers call *color,* simply another way of describing the overall quality or appearance of text on a page. If you want to see a document's typographic color, make your eyes go slightly out of focus. Here's a good way to understand the concept of typographic color: Find a magazine page that has a good amount of text on it. Stare at the page for two minutes or so. Then focus on something halfway between you and the page. You'll see the text blur. The resulting gray level and consistency is *color.* Why is a document's color so important? Because it affects both the document's mood and readability. For most publishing applications, a light to medium color is preferable because it is easier on the eye.

The influence of typeface

Factors in addition to character spacing influence color. The most fundamental factor is the typeface. An airy, light typeface such as Baskerville Old Face has a light color, while a solid, heavy typeface such as Franklin Gothic Heavy has a dark color. Figure 40-5 shows the same text in these two typefaces. Notice how the text on the right, in Baskerville, looks lighter than the Caslon 224 text on the left. The example shown in the figure clearly demonstrates that type fonts are major contributors to typographic color. Some typefaces are light; some are heavy. Regardless of a typeface's intrinsic weight, InDesign includes character spacing controls that let you modify a font's effect on typographic color.

Two decades ago, when they first began buying homes, the Donegans decided that creating a beautiful garden would be a weekend pastime they could share. "I hated boring yards!" Lorene, a writer who specializes in 19th century New York history, recalls. "Even though the yard was nearly two acres, we knew it could be a magic place."

Lorene and Joe shared a vision of natural foliage mixed with fragrant native flowers, with a border of wild raspberries. Together, the couple created a tranquil, comfortable garden that includes both annuals – many in raised beds – and perennials. Roses in many vivid colors add the final touch.

A major task for the retired couple each spring is the raking and removal of more than 100 garbage bags full of leaves, applied as a winter compost cover the previous fall to the many rose bushes. Eventually, the decomposing leaves become mulch used on perennials, except in winter, when the soil at the base of some bushes is kept bare.

Two decades ago, when they first began buying homes, the Donegans decided that creating a beautiful garden would be a weekend pastime they could share. "I hated boring yards!" Lorene, a writer who specializes in 19th century New York history, recalls. "Even though the yard was nearly two acres, we knew it could be a magic place."

Lorene and Joe shared a vision of natural foliage mixed with fragrant native flowers, with a border of wild raspberries. Together, the couple created a tranquil, comfortable garden that includes both annuals — many in raised beds — and perennials. Roses in many vivid colors add the final touch.

A major task for the retired couple each spring is the raking and removal of more than 100 garbage bags full of leaves, applied as a winter compost cover the previous fall to the many rose bushes. Eventually, the decomposing leaves become mulch used on perennials, except in winter, when the soil at the base of some bushes is kept bare.

Figure 40-5: Different typefaces produce different shades of typographic color.

Learning about Typefaces

The two basic types of typefaces are serif and sans serif. A serif typeface has horizontal lines (called *serifs*) extending from the edges of the character, such as at the bottom of a *p* or at the top of an *I*. A sans serif typeface does not have these lines (*sans* is French for *without*). There are more types of typefaces than just serif and sans serif, but these are all in the minority. Calligraphic, block, and other nonserif/non–sans serif typefaces usually have other elements that serve the purpose of serifs — extensions to the characters that add a distinctive character to the typeface. Another distinct type of typeface is the pi font, which is a font made up of themed symbols (anything from math to Christmas ornaments). The name *pi font* comes from the Greek letter pi (π), a common mathematical symbol.

Cross-Reference   For more on special characters such as symbols, see Chapter 41.

Typeface variations

A typeface usually has several variations, the most common of which are roman, italic, bold-face, and boldface italic for serif typefaces; and medium, oblique, boldface, and boldface oblique for sans serif typefaces. Italic and oblique differ in that italics are a curved variant of the typeface, with the serifs usually heavily curved, while an oblique is simply a slanted version of the typeface. Other variations that involve type weight include thin, light, book, demi-bold, heavy, ultrabold, and black. Compressed, condensed, expanded, and wide describe type scale.

InDesign will show all variations available for a font, as long as those variations are stored in the font file, not as a series of separate files. For example, if you have a font file named Big Bold and a separate font file named Big Semibold, they appear as two separate fonts in InDesign's menus and dialog boxes. But if you have a font file called Big that contains Big Normal, Big Light, Big Semibold, Big Bold, Big Ultra, and Big Compressed, all will appear as options for the font Big.

Understanding Typeface Formats

Typefaces come in several formats, with two predominating. InDesign supports them all, as long as your operating system or font-management utility does.

✦ **PostScript Type 1.** This is the publishing industry's standard for fonts. Anyone outputting to an imagesetter or other prepress device must use these fonts. PostScript Type 1 font support is native to Mac OS X. Windows does not support PostScript natively and so requires a font-management utility like Adobe Type Manager, Extensis Font Reserve, or Extensis Suitcase to work with PostScript fonts. Note that Adobe has ATM Light available for free download from its Web site at www.adobe.com.

✦ **TrueType.** Codeveloped by Microsoft and Apple Computer, this is the standard font format of Windows, and it also is supported natively on the Mac OS. However, TrueType fonts are not supported by most imagesetters and prepress devices, and their use in your layouts can cause output problems. Do not use them in any professionally published document.

✦ **OpenType.** This new version of PostScript, codeveloped by Adobe and Microsoft, combines some TrueType technology and is meant to eventually replace both Type 1 and TrueType. Its biggest asset is that it supports a wide range of international characters, symbols, and character variations within the same font, such as true small caps and ligatures — called *glyphs* as a group. Mac OS X, Windows 2000, and Windows XP support it natively, but you'll need to make sure that your imagesetter or other prepress device can handle them — at the time of this writing, many cannot. Over time, however, support for OpenType continues to increase. InDesign has strong support for OpenType, making all character and glyph attributes available in character formatting.

Note that Windows will display an icon letting you know what format a font is in, as the figure here shows. The code T1 stands for PostScript Type 1, TT for TrueType, and O for Open Type.

What's in a face?

Each of these variants, as well as each available combination of variants (for example, compressed light oblique), is called a *face*. Some typefaces have no variants; these are typically calligraphic typefaces, such as Park Avenue and Zapf Chancery, and symbol typefaces (pi fonts), such as Zapf Dingbats and Sonata. In Figure 40-6, you see samples of several typefaces and some of their variants. By using typeface variants wisely, you can create more-attractive and more-readable documents.

A font is a typeface by any other name

Desktop-publishing programs popularized the use of the term *font* to describe what traditionally was called a typeface. In traditional terms, a typeface refers to a set of variants for one style of text, such as Times Roman. A face is one of those variants, such as Times Roman

Italic. A font, in traditional terms, is a face at a specific point size, such as 12-point Times Roman Italic. (Until electronic typesetting was developed, printers set type using metal blocks that were available only in a limited range of sizes.) The word *font* today means what *typeface* used to mean, and almost no one uses *font* any more for its original meaning.

Figure 40-6: A variety of typefaces and their variants

The heart of a document is its typography. Everything else can be well laid out and illustrated, but if the text is not legible and appealing, all that other work is for naught. If you don't believe type is central, then consider this: You've surely seen engaging documents with no artwork, but have you ever seen artwork carry the day if the type is ugly or scrunched? I didn't think so.

Selecting the Right Typefaces

If you've ever seen a type chart, you already know that thousands of typefaces are available, each with a different feel. Matching the typeface's feel to the effect that you want for your document is a trial-and-error process. Until you are experienced at using a wide variety of typefaces (and even then), experiment with different typefaces on a mock-up of your document to see what works best.

Defining a standard set

I recommend that you take the time necessary to define a standard set of typefaces for each group of publications. You may want all employee newsletters in your company to have a similar feel, which you can achieve by using common body text and headline typefaces, even if layout and paragraph settings differ. The key to working with a standard set of typefaces is to avoid limiting the set to only a few typefaces. Selecting more typefaces than any one document might use gives you enough flexibility to be creative while providing an obviously standard appearance. You also can use the same typeface for different purposes. For example, you might use a newsletter's headline typeface as a kicker in a brochure. A consistent — but not constrained — appearance is a good way to establish an identity for your company.

Understanding Typeface Names

The many variants of typefaces confuse many users, especially because most programs use only the terms *roman* (or *normal* or plain), *italic* (or *oblique*), *bold,* and *bold italic* (or bold oblique) to describe available variations. When a typeface has more than these basic variations, programs usually split the typeface into several typefaces.

For example, in some programs, Helvetica comes as Helvetica, with medium, oblique, boldface, and boldface oblique faces; Helvetica Light/Black, with light, light oblique, black, and black oblique faces; Helvetica Light/Black Condensed, with condensed light, condensed light oblique, condensed black, and condensed black oblique faces; Helvetica Condensed, with condensed medium, condensed oblique, condensed boldface, and condensed boldface oblique faces; and Helvetica Compressed, with compressed medium and condensed oblique faces. When there are this many variations, you have to choose from among several Helvetica typefaces, and you have to know that, for example, selecting bold for Helvetica Condensed results in Helvetica Condensed Bold type.

For some typefaces, the variants are even more confusing. For example, in text, Bookman is usually printed in light face, which is lighter than the medium face. So when you select plain, you really select Bookman Light. And when you select bold, you really select Bookman Demibold. Bookman Medium and Bookman Bold are too heavy for use as body text, which is why the typeface comes in the light/demi combination of faces. Fortunately, the issue of what face a program designates as plain, italic, and the rest rarely comes into play. You usually encounter a problem only in one of the following situations:

✦ When you are exchanging files between PCs and Macs — because some vendors use slightly different names for their typefaces on different platforms. The Type ➪ Find Font option lets you correct this problem by replacing one typeface name with another in your document.

✦ When you are working with a service bureau that has typeface names that are different, or whose staff uses the traditional names rather than the desktop-publishing names.

✦ When you are working with artists or typesetters to match a typeface. Typically, the problem is a lack of familiarity with the different names for a typeface. The best way to reach a common understanding is to look at a sample of the typefaces being discussed.

You may have noticed that many people use serif typefaces for body copy and sans serif typefaces for headlines, pull-quotes, and other elements. But there is no rule you should worry about following. You can easily create engaging documents that use serif typefaces for every element. All–sans-serif documents are possible, but they are rare because sans serif typefaces tend to be hard to read when used in many pages of text. (Exceptions include typefaces such as News Gothic and Franklin Gothic, which were designed for use as body text.) No matter which typefaces you use, the key is to ensure that each element calls an appropriate amount of attention to itself.

Some basic guidelines

If you're feeling confused about which typeface is right for you, here are some basic guidelines:

✦ **Use a roman, medium, or book weight typeface for body text.** In some cases, a lightweight typeface works well, especially for typefaces such as Bookman and Souvenir, which tend to be heavy in the medium weights.

✦ **Output some samples before deciding on a light typeface for body text because many light typefaces are hard to read when used extensively.** Also, if you intend to output publications on an imagesetter (at 1,270 dpi or finer resolution), make sure that you output samples on that imagesetter because a light font may be readable on a 300- or 600-dpi laser printer but too light on a higher-resolution printer that can reproduce thin characters more faithfully than a laser printer. (The laser printer may actually print a light typeface as something a bit heavier: Because the width of the text's stroke is not an even multiple of the laser printer's dots, the printer has no choice but to make the stroke thicker than it should be.) Although 1,200-dpi laser printers are increasingly common, and make more accurate proofs than a 300- or 600-dpi model, note that imagesetters are still more accurate because they use smooth paper, which allows less distortion than the standard bond paper used in laser printers.

✦ **Use a heavier typeface for headlines and subheads.** A demibold or bold usually works well. Avoid using the same typeface for headlines and body text, even if it is a bolder variant. On the other hand, using the same typeface for subheads and headlines, even if in a different variant, helps ensure a common identity. (And if you mix typefaces, use those that have similar appearances. For example, use round typefaces with other round typefaces and squared-off typefaces with other squared-off typefaces.)

✦ **If captions are long (more than three lines), use a typeface with the same weight as body text.** If you use the same typeface as body text, differentiate the caption visually from body text. Using a boldface caption lead-in (the first words are boldface and act as a title for the caption) or putting the caption in italics distinguishes the caption from body text without being distracting. If captions are short (three lines or fewer), consider using a heavier face than body text or a typeface that is readily distinguished from your body text.

✦ **As a general rule, avoid using more than three typefaces (not including variants) in the main document elements (headlines, body text, captions, pull-quotes, and other elements that appear on most pages).** However, some typefaces are very similar, so you can use them as a group as if they were one. Examples include Helvetica, Univers, and Arial; Futura, Bauhaus, and Avant Garde; Times and its many relatives (including Times New Roman and Times Ten); Galliard and New Baskerville; Souvenir and Korinna; Benguiat, Americana, Garamond, Stone Serif, and Cheltenham; New Baskerville and Esprit; and Goudy Old Style and Century Old Style. You can treat the individual typefaces within these groups almost as variants of one another, especially if you use one of the individual typefaces in limited-length elements such as kickers, pull-quotes, and bylines.

✦ **Use italics for kickers, bylines, sidebar headlines, and pull-quotes.**

Summary

Typography is an often unappreciated component of a layout's visual style and character. Typefaces have distinct looks that can support or even create the publication's fundamental tone. The spacing of characters can also play a key role in the visual tone, or color, of typography.

Because fonts come in several formats, it's key to coordinate font usage with service bureaus and internal production departments. Generally speaking, only PostScript fonts should be used for files that will be output at a service bureau or production department. The common TrueType format should be reserved for personal and local documents printed from your own computer because most professional-class printers and typesetters do not support this format.

✦   ✦   ✦

Using Special Characters

InDesign has 18 different language versions available, covering American English, Brazilian Portuguese, British English, Castilian Spanish, central and eastern European (Czech, Greek, and Polish in one edition), Czech, Danish, Dutch, Finnish, French, German, Greek, Italian, Japanese, Middle Eastern Arabic, and Hebrew (in one edition), Norwegian, Polish, and Swedish. For North American users who want to use special characters — foreign letters, accents, and special symbols such as ¢, £, ©, and • — InDesign takes advantage of the Mac and Windows font standards to provide access to those glyphs as well. Typically, there are shortcuts to access such common glyphs, but for uncommon or specialty glyphs, you'll need to use specialized fonts, whether foreign-language or pi (symbol) fonts.

Tip InDesign lets you insert glyphs from the current font by choosing Type ⇨ Glyphs. But if you deal with such characters, you probably need to access them in other programs. In that case, a great tool for accessing special characters on the Macintosh is PopChar X, which adds a spot next to the Apple logo that, when clicked, opens a palette of all available characters for the current font. (Go to www.InDesignCentral.com for a link to this software.) Windows comes with a similar utility, Character Map, that is available by choosing Start ⇨ Accessories ⇨ Character Map. There's also a version of PopChar for Windows that's a bit easier to access than Character Map.

For quick access to frequently used glyphs (from multiple fonts), InDesign CS2 lets you create glyph sets.

To create glyph sets:

1. **Click New Glyph Set from the Glyphs pane's palette menu, as shown in Figure 41-1.** Choose Window ⇨ Type & Tables ⇨ Glyphs to open the pane.

2. **Type a name in the New Glyph Set dialog box, and click OK.**

3. **In the Glyphs pane, select the special character you want to add to your new set.** You may need to change the font and style using the pop-up menus at the bottom of the pane.

4. **In the pane's palette menu, choose Add to Glyph Set ⇨ *set name* to add the symbol to the chosen set.**

5. **Repeat Steps 3 and 4 for each glyph you want to add.**

6. **When done adding glyphs, choose Edit Glyph Set ⇨ *set name* to edit the glyph set.** This will open the Edit Glyph Set dialog box shown in Figure 41-2.

7. **If you want a specific font to be used for a glyph (which you'll need to do for symbols chosen from pi fonts, as opposed to common symbols like ™ available in most fonts), make sure that the Remember Font with Glyph option is selected.** You can also choose or change the font using the Font and Style pop-up menus in the dialog box.

8. **To delete a glyph, select it in the dialog box, and then click Delete from Set.**

9. **Click OK when done.**

Figure 41-1: Creating a new glyph set

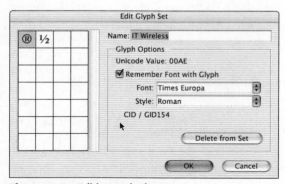

Figure 41-2: Editing a glyph set

To access a glyph set, simply click the desired glyph set from the Show pop-up menu in the Glyph pane. Make sure the Type tool is active and that the text cursor is active in a text frame or path. Double-click the desired glyph in the Glyphs pane; InDesign will insert it at the text cursor location.

Working with OpenType Variants

InDesign takes strong advantage of OpenType—but only if you let it. The OpenType font standard has been around for several years, but it is not used very much. One reason is that it requires publishers to replace their older fonts, which costs money for enhancements that everyone has lived without for years.

But OpenType offers compelling value, at least for some fonts. What OpenType provides is a greater variety of glyphs and glyph attributes than a standard font. For example, small caps, old-fashioned numerals (the kinds with superiors and denominators), true fractions, true superiors (used for footnotes and mathematics), and true ordinals (the raised or superscript *th* in *4th*) are just some of the examples. What's key is that you don't have to manually style such attributes for every occurrence, as you do with the so-called expert-collection fonts. Instead, InDesign will automatically apply the available attributes to selected text or to text whose character style engages specified OpenType features. (Note that any OpenType attribute in brackets is one unavailable for the current font.)

The results can be striking, as Figure 41-3 shows.

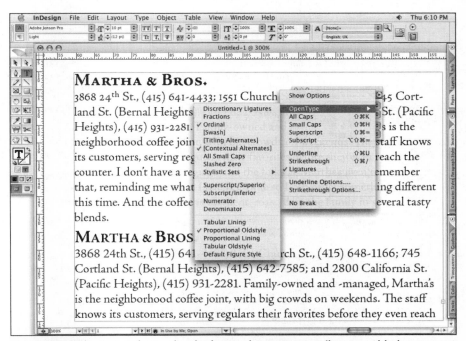

Figure 41-3: The text at the top has had several OpenType attributes enabled, as seen in the palette menu. The text at the bottom shows the same text with the normal attributes for the same font.

There are several types of OpenType attributes:

✦ **Discretionary ligatures.** This creates ligatures.

✦ **Fractions.** This substitutes true fractions such as ½ for the text *1/2*.

✦ **Ordinal.** This raises the *st*, *nd*, and *th* portions of ordinal numbers such as *1ˢᵗ*, *22ⁿᵈ*, and *345ᵗʰ*.

✦ **Swash.** This adds embellishments in front of the first character or at the end of the last letter of a word.

✦ **Titling Alternates.** This uses variants of a font for use in titles. These variants are usually a little clearer than the body-text version so they work better as titles where surrounding white space can make the normal variations within body text look strange.

✦ **Contextual Alternates.** This uses variants for specific characters to improve legibility in some contexts. For example, a contextual alternate for *t* might drop the left-side bar in the *t* so it doesn't bump against an adjacent letter.

✦ **All Small Caps.** This replaces all the text with true small caps, not the scaled-down version that the standard InDesign small-caps feature uses. True small caps are usually a little thicker than their scaled-down version, so they have the same visual weight as lowercase letters.

✦ **Slashed Zero.** This adds a slash over a 0 character for fonts that support it. The slashed zero is often used in European writing to differentiate from the letter *O*.

✦ **Superscript/Superior.** This replaces scaled-down raised text that InDesign uses to create superscripts with thicker characters placed where the font designers think works best. As with true small caps, this results in superscripts that have more visual weight.

✦ **Subscript/Inferior.** This replaces scaled-down lowered text that InDesign uses to create subscripts with thicker characters placed where the font designers think works best. As with true small caps, this results in subscripts that have more visual weight.

✦ **Numerator.** This is used to build a fraction when the font does not have predefined ones, such as for ⅓.

✦ **Denominator.** This is used to build a fraction when the font does not have predefined ones, such as for ¼.

✦ **Stylistic Sets.** This lets you choose which sets of variants within a font to use. A very few OpenType fonts, such as Poetica Std, use stylistic sets, which provide multiple variations of the same characters, letting you choose which variants to use.

✦ **Tabular Lining.** This uses standard numeric characters (which start on the baseline and have no descenders or ascenders) spaced evenly for proper alignment in tables.

✦ **Proportional Oldstyle.** This uses old-fashioned numerals with ascenders and descenders that are spaced like any other characters, based on their width, shape, and visual weight.

✦ **Proportional Lining.** This uses standard numerals spaced like any other characters, based on their width, shape, and visual weight.

✦ **Tabular Oldstyle.** This uses old-fashioned numerals spaced evenly for natural alignment in tables.

✦ **Default Figure Style.** This does whatever the font's designers want it to do by default (one of the above four settings).

The top text in Figure 41-3 shows the use of true small caps (in the name *Martha & Bros.*), ordinal numbers (the raised *th* in *24th*), and proportional old-style numerals (look at the address and phone numbers). The bottom text shows the same text without these effects.

Figure 41-4 shows the same text with a font that supports discretionary ligatures, contextual alternates, and swashes:

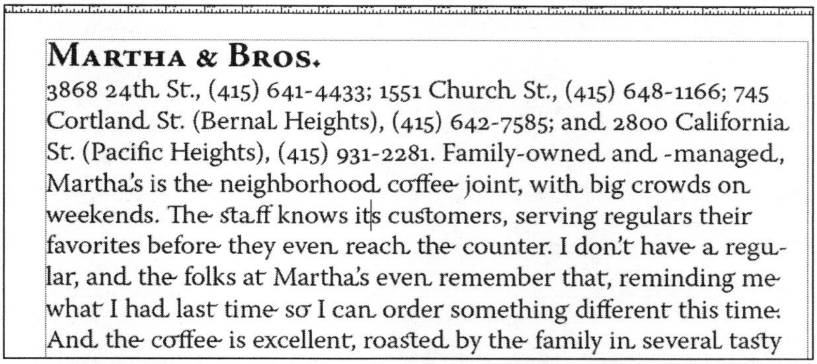

MARTHA & BROS.
3868 24th St., (415) 641-4433; 1551 Church St., (415) 648-1166; 745 Cortland St. (Bernal Heights), (415) 642-7585; and 2800 California St. (Pacific Heights), (415) 931-2281. Family-owned and -managed, Martha's is the neighborhood coffee joint, with big crowds on weekends. The staff knows its customers, serving regulars their favorites before they even reach the counter. I don't have a regular, and the folks at Martha's even remember that, reminding me what I had last time so I can order something different this time. And the coffee is excellent, roasted by the family in several tasty

Figure 41-4: The same text as in Figure 41-3, but using a different font that supports discretionary ligatures, contextual alternatives, and swashes (look for the embellishments that appear between characters and at the beginning and end of words).

✦ You can see contextual ligatures in many *st* combinations, such as the word *staff* on the sixth line (which begins with the word *weekend*).

✦ You can see a contextual alternate by looking at the *t* in the abbreviation *St.* that begins the fourth line. Compare that embellished *t* with the *t* in the word *Heights* on the same line: the alternate used in *St.* extends the *t*'s bar to extend over the adjacent period, while the normal *t* in *Heights* does not.

✦ In this figure, many words use swashes at the end or beginning, such as in the last line's *And the coffee*, *roasted*, *the*, and *in several* text fragments.

Shortcuts for Symbols

Symbols are commonly used in all sorts of documents, from legal symbols to scientific ones. That's why most fonts have a selection of popular symbols built in. Table 41-1 shows the common symbols for Windows and Macintosh fonts (In Windows, shortcuts that begin with Alt and are followed by a number are entered this way: Hold Alt down, and then type in a number using the numeric keypad, then release Alt.).

Table 41-1: Shortcuts for Symbols

Character	Mac Shortcut	Windows Shortcut
Legal		
Copyright (©)	Option+G	Shift+Alt+C *or* Ctrl+Alt+C *or* Alt+0169
Registered trademark (®)	Option+R	Shift+Alt+R *or* Alt+0174
Trademark (™)	Option+2	Shift+Alt+2 *or* Alt+0153
Paragraph (¶)	Option+7	Shift+Alt+7 *or* Ctrl+Alt+; *or* Alt+0182
Section (§)	Option+6	Shift+Alt+6 *or* Alt+0167
Dagger (†)	Option+T	Shift+Alt+T *or* Alt+0134
Double dagger (‡)	Option+Shift+T	Alt+0135
Currency		
Cent (¢)	Option+4	Alt+0162
Euro (€)	Option+Shift+2	Alt+Ctrl+5
Pound sterling (£)	Option+3	Alt+0163
Yen (¥)	Option+Y	Ctrl+Alt+- (hyphen) *or* Alt+0165
Punctuation		
En bullet (•)	Option+8	Alt+8 *or* Alt+0149
Thin bullet (·)	not supported*	Alt+0183
Ellipsis (…)	Option+; (semicolon)	Alt+0133
Measurement		
Foot (')	Control+'	Ctrl+'
Inch (")	Control+Shift+'	Ctrl+Alt+'
Mathematics		
One-half fraction (½)	*not supported*	Ctrl+Alt+6 *or* Alt+0189
One-quarter fraction (¼)	*not supported*	Ctrl+Alt+7 *or* Alt+0188
Three-quarters fraction (¾)	*not supported*	Ctrl+Alt+8 *or* Alt+0190
Infinity (∞)	Option+5	*not supported*
Multiplication (×)	*not supported*	Ctrl+Alt+= *or* Alt+0215
Division (÷)	Option+/	Alt+0247
Root (√)	Option+V	*not supported*

Character	Mac Shortcut	Windows Shortcut
Mathematics		
Greater than or equal to (≥)	Option+. (period)	*not supported*
Less than or equal to (≤)	Option+, (comma)	*not supported*
Inequality (≠)	Option+=	*not supported*
Rough equivalence (≈)	Option+X	*not supported*
Plus or minus (±)	Option+Shift+=	Alt+0177
Logical not (¬)	Option+L	Ctrl+Alt+\ *or* Alt+0172
Per mil (‰)	Option+Shift+R	Alt+0137
Degree (°)	Option+Shift+8	Alt+0176
Function (ƒ)	Option+F	Alt+0131
Integral (∫)	Option+B	*not supported*
Variation (∂)	Option+D	*not supported*
Greek beta (ß)	Option+S	*not supported*
Greek mu (µ)	Option+M	Alt+0181
Greek Pi (Π)	Option+Shift+P	*not supported*
Greek pi (π)	Option+P	*not supported*
Greek Sigma (Σ)	Option+W	*not supported*
Greek Omega (Ω)	Option+Z	*not supported*
Miscellaneous		
Apple logo ( )	Option+Shift+K	*not supported*
Light (¤)	*not supported*	Ctrl+Alt+4 *or* Alt+0164
Open diamond (◊)	Option+Shift+V	*not supported*

Shortcuts for Foreign Characters

Although most American publishers don't produce work in other languages, they may still use accents in their work. And, of course, many publishers do publish in other languages, such as Spanish, French, German, and Portuguese, because they do business with customers in multiple countries. Even all-English publishers may choose to use accents in foreign words like *café* to help pronunciation and show a bit of international flair.

See Table 41-2 for foreign-language characters. Note that Windows shortcuts involving four numerals (such as Alt+0157) should be entered from the numeric keypad while holding the Alt key.

Tip   If your font doesn't have the accented characters you need, you may be able to create them by kerning accent marks over the letters. See Chapter 17 for detailed information on kerning.

Table 41-2: Shortcuts for Accents and Foreign Characters

Character	Mac Shortcut	Windows Shortcut
acute (´)*	Option+E *letter*	' *letter*
cedilla (¸)*	*see Ç and ç*	' *letter*
circumflex (ˆ)*	Option+I *letter*	^ *letter*
grave (`)*	Option+` *letter*	` *letter*
tilde (˜)*	Option+N *letter*	~ *letter*
trema (¨)*	Option+U *letter*	" *letter*
umlaut (¨)*	Option+U *letter*	" *letter*
Á	Option+E A	' A *or* Alt+0193
á	Option+E a	' a *or* Alt+0225
À	Option+` A	` A *or* Alt+0192
à	Option+` a	` a *or* Alt+0224
Ä	Option+U A	" A *or* Alt+0196
ä	Option+U a	" a *or* Alt+0228
Ã	Option+N A	~ A *or* Alt+0195
ã	Option+N a	~ a *or* Alt+0227
Â	Option+I A	^ A *or* Alt+0194
â	Option+I a	^ a *or* Alt+0226
Å	Option+Shift+A	Alt+0197
å	Option+A	Alt+0229
Æ	Option+Shift+'	Alt+0198
æ	Option+'	Alt+0230 *or* Ctrl+Alt+Z
Ç	Option+Shift+C	' C *or* Alt+0199
ç	Option+C	' c *or* Alt+0231 *or* Ctrl+Alt+,
Ð	*not supported*	Alt+0208
đ	*not supported*	Alt+0240

Character	Mac Shortcut	Windows Shortcut
É	Option+E E	' E *or* Alt+0201
é	Option+E e	' e *or* Alt+0233
È	Option+` E	` E *or* Alt+0200
è	Option+` e	` e *or* Alt+0232
Ë	Option+U E	" E *or* Alt+0203
ë	Option+U e	" e *or* Alt+0235
Ê	Option+I E	^ E *or* Alt+0202
ê	Option+I e	^ e *or* Alt+0234
Í	Option+E I	' I *or* Alt+-205
í	Option+E i	' i *or* Alt+0237
Ì	Option+ ` I	` I *or* Alt+0204
ì	Option+` i	` i *or* Alt+0236
Ï	Option+U I	" I *or* Alt+0207
ï	Option+U i	" I *or* Alt+0239
Î	Option+I I	^ I *or* Alt+0206
î	Option+I i	^ I *or* Alt+0238
Ñ	Option+N N	~ N *or* Alt+0209
ñ	Option+N n	~ n *or* Alt+0241
Ó	Option+E O	' O *or* Alt+0211
ó	Option+E o	' o *or* Alt+0243 *or* Ctrl+Alt+O
Ò	Option+` O	` O *or* Alt+0210
ò	Option+` o	` o *or* Alt+0242
Ö	Option+U O	" O *or* Alt+0214
ö	Option+U o	" o *or* Alt+0246
Õ	Option+N O	~ O *or* Alt+0213
õ	Option+N o	~ o *or* Alt+0245
Ô	Option+I O	^ O *or* Alt+0212
ô	Option+I o	^ o *or* Alt+0244
Ø	Option+Shift+O	Alt+0216
ø	Option+O	Alt+0248 *or* Ctrl+Alt+L
Œ	Option+Shift+Q	Alt+0140
œ	Option+Q	Alt+0156

Continued

Table 41-2 *(continued)*

Character	Mac Shortcut	Windows Shortcut
Þ	*not supported*	Alt+0222
þ	*not supported*	Alt+0254
ß	not supported	Ctrl+Alt+S or Alt+0223
Š	*not supported*	Alt+0138
š	*not supported*	Alt+0154
Ú	Option+E U	' U or Alt+0218
ú	Option+E u	' u or Alt+0250 *or* Ctrl+Alt+U
Ù	Option+` U	` U or Alt+0217
ù	Option+` u	` u or Alt+0249
Ü	Option+U U	" U or Alt+0220
ü	Option+U u	" u or Alt+0252
Û	Option+I U	^ U or Alt+0219
û	Option+I u	^ u or Alt+0251
Ý	*not supported*	' Y or Alt+0221
ý	*not supported*	' y or Alt+0253
Ÿ	Option+U Y	" Y or Alt+0159
ÿ	Option+U y	" y *or* Alt+0255
Ž	*not supported*	Alt+0142
ž	*not supported*	Alt+0158
Spanish open exclamation (¡)	Option+1	Ctrl+Alt+1 *or* Alt+-0161
Spanish open question (¿)	Option+Shift+/	Ctrl+Alt+/ *or* Alt+0191
French open double quote («)	Option+\	Ctrl+Alt+[*or* Alt+0171
French close double quote (»)	Option+Shift+\	Ctrl+Alt+] *or* Alt+0187

* On the Mac, enter the shortcut for the accent and then type the letter to be accented. For example, to get é, type Option+E and then the letter e. In Windows, if the keyboard layout is set to United States-International — via the Keyboard icon in the Windows Control Panel — you can enter the accent signifier and then type the letter (for example, type ` and then the letter e to get è). To avoid an accent (for example, if you want the begin a quote — such as "A man" rather than have Ä man" — type a space after the accent character — for example, " then space, then A, rather than " then A.

European Languages and Accented Characters

Using accents in foreign words is great, but many Americans use them incorrectly, which is embarrassing. Although I can't tell you how to properly spell and accent every foreign word (a good dictionary for that language can!), I can tell you which accented characters are used in European languages. If you're using a word from one of the languages here and that word uses an accented character not shown for the language, you either have the wrong accent or that word is actually from a different language. I've also indicated which countries use the euro currency symbol (€) by including that symbol in their lists, and special currency symbols for other nations.

Many of the characters shown here are not available in standard PostScript and TrueType fonts. Most are available in OpenType fonts, though not in every case. You may need a special font for the specific language to get all the characters.

Albanian: ç, ë

Basque (Euskara): ñ, €

Breton: â, ê, è, ñ, ô, ù, ü, €

Catalan: à, ç, è, é, í, ï, l·, ò, ó, ú, ü, €

Croatian: c, č, đ, š, ž

Czech: á, č, d', é, ě, í, ň, ř, š, ť, ú, ů, ý, ž

Danish: å, æ, é, ø, ú

Dutch: á, â, è, é, ê, ë, í, ï, ij, ó, ô, ö, ú, û, €

English, American and Canadian: $, ¢

English, British: ö, £

English, Old: ð, þ

Estonian: ä, õ, ö, s, ž

Faroese: á, æ, ð, í, ó, ø, ú, ý

Finnish: ä, ö, €

French: à, â, æ, è, é, ê, ë, ç, î, ï, ô, ö, œ, ù, û, ü, ÿ, «, », €

Frisian: â, ê, î, ô, ú, û

Gaelic (Scots): à, á, è, é, ì, ò, ó, ù, £

German: ä, ö, ß, ü, €

Hungarian: á, é, i', ó, ö, ő, ú, ü, ű

Icelandic: á, æ, é, ð, í, ó, ö, þ, ú, ý

Continued

Continued

Irish: á, é, í, ó, ú, €

Italian: à, è, ì, í, ò, ó, ù, €

Latvian: a, č, ē, ģ, ī, ļ, ņ, š, ū, ž

Lithuanian: a, č, ę, è, į, š, ų, ū, ž

Luxembourgean: ä, ë, é, ï, ö, ü, €

Maltese: à, ċ, è, ġ, ħ, î, ì, ò, ù, ż

Norwegian: å, ø, æ

Occitan (Provençal): á, à, ç, é, è, í, ó, ò, ú, €

Polish: ą, ć, ę, ł, ń, ó, ś, ź, ż

Portuguese: à, á, â, ã, é, ê, ç, í, ñ, ó, ô, ô, õ, Ú, ü, €

Rhaeto-Roman: à, è, é, ì, î, ò, ù

Romanian: â, ă, î, ş, ţ

Slovak: á, ä, č, ď, é, í, Í, ľ, ń, ó, ô, ŕ, š, ť, ú, ý, ž

Slovenian: c, š, ž

Spanish (Castilian, Galician): á, é, í, ñ, ó, ú, ü, ¿, ¡, €

Swedish: å, ä, é, ö

Turkish: â, ç, ğ, î, ı, ö, ş, û, ü

Welsh: à, á, â, ä, è, é, ê, ë, ì, í, î, ï, ò, ó, ô, ö, ù, ú, û, ü, ŷ, ý, ŷ, ÿ, £

A great source for information on foreign characters and fonts is the Yamada Language Center, accessible on the Web at `http://babel.uoregon.edu/yamada/fonts.html`.

Summary

Windows and Macintosh fonts come with a wealth of special characters called glyphs, but they are usually accessible only with special codes or shortcuts. Plus, not all fonts support all glyphs. Similarly, the Mac OS and Windows support different glyphs. This makes it important to use the same symbol fonts on both platforms and to be sure that you know the glyphs you use are available in all the fonts you use.

✦   ✦   ✦

Color Fundamentals

You see color every day, so it probably seems like working with it should come naturally. But color is a complex issue in printing, involving both physics and chemistry. The inks that produce color are designed chemically to retain those colors and to produce them evenly, so your images don't look mottled or faded. How light reflects off of ink and paper to your eye determines the color you see, and many factors (particularly different textures of paper) can affect the physics of how the light carries the color.

You also have implementation issues to consider: How many colors can your printing press produce, and how much will it cost? When do you decide to go for the exact pure color, and when do you decide to go with a close-enough version that costs less to print?

This chapter explains the basic theory behind color and InDesign's use of it. Although color is part of your everyday life, in order to get it to look the way you want in your printed pieces you need a solid understanding of how it works.

In This Chapter

Getting acquainted with color terminology

Making sense of process and spot colors

Working with color models in InDesign

Defining Color Terms

Color is an expansive (and sometimes confusing and esoteric) concept in the world of publishing. The following definitions, however, should start you on your way to a clear understanding of the subject:

Cross-Reference Chapter 8 covers defining and using color in InDesign.

+ **Build:** Attempts to simulate a color-model color by overprinting the appropriate percentages of the four process colors.

+ **CIE LAB:** A standard that specifies colors by one lightness coordinate and two color coordinates — green-red and blue-yellow. The first part of the name means Commission Internationale de l'Éclairage (International Committee on Illumination), an international standards group, and the second part refers to the mathematical approach used to describe the colors in a cubic arrangement: luminance, *a*-axis, and *b*-axis.

+ **CMYK:** A standard that specifies colors as combinations of cyan, magenta, yellow, and black. These four colors are known as *process colors*.

✦ **Color gamut:** The range of colors that a device, such as a monitor or a color printer, can produce. Each color model has a different color gamut.

✦ **Color model:** An industry standard for specifying a color, such as CMYK or Pantone.

✦ **Color separation:** A set of four photographic negatives — one filtered for each process color — shot from a color photograph or image. When overprinted, the four negatives reproduce that original image.

✦ **Color space:** A method of representing color in terms of measurable values, such as the amount of red, yellow, and blue in a color image. The color space RGB represents the red, green, and blue colors on video screens.

✦ **Four-color printing:** The use of the four process colors in combination to produce most other colors.

✦ **Hexachrome:** Pantone's six-color alternative to CMYK. It adds green and orange inks for more accurate color reproduction in those hues, as well as enhanced versions of black, magenta, cyan, and yellow inks. (InDesign does not support Hexachrome unless you use a third-party utility.)

✦ **Process color:** Any of the four primary colors in publishing — cyan, magenta, yellow, and black (known collectively as CMYK). A six-color, high-fidelity variant produced by Pantone is called Hexachrome.

✦ **RGB:** The standard used by monitors, and the abbreviation from the three colors in it: red, green, and blue. One of the biggest hurdles to producing color documents that look as you'd expect is that computers use RGB while printers use CMYK, and the two don't always produce colors at the same hue.

✦ **Spot color:** A single color applied at one or more places on a page, such as for a screen or as part of an illustration. You can use more than one spot color per page. Spot colors can also be process colors.

✦ **Swatchbook:** A table of colors collected together as a series of color samples. The printer uses premixed ink based on the color model identifier you specify; you look up the numbers for various colors in the table of colors in a swatchbook.

Understanding Process and Spot Color

Let's briefly explore the differences between spot and process colors, the two primary ways of indicating color in print documents.

Identifying methods of color printing

Several forms of color are used in printing, but the two most-used ones are process color and spot color.

Process color is the use of four basic colors — cyan, magenta, yellow, and black (known collectively as CMYK) — that are mixed to reproduce most color tones the human eye can see. A separate negative is produced for each of the four process colors. This method, often called *four-color printing,* is used for most color publishing.

Spot color is any color ink — whether one of the process colors or some other hue — used for specific elements in a document. For example, if you print a document in black ink but print the company logo in red, the red is a spot color. A spot color is often called a *second color* even though you can use several spot colors in a document. Each spot color is output to its own negative (and not color-separated into CMYK). Using spot color gives you access to special inks that are truer to the desired color than any mix of process colors can be. These inks come in several standards. Basically, spot-color inks can produce some colors that are impossible to achieve with process colors, such as metallics, neons, and milky pastels. You even can use varnishes as spot colors to give layout elements a different gleam from the rest of the page. Although experienced designers sometimes mix spot colors to produce special shades not otherwise available, you probably won't need to do so.

There are several advantages to spot colors. You can use colors like metallic inks that are impossible to create with CMYK. Also, your printed results will be more consistent than with CMYK separations, which can suffer from *color shift* (variation in the hue produced) over the length of a long printed piece. But spot colors work only in objects that have distinct, continuous hue — such as a solid brick red — that can be printed with just one ink. To produce any image with multiple colors, such as a photograph, you need to use multiple inks, and because printing presses can traditionally print only four to eight colors on a page, you have to mix colors to create the range of hues in such multicolor objects.

Mixing spot and process colors

Some designers use both process and spot colors in a document in a procedure known as using a *fifth color*. Typically, the normal color images are color-separated and printed using the four process colors, while a special element (such as a logo in metallic ink) is printed in a spot color. The process colors are output on the usual four negatives; the spot color is output on a separate, fifth negative and printed using a fifth plate, a fifth ink roller, and a fifth inkwell. You can use more than five colors, however; you're limited only by your budget and the capabilities of your printing plant. (Most commercial printers can handle six colors for each run through the press, and larger ones often can handle as many as eight colors.)

Converting spot color to process color

InDesign can convert spot colors to process colors. This handy capability lets designers specify the colors they want through a system with which they're familiar, such as Pantone, without the added expense of special spot-color inks and extra negatives. Conversions are never an exact match, but guidebooks are available that can show you in advance the color that will be created. And with Pantone Process variation, which InDesign supports, designers can pick a Pantone color that will color-separate predictably.

You can set InDesign to convert some spot colors in a document to process colors while leaving others alone. (For example, you would keep a metallic silver as a spot color so it prints with a metallic ink, rather than be converted to a grayish color that is the closest the CMYK colors can produce to simulate a silver. But you would convert common colors like deep blue, purple, and green to process colors, because the CMYK inks can combine fairly accurately to reproduce them.) You can also leave all spot colors as spot colors or convert all spot colors to process colors.

Working with Color Models

Once you understand color terminology — and the difference between process and spot colors — you can start thinking about the type of colors you create in InDesign. (You define colors in the Swatches pane.) The color models fall into two broad classes:

✦ Those that let you define a color by selecting a color from a *color wheel* (which represents a spectrum of available colors) or by entering specific values for the color's *constituent colors* (the colors that make up the color), which include CMYK, RGB, LAB, and Multi-Ink.

✦ Those that have a predefined set of colors, which you select from a palette of swatches. These swatches include ANPA, Focoltone, Trumatch, DIC (Dainippon Ink & Chemical), Toyo seven variants of Pantone, and four variants of HKS. There are also two sets of colors meant for use on the Web.

 Note   Most North American publishers use Pantone color models. Focoltone, HKS, and Trumatch tend to be used in Europe. DIC, Focoltone, and Toyo tend to be used in Asia. ANPA is used by North American newspapers. And everyone uses CMYK.

Keep in mind that the colors displayed are only on-screen representations; the actual colors may be different. The differences are particularly noticeable if your monitor is running in 8-bit (256 hues) color mode. Check the actual color in a color swatchbook for the model you are using. (Art and printing supply stores usually carry these swatchbooks. See the sidebar "Using Color Swatchbooks" for lists of other sources.) You can also calibrate your monitor display with tools from X-Rite (www.xrite.com); this keeps the colors as close as possible to actual output.

 Tip   InDesign uses the same swatch format as Illustrator, so you can add color models to InDesign created in or for Illustrator. Use the Other Library option in the New Swatch dialog box to select these other color models (from the Swatches pane, select New Swatch from the palette menu to open the New Swatch dialog box). InDesign CS2 also adds support for the new Adobe Swatch Exchange format that all Adobe Creative Suite 2 applications support for color exchange.

Paper Variation Models

Both the Pantone and HKS color models recognize that the type of paper on which you print affects how a color appears, so they have variations based on popular paper types. Here's how they work:

✦ **Pantone Process Coated:** Use this variant when you color-separate Pantone colors and your printer uses the standard Pantone-brand process-color inks on coated paper. Colors in this variant have the code DS added *before* the numerals in their names and the code C *after* the numerals.

✦ **Pantone Solid Coated:** Use this variant when your printer uses actual Pantone-brand inks (as spot colors) when printing to coated paper stock. Colors in this variant have the code C appended to their names.

Using Color Swatchbooks

Anyone who uses a lot of color should have a color swatchbook handy. You probably can get one at your local art supply store or from your commercial printer (prices typically range from $50 to $100, depending on the color model and the type of swatchbook). But if you can't find a swatchbook, here's where to order the most popular ones:

✦ **Pantone:** Several Pantone swatchbooks are available, including ones for coated and uncoated paper, and for spot-color output and process-color output. If you are converting (called *building* in publishing parlance) Pantone colors to CMYK for four-color printing, I particularly recommend the *Pantone Process Color Imaging Guide: CMYK Edition* or the *Pantone Process Color System Guide* swatchbooks. Pantone, 590 Commerce Blvd., Carlstadt, NJ 07072-3098; phone: 201-935-5500; fax: 201-935-3338; Internet: www.pantone.com.

✦ **Hexachrome:** Pantone also created the Hexachrome standard and sells Hexachrome swatchbooks, as well as the $299 HexWare software that adds Hexachrome output capability to Adobe Photoshop and Illustrator. Because InDesign uses Illustrator color swatch files, you can add Hexachrome support to InDesign via HexWare. (See the contact information for Pantone in the preceding bullet.)

✦ **Trumatch:** Based on a CMYK color space, Trumatch suffers almost no matching problems when converted to CMYK. Variants of the swatchbooks for coated and uncoated paper are available. Trumatch, 50 E. 72nd St. #15B, New York, NY 10021; phone: 800-878-9100; fax: 212-517-2237; Internet: www.trumatch.com.

✦ **ANPA:** Designed for reproduction on newsprint, these colors also are designed in the LAB color space. Newspaper Association of America, 1921 Gallows Rd., Suite 600, Vienna, VA 22182-3900; phone: 703-902-1600; fax: 703-917-0636; Internet: www.naa.org.

✦ **Focoltone:** Like Trumatch, this color model is based on the CMYK color space. A & P Publishing Network, No. 6 Aljunied Ave. 3 #01-02, Singapore 389932; phone: +65-6746-0188; fax: +65-6746-1890; Internet: www.apmedia.com.

✦ **HKS:** This new-to-InDesign color model is used mainly in Germany and other European countries, with variants for industrial printing such as on plastics. It uses various combinations of cyan, magenta, and yellow with black overlays to achieve different shades. Hostmann-Steinberg, Bremer Weg 125, D-29223 Celle, Germany; phone: +49-5141-591-0; fax: +49-5141-591-202; Internet: www.hks-colour.de.

✦ **Dainippon Ink & Chemical (DIC):** Like Pantone, the DIC color set is a spot –color–based system. Dainippon Ink & Chemical Americas, 222 Bridge Plaza South, Fort Lee, NJ 07024; phone: 201-592-5100; fax: 201-592-8232; Internet: http://dicwww01.dic.co.jp/eng/index.html.

✦ **Toyo:** Similar to Pantone in that it is based on spot-color inks, this model is popular in Japan. Toyo Ink America, 710 W. Belden, Addison, IL 60101; phone: 630-930-5100; Internet: www.toyoink.com.

✦ **Pantone Solid Matte:** This is the same as Pantone Coated but for paper with a matte finish. Colors in this variant have the code M appended to their names.

✦ **Pantone Solid Uncoated:** This is the same as Pantone Solid Coated but for uncoated paper. Colors in this variant have the code U appended to their names.

✦ **Pantone Coated:** This is the generic Pantone coated color model, for use on any kind of paper. Colors in this variant have the code CVC appended to their names.

✦ **Pantone Process:** This is the generic Pantone process color model, for use on any kind of paper. Colors in this variant have the code CVS appended to their names.

✦ **Pantone Uncoated:** This is the generic Pantone uncoated color model, for use on any kind of paper. Colors in this variant have the code CVU appended to their names.

✦ **HKS E:** Use this HKS variant for continuous-form stationery. Colors in this variant have the code E appended to their names.

✦ **HKS K:** Use this HKS variant for glossy art paper (highly coated). Colors in this variant have the code K appended to their names.

✦ **HKS N:** Use this HKS variant for natural paper (uncoated). Colors in this variant have the code N appended to their names.

✦ **HKS Z:** Use this HKS variant for newsprint. Colors in this variant have the code Z appended to their names.

Note   When printing on uncoated stock with any colors designed for use on coated stock, you will usually get weaker, less-saturated color reproduction.

Summary

Using color in publishing involves complex decisions. There are many ways to define colors, but they don't all result in the same colors when you finally print your documents. That's why choosing the color models for your documents up front is important.

Color can also be expensive to print, so you may need to weigh when you use color and how you apply it. A spot color—a single ink—is cheaper to print than full color (produced by combining four or six process colors) but, of course, gives you less visual flexibility. You can also mix spot colors with process colors to add special colors such as pastels and metallics that process colors cannot produce.

✦   ✦   ✦

Appendixes

✦ ✦ ✦ ✦

In This Part

Appendix A
Installing or Upgrading
InDesign

Appendix B
What's New in
InDesign CS2

Appendix C
Switching from
QuarkXPress

Appendix D
Switching from
PageMaker

Appendix E
Using Adobe
InCopy CS2

Appendix F
More Resources

Appendix G
Shortcuts Cheat Sheet

✦ ✦ ✦ ✦

Installing or Upgrading InDesign

Installing InDesign CS2 is surprisingly easy. Before installing or upgrading, make sure your system meets the InDesign CS2 system requirements (most computer systems since 1997 will). Then use the steps in this appendix to make quick work of the installation process. If you're upgrading from an earlier version, you'll actually perform a new installation. But read the section on upgrading at the end of this appendix for information about making the transition to InDesign CS2.

InDesign CS2 System Requirements

InDesign CS2 does not require extraordinary resources — if you have a Mac or PC that runs one of the required operating systems, you can run InDesign CS2. Just be sure to have enough hard-drive space and memory to be able to work with large images, many fonts, and multiple projects, as well as to have multiple applications like Adobe Photoshop open at the same time.

Here are the official requirements:

- ✦ For Macintosh systems, a PowerPC G3, G4, or G5 processor running Mac OS X version 10.2 (Jaguar) or later

- ✦ For Windows systems, an Intel Pentium II, III, or 4, or AMD K6, Athlon, Athlon XP, or Athlon 64 processor running Windows 2000 Service Pack 2 or later, or running Windows XP or later

- ✦ At least 350MB of free hard-drive space on the Mac and 312MB of free hard-drive space in Windows for installation (installation also requires free disk space on the startup drive, even if you install InDesign CS2 software on a different drive)

- ✦ 128MB of RAM

- ✦ Eight-bit color depth (256 colors) at 1024-×-768 monitor resolution

- ✦ For PostScript printing, Adobe PostScript Language Level 2 or Adobe PostScript 3

- ✦ For the eBook and other multimedia features, QuickTime 6

Note InDesign CS2 runs only on Mac OS X 10.2 and later (and only in native mode, not in Classic mode), Windows 2000, and Windows XP. You must use InDesign 2 for earlier versions of Mac and Windows.

Cross-Reference See Chapter 38 for advice on the computer, operating system, and amount of RAM you need to run InDesign, as well as advice on hardware peripherals and software options.

Installing InDesign CS2

Both the Mac OS and Windows installers for InDesign CS2 provide easy-to-follow on-screen instructions. Before beginning the installation process, make sure you have your serial number provided by Adobe.

Tip Both installers provide a Custom Install option that lets you decide what to install with InDesign. Even if you're not sure whether you want all the InDesign plug-ins, filters, and the other items, you may want to install them anyway. Installing more than you absolutely need is better than not having a feature or information available when you need it. (You can always disable plug-ins and filters via InDesign ➪ Configure Plug-ins on the Mac or Help ➪ Configure Plug-ins in Windows, as covered in Chapter 36.)

1. **Insert the CD in the CD-ROM drive or access the CD over the network.** If necessary, double-click the CD icon to open the CD.

2. **Double-click the installer program.** On the Mac, you may be asked for a system password to allow the installation of new software.

3. **The InDesign installer will ask you what language to install, US English or International English; choose one and click Continue.** International English is British English, used in the United Kingdom, Canada, Australia, and most former British colonies.

4. **Read the License Agreement, and click Accept to continue.** If you want to file this information, click Print to create a hard copy.

5. **In the next dialog box, type your name, company (leave blank if you're an individual, such as a self-employed designer), and your serial number, and then click Continue.** A new dialog box appears where you can confirm your name, company, and serial number. If correct, click Continue; if incorrect, click Back. You'll also be given the chance to register your copy of InDesign or to skip registration for a later time.

6. **The next dialog box gives you the opportunity to decide where to install InDesign; select the location and click Next.**

   • By default, the installer places InDesign in the Applications folder (Mac) or Program Files\Adobe folder (Windows) on your startup hard drive. If you want to change the location (for example, to your Applications folder), choose Select Folder from the Install Location menu. Select or create another folder, and click Select.

- If you're short on hard-drive space — or you're very confident that the installation includes items you don't need — click Custom Install from the menu at the top of the dialog box. Click the arrow next to InDesign CS2 to see all the options. Deselect any items that you don't want to install. If you need more information about an item to make this decision, click the **i** button next to the item.

7. **When you've decided what to install and where to install it, click Install.** The installation should take only a few minutes.

8. **When the installation is complete, an alert tells you that you will need to activate your software to be able to use it beyond 30 days.** It takes just a few seconds to run through that activation process, which downloads a unique ID from Adobe's servers to your computer, so if someone else installs InDesign from the same CD you did, the Adobe server will see the additional installation and check further. You can upgrade major pieces of hardware without requiring reactivation, and you may install the software on two computers (typically a desktop and a laptop) per the Adobe software license. If the Adobe server thinks you are trying to install a third copy, it will require you to call Adobe for reactivation, so a technician can determine whether you are simply trying to reinstall the program on a replacement computer or if you really are installing a third copy. (If you don't activate during installation, you have just 30 days to so afterwards. Choose Help ⇨ .Activate to run the activation program.)

New Feature   Product activation is new to InDesign CS2.

9. **The installer will also ask if you want to register online. If you have an Internet connection and are ready to register, click Yes.** This launches your default browser and takes you through the registration process. After you register online, an alert may prompt you to restart your computer, depending on whether system-level files were installed. Unlike activation, registration is optional, and lets Adobe know who is entitled to technical support.

When you first launch InDesign after installing it, you'll get the dialog box that appears in Figure A-1. Its options include creating new documents, opening documents, and seeing information on new features. If you don't want one of these options, you can just go to the program by clicking Close. This is similar to quick-start dialog boxes in other programs, such as Microsoft PowerPoint, aimed at novice users. If you want to disable it so you go straight into InDesign, just deselect the check box.

New Feature   This quick-start dialog box is new to InDesign CS2.

After you install InDesign CS2, there's one more setup step you should take: Tell InDesign CS2 how often to check for program updates via the Web. To do so, choose Help ⇨ Update. InDesign will look for any new updates, and then display a dialog box that has a button labeled Preferences. Click Preferences to open a dialog box in which you enable monthly update checks and tell InDesign whether to automatically install them or ask your permission first. You also select which Adobe software you want to have these settings applied to (not just InDesign).

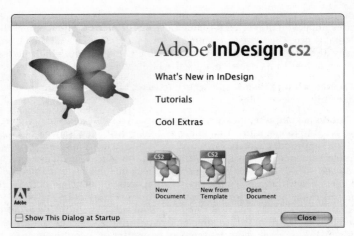

Figure A-1: This new quick-start dialog box loads each time you open InDesign, unless you disable it.

Working with Activation

The activation system is new to many Adobe products, including InDesign CS2. Although it is easy to activate your software, there are some issues you need to understand about activation *after* you are using your software:

✦ Adobe's standard licenses let you run its software on two computers (but not simultaneously on both), such as on a desktop and on a notebook. This means you can install and activate the software twice. It also means that if you install it on a computer, and then have a major system crash and need to install it over again on a reformatted drive, that second installation and activation counts as an additional use of the license. If you had previously installed the software on a second computer, Adobe would think this reinstallation was a new installation on a third system and require that you call Adobe. Because Adobe's phone-in support has limited hours, you might not be able to use InDesign for a day or so in such a situation.

✦ If you need to uninstall InDesign, you will be given the choice to remove the activation or leave it installed. Remove the activation if you are transferring your software to a new computer. That way, when you install InDesign on that new computer, Adobe will know that you've moved InDesign and that you're not trying to use it on an additional computer — Adobe's server will simply note that you changed the computer authorized to run InDesign. If you plan to reinstall the software on the same computer, then go ahead and leave the activation installed.

✦ You can transfer your activation from one computer to another as described, or you can use this method: Choose Help ➪ Transfer Activation to run a program that deactivates the current computer, so you can reinstall InDesign on another computer. Note that this method leaves InDesign installed on the original computer, but you won't be able to run it once it's deactivated.

Upgrading from Prior Versions of InDesign

Actually, all installations of InDesign CS2 are new installations. The installer creates a new folder and places your new copy of InDesign in it — regardless of whether you were using a previous version of InDesign. The only difference between purchasing a new product and upgrading is the price you pay for the software.

Installing new software has its good points and bad points. On the plus side, your existing, earlier-version copy of InDesign is available for future use. You never know when you'll need it — for example, for that new client who is still using InDesign 2, for which there is no back-saving capability from InDesign CS2 (or CS) — so it can be worth keeping on your machine or at least storing on a CD or Zip disk. The drawback is, of course, that you need space in which to store this old software.

For Mac-based organizations that have Mac OS 9–based systems, or that want to run Mac Classic mode from Mac OS X for compatibility with other software (including plug-ins), having both InDesign CS2 and an earlier version (such as Version 2) is a good idea. After all, InDesign CS2 does not run on Mac OS 9 or earlier.

A bigger drawback to the fact that InDesign CS2 requires a new installation is that InDesign CS2 won't have any of the custom settings you've selected in your earlier version of InDesign — you often don't realize how many preferences you've set over time until you switch to a new version of the software.

If you did put some effort into customizing InDesign, when you start using InDesign CS2, do the following:

✦ Reset your preferences in the Preferences dialog box (InDesign ➪ Preferences on the Mac and Edit ➪ Preferences in Windows, or ⌘+K or Ctrl+K).

✦ Copy any color swatch libraries from the previous version of InDesign (as well as from Adobe Illustrator) to the Swatch Libraries folder in the Presets folder in your InDesign application folder.

✦ With no document open, set any preferences such as styles and color definitions that you want to be used in all future documents. You can also load such settings from other documents using the Load menu option in the various panes' palette menus.

Although the customizing process can be tedious, it's definitely preferable to performing repetitive tasks such as creating the same style for each document.

✦　　✦　　✦

What's New in InDesign CS2

In its fifth major version (after 1.0, 1.5, 2.0, and 3.0 [CS]), InDesign 4.0 — known formally as InDesign CS2 — has become a very strong page-layout program offering a broad range of flexible, powerful tools.

Most InDesign users discovered the program in its CS version. You'll find a host of new features and updated features in this latest release. Although the chapters in this book identify new features as they come up in discussing publishing techniques, this appendix brings the whole list to you in one place for easy browsing. The new features are arranged in the same order as this book because that reflects the basic workflow of publishing and the major functional divisions.

InDesign Interface

Operating-system interaction

The Links pane now lets you find a file on your computer, opening its folder in a separate window through the Reveal in Finder/Reveal in Explorer and Reveal in Bridge/Reveal in Bridge menu options.

InDesign CS2 gives you two ways to work with files, through the standard Windows and Macintosh folder structures or through the revised Adobe Version Cue CS2 structure, which is designed to help multiuser environments work in shared folders.

Version Cue is now turned on by default, which changes all dialog boxes for opening, importing, exporting, and saving files to let you access files in Version Cue folders, in which you can save multiple versions of the same file. As part of this, InDesign CS2 also adds the Version Cue pop-up menu that lets you see other versions and alternates, revert to the project's version of the file, and show the source file in the Adobe Bridge browser window or in the Finder (Mac) or Explorer (Windows) interface. At the left of the pop-up menu is an information display that indicates the document's current Version Cue status.

Adobe now requires that InDesign be activated over the Web, which writes a unique serial number on your computer's hard drive so Adobe can detect any pirated copies.

Automatic file updating has been moved to the Updates menu option in the Help menu from the Preferences dialog box and now lets you set up automatic updates for all Adobe Creative Suite 2 programs.

Tools, palettes, and panes

Essentially a renamed version of PageMaker's Crop tool, the Position tool combines some aspects of the Selection tool with some aspects of the Direct Selection tool: As with the Selection tool, you can resize an object's frame by clicking and dragging its handles. And as with the Direct Selection tool, you can click a graphic and reposition it (crop it) within the frame by dragging.

The PageMaker Toolbar palette provides a row of icons for quick access to a variety of functions, mimicking a similar feature in PageMaker 7.

New panes are Object Styles and Data Merge. Several panes are now accessed through submenus in the Window menu: The Align, Navigator, Pathfinder, and Transform panes are now submenu options in the Objects & Layout menu, while Trap Presets has joined the Flattener and Separations panes as submenus in the Output menu (formerly the Output Preview menu). The Data Merge pane joins the Script Label and Scripts panes as submenus in the Automation menu (the former Scripting menu). Meanwhile, the Text Wrap pane has moved from the Type & Tables submenu to the Window menu.

The Pathfinder tools are now available from the Object menu, in addition to the Pathfinder pane. The Pathfinder pane also adds the new shape-conversion controls.

The Control palette has gained many new buttons, offering quick access to more functions than in previous versions. The buttons displayed depend on what is selected. Examples of new buttons are those that open the Quick Apply palette and the Adobe Bridge application, as well as those that apply object styles, clear style attributes, automatic bulleted and numbered lists, baseline-grid alignment, and language.

Views settings, guides, and grids

Frame-based baseline grids for text frames are new to InDesign CS2. You set a baseline grid as part of your text frame options by choosing Object ⇨ Text Frame Options, or by ⌘+B or Ctrl+B, and going to the Baseline Options pane. Setting up a frame-based grid is otherwise just like setting up a page's baseline grid.

InDesign CS2 lets you lock column guides independently of ruler guides. Choose View ⇨ Grids & Guides ⇨ Lock Column Guides to ensure they can't be moved. Choose View ⇨ Grids & Guides ⇨ Unlock Column Guides to make them movable again.

You can now set the baseline grid to start at the top of the page or at the top margin.

InDesign CS2 has moved the Hide/View Master Options command from the View menu to the Pages pane's palette menu.

Preferences

InDesign CS2 lets you set anti-aliasing (font smoothing) for text in the Story Editor.

The Type and Advanced Type panes are new, taking the place of the Text pane in InDesign CS and expanding its controls. The Appearance of Black pane takes the Print Options section from the old General pane and adds additional control. The Autocorrect pane is entirely new to InDesign CS2. The Updates pane has gone away, and its settings are now handled by clicking Preferences in the Updates dialog box (Help ➪ Updates).

InDesign CS2 lets you choose the default values for points: 72 points to the inch (the PostScript default), 72.27 points to the inch (the pre-desktop-publishing standard), 72.23, and 72.3. You may also type any number from 60 through 80 in the Points/Inches field. Note that changing the points-to-inch value will change the size of your printed output, as it changes the definition of a point.

InDesign CS2 can display previews of fonts when you select fonts through the Control palette, various text-oriented panes, and the Type menu. You turn on this capability in the Type pane of the Preferences dialog box, as covered in Chapter 3.

A new option is the ability to control image display while scrolling. You can set InDesign CS2 to reduce image quality while scrolling to speed up scrolling.

Document and Object Functions

Page actions

InDesign CS2 adds a faster way to add and manipulate pages if you don't happen to have the Pages pane already open: Choose Layout ➪ Pages, and then select the appropriate option, such as Add Pages, from the submenu. The resulting dialog boxes match those accessed from the Pages pane.

InDesign CS2 also adds a new palette menu option — Move Pages — to the Pages pane.

You can now apply a master page to the currently displayed page(s) by choosing Layout ➪ Pages ➪ Apply Master to Page(s).

File exchange and sharing

The capability to create files compatible with a previous version (InDesign CS) is new to InDesign CS2.

InDesign CS2 adds a Save as Alternate option if you are using the Version Cue–enabled Save dialog box. This lets you save alternate versions of a document that you can later decide to use instead of the main version, if you are using the Version Cue version-management and collaborative file-management tools.

Object handling

InDesign CS2 lets you create object styles, and collections of attributes for frames, lines, and other objects that are similar in context to the collections of text formatting saved in paragraph styles and character styles.

You can now choose anchor objects to specific points in text, so they move with the text as it reflows in your document. Anchored objects can be inline (embedded in the text) or external to the text in independent frames. InDesign CS2 also imports such anchored objects from Microsoft Word. Whether created in InDesign or Word, you can modify their settings in InDesign.

InDesign CS2 keeps a history of your transformations, so you can apply them again. Choose Object ➪ Transform Again ➪ Transform Again (Option+⌘+3 or Ctrl+Alt+3) to repeat the previous transformation on the selected object (it can be a different object than you most recently applied a transformation to). Or choose Object ➪ Transform Again ➪ Transform Sequence Again (Option+⌘+4 or Ctrl+Alt+4) to apply all recent transformations to a selected object. That sequence of transactions stays in memory until you perform a new transformation, which then starts a new sequence, so you can apply the same transformation to multiple objects.

The Fit Frame Proportionally submenu in Object ➪ Fitting is new to InDesign CS2. It guarantees that there will be no space between the graphic and the frame. (The Fit Frame to Content option that was available in previous versions and remains available in InDesign CS2 can result in such space at the bottom and/or right sides of a graphic.)

The new Convert Shape option in the Object menu lets you convert frames to other shapes, such as from a rectangle to a triangle. These options have also been added to the Pathfinder pane.

InDesign CS2 adds a new option to a library palette's palette menu: Update Library Item. This will replace the selected library item with whatever object is selected in your layout.

Text Functions

Text import

InDesign CS2 can open QuarkXPress Passport 3.3–4.1 files (the multilingual format) in addition to the standard single-language QuarkXPress 3.3–4.1 formats, plus it can now open PageMaker Version 6.0 files, not just versions 6.5 and 7.0.

InDesign CS2 has substantially increased the controls for the importation of Word and RTF files, including how to handle table formatting, footnotes, and style-sheet conflicts. Also, for Word and RTF file import, you can now save import settings as presets for reuse and sharing with others.

Newly supported Word and RTF text attributes when importing into InDesign CS2 include character styles, footnotes, and text boxes. For Excel files, InDesign CS2 imports inline graphics as well.

If you paste text that's been cut or copied from within InDesign, you now have two options for pasting it: File ➪ Paste (or ⌘+V or Ctrl+V) or the new File ➪ Paste without Formatting. This option lets you choose each time you paste text whether to preserve formatting or not.

Similarly, if you want InDesign CS2 to remove formatting when you choose paste text from other applications, instead of remembering to use File ➪ Paste without Formatting, instead go to the Type pane of the Preferences dialog box (InDesign ➪ Preferences or ⌘+K on the Mac and Edit ➪ Preferences or Ctrl+K in Windows) and select the Text Only option for the When Pasting Text and Tables from Other Applications setting. (InDesign CS offered a similar capability, but had placed it in the File Handling pane of the Preferences dialog box.)

Text editing

Automatic bulleted and numbered lists are new to InDesign CS2.

InDesign CS2 lets you create and manage footnotes and end notes.

InDesign CS2 supports data merge, which lets you create a single document that is then automatically customized for multiple recipients, such as a form letter, or that lets you repeat specific formatting for a database of text, such as for mailing labels.

You can set up drag-and-drop text editing in the Story Editor and in the standard layout view.

InDesign CS2 also lets you control the Story Editor's view settings from a trio of options accessed by choosing View ⇨ Story Editor.

When you paste text, InDesign is smart enough to know to remove extra spaces or add them around the pasted text. You can disable this by deselecting the Adjust Spacing Automatically When Cutting and Pasting Words option in the Type pane of the Preferences dialog box.

In the Story Editor, InDesign CS2 highlights overset text with a red border.

Paragraph and character formatting

The Towards Spine and Away from Spine paragraph-alignment options are new to InDesign CS2. Towards Spine is similar to Left Justify or Right Justify except that InDesign automatically chooses a left or right alignment based on where the spine is in a facing-pages document. Essentially, this automatically creates right-aligned text on left-hand pages and left-aligned text on right-hand pages. Away from Spine is the same as Towards Spine, except that the alignment is reversed: Text aligns to the left on left-hand pages and to the right on right-hand pages.

The ability to select which specific styles to load from another InDesign document is new to InDesign CS2. The ability to choose how to handle style conflicts is also new to InDesign CS2 and puts it on par with QuarkXPress.

InDesign CS2 has a default paragraph style called [Basic Paragraph] that is applied to any text entered in a new frame, as well as any imported text that has no styles associated with it. You can modify the [Basic Paragraph] just like any other style.

InDesign CS2 no longer displays [No Paragraph Style] or [No Character Style] in its Paragraph Styles and Character Styles panes. Instead, to remove styles from text, choose Break Link to Style in the palette menu. In the Character Style pane, you can also select [None] in the list of styles.

InDesign CS2 gives you the option of replacing a deleted style with another style. You can also choose [No Paragraph Style] or [None] (for character styles) if you no longer want a style applied. In that case, select the Preserve Formatting option to convert the unapplied style's formatting to local formatting, or deselect it to make the text lose that formatting as well as its style.

The new Clear Overrides option in the Paragraph Styles pane's palette menu removes any local formatting applied to the selected paragraphs. There's also a Clear Overrides button at the bottom of the Paragraph Styles pane. Both are simply more obvious alternatives to pressing and holding Option+Shift or Alt+Shift when clicking on a style name.

If your selected paragraphs have more than one paragraph style applied within the group, the Paragraph Styles pane displays the text *(Mixed)* at the lower left. The same holds true for the Character Styles pane if your text selection has more than one character style applied within the selection.

Spelling, hyphenation, and indexing

InDesign CS2 lets you associate multiple user dictionaries with a language, and the list of such dictionaries is new to this version. You can also determine which dictionaries to use during spelling checks.

The program supports dynamic spelling, where suspected misspellings and wrong capitalizations are displayed as you type and in your layout for imported text.

User-defined spelling-check exceptions can now be case-sensitive.

The Hyphenate Last Word option is new to InDesign CS2, letting you control whether the last word in a paragraph is hyphenated.

New to InDesign CS2 is the ability to autocorrect text, which lets you specify common misspellings you want InDesign to correct automatically as you type. You can also use this feature to replace codes or other text strings (such as replacing -- with —).

InDesign CS2 changes how multiparagraph text selections are indexed. InDesign CS2 indexes each paragraph in that selection. The idea is that you can create lists this way.

InDesign uses new keyboard shortcuts for adding selected text as entries to the index: Option+Shift+⌘+[or Ctrl+Alt+Shift+[to add it as is and Option+Shift+⌘+] or Ctrl+Alt+Shift+] to add it in reverse-name order.

Color Functions

In InDesign CS2, color management is always on, a change from previous versions.

InDesign CS2 automatically synchronizes the color calibration settings with other Adobe Creative Suite 2 applications to ensure consistent settings in Illustrator, Photoshop, Acrobat, and InDesign. Use the Adobe Bridge program that comes with the full Adobe Creative Suite to choose a common color management system for all your CS2 software. You'll see a note in each CMS-related dialog box letting you know if this synchronization is active.

You can import and save Adobe Swatch Exchange files — which hold color swatch definitions — among Adobe Creative Suite 2 programs, including InDesign.

InDesign CS2 now lets you double-click the Stroke and Fill buttons on the Tools palette to create colors, using a Photoshop-style color picker. You can add any colors created this way to the Swatches pane by clicking the Add Swatch button. Otherwise, you run the same risk as creating colors through the Color pane: having unamed colors whose output you can't control when printing.

InDesign CS2 can be set to automatically display, export, and print black elements as rich black, which makes the black darker.

InDesign CS2 changes the options and layout of the Color Management pane. What had been called the Source Space section is now the Print section, while the previous Print Space section has been renamed the Options section and offers a different way to specify color output. Essentially, you no longer can specify an output intent or color reference dictionary (CRD) — these are now part of the profiles you assign to your document and not individually changeable. But you also have new controls over CMYK number management and paper color simulation, as described later in this section.

Support for the ANPA color model is new to InDesign CS2.

Graphics Functions

Image import and editing

When importing JPEG files, InDesign CS2 now automatically scales the image to fit in the page. This helps deal with digital-camera graphics that tend to be very large, so when imported end up taking much more than the width of a page. While you'll likely still need to scale the image to fit your layout, you can at least see the whole image before doing so.

InDesign CS2 now can differentiate layers in an Illustrator, Photoshop, or PDF graphic, letting you decide which one(s) to display in your layout.

Adobe has added a Purchase This Image menu option to the Links pane's palette menu. This lets you directly buy clip art from several vendors that have partnered with Adobe.

Strokes and paths

InDesign CS2's Pathfinder tool now correctly handles path junctions that have corner effects applied. Before, the Pathfinder tool didn't notice the corner effects, so joined paths could look odd. Now, it recognizes that there are corner effects and joins the paths appropriately so the corner effects are correctly applied to any new corners.

The Object menu now contains a Paths option with three suboptions: Open Path, Close Path, and Reverse Path. (The Reverse Path option had existed in the Object menu in InDesign CS, but the other two options are new to InDesign CS2). The Open Path option converts a closed shape into an open path, while the Close Path option converts an open path to a closed shape.

Output Functions

InDesign CS2 has greatly simplified the Print dialog box's Color Management pane, removing many overrides for options set in the Color Settings dialog box.

In the Print dialog box's Ink Manager dialog box, InDesign CS2 offers the Use Standard Lab Values for Spots option to force InDesign to substitute the basic CMYK process colors for the similar colors defined by the Pantone and HKS color models. In most cases, they're almost identical, so no one will notice, but check with your printer first because the type of paper you use or other factors may cause a different output than expected. Note that this option is selected by default.

InDesign CS2 lets you export multiple pages to the JPEG format; each page is saved into its own file. You choose which pages to save in the Export JPEG dialog box that appears after you click Save in the Export dialog box.

Support for the Scalable Vector Graphics (SVG) format is also new to InDesign CS2; this fairly new World Wide Web Consortium format is meant to become a sort of EPS for the Web, though it's not yet widely supported. As with JPEG export, you will get a dialog box letting you select which pages to export once you click Save in the Export dialog box.

Other Functions

PDF files

InDesign CS2 can import multiple pages from a multipage PDF file. InDesign CS2 can also differentiate layers in a PDF file, letting you decide which one(s) to display in your layout.

InDesign CS2 can retain PDF objects placed in the Clipboard so they are accessible after you quit InDesign.

The ability to open PDF creation setting (job option) files is new to InDesign CS2, as is the ability to create your own in InDesign and save them for use by other Adobe Creative Suite 2 and Acrobat Distiller users.

InDesign CS2 supports Acrobat 7's PDF 1.6 format.

XML files

You can now export components in your InDesign document as XML snippets by choosing InDesign Snippets in the Export dialog box's Format pop-up menu. InDesign will export to a snippet file any selected objects. You can place those objects in an InDesign layout by placing them (File ⇨ Place, or ⌘+D or Ctrl+D), as you would any graphic or text file. (If no objects are selected, InDesign Snippet will not appear as a choice in the Format pop-up menu.) Note that InDesign Snippet files are given the filename extension .inds.

InDesign CS2's XML functionality supports table elements such as table cells, cell content, and table structure during import and export.

It also supports the definition of style attributes (for example, `<Title: aid:pstyle= "ChapterStyle"/>` to define and apply the style `ChapterStyle` to the element names `Title`) in an imported XML file and will import and apply those attributes to imported content.

The following are new options in the InDesign CS2 Import XML dialog box: Delete Elements, Frames, and Content That Do Not Match Imported XML; Only Import Elements That Match Existing Structure; Repeated Text Elements Inherit Formatting; and Do Not Import Contents of Whitespace-Only Elements. To access these controls, the Show XML Import Options option must be selected in the Import CML dialog box.

✦   ✦   ✦

Switching from QuarkXPress

Learning to use new software, or even learning to use an upgrade of a familiar application, can be so intimidating that many users resist passionately. Even if an application is woefully out of date and lacking in functionality, you cling to it knowing you can accomplish your mission—even with workarounds—with less frustration than the untried, but powerful, new application. Users are particularly passionate about their choice of page-layout software—which is usually QuarkXPress—probably because they're involved with it for 8 to 12 hours a day. (A QuarkXPress user once said he spent more time with QuarkXPress than with his wife, so you can see where the dedication is coming from.)

But times, circumstances, and jobs change. Eventually, your old software won't run on your zippy new machine or you switch jobs or you simply prefer another vendor. No matter what circumstances led you to choosing InDesign, this appendix is designed to help you let go and move forward, showing you the differences between your old layout application and InDesign, and pointing out a few benefits of InDesign as well.

Note All references to QuarkXPress apply to versions 4.x, 5.x, and 6.x unless I provide a specific version number.

So you can continue working with existing designs, in its very first version of InDesign, Adobe made sure it could open QuarkXPress files, recognizing the preeminence of QuarkXPress in the publishing world. Since then, Quark modified the QuarkXPress file format (starting in version 5) to prevent InDesign from opening its files, but because most QuarkXPress users have stayed with version 4, the InDesign ability to open QuarkXPress files remains valuable.

Opening QuarkXPress Documents

The Open command (File ⇨ Open, or ⌘+O or Ctrl+O) lets you select and open documents and templates saved in QuarkXPress and QuarkXPress Passport versions 3.3 through 4.11 on Macintosh or Windows. (QuarkXPress Passport is the multilingual version of QuarkXPress.) You also can import QuarkXPress-created XML files into InDesign as XML documents. But you can't open libraries or books from any version of QuarkXPress, nor documents or templates from QuarkXPress 5 and later.

Tip

Be sure to use QuarkXPress's Collect for Output function to copy all linked graphics to a single folder. This also ensures that all graphics files are available. If you don't do this, InDesign may not get all the linked graphics from the source QuarkXPress file.

All the text, graphics, items, master pages, style sheet, and more in the QuarkXPress document are converted to their InDesign equivalents. If the document contains items, content, or formatting that can't be converted, an alert notifies you of the issues. Once the document is converted, it appears as a new, untitled document.

New Feature

InDesign CS2 lets you open QuarkXPress Passport 3.3 and 4.x files directly. You no longer have to first save them in QuarkXPress as single-language documents.

Once you open a QuarkXPress file in InDesign, you can save it as an InDesign file only. InDesign will automatically append the .indd filename extension to the QuarkXPress filename, so unless you explicitly change the filename extension when saving, there's no chance of accidentally overwriting that original QuarkXPress file.

Conversion Issues

Now that you know that InDesign is supposed to open QuarkXPress files, let's take a look at how well it actually does it. Yes, you can open QuarkXPress 3.3 and 4.x documents, save them as InDesign documents, and continue working with them. But the documents don't convert perfectly: You're likely to lose some formatting because InDesign doesn't have equivalent formatting, or its options work differently. In general, you can expect to use a QuarkXPress document as a starting point for a design — usually with a little repair work — but you should not expect to simply open a QuarkXPress document and have it look and print exactly the same way.

Tip

After realizing which QuarkXPress features are not supported or converted well, and considering how your own QuarkXPress documents are created, you can decide on a document-by-document basis whether conversion is worth the effort. In some cases, it might be easier to simply reconstruct a document, while in other cases you might be able to start working almost immediately.

When you convert QuarkXPress documents to InDesign, you can expect the following:

✦ Master pages are converted, including all items, content, and guides.

✦ All line and frame styles are converted to dashed or plain strokes.

✦ Text boxes are converted to text frames; picture boxes are converted to graphics frames.

✦ Text paths are converted.

✦ Because InDesign favors looser default text spacing than QuarkXPress, many stories will no longer fit in their text frames.

✦ All paragraph and character style sheets are converted to InDesign styles.

✦ Incremental auto-leading (such as **+4**, which adds 4 points to the largest font size on the line) is converted to InDesign's standard auto-leading.

✦ The Next Column (keypad Enter) or Next Box (Shift+keypad Enter) characters (which you use to bump text to the next column or next text box rather than resizing the box) are retained.

✦ The Bold and Italic type styles are converted to the appropriate typeface (if available), and Underline, Strike Thru, Superscript, Subscript, All Caps, and Small Caps are converted. Superior, Word Underline, Outline, and Shadow revert to plain text.

✦ Keyboard shortcuts assigned to character and paragraph styles are not retained, though you can assign keyboard shortcuts to your styles within InDesign.

✦ Index tags are not maintained, and you may have difficulty opening chapters of a book.

✦ If a picture is missing or modified in QuarkXPress, it won't appear in the InDesign document. If you want to retain the picture, you'll need to update the links in QuarkXPress (Utilities ⇨ Usage ⇨ Pictures) before converting it.

✦ Pasted (embedded) pictures, pictures imported using OLE or Publish and Subscribe, and pictures created with third-party XTensions will not convert.

✦ The customizable dashes in QuarkXPress are converted to solid and dashed lines; note that custom stripes do convert properly.

✦ Clipping paths created in QuarkXPress or imported with an image into QuarkXPress are not converted, so the image's display will change.

✦ The Same as Clipping Runaround feature in QuarkXPress leaves a runaround shape based on the clipping path in InDesign — but if you've resized the image in QuarkXPress, the runaround path stays at 100 percent in InDesign.

✦ Items for which Suppress Printout is checked are placed on a separate layer called Nonprinting layer. To view these objects in InDesign, view the layer.

✦ If a group contains an item for which Suppress Printout is selected, all the items are ungrouped and the suppressed items are placed on the nonprinting layer.

✦ Rotated items, typically when grouped, often are unrotated after conversion by InDesign.

✦ Pictures imported into QuarkXPress by holding ⌘ or Ctrl to import color images as grayscale or grayscale images and black and white lose that conversion and appear I their original color or grayscale in InDesign.

✦ The ICC-compliant color profiles used in QuarkXPress 4.0 and greater are retained, but the EfiColor profiles used in QuarkXPress 3.3 are not retained.

✦ Colors in QuarkXPress 3.3 documents are converted to InDesign swatches according to their CMYK values (except for HSB colors, which are converted to RGB swatches).

✦ Colors in QuarkXPress 4.*x* documents are converted to InDesign swatches according to their RGB values (except for HSB and LAB colors, which are converted to RGB swatches). Hexachrome colors are not converted.

✦ Blends are converted to linear or circular gradients.

InDesign will highlight any conversion issues as you open a QuarkXPress document, as Figure C-1 shows. You can save the warning's text to a text file by clicking the Save button, so you will have a reference to the issues to refer to later.

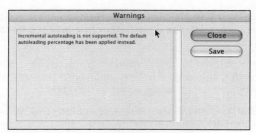

Figure C-1: The warning dialog box that InDesign presents when it cannot convert an element in a QuarkXPress file

Understanding Tool Differences

For the QuarkXPress veteran, the toughest thing about switching to InDesign is the set of tools. In your world, you've been using the Item tool (which you might call the pointer) and the Content tool (the little hand) for almost everything. Not only did you use them all the time, but the Item tool or Content tool was selected automatically for you most of the time (because object-creation tools snap back to the last-used selection tool). Over time, the two tools have evolved into almost one, so you might have been using the Content tool all the time, pressing ⌘ or Ctrl when you needed to manipulate an entire item.

You need to forget about this way of working entirely. In InDesign, you'll be switching tools constantly. When you create an object, its tool remains selected so you can't move or resize the objects immediately after creation. The Selection tool only lets you move and resize objects, while the Direct Selection tool lets you reshape objects and work with graphics.

The difference between the Selection tool and Direct Selection tool takes some getting used to for QuarkXPress users. In terms of working with content, the Direct Selection tool is much like QuarkXPress's Content tool, but it also lets you edit the frame as if it were a Bézier object. For example, if the Direct Selection tool is selected and you click and drag a point on the frame, you'll move that point and thus change the shape of the object — a rectangle would be converted into a polygon, because the lines immediately adjacent to the moved point will move with the point while the rest of the frame will not be affected. In QuarkXPress, if the Content tool is selected and you click and drag a point on the frame, you'll resize the frame (perhaps non-proportionally) but the entire side(s) adjacent to the point will move with the point, so a rectangle would still be a rectangle. To change a frame in the way that QuarkXPress does with both the Content and Item tools, use the Selection tool in InDesign.

Think of the Type tool as a combination of the Rectangle Text Box tool and the Content tool for text. You must have the Type tool to work with text, but there's no moving or resizing of text frames while you're using it. However, you can hold ⌘ or Ctrl to temporarily change from the Type tool to the Selection tool. This is the same as pressing ⌘ or Ctrl while using the QuarkXPress Content tool, which allows you to manipulate the entire item. Release ⌘ or Ctrl to return to the Type tool.

This need to switch between the Type and Selection tools will seem restrictive to you at first — but the key is to embrace InDesign's single-letter shortcuts for selecting tools. (InDesign also provides QuarkXPress-like keyboard commands for temporarily activating tools, but it's easier to press a single letter to switch tools.)

As long as the Type tool isn't selected, you can activate any tool by pressing the letter that appears next to it in the tool's Tool Tip. In particular, you'll want to memorize the following:

✦ Press V for the Selection tool.

✦ Press A for the Direct Selection tool.

✦ Press T for the Type tool.

✦ Press H for the Hand tool (you can also press the spacebar; when editing text, you can press Option or Alt).

✦ Press Z for the Zoom tool (you can also press ⌘+spacebar or Ctrl+spacebar and then click the mouse to zoom in, and Option+⌘+spacebar or Ctrl+Alt+spacebar and then click the mouse to zoom out).

If you're also a Photoshop user, the single-letter shortcuts might be familiar to you, but it's an odd concept for a QuarkXPress-only user. Once you get the hang of it, however, you'll appreciate how fast and easy it is to switch tools.

A few overall interface differences between QuarkXPress and InDesign might hang you up initially. Keep in mind that many menu commands simply display a pane (which may already be open) rather than showing a dialog box. Get used to deciphering icons or using Tool Tips on the panes because there are not as many dialog boxes containing named fields as you're used to in QuarkXPress's Character Attributes, Paragraph Attributes, and Modify dialog boxes. Contextual menus are implemented on a broader scale than in QuarkXPress, so you can Control+click or right+click objects, rulers, and more to make changes quickly.

InDesign CS2 also offers docking panes, whose tabs can be aligned to the lefthand and righthand screen edges so they're not in the way. You can drag these docked panes to your document to make them floating panes à la QuarkXPress. Note that InDesign's panes can be rearranged and combined into multipane palettes by dragging them on top of each other; QuarkXPress's palettes are fixed and cannot be combined. Because InDesign has so many panes, it needs a way to manage them. Unlike QuarkXPress, InDesign lets you save these interface settings using its Workspaces feature (Window ➪ Workspace, whose submenu lets you select, create, and delete these workspaces).

InDesign uses all of QuarkXPress's measurement abbreviations, as well as its own. For example, InDesign accepts QuarkXPress's use of " to indicate inches, as well as InDesign's own standard of *in* and *inch*.

Tip   InDesign offers a set of keyboard commands similar to those in QuarkXPress (Edit ➪ Keyboard Shortcuts). I recommend that you avoid this set and learn the commands in InDesign. This will help you in communicating about InDesign and working with other Adobe software.

Converting Keyboard Shortcuts

If you're switching from QuarkXPress and committed to learning InDesign's keyboard shortcuts, skim Table C-1 to see the primary differences.

Table C-1: Keyboard Shortcuts Translated from QuarkXPress to InDesign

Action	QuarkXPress Shortcut	InDesign Equivalent
Zoom in	Control or Ctrl	⌘+spacebar or Ctrl+spacebar
Zoom out	Control+Option or Ctrl+Alt	Option+⌘+spacebar or Ctrl+Alt+spacebar
Page grabber hand	Option or Alt	H, or Option or Alt
Preferences	Option+Shift+⌘+Y or Ctrl+Alt+Shift+Y	⌘+K or Ctrl+K
Get Text/Picture	⌘+E or Ctrl+E	⌘+D or Ctrl+D for Place
Paragraph formats	⌘+Shift+F or Ctrl+Shift+F	Option+⌘+T or Ctrl+Alt+T
Character formats	⌘+Shift+D or Ctrl+Shift+D	⌘+T or Ctrl+T
Style Sheets palette	F11	F11 (Character Styles), Shift+F11 (Paragraph Styles)
Spelling (word)	⌘+L or Ctrl+W	⌘+I or Ctrl+I
Modify dialog box	⌘+M or Ctrl+M	*No equivalent*
Delete selection	⌘+K or Ctrl+K	Delete or Backspace
Duplicate	⌘+D or Ctrl+D	Option+Shift+⌘+D or Ctrl+Alt+Shift+D
Step and Repeat	Option+⌘+D or Ctrl+Alt+D	Shift+⌘+V or Ctrl+Shift+V
Lock/Unlock	F6	⌘+L or Ctrl+L (lock), Option+⌘+L or Ctrl+Alt+L (unlock)
Ungroup	⌘+U or Ctrl+U	Shift+⌘+G or Ctrl+Shift+G
Space Align	⌘+, or Ctrl+,	F8
Send to Back	Shift+F5	Shift+⌘+[or Ctrl+Shift+[
Send Backward	Option+Shift+F5 or Ctrl+Shift+F5	⌘+[or Ctrl+[
Bring to Front	F5	Shift+⌘+] or Ctrl+Shift+]
Bring Forward	Option+F5 or Ctrl+F5	⌘+] or Ctrl+]

Document Differences

By and large, documents in InDesign and QuarkXPress are the same. You have master pages, layers, and pages. You can also set bleeds for objects that go beyond the page boundary. But there are some differences:

✦ InDesign lets you specify a slug area, which reserves space during printing for the printer's marks.

✦ QuarkXPress 6 permits several layouts in one document file, called a *project,* so you can mix layouts with different page sizes. InDesign does not permit that.

✦ The InDesign master text frame is not the same as QuarkXPress's automatic text box on a master page. You cannot flow text into a QuarkXPress automatic text box while you're working on a master page; instead, an empty text box is placed on each of your layout pages for you automatically. Although you can have QuarkXPress flow text into automatic text boxes across pages as you add pages to your layout, you can also place text in these boxes individually, without them being linked. An InDesign master text frame is linked automatically from page to page and is not meant for holding text that does not flow from page to page.

✦ QuarkXPress 5 and 6 support Web documents, which InDesign CS2 does not. InDesign CS2 also cannot export layouts to the Web's HTML format.

✦ InDesign can generate TOCs only based on paragraph styles, not on character styles. This means you can't create other kinds of lists, such as a list of companies in a magazine article or research report, based on the use of character styles. InDesign doesn't have a flexible Lists feature as QuarkXPress does, just the Table of Contents feature that is essentially a subset of QuarkXPress's Lists feature. However, you can use the InDesign Table of Contents feature to create some lists besides TOCs. Also, the level of formatting you can achieve over TOC entries in InDesign is greater than in QuarkXPress.

✦ The InDesign index features are similar to those in QuarkXPress, though the InDesign Index pane and QuarkXPress Index palette have very different interfaces.

✦ The corner-style feature in InDesign (Object ⇨ Corner Effects) is similar to the text-box and picture-box variants in QuarkXPress, which offer the same selection of corners except for the Fancy option. In QuarkXPress, you create, or convert, a box to a variant that has one of these corner effects, while in InDesign, you apply the corner effect to a frame.

✦ InDesign's nested frames are similar to QuarkXPress's constrained boxes — the biggest difference is that, to nest a frame in InDesign, you paste a frame into another (Edit ⇨ Paste Into, or Option+⌘+V or Ctrl+Alt+V). In QuarkXPress, you choose Item ⇨ Constrain.

Working with Objects Rather Than Items

In QuarkXPress, you're used to items such as text boxes, picture boxes, lines, and maybe text paths. In InDesign, you have paths and frames, with the only difference being that frames contain graphics or text. You can, therefore, make a one-to-one relationship between text boxes and text frames, and picture boxes and graphics frames. Just keep in mind that, with InDesign, you're not restricted to using frames for content; you can fill any path, even an open one, with text or graphics and have it become a frame. And if you don't make a frame (or the right kind of frame) up front, you can still import graphics and text in InDesign (unlike in QuarkXPress, which requires you to change the box type first).

While selecting and manipulating objects with tools, remember the following:

✦ Use the Selection tool to move objects or resize frames. It's kind of like QuarkXPress's Item tool.

✦ Use the Direct Selection tool to reshape objects, work with graphics, and change the endpoints of lines. It's kind of like QuarkXPress's Content tool.

New Feature   The Position tool is new to InDesign CS2.

✦ You can use the Position tool (a variation of PageMaker's Crop tool) to resize and move images and their frames, or reposition content in relation to their frames. It also blurs the QuarkXPress Content/Item dichotomy, acting like the Item tool in terms or resizing and moving frames, and like the Content tools when it comes to repositioning the contents.

✦ When reshaping objects, you can use the Pen tool, Add Anchor Point tool, and Remove Anchor Point tool in addition to the Direct Selection tool.

✦ You can't just click master-page objects to select them on the document pages. Instead, use Shift+⌘+click or Ctrl+Shift+click to select them.

When modifying objects, remember the following:

✦ InDesign CS2 has a more-capable clone of QuarkXPress's Measurements palette, called the Control palette in InDesign (Window ➪ Control, or Option+⌘+6 or Ctrl+Alt+6). You can also use the Transform pane in InDesign (Window ➪ Object & Layout ➪ Transform or F9). Use these tools for the equivalent of QuarkXPress's Modify dialog box's Box and Line panes.

✦ In InDesign CS2, when you scale a frame's contents using the Control palette or Transform pane, the scale value may jump back to 100% in the palette or pane, even though the contents will indeed be at the new size. This occurs when you have the Selection tool selected, because that causes InDesign to report the scale of the frame (stroke), not of the contents. If you switch to the Direct Selection tool, you'll see the proper scale for the contents in the Control palette or Transform pane.

✦ To specify runaround, choose Window ➪ Text Wrap, or press Option+⌘+W or Ctrl+Alt+W, to open the Text Wrap pane.

✦ To specify attributes of text frames, choose Object ➪ Text Frame Options, or press ⌘+B or Ctrl+B, to open the Text Frame Options dialog box.

✦ The InDesign Shear tool is not the same as the QuarkXPress Skew tool; Shear both slants and rotates an object, while Skew just slants it. To simulate the QuarkXPress Skew tool, hold the Shift key while you move the mouse horizontally when using the InDesign Shear tool. This ensures that there is no rotation. You can also use the Shear X fields in the Control palette or Transform pane to only slant an object.

Working with Text

InDesign works with text very differently than QuarkXPress in many cases, even though the fundamental capabilities are the same in both programs. Veteran QuarkXPress users will be frustrated initially with InDesign's more-laborious approach to text flow and formatting, but will eventually appreciate some of InDesign's more powerful capabilities such as stroke formatting and nested styles.

Flowing text

Once you learn how to flow text in InDesign, you'll find it's easier and more flexible than QuarkXPress. It's easy to get stuck and to restrict yourself to QuarkXPress techniques. To prevent that, keep these differences in mind:

✦ To import a text file, use File ➪ Place, or ⌘+D or Ctrl+D. You can also click and drag files and text from the desktop or any application that supports drag and drop.

✦ You do not need to create or select a text frame before you import text; you'll be able to create or select a text frame after choosing the file to import.

✦ InDesign does not have linking tools. To flow text from frame to frame, use a selection tool to click the out ports and in ports on text frames. (Make sure View ➪ Show Text Threads is selected.)

✦ To flow text and add pages automatically, click Master Text Frame in the New Document dialog box (File ➪ New ➪ Document, or ⌘+N or Ctrl+N). Then, you'll need to press Shift+⌘+click or Ctrl+Shift+click the master text frame on a document page. Finally, Option+click or Alt+click the loaded text icon.

See Chapter 15 for complete information about flowing text.

Editing text

A few minor differences exist when it comes to editing and selecting text:

✦ In QuarkXPress, clicking three times in text selects the line, and clicking four times selects the entire paragraph. In InDesign, clicking three times selects the paragraph.

✦ To type special characters such as ñ, •, or ¶, you can choose Type ➪ Glyphs rather than use system utilities or key combinations.

✦ The control for showing invisible characters such as spaces, tabs, and paragraph returns is Type ➪ Show Hidden Characters, or press Option+⌘+I or Ctrl+Alt+I.

✦ InDesign lets you select from various Western European languages for spell checking and hyphenation. You first apply a Language to text selections via the Character or Character Styles panes. The Passport edition of QuarkXPress has a similar feature to specify the hyphenation and spelling language, but not the standard version of QuarkXPress.

✦ InDesign 2 and CS didn't support "smart space" the way QuarkXPress 4 and later do, so when you double-click to select, and then cut and paste a word, you won't also select the trailing space. InDesign CS2 has fixed this problem.

Formatting text

In general, formatting text in InDesign will feel comfortable to QuarkXPress users. You'll miss those nice, big Character and Paragraph Attributes dialog boxes (featuring real words, not icons!), but you have most of the same power. Review these differences, and keep them in mind while formatting text:

✦ Use the Character pane (Type ➪ Character, or ⌘+T or Ctrl+T) to format highlighted characters. You'll notice there are no type style buttons — InDesign requires you to choose the appropriate version of a typeface rather than attributes such as bold and italic, while other type styles are listed in the Character pane's palette menu.

✦ Leading is a character-level format in InDesign; therefore the controls are in the Character pane rather than the Paragraph pane as you might have come to expect. Fortunately, you can change the leading behavior by selecting the Text pane of the Preferences dialog box and clicking the Apply Leading to Entire Paragraphs option. Clicking this box will make InDesign match the behavior of leading in QuarkXPress. Leading is always measured from baseline to baseline in InDesign.

✦ Unlike QuarkXPress, you can stroke and fill characters in InDesign.

✦ Use the Paragraph pane (Type ➪ Paragraph, or Option+⌘+T or Ctrl+Alt+T) to format selected paragraphs; the palette menu includes additional commands for adding rules and controlling hyphenation.

✦ InDesign lets you apply OpenType settings to OpenType fonts, using the palette menus of the Character pane or the Control palette, or the OpenType Features pane of the Character Styles pane. QuarkXPress can use OpenType fonts but apply only standard formatting to them.

✦ InDesign does not have H&J sets, so set up your hyphenation using the Paragraph pane and save your settings in paragraph styles.

✦ Use the Tabs pane (Type ➪ Tabs, or Shift+⌘+T or Ctrl+Shift+T) to set tabs for selected paragraphs.

✦ To create styles, use the New Character Style and New Paragraph Stylecommands in the palette menus on the Character pane (Type ➪ Character Styles, or Shift+F11) and the Paragraph pane (Type ➪ Paragraph Styles, or F11). To share styles with other documents, use the Load commands in the same menus.

✦ Click Type ➪ Find Font to replace fonts throughout your document; this works like the Font Usage dialog box in QuarkXPress (Utilities ➪ Usage ➪ Fonts).

✦ Unlike Windows QuarkXPress, InDesign for Windows supports automatic ligatures in Windows fonts that have them.

✦ InDesign has no equivalent to QuarkXPress's fraction-building tool.

✦ InDesign has no equivalent to QuarkXPress's Underline Styles. Instead, specify custom underlines and strikethroughs as part of a character style. To add stripes and dashed lines, open the Strokes pane (Window ➪ Stroke or F10) and select the Stroke Styles option from the palette menu.

✦ Those converting to QuarkXPress may be surprised at the seemingly large kerning and tracking values produced by all of the program's kerning and tracking methods. Keep in mind that InDesign lets you adjust space in 0.001-em units ($\frac{1}{1,000}$ of an em). In QuarkXPress, for example, the kerning unit is 0.005 ems ($\frac{1}{200}$ of an em). So QuarkXPress users should not be surprised to see kerning and tracking values that are 10 to 20 times greater than you're used to — you're working with multiples of finer increments.

New Feature   InDesign 2 and CS imported all styles when you use one of the Load commands. They did not let you select specific styles for import, as QuarkXPress does. That can add a lot of irrelevant styles to your InDesign document, unfortunately. InDesign CS2 fixes this flaw.

Working with Tables

Recent editions of QuarkXPress and InDesign have added significant table formatting capabilities. Among the differences:

✦ InDesign does a good job of importing Word tables and Excel spreadsheets as tables, unlike QuarkXPress versions through 6.0, which does not support tables during import without extra-cost add-on software. Also, InDesign can export tables in RTF format, allowing Word users to see and edit tables that you build in InDesign. This is very helpful for migrating tabular data into and out of InDesign for revision by Word users.

✦ InDesign tables and QuarkXPress tables have several differences. Although both treat tables as collections of cells, InDesign offers more formatting options for cell strokes than QuarkXPress does. InDesign has more controls for text and row placement than QuarkXPress offers. InDesign also imports Word, Excel, and RTF tables, while QuarkXPress does not. But QuarkXPress offers more control over the flow of text among cells in a table. InDesign doesn't let you flow text from one cell to another, for example, much less control the order of that flow.

✦ In one way, InDesign is savvier about text-to-table conversion than QuarkXPress is because InDesign lets you choose any string as the column or row separator during conversion (just enter that string in the appropriate field). But in another way, InDesign is less savvy: QuarkXPress lets you "pivot" data during conversion, so you can swap columns and rows for a better fit.

Working with Graphics

Importing and manipulating graphics in InDesign is very similar to QuarkXPress. As long as you remember to use the Direct Selection tool to select a graphic rather than its frame, you and the InDesign graphics features will get along fine. Differences between the programs include the following:

✦ To import a graphics file in InDesign, use File ➪ Place, or ⌘+D or Ctrl+D. You can also click and drag files in from the desktop or other programs if InDesign supports their file formats.

✦ InDesign cannot convert color bitmap images to grayscale during import (while retaining the original file's colors) as QuarkXPress can. Thus, in InDesign, you'll need to convert the files in Photoshop or turn off color separation when printing.

✦ You do not need to create or select a graphics frame before you import a graphic; you'll be able to create or select a graphics frame after choosing the file to import.

✦ Use the Control palette (Window ➪ Control, or Option+⌘+6 or Ctrl+Alt+6) or the Transform pane (Window ➪ Object & Layout ➪ Transform or F9) to rotate, scale, and skew graphics. You can create clipping paths by clicking Object ➪ Clipping Paths or pressing Option+Shift+⌘+K or Ctrl+Alt+Shift+K.

✦ To automatically scale a graphic to fit within its frame — proportionally or not — use the Fitting commands in the Object menu or their keyboard commands. As a bonus, you get a Fit Frame to Picture command, a task you have to perform manually in QuarkXPress.

✦ The InDesign Stroke Styles feature (accessed via the Strokes pane's palette menu) looks and works very much like the QuarkXPress Dashes & Stripes feature. The major difference is that InDesign has a separate option for dotted lines.

✦ Although InDesign doesn't have background, frame, and contents buttons in its Swatches pane to let you select where color is applied, as QuarkXPress does, InDesign lets you determine what component of the image gets the color based on how you apply the color: Click and drag a color swatch onto an object to change the foreground color. Click a graphics frame and then the Fill or Stroke button in the Tools palette, and then select a color from the Swatches pane to change the background or frame color, respectively. Furthermore, you can use the Control palette's Select Container and Select Contents buttons to choose whether the image background or contents, respectively, are colored when you click a swatch.

✦ InDesign offers a customizable drop-shadow tool (Object ➪ Drop Shadow, or Option+⌘+M or Ctrl+Alt+M) that lets you determine the shadow angle, distance, and lighting effects. QuarkXPress's drop shadow is fixed to one setting. Although InDesign's drop shadow can be applied to any object, not just a text frame, it cannot be applied to selected text. By contrast, QuarkXPress's drop shadow can be applied only to selected text as a character attribute.

✦ InDesign lets you feather the edges of objects, to create soft outlines and other lighting-oriented effects, by clicking Object ➪ Feather. QuarkXPress has no equivalent.

✦ QuarkXPress has no equivalent to InDesign's transparency settings, which let you make objects transparent or semitransparent, allowing a wide variety of special effects. QuarkXPress users instead must rely on such settings in Adobe Photoshop and Illustrator for imported pictures and do without them for objects created in QuarkXPress. InDesign also provides controls for how overlapping transparent objects are output because they can sometimes interfere with printing.

✦ To track the location of graphics files, use the Links pane (Window ➪ Links, or Shift+⌘+D or Ctrl+Shift+D).

✦ InDesign's relink function is not as smart as QuarkXPress's equivalent Picture Usage. If you have multiple broken links to the same file in an InDesign document, you must relink each one manually from the Links pane. QuarkXPress will automatically fix all links to the same file as soon as you correct any link to it. That's another reason to use InDesign's automatic fix when you open a document and InDesign identifies that links are broken or out of date. (You can relink a group of files at once by selecting them all in the Links pane (Window ➪ Links, or Shift+⌘+D or Ctrl+Shift+D), and choosing Relink in the palette menu to relink them all at once.)

✦ QuarkXPress uses a very different approach to changing direction points from smooth to corner: It has iconic buttons in its Measurements palette that let you easily convert segment and corner types. The InDesign approach is more efficient in that it uses one tool and relies on a mouse-based tool (because you're likely using the mouse when you edit a shape), but it does require a bit more getting used to initially.

✦ The Pathfinder in InDesign options to connect paths is similar to QuarkXPress's Merge options for paths.

Manipulating Pages

You'll find the controls for working with document pages and master pages to be quite similar to QuarkXPress — if not slightly better. Once you realize the differences and start working, you can take advantage of InDesign's improvements. The differences mostly relate to guides and using the InDesign Pages pane rather than the QuarkXPress Document Layout palette (the Page Layout palette in QuarkXPress 6):

✦ InDesign provides three methods for creating guides: Click and drag them off the ruler as you do in QuarkXPress, double-click the ruler where you want a guide, or choose Layout ➪ Create Guides.

✦ To delete guides, you need to select them and click Delete. (To select all guides on a page, press Option+⌘+G or Ctrl+Alt+G.)

✦ Use the Pages pane (Window ➪ Pages or F12) as you would the QuarkXPress Document Layout palette (called the Page Layout palette in QuarkXPress 6). To place more than two pages side by side, you'll need to use the Keep Spreads Together command in the pane's palette menu.

✦ If you're missing the QuarkXPress Page menu, look for your favorite commands in the InDesign Layout menu and in the Pages pane's palette menu. There's a bonus in the Type menu: a command so you don't have to remember the shortcut (Option+Shift+⌘+N or Ctrl+Alt+Shift+N): Choose Type ➪ Insert Special Character ➪ Auto Page Number.

✦ You can base one master page on another, the same way you can base styles on each other. QuarkXPress does not offer this capability.

✦ To share master pages among documents, you can click and drag a master page icon into another document window. QuarkXPress cannot do this.

Working with Color

Not to intimidate you, but color will confound you (although Photoshop users will have an easier transition). Basically, try to forget everything you know about creating and applying colors in QuarkXPress. Here's what you need to know to work with colors in InDesign:

✦ Most of your work with colors happens through the Swatches pane (Window ➪ Swatches or F5) — not through the Colors pane as QuarkXPress users might think.

✦ To create colors, use the New Swatches command in the Swatches pane's palette menu. You cannot create Hexachrome colors in InDesign.

✦ To apply colors, first click the Stroke or Fill button on the Tools palette to specify where the color goes on the selected object. Then click a color in the Swatches pane.

✦ Use the Swatches or Colors pane (Window ➪ Colors or F6) to specify a shade (tint) of a color.

✦ InDesign's [Paper] color is equal to the QuarkXPress White color. Both programs use the color None for transparency, but InDesign provides None in both the Swatches pane and as a button on the Tools palette.

✦ To share colors among documents, click and drag a colored object into another document window.

Printing and Output

InDesign and QuarkXPress offer many of the same output capabilities, such as print styles (called *print presets* in InDesign), PDF export, color calibration, and color separation support. But there are some notable differences beyond the different organization of their Print dialog boxes:

✦ You cannot print hidden layers in InDesign as you can in QuarkXPress 6. You must make them visible before printing.

✦ To suppress printout of individual objects, use the Attributes pane (Window ➪ Attributes) and choose Nonprinting. You can also hide layers using the Layers pane (Window ➪ Layers or F7), which works pretty much like QuarkXPress's Layers feature.

✦ InDesign's Thumbnails option is more flexible than QuarkXPress's, letting you choose the number of thumbnails per page.

✦ Note that InDesign does not have any options to change image contrast or line-screen element for grayscale and black-and-white images, as QuarkXPress does. You'll need to apply such effects in an image editor.

✦ InDesign and QuarkXPress offer similar levels of color output controls, but InDesign does have several options QuarkXPress does not. One is setting ink density, another is automatic calculation of screen angles for spot colors. A third is the ability to more accurately preview documents with overprinting colors. InDesign also can apply black-point compensation as part of its color calibration during output. And InDesign lets you save your color-management preferences for use in other documents.

✦   ✦   ✦

Switching from PageMaker

PageMaker is now an officially dead product, with Adobe confirming this reality in 2004. This should surprise no one: There has been no PageMaker revision since version 7.0 came out in 2001, not even one to make it Mac OS X–native. So PageMaker users need to move to either InDesign or longtime rival QuarkXPress. However, most PageMaker users who would have switched to QuarkXPress have already done so. Most of the remaining users simply don't like the QuarkXPress structured approach to layouts, preferring PageMaker's more free-form style.

InDesign knows the PageMaker mentality, having adopted much of the PageMaker free-form approach since its very first version. (As InDesign has been updated, it has also taken on more of the structured QuarkXPress approach — but without removing its PageMaker-like roots.) So InDesign is a natural upgrade for PageMaker users.

Opening PageMaker Documents

The Open command (File ⇨ Open, or ⇨+O or Ctrl+O) lets you select and open documents (what PageMaker calls *publications*) and templates saved in PageMaker 6.0, 6.5, or 7.0 format on Macintosh or Windows. (You can't open libraries, though.) All the text, graphics, elements, layers, master pages, styles, and more in the PageMaker document are converted to their InDesign equivalents. If formatting can't be converted, an alert notifies you of the issues. After the document is converted, it appears as a new, untitled document.

Cross-Reference See Chapter 4 for complete information about opening files.

Because InDesign and PageMaker are similar, documents from PageMaker usually convert reliably. However, you still shouldn't count on PageMaker documents appearing and printing exactly the same way once they're converted in InDesign. You may need to do a little repair work, depending on the type of formatting you use.

Tip Be sure to copy all linked graphics to a single folder. (Do this by saving the publication to a new folder, with the All Linked Files option selected in the Save dialog box.) If you don't do this, InDesign may not get all the linked graphics from the source PageMaker file.

When you convert PageMaker documents to InDesign, you can expect the following:

✦ Master pages are converted, including all elements and content.

✦ Guides on master pages are placed on a separate layer called Guides.

✦ All line and stroke styles are converted to dashed or plain strokes.

✦ All styles are converted to InDesign styles.

✦ The Bold and Italic type styles are converted to the appropriate typeface (if available), Underline and Strikethrough are converted, while Outline, Shadow, and Reverse revert to plain text.

✦ Index tags are not maintained.

✦ If an imported graphic's link is not intact, it won't appear in the InDesign document. If you want to retain the graphic, you'll need to update the links in PageMaker (File⇨ Links Manager) before converting it.

✦ Pasted (embedded) graphics and graphics imported using OLE or Publish and Subscribe will not convert.

✦ Items for which Suppress Printout is checked are placed on a separate layer called Non-printing layer. To view these objects in InDesign, view the layer.

✦ If a group contains an item for which Suppress Printout is checked, all the items are ungrouped and the suppressed items are placed on the non-printing layer.

✦ PageMaker fill patterns are not supported.

✦ Tracking values will be modified to InDesign's settings.

✦ Color profiles are converted.

✦ Colors are converted to InDesign swatches according to their CMYK values (except for HLS colors, which are converted to RGB swatches).

Differences from PageMaker

As you might expect, because both PageMaker and InDesign come from the Adobe world, the transition from PageMaker to InDesign isn't that tough. The basic methods for working with frames, lines, and pages are the same in both programs. What you will get with InDesign is more control, with improved tools for drawing, formatting text, and manipulating objects. And there's not much to miss about PageMaker, either.

 Cross-Reference   If you're switching from PageMaker on Mac OS 9 to InDesign CS on Mac OS X, you should also get a good Mac OS X reference. A good start is the online bonus chapter "Switching to Mac OS X," available at www.InDesignCentral.com.

Using tools and setting preferences

The basic selection, object-creation, and navigation tools in InDesign are similar to those in PageMaker. You need to remember that InDesign CS2 has *three* selection tools: the Selection tool for moving and resizing objects, the Direct Selection tool for reshaping objects and working with graphics, and the new Position tool, which is essentially the same as PageMaker's Crop tool.

New Feature The Position tool is new to InDesign CS2, though it was available as part of the $49 PageMaker Plug-in Pack for InDesign CS.

Because you'll be switching tools often, as you did in PageMaker, get in the habit of using the keyboard shortcuts. (Table D-1, later in this chapter, shows InDesign keyboard shortcuts that differ from PageMaker shortcuts. It's not a long list because the two programs share many shortcuts as part of Adobe's strategy to have a common interface across its creative programs, with the exception of Adobe Acrobat.) As long as the Type tool isn't selected, you can hop from tool to tool by simply pressing a letter on the keyboard. In particular, you'll want to memorize the following:

- ✦ Press V for the Selection tool.
- ✦ Press A for the Direct Selection tool.
- ✦ Press T for the Type tool.
- ✦ Press H for the Hand tool. (You can also press the spacebar; when editing text, you press Option or Alt instead of the spacebar.)
- ✦ Press Z for the Zoom tool (you can also press ⌘+spacebar or Ctrl+spacebar to zoom in and Option+⌘+spacebar or Ctrl+Alt+spacebar to zoom out). Remember you can zoom to 1600 percent in InDesign!

Note There is no keyboard shortcut for the new Position tool.

InDesign includes significantly more preferences than PageMaker. You'll definitely want to explore all the panes in the Preferences dialog box (click InDesign ⇨ Preferences on the Mac or Edit ⇨ Preferences in Windows, or press ⌘+K or Ctrl+K). You might find some power you've never had before (although you will be disappointed to see values for Superscript, Subscript, and Small Cap relegated to a document-wide preference in InDesign rather than something you can set as a character attribute for local formatting as they were in PageMaker).

InDesign also allows multiple levels of undo of actions performed in the current document. PageMaker required that you revert to the last mini-saved version. Both programs also let you revert to the last saved version of the file.

Working with objects rather than elements

As with other aspects of InDesign, when you work with objects, you gain more than you lose. The types of objects are similar: text frames, graphics frames, and lines. PageMaker is limited to creating closed frames and straight lines.

While selecting and manipulating objects with tools, remember the following:

- ✦ Use the Selection tool to move objects or resize frames.
- ✦ Use the Direct Selection tool to reshape objects, change the endpoints of lines, and work with objects in groups. The Direct Selection tool also works like PageMaker's Crop tool, letting you move graphics within a frame.
- ✦ You get Bézier curves in InDesign! Using the Pen tool, Add Anchor Point tool, and Remove Anchor Point tool, you can draw and manipulate curves to your heart's content.
- ✦ You can't just click master page objects: Press Shift+⌘+click or Ctrl+Shift+click to select them.

When modifying objects, remember the following:

✦ Look in the Object menu for familiar Elements menu commands.

✦ InDesign CS2 now uses a more powerful version of the PageMaker Control palette.

✦ To specify runaround, choose Window ⇨ Text Wrap or press Option+⌘+W or Ctrl+Alt+W to display the Text Wrap pane.

✦ To specify attributes of text frames, use the Object ⇨ Text Frame Options command, or ⌘+B or Ctrl+B.

✦ What PageMaker called *rounded corners* are called *corner effects* in InDesign.

✦ To align objects in InDesign, use the Align pane or the controls in the Control palette. In PageMaker, you used the Align menu commands.

✦ To suppress printout of objects, put them on a different layer and hide the layer.

Working with text

When it comes to working with text, PageMaker users will feel comfortable, thanks to InDesign's Edit Story mode (choose Type ⇨ Edit Story, or press ⌘+Y or Ctrl+Y based on a feature that PageMaker users have long enjoyed.

If the display of graphics makes it difficult for you to edit text, go to the Display Preferences pane of the Preferences dialog box (choose InDesign ⇨ Preferences on the Mac or Edit ⇨ Preferences in Windows, or press ⌘+K or Ctrl+K). Chapter 3 covers this pane.

Other differences between PageMaker and InDesign include:

✦ To type special characters such as ñ, •, or ¶, you can choose Type ⇨ Glyphs or Type ⇨ Insert Special Character rather than use system utilities or key combinations.

Tip   Use the Keyboard Shortcuts feature (Edit ⇨ Keyboard Shortcuts) to assign a keyboard command to the Insert Character command if you find yourself using it often.

✦ In PageMaker's Edit Story mode, you are only able to see invisible characters such as spaces and tabs. But you can see all hidden characters all the time in InDesign by choosing Type ⇨ Show Hidden Characters.

✦ Use the Character pane (Window ⇨ Type & Tables ⇨ Character, or ⌘+T or Ctrl+T) to format highlighted characters. You'll notice there are no type-style buttons — InDesign requires you to choose the appropriate version of a typeface rather than apply bold and italic to the general typeface. Other type styles are listed in the Character pane's palette menu.

✦ Unlike PageMaker, you can stroke and fill characters in InDesign.

✦ Use the Paragraph pane (Window ⇨ Type & Tables ⇨ Paragraph, or Option+⌘+T or Ctrl+Alt+T) to format selected paragraphs. The palette menu includes additional commands for adding rules and controlling hyphenation.

✦ Use the Tabs pane (Window ⇨ Type & Tables ⇨ Tabs, or Shift+⌘+T or Ctrl+Shift+T) to set tabs for selected paragraphs.

✦ To create styles, use the New Character Style and New Paragraph Style commands in the palette menus of the Character pane (Window ⇨ Type & Tables ⇨ Character Styles, or

Shift+F11) and the Paragraph pane (Window ➪ Type & Tables ➪ Paragraph Styles or F11). To share styles with other documents, use the Load commands in the same menus.

✦ PageMaker offers just paragraph styles, while InDesign offers both paragraph and character styles.

✦ When you apply styles in PageMaker, local formatting is retained. InDesign styles have the opposite effect — they wipe out all local formatting when applied.

New Feature

InDesign CS2 adds bulleting and numbering features based on the same features in PageMaker, though they were available as part of the $49 PageMaker Plug-in Pack for InDesign CS. They work very similarly in InDesign CS2 to how they worked in PageMaker, and are covered in Chapter 18.

Table D-1: Keyboard Shortcuts Translated from PageMaker to InDesign

PageMaker Shortcut	Result	InDesign Equivalent
F10 or Shift+F7	Page grabber hand	H, or Option or Alt
⌘+M or Ctrl+M	Paragraph Specifications dialog box	Option+⌘+T or Ctrl+Alt+T
⌘+B or Ctrl+B	Styles pane	F11 (Character Styles), Shift+F11 (Paragraph Styles)
⌘+I or Ctrl+I	Indents/tabs dialog box	Shift+⌘+T or Ctrl+Shift+T
⌘+E or Ctrl+E	Edit in Story Editor	⌘+Y or Ctrl+Y
⌘+L	Spell-check	⌘+I or Ctrl+I
⌘+' (apostrophe) or Ctrl+' (apostrophe	Control palette	Option+⌘+6 or Ctrl+Alt+6
⌘+J or ⌘+J	Colors pane	F12 (Swatches pane)
⌘+8 or Ctrl+8	Layers pane	F7
Option+⌘+8 or Ctrl+Alt+8	Master Pages pane	F12 (Pages pane)
⌘+9 or Ctrl+9	Hyperlinks pane	none
⌘+U or Ctrl+U	Fill and Stroke dialog box	F10 (Stroke pane)
Shift+⌘+E	Align dialog box	none
Option+⌘+E	Text Wrap dialog box	Option+⌘+W or Ctrl+Alt+W

Working with graphics

InDesign and PageMaker are very much alike when it comes to importing and manipulating graphics. Differences include the following:

✦ You can click and drag graphics files into a layout in addition to using the Place command (File ➪ Place, or ⌘+D or Ctrl+D).

✦ You now get to create clipping paths; use the Object ➪ Clipping Path command.

✦ InDesign can automatically scale pictures or frames for you. Use the Object ⇨ Fitting commands: Fit Content to Frame, Fit Frame to Content, Center Content, and Fit Content Proportionally.

✦ To track the location of graphics files, use the Links pane (Window ⇨ Links, or Shift+⌘+D or Ctrl+Shift+D).

Manipulating pages

The one feature you'll miss about PageMaker is those neat little page icons in the lower-left corner of the document window. In shorter documents especially, the icons provided a quick, easy method for jumping to pages. Get used to using the Page text field and arrows at the bottom of the document window or the icons in the Pages pane instead.

Other differences between InDesign and PageMaker's page handling include the following:

✦ To create columns in PageMaker, you create the text blocks after you create your document. In InDesign, you can create a document with columns already in place using the options in the New dialog box.

✦ Conversely, in PageMaker, you can set up page-numbering settings when you create a new document, while in InDesign you set up page numbers and sections after the document has been created.

✦ InDesign provides three methods for creating guides: clicking and dragging them off the ruler as you do in PageMaker, double-clicking the ruler where you want a guide, or choosing Layout ⇨ Create Guides.

✦ To delete guides, you need to select them and click Delete. (To select all guides on a page, press Option+⌘+G or Ctrl+Alt+G.) Make sure that guides are not locked (View ⇨ Grids & Guides ⇨ Lock Guides, or Option+⌘+; [semicolon] or Ctrl+Alt+; [semicolon]).

✦ Use the Pages pane (Window ⇨ Pages or F12) to create and apply master pages; to add, move, and delete document pages; and to display different pages.

✦ You can now place more than two pages side by side. Choose the Keep Spread Together command in the Pages pane's palette menu to ensure they stay together if you add more pages later before them.

✦ Some of your favorite commands from the Layout menu seem to be missing (such as Insert Pages), but you can access similar commands from the Pages pane's palette menu.

✦ You can base one master page on another, the same way you can base styles on each other.

✦ To share master pages among documents, you can click and drag a master page icon into another document window.

Working with color

Although creating colors is somewhat different in InDesign, applying colors is fairly similar. You can create colors in the same color models, and you can manage colors in a similar way. Differences between PageMaker and InDesign include the following:

✦ Most of your work with colors happens through the Swatches pane (Window ⇨ Swatches or F5), not through the Colors pane as PageMaker users might think.

✦ To create colors, use the New Color Swatch command in the Swatches pane's palette menu.

✦ To apply colors, first click the Stroke or Fill button on the Tools palette to specify where the color goes on the selected object. Then click a color in the Swatches pane.

✦ Use the Colors pane (Window ➪ Colors or F6) to specify a shade (tint) of a color, or create reusable tints by choosing the New Tint Swatch command in the Swatches pane's palette menu.

✦ Apply the color [None] to strokes and fills for transparency; you can also click the Apply None button on the Tools palette.

✦ To share colors among documents, click and drag a colored object into another document window.

The PageMaker toolbar

In addition to adding the Position tool to InDesign CS2 that acts like PageMaker's Crop tool, InDesign CS2 also adds the PageMaker Toolbar, which provides 31 iconic buttons to permit quick access to various operations. You open and close this toolbar by choosing Window ➪ PageMaker Toolbar. Figure D-1 shows the toolbar and identifies each button's function.

New Feature The PageMaker toolbar is new to InDesign CS2, though it was available as part of the $49 PageMaker Plug-in Pack for InDesign CS.

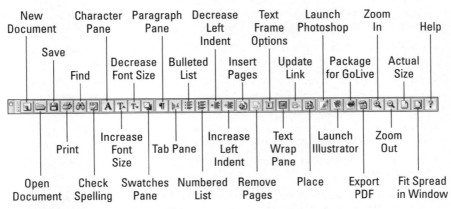

Figure D-1: The PageMaker toolbar

The functions are self-explanatory. Note that some require that an object or a block of text be selected (for example, Update Link, Increase Left Indent, and Numbered List) while others do not (for example, Save, Help, and Export PDF).

✦   ✦   ✦

Using Adobe InCopy CS2

Publishing is almost always a workgroup activity involving writers, editors, copy editors, layout artists, and production editors. Even when a person has multiple roles, most publications still involve multiple people. And that means that files go back and forth as edits are made, layouts are created, and text and other elements are adjusted to fit the available space. Like rival QuarkXPress, InDesign has a companion product called InCopy to facilitate this back and forth. InCopy is not as powerful as InDesign — it's not a layout tool — but it does let copy editors, editors, and other wordsmiths work on InDesign layouts to make sure headlines fit, stories fit, and captions can be written in context without needing a full copy of InDesign.

InCopy works best in a networked environment, where everyone shares files from a common folder. That way, a copy editor can work on a layout without worrying that the designer might be working on a local copy at the same time, for example.

InCopy is both a separate program that runs by itself for text editing of stories in an InDesign layout and a plug-in that works within InDesign to provide shared editing capabilities.

Using InCopy within InDesign

InCopy does more than install on a user's system. It changes how InDesign works, adding a new menu and pane, both called Notes, and several new menu options in the File and Edit menus. It also adds a Notes tool to the Tools palette.

Working with notes

The Notes feature inserts comments into text. To use it, click the Text tool inside a text box. You can now choose New Note to add a note, which is indicated in the file with a green dual-triangle character called a *note anchor*, as shown in Figure E-1. (The Notes menu duplicates options in the Notes pane's palette menu, shown in Figure E-1.)

Caution If you select a string of text, InDesign won't display the New Note menu option; instead, it displays the Convert to Note option to make that text into a note. That's great if someone types a note directly into text, but it can be dangerous if you are trying to highlight an entire word, as you would do when adding notes in Adobe Acrobat. You can convert a note back to text by choosing Convert to Text from the palette menu or from the Notes menu.

You can use the Notes pane's palette menu or the Notes menu in InDesign to navigate through notes (choose Previous Note or Next Note), control notes' display (Expand Notes in Story and Collapse Notes in Story), remove notes (choose Delete Note, Remove Notes from Story, or Remove All Notes), move to the note's anchor (choose Go to Note Anchor), or split a note into multiple notes (choose Split Note). If your document displays hidden text (Type ➪ Show Hidden Characters, or Option+⌘+I or Ctrl+Alt+I), the note anchor appears as a yellow hourglass figure in text (it will, of course, not print).

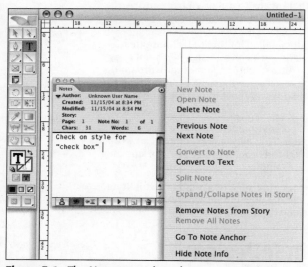

Figure E-1: The Notes pane, its palette menu, and the modified Tools palette

The InCopy plug-in also adds a Notes pane to the Preferences dialog box (choose InDesign ➪ Preferences on the Mac or Edit ➪ Preferences in Windows, or press ⌘+K or Ctrl+K). Figure E-2 shows the pane. In addition to changing the note anchor's color, you can also tell InDesign whether to spell-check notes, search notes in find/change operations, and display a user color behind notes in text. (Each user who edits a file gets assigned a unique color for easy identification, à la Microsoft Word's Track Changes feature.)

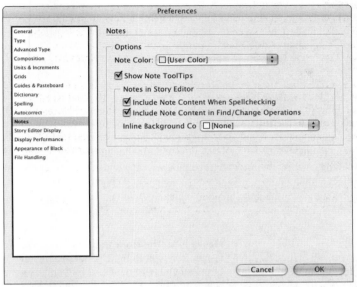

Figure E-2: The Notes pane of the Preferences dialog box

Working with other users

Before an InCopy user can work on a layout, an InDesign user has to InCopy-enable that layout. That means exporting the layout's stories to the InCopy Interchange format (InCopy files have a filename extension of .incx.), which you do by choosing Edit ➪ InCopy ➪ Export, which lets you then choose to export the selection, layer, all stories, or all graphics. Or all graphics and stories. (A story is all text in a text frame or path and any frames and/or paths linked to it.)

After navigating to the folder where you want to store the InCopy file, click Export, and then click OK.

If you had not done so already, you'll be asked to provide a user name, which InCopy uses to track the author of every change. Type a name, and then click OK, as shown in Figure E-3. (You can set up your user name in InDesign by choosing File ➪ User.)

Creating an InCopy file also makes the stories unavailable in the InDesign layout for further work. But you can keep working on the layout, such as resizing frames, adding graphics, and even changing the text's color. If you want to work on the text, you need to *check out* the story, making it available to you but to no one else. To do so, click on the frame containing the story you want to edit, and then choose Edit ➪ InCopy ➪ Check Out Story (⌘+F9 or Ctrl+F9). When done, choose either Edit ➪ InCopy ➪ Check In Story (Shift+⌘+F9 or Ctrl+Shift+F9) or Edit ➪ InCopy ➪ Check In All (Option+Shift+⌘+F9 or Ctrl+Alt+Shift+F9) to return the stories to use by others. (Or choose Edit ➪ InCopy ➪ Cancel Check Out to undo all your changes and leave the story unchanged.)

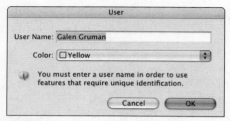

Figure E-3: Setting up a user name for
InCopy's edit tracking

If someone else is working on a story, you can have InDesign apply the current changes to the layout on your screen by choosing Edit ⇨ InCopy ⇨ Update Story (⌘+F5 or Ctrl+F5).

When you are working on a story, InDesign displays an icon indicating its status, as Figure E-4 shows.

Figure E-4: The icons that indicate a story's status, from left to right: Checked In, Checked Out, Checked Out by Someone Else, and Checked In but Out of Date

Caution   When you choose Export All Stories, InDesign exports every story it finds. And by *story*, InDesign means any text in any text frame. So, if your headlines are in separate frames and not linked to their body copy frames, the headlines will each be a separate story. Ditto for any captions or text in figures. This can create dozens of files in your project folder. So it's usually better not to choose Export All Stories and instead export each story individually that you want to be editable.

Using InCopy Alone

The stand-alone InCopy application looks and works very much like the InDesign Story Editor. You'll also find a bevy of familiar panes — Notes, Scripts, Swatches, Tags, Tools, and the various text-editing panes — in the Window menu. You'll also find the standard Edit and Type menu options to change text attributes and do spell-checking. Plus, you'll find many of the standard InDesign preferences panes.

What's different? Plenty.

Story views

First, there are three panes in which to view the story. The Story pane is the plainest view, essentially the same as the InDesign Story Editor. Here, you work on text as if you are in a word processor, with applied styles shown at left. Figure E-5 shows this view. The Layout pane shows the story as it appears in InDesign. The Galley pane is like the Story pane, except that each line breaks as it does in InDesign, so you can see where lines end and whether the last lines in paragraphs have room for more text or whether small text deletions could easily eliminate a short last line during copy fitting.

What's New in InCopy

InCopy CS2has several changes since its previous versions, as InDesign has:

✦ InCopy CS2 now uses the InDesign Interchange (.inx) format, so it can store file geography in addition to text. It can save in both the InDesign CS and CS2 interchange formats for backward compatibility.

✦ InCopy CS2 can now open Microsoft Word, Rich Text Format (RTF), and ASCII text (.txt) files directly.

✦ InCopy CS2 lets you set a marker in text that you can then quickly find, so you can easily return to where you left off. Choose Edit ➪ Position Marker ➪ Insert Marker (Shift+⌘+[or Ctrl+Shift+[) to insert the marker and Edit ➪ Position Marker ➪ Go to Marker (Shift+⌘+] or Ctrl+Shift+]) to find it. Choose Edit ➪ Position Marker ➪ Remove Marker to delete it.

✦ InCopy CS2 lets you create text macros, so you can insert long strings of texts by typing just a few characters.

✦ InCopy CS2 gives you more control over what parts of a document are exported to an InCopy file, supporting graphics as well as text. The menu option for this, Edit ➪ InCopy, has changed slightly from the previous version.

✦ InCopy CS2 now lets you create a type area in addition to the page size when creating a new document, letting you create a stand-alone copyfit area.

✦ When InCopy CS2 is installed, the Story List pane now appears in InDesign as well as in InCopy.

✦ InCopy CS2 now lets you place graphics in existing frames (or as anchored graphics into text) and make basic modifications to them, such as positioning the graphic within the frame.

✦ The Story List pane has been renamed the Assignments pane in InCopy CS2, while the Story Info pane has been renamed the Change Info pane.

✦ InCopy CS2 has changed many shortcuts, as well as added new ones.

Some enhancements mirror those in InDesign CS2:

✦ InCopy CS2 now has greater control over Word and RTF files, as well as support for their and InDesign's anchored text frames.

✦ InCopy CS2 now allows drag-and-drop text editing.

✦ InCopy CS adds a Layers pane.

✦ InCopy CS2 supports dynamic spell-checking and automatic text correction, as well as multiple dictionaries per document.

✦ InCopy CS2 adds the Quick Apply palette to apply object, character, and paragraph styles entirely through keyboard interaction.

✦ InCopy can paste unformatted text and can add or remove spaces around pasted text as needed.

✦ InCopy CS2 includes the Story Editor enhancements such as an indicator for overset text in galley view, anti-aliased text for smoother on-screen text display, and a vertical depth ruler.

✦ InCopy CS2 supports the new Towards Spine and Away from Spine paragraph alignments, last-line right indent, automatic bullets and numbering, footnotes, and other changes made to paragraph styles, character styles, local paragraph formatting, and local character formatting.

Note   To edit stories from an InDesign file, you must first export that story to its own InCopy Interchange (.incx) file, as described earlier in this appendix. The reason that InCopy has all these separate story files is so multiple users can work on the same layout, but on different stories, at the same time.

Note   Note the Story and Galley panes, as well as the Assignments pane, will show all InCopy stories associated with an InDesign file—InCopy CS adds them all automatically if you open any of them. In any of these panes, you can display and hide stories by clicking the triangles to the left of the story name.

Story checkout, checking, and saving

When you open an InCopy Interchange file in InCopy, you need to check stories out to edit them and check them in to make them available to others, as described in the previous section. To check out stories, go to the story in any of the panes, and then choose File ⇨ Check Out Story, or press ⌘+Y or Ctrl+Y. You check stories back in by choosing File ⇨ Check In Story, or pressing Option+⌘+W or Ctrl+Alt+W, or by choosing File ⇨ Check In All, or pressing Option+Shift+⌘+W or Ctrl+Alt+Shift+W. The Assignments pane (Window ⇨ Assignments, or Option+⌘+F10 or Ctrl+Alt+F10) shows which stories are already checked out.

You can also choose File ⇨ Cancel Checkout to make a story available to others without saving any changes you made. Choose File ⇨ Revert Story instead to undo changes made since the last save but keep the story checked out for your use.

To save a story, you have five options in the File menu:

✦ Save Story, or ⌘+S or Ctrl+S, to save the current story.

✦ Save Story As, or Shift+⌘+S or Ctrl+Shift+S, to save the current story with a new name or in a new location. Such a story will have to be imported into the InDesign layout.

✦ Save Story Copy, or Option+⌘+S or Ctrl+Alt+S, to save a copy of the current story, such as for archiving story versions.

✦ Save a Version saves a version of the text file, so you can work with different versions and later choose one, as Chapter 35 explains.

✦ Save All Stories, or Option+Shift+⌘+S or Ctrl+Alt+Shift+S, to save all stories—this helps ensure all changes are made to the InDesign document, no matter what stories the changes occurred in.

Revisions tracking

InCopy can track who made what changes to InDesign files. To enable such revisions tracking, choose Changes ⇨ Track Changes in Current Story, or press ⌘+Y or Ctrl+Y. If multiple stories are open, you can choose Changes ⇨ Enable Tracking in All Stories.

When reviewing changes, you can move from change to change by choosing Changes ⇨ Next Change, or pressing ⌘+down arrow or Ctrl+down arrow. You can move backward by choosing Changes ⇨ Previous Change, or pressing ⌘+up arrow or Ctrl+up arrow. You can accept individual changes by choosing Changes ⇨ Accept Change, or pressing Shift+⌘+O or Ctrl+Shift+O, and you can accept all changes by choosing Changes ⇨ Accept All Changes, or Option+Shift+⌘+O or Ctrl+Alt+Shift+O.

Zoom tool

Hand tool

Position tool

Note tool

Type tool

Tools palette

Command   Info   Track Changes
Bar palette Column   Toolbar palette

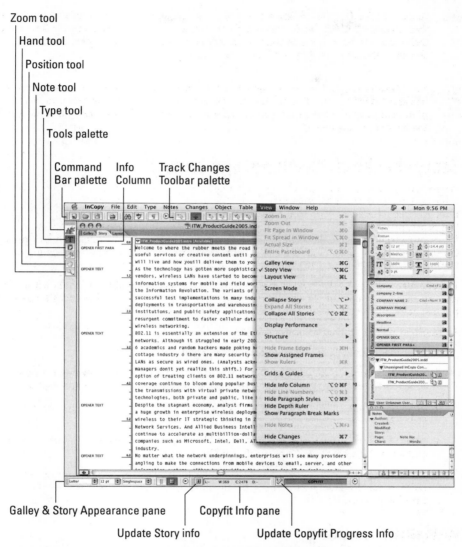

Galley & Story Appearance pane   Copyfit Info pane

Update Story info   Update Copyfit Progress Info

Figure E-5: Adobe InCopy CS2, with a layout viewed in the Story pane

Likewise, you can reject changes individually by choosing Changes ⇨ Reject Change, or pressing Shift+⌘+; (semicolon) or Ctrl+Shift+; (semicolon), or globally by choosing Changes ⇨ Reject All Changes, or pressing Option+Shift+⌘+; (semicolon) or Ctrl+Alt+Shift+; (semicolon).

When reviewing changes, you can get information on who made the change and when by having the Change Info pane open (Window ⇨ Change Info, or Shift+⌘+F3 or Ctrl+Shift+F3).

Tip

You can hide changes as you make them by choosing View ⇨ Hide Changes, or pressing ⌘+7 or Ctrl+7. To review changes, you'll need to make changes visible.

Note   You can also use the Track Changes Toolbar pane to move among revisions and accept or reject changes. The iconic palette offers the following buttons from left to right: Track Changes in Current Story, Show/Hide Changes, Previous Change, Next Change, Accept Change, Reject Change, Accept All Changes, and Reject All Changes.

Special features

The editing and formatting features are almost the same as in InDesign, so this appendix does not cover them. Likewise, the Notes features are the same as described earlier in this appendix. But there are some specific InCopy features you should know about:

✦ You can transpose two letters by inserting the text-insertion pointer between them and choosing Edit ⇨ Transpose (Option+⌘+4 or Ctrl+Alt+4).

✦ You can create text macros in the Text Macros pane (Window ⇨ Text Macros, or Shift+F10). You add a macro by choosing New Macro from the palette menu or by pressing Option+⌘+F8 or Ctrl+Alt+F8.

✦ You can look up a word in an electronic thesaurus to find better alternatives. Choose Window ⇨ Thesaurus or press Option+⌘+F7 or Ctrl+Alt+F7 to open the pane. If a word is selected, click the Load Word icon (the eyedropper icon) from the bottom of the pane to add it. Click the Lookup Word button (the magnifying-glass icon) to look up alternatives. If you want one of the alternatives, select it and then click the Change Word button (the dual-curved-arrows icon).

✦ The Command Bar palette (Window ⇨ Command Bar, or Shift+⌘+F2 or Ctrl+Shift+F2) provides iconic button access for, from left to right, New Document, Open Document, Save, Print, Find, Check Spelling, and Show/Hide Hidden Characters.

✦ The Galley & Story Appearance pane likewise provides Font, Size, and text preview Spacing pop-up menus to change the Story and Galley panes' text display, plus iconic controls to Show/Hide Line Numbers and Show/Hide Paragraph Styles. You can also change these settings, plus the text cursor display, through the Galley & Story Display pane in the Preferences dialog box (choose InCopy ⇨ Preferences on the Mac or Edit ⇨ Preferences in Windows, or press ⌘+K or Ctrl+K). The pane is identical to the Story Editor preferences pane covered in Chapter 14. The show/hide options in the Galley & Story Appearance pane are also available in the View menu.

✦ The Copyfit Info pane shows how many lines a story is over what fits in its text frame(s) and/or path(s), using the bar at its far right. As you delete text, the progress bar gets smaller and smaller until there is no runover. The pane also tracks the number of lines, words, characters, and column depth. The Update Copyfit Progress Info button (the ruler icon) checks the current InDesign layout to see if changes to the layout have solved or created copyfitting problems, in which text overflows its text frame(s). The pane also has the Update Story Info button (the downward arrow) at far left that updates the Change Info pane (File ⇨ Change Info, or Shift+⌘+F3 or Ctrl+Shift+F3) with the name of the current reviser.

These last three panes, as well as the Track Changes Toolbar palette, are shown in Figure E-5.

✦   ✦   ✦

More Resources

Technology doesn't stand still, especially in an area as dynamic as publishing where multiple products work together. That's why I've created an independent Web site that helps InDesign users stay current on tools and techniques. The www.InDesignCentral.com site provides the following resources:

- ✦ **Tools:** Links to plug-ins, scripts, utilities, and Adobe downloads

- ✦ **Tips:** My favorite tips, as well as reader tips

- ✦ **Resources:** Print publishing links, Web publishing links, Mac OS X links, and Windows 2000/XP links

- ✦ *InDesign Bible* **series:** Excerpts from the books, including color versions of the screenshots from the chapters that cover color, as well as updates from after the books' release

Figure F-1 shows the site's home page.

Wiley Publishing, the publisher of this book, also offers a wide range of books to help layout artists and publications designers exploit the publishing tools to the fullest:

- ✦ *Adobe InDesign CS2 For Dummies* by Barbara Assadi and Galen Gruman is a great way to quickly get up to speed on the newest version of InDesign.

- ✦ *Photoshop CS2 Bible* by Deke McClelland and Laurie Ulrich Fuller provides an in-depth look at how to make the most of Photoshop's extensive image-editing capabilities.

- ✦ *Photoshop CS2 Bible, Professional Edition* by Deke McClelland and Laurie Ulrich Fuller goes even further, adding new and expanded coverage of high-end topics, such as creating and optimizing Web graphics, using filters, working with convolution kernels and displacement maps, harnessing actions and batch processing, and adjusting color.

- ✦ *Illustrator CS2 Bible* by Ted Alspach and Brian Underdahl includes in-depth coverage on using Illustrator for print and Web graphics, as well as information on how to integrate Illustrator with Photoshop.

- ✦ *Illustrator CS2 For Dummies* by Ted Alspach is a great way to quickly get up to speed on the newest version of Illustrator.

- ✦ *Adobe Acrobat 7 PDF Bible* by Ted Padova features complete coverage of using Acrobat and PDF for print prepress, the Internet, CD-ROMs, and all the new media.

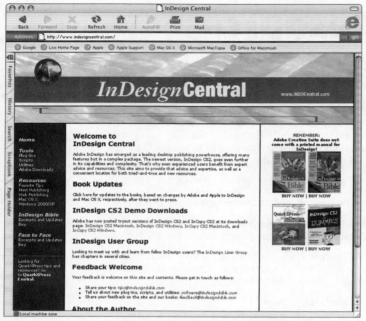

Figure F-1: The home page for the InDesignCentral Web site

✦ *Adobe Creative Suite 2 Bible* by Ted Padova, Kelly L. Murdock, and Wendy Halderman provides an all-in-one resource for users of Adobe's cornerstone tools (Photoshop, Illustrator, Acrobat Professional, and InDesign).

✦ *QuarkXPress to InDesign: Face to Face* by Galen Gruman provides a visual, side-by-side comparison of how to achieve in InDesign 2, CS, and CS2 the steps you would take in QuarkXPress versions 4, 5, and 6.

✦ *QuarkXPress 6 Bible* by Galen Gruman and Barbara Assadi provides detailed advice on using QuarkXPress for a variety of publications.

✦ *QuarkXPress 6 For Dummies* by Barbara Assadi and Galen Gruman provides a quick look at key QuarkXPress features, a handy way for experienced users of previous versions to quickly get up to speed.

✦ *Digital Photography: Top 100 Simplified Tips & Tricks* by Gregory Georges provides clear, illustrated instructions for 100 tasks that reveal cool secrets, teach time-saving tricks, and explain great tips to make you a better digital photographer.

✦ *Total Digital Photography: The Shoot to Print Workflow Handbook* by Serge Timacheff and David Karlins offers complete, end-to-end workflow advice from shoot to print in a full-color presentation.

✦   ✦   ✦

Shortcuts Cheat Sheet

Shortcuts are essential to making the most of InDesign. Sure, you can access everything from a menu or pane, but shortcuts make the work much faster. This appendix covers InDesign's keyboard shortcuts and working with contextual menus, which lets you use the mouse to find out what options are available for specific objects.

Because there are so many keyboard shortcuts, I've broken them into functional areas to help you find them more easily in the following table.

Action or Command	Macintosh	Windows
Opening/Closing/Saving		
New document	⌘+N	Ctrl+N
New default document	Option+⌘+N	Ctrl+Alt+N
Open document	⌘+O	Ctrl+O
Open library	Option+Shift+⌘+L	Ctrl+Alt+Shift+L
Close document	⌘+W	Ctrl+W or Ctrl+F4
Close all documents	Option+Shift+⌘+W	Ctrl+Alt+Shift+W
Quit program	⌘+Q	Ctrl+Q or Alt+F4
Save document	⌘+S	Ctrl+S
Save document as	Shift+⌘+S	Ctrl+Shift+S
Save copy of document	Option+⌘+S	Ctrl+Alt+D
Export document to PDF or EPS	⌘+E	Ctrl+E
Place text and graphics	⌘+D	Ctrl+D
Viewing		
Hide/show panes	Tab	Tab
Hide/show all panes but Tools palette	Shift+Tab	Shift+Tab
Zoom in	⌘+=	Ctrl+=
Zoom out	⌘+− (hyphen)	Ctrl+− (hyphen)
Fit page/spread in window	⌘+0	Ctrl+Alt+=
Fit spread in window	Shift+⌘+0	Ctrl+Alt+0
Fit entire pasteboard in window	Option+Shift+⌘+0	Ctrl+Alt+Shift+0
Display actual size	⌘+1	Ctrl+1
Display at 50%	⌘+5	Ctrl+5
Display at 200%	⌘+2	Ctrl+2
Display at 400%	⌘+4	Ctrl+4
Overprint preview	Option+Shift+⌘+Y	Ctrl+Alt+Shift+Y
Switch between current and previous view	Option⌘+2	Ctrl+Alt+2
Set magnification	Option⌘+5	Ctrl+Alt+5
Set all pages to same view	⌘+percent in view percent menu	Ctrl+percent in view percent menu
Switch to previous document window	Shift+⌘+F6	Ctrl+Shift+F6
Switch to next document window	⌘+Y	Ctrl+F6
Show/hide text threads	Option+⌘+Y	Ctrl+Alt+Y

Action or Command	Macintosh	Windows
Show/hide frame edges	⌘+H	Ctrl+H
Show/hide rulers	⌘+R	Ctrl+R
Show hidden characters	Option+⌘+I	Ctrl+Alt+I
Preference/Setup		
Preferences dialog box	⌘+K	Ctrl+K
Document setup	Option+⌘+P	Ctrl+Alt+P
Tools		
Selection tool	V	V
Direct Selection tool	A	A
Type tool	T	T
Text Path tool	Shift+T	Shift+T
Pen tool	P	P
Ellipse tool	L	L
Rectangle tool	M	M
Rectangle Frame tool	F	F
Rotate tool	R	R
Scale tool	S	S
Shear tool	O	O
Scissors tool	C	C
Hand tool	H	H
Temporary Hand tool	Shift+spacebar	Shift+spacebar
Zoom tool	Z	Z
Temporary zoom-in tool	⌘+spacebar	Ctrl+spacebar
Temporary zoom-out tool	Option+⌘+spacebar	Ctrl+Alt+spacebar
Gradient tool	G	G
Fill button	X	X
Stroke button	X	X
Swap Fill/Stroke button	Shift+X	Shift+X
Default Fill/Stroke button	D	D
Apply Color button	, (comma)	, (comma)
Apply Gradient button	. (period)	. (period)
Apply None button	/	/

Continued

Action or Command	Macintosh	Windows
Panes		
Apply value in field	Option+Enter	Shift+Return
Show Control palette	Option+⌘+6	Ctrl+Alt+6
Show Links pane	Shift⌘+D	Ctrl+Shift+D
Show Layers pane	F7	F7
Show Pages pane	F12	F12
Show Swatches pane	F5	F5
Show Color pane	F6	F6
Show Transform pane	F9	F9
Show Character pane	⌘+T	Ctrl+T
Show Paragraph pane	Option+⌘+T	Ctrl+Alt+T
Show Character Styles pane	Shift+F11	Shift+F11
Show Paragraph Styles pane	F11	F11
Show Object Styles pane	⌘+F7	Ctrl+F7
Show Quick Apply palette	⌘+Return	Ctrl+Enter
Show Text Wrap pane	Option+⌘+W	Ctrl+Alt+W
Open Text Frame Options dialog box	⌘+B	Ctrl+B
Show Index pane	Shift+F8	Shift+F8
Show Table pane	Shift+F9	Shift+F9
Show Tabs pane	Shift+⌘+T	Ctrl+Shift+T
Show Align pane	Shift+F7	Shift+F7
Show Stroke pane	F10	F10
Show Transparency pane	Shift+F10	Shift+F10
Show Info pane	F8	F8
Guides		
Show/hide guides	⌘+; (semicolon)	Ctrl+; (semicolon)
Lock/unlock guides	Option+⌘+; (semicolon)	Ctrl+Alt+; (semicolon)
Snap to guides on/off	Shift+⌘+; (semicolon)	Ctrl+Shift+; (semicolon)
Show/hide baseline grid	Option+⌘+"	Ctrl+Alt+"
Show/hide document grid	⌘+"	Ctrl+"
Snap to document grid on/off	Shift+⌘+"	Ctrl+Shift+"
Select all guides	Option+⌘+G	Ctrl+Alt+G
Create zero-point guidelines	⌘+click zero point when dragging guides	Ctrl+click zero point when dragging guides

Action or Command	*Macintosh*	*Windows*
Adding and Navigating Pages		
Add new page	Shift+⌘+P	Ctrl+Shift+P
Go to first page	Shift+⌘+PgUp	Ctrl+Shift+Page Up
Go back one page	Shift+PgUp	Shift+Page Up
Go forward one page	Shift+PgDn *or* ⌘+PgDn	Shift+Page Down *or* Ctrl+keypad PgDn
Go to last page	Shift+⌘+PgDn	Ctrl+Shift+Page Down
Go to last page viewed	⌘+PgUp	Ctrl+keypad PgUp
Go forward one spread	Option+PgDn	Alt+Page Dn
Go back one spread	Option+PgUp	Alt+Page Up
Object Selection		
Select master page	Shift+⌘+click	Ctrl+Shift+click
Select topmost object	Option+Shift+⌘+]	Ctrl+Alt+Shift+]
Select object above current object	Option+⌘+]	Ctrl+Alt+]
Select bottommost object	Option+Shift+⌘+[	Ctrl+Alt+Shift+[
Select object below current object	Option+⌘+[	Ctrl+Alt+[
Go to last frame in thread	Option+Shift+⌘+PgDn	Ctrl+Alt+Shift+Page Down
Go to next frame in thread	Option+⌘+PgDn	Ctrl+Alt+Page Down
Go to first frame in thread	Option+Shift+⌘+PgUp	Ctrl+Alt+Shift+Page Up
Go to previous frame in thread	Option+⌘+PgUp	Ctrl+Alt+Page Up
Moving Objects		
Move selection 1 point	Left, right, up, and down arrows	Left, right, up, and down arrows
Move selection 10 points	Shift+left, right, up, and down arrows	Shift+left, right, up, and down arrows
Bring object to front	Shift+⌘+]	Ctrl+Shift+]
Bring object forward	⌘+]	Ctrl+]
Send object to back	Shift+⌘+[	Ctrl+Shift+[
Send object backward	⌘+[	Ctrl+[
Object Commands		
Cut	⌘+X	Ctrl+X
Copy	⌘+V	Ctrl+V
Paste	⌘+P	Ctrl+P

Continued

Action or Command	Macintosh	Windows
Paste into	Option+⌘+V	Ctrl+Alt+V
Paste in place	Option+Shift+⌘+V	Ctrl+Alt+Shift+V
Paste without formatting	Shift+⌘+V	Ctrl+Shift+V
Clear	Delete	Backspace or Del
Duplicate object	Option+Shift+⌘+D	Ctrl+Alt+Shift+D
Step and repeat	Shift+⌘+U	Ctrl+Shift+U
Resize proportionately	Shift+drag	Shift+drag
Resize frame and content	⌘+drag	Ctrl+drag
Center content	Shift+⌘+E	Ctrl+Shift+E
Fill frame proportionally	Option+Shift+⌘+C	Ctrl+Alt+Shift+C
Fit content proportionally	Option+Shift+⌘+E	Ctrl+Alt+Shift+E
Fit content to frame	Option+⌘+E	Ctrl+Alt+E
Fit frame to content	Option+⌘+C	Ctrl+Alt+C
Decrease size/scale by 1%	⌘+, (comma)	Ctrl+, (comma)
Decrease size/scale by 5%	Option+⌘+, (comma)	Ctrl+Alt+, (comma)
Increase size/scale by 5%	Option+⌘+. (period)	Ctrl+Alt+. (period)
Duplicate	Option+drag, or Option+left, right, up, and down arrows	Alt+drag, or Alt+left, right, up, and down arrows
Group	⌘+G	Ctrl+G
Ungroup	Shift+⌘+G	Ctrl+Shift+G
Lock	⌘+L	Ctrl+L
Unlock	Option+⌘+L	Ctrl+Alt+L
Drop shadow	Option+⌘+M	Ctrl+Alt+M
Transform Again	Option+⌘+3	Ctrl+Alt+3
Transform Sequence Again	Option+⌘+4	Ctrl+Alt+4
Graphics Handling		
Convert text to outlines	Shift+⌘+O	Ctrl+Alt+O
Create outlines without deleting text	Option+Shift+⌘+O	Ctrl+Alt+Shift+O
Image color settings	Option+Shift+⌘+D	Ctrl+Alt+Shift+D
Make clipping path	Option+Shift+⌘+K	Ctrl+Alt+Shift+K
Make compound path	⌘+8	Ctrl+8
Release compound path	Option+⌘+8	Ctrl+Alt+8

Action or Command	*Macintosh*	*Windows*
Text Selection		
Select all	⌘+A	Ctrl+A
Deselect all	Shift+⌘+A	Ctrl+Shift+A
Select word	double-click	double-click
Select one word to left	Shift+⌘+left arrow	Ctrl+Shift+left arrow
Select one word to right	Shift⌘+right arrow	Ctrl+Shift+right arrow
Select range	Shift+left, right, up, and down arrows	Shift+left, right, up, and down arrows
Select paragraph	triple-click	triple-click
Select one paragraph before	Shift+⌘+up arrow	Ctrl+Shift+up arrow
Select one paragraph after	Shift+⌘+down arrow	Ctrl+Shift+down arrow
Select to start of story	Shift+⌘+Home	Ctrl+Shift+Home
Select to end of story	Shift+⌘+End	Ctrl+Shift+End
Moving within Text		
Move left one word	⌘+left arrow	Ctrl+left arrow
Move right one word	⌘+right arrow	Ctrl+right arrow
Move to start of line	Home	Home
Move to end of line	End	End
Move to previous paragraph	⌘+up arrow	Ctrl+up arrow
Move to next paragraph	⌘+down arrow	Ctrl+down arrow
Move to start of story	⌘+Home	Ctrl+Home
Move to end of story	⌘+End	Ctrl+End
Text/Paragraph Formats		
Bold	Shift+⌘+B	Ctrl+Shift+B
Italic	Shift+⌘+I	Ctrl+Shift+I
Normal	Shift+⌘+Y	Ctrl+Shift+Y
Underline	Shift+⌘+U	Ctrl+Shift+U
Strikethrough	Shift+⌘+/	Ctrl+Shift+/
All caps on/off	Shift+⌘+K	Ctrl+Shift+K
Small caps	Shift+⌘+H	Ctrl+Shift+H
Superscript	Shift+⌘+=	Ctrl+Shift+=
Subscript	Option+Shift+⌘+=	Ctrl+Alt+Shift+=

Continued

Action or Command	Macintosh	Windows
Update character style based on selection	Option+Shift+⌘+C	Ctrl+Alt+Shift+C
Update paragraph style based on selection	Option+Shift+⌘+R	Ctrl+Alt+Shift+R
Drop caps and nested styles	Option+⌘+R	Ctrl+Alt+R
Paragraph rules	Option+⌘+J	Ctrl+Alt+J
Set horizontal scale to 100%	Shift+⌘+X	Ctrl+Shift+X
Set vertical scale to 100%	Option+Shift+⌘+X	Ctrl+Alt+Shift+X
Increase point size by 1 point	Shift+⌘+. (period)	Ctrl+Shift+. (period)
Increase point size by 10 points	Option+Shift+⌘+. (period)	Ctrl+Alt+Shift+. (period)
Decrease point size by 1 point	Shift+⌘+, (comma)	Ctrl+Shift+, (comma)
Decrease point size by 10 points	Option+Shift+⌘+, (comma)	Ctrl+Alt+Shift+, (comma)
Text Alignment and Spacing		
Align left	Shift+⌘+L	Ctrl+Shift+L
Align right	Shift+⌘+R	Ctrl+Shift+R
Align center	Shift+⌘+C	Ctrl+Shift+C
Justify full	Shift+⌘+F	Ctrl+Shift+F
Justify left	Shift+⌘+J	Ctrl+Shift+J
Justify right	Option+Shift+⌘+R	Ctrl+Alt+Shift+R
Justify center	Option+Shift+⌘+C	Ctrl+Alt+Shift+C
Autohyphenation on/off	Option+Shift+⌘+H	Ctrl+Alt+Shift+H
Hyphenation on/off (selected text)	Option+⌘+H	Ctrl+Alt+H
Set spacing and justification	Option+Shift+⌘+J	Ctrl+Alt+Shift+J
Set keep options	Option+⌘+K	Ctrl+Alt+K
Increase leading by 2 points	Option+up arrow	Alt+up arrow
Decrease leading by 2 points	Option+down arrow	Alt+down arrow
Increase leading by 10 points	Option+⌘+up arrow	Ctrl+Alt+up arrow
Decrease leading by 10 points	Option+⌘+down arrow	Ctrl+Alt+down arrow
Use autoleading	Option+Shift+⌘+A	Ctrl+Alt+Shift+A
Increase kerning/tracking by 20 units	Option+right arrow	Alt+right arrow
Increase kerning/tracking by 100 units	Option+⌘+right arrow	Ctrl+Alt+right arrow
Decrease kerning/tracking by 20 units	Option+left arrow	Alt+left arrow
Decrease kerning/tracking by 100 units	Option+⌘+left arrow	Ctrl+Alt+left arrow

Action or Command	Macintosh	Windows
Clear all kerning/tracking (set to 0)	Shift+⌘+Q	Ctrl+Shift+Q
Increase baseline shift by 2 points	Option+Shift+up arrow	Alt+Shift+up arrow
Increase baseline shift by 10 points	Option+Shift+⌘+up arrow	Ctrl+Alt+Shift+up arrow
Decrease baseline shift by 2 points	Option+Shift+down arrow	Alt+Shift+down arrow
Decrease baseline shift by 10 points	Option+Shift+⌘+down arrow	Ctrl+Alt+Shift+down arrow
Align to grid on/off	Option+Shift+⌘+G	Ctrl+Alt+Shift+G
Table Editing		
Insert table	Option+Shift+⌘+T	Ctrl+Alt+Shift+T
Insert column	Option+⌘+9	Ctrl+Alt+9
Insert row	⌘+9	Ctrl+9
Select table	Option+⌘+A	Ctrl+Alt+A
Select column	Option+⌘+3	Ctrl+Alt+3
Select row	⌘+3	Ctrl+3
Select cell	⌘+/	Ctrl+/
Delete column	Shift+Delete	Shift+Backspace
Delete row	⌘+Delete	Ctrl+Backspace
Table setup	Option+Shift+⌘+B	Ctrl+Alt+Shift+B
Set cell text options	Option+⌘+B	Ctrl+Alt+B
Find/Change Text, Spelling, and Indexing		
Edit in Story Editor	⌘+Y	Ctrl+Y
Find/change	⌘+F	Ctrl+F
Find next	Option+⌘+F	Ctrl+Alt+F
Search for selected text	Shift+F1	Shift+F1
Add selected text to Find What field	⌘+F1	Ctrl+F1
Add selected text to Change To field	⌘+F2	Ctrl+F2
Change current selection	⌘+F3	Ctrl+F3
Change current selection and search forward	Shift+⌘+F3	Ctrl+Shift+F3
Check spelling	⌘+I	Ctrl+I
Add new index entry	Option+Shift+⌘+]	Ctrl+Alt+Shift+]
Add new index entry (reversed)	Option+Shift+⌘+[	Ctrl+Alt+Shift+[
New index/open index entry dialog box	⌘+U	Ctrl+U

Continued

Action or Command	Macintosh	Windows
Special characters		
Bullet (•)	Option+8	Alt+8
Ellipsis (…)	Option+; (semicolon)	Alt+; (semicolon)
Copyright (©)	Option+G	Alt+G
Registered trademark (®)	Option+R	Alt+R
Trademark (™)	Option+2	Alt+2
Paragraph (¶)	Option+7	Alt+7
Section (§)	Option+6	Alt+6
Switch between keyboard and typographic quotes	Option+Shift+⌘+"	Ctrl+Alt+Shift+"
Em dash (—)	Option+Shift+– (hyphen)	Alt+Shift+– (hyphen)
En dash (–)	Option+– (hyphen)	Alt+– (hyphen)
Nonbreaking hyphen	Option+⌘+– (hyphen)	Ctrl+Alt+– (hyphen)
Discretionary hyphen	Shift+⌘+– (hyphen)	Ctrl+Shift+– (hyphen)
Em space	Shift+⌘+M	Ctrl+Shift+M
En space	Shift+⌘+N	Ctrl+Shift+N
Thin space	Option+Shift+⌘+M	Ctrl+Alt+Shift+M
Hair space	Option+Shift+⌘+I	Ctrl+Alt+Shift+I
Nonbreaking space	Option+⌘+X	Ctrl+Alt+X
Soft return	Shift+Enter	Shift+Return
Column break	keypad Enter	keypad Enter
Frame break	Shift+keypad Enter	Shift+keypad Enter
Page break	⌘+keypad Enter	Ctrl+keypad Enter
Indent to here	⌘+\	Ctrl+\
Right-indent tab	Shift+Tab	Shift+Tab
Insert current page number	Option+Shift+⌘+N	Ctrl+Alt+Shift+N
Printing and Output		
Print document	⌘+P	Ctrl+P
Preflight document	Option+Shift+⌘+F	Ctrl+Alt+Shift+F
Package document	Option+Shift+⌘+P	Ctrl+Alt+Shift+P
Miscellaneous		
Help	Help	F1
Undo	⌘+Z	Ctrl+Z
Redo	Shift+⌘+Z	Ctrl+Shift+Z

✦   ✦   ✦

Index